An Introduction to C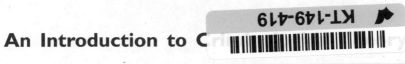

For Kristan, Thomas and Oliver

An Introduction to Criminological Theory

Third Edition

Roger Hopkins Burke

Routledge
Taylor & Francis Group

LONDON AND NEW YORK

Published by Willan Publishing 2001

This edition published by Taylor & Francis 2011
2 Park Square
Milton Park
Abingdon
Oxon
OX14 4RN

Published simultaneously in the USA and Canada by:
711 Third Avenue
New York
NY10017 (8th Floor)

First published 2001
Second Edition 2005
Third Edition 2009

ISBN 978-1-84392-407-4 paperback
ISBN 978-1-84392-569-9 hardback

British Library Cataloguing-in-Publication Data

A catalogue record for this book is available from the British Library

Project managed by Deer Park Productions, Tavistock, Devon
Typeset by GCS, Leighton Buzzard, Bedfordshire, LU7 1EU
Printed and bound by T.J. International, Padstow, Cornwall

Contents

Acknowledgements

I would like to offer my sincerest thanks to those who have offered advice and support during the researching and writing of the third edition of this book. It has again been most appreciated. Thanks to all my colleagues at Nottingham Trent University and in particular those in the Criminology Team: Mike Ahearne, Natasha Chubbock, Chris Crowther-Dowey, Terry Gillespie, Paul Hamilton, Phil Hodgson, Matt Long, Roger Moore, Paul Sparrow, Mike Sutton, Andromachi Tseloni and Andy Wilson. Thanks as usual to Brian Willan – who remains for me an ideal publisher – and his staff at Willan Publishing. Last, and very far from least, thanks to my wife Kristan, and our two wonderful and talented boys, Thomas, now 11 and Oliver 8 who as always like to see their names in print.

1. Introduction: crime and modernity

This is a book about the different ways in which crime and criminal behaviour have been explained in predominantly modern times. It will be seen that there are different explanations – or theories – which have been proposed at various times during the past 200 years by among others legal philosophers, biologists, psychologists, sociologists and political scientists. Moreover, these theories – in particular the earlier variants – have tended to reflect the various concerns and professional interests of the discipline to which the theorist or theorists has belonged. For example, biologists sought explanations for criminality in terms of the physiology of the individual criminal, while psychologists directed our attention to the mind or personality of the person. Increasingly, explanations have come to incorporate elements from more than one discipline. Thus, for example, some biologists came to recognise that individuals with the same physiological profiles will behave differently depending on the circumstances of their socialisation.

Most of the theories discussed in this book nevertheless share one common characteristic. They are all products of a time period – approximately the past two centuries – and a way of life that has come to be termed the modern age. As such these different explanations of crime and criminal behaviour are themselves very much a reflection of the dominant ideas that have existed during this era. It is therefore a useful starting point to briefly consider how crime and criminal behaviour was explained and dealt with in the pre-modern period.

Pre-modern crime and criminal justice

Prior to the modern age crime and criminal behaviour in Europe had been explained for over a thousand years by spiritualist notions (Vold, Bernard and Snipes, 1998). The influential theologian St Thomas Aquinas (1225–74) had argued that there is a God-given 'natural law' that is revealed by observing – through the eyes of faith – the natural tendency of people to do good rather than evil. Those who violate the criminal law are therefore not only criminals but also 'sinners' and thus crime not only harms victims but also the offender because it damages their essential 'humanness' or natural tendency to do good (Bernard, 1983). Central to spiritualist thought was *demonology*, where it was proposed that criminals were possessed by demons that forced them to do wicked things beyond their control. Criminal activity is rarely attributed these days to the influence of devils from hell – well at least by criminologists and criminal justice system practitioners – but the logic underlying this idea that criminals are driven by forces beyond their control, is still with us. What can arguably be regarded as a modified variant of this form of thought – but where the explanatory power of spirituality has been replaced by that of science – is the focus of the second part of this book.

Pre-modern European legal systems were founded on spiritualist explanations of crime and what little written law that did exist was applied through judicial interpretation and caprice, and in the main to those who were not of the aristocracy. Because crime was identified with sin – and the criminal could therefore be considered to be possessed by demons – the state had the moral authority to use horrible tortures and punishments. Those accused of crime often faced secret accusations, torture and closed trials with arbitrary and harsh sanctions applied to the convicted. The emphasis of punishment was moreover on the physical body of the accused for the bulk of the population possessed little else on which the power to punish could be usefully exercised. Foucault (1977: 3) provides an account of a public execution reserved for the greatest of all crimes under the French *ancien regime*, regicide:

> The flesh will be torn from the breasts, arms, thighs and calves with red-hot pincers, his right hand, holding the knife with which he committed the said parricide, burnt with sulphur, and, on those places where the flesh will be torn away, poured molten lead, boiling oil, burning resin, wax and sulphur melted together and then his body drawn and quartered by four horses and his limbs and body consumed by fire.

Pre-modern punishment frequently involved torture and in some jurisdictions the possibility of being tortured to death remained a penal option into the nineteenth century. Penal torture had not been used in England since the eighteenth century, except in exceptional cases for treason; Scotland, on the other hand, retained in legal theory, although certainly not in practice, hanging, drawing and quartering for treason until 1948.

Little use was made of imprisonment as a punishment in the pre-modern era. Prisons were most commonly places for holding suspects and offenders prior to trial or punishment, except in cases of debt when they were used to hold debtors until their financial affairs could be resolved. It would appear that those who framed and administered the law enacted and exercised the criminal codes on the premise that it was only the threat of savage and cruel punishments, delivered in public and with theatrical emphasis, that would deter the dangerous materially dispossessed classes who constituted 'the mob'.

It seems that from the seventeenth to the early eighteenth century the English ruling class or aristocracy sought to protect their property interests through the exercise of the criminal law (Koestler and Rolph, 1961). Thus, a vast number of property crimes came to be punished by death in accordance with a body of legislation enacted during that period and which later came to be known as the 'the bloody code'. Hanging was the standard form of execution and was the typical punishment for offences ranging from murder to stealing turnips, writing threatening letters or impersonating an outpatient of Greenwich Hospital (Radzinowicz, 1948). By 1800 there were more than 250 such capital offences and executions were usually carried out *en masse* (Lofland, 1973).

The full weight of the law was nevertheless not always applied. The rural aristocracy – who sat as judges and 'justices of the peace' – used their prerogative of clemency and leniency in order to demonstrate their power over the 'lower orders'. Hence, evidence of 'respectability' in the form of references from a benevolent landowner, confirmation of significant religious observance and piety, or the simple discretionary whim of a JP could lead to a lesser sentence. These alternatives included transportation to a colony, a non-fatal, if brutal, corporal punishment or even release (Thompson, 1975).

In short, the administration of criminal justice was chaotic, predominantly non-codified, irrational and irregular, and at the whim of individual judgement. It was the emergence and establishment of the modern era and the subsequent new ways of seeing and responding to the world that provided the preconditions for a major break in the way in which crime and criminal behaviour was both conceptualised and dealt with.

The rise of modern society

The idea of the modern originated as a description of the forms of thought and action that began to emerge with the decline of medieval society in Western Europe. The authority of the old aristocracies was being seriously questioned, both because of their claims to natural superiority and their corrupt political practices. A new and increasingly powerful middle class was benefiting from the profits of trade, industry and agricultural rationalisation. In the interests of the latter, the enclosure movement dispossessed many of the rural poor from access to common lands and smallholding tenancies, causing great hardship to those involved, yet, at the same time, producing a readily available pool of cheap labour to satisfy the demands of the Industrial Revolution. The aggregate outcome of these fundamental social changes was that societies were becoming increasingly industrialised and urbanised, causing previous standard forms of human relationships based on familiarity, reputation and localism to give way to more fluid, often anonymous interactions which significantly posed problems for existing forms of social control.

The notion of the modern essentially involved a secular rational tradition with the following origins. First, there was the emergence of humanist ideas and Protestantism in the sixteenth century. Previously the common people had been encouraged by the established church to unquestioningly accept their position in life and look for salvation in the afterlife. It was with the rise of the 'protestant ethic' that people came to expect success in return for hard work in this world. At the same time assumptions about the natural superiority – or the divine right – of the powerful aristocracy came to be questioned. Second, there was the scientific revolution of the seventeenth century where our understanding of the world around us was first explained by reference to natural laws. Third, there was the eighteenth century philosophical Enlightenment where it was proposed that the social world could similarly be explained and regulated by natural laws and political systems should be developed that embraced new ideas of individual rationality and free will. Indeed, inspired by such ideas and responding to dramatically changing economic and political circumstances, revolutions occurred in the American colonies and in France. These were widely influential and ideas concerning human rights were championed in many European countries by the merchant, professional and middle classes. Subsequently, there were significant changes in the nature of systems of government, administration and law. Fourth, there was the increasingly evident power of industrial society and the prestige afforded to scientific explanation in the nineteenth and twentieth centuries that seemed to confirm the superiority of the modernist intellectual tradition over all others (Harvey, 1989).

The principal features that characterise the idea of modern society can thus be identified in three main areas. First, in the area of economics there was the development of a market economy involving the growth of production for profit, rather than immediate local use, the development of industrial technology with a considerable extension of the division of labour and wage labour became the principal form of employment. Second, in the area of politics there was the growth and consolidation of the centralised nation state and the extension of bureaucratic forms of administration, systematic forms of surveillance and control, the development of representative democracy and political party systems. Third, in the area of culture there was a challenge to tradition in the name of rationality with the emphasis on scientific and technical knowledge.

The modern world was consequently a very different place to its pre-modern predecessor. Not surprisingly, therefore, modern explanations of crime and criminal behaviour – and the nature of criminal justice interventions – were different from those that existed in pre-modern times. A word of caution should nevertheless be considered at this point. Contemporary criminologist David Garland (1997: 22–3) notes similarities between traditional accounts of criminality – whether they were religious or otherwise – and those of the modern era:

> Stories of how the offender fell in with bad company, became lax in his habits and was sorely tried by temptation, was sickly, or tainted by bad blood, or neglected by unloving parents, became too fond of drink or too idle to work, lost her reputation and found it hard to get employment, was driven by despair or poverty or simply driven to crime by avarice and lust – these seem to provide the well-worn templates from which our modern theories of crime are struck, even if we insist upon a more

neutral language in which to tell the tale, and think that a story's plausibility should be borne out by evidence as well as intuition.

Garland notes that there were plenty of secular explanations of the roots of crime to place alongside the spiritual in pre-modern society. What was lacking was a developed sense of differential explanation. Crime was widely recognised as a universal temptation to which we are all susceptible, but when it came to explaining why it is that some of us succumb and others resist, explanations tended to drift off into the metaphysical and spiritual. Furthermore, we should note that 'traditional' ways of explaining crime have not entirely disappeared with the triumph of modernity, though they may nowadays be accorded a different status in the hierarchy of credibility. We do nevertheless continue to acknowledge the force of moral, religious and 'commonsensical' ways of discussing crime.

Defining and the extent of crime

It will become increasingly apparent to the reader of this book that developments in what has come to be termed criminological theorising have tended to reflect the economic, political and cultural developments that have occurred in modern society. In fact, definitions of crime and thus criminality are also closely linked to such socio-political factors and how we view the nature of society.

Crime includes many different activities such as theft, fraud, robbery, corruption, assault, rape and murder. We might usefully ask what these disparate activities – and their even more disparate perpetrators – have in common. Some might simply define crime as 'the doing of wrong' and it is a commonly used approach related to notions of morality. Yet not all actions or activities that might be considered immoral are considered crimes. For example, poverty and social deprivation might be considered 'crimes against humanity' but are not usually seen to be crimes. Conversely, actions that are crimes, for example, parking on a yellow line or in some cases tax evasion are not seen as immoral (Croall, 1998).

The simplest way of defining crime is that it is an act that contravenes the criminal law. This is nevertheless a problematic definition, for many people break the criminal law but are not considered to be 'criminals'. In English law, for example, some offences such as murder, theft or serious assaults are described as *mala in se* or wrong in themselves. These are often seen as 'real' crimes in contrast to acts that are *mala prohibita*, prohibited not because they are morally wrong but for the protection of the public (Lacey, Wells and Meure, 1990). Thus the criminal law is used to enforce regulations concerning public health or pollution not because they are morally wrong but because it is considered to be the most effective way of ensuring that regulations are enforced.

Legal definitions also change over time and vary across culture. Thus, for example, in some countries the sale and consumption of alcohol is a crime while, in others the sale and consumption of opium, heroin or cannabis is perfectly legal. For some years there have been arguments in Britain for the use of some soft drugs such as cannabis to be legalised and in 2004 the latter was downgraded from 'Class B to C', which meant that the police can no longer automatically arrest those caught in possession, although it remained illegal (Crowther, 2007). The government subsequently reclassified cannabis from Class C to Class B in January 2009. They did this to reflect the fact that skunk, a much stronger version of the drug, now accounts for more than 80 per cent of cannabis available on our streets, compared to just 30 per cent in 2002 (Home Office, 2009). On the other hand, there has been a demand for other activities to be criminalised and in recent years these have included 'stalking', racially motivated crime and knowingly passing on the Aids virus. The way that crime is defined is therefore a social construction and part of the political processes.

This construction can be exemplified by considering what is included and excluded. Thus, Mars (1982) observes that 'crime', 'theft' and 'offence' are 'hard' words that can be differentiated from 'softer' words such as 'fiddle' or 'perk' that are often used to describe and diminish criminal activities conducted in the workplace. In the same context, the terms 'creative accounting' or 'fiddling the books' do not sound quite as criminal as 'fraud'. Furthermore, incidents in which people are killed or injured in a train crash or as a result of using unsafe equipment are generally described as 'accidents' or 'disasters' rather than as 'crimes', albeit they often result from a failure of transport operators or managers to comply with safety regulations (Wells, 1993). Thus, different words denote different kinds of crime, with some activities being totally excluded from the social construction of crime (Croall, 1998).

Crime is usually associated with particular groups such as young men or the unemployed, some of whom become 'folk devils', and are identified with certain kinds of offences. This social construction of crime is reflected in media discussions and portrayals of what constitutes the 'crime problem'. Thus, for example, rising crime rates or policies are introduced to 'crack down' on crimes such as burglary or violent street crime rather than on environmental crimes such as pollution, corporate crimes or major frauds.

The vast majority of criminological research – and thus the explanations or theories of criminal behaviour that emanate from those studies and which are discussed in this book – have been conducted on those from the lower socio-economic groups and their activities. For it is concerns about this apparently 'dangerous class' that have dominated criminological thought since at least the beginning of modern society. The substitution of determinate prison sentences for those of capital punishment and transportation came to mean in reality the existence of a growing population of convicted criminals that frightened many in 'respectable society'. It is therefore perhaps not surprising that both the law and criminology has subsequently targeted this group.

The problem of 'white collar', business or corporate crime has nevertheless been recognised since at least the beginning of the twentieth century, although it has continued to be neglected and under-researched by criminologists (Clinard and Yeager, 1980; Kramer, 1984; Croall, 1992, 2001). Moreover, there has also been a tendency for much of the research conducted in this area to be atheoretical with white collar and corporate crime seen as a phenomenon completely separate from the 'normal', that is, predatory 'street' crime. This criminological neglect does appear at first sight somewhat surprising.

It has been estimated that, for example, in the USA the economic losses from various white collar crimes are about ten times those from 'ordinary' economic crime (Conklin, 1977) with corporate crime killing and maiming more than any violence committed by the poor (Liazos, 1972). In the same country 100,000 people have died each year from occupationally related diseases that have mostly been contracted as a result of wilful violation of laws designed to protect workers (Swartz, 1975), defective products have killed another 30,000 US citizens annually (Kramer, 1984), while US manufacturers have been observed to dump drugs and medical equipment in developing countries after they have been banned from the home market (Braithwaite, 1984). Croall (1992, 2001) observes that the activities of the corporate criminal are not only greater in impact than those of the ordinary offender, but they are also longer lasting in effect.

There has been a real problem in actually defining the concept of white collar or corporate crime (Geis and Maier, 1977). Sutherland (1947) had proposed that 'white collar crime may be defined approximately as a crime committed by a person of respectability and high social status in the course of his occupation'. This is nevertheless a restricted definition. White collar crime can occur when an individual commits crime against an organisation within which they work or, for example, when a self-employed person evades income tax. Corporate crime, on the other hand, involves illegal acts carried out in the furtherance of the goals of an organisation and is therefore a particular form of white-collar crime. Schraeger and Short (1978: 409) propose that organisational crime should be defined as

> ... illegal acts of omission of an individual or a group of individuals in a legitimate formal organisation in accordance with the operative goals of the organisation which have a serious physical or economic impact on employees, consumers or the general public.

This is a definition that goes beyond that of economic impact and includes crimes of omission – failure to act – as well as those of commission. Others go further and include serious harms, which, though not proscribed, are in breach of human rights (Schwendinger and Schwendinger, 1970). In this book we will consider how the various explanations – or theories – of criminal behaviour that have usually been developed and applied to the socio-economically less powerful can – and have on occasion – been applied to these crimes of the powerful and the relatively powerful.

The structure of the book

This book is divided into five parts. The first three parts consider a different model – or tradition – of explaining crime and criminal behaviour that has been developed during the modern era. Different explanations – or theories – can generally be located in terms of one of these models and these are here introduced chronologically in order of their emergence and development. It is shown how each later theory helped to revive, develop and/or rectify identified weaknesses in the ideas and prescriptions of their predecessors within that tradition.

A word of caution needs to be signposted at this juncture. Explanations of criminal behaviour have become increasingly complex as researchers have become aware that crime is a more complicated and perplexing matter than their criminological predecessors had previously recognised. Thus, some readers might consider that a particular theory introduced as being central to the development of a particular tradition might also be considered in terms of a different model. In such instances attention is directed to that ambiguity. For clearly, as each tradition has developed there has been an increasing recognition by researchers of a need to address previously identified weaknesses internal to the model. The solution has invariably encompassed recognition of the at least partial strengths contained within alternative approaches. Hence, biologists have come increasingly to recognise the influence of environmental factors while some psychologists have embraced the previously alien notion of individual choice. Some more recent theoretical initiatives are in fact impossible to locate in any one of the three models. In short, their proponents have consciously sought to cross model boundaries by developing integrated theoretical approaches. These developments provide the focus of the fourth part of the book. The fifth and final part of the book addresses a range of contemporary criminological issues, forms of deviance, criminality and the nature of the societal response which do not fit easily in any one particular theoretical tradition.

Part One introduces the rational actor model. Central to this tradition is the notion that people have free will and make the choice to commit crime in very much the same way as they choose to indulge in any other form of behaviour. It is a tradition with two central intellectual influences. First, *social contract* theories challenged the notion of the 'natural' political authority which had previously been asserted by the aristocracy. Human beings were now viewed as freely choosing to enter into contracts with others to perform interpersonal or civic duties (Hobbes, 1968 originally 1651; Locke, 1970 originally 1686, 1975 originally 1689; Rousseau, 1964 originally 1762, 1978 originally 1775). Second, *utilitarianism* sought to assess the applicability of policies and legislation to promote the 'happiness' of those citizens affected by them (Bentham, 1970 originally 1789; Mill, 1963–84 originally 1859).

Chapter 2 considers the ideas of the Classical School that provide the central theoretical foundations of the rational actor tradition. From this perspective, it is argued that people are rational creatures who seek pleasure while avoiding pain and consequently, the level of punishment inflicted must outweigh any pleasure that might be derived from a criminal act in order to deter people from resorting to crime. It was nevertheless a model of criminal behaviour that was to go into steep decline for many years. The increasing recognition that children, 'idiots' and the insane do not enjoy the capacity of perfect rational decision-making seemed best explained by the predestined actor model of human behaviour – or positivism – that is the focus of the second part of this book. The Classical school has however had a major and enduring influence on the contemporary criminal justice process epitomised by notions of 'due process' (Packer, 1968) and 'just deserts' (Von Hirsch, 1976).

Chapter 3 considers the revival of the rational actor tradition that occurred with the rise of the political 'new right' – populist or neoconservatives – both in the USA and the UK during the 1970s. This emerging body of thought was highly critical of both the then orthodox predestined actor model with its prescriptions of treatment rather than punishment and the even more radical 'victimised' actor model – the focus of the third part of this book – with its proposals of forgiveness and non-intervention (Morgan, 1978; Dale, 1984; Scruton, 1980, 1985). These rational actor model revivalists argued that crime would be reduced if the costs of involvement were increased so that legal activities become comparatively more attractive (Wilson, 1975; Wilson and Herrnstein, 1985; Felson, 1998).

Chapter 4 discusses those theories that have come to prominence with the revival of the rational actor tradition. First, modern deterrence theories have addressed the principles of certainty, severity and promptness in terms of the administration of criminal justice (Zimring and Hawkins, 1973; Gibbs, 1975; Wright, 1993). Second, contemporary rational choice theories have proposed that people make decisions to act based on the extent to which they expect that choice to maximise their profits or benefits and minimise the costs or losses. Hence, decisions to offend are based on expected effort and reward compared to the likelihood and severity of punishment and other costs of crime (Becker, 1968; Cornish and Clarke, 1986). Routine activities theorists have developed a more sophisticated variant of this argument to propose that the likelihood of a crime increases when there are one or more motivated persons present, a suitable target or potential victim available, and an absence of capable guardians to deter the offender (Cohen and Felson, 1979).

Part Two introduces the predestined actor model. Proponents of this perspective fundamentally reject the rational actor emphasis on free will and replace it with the doctrine of determinism. From this *positivist* standpoint, criminal behaviour is explained in terms of factors, either internal or external to the human being that cause – or *determine* – people to act in ways over which they have little or no control. The individual is thus in some way predestined to be a criminal.

There are three basic formulations of the predestined actor model: biological, psychological and sociological. All three variants nevertheless incorporate the same fundamental assumptions, and although each is discussed separately, it will become increasingly apparent to the reader that they are not mutually exclusive; for example, biologists came to embrace sociological factors, while at times it is often difficult to differentiate between biological and psychological explanations.

Three factors were central to the emergence of the predestined actor model. First, there was the replacement of theology as the central explanation of the essence of humanity with science. In particular, the theory of evolution proposed that human beings were now subject to the same natural laws as all other animals (Darwin, 1871). Second, there was development of *social* evolutionism and the view that human beings develop as part of a process of interaction with the world they inhabit (Spencer, 1971 originally 1862–96). Third, there was the philosophical doctrine of positivism and the proposition that we may only obtain knowledge of human nature and society by using the methods of the natural sciences (Comte, 1976 originally 1830–42).

Chapter 5 considers biological variants of the predestined actor model and starts with an examination of the early theories of 'the Italian School' where the central focus is on the notion that the criminal is a physical type distinct from the non-criminal (Lombroso, 1875; Ferri, 1895; Garofalo, 1914). There follows consideration of increasingly sophisticated variants on that theme. First, there is an examination of those theories that consider criminal behaviour to be inherited in the same way as physical characteristics. Evidence to support that supposition has been obtained from three sources: studies of criminal families (Dugdale, 1877; Goddard, 1914; Goring, 1913), twins (Lange, 1930; Christiansen, 1968, 1974; Dalgard and Kringlen, 1976; Cloninger and Gottesman, 1987; Rowe and Rogers, 1989; Rowe, 1990) and adopted children (Hutchings and Mednick, 1977; Mednick *et al.*, 1984). Second, consideration is given to those theories that link criminal behaviour to abnormalities in the genetic structure of the individual (Klinefelter, Reifenstein and Albright, 1942; Price and Whatmore, 1967; Ellis, 1990; Jones, 1993) and, third, later versions of the body type thesis (Hooton, 1939; Sheldon, 1949; Glueck and Glueck, 1950; Gibbons, 1970; Cortes and Gatti, 1972). Fourth, neurological and brain injuries (Mark and Ervin, 1970; Mednick and Volavka, 1980; Volavka, 1987) and, fifth, different categories of biochemical explanation are scrutinised (Schlapp and Smith 1928; Dalton, 1961, 1964; Rose *et al.*, 1974; Keverne, Meller and Eberhart, 1982; Olwens, 1987; Schalling, 1987; Virkkunen, 1987; Ellis and Crontz, 1990; Baldwin, 1990; Fagan, 1990; Fishbein and Pease, 1990; Pihl and Peterson, 1993). Biological positivists propose that offenders should receive some form of treatment rather than punishment and there thus follows an examination of the treatment options of surgical intervention, chemotherapy and electro-control.

Chapter 6 considers psychological variants of the predestined actor model. These all have in common the proposition that there are patterns of reasoning and behaviour specific to offenders that remain constant regardless of the different environmental experiences of individuals. There is a criminal mind. Three different psychological perspectives are identified. First, the psychodynamic approach has its roots in the notion of psychosexual development and the idea of a number of complex stages of psychic development (Freud, 1920, 1927). This approach was later developed through latent delinquency theory, which proposed that the absence of an intimate attachment with parents could lead to later criminality (Aichhorn, 1925; Healy and Bronner, 1936). Maternal deprivation theory was to propose that a lack of a close mother/child relationship in the early years of life could lead to criminal behaviour (Bowlby, 1952). Other researchers have proposed that the nature of child rearing practice is closely linked to later behavioural patterns (Glueck and Glueck, 1950; McCord, McCord and Zola, 1959; Bandura and Walters, 1959; Hoffman and Saltzstein, 1967) while other theories propose that much criminality is a product of 'broken families' (Burt, 1945; Mannheim, 1948; Wootton, 1959; West, 1969; Pitts, 1986; Kolvin et al., 1990; Farrington, 1992). Second, behavioural learning theories have their origins in the notion that all behaviour is learned from an external stimulus (Skinner, 1938). Criminals thus develop abnormal, inadequate, or specifically criminal personalities or personality traits that differentiate them from non-criminals. These theories – based on the concept of conditioned learning – propose that there are dimensions of personality that can be isolated and measured and thus criminal behaviour predicted (Eysenck, 1970, 1977; Smith and Smith, 1977; McEwan, 1983; McGurk and McDougall, 1981; Farrington, 1994). Antisocial personality disorder proposes that similar techniques can be used to detect individuals who are 'psychopaths' (Cleckley, 1976; Hare, 1980; Feldman, 1977; Hare and Jutari, 1986; Hollin, 1989) and predict future dangerousness (Kozol, Boucher and Garofalo, 1972; Monahan, 1981; Loeber and Dishion, 1983; Holmes and De Burger, 1989; Omerod, 1996). Third, cognitive theories are explicitly critical of the determinist nature of the previous two psychological traditions (Tolman, 1959; Piaget, 1980; Skinner, 1981). Social learning theory thus proposes that behaviour is learned through watching what happens to other people and then making *choices* to behave in a particular way (Sutherland, 1947; Akers et al., 1979; Akers, 1985, 1992). In this way psychology can be seen to have moved away from its roots in the predestined model to incorporate notions from the rational actor model.

Chapter 7 considers sociological variants of the predestined actor model. These provided a direct challenge to those variants of the tradition that had focused on the characteristics – whether biological or psychological – of the deviant individual. Thus, in contrast, crime is explained as being a product of the social environment, which provides cultural values and definitions that govern the behaviour of those who live within them. Deviant or criminal behaviour is said to occur when an individual – or a group of individuals – behave in accordance with definitions that conflict with those of the dominant culture. Moreover, such behaviour is transmitted to others – and later generations – by frequent contact with criminal traditions that have developed over time in disorganised areas of the city (Durkheim, 1964 originally 1895; Shaw and McKay, 1972 originally 1931). Later anomie or strain theories develop the positivist sociological tradition to propose that most members of society share a common value system that teaches us both the things we should strive for in life and the approved way in which we can achieve them. However, without reasonable access to the socially approved means, people will attempt to find some alternative way – including criminal behaviour – to resolve the pressure to achieve (Merton, 1938). Delinquent subculture theories develop that argument further by observing that lower-class values serve to create young male behaviours that are delinquent by middle-class standards but which are both normal and useful in lower-class life. Thus, crime committed by groups of young people – or gangs – that seriously victimises the larger community is in part a by-product of efforts of lower-class youth to attain goals valued within their own subcultural social world (Cohen, 1955; Miller, 1958; Cloward and Ohlin, 1960; Spergel, 1964; Matza, 1964; Mays, 1954; Morris, 1957; Downes, 1966; Wilmott, 1966; Parker, 1974; Pryce, 1979). Later deviant subculture theorists – with clear theoretical foundations in the victimised actor model – propose that involvement in particular subcultures whether these be 'mainstream' (Willis, 1977; Corrigan, 1979) or 'spectacular' (Hebdige, 1976, 1979; Brake, 1980, 1985) is determined by economic factors. Postmodern approaches develop that perspective but recognise an element of albeit limited and constrained choice for some young people (Hopkins Burke and Sunley, 1996, 1998).

Chapter 8 considers how proponents of the predestined actor model have considered female criminality. Lombroso and Ferrero (1885) provides a fundamentally biologically determinist account and later studies in this tradition rely implicitly on his assumptions about the physiological and psychological nature of women (Thomas 1907, 1923; Davis, 1961, originally 1937; Pollak, 1950). The Freudian perspective is fundamentally grounded in explicit biological assumptions about the nature of women encapsulated by his famous maxim that 'anatomy is destiny' (Lerner, 1998); while, Kingsley Davis' (1961, originally 1937) influential structural functionalist study of prostitution is founded on crucial assumptions about the 'organic nature of man and woman'. Sociological theories tend to be explanations of male patterns of behaviour and appear to have at first sight little or no relevance for explaining female criminality (Leonard, 1983).

Part Three introduces the victimised actor model. This is a tradition that proposes – with increasingly radical variants – that the criminal is in some way the victim of an unjust and unequal society. Thus, it is the behaviour and activities of the poor and powerless sections of society that are targeted and criminalised while the dubious activities of the rich and powerful are simply ignored or not even defined as criminal.

There are two factors central to the emergence of the victimised actor model. First, there emerged during the mid-twentieth century within the social sciences an influential critique of the predestined actor model of human behaviour. Symbolic interactionism (Mead, 1934), phenomenology (Schutz, 1962) and ethnomethodology (Garfinkel, 1967) all questioned the positivist insistence on identifying and analysing the compelling *causes* that drive individuals towards criminal behaviour while at the same time being unable to describe the social world in a way that is meaningful to its participants. Positivists were observed to have a restricted notion of criminality that was based on a tendency to accept the conventional morality of rules and criminal laws as self-evident truths and where a particular action is defined as a crime because the state has decreed it to be so. Second, there developed a critique of the orthodox predestined actor model notion that society is fundamentally characterised by consensus. Pluralist conflict theorists proposed that society consists of numerous interest groups all involved in an essential struggle for resources and attention with other groups (Dahrendorf, 1958). More radical theories – informed by various interpretations of Marxist social and economic theory – view social conflict as having its roots in fundamental discord between social classes struggling for control of material resources (Taylor, Walton and Young, 1973).

Chapter 9 considers social reaction – or labelling – theories (Lemert, 1951; Kitsuse, 1962; Becker, 1963; Piliavin and Briar, 1964; Cicourel, 1968). These propose that no behaviour is inherently deviant or criminal, but only comes to be considered so when others confer this label upon the act. Thus, it is not the intrinsic nature of an act, but the nature of the social reaction that determines whether a 'crime' has taken place. Central to this perspective is the notion that being found out and stigmatised, as a consequence of rule breaking conduct, may cause an individual to become committed to further deviance, often as part of a deviant subculture. The labelling perspective has also been applied at a group level and the concept of 'deviancy amplification' suggests that the less tolerance there is to an initial act of group deviance, the more acts will be defined as deviant (Wilkins, 1964). This can lead to a media campaign that whips up a frenzy of popular societal indignation – or a 'moral panic' – about a particular activity that is seen to threaten the very fabric of civilisation. For example, 'lager louts', 'football hooligans', 'new age travellers', 'ravers' and even 'dangerous dogs' have all been the subjects of moral panics in recent years. Once labelled as such, those engaged in the particular activity, become ostracised and targeted as 'folk devils' by the criminal justice system reacting to popular pressure (Young, 1971; Cohen, 1973).

Among the critics of the labelling perspective are those who argue that they simply do not go far enough. By concentrating their attention on the labelling powers of front-line agents of the state working in the criminal justice system, the capacity for powerful groups to make laws to their advantage and to the disadvantage of the poor and dispossessed is ignored.

These issues are addressed in Chapter 10, which considers conflict and radical theories. For both sets of theorists, laws are formulated to express the values and interests of the most powerful groups in society while at the same time placing restrictions on the behaviour and activities common to the less powerful, thus disproportionately 'criminalising' the members of these groups. The more radical variants propose that it is the very conditions generated by the capitalist political economy that generate crime (Vold, 1958; Turk, 1969; Quinney, 1970; Chambliss, 1975). These latter ideas were further developed in the UK in the late 1960s and early 1970s by the 'new criminology' that sought an explanation of criminal behaviour based on a theoretical synthesis of Marxism and labelling perspectives (Taylor, Walton and Young, 1973; Hall et al., 1978).

Criticisms of radical criminology have originated from three primary sources. First, traditional Marxists have questioned the manipulation of this theoretical tradition to address the issue of crime (Hirst, 1980). Second, there was the important recognition by the populist conservatives – or right realists – that most predatory crime is committed by members of the poorer sections of society against their own kind and in doing so changing the whole nature of political debate on the crime problem. Third, there was the increasing recognition of this latter reality by sections of the political left and the consequent development of a populist socialist response that is the focus of the final chapter of the fourth part of this book.

Chapter 11 considers the gendered criminal. Feminists propose that it is men who are the dominant group in society and it is privileged males who make and enforce the rules to the detriment of women. Feminism is nevertheless not a unitary body of thought and this chapter thus commences with a brief introduction to the different contemporary manifestations of feminism. There follows a feminist critique of the predestined actor model explanations of female criminality (Smart, 1977; Heidensohn, 1985) and an examination of the impact of feminist critiques in four critical areas: the female emancipation leads to crime debate (Adler, 1975; Simon, 1975), the invalidation of the leniency hypothesis (Pollak, 1950), the emergence of gender-based theories (Heidensohn, 1985) and the recognition and redefinition of previously non-problematic activities such as domestic violence and intrafamilial child molestation as serious crimes that need to be taken seriously (Hanmer and Saunders, 1984; Dobash and Dobash, 1992). The chapter concludes with an examination of the notion of masculinity which feminist discourse has encouraged a small but growing group of male writers to 'take seriously' (Connell 1987, 1995; Messerschmidt, 1993; Jefferson, 1997).

Chapter 12 considers critical criminology which is one of two contemporary variants of the radical tradition in criminology. There are a number of different versions but in general critical criminologists define crime in terms of oppression where it is members of the working class, women and ethnic minority groups who are the most likely to suffer the weight of oppressive social relations based upon class division, sexism and racism (Cohen, 1980; Box, 1983; Scraton, 1985; Sim, Scraton and Gordon, 1987; Scraton and Chadwick, 1996 originally 1992). The contemporary notion of relative deprivation has been developed – with its roots in anomie theory – and its proposition that crime is committed by members of the poorer sections of society who are excluded from the material good things in life enjoyed by those with economic advantage. They have also importantly drawn our attention to the crimes of the powerful that – as we observed above – have been inadequately addressed by traditional explanations of crime and criminal behaviour.

Critical criminologists have nevertheless been criticised by the other contemporary wing of the radical tradition – the populist socialists or 'left realists' – who consider them to be 'left idealists' with romantic notions of criminals as revolutionaries or latter-day 'Robin Hoods' stealing from the rich to give to the poor, while failing adequately to address the reality that much crime is committed by the poor on their own kind. Critical criminologists have nonetheless widened the horizons of the discipline to embrace the study of zemiology or those social harms that are often far more damaging to society than those restricted activities which have been defined as criminal (Schwendinger and Schwendinger, 1970; Shearing, 1989; Tifft, 1995).

Part Four introduces various attempts at integrating different theories both within one of the theoretical traditions outlined in the first three parts of this book and across model boundaries. It is observed that there are three ways in which theories can be developed and evaluated. First, each theory can be considered on its own. Second, there can be a process of theory competition where there is a logical and comprehensive examination of two different perspectives and a consideration of which one most successfully fits the data at hand (Liska, 1987). The third way is by theoretical integration where the intention is to identify commonalties in two or more theories in order to produce a synthesis that it is superior to any one individual theory (Farnsworth, 1989).

Chapter 13 considers those sociobiological theories that have attempted a synthesis of biological and sociological explanations. Biosocial theorists argue that the biological characteristics of an individual are only part of the explanation of criminal behaviour and thus, factors in the physical and social environment of the offender are also influential. It is proposed that all individuals must learn to control natural urges toward antisocial and criminal behaviour (Mednick, 1977; Mednick, Moffit and Stack, 1987). Environmentally influenced behaviour explanations address those incidents where outside stimuli such as drug and alcohol use has instigated or enhanced a propensity towards certain forms of behaviour (Fishbein and Pease, 1996).

The sociobiological perspective has been developed by the 'right realist' criminological theorists, Wilson and Herrnstein (1985), who have developed a theory combining gender, age, intelligence, body type and personality factors and have considered these in the context of the wider social environment of the offender. They propose that the interplay between these factors provides an explanation of why it is that crime rates have increased in both periods of economic boom and recession observing that the relationship between the environment and the individual is a complex one. Among the most contentious sociobiological criminological theories to emerge in recent years have been those that propose that rape has evolved as a genetically advantageous behavioural adaptation (Thornhill and Palmer, 2000). Moreover, there has been significant recent interest by sociobiologists in the USA in antisocial behaviour that is seen to emerge early in childhood, persists into adulthood and which is difficult or even impossible to rehabilitate (Aguilar et al., 2000).

Chapter 14 discusses environmental theories which are part of a long established tradition with their foundations firmly located in the sociological version of the predestined actor model. Later British area studies were to incorporate notions from the victimised actor model, primarily a consideration of the effects of labelling individuals and groups of residents as different or bad (Damer, 1974; Gill, 1977). Later North American studies sought to incorporate the discipline of geography to provide a more sophisticated analysis of the distribution of crime and criminals (Brantingham and Brantingham, 1981). However, this was not to be simply a geographical determinist account. For, in adopting the recognition that crime happens when the four elements of a law, an offender, a target and a place concur, the perspective is brought into contact with those contemporary opportunity theories that characterise recent developments within the rational actor model (Cohen and Felson, 1979). Environmental management theories certainly presuppose the existence of a rational calculating individual whose activities can be restricted or curtailed by changing his or her surroundings (Wilson and Kelling, 1982).

Chapter 15 examines social control theories which again have a long and distinguished pedigree with their origins in both the rational actor and predestined actor models (Hobbes, 1968 originally 1651; Durkheim, 1951 originally 1897; Freud, 1927) with both social and psychological factors employed in order to explain conformity and deviance. Early social theory had proposed that inadequate forms of social control were more likely during periods of rapid modernisation and social change because new forms of regulation could not evolve quickly enough to replace declining forms of social integration (Durkheim, 1951 originally 1897). Early social control theorists – such as the Chicago School – had taken this argument further and proposed that social disorganisation causes a weakening of social control making crime and deviance more *possible*. Other control theorists nevertheless attached more importance to psychological factors in their analysis of deviance and conformity (Nye, 1958; Matza, 1964; Reckless, 1967). Later control theories are based on the fundamental assumption that criminal acts take place when an individual has weakened or broken bonds with society (Hirschi, 1969).

In an attempt to remedy identified defects in control theory, different writers have sought to integrate control theory with other perspectives. First, a model expanding and synthesising strain, social learning and control theories begins with the assumption that individuals have different early socialisation experiences and that these lead to variable degrees of commitment to – and integration into – the conventional social order (Elliot, Ageton and Canter, 1979). Second, an integration of control theory with a labelling/conflict perspective – from the victimised actor tradition – seeks to show how 'primary' deviants become 'secondary' deviants. This it is argued is an outcome of the selective targeting of the most disadvantaged groups in society – by the criminal justice system – acting in the interests of powerful groups (Box, 1981, 1987). Third, a further highly influential approach builds upon and integrates elements of control, labelling, anomie and subcultural theory and proposes that criminal subcultures provide emotional support for those who have been stigmatised and rejected by conventional society (Braithwaite, 1989).

Gottfredson and Hirschi (1990) subsequently sought to produce a 'general theory of crime' that combines rational actor notions of crime with a predestined actor model (control) theory of criminality. In accordance with the rational actor tradition, crime is defined as acts of force or fraud undertaken in pursuit of self-interest, but it is the predestined actor notion of – or lack of – social control that provides the answer as to exactly who will make the choice to offend when appropriate circumstances arise.

More recent developments in the social control theory tradition have been power control theory which has sought to combine social class and control theories in order to explain the effects of familial control on gender differences in criminality (Hagan, Gillis and Simpson, 1985, 1987, 1990; Hagan, 1989); control balance theories that define deviancy as simply any activity which the majority find unacceptable and/or disapprove of and occurs when a person has either a surplus or deficit of control in relation to others (Tittle, 1995, 1997, 1999, 2000); and differential coercion theory which seeks to extend our existing understanding of the coercion-crime relationship (Colvin, 2000).

Chapter 16 concludes the fourth part of the book with a consideration of 'left realism' – a perspective that had originated as a direct response to two closely related factors. First, a reaction among some key radical criminologists on the political left to the perceived idealism of critical criminology and its inherent apology for criminals and criminal behaviour and second, the rise of the populist conservatives and their 'realist' approach to dealing with crime. Thus, 'left realists' came to acknowledge that crime is a real problem that seriously impinges on the quality of life of many poor people and must therefore be addressed. From this perspective – a comprehensive solution to the crime problem – a 'balance of intervention' – is proposed (Young, 1994). On the one hand, crime must be tackled and criminals must take responsibility for their actions; on the other hand, the social conditions that encourage crime must also be tackled.

Left realism is not really an integrated theory of crime but rather an approach that recognises that there is something to be said for most theories of crime and for most forms of crime prevention with the distinct suggestion that insights can be incorporated from each of the three models of crime and criminal behaviour introduced in this book. It is a strategy that has been very influential with the 'New' Labour Government elected in the UK in 1997 which was demonstrated by the oft-quoted remark of Prime Minister Tony Blair first made while previously the Shadow Home Secretary, 'tough on crime, tough on the causes of crime'.

The chapter includes a case study that considers the issue of social exclusion, criminality and the 'underclass' from different theoretical standpoints introduced in the book. First, the behavioural perspective – normally associated with the populist or neoconservatives – argues that state welfare erodes individual responsibility by giving people incentives not to work and provide for themselves and their family. Moreover, it is observed that those 'controls' that stop individuals and communities from behaving badly – such as stable family backgrounds and in particular positive male role models – have ceased to exist for many members of this identified 'underclass' (Murray, 1990, 1994). Second, structural explanations – normally associated with sociological variants of the predestined actor model, critical criminologists and left idealists – observe the collapse of the manufacturing industry, traditional working class employment and the subsequent retreat of welfare provision in modernist societies as providing the structural preconditions for the creation of a socially excluded class (Dahrendorf, 1985; Campbell, 1993; Jordan, 1996; Crowther, 1998). Third, a process model – which has a resonance with left realism – suggests that we identify and address the structural preconditions for the emergence of a socially excluded underclass while at the same time considering and responding to the behavioural subcultural strategies developed by those finding themselves located in that socio-economic position (Hopkins Burke, 1999a).

Part Five considers the implications for explaining crime and criminal behaviour posed by the fragmentation of the modernity that had provided the socio-economic context for the theories we encounter in the first four parts of this book. The outcome of that fragmentation has been a new socio-economic context that has been termed the postmodern condition by some social scientists (Lyotard, 1984; Baudrillard, 1988; Bauman, 1989, 1991, 1993) where there is recognition of the complexity of contemporary society and the moral ambiguities and uncertainties that are inherent within it, and where it is proposed that there are a range of different discourses that can be legitimate and hence right for different people, at different times, in different contexts.

Chapter 17 considers the morally ambiguous nature of crime and criminal behaviour in the postmodern condition. It is observed that the essential problem for the development of legislation and legitimate explanations of criminality in this fragmented social formation and era of moral uncertainty is the difficulty of making any objective claims for truth, goodness and morality. The only well-developed attempt to rethink the central issues and themes of criminology in terms of postmodern theories is the constitutive criminology originally developed by Henry and Milovanovic (1996, 1999, 2000, 2001) and in which two main theoretical inputs can be identified: the post-Freudian Jacques Lacan and chaos theory. Henry and Milovanovic (1996) define crime as the power to deny others and they argue that conventional crime control strategies actually encourage criminality. In contrast, they seek the development of 'replacement discourses' which encourage positive social constructions and challenge the omnipresence of power (Henry and Milovanovic, 1996). The chapter concludes with a consideration of anarchist criminology which unlike most modernist intellectual orientations, does not seek to incorporate reasoned or reasonable critiques of law and legal authority but, in contrast, argues that progressive social change requires the pursuit of the 'unreasonable' and the 'unthinkable' (Ferrell, 1998). Anarchist criminologists thus launch aggressive and 'unreasonable' critiques against a law and legal authority which they observe undermines human community and constrains human diversity (Mazor, 1978; Ferrell, 1996, 1998).

Chapter 18 considers cultural criminology and the schizophrenia of crime. The former seeks to explain crime and criminal behaviour and its control in terms of culture and it is argued that the various agencies and institutions of crime control are cultural products which can only be understood in terms of the phenomenological meanings they carry (Presdee, 2004). Cultural criminology thus uses everyday existences, life histories, music, dance and performance in order to discover how and why it is that certain cultural forms become criminalised (O'Malley and Mugford, 1994; Ferrell and Sanders, 1995; Ferrell, 1999), while Katz (1988) writes about the 'seductions of crime' in which disorder becomes in itself a 'delight' to be sought after and savoured and argues that the causes of crime are constructed by the offenders themselves in ways which are compellingly seductive. Presdee (2000) develops this sense of the inter-relationship between pleasure and pain with his notion of 'crime as carnival' where he argues that the latter is a site where the pleasures of playing at the boundaries of illegality are temporarily legitimated at the time of carnival.

Hopkins Burke (2007) uses the term 'the schizophrenia of crime' to refer to the apparently contradictory contemporary duality of attitude to criminal behaviour where there is both a widespread public demand for a rigorous intervention against criminality, while at the same time, criminality is seen to be widespread to the virtual point of universality with most people having committed criminal offences at some stage in their life. It is observed that in a world where crime has become 'normal and non pathological' (Garland, 1996) the boundaries between criminals and non criminals – and legal and illegal activities – have become increasingly difficult to disentangle (Young, 1999, 2001) while, at the same time, the classic crime control strategies of modernity have become increasingly more problematic not least with the increasing globalisation of deviance. The chapter thus concludes with a discussion of the globalisation of deviant youth subcultures in the guise of a significant fast growing club culture (Carrington and Wilson, 2002) which has clear identifiable roots in the notions of the postmodern condition, the carnival of crime and beyond.

Chapter 19 considers further the relationship between crime and the increasing globalisation of crime in the context of what has come to be termed 'the risk society' (Beck, 1992). The chapter commences by considering new modes of governance which in criminology is a concept that has been used to signify changes in the control of crime. It is observed that for most of the twentieth century crime control was dominated by the 'treatment model' prescribed by the predestined actor model of crime and criminal behaviour and which was closely aligned to benevolent state which was obliged to intervene in the lives of offenders and seek to diagnose and cure their criminal behaviour. It was thus the apparent failure of that interventionist modernist project epitomised by chronically high crime rates and the seeming inability of the criminal justice system to do anything about it that was to lead to a rediscovery of the rational actor model and an increased emphasis on preventive responses (Crawford, 1997; Garland, 2001). Feeley and Simon (1994) propose these changes to be part of a paradigm shift in the criminal process from the 'old penology' to a 'new penology' which is concerned with developing techniques for the identification, classification and management of groups and categorising them in accordance with the levels of risk they pose to society. Some consider these trends to be indicative of a broader transition in the structural formation from an industrial society towards a risk society (Beck, 1992) and Ericson and Haggerty (1997) observe that in this context we are witnessing a transformation of legal forms and policing strategies characterised by surveillance.

The chapter further considers the issue of the globalisation of crime and criminality and it is observed that dealing in illicit drugs, illegal trafficking in weapons and human beings, money laundering, corruption, violent crimes, including terrorism, and war crimes are characteristic of such developments (Braithwaite, 1979; UNDP, 1999; Bequai, 2002; Eduardo, 2002). The growing influence of global organised crime is estimated to gross $1.5 trillion a year and has provided a significant rival to multinational corporations as an economic power (UNDP, 1999). Findlay (2000) explains the global explosion in criminality in terms of the market conditions that he observes to be the outcome of the internationalisation of capital, the generalisation of consumerism and the unification of economies that are in a state of imbalance. He proposes that power and domination are simply criminogenic.

Globalisation has greatly facilitated the growth of international terrorism with the development of international civil aviation having made hijacking possible, television has given terrorists worldwide publicity and modern technology has provided an amazing range of weapons and explosives (Eduardo, 2002). The chapter thus concludes with an extensive discussion of terrorism and state violence and observes that the widespread development of terrorist activities throughout the world during the past decade has signified the end of any positive notion of postmodernism. For such societies could only function effectively if there is a reciprocal acceptance of diverse values from all participant groups.

Chapter 20 concludes the book by presenting the case for radical moral communitarian criminology. For while regular recent terrorist atrocities have ended any legitimate notion of a postmodern society there is no justifiable basis for a return to the unquestioned moral certainty of high modernity. It is the work of Emile Durkheim (1933) and his observations on the moral component of the division of labour in society that provides the theoretical foundations of a 'new' liberalism – or radical moral communitarianism – which provides a legitimate political vision which actively promotes both the rights and responsibilities of both individuals and communities *in the context of an equal division of labour*. It is observed that it this highly significant element that deviates significantly from the orthodox version of communitarianism promoted by Amitai Etzioni (1993, 1995a, 1995b) and which has been embraced and distorted in the UK by New Labour with its enthusiasm for a strong dictatorial central state apparatus with which to enforce its agenda. It is accepted that some may well consider these propositions to be fanciful and idealistic but, at the same time, it is observed that the enormous economic ructions that are seen to be engulfing the planet at the time of writing could well provide the socio-economic context for the development of a radical moral communitarianism.

Suggested further reading

For some contrasting accounts from very different perspectives of pre-modern criminal justice and attempts to explain the causes of crime see Foucault (1977), Hay (1981) and Thompson (1975). Garland (1997) provides something of a pragmatic antidote to those who seek to identify distinct ruptures between pre-modern and modern thinking. For an introduction to the notion of modern society and modernity albeit in the context of his discussion of postmodernity see Harvey (1989). Croall (1998) provides an excellent introduction to the different forms of crime in existence and the extent of criminality with a particular emphasis on business and corporate crime.

Part One

The rational actor model of crime and criminal behaviour

The average citizen hardly needs to be persuaded of the view that crime will be more frequently committed if, other things being equal, crime becomes more profitable compared to other ways of spending one's time. Accordingly, the average citizen thinks it obvious that one major reason why crime has gone up is that people have discovered it is easier to get away with it; by the same token, the average citizen thinks a good way to reduce crime is to make the consequences of crime to the would-be offender more costly (by making penalties swifter, more certain, or more severe), or to make the value of alternatives to crime more attractive (by increasing the availability and pay of legitimate jobs), or both ... These citizens may be surprised to learn that social scientists that study crime are deeply divided over the correctness of such views.

(Wilson, 1975: 117)

The first identifiable tradition of explaining crime and criminal behaviour to emerge in modern society is the rational actor model. It has its origins in a range of philosophical, political, economic and social ideas that were developed and articulated during the seventeenth and eighteenth centuries and which were fundamentally critical of the established order and its religious interpretations of the natural world. Two major sets of ideas provide the intellectual foundations of a major period of social change: social contract theories and utilitarianism.

The essence of social contract theories is the notion that legitimate government is only possible with the voluntary agreement of free human beings who are able to exercise free will. It was the key writers in this tradition – Thomas Hobbes, John Locke and John-Jacques Rousseau – and their criticisms of the exercise of arbitrary powers by monarchs, established churches and aristocratic interests that created the preconditions for the specific attacks on pre-modern legal systems and practices which were later mounted by Jeremy Bentham and Cesare Beccaria and which provided the foundations of the rational actor model of crime and criminal behaviour.

Thomas Hobbes (1588–1678) emphasised that it is the exercise of human free will that is the fundamental basis of a legitimate social contract. Compliance can be enforced by the fear of punishment, but only if entry into the contract and the promise to comply with it has been freely willed, given and subsequently broken. Hobbes held a rather negative view of humanity and proposed a need for social institutions – the origins of the very idea of modern criminal justice systems – to support social contracts and to enforce laws. He claimed that in a 'state of nature' – or without outside intervention in their lives – people would be engaged in a 'war of all against all' and life would tend to be 'nasty, brutish and short'. He thus proposed that people should freely subject themselves to the power of an absolute ruler or institution – a 'Leviathan' – which, as the result of a political-social contract would be legitimately empowered to enforce the contracts that subjects make between themselves (Hobbes, 1968 originally 1651).

John Locke (1632–1704) had a more complex conception of what people are like 'in the state of nature' and argued that there is a natural law that constitutes and protects essential rights of life, liberty and property: key assumptions that, subsequently, were to significantly shape the constitutional arrangements of the USA. Locke proposed that the Christian God has presented all people with common access to the 'fruits of the earth', but at the same time individual property rights can be legitimately created when labour is mixed with the fruits of the earth, for example by cultivating crops or extracting minerals. People nevertheless have a natural duty not to accumulate more land or goods than they can use and if this natural law is observed then a rough equality can be achieved in the distribution of natural resources. Unfortunately, this natural potential towards egalitarianism had been compromised by the development of a money economy that has made it possible for people to obtain control over more goods and land than they can use as individuals.

Locke saw the transition from a state of nature to the development of a political society as a response to desires, conflict and ethical uncertainty brought about by the growth of the use of money and the material inequalities that consequently arose. The expansion of political institutions is thus necessary to create a social contract to alleviate the problems of inequality generated by this distortion of natural law. For Locke, social contracts develop through three stages. First, people must agree unanimously to come together as a community, and to pool their natural powers, so as to act together to secure and uphold the natural rights of each other. Second, the members of this community must agree, by a majority vote, to set up legislative and other institutions. Third, the owners of property must agree, either personally or through political representatives, to whatever taxes that are imposed on them.

Locke disagreed with Hobbes' view that people should surrender themselves to the absolute rule of a Leviathan and argued that people gain their natural rights to life and liberty from the Christian God and hold them effectively in trust. These rights are not therefore theirs to transfer to the arbitrary power of another. Furthermore, he argued that government is established to protect rights to property and not to undermine them. It cannot therefore take or redistribute property without consent. It is not the task of human legislation to replace natural law and rights but to give them the precision, clarity and impartial enforceability that are unattainable in the state of nature.

Although, Locke had a relatively optimistic view of human potential in the state of nature, he nevertheless observed the inevitable potential for conflict and corruption that occurs with the increasing complexity of human endeavour and the 'invention' of money. If natural rights are to be preserved, what is required is the consensual development of institutions to clarify, codify and maintain these rights to life, liberty and property. In short, these institutions should constrain all equally in the interests of social harmony (Locke, 1970 originally 1686).

Jean-Jacques Rousseau (1712–1778) was a severe critic of some of the major aspects of the emerging modern world arguing that the spread of scientific and literary activity was morally corrupting. He emphasised that human beings had evolved from an animal-like state of nature in which isolated, somewhat stupid individuals lived peacefully as 'noble savages'. Rousseau (1964 originally 1762) originally claimed that humans were naturally free and equal, animated by the principles of self-preservation and pity. However, as humans came together into groups and societies, engaging in communal activities that gave rise to rules and regulations, the 'natural man' evolved into a competitive and selfish 'social man', capable of rational calculation and of intentionally inflicting harm on others. Rousseau thus had a pessimistic view of social change and was unconvinced that the human species was progressing. Civilisation was not a boon to humanity; it was 'unnatural' and would always be accompanied by costs that outweighed the benefits.

With his later work, Rousseau (1978 originally 1775) appeared a little more optimistic about the future of humanity. He still asserted that at the beginning of history people were admirable, fundamentally equal, free individuals and that moral corruption and injustice arose as people came to develop more complex forms of society and become dependent on one another, thus risking exploitation and disappointment. He was however now prepared to propose political solutions to the moral corruption of society, arguing the necessity of establishing human laws that consider all individuals equally and give each a free vote on the enactment of legislation.

Rousseau developed the concept of the *general will*, observing that in addition to individual self-interest, citizens have a collective interest in the well-being of the community. Indeed, he traced the foundations of the law and political society to this idea of the 'general will' – a citizen body, acting as a whole, and freely choosing to adopt laws that will apply equally to all citizens.

Rousseau's work presented a radical democratic challenge to the French monarchical *ancien regime* proposing that it was the 'citizen body' – not kings – that were 'sovereign' and government should represent their interests. It was only in this way that individuals could freely vote for, and obey, the law as an expression of the common good, without contradicting their own interests and needs.

Rousseau considered that he had resolved the dilemma of human selfishness and collective interests posed by Hobbes. Moreover, he had done this without denying the potential existence of a positive and active form of civic freedom, based on self-sacrifice for a legitimate political community.

Social contract theories provide an overwhelming critique of pre-modern forms of government and are highly relevant to the development of the rational actor model of crime and criminal behaviour. First, there is the claim that human beings once lived in a state of 'innocence', 'grace' or 'nature'. Second, there is the recognition that the emergence of humanity from its primitive state involved the application of *reason* – an appreciation of the meaning and consequences of actions – by responsible individuals. Third, the human 'will' is recognised as a psychological reality, a faculty of the individual that regulates and controls behaviour, and is generally free. Fourth, society has a 'right' to inflict punishment although this right has been transferred to the political state, and a system of punishments for forbidden acts, or a 'code of criminal law'.

Thus, human beings are viewed as 'rational actors', freely choosing to enter into contracts with others to perform interpersonal or civic duties. Laws can legitimately be used to ensure compliance if they have been properly approved by citizens who are party to the social contract.

A further major intellectual contribution to the development of the rational actor model was the philosophical tradition termed *utilitarianism*. Essentially this assesses the rightness of acts, policies, decisions and choices by their tendency to promote the 'happiness' of those affected by them. The two most closely associated adherents and developers of the approach were the political philosophers Jeremy Bentham and John Stuart Mill.

Jeremy Bentham (1748–1832) proposed that the actions of human beings are acceptable if they promote happiness, and they are unacceptable if they produce the opposite of happiness. This is the basis of morality. His most famous axiom is the call for society to produce 'the greatest happiness of the greatest number'. 'Happiness' is understood to be pleasure and unhappiness is pain, or the absence of pleasure. The moral principle arising from this perspective is that if individuals use their reason to pursue their own pleasure then a state of positive social equilibrium will naturally emerge.

For Bentham, pleasures and pains were to be assessed, or 'weighed', on the basis of their intensity, duration and proximity. Moreover, such a calculus was considered to be person-neutral – that is, capable of being applied to the different pleasures of different people. The extent of the pleasure – or the total number of people experiencing it – was also a part of the calculation of the rightness of the outcome of an act. The overall aim was to provide a calculation whereby the net balance of pleasure over pain could be determined as a measure of the rightness of an act or policy.

John Stuart Mill (1806–1873) generally accepted the position of Bentham including his emphasis on hedonism as the basic human trait that governs and motivates the actions of every individual. Mill nevertheless wanted to distinguish qualities – as well as quantities – of pleasures and this posed problems. For it is unclear whether a distinction between qualities of pleasures – whether one can be considered more worthwhile than another – can be sustained or measured. Mill emphasised, first, that pure self-interest was an inadequate basis for utilitarianism, and suggested that we should take as the real criterion of good, the social consequences of the act. Second, he proposed that some pleasures rank higher than others, with those of the intellect superior to those of the senses. Importantly, both social factors and the quality of the act were seen as important in seeking an explanation for human behaviour.

Mill has proved to be a formidable and influential philosophical force but it is Bentham who has had the greatest impact on the development of the rational actor model of crime and criminal behaviour. He essentially provided two central additions to social contract theory. First, there is his notion that the principal control over the unfettered exercise of free will is that of fear; especially the fear of pain. Second, there is the axiom that punishment is the main way of creating fear in order to influence the will and thus control behaviour.

2. Classical criminology

Classical criminology emerged at a time when the naturalistic approach of the social contract theorists we encountered above was challenging the previously dominant spiritualist approach to explaining crime and criminal behaviour and it was Cesare Beccaria in Italy and Jeremy Bentham in Britain writing in the late eighteenth century who established the essential components of the rational actor model.

The Classical theorists

Cesare Beccaria (1738–1794) was an Italian mathematician and the author of *Dei delitti e delle pene (On Crimes and Punishment)* (1963, originally 1767), a highly influential book which was translated into 22 languages and had an enormous impact on European and US legal thought. In common with many of his contemporary intellectuals – and inspired by social contract theories – Beccaria was strongly opposed to the many inconsistencies that existed in government and public affairs, and his major text was essentially the first attempt at presenting a systematic, consistent and logical penal system.

Beccaria considered that criminals owe a 'debt' to society and proposed that punishments should be fixed strictly in proportion to the seriousness of the crime. Torture was considered a useless method of criminal investigation, as well as being barbaric. Moreover, capital punishment was considered to be unnecessary with a life sentence of hard labour preferable, both as a punishment and deterrent. The use of imprisonment should thus be greatly extended, the conditions of prisons improved with better physical care provided and inmates should be segregated on the basis of gender, age and degree of criminality.

Beccaria was a very strong supporter of 'social contract' theory with its emphasis on the notion that individuals can only be legitimately bound to society if they have given their consent to the societal arrangements. It is nevertheless the law that provides the necessary conditions for the social contract and punishment exists only to defend the liberties of individuals against those who would interfere with them. Beccaria's theory of criminal behaviour is based on the concepts of free will and hedonism where it is proposed that all human behaviour is essentially purposive and based on the pleasure-pain principle. Beccaria argues that punishment should reflect that principle and thus fixed sanctions for all offences must be written into the law and not be open to the interpretation, or the discretion, of judges. The law must apply equally to all citizens while the sole function of the court is to determine guilt. No mitigation of guilt should be considered and all that are guilty of a particular offence should suffer the same prescribed penalty. This extremely influential essay can be summarised in the following thirteen propositions:

1. In order to escape social chaos, each member of society must sacrifice part of their liberty to the sovereignty of the nation-state.
2. To prevent individuals from infringing the liberty of others by breaking the law, it is necessary to introduce punishments for such breaches.
3. 'The despotic spirit' – or the tendency to offend – is in everyone.
4. Punishments should be decided by the legislature not by the courts.
5. Judges should only impose punishment established by the law in order to preserve consistency and the certainty of punishment.
6. The seriousness of the crime should be judged not by the intentions of the offender but by the harm that it does to society.
7. Punishment must be administered in proportion to the crime that has been committed and should be set on a scale – or a tariff – with the most severe penalties corresponding to offences which caused the most harm to society. The most serious crimes are considered to be those that threaten the stability of society.
8. Punishment which follows promptly after a crime is committed will be more just and effective.
9. Punishment has to be certain to be effective.
10. Laws and punishments have to be well publicised so that people are well aware of them.
11. Punishment is imposed for the purpose of deterrence and therefore capital punishment is unnecessary and should not be used.
12. The prevention of crime is better than punishment.
13. Activities which are not expressly prohibited by law therefore not illegal and thus permissible.

It is important to recognise that Beccaria's ideas have had a profound effect on the establishment of the modern criminal law and, while they may not be expressed in quite the same way, it is easy to detect resonances of his views in any popular discussion on crime. The doctrine of free will is built into many legal codes and has strongly influenced popular conceptions of justice.

Jeremy Bentham was a leading disciple of Beccaria. As a philosopher – as we saw above – he is classed as a utilitarian, or a *hedonistic utilitarian*, due to his emphasis on the human pursuit of pleasure. He was very much influenced by the philosophical materialism of John Locke which had denied the existence of innate ideas and traditional, established religious notions of original sin.

He consequently ascribed criminal behaviour to incorrect upbringing or socialisation rather than innate propensities to offend. For Bentham, criminals were not incorrigible monsters but 'forward children', 'persons of unsound mind', who lacked the self-discipline to control their passions according to the dictates of reason.

Bentham's ideas are very similar to those of Beccaria and his most famous principle – 'the greatest happiness for the greatest number' – is the fundamental axiom of all utilitarian philosophy. People are rational creatures who will seek pleasure while trying to avoid pain. Thus, punishment must outweigh any pleasure derived from criminal behaviour, but the law must not be as harsh and severe as to reduce the greatest happiness. Moreover, the law should not be used to regulate morality but only to control acts harmful to society which reduce the happiness of the majority. He agreed with Beccaria about capital punishment, that it was barbaric and unnecessary, but disagreed about torture, allowing that on occasion it might be 'necessary' and thus have utility. This is a significant point worth reflecting on. If the intention is to get someone – anyone – to admit to having committed a criminal act then the use of torture will be useful but if the purpose is to ensure that you have found the right offender then it is of no use. This seems to be the point being made by Beccaria. If, on the other hand, you wish to obtain urgently some *important* information from someone who you have good reason to believe is withholding this – as for example, in the case of a planned terrorist atrocity – then the rationale for torture is rather different. This seems to be the utilitarian point being made by Bentham. Moreover, we might note that although Bentham believed in the doctrine of free will, there is a strong hint in his work that suggests criminality might be learned behaviour.

Bentham spent a considerable amount of time and energy designing a prison, an institution to reflect and operationalise his ideas on criminal justice. Prisons were not much used as a form of punishment in pre-modern times, being reserved for holding people awaiting trial, transportation or some other punishment. They were usually privately administered, chronically short of money, undisciplined and insanitary places.

In 1791 Bentham published his design for a new model prison called a Panoptican. The physical structure of this edifice was a circular tiered honeycomb of cells, ranged round a central inspection tower from which each could be seen by the gaolers. He proposed that the constant surveillance would make chains and other restraints superfluous. The prisoners would work sixteen hours a day in their cells and the profits of their labour would go to the owner of the Panoptican. Bentham described the prison as a 'mill for grinding rogues honest' and it was to be placed near the centre of the city so that it would be a visible reminder to all of the 'fruits of crime'. Furthermore, said Bentham, such an institution should act as a model for schools, asylums, workhouses, factories and hospitals that could all be run on the 'inspection principle' to ensure internal regulation, discipline and efficiency.

Underpinning all of these institutions of social control was a shared regime and common view of discipline and regimentation as mechanisms for changing the behaviour of the inmates. The rigorous regime proposed as the basis of these institutions was itself part of a more general discipline imposed on the working class in the factories and mills:

> [The prison] took its place within a structure of institutions so interrelated in function, so similar in design, discipline and language of command that together the sheer massiveness of their presence in the Victorian landscape inhibited further challenge to their logic.
>
> It was no accident that the penitentiaries, asylums, workhouses, monitorial schools, night refuges and reformatories looked alike or that their charges marched to the same disciplinary cadence. Since they made up a complementary and independent structure of control, it was essential that their diets and deprivations be calibrated in an ascending scale, school-workhouse-asylum-prison, with the pain of the last serving to undergird the pain of the first.
>
> Nor was it accidental that these state institutions so closely resembled the factory ... the creators of the new factory discipline drew inspiration from the same discourse in authority as the makers of the prison: nonconformist asceticism, faith in human improvability through discipline, and the liberal theory of the state.
>
> (Ignatieff, 1978: 214–15)

The Panoptican, in its strict interpretation, was never built in England but two American prisons were built based on such a model but these institutions did not prove to be a success in terms of the original intentions of the builders and they had to be taken down and rebuilt. A variation on the theme, London's Millbank Prison, built in 1812, was also poorly conceived, built and administered, and was eventually turned into a holding prison rather than a penitentiary. Bentham's proposal also called for the provision of industrial and religious training and pre-release schemes, and suggested the segregation and classification of prisoners in order to avoid 'criminal contamination'.

Michel Foucault (1977) and Michael Ignatieff (1978) have both traced the development of the prison as a concept and as a physical institution observing that it was one of many 'carceral' institutions developed around the time in order to rationalise and discipline human activity along the lines of early modern thought. Foucault provides the following extract from rules drawn up for the House of Young Prisoners in Paris:

> At the first drum-roll, the prisoners must rise and dress in silence, as the supervisor opens the cell doors. At the second drum-roll, they must be dressed and make their bed. At the third, they must line and proceed to the chapel for Morning Prayer. There is a five-minute interval between each drum-roll....
>
> (Foucault, 1977: 6)

These imposing new penal institutions soon competed for domination of the new urban skylines with the great palaces, cathedrals and churches which had long provided the symbols of the concerns of an earlier age. While the original Panoptican idea was not widely implemented, a variation on the theme developed and built from the early part of the nineteenth century still forms a substantial part of the prison estate in many countries. After a number of aborted experimental institutions had failed, a new model prison was built in North London, inspired by the Quaker prison reformer John Howard. Pentonville prison provided a template for over fifty similar prisons in Britain and for many others throughout the world.

While his writings focused on reform of the penal system, Bentham was also concerned to see crime prevented rather than punished, and to this end made suggestions that alcoholism should be combated and that those with no means of sustenance should be cared for by the state.

The limitations of Classicism

The philosophy of the Classical theorists was reflected in the *Declaration of the Rights of Man* in 1789 and the *French Penal Code* of 1791, the body of criminal law introduced in the aftermath of the French Revolution. The authors of these documents had themselves been inspired by the writings of the major Enlightenment philosophers, notably Rousseau. It was nevertheless attempts such as these to put these ideas of the Classical School into practice that exposed the inherent problems of its philosophy of criminal justice. The Classical theorists had deliberately and completely ignored differences between individuals. First offenders and recidivists were treated exactly alike and solely on the basis of the particular act that had been committed. Children, the 'feeble-minded' and the insane were all treated as if they were fully rational and competent.

This appearance in court of people who were unable to comprehend the proceedings against them did little to legitimise the new French post-revolutionary criminal code and consequently, this was revised in 1810, and again in 1819, to allow judges some latitude in deciding sentences. It was thus in this way that the strict, formal, philosophical elegance of the Classical model was to be breached. It was to become increasingly recognised that people are not equally responsible for their actions and as a result a whole range of experts gradually came to be invited into the courts to pass opinion on the degree of reason that could be expected of the accused. Judges were now able to vary sentences in accordance with the degree of individual culpability argued by these expert witnesses and it was this theoretical compromise that was to lead to the emergence of a modified criminological perspective that came to be termed the *neo-Classical School*.

The neo-Classical compromise

Neo-Classicists such as Rossi (1787-1848), Garraud (1849–1930) and Joly (1839–1925) modified the rigorous doctrines of pure Classical theory by revising the doctrine of free will. In this modified form of the rational actor model, ordinary sane adults were still considered fully responsible for their actions and all equally capable of either criminal or non-criminal behaviour. It was nevertheless now recognised that children – and in some circumstances, the elderly – were less capable of exercising free choice and were thus less responsible for their actions. Moreover, the insane and 'feeble-minded' might be even less responsible. We can thus observe here the beginnings of the recognition that various innate predisposing factors may actually determine human behaviour which is a significant perception that was to provide the fundamental theoretical foundation of the predestined actor model that is the focus of the second part of this book.

It was these revisions to the penal code that admitted into the courts for the first time, non-legal 'experts' including doctors, psychiatrists and, later, social workers. They were gradually introduced into the criminal justice system in order to identify the impact of individual biological, psychological and social differences with the purpose of deciding the extent to which offenders should be held responsible for their actions. The outcome of this encroachment was that sentences became more individualised, dependent on the perceived degree of responsibility of the offender and on mitigating circumstances.

It was now recognised that a particular punishment would have a differential effect on different people and as a result punishment came increasingly to be expressed in terms of punishment appropriate to rehabilitation. Though, as those eminent proponents of the more radical variant of the victimised actor model, Taylor, Walton and Young (1973: 10) were later to observe:

> There was however, no radical departure from the free will model of man involved in the earlier Classical premises. The criminal had to be punished in an environment conducive to his making the correct moral decisions. Choice was (and still is) seen to be a characteristic of the individual actor – but there is now recognition that certain structures are more conducive to free choice than others.

The neo-Classicists thus retained the central rational choice actor model notion of free will, but with the modification that certain circumstances may be less conducive to the unfettered exercise of free choice than others. Indeed, it can be convincingly argued that most modern criminal justice systems are founded on this somewhat awkward theoretical compromise between the rational actor model of criminal behaviour and the predestined actor model that we will encounter in the second part of the book. This debate between free will and determinism is perhaps one of the most enduring in the human and social sciences.

In summary, it is possible to identify the following central attributes of the Classical and neo-Classical Schools that provide the central foundations of the rational actor model:

1. There is a fundamental focus on the criminal law and the simple adoption of a legal definition of crime. This leaves the perspective crucially exposed

to the criticism that legal definitions of crime are social constructions which change over time and with geographical location.

2. There is the central concept that the punishment should fit the crime rather than the criminal. This leaves it exposed to the criticism that it fails to appreciate the impact of individual differences in terms of culpability and prospects for rehabilitation.

3. There is the doctrine of free will according to which all people are free to choose their actions and this notion is often allied to the hedonistic utilitarian philosophy that all people will seek to optimise pleasure but avoid pain. From this perspective, it is assumed that there is nothing 'different' or 'special' about a criminal that differentiates them from other people. It is a doctrine thus exposed to the criticism that it fails to appreciate that the exercise of free will may be constrained by biological, psychological or social circumstances.

4. There is the use of non-scientific 'armchair' methodology based on anecdote and imaginary illustrations in place of empirical research and it was thus an administrative and legal criminology, concerned more with the uniformity of laws and punishment rather than really trying to explain criminal behaviour.

The rational actor model was to go out of fashion as an explanatory model of crime and criminal behaviour at the end of the nineteenth century and was to be replaced predominantly by the new orthodoxy of the predestined actor model in its various guises. It nevertheless continued to inform criminal justice systems throughout the world.

The enduring influence of Classicism

The enduring influence of the Classical school is evident in the legal doctrine that emphasises conscious intent or choice, for example, the notion of *mens rea* or the guilty mind. In sentencing principles, for example, the idea of culpability or responsibility; and in the structure of punishment, for example, the progression of penalties according to the seriousness of the offence or what is more commonly known as the 'sentencing tariff'.

Philosophically, the ideas of the Classical school are reflected in the contemporary 'just deserts' approach to sentencing. This involves four basic principles. First, only a person found guilty by a court of law can be punished for a crime. Second, anyone found to be guilty of a crime must be punished. Third, punishment *must not be more* than a degree commensurate to – or proportional to – the nature or gravity of the offence and culpability of the offender. Fourth, punishment *must not be less* than a degree commensurate to – or proportional to – the nature or gravity of the offence and culpability of the criminal (von Hirsch, 1976).

Such principles have clear foundations in the theoretical tradition established by Beccaria and Bentham. There is an emphasis on notions of free will and rationality, as well as proportionality and equality, with an emphasis on criminal behaviour that focuses on the offence not the offender, in accordance with the pleasure-pain principle, and to ensure that justice is served by equal punishment for the same crime. 'Just deserts' philosophy eschews individual discretion and rehabilitation as legitimate aims of the justice system. Justice must be both done and seen to be done and is an approach which is closely linked with the traditional Classical school notion of 'due process'.

Packer (1968) observes that the whole contemporary criminal justice system is founded on a balance between the competing value systems of *due process* and *crime control*. The former maintains that it is the purpose of the criminal justice system to prove the guilt of a defendant beyond a reasonable doubt in a public trial as a condition for the imposition of a sentence. It is based on an idealised form of the rule of law where the state has a duty to seek out and punish the guilty but must prove the guilt of the accused (King, 1981). Central to this idea is the presumption of innocence until guilt is proved.

A due process model requires and enforces rules governing the powers of the police and the admissibility and utility of evidence. There is recognition of the power of the state in the application of the criminal law but there is a requirement for checks and balances to be in place to protect the interests of suspects and defendants. The use of informal or discretionary powers is seen to be contrary to this tradition.

A strict due process system acknowledges that some guilty people will go free and unpunished but this is considered acceptable in order to prevent wrongful conviction and punishment while the arbitrary or excessive use of state power is seen to be a worse evil. Problematically, a high acquittal rate gives the impression that the criminal justice agencies are performing inadequately and the outcome could be a failure to deter others from indulging in criminal behaviour.

A crime control model, in contrast, prioritises efficiency and getting results with the emphasis on catching, convicting and punishing the offender. There is almost an inherent 'presumption of guilt' (King, 1981) and less respect for legal controls that exist to protect the individual defendant. These are seen as practical obstacles that need to be overcome in order to get on with the control of crime and punishment. If occasionally some innocent individuals are sacrificed to the ultimate aim of crime control then that is acceptable. Such errors should nevertheless be kept to a minimum and agents of the law should ensure through their professionalism that they apprehend the guilty and allow the innocent to go free.

In the crime control model the interests of victims and society are given priority over those of the accused and the justification for this stance is that swifter processing makes the system appear more efficient and that it is this that will deter greater criminality. In other words, if you offend you are likely to be caught and punished and it is therefore not worth becoming involved in criminality. The primary aim of crime control is thus to punish the guilty and deter criminals as a means of reducing crime and creating a safer society.

It was observed above that the rational actor model had gone out of fashion as an explanatory model of criminal behaviour with the rise of the predestined actor tradition at the end of the nineteenth century. It was nevertheless to return very much to favour with the rise of the 'new' political right – or populist conservatism – during the last quarter of the twentieth century. It was however a revival where the purist Classical tradition of 'due process' promoted in particular by Beccaria was to be very much superseded by the interests of the proponents of the crime control model of criminal justice.

Suggested further reading

The best exposition and introduction of the core ideas of the Classical school and the fundamental concepts of the rational actor model is still provided by the most accessible original account by Beccaria (1963). King (1981), Packer (1968) and von Hirsch (1976) provide essential demonstrations of the enduring and revitalised influence of the Classical School and rational actor thinking on the contemporary legal system and jurisprudence.

3. Populist conservative criminology

The rational actor model ceased to be a popular means of explaining crime and criminal behaviour for most of a twentieth century dominated by the pre-destined actor model of crime and criminal behaviour that we will encounter in the following second part of this book. It was nevertheless to return very much to favour with the emergence of the 'new political right' – populist or neoconservatives[1] – during the 1970s and 1980s.

The rise of the political new right

During the 1970s conservative intellectuals in both the USA and the UK mounted a vigorous moral campaign against various forms of 'deviance' and in 1979 Margaret Thatcher was to make crime a major and successful election issue for the first time in post-war Britain. Her general concern was to re-establish what she considered to be 'Victorian values' and to this end targeted the supposed debilitating permissive society of the 1960s and its perceived legitimisation in 'soft' social science. For this political 'new right', the economic, technological and managerial achievements of the modern world should be safeguarded and expanded, but at the same time there should be a comprehensive assault mounted on its cultural and ethical components. Indeed, it was perceived to be this modernist culture with its emphasis on subjective values and individual self expression that was crucially undermining the motivational requirements of an efficient economy and rational state administration. In short, individuals were seen as increasingly unwilling to achieve and even less prepared to obey (Habermas, 1989). Populist conservatives thus sought a revival in past tradition, in the values of the state, schools, family, and implicitly, in the unquestioned acceptance of authority.

In criminology this perceived liberal indulgence was epitomised by the other two explanatory models discussed in this book. First, there is the enduring dominant orthodoxy of the twentieth century – the 'predestined actor' model – with its focus on discovering the causes of crime and, having once located them offering treatment and rehabilitation rather than punishment. Second, there are the more radical variants of the 'victimised actor' model with their critique of an unfair and unequal society and their policy assumptions of understanding, forgiveness and non-intervention that were gaining increasing popularity with the idealistic but at that time still electorally viable political left.

Moreover, right-wing intellectuals observed that it was not merely that left wing and liberal thought had simply failed to *see* problems inherent in 'soft' approaches to crime, discipline, education, and so forth. This so-called progressive theorising had itself provided a basis for the *acceleration* of the permissive syndromes in question. High levels of criminality and disorder were therefore blamed not only on the weakening sources of social authority, the family, schools, religion and other key institutions, but even more so on the corrosive influence of the surrounding culture with its emphasis on rights rather than obligations and the celebration of self expression to the point of self indulgence instead of promoting self control and self constraint (Tzannetakis, 2001). The new right argued that in such a spiralling, de-moralising culture, it was clear that crime and violence would inevitably increase. Thus, real problems and sociological apologies alike had to be confronted, and an attempt made to reassert the virtue and necessity of authority, order and discipline (Scruton, 1980, 1985).

In social policy in general (Morgan, 1978) and in the area of crime and deviance in particular (Dale, 1984), an assault was mounted on liberal and radical left trends. Empirical justification for this attack on the self-styled forces of socially progressive intervention came from the publication of an influential paper by Robert Martinson (1974) which purported to show that rehabilitation programmes in prison simply 'do not work' and thus the whole rationale for the existence of a welfare-oriented probation service, in particular, was called into question. Consequently, we were to see the enthusiastic reintroduction of the idea of retributive punishment – serious crimes are simply evil, after all – and arguments for the protection of society from danger. From this populist conservative perspective, punishment is essentially about devising penalties to fit the crime and ensuring that they are carried out, thus reinforcing social values.

In short, this concern to treat the miscreant as an offender against social morality and not as a candidate for reform can be seen as a contemporary form of the rational actor model – but one with a distinctly retributive edge.

James Q. Wilson and 'right realism'

James Q. Wilson first published *Thinking About Crime* in the USA in 1975 which was some years after the election of a Republican president, Richard M. Nixon, with a mandate to 'get tough' on offenders by strengthening the criminal justice system, installing a tough Attorney General and giving the police more powers. The foremost proponent of right realism, Wilson discusses crime from the standpoint of new right philosophy and politics but nevertheless – certainly in his earlier work – rejects much of the traditional conservative approach to crime control as well as that offered by the political left. Later Republican President Ronald Reagan (1981-89) appointed Professor Wilson to be his special adviser on crime and a harder more retributive element can be detected in this later variant of 'right realism'.

Wilson accepts liberal arguments that increased police patrols, longer prison sentences for offenders and changes of personnel in central government posts could have little effect on crime levels. He was nevertheless scornful of those arguments that denied the existence of crime as a real problem. On the contrary – and this is a central contention of right realism – crime is quite simply an evil that requires a concerted and rigorous response.

Thus, Wilson and George Kelling (1982, 1989) argue that the police are most effectively used not to reduce crime but maintain social order. Kelling (1999) subsequently summed up this position, thus: 'you ignore minor offences at great cost' and 'disorder not only creates fear but ... is a precursor to serious crime'. Conversely, the maintenance of order allows community control mechanisms to flourish and encourages law-abiding behaviour. It is therefore the constructive function of the police to provide an environment in which criminality is unable to flourish. The focus should be less on simple breaches of the criminal law but more on regulating street life and incivilities – such as prostitution, begging, gang fights, drunkenness and disorderly conduct – which in themselves may not be that harmful, but which in aggregate are detrimental to the community and therefore need to be controlled (see Hopkins Burke, 1998b, 2004b; Karmen, 2004).

Wilson is suspicious of those proponents of the predestined actor model of criminal behaviour who call for treatment not punishment. Not that right realists abandon all such explanations of criminal behaviour. Wilson and Richard Herrnstein (1985) have thus devised a bio-social explanation including biological and psychological components to explain why some individuals are more prone to criminality. They propose that the inclination of people to commit crimes varies in accordance with the extent they have internalised a commitment to self control. This is all dependent on the level of investment a society has made in promoting self-control, through its socialisation mechanisms, as well as on the, not necessarily unchangeable, genetic and biological characteristics of individuals. This perspective attacks certain types of family – particularly the single-parent variant – for ineffective socialisation, while at the same time the ability to learn is affected by the constitution of the individual and the effectiveness of the input from family, peers, school and work. The conclusion is that it is biology that establishes the population that are at risk of becoming criminal, whilst it is socialisation, or its failure, that helps to decide whether this will be realised. This socio-biological argument is discussed in more detail in Chapter 13.

Wilson thus uses the predestined model factors we will encounter in the second part of the book – such as biology and conditioning – in his initial analysis of criminal behaviour but because this does not offer pragmatic policy suggestions does not pursue this line of reasoning. For, it is not – or at least not *yet* – possible to alter the biology of an individual in the way which would be necessary were his assumptions to be correct. Moreover, it would not be easy to rapidly improve the socialisation offered by families, or quickly rid society of single-parent families, although both in Britain and the USA this has been a policy objective of the populist conservatives, and one which has been tackled to some extent as part of the welfare agenda. Thus, the aim is to reduce criminality through pragmatic intervention and by making the benefits of leading an honest and considerate existence more attractive to those who would otherwise take the wrong direction in life.

Right realism emphasises the findings of victim surveys that show that the burden of crime falls disproportionately on the poor, the disadvantaged and those least able to defend their selves. They however deny absolutely the notion – proposed by the radical variants of the victimised actor model that we will encounter in the third part of this book – of a struggle of an oppressed class against an unjust society. Right realists stress the point that both perpetrators and victims of predatory crime tend to come from the same community.

Wilson (1975: 21) observes the individualistic nature of offending and adopts a utilitarian explanation for human action:

If the supply and value of legitimate opportunities (i.e. jobs) was declining at the very time that the cost of illegitimate opportunities (i.e. fines and jail terms) was also declining, a rational teenager might well have concluded that it made more sense to steal cars than to wash them.

The implication of this utilitarian argument would seem to support both increasing the benefits of 'non-crime' (by providing more and better jobs) and increasing the costs of crime (by the use of imprisonment). Wilson nevertheless concentrates on the latter half of the equation. In short, populist conservative crime control strategies – as we shall see below – tend to place far more emphasis on the stick than the carrot.

Right realists also differ from previous conservatives in the way they believe that punishment should be applied. Recognising that the USA imprisons a very large proportion of its population for longer periods than other countries who have far lower crime rates, Wilson stresses the certainty of punishment more than its severity. Thus, it is proposed that one of the reasons increased police activity does not itself reduce crime is that the value of an arrest depends on whether a conviction results and on the subsequent actions of the criminal justice system. Wilson observes that, once the chances of being caught, convicted and imprisoned are accounted for, a given robbery is four times more likely to result in imprisonment in the UK than in California and six times more likely in Japan.

It is argued that offenders do not decide to transgress on the basis of the length of sentence, but first of all on the probability of the sentence being applied and thus 'consequences gradually lose their ability to control behaviour in proportion to how delayed or improbable they are' (Wilson and Herrnstein, 1985: 49). Felson (1998: 9) – another criminologist widely associated with right realism and whose work is discussed in more detail in the following chapter – provides a neat and often quoted analogy:

What happens when you touch a hot stove: you receive a quick, certain, but minor pain. After being burned once, you will not touch a hot stove again. Now think of an imaginary hot stove that burns you only once every 500 times you touch it, with the burn not hurting until five months later. Psychological research and common sense alike tell us that the imaginary stove will not be as effective in punishing us as the real stove.

The solution, according to Wilson, involves catching more offenders – by increasing police effectiveness – and improving the consistency of the criminal justice system. A poor police/public relationship in the very areas where crime is most prevalent compromises the effectiveness of the police. Poor relations lead to a blockage of information and co-operation flow from the public to the police together with hostility, mistrust and even protection for offenders by their victims.

The US criminal justice system – although it passes longer prison sentences – convicts fewer of those it tries for predatory crime than do other countries. Wilson and Herrnstein (1985) consequently argue *against* long sentences, observing that undue severity might persuade the prisoner that he has been treated inequitably, and prompt him to exact revenge by further offending. Moreover, the longer the available sentence, the less likely judges are to impose them, thus the certainty principle is flouted further.

On the issue of the deterrent value of sentencing, Wilson and Herrnstein adopt a traditional rational actor model stance. They lament the irrationality of the criminal justice system, which they argue, reflects the view of judges that prison does not act as a deterrent and, in support of their argument, they cite the low proportion of recidivists who are sent to prison. They thus call for fixed-term sentences for offences, regardless of the age of the offender and other attributes, such as the scope for rehabilitation.

It is observed that differential sentences for the same crime reflect a wish to change the behaviour of the offender. If the aim is to deter others, the sentence must be fixed and certain. Moreover, differential sentencing causes a moral dilemma. Those who are perceived less likely to reoffend receive shorter sentences, which in practice means that young, poor black offenders from unstable family backgrounds are sent to prison for longer than older, white middle-class offenders from stable family backgrounds who have committed the same offence.

Right realists nevertheless argue for the use of imprisonment as an incapacitator. Recidivists, they note, commit most known crime and, therefore, if offenders in particular categories are certain to be locked up, even for a short period, then the rate of offending in those categories must fall. However, this loss of liberty need not necessarily take the form of conventional imprisonment. Incarceration overnight, or at weekends only, would have the same effect, just so long as it is certain to be applied and rigorously imposed. This neo-Classical approach to deterrence, sentencing and incapacitation are neatly encapsulated in the conclusion of *Thinking About Crime* thus:

Wicked people exist. Nothing avails except to keep them apart from innocent people. And many people, neither wicked nor innocent, but watchful, dissembling, and calculating of their opportunities, ponder our reaction to wickedness as a cue to what they might profitably do.

(Wilson, 1975: 235-6)

Right realism and social control

Right realism has emphasised the necessity of upholding public order and public morality in the fight against crime. In contrast to liberal demands for the legalisation – or at least decriminalisation – of apparently non problematic street offences such as prostitution and recreational drug-taking, right realists propose that these should be more rigorously controlled. Moreover, in the fight against drugs they see little point in increased interventions against the dealers and the addicts who are beyond help, but propose a concerted intervention against small-time users identified as attacking the fibre of the community (Wilson, 1985).

Wilson and Kelling (1989) propose that the police should intervene against behaviour that in itself is not strictly criminal, advocating action against empty properties, rowdy children and groups of young people on the streets, litter, noise harassment, intimidation and other incivilities which they consider to be indicators of social decline. Such action is justified because it provides the welcoming preconditions for high crime rates. Thus, right realists make no demands for changes in the structural conditions in society but rather for the behaviour of individuals to be controlled because it is these incivilities that interfere most with the enjoyment of life for many – particularly poor – people.

It is argued that interventions designed to restore order – and to control crime – should be focused on those areas at high risk of becoming, or just beginning to turn into, high crime rate areas. Those areas where crime is already endemic should not have resources devoted to them. The emphasis should be on areas where behaviour can be changed and there is still a possibility of restoring order. In the more problematic localities there should be a more comprehensive assault on criminality itself. The police should detect and prosecute offenders with a particularly vigorous response for repeat offenders advocated. It was this latter proposal that led to the 'three strikes and you're out' policy in the US whereby following a third offence – however trivial – an offender would receive a very long prison sentence. In 2002 a total of 6,700 people were serving 25 years to life under 'third strike' legislation. More than 3,350 of them were non-violent offenders, with 350 serving 25 years for petty theft. Forty-four per cent were black and 26 per cent Latino (Campbell, 2002).

Right realism can be considered very much a contemporary revival of the rational actor model of crime and criminal behaviour. It is the central proposition of their thesis that crime is the result of individual choice and can be prevented or contained by pragmatic means which make the choice of criminal behaviour less likely; reducing the opportunity; increasing the chances of detection; increasing perceptions of detection partly through rigorous policing, especially of disorder; and most importantly, definite punishment; the threat of severe, certain and swiftly imposed punishment. Imprisonment is seen to be particularly effective in neutralising or incapacitating offenders and frightening others into adopting law abiding lifestyles.

Right realism and its propositions on incapacitation have been extremely influential in the USA as the following figures suggest: the prison population in the USA exceeded two million people for the first time in 2002; it is the biggest prison population in the world, and has the highest number of inmates as a proportion of its population. A report from the US Justice Department has estimated that 12 per cent of black men in their 20s and early 30s were in prison, but only 1.6 per cent of white males in the same age group. The overall increase – almost double the number in 1990 – has been credited to the 'get tough sentencing policy that has led to longer sentences for drug offenders and other criminals'. One in every 142 people living in the USA was in prison. (BBC News, 2003a). Penal incapacitation is not restricted to the USA: on 30 January 2004 the prison population in England and Wales stood at 73,688 an increase of 2,729 over the previous year and 25,000 over the previous ten years (Prison Reform Trust, 2004).

An enthusiasm for retribution in US criminal justice policy in recent years is epitomised by the reintroduction during the past 30 years of capital punishment. This policy-shift is in itself contrary to the early rational actor tradition established by Beccaria who considered such punishment to be uncivilised and inappropriate to a modern criminal justice system; nevertheless, the parallel predilection for responding to children as rational adults is undoubtedly vintage rational actor thinking. An Amnesty International report published in September 2002 observed that in the previous decade two-thirds of known executions of under-age offenders – or children – had been conducted in the USA. It was observed that, of the 190 member states of the United Nations, only the USA and Somalia had failed to ratify the Convention on the Rights of the Child which bans such executions (BBC News, 2002a).

A critique of right realism

The right realist perspective on explaining crime and criminal behaviour and the policy implications that arise from these can be summarised in the following ten propositions:

1. Crime is not determined by social conditions but by tendencies within individuals.
2. Searching for the causes of crime is a distraction and a waste of time.
3. Individuals choose to commit crime. Thus fewer will choose criminal behaviour if governments create more effective and appropriate punishments.
4. Improving social conditions will not reduce crime rates.

5. Rehabilitation is an ineffective way of responding to offenders.
6. Crime is a problem and 'the fear of crime' has a rational basis.
7. We need to be realistic about what can be achieved in the war against crime and acknowledge the limitations of the current knowledge-base.
8. We should not object to the achievement of marginal gains but discount utopian grand solutions.
9. Crime is a violation of the law because the latter is an embodiment of the morals of society which in turn reflect absolute religious notions of right and wrong. Crime is an offense against morality.
10. Crime may be prevented by the repeated assertion of strong social authority founded on traditional morality.

There are nevertheless a number of significant criticisms that can be made of right realist criminology. First, the perspective prioritises a total focus on street criminality and the maintenance of social order to the virtual exclusion of the white collar and corporate crimes that are so costly to the economy (Conklin, 1977; Croall, 1992, 2001; see Chapter 1). There is an apparent assumption that most people only experience and have an awareness of street crimes, although it is important here to recognise that it is these very offences that are the most visible and impact most directly on individuals. Mis-sold pension plans, the sale of under-tested and unlicensed pharmaceuticals to distant developing nations and the dumping of polluted effluent into rivers are all examples of crimes that have a considerable aggregate impact on society,[2] but it is being robbed in the street and returning home to find it burgled and trashed that impacts most immediately on individuals and engenders the greatest 'fear of crime' (Kershaw et al., 2000). It is that reality that has been recognised by criminological realists and politicians of both right and left persuasions. Indeed, it could be argued that it is that very recognition that makes them 'realists'.

Second, in searching for explanations of criminal behaviour right realists ignore all social economic and structural variables – such as poverty and other measures of social exclusion – and focus their attention solely on the behavioural conditioning and inadequate socialisation of the individual. Nonetheless, the proposed explanatory link between incivilities, disorder and criminality has been difficult to empirically substantiate. In the UK, for example, Matthews (1992) found that various social indicators such as levels of poverty and the general level of available public services available were far more significant than incivilities to the process of urban decline.

Third, the areas with the worst social problems and highest levels of criminality are not deemed worth saving (Wilson and Kelling, 1989). When their inhabitants transgress against the law, they are targeted with vigorous crime control strategies and given harsh punishments; when they do not they are left unprotected in high crime areas, further marginalised and disadvantaged. Moreover, right realists consider that it is these people themselves who are responsible for their own predicament because they have failed to both correctly socialise their children and use the appropriate controlling mechanism – that is, invariably, corporal punishment – to condition behaviour.

Fourth, the policing of public order offences such as begging and vagrancy allows intervention on grounds of often dubious legality and is simply unfair because it is particular disadvantaged groups such as homeless beggars that are targeted (Hopkins Burke, 1998c, 2000).

Fifth, it has been argued that crime clear-up rates are the only true indicators of police performance and moving towards a social order model reduces the possibility of accurately measuring their efficiency (Kinsey, Lea and Young, 1986). More worryingly, if the police are allowed a more flexible role to control a whole range of incivilities, it becomes very difficult to ensure their accountability and professionalism (see Smith, 2004).

Sixth, this right realist rediscovery and adaptation of the rational actor model, with its central proposition that criminal behaviour is simply a rational choice made by those brought up in a world bereft of correct moral values, has led to the targeting and demonisation of whole groups of people – such as New Age travellers, drug users and groups of young 'marauding' males – it is argued, by an intrusive and punitive 'law and order' state response with all these aforementioned categories of humanity deemed worthy of severe and vindictive punishment (see Hogg and Brown, 1998).

An early right realist and contemporary of the early James Q. Wilson who indeed had proposed a similar set of ideas – Ernest Van Den Haag (1975) – was most implicit about the wider political significance of right realism and thus completely dismissive of the above six objections. A rigorous supporter and defender of the inevitability and indeed necessity of capitalism, Van Den Haag observes that the basic rationale of the system is the creation of 'winners' and 'losers'. If we accept that analysis, we then also have to accept that the winners must be allowed to enjoy the fruits of their enterprise and risk-taking without these rewards being illegally taken away by the losers. In short, for capitalism to continue as a (successful) form of economic production, those responsible for the creation/accumulation of wealth – and in its widest sense that includes all those significantly employed core members of a polarised society (Jordan, 1996) with ready access to the opportunities and rewards offered by a meritocratic society – must be protected from the activities of criminals and a socially excluded 'underclass', which is discussed in more detail later in this book and which threatens our well-being material and otherwise. Moreover, it is members of this core group in society that provides electoral majorities for maintaining these policies.

Suggested further reading

For a discussion of the failings of the then dominant predestined actor model and the – at the time – quite influential victimised actor model as a precursor to the rise of the popular conservatism and right realism see Dale (1984), Morgan (1978) and Scruton (1980). Wilson (1985), Wilson and Herrnstein (1985) and Wilson and Kelling (1982, 1989) are essential key texts associated with right realism. Good critiques of different aspects of the populist conservative criminological agenda are offered by: Kinsey, Lea and Young (1986), Matthews and Young (eds) (1992) and Hogg and Brown (1998).

Notes

1 I have used the term populist conservatives here as that is more descriptive of the electorally successful new right politics of the Thatcher (and less so Major) Governments during the period 1979–97. The term neo-conservatives has gained considerable recognition in the USA but in both constituencies electoral success was based on widespread popularity with groups not previously considered conservative. Thus, the terms 'populist' and 'neo' conservative can be here used interchangeably.
2 Of course corporate crimes do impact very much on individuals. For a discussion of the victims of mis-sold pensions see Spalek (2004) while this is an extremely important contemporary issue in view of the continuing and deepening economic crisis that has enveloped the world since the 'credit crunch' seemingly instigated by highly dubious banking policies and strategies.

4. Contemporary rational actor theories

Interest in the rational actor model of crime and criminal behaviour was revived both in the UK and the USA during the rise of the political new right – or populist conservatives – during the 1970s and 1980s. The second decade of that time period was to see the influential emergence of the 'nothing works' (Martinson, 1974) agenda at the British Home Office which seriously questioned the effectiveness of rehabilitation – proposed by the then dominant paradigmatic orthodoxy of the predestined actor model of crime and criminal behaviour – as a crime control strategy. This chapter considers three groups of contemporary rational choice theories that have come very much to prominence with that revival: (i) contemporary deterrence theories (ii) rational choice theories and (iii) routine activities theory.

Contemporary deterrence theories

At the core of contemporary deterrence theories are the principles of certainty, severity and celerity of punishment, proportionality, specific and general deterrence (Zimring and Hawkins, 1973; Gibbs, 1975; Wright, 1993). The deterrence doctrine proposes that in order to deter, punishment must be both swift and certain, the notion of celerity concerns the swiftness with which sanctions are applied after the commission of a crime, while certainty refers to the probability of apprehension and punishment. If the punishment is severe, certain and swift, people will, it is proposed, rationally calculate that there is more to be lost than there is to be gained from committing crime. Moreover, it is argued that certainty is more effective in deterring crime than severity of punishment. The more severe the available punishment, the less likely it is to be applied. On the other hand, the less certain the punishment, the more severe it will need to be to deter crime (Akers, 1997).

Deterrence is said to operate in one of two ways. First, in the case of 'general deterrence' the punishment of offenders by the state is seen to serve as an example to the general population who will be frightened into non-participation in criminal behaviour (Zimring and Hawkins, 1973). Second, in the case of 'specific deterrence', it is proposed that the apprehended and punished offender will refrain from repeat offending because they realise that they are certain to be caught and severely punished. The ultimate form of individual deterrence is considered to be the death penalty, although research evidence on the deterrent effectiveness of capital punishment has remained ambiguous.

Among the earliest studies of deterrence were examinations of murder rates in various geographical localities before and after the abolition of capital punishment. Ehrlich (1975) used a subsequently much criticised econometric version of rational choice theory to propose that every execution carried out in the USA deterred seven or eight other murders. His findings were nevertheless in contrast to those of studies previously conducted in that country and which had found that the availability of the death penalty in state legislation had no effect on the murder rate (Sellin, 1959; Bedau, 1964). Moreover, following the abolition of capital punishment for murder in England and Wales in 1965, research suggested no identifiable impact on the rate of homicide (Beyleveld, 1979; Morris and Blom Cooper, 1979).

It has often been suggested that murder – particularly in a domestic context – is a crime where the offender is highly unlikely to make a rational choice before committing the act. If that is the case, the potential consequences will be irrelevant and deterrence is unlikely. In this context Walker (1985) argues that capital punishment is no more effective a deterrent than a sentence of life imprisonment.[1]

We have seen that proponents of the rational actor model assume that potential offenders calculate the rewards and risks associated with crime and research supports the suppositions of the right realists – discussed in the previous chapter – which suggest that the likelihood of detection is a more important part of that calculus than the potential level of punishment (Beyleveld, 1978, 1979). Certainly the chances of being caught in the commission of an offence by a passing police patrol have been found to be extremely low in the UK (Bottomley and Coleman, 1981) while the detection rates for burglary, for example, vary between 9 per cent and 46 per cent depending on the locality. The extent to which people believe that they might be caught is therefore probably a more important variable. Gill and Matthews (1994, see also Matthews, 1996) conducted a study of convicted bank robbers and interestingly found that none of their research subjects had even considered the possibility that they would be caught before setting out on their criminal enterprises even though all had previous criminal convictions.

Even if punishment does deter effectively, a number of ethical objections can be raised to the use of sentences for this purpose. Beyleveld (1978) suggests that the types of punishment needed to deter a potential offender will vary substantially between different people, different crimes and different circumstances. Therefore, in order to deter crime, it might well be necessary to set sentences at a level totally out of all proportion to the seriousness of the offence (Wright, 1982). This is rather at odds with the central rational choice actor model concept that the punishment should fit the crime. Moreover, when a particular offender has not been deterred then he or she must receive the threatened punishment. The consequences of such punishment may be simply counterproductive (Wright, 1982).

Martin and Webster (1971) have argued that conviction and punishment may simply push an individual into a situation where he or she has little to lose from further offending. The opportunity to live by legitimate means may be reduced and the individual with previous convictions is pushed towards further illegitimate activity regardless of the consequences. This is an argument similar to that proposed by the labelling theorists working in the victimised actor model tradition that we will encounter in the third part of this book. Central to that perspective is the notion that being caught and stigmatised may lead to an offender becoming committed to further offending behaviour.

Wright (1982) suggests that the possibility of severe punishment encourages offenders to try harder to avoid detection and conviction and this can lead to violent escapes and to time being wasted by not guilty pleas in court that have no realistic chance of success. Moreover, child sex offenders who could benefit from treatment might be deterred from seeking it.

The use of punishment as a deterrent is based on the core rational actor model assumption that people choose to commit crime. Imposing deterrent sentences on those individuals who have little or no control over their impulses – or who break the law unwittingly – would appear to be morally indefensible although it can be legitimately argued that deterrence remains a valid option in the case of intentional calculating offenders (Walker, 1980) although there remains considerable debate as to the existence of such individuals. Critics of contemporary deterrence theories focus on this limited conception of human action on which this perspective is founded and argue the need to develop a considerably more sophisticated theory of human behaviour which explores the external and internal constraints on why people do or do not engage in criminal activity (see Piliavin *et al.*, 1986; Klepper and Nagin, 1989; Grasmick and Bursik, 1990; Matravers, 1999). For it is proposed that such a theory must recognise the significant number of motivational states – rational and irrational – that can result in the commission of a crime. It is clearly evident that many petty criminals are incapable of accurately balancing the costs and benefits of crime before committing an offence and many young men get involved in street fights with others like themselves without any thought for the consequences of their actions. Keane, Maxim and Teevan (1993) argue that such people do not in any sense act in a rational manner because their low self control – or overwhelming demand for immediate gratification – quite simply excludes the possibility of calculating behaviour. If this supposition is correct then punishment in these circumstances is almost never likely to deter, no matter how certain, severe or quickly it is implemented.

The high recidivism rate further challenges the usefulness of contemporary deterrence theories. Reoffending rates for young people leaving custody are particularly high. Thus, for males aged 14–17, the rate of reconviction within two years of discharge from prison in 1998 was 84 per cent. Of those who were reconvicted, 36 per cent were again sentenced to custody for their first subsequent conviction (Nacro, 2003). Moreover, it would be incorrect to assume that no offences are committed by offenders while they are in custody. Assaults, both on other inmates and staff are common. During 2000–1 there were 6,388 recorded assaults across the Prison Service, and by this measure the worst five performing establishments were all young offender institutions (Prison Reform Trust, 2002). Similarly, the widespread use of drug testing within the 'secure estate' suggests that detention does not prevent access to illegal substances. Furthermore, the potential of incapacitation to reduce overall levels of crime is extremely limited. The Home Office (2001) has estimated that it would take a 15 per cent increase in the level of custody to effect a 1 per cent reduction in offending.

Rational choice theory

The considerable revival of interest in the rational actor model of crime and criminal behaviour has been clearly demonstrated by the considerable government enthusiasm for situational crime prevention measures which were energetically promoted as governments essentially lost patience with the failure of criminologists to solve the apparently never-ending explosion in the crime figures. Certainly, spending in the UK since the late 1970s was to become devoted more to finding and evaluating pragmatic solutions to particular offences rather than to developing criminological theory. At the same time most professional crime prevention practitioners that were to enjoy government patronage came to accept the central nostrum that crime is an outcome of the opportunity to offend. Regardless of offender motivation, removal of that opportunity, it is argued, will reduce the incidence of crime. Consequently whole ranges of measures were to be introduced in order to remove or reduce the opportunity to offend.

Situational crime prevention methods aim to reduce a wide range of crimes. Target hardening in its simplest form can amount to no more than closing a door after leaving a room or building unoccupied. At a more sophisticated level, it can take the form of toughened glass 'anti-bandit' screens, specially designed security fencing and armoured safes. If a target can be removed completely instead of simply being protected even more impressive results are possible. Such strategies include the centralisation of cash transactions and the issue of tokens for use with gas and electricity meters. Where valuable targets cannot actually be removed, an alternative strategy lies in reducing their attraction to thieves. For example, credit and debit cards were much more attractive to thieves before the UK Government sponsored Chip and PIN system[2] in the use of guarantee cards. Some straightforward situational crime prevention initiatives can be remarkably cost-effective and successful, for example, Painter and Farrington (1999, 2001) demonstrated that a scheme to introduce street lamping both substantially reduced criminality and paid for itself within a year.

Proponents of the effectiveness of formal surveillance argue that potential offenders will be deterred by the threat of being seen, and propose that agencies – such as the police and private security companies – that engage in observation activities will deter offenders (Mayhew, 1984). On the other hand, the concept of natural surveillance is founded on the notion that by observing their environment as they go about their everyday business, people can provide themselves with some protection against crime. Moreover, commercial organisations can seek to protect themselves by the careful positioning of their employees.

These pragmatic strategies for reducing the opportunity to offend are theoretically informed by more recent variants of the rational actor model. In his memoir of a criminal career in the early twentieth century USA, Jim Phelan (1940: 178) observed that:

> The robber is a tradesman who, from economics or other motivation, chooses a trade with greater rewards and dangers than navvying. All men in dangerous jobs ... will readily understand the thief-convict ... Yet no one speaks of hereditary test-piloting. No semi-neurotics rush into print about the movie-stuntman's characteristic nose or jaw.
>
> (Phelan, 1940: 178)

From this perspective, involvement in crime – well at least property crime – is the outcome of a career decision, it is a chosen way of life, a way of making your living, one of a range of options. There is no need for complex cultural and structural biological arguments – such as we will encounter in the second part of this book – to explain it. The key premises of rational choice theory can thus be summarised in the following five propositions.

1 Most criminals are normal-reasoning people. The mode of reasoning used by all adults – with perhaps the exception of the mentally ill, is rational.

2 Rationality is a mode of thinking in which individuals are able to accurately distinguish *means* and *ends*. What they want and the ways that are available to them for obtaining those ends. For example: ends – possessing a certain amount of money for a certain amount of work; and means – paid employment, buying a lottery ticket, stealing it.

3 For each of the different means *available* to them, rational actors are also able to calculate the likely costs (things they do not want to happen) and benefits (how many or how much of their ends they can achieve) of following a course of action.

4 If benefits outweigh costs, *do it*. If costs outweigh benefits, *don't do it*.

5 So, according to rational choice theory, it is not necessary to consider prior causes, antecedents and structures. All that matters are the rational judgements and calculations facing a given person, with their particular set of ends and preferences, in a given situation.

Earlier and less sophisticated variants of rational choice theory had tended to follow the summarised key propositions above and compare the decision-making process adopted by offenders with straightforward economic choice. Thus, Gary Becker (1968) proposed that the potential offender calculates the legitimate opportunities of earning income available, the amount of reward they offer, the amounts offered by illegal methods, the probability of arrest, and the likely punishment. The person chooses the activity – legal or illegal – that offers the best return. Suggested preventive strategies – such as those proposed by the right realists encountered in the previous chapter – would involve reform of the law and its administration in order to alter the equation and make crime appear less attractive.

It is perhaps not surprising that these early theories have been accused of implying too high a degree of rationality by comparing criminal choices too closely with marketplace decisions, and, at the same, failing to explain expressive non-economically motivated criminal activity such as vandalism (Trasler, 1986). In the first instance, it can nevertheless be argued that the amateurish criminal who makes wildly inaccurate estimates is no less a rational being than a consumer who runs up huge debts (Sullivan, 1973) and, in the second case, Clarke (1987) observes that while the motivation behind some expressive crimes may be pathological, their planning and execution may be highly rational. Expressive crimes such as vandalism are actually well explained by the related concept of crime as a function of opportunity and routine activities (Cohen and Felson, 1979). Such offences are usually unplanned and most likely to occur in places where the potential perpetrators are likely to find themselves in the normal course of their lives. A crime such as arson, for example, may have a financial motive, but it is more likely to be committed for expressive reward, to gain the approval of peers, to 'get back at' a target (such as a school) (see Knights, 1998) or simply to alleviate boredom.

A more sophisticated and highly influential variant of rational choice theory has been subsequently developed notably through the work of Clarke and Cornish. From their perspective crime is defined as 'the outcome of the offender's choices or decisions, however hasty or ill-considered these might be' (Clarke, 1987: 118). In other words, offenders invariably act in terms of a *limited* or *bounded* form of rationality. They will not always obtain all the facts needed to make a wise decision and the information available will not necessarily be weighed carefully but it is an approach that avoids the inherent tendency within the predestined actor model to treat criminals as a category of humanity apart from law-abiding citizens. As Paul Ekblom (2001: 264) succinctly observes:

[It is an approach] that does not rely on past improvements in society, treatment regimes for offenders or early interventions in children's socialisation to reduce current criminality; or on the sheer aversive intensity of sanctions anticipated at some remote time in the future to deter or incapacitate present offending. It does not directly aim to change *offenders'* [emphasis in original] propensities or motives for crime at all. It takes these as given and, proceeding from an analysis of the circumstances engendering particular crimes, it introduces specific changes to influence the offender's *decision* or *ability* [emphasis in the original] to commit these crimes at given places and times.

Thus, from the rational choice perspective, crime is simply rational action performed by fairly ordinary people in response to particular pressure, opportunities and situational inducements (Hough, Clarke and Mayhew, 1980; Trasler, 1986). Clarke (1987) is nonetheless not entirely dismissive of the predestined actor model suggesting that most of the factors seen as predisposing an individual to commit crime can be interpreted in terms of their influence on offender cognitive decision-making. This suggestion that individuals respond to situations in different ways because they bring with them a different history of psychological conditioning and this is examined further in the final section of Chapter 6.

Bennett (1986) observes that an offence rarely happens because of a single decision to act. A series of decisions will probably be made, starting with the original choice to offend, somewhere at some time, and ending with the final decision to act against a particular target. Therefore, both dispositional *and* situational factors are involved. Others note the operation of a conscious selection process at the scene of burglaries (Brantingham and Brantingham, 1984; Mayhew, 1984), while situational factors would clearly be expected to exert more influence nearer the criminal event taking place (Bennett, 1986; Heal and Laycock, 1986). If these suppositions are correct, there are clear implications for crime prevention practitioners in deciding when and where to intervene in the sequence of decisions that the potential offender has to make.

Early variants of rational choice theory had considered the issue of offender motivation to be irrelevant, although later variations propose that offenders choose to act in a certain way because these actions appear to them rational in the circumstances in which they find themselves and in terms of their knowledge base and cognitive thought processes (Clarke, 1987, 1999). Sutton (1995, 1998) proposes that it is the existence of stolen goods markets that provides the crucial motivation for theft. Indeed, much of the motivation for seeking out those markets is invariably provided by the large increase in drug addiction in recent years. Bennett, Holloway and Williams (2001), for example, detected a considerable correlation between heroin and crack cocaine use and offending behaviour, finding that those who used both drugs regularly spent on average £290 a week or £15,000 a year, were rarely employed and invariably needed to steal to fund their habit.

Sutton (2004) observes that while there is no doubt that supply to stolen goods markets is provided by those with a motivation to steal, the demand for the goods is – in at least many cases – stimulated by respectable people prepared to ask few questions in the right circumstances. He thus notes that many respectable members of society will be only too willing to buy a 42" plasma screen television set if offered for a totally unrealistic price as long as it comes unused in a box. If it has been clearly used and comes with a child's fingerprints clearly visible on the screen they will be far less enthusiastic. The suggestion is that goods apparently stolen from a factory or 'off the back of a lorry' are somehow acceptable to many 'respectable' members of society but when they are clearly the outcome of a household burglary they are far less so.

The offence of handling stolen goods has long been a low priority for a resource-stretched public police service and the criminal justice system. Sutton (2004) suggests that judges and their advisors should consider the social harm stolen goods markets do in stimulating the incidence and prevalence of theft – and the unintended consequences of providing subsidies for the illicit sex and drugs industries – and that they should be considerably less tolerant of the local 'fence' thus substantially reducing criminal opportunity. We might nevertheless speculate whether the eradication of stolen goods markets would substantially reduce drug-addicted motivation or simply displace addicts to other means of obtaining cash such as prostitution – male as well as female – or armed robbery (Hopkins Burke, 2004b).

Routine activities theory

Routine activities theory is, to some extent, a development and subdivision of rational choice theory which proposes that for a personal or property crime to occur, there must be at the same time and place a perpetrator, a victim, and/or an object of property (Felson, 1998). The crime event can take place if there are other persons or circumstances in the locality that encourage it to happen but, on the other hand, the offence can be prevented if the potential victim or another person is present who can take action to deter it.

Cohen and Felson (1979) took these basic elements of time, place, objects, and persons to develop a 'routine activities' of crime events. They are placed into three categories of variables that increase or decrease the likelihood that persons will be victims of 'direct contact' predatory – personal or property – crime. The first variable is the presence in the locality of *motivated offenders* which are perceived to be predominantly young males. Second, there is the necessity of available *suitable targets*, in the form of a person or property. The term target was used in preference to that of victim because the acquisition of property or money was seen to be the focus of the great majority of criminal behaviour. Suitability of the target is characterised by four attributes (VIVA):

- Value calculated from the subjective rational perspective of the offender
- Inertia, the physical aspects of the person or property that impede or disrupt its suitability as a target
- Visibility, which identifies the person or property for attack
- Accessibility which increases the risk of attack.

The third variable is the absence of 'capable guardians' against crime. Thus, the likelihood of a crime taking place increases when there is one or more persons present who are motivated to commit a crime, a suitable target or potential victim that is available, and the absence of formal or informal guardians who could deter the potential offender. In short, 'the risk of criminal victimisation varies dramatically among the circumstances and locations in which people place themselves and their property' (Cohen and Felson, 1979: 595).

Cohen and Felson observe that it is the fundamental changes in daily activities related to work, school, and leisure since World War II that have placed more people in particular places at particular times. This has both increased their accessibility as targets of crime and at the same time keeps them away from home as guardians of their own possessions and property.

In his more recent work, Felson (1998) has come to place less emphasis on the significance of formal guardians – such as the police – because he has reached the conclusion that crime is a private phenomenon largely unaffected by state intervention. He now emphasises the natural crime prevention and deterrence that occurs in the informal control system, the 'quiet and natural method by which people prevent crime in the course of daily life' (Felson, 1998: xii–xiii). Ordinary people, oneself, friends, family, or even strangers are the most likely capable guardians.

Felson (1998) has also subsequently applied routine activities theory to four crime categories other than the property variants:

- exploitative (robbery, rape)
- mutualistic (gambling, prostitution, selling and buying drugs)
- competitive (fighting)
- Individualistic (individual drug use, suicide).

In doing so he has identified a fourth variable that enables a criminal event to take place – the absence of an *intimate handler*, a significant other, for example, a parent or girlfriend – that can impose informal social control on the offender. A potential offender must escape the 'intimate handler' then find a crime target without being under the surveillance of this 'capable guardian'.

Cohen and Felson (1979) relate crime rates to a 'household activity ratio', that is, the percentage of all households that are not husband–wife families or where the wife is employed outside the home. Such households are considered more vulnerable to crime victimisation because their members are away from home more and less able to function as guardians of their property. Moreover, they are more likely to possess more desirable goods to be stolen, while at the same time they are more exposed to personal crime away from home. Controlling for age composition and unemployment, Cohen and Felson found that the changes in household activity were correlated with changes in the rates of all major predatory violent and property crimes.

Cohen, Kluegel and Land (1981) have developed a more formalised version of routine activities theory and renamed it 'opportunity' theory. This considers elements of exposure, proximity, guardianship and target attractiveness as variables that increase the risk of criminal victimisation. But these are not measured directly. These are assumed from variations in age, race, income, household consumption, labour force participation, and residence in different areas of the city obtained from US crime victimisation surveys. Their findings nevertheless support most of their propositions.

Cromwell *et al.* (1995) studied the responses of the formal and informal control systems to the devastation of Hurricane Andrew that occurred in Florida in 1982 and they found that the natural disaster temporarily increased the vulnerability of persons and property as crime targets. For a short time, there was nearly a complete loss of police protection in some of the neighbourhoods and motivated offenders with previous records were attracted to the areas in the aftermath of the storm while at the same time some local people took criminal advantage of the situation. There was however little looting and crime rates actually went down during the time when the community was most vulnerable only to increase again after the initial impact period. Cromwell *et al.* explain these findings as being most likely the result of neighbours watching out for neighbours, citizens guarding their own and other property – sometimes with firearms – citizens' patrols, and other steps taken to aid one another in the absence of government and formal control.

The fact that some people may be motivated to commit crime when targets are made vulnerable by such events as natural disasters raises important questions about the concept of the motivated – or potential – offender that purist versions of the rational actor model are ill-equipped to answer. Quite simply does the concept of motivated offender in routine activities theory refer only to someone who has an inherent predisposition to offend? Or does it include anyone who is enticed by the opportunity for quick gain itself, even though he or she may not have previously existing criminal intentions?

Akers (1997) observes that routine activities theory is simply a way of explaining why people become victims of crime. It fails categorically to explain why it is that some people engage in criminal behaviour and others do not. There is a taken-for-granted assumption that such people exist and that they commit crimes in certain places and at times when the opportunities and potential victims are available. It tells us absolutely nothing about these people and their motivations. It is the predestined actor model discussed in the following second part of this book that offers numerous suggestions.

There have nevertheless been some useful and interesting applications and developments in the use of routine activities theory both in the USA and the UK in recent years which have been helpful in explaining why it is that certain groups are more likely to become victims of crime. Thus, Boudreaux, Lord and Jarvis (2001) review existing research on the topics of child abduction and child homicide and identify and assess potential victim risk factors through a discussion of victim access, vulnerability, and routine activities theory. Freisthler, Midanik and Gruenewald (2004) use the concept to provide a partial explanation for the substantial growth in recorded cases of child abuse in the USA since the early 1970s identifying a close correlation with a parallel growth in substance – in particular alcohol – abuse during the same time period. Pizarro, Corsaro and Yu (2007) consider the journey to murder and show that there are statistically significant differences among homicide types in terms of the length of the journey of victims and suspects to the incident location and in their motives for actually going there. The findings of the researchers suggest that the demographic and lifestyle characteristics of victims and suspects have an impact on their journey to crime and victimisation.

In the UK, Nick Tolson (2007) has used routine activities theory as the basis of his Clergy Lifestyle Theory which he has used to assess the risk of violence to members of the clergy with the practical purpose of improving their safety and security. Since 1996 there have been a total of five vicars murdered and many others seriously injured. Gabe (2001) found that 12 per cent of clergy suffer from physical violence and that 70 per cent suffer from some form of violence and found these figures to be significantly higher than for other professional groups who work in the community. Moreover, while the majority of assaults inflicted on probation officers and GPs – other professional groups with a high rate of victimisation – had occurred in their main place of work, the majority of assaults on members of the clergy were reported to have taken place in their homes, in the street or on local estates rather than in church buildings. At the same time, most GPs and probation officers knew their assailant while almost half the clergy who had experienced an assault said that they did not know their assailant. Thus, an attack could occur at virtually any time or location in their everyday lives while at the same time any stranger they encountered was potentially an assailant. Tolson (2006) found that 48 per cent of the clergy in his sample had suffered at least one violent incident in the preceding twelve months. Tolson (2007) found that there is much similarity in how the clergy live their lives and almost all are on their own at certain points of the day, they travel, visit and, on occasion, pray on their own, which, in certain situations can mean that they are at very high risk of violence should they encounter the 'motivated offender' whoever they might be.

The rational actor reconsidered

The Classical theorists had emphasised the rationally calculating, reasoning human being who could be deterred from choosing to commit criminal behaviour by the threat of fair and proportionate punishment. Moreover, they had proposed that all citizens should be treated equally in terms of a codified and rationalised legal system. In terms of the influential social contract theories of the time – epitomised and institutionalised by the initial aftermath of the French and American Revolutions at the end of the eighteenth century – human beings were (mostly) all seen to be *equal* citizens. In this purist initial version of the rational actor model of crime and criminal behaviour the implicit emphasis was very much on a due process criminal justice model epitomised by such notions as the 'rights of man' and the 'rule of law'.

This purist version was both amended and fell into decline for three closely interlinked reasons. First, it became clear that not all are equally rational calculating human beings: a recognition that was to herald the end of what in practice had been a rather short-lived notion that all human beings are equal. Second, there was an increasing awareness that a rational due process criminal justice intervention was having little effect on the crime statistics, not least because there was a growing group of recidivists who were apparently not deterred by this strategy. Third, the latter discovery neatly coincided with the rise of the predestined actor model – the focus of the following part of this book – and its central supposition that criminals are a separate entity from law-abiding citizens.

Thus, the revised version of the rational actor model – that came to the fore with the rise of the political 'new right' in the last quarter of the twentieth century – *implicitly* accepted the predestined actor notion that there are different categories of human beings while denying the central notion of that model that proposed treatment or rehabilitation in preference to punishment. Criminal motivation or the predisposition of the offender was immaterial. The emphasis was now on deterrence and – if the person failed to heed that warning and was not to be deterred or scared off – punishment. The issue of motivation was of no importance as long as criminal behaviour ceased to occur. Hopkins Burke and Pollock (2004) nevertheless challenge the supposed irrelevance of addressing the issue of offender motivation in their discussion of hate – or bias – crime and they define the perpetrators of such offences to be:

> ... those unaccepting of the heterogeneous nature of the contemporary societies in which they live and primarily characterise social groups according to their visible ethnic, racial or sexual identity rather than their personal attributes. Thus, a key component of hate victimisation is the existence of bias and prejudice based upon 'what' someone is, rather than 'who' they actually are.
>
> (Hopkins Burke and Pollock: 2004: 2)

They acknowledge that the introduction of specific legislation and targeted situational crime prevention measures have had some considerable impact on reducing the incidence of hate crimes and recognise that for many – and this appears to be a widespread and influential discourse – the impact of this contemporary rational actor intervention strategy has brought a satisfactory outcome. The validity of ignoring hate motivation is on the other hand fundamentally questioned:

> An ethnic minority colleague of ours recently summed up this apparent contemporary race-relations orthodoxy by observing that 'if they aren't saying it and they aren't doing it then that's ok'. But is it ok? These dimensions of intervention [legal and situational crime prevention] do not eradicate hatred itself, and the colleague had undoubtedly also seen the look in their eyes which betrayed their real thoughts. It could well be that as an outcome of a change in structural circumstances – for example, the arrival of a group of immigrants or asylum seekers in the locality, the chance meeting of a new friend or colleague with similar latent views, perhaps while on holiday or after the consumption of a few 'social' drinks, or as the outcome of surfing the Internet – that latent

hate crime motivation could well be transformed into something more insidious.

(Hopkins Burke and Pollock, 2004: 18)

Hate crimes do not appear to be at the top of the crime control agenda of populist conservative politicians seeking election but in dealing with offenders in general, and predatory street offenders in particular, they seem to be only too willing to accept the notion proposed by James Q. Wilson that there are simply evil people – or perhaps more accurately a class or underclass of evil people – who need to be rigorously targeted by the agencies of the criminal justice system. Thus, with this revised formulation of the rational actor model there has been an emphasis on a crime control model criminal justice intervention that promotes the detection and punishment of those offenders who cannot be deterred as the main priority. The huge increase in the prison population in both the USA (BBC News, 2003) and the UK (Prison Reform Trust, 2004) during the past twenty years appears to be testimony to the success of this crime prevention strategy.

If the prescriptions of the rational actor model are in any way accurate then the prisons should be clearly full of people who have made (for them) rationally calculating decisions to commit criminal offences. Yet the reality is very different. Statistics suggest that prisons are full of people with (often chronic) mental health problems who seem incapable of making any rational choice. In the most recent large-scale survey of UK prisons, it was found that over one-third of men serving prison sentences had a significant mental health problem (such as anxiety or depression); nearly one in ten had experienced some form of psychosis, while one in four had attempted suicide in prison. Over three-quarters of men on remand and nearly two-thirds of male inmates met the diagnosis of having a personality disorder (Mind, 2006). The suicide rate among male prisoners is six times higher than among men in the general population and in 2003 there were 94 suicides in prisons in England and Wales, 80 of which were men with 19 per cent under 21 years of age. Many aspects of prison life undermine the health and well-being of those in custody, and exacerbate pre-existing mental health problems. As Juliet Lyons (2005) from the Prison Reform Trust observes,

If you had to invent a way to deepen mental health problems and create a health crisis, an overcrowded prison, and particularly the bleak isolation of its segregation unit, would be it.

It is thus clear that prisons are full of prisoners who cannot be considered fully rational calculating actors and thus the limitations of the rational actor model first identified two hundred years ago are still relevant today. In the following second part of this book we will consider the predestined actor model of criminal behaviour which makes alternative suggestions as to how such people should be dealt with.

Suggested further reading

For a comprehensive introduction to the notion of 'deterrence' in contemporary criminal justice and jurisprudence observed from a US perspective, see Gibbs (1975), Zimring and Hawkins (1973), and Piliavin *et al.* (1986). Walker (1980, 1985) and Grasmick and Bursik (1990) provide the equivalent in a UK context. Matravers (ed.) (1999) provides a series of essays on punishment and political theory. For further discussion of contemporary rational choice theory and situational crime prevention, see: Clarke (1980, 1987, 1999), Clarke and Mayhew (1980), Cornish and Clarke (1986) and Mayhew *et al.* (1976). Cohen and Felson (1979) and Felson (1998) are key routine activities theory texts.

Notes

1 There was moratorium on the use of the death penalty in the USA for a period of four years during the 1970s until the case of Gary Gilmore who actively sought death following his conviction for murder and refused all avenues of legal appeal to stay his execution. He was executed on 17 January 1977. It was a case which received world-wide publicity and was immortalised by the British punk rock band 'The Adverts' and their hit record 'Looking through Gary Gilmore's Eyes' having been banned by the BBC for being in bad taste.
2 Banks and retailers replaced magnetic stripe equipment with that based around smartcards which contain an embedded microchip and are authenticated automatically using a PIN. When a customer wishes to pay for goods using this system, the card is placed into a 'PIN pad' terminal (often by the customer themselves) or a modified swipe-card reader, which accesses the chip on the card. Once the card has been verified as authentic, the customer enters a 4-digit PIN, which is checked against the PIN stored on the card. If the two match, the transaction is completed. This technology is nevertheless not without its problems.

Part Two

The predestined actor model of crime and criminal behaviour

The method which we ... have inaugurated is the following. Before we study crime from the point of view of a juristic phenomenon, we must study the causes to which the annual recurrence of crimes in all countries is due. These are natural causes, which I have classified under the three heads of anthropological, telluric and social. Every crime, from the smallest to the most atrocious, is the result of the interaction of these three causes, the anthropological condition of the criminal, the telluric environment in which he is living, and the social environment in which he is born, living and operating. It is a vain beginning to separate the meshes of this net of criminality.

(Ferri, 1968: 71–2, originally 1901)

It was shown in the first part of this book that the rational actor model of crime and criminal behaviour proposes that human beings possess free will which enables them to make rational decisions about what actions they should take whether these are legal or illegal. It is also proposed that as rational calculating human beings they should be held fully accountable for their actions. These ideas – as we have seen – had been highly influential in changing criminal justice policies during the late eighteenth and early nineteenth centuries particularly in France. However, with the publication of the first national crime statistics in that country in 1827 it became clear that these data were astonishingly regular. Furthermore, some places had higher rates than others and these differences remained relatively constant from year to year. Rational actor model proponents had expected random changes in the number of crimes. The regularity of the new crime statistics suggested that rather than being entirely the product of free will, criminal behaviour must be influenced by other factors.

It was also clear that crime rates were increasing rather than decreasing and so was the rate of recidivism or repeat offending. People who had received the prompt proportionate punishment administered by the new French criminal code were committing more offences rather than less which suggested that the rational actor model notion that changes in punishment policies alone could reduce crime was simply wrong.

These recognitions were to be highly influential in the rise of the predestined actor model of crime and criminal behaviour which is a tradition with its origins in a very different view of society and human nature than that proposed by the rational actor model. It emerged during the nineteenth century during a period of rapid industrialisation and the consolidation of capitalism as the dominant mode of production in Europe and – at that time – when there was a major concentration of previously rural-based peasants into the fast expanding large cities, the creation and expansion of the factory system and the introduction of new productive technologies. These changes saw the flow of labour into employment in the industrial sphere and the emergence of a new social class – the working class or the proletariat.

The rise of the urban working class was accompanied by major industrial, social and political conflict. Life was hard and brutal for these people. Child labour was common and there was a thin dividing line between conditions experienced by those working for a living and those condemned to the poorhouse. Living and working conditions were harsh, dirty and crowded. At the same time, the capitalist class was amassing huge fortunes and adopting opulent lifestyles. The contrast in circumstances and opportunities between the two classes was immense.

It was at this time that the working class began to organise itself industrially and politically and although banned by law, workers began to combine into trade unions while there was a growing sympathy for fledgling socialist notions of a 'classless society'. This was all reflected in the proliferation of alternative working-class publications, pamphlets and daily press, and in the formation of socialist parties. It was also a time of new thinking about the nature of human beings and of society in general.

Proponents of the predestined actor model – or positivist school of criminology – rejected the rational actor model emphasis on free will and replaced it with the doctrine of determinism and from this perspective it was argued that criminal behaviour could be explained in terms of factors, either internal or external to the human being, which cause people to act in a way over which they have little or no control. Thus, in some way, it is the destiny of the individual to become a criminal.

There are three basic formulations of the predestined actor model: biological positivism (the focus of Chapter 5), psychological positivism (Chapter 6) and sociological positivism (Chapter 7). All three versions are nevertheless founded on the same fundamental assumptions, and although each is discussed separately, it will become increasingly apparent to the reader that they are not mutually exclusive. Chapter 8 considers how each of these three formulations has explained female criminal behaviour.

Three sets of ideas provide the intellectual foundations of the predestined actor model. First, there is the notion of evolution and science. Before the latter half of the nineteenth century, explanations of the essence of humanity had been fundamentally provided by theology but from that time onwards such questions became increasingly the preserve of science, in particular, biology.

The biggest influence on the development of biology was the work of the great English naturalist Charles Darwin (1809–82) whose major works *The Origin of Species* (1968, originally 1859), *The Descent of Man* (1871) and *Expression of Emotion in Man and Animals* (1872), are widely considered to mark the end of 'pre-scientific' thinking about the causes of human behaviour. In a world dominated by religious stricture and biblical explanation it was simply assumed that human beings are a species distinct from the rest of the animal world with the free will to choose a course of action based on their assessment of the pleasures and pains that various alternatives are likely to provide. It was Darwin's theory of evolution that was to first seriously challenge such views.

According to evolutionary biology, humans are animals subject to the laws of nature like all other animals and it is these rather than free will or choice that must therefore govern human behaviour. The task of scientists interested in criminal behaviour is to isolate and identify those causal forces that determine conduct and, inevitably, the first place they looked for such forces was in the biological constitution of the offender.

The second set of ideas was provided by social evolutionism of which Herbert Spencer (1820–1903) was the major theorist. In the 1850s he had produced a series of essays – especially 'The Development Hypothesis' and 'Progress: It's Law and Cause' that drew from biology the elements of a general evolutionary *Naturphilosophie*. This was to be the basis of his multi-volume *System of Synthetic Philosophy* (1862–96), which first expounded a set of general evolutionary principles that he then applied to biology, psychology, sociology and ethics. In sociology, in particular, Spencer broke new ground in comparative data collection and synthesis.

Spencer was an evolutionist before Darwin. He had always held the view that human characteristics are inherited and it was this aspect of his work that was to be the biggest influence on the development of the predestined actor model of crime and criminal behaviour. Spencer nevertheless went much further than Darwin explaining evolution as the product of the progressive adaptation of the individual character to the 'social state' or society and in this respect his sociology rests on definite psychological foundations. His major contribution to the development of sociology is however his recognition that human beings develop as part of a process of interaction with the social world they inhabit. This significant thesis that environmental factors influence the development of the human being was – as we shall see – to be increasingly important and latterly fundamental to the development of the predestined actor model.

The third set of ideas focused on the positivist method devised by the philosopher and social visionary Auguste Comte (1798–1857) who perhaps is best known for giving a name to the discipline of sociology which he nevertheless outlined rather than practised. The foundation of his thought was his search in chaotic times – exemplified by the major transition from predominantly agrarian to urban societies throughout Western Europe – for principles of cultural and political order that were consistent with this apparently forward march of society. In his later writings, especially the *Discours sur L'esprit Positif* ('Discourse on the Positive Spirit'), the *Systeme de la Politique Positif* ('System of Positive Polity') and the *Catechism of Positive Religion*, Comte provided the design for a new social order. This work provides the theoretical foundations of the social positivism that is the focus of Chapter 7.

For Comte (1976), positivism is the doctrine that the methods of the natural sciences provide the only means of obtaining knowledge of human nature and society. This knowledge has to be constructed out of evidence obtained from the senses – from empirical data – although there is to be a role for theoretical conceptualisation in order to make sense of this data. Thus, from the positivist standpoint, truth can never be attained through abstract speculation or pure intellectual philosophising. On the contrary, the laws that govern all events in the world – for all are caused in regular discoverable ways – are available to the rigorous observer. Having obtained their empirical data, the scientist can then formulate these laws in order to subject them to test and verification.

None of this was new – British empirical philosophers, such as, David Hume, had said as much for two hundred years – but what *was* radical was the application of positivism to the discovery of *social* laws. The implications of this theoretical revolution were colossal, for the application of positivist knowledge could provide the means for the peaceful reconstruction of the social order by the elite of enlightened scientists and intellectuals. It was this aspect of his work that undoubtedly influenced the early biological criminologists discussed in the following chapter.

5. Biological positivism

The foundations of the biological variant of the predestined actor model of crime and criminal behaviour – or biological positivism – can be located primarily in the work of Cesare Lombroso, Enrico Ferri and Raffaele Garofalo. These early and highly influential biological criminologists – or the Italian School as they are usually collectively known – argued that criminology should focus primarily on the scientific study of criminals and criminal behaviour. Both their methodology – and clearly some of their findings – might seem highly simplistic and even laughable by the standards of today but they nevertheless established an enduring scientific tradition which has become increasingly sophisticated over the years and at the time of writing is enjoying something of an explanatory renaissance.

Early biological theories

Cesare Lombroso (1836–1909) was both a psychiatrist at the University of Turin and a physician employed in the Italian penal system. In 1875 he published his most famous work *L'Uomo Delinquente* (*On Criminal Man*) and the primary – and most significant – theme in this early work is that criminals represent a physical type distinct from non-criminals. Said to represent a form of degeneracy apparent in physical characteristics suggestive of earlier forms of evolution, criminals are *atavistic*, throwbacks to earlier forms of evolutionary life. Ears of unusual size, sloping foreheads, excessively long arms, receding chins and twisted noses are indicative signs of criminality. Although essentially a biological positivist, we should nevertheless note that in the later editions of his work, Lombroso came increasingly to pay attention to environmental factors such as climate, poverty, immigration and urbanisation.

Lombroso now classified criminals in four main categories. First, *born criminals* are simply those who can be distinguished by their physical atavistic characteristics. Second, *insane criminals* are those including idiots, imbeciles, paranoiacs, epileptics and alcoholics. Third, *occasional criminals* or *criminaloids* are those who commit crimes in response to opportunities when these might be available – as identified by rational actor theorists – but importantly in contrast to that alternative tradition have innate traits that predispose them to commit criminal behaviour. Fourth, *criminals of passion* are those motivated to commit crime because of anger, love or honour.

Lombroso made little reference to female offenders and considered their criminality to be predominantly restricted to prostitution and abortion, and observed that a man was invariably responsible for instigating their involvement in these crimes. This stereotypical view – that women engage in prostitution because of their sexual nature – nevertheless totally disregarded the obvious motivation of economic necessity, and was to remain an enduring and influential explanation of female criminal behaviour until very recently and is discussed in more detail in Chapters 8 and 11.

Lombroso undoubtedly used primitive methodology based on very limited data and a very simplistic use of statistics. Moreover, he did not have a general theory of crime that would enable him to organise his data in any meaningful way (Taylor, Walton and Young, 1973). Criminals were simply those who had broken the law and the problem thus appeared deceptively straightforward. All one needed to do was locate the differences between people that produce variances in their tendencies to violate the law.

Early biological proponents of the predestined actor model fundamentally assumed that offenders differ in some way from non-offenders. They then problematically observed that offenders appeared to differ among themselves and committed different types of crime. Moreover, offenders who committed the same type of crime appeared alike in terms of important characteristics. The solution to this problem was to subdivide the criminal population into types – each of which would be internally comparable with respect to the causes of crime – and different from other types on the same dimensions.

Most today consider the approach of Lombroso to have been simplistic and naïve but we should observe that he did make three important contributions to the development of modern criminological theory. First, he directed the study of crime away from the armchair theorising that had characterised the early proponents of the rational actor model towards the scientific study of the criminal. Second, although his methodology was rather primitive, he demonstrated the importance of examining clinical and historical records. Third, and most significantly, he recognised the need for multi-factor explanations of crime that include not only hereditary, but social, cultural and economic factors. These latter important factors were also emphasised by his successors in the early biological tradition Enrico Ferri and Raffaele Garofalo.

Enrico Ferri (1856–1929) was thus not simply a biological positivist but significantly argued that criminal behaviour could be explained by studying the interaction of a range of factors: *physical factors* such as race, geography and temperature; *individual factors* such as age, sex and psychological variables; and *social factors* such as population, religion and culture (Ferri, 1895). He rather radically proposed that crime could be controlled by improving the social conditions of the poor and to that end advocated the provision of subsidised housing, birth control and public recreation facilities and it was a vision that fitted well with the socialist views of Ferri. In the 1920s he was invited to write a new penal code for Mussolini's Fascist state, but his positivistic approach was rejected for being too much of a departure from rational actor model legal reasoning. Sellin (1973) observes that Ferri was attracted to Fascism because it offered a reaffirmation of the authority of the state over the excessive individualism that he had always rejected.

Raffaele Garofalo (1852–1934) was both an academic and a practising lawyer remembered for his doctrine of 'natural crimes' where he argued that because society is a 'natural body', crimes are offences 'against the law of nature'. Criminal behaviour is therefore unnatural. The 'rules of nature' are the rules of right conduct revealed to human beings through their powers of reasoning. For Garofalo, the proper rules of conduct come from thinking about what rules should be allowed or prohibited and he identified acts that he argued no society could refuse to recognise as criminal and, consequently, repress by punishment.

Garofalo argued that these *natural crimes* violated two basic human sentiments which are found among people of all ages, namely the sentiments of *probity* and *pity*. Pity is the sentiment of revulsion against the voluntary infliction of suffering on others, while probity refers to respect for the property rights of others. Garofalo argued that these sentiments are basic moral sensibilities that appear in the more advanced forms of civilised society and proposed that some members of society may have a higher than average sense of morality because they are superior members of the group. True criminals, on the other hand, lack properly developed altruistic sentiments and have psychic or moral anomalies that can be inherited.

Garofalo identified four criminal categories, each one distinct from the others because of deficiencies in the basic sentiments of pity and probity. The first category, *murderers* are totally lacking in both pity and probity and will kill and steal whenever the opportunity arises. Lesser criminals are however more difficult to identify and this category is subdivided on the basis of whether criminals lack sentiments of either pity or probity. Thus, the second category, *violent criminals* lack pity and can be influenced by environmental factors such as the consumption of alcohol, or the fact that criminality is endemic to their particular population. The third category, *thieves* suffer from a lack of probity, a condition that might be more the product of social factors than is the case for criminals in the other categories. His fourth category contains *sexual criminals*, some of whom will be classified among the violent criminals because they lack pity. Others require a separate category because their actions stem from a low level of moral energy rather than a lack of pity.

The penological implications of the respective theories of Lombroso and Garofalo are substantially different. Lombroso had wanted to provide treatment for – and change – deviants so that they could be reintegrated back into society. Garofalo reasoned that criminal behaviour demonstrated a failure to live by the basic human sentiments necessary for the survival of society. Criminals should therefore be eliminated in order to secure that survival. Life imprisonment or overseas transportation was proposed for lesser criminals.

Significantly, both Garofalo and Ferri were prepared to sacrifice basic human rights to the opinion of 'scientific experts' whose decisions would take no account of the opinions of either the person on whom they were passing judgement or the wider general public. Their work was thus acceptable to the Mussolini regime in Italy, because it provided scientific legitimisation to ideas of racial purity, national strength and authoritarian leadership (Vold, 1958). It will be seen in the following sections that later biological explanations of crime and criminal behaviour became – and indeed have *become* – increasingly more sophisticated. The logical conclusions that can be reached from the implications of the tradition established by Garofalo and Ferri nevertheless remain the same. If an incurable criminal type exists and can be identified then the logical solution is surely to isolate and remove such individuals permanently from society. Some would indeed suggest that this process of isolation take place before the individual has the opportunity to offend. The notion of treatment should not be automatically assumed to be a soft option to the punishment intervention advocated by proponents of the rational actor model. The term treatment can have much more sinister connotations with serious civil rights implications. We should thus perhaps be grateful that the latter apparently more sophisticated biological variants of the predestined actor model remain inherently problematic.

Inherited criminal characteristics

An idea arose at the end of the nineteenth century that criminality is inherited in the same way as physical characteristics and evidence to support this supposition has subsequently been obtained from three sources: (i) criminal family studies; (ii) twin studies and (iii) adopted children studies.

Criminal family studies

Criminal family studies have their origins in the work of Dugdale (1877) who traced 709 members of the Juke family and found that the great majority were either criminals or paupers. Goddard (1914) subsequently traced 480 members of the Kallikak family and found that a large number of them had been criminals. Interestingly, while both researchers had observed social as well as inherited criminal characteristics as causes of crime, both emphasised the link between criminality and 'feeblemindedness'. Indeed, following the invention of intelligence tests (IQ tests) by Alfred Binet in 1905, inherited feeblemindedness was commonly proposed as a principal cause of crime, although it was to go out of fashion for some considerable time from the 1920s onwards.

Goring (1913) reported a fairly sophisticated study of 3,000 prisoners, with a history of long and frequent sentences, and a control group of apparently non-criminals. The prisoners were found to be inferior to the control group in terms of physical size and mental ability while strong associations between the criminality of the children and their parents and between brothers were found. Moreover, it was found that children who were separated from their parents at an early age, because the latter were imprisoned, were as likely, or more likely, to become criminals compared with other children not separated in this way. Thus, contact with a criminal parent did not seem a significant factor associated with criminal conduct. Goring thus claimed that the primary source of criminal behaviour is inherited characteristics rather than environmental factors.

Three principal weaknesses can be identified in Goring's study. First, there is a failure to measure satisfactorily the influence of environmental effects on criminal behaviour. Second, a comparison of stealing and sex offences is based on the assumption that parental contagion is restricted entirely to techniques of crimes and fails to consider the possibility that the transmission of values is more important. Third, the study was restricted to male criminals, although the ratio of 102 brothers to six sisters imprisoned is mentioned. It would seem logical that if criminality is inherited females should be affected to a similar extent as males unless it is a sex-linked condition. Twin and adoption studies have attempted to provide a more sophisticated examination of the relationship between criminality and heredity (Sutherland and Cressey, 1978).

Twin studies

There are clear genetic differences between identical (monozygotic) twins and fraternal (dizygotic) twins. Identical twins occur when a single fertilised egg produces two embryos. They are thus genetically identical. Fraternal twins are the outcome of two different eggs being fertilised at the same time and they are as genetically different as children born after separate pregnancies. It is obvious that differences in the behaviour of identical twins cannot be explained by different inherited characteristics but, on the other hand, various studies have proposed that similarities in their conduct can be explained by shared heredity.

Lange (1930) examined a group of 30 men, comprising 13 identical twins and 17 fraternal twins, all of who had a prison record and found that in 77 per cent of cases for the identical twins, the other brother had such a record. However, for the fraternal twins, only 12 per cent of the second twins had a prison record. This percentaged relationship is referred to as a criminal concordance. Two hundred pairs of ordinary brothers – near to each other in age – were also compared. Where one brother had a criminal record, the same applied to the other brother in only 8 per cent of cases. Lange thus concluded that heredity plays a major part in the causation of criminal behaviour.

Christiansen (1968) examined official registers to discover how many of 6,000 pairs of twins born in Denmark between 1881 and 1910 had acquired a criminal record and found that in the 67 pairs of identical male twins – where at least one brother had a criminal record – the criminal concordance was 35.8 per cent. There were 114 pairs of fraternal male twins where at least one brother was a convicted criminal, but the criminal concordance was only 12.3 per cent. The criminal concordance was found to be higher for both categories where more serious offences had been committed.

A problem with twin studies is a lack of clarity about the sort of characteristics that are supposed to be passed on and this is important, as variations might reveal themselves in quite different forms of behaviour (Trasler, 1967). For example, some pairs of twins in Lange's study had committed very different types of offences from each other and it could well be the case that a predisposition to offend is inherited but the actual form of offending is determined by other factors.

Christiansen did not however claim that inherited characteristics were the only – or for that matter the dominant – factor that led to the higher concordance for identical twins. He was of the opinion that twin studies could increase our understanding of the interaction between the environment and biological traits and, in fact, he used variations in concordance rates in urban and rural areas to suggest that environmental factors might play a greater part in an urban setting. It is, nevertheless, a central criticism of such studies that they cannot accurately assess the balance between the effects of inherited characteristics and those of the environment. Twins are more likely than ordinary siblings to share similar experiences in relation to family and peers and it is possible that such similarities will be greater in the cases of identical twins.

Dalgard and Kringlen (1976) studied 139 pairs of male twins where at least one brother had a criminal conviction and concordances of 25.8 per cent and 14.9 per cent were found for identical and fraternal twins, respectively. However, when the researchers controlled for mutual closeness, no appreciable difference in concordance rates was found between the types of twins and they thus concluded that hereditary factors were not significant in explaining crime. However, Cloninger and Gottesman (1987) reviewed the same data and reached a very different conclusion observing that if Dalgard and Kringlen had been correct, then the environmental effects would cause psychologically close identical twins to act the same as each other, and psychologically distant identical twins to act differently. This did not happen.

A more recent twin study supports both inherited characteristics and environmental explanations of criminality. Rowe and Rogers (1989) collected data from self-report questionnaires involving 308 sets of twins in the Ohio State school system in the USA and concluded that inherited characteristics partly determine the similarity of behaviour of same-sex and identical twins. They nevertheless recognised that interaction between siblings could cause initially discordant siblings to become concordant in their levels of offending. Moreover, as twins are brought up together as a general rule, it becomes virtually impossible to reach any firm conclusion as to the role of inherited characteristics alone (Rowe, 1990). Studies of adopted children have sought to overcome that inherent methodological problem.

Adopted children studies

In the case of adopted children – where contact with a criminal parent has obviously been limited – any association between criminal behaviour can be attributed to inherited characteristics with a greater degree of certainty. Hutchings and Mednick (1977) carried out a study of male adoptees born in Copenhagen between 1927 and 1941 and found that 48 per cent of young males with a criminal record and 37.7 per cent with a record of minor offences had a birth father with a criminal record. Among young males without a criminal record, 31.1 per cent had a birth father with such a record. The study discovered that an adoptee was more likely to have a record where both the birth and adoptive father had previous convictions.

In a further comparison, 143 of the adoptees with criminal records were matched with a control group containing the same number of adoptees without convictions. Among the sample group, 49 per cent were found to have criminal birth fathers, 18 per cent had criminal birth mothers and 23 per cent had criminal adoptive fathers. Among the control group 28 per cent were found to have criminal birth fathers, 7 per cent had criminal birth mothers and 9.8 per cent had criminal adoptive fathers. On the basis of these findings a very strong link between inherited characteristics and criminal behaviour was proposed.

The research was later replicated in a wider study that encompassed all non-familial adoptions in Denmark between 1924 and 1947 (Mednick *et al.*, 1984). A similar though slightly less strong correlation between birth parents and their adoptee children was found and again the most significant results were when both birth and adoptive parents were criminal. The researchers concluded that there was an inherited characteristic element that was transmitted from the criminal parents to their children that increased the likelihood of the children becoming involved in criminal behaviour. It is nevertheless important to note that adoption agencies try to place children in homes situated in similar environments to those from which they came and it remains a possibility that it is upbringing not inherited characteristics that cause criminal behaviour. On the other hand, some people may be genetically endowed with characteristics that render them more likely to 'succumb to crime' (Hutchings and Mednick, 1977: 140). Exactly what these inherited crime inducing characteristics might actually be is not really considered.

Intelligence and criminal behaviour

In more recent years there have been attempts to rehabilitate notions of a link between intelligence and criminal behaviour. This interest in intelligence is based on a controversial position – taken in the late 1960s – that proposed intelligence to be genetically based, and that differences in IQ can be used to explain different criminal propensities between ethnic groups (see Shockley, 1967; Jensen, 1969). Robert Gordon (1986) argued from this perspective that IQ is actually the best predictor of offending behaviour among various groups.

Hirschi and Hindelang (1977) reviewed studies on IQ and offending behaviour and found that – as a predictor of offending behaviour – IQ is at least as good as any of the other major social variables. Furthermore, they noted that IQ is also strongly related to social class and ethnic group. Because offending behaviour is viewed as the province of lower class young people from ethnic minorities, this relationship implies that such people have lower IQs and this argument has received a great deal of understandable criticism. For example, Menard and Morse (1984) observed that IQ is merely one of the ways in which juveniles are disadvantaged in US society and proposed that it is societal and institutional response to these disadvantages that are the real explanation for offending behaviour.

In general, critics of IQ tests have noted that the way in which the tests are constructed provides advantages to those who are middle class and white, while it is argued that the tests do not measure innate intelligence, but rather some other ability, such as a facility in language or cultural concepts.

Genetic structure

A further category of biological explanations of crime and criminal behaviour considers abnormalities in the genetic structure of the offender. Crucial abnormalities identified are those related to the sex chromosomes. People usually have 23 pairs of chromosomes, 46 in all and the sex of a person is determined by one of these pairs. The normal complement in a female is XX and in a male XY but in some men an extra chromosome has been found to be present.

Klinefelter, Reifenstein and Albright (1942) found that sterile males often display a marked degree of feminisation and sometimes with low intelligence and increased stature. It was subsequently discovered that these men with 'Klinefelter's syndrome' had an extra X chromosome. In 1962, Court Brown conducted a study of Klinefelter males in psychiatric institutions and discovered an abnormally high incidence of criminal behaviour among his subjects and suggested that these men are over-represented among the population of homosexuals, transvestites and transsexuals. It is of course important to recognise that such activities are no-longer illegal.

Later studies considered incarcerated criminals and focused on individuals with an XYY complement of sex chromosomes, in order to test the hypothesis that they might be characterised by 'extra maleness', and thus be more aggressive. Casey in 1965 and Neilson in 1968 conducted the first major studies at the Rampton and Moss Side secure hospitals, respectively and found that men with an extra Y chromosome tend to be very tall, generally of low intelligence and often present EEG abnormalities (EEG is discussed below). Moreover, many of these early examples were found to have histories of criminal and aggressive behaviour with theft and violent assault their characteristic offences.

Price and Whatmore (1967) noted that subjects with an extra Y chromosome tend to be convicted at an earlier age than other offenders, come from families with no history of criminality, tend to be unstable and immature without displaying remorse and have a marked tendency to commit a succession of apparently motiveless property crimes. Witkin, Mednick, and Schulsinger (1977) explain the over-representation of such men in institutions to be the result of their slight mental retardation.

A range of criticisms has been made of these genetic structure theories. First, almost all the research has been concentrated on inmates in special hospitals and has revealed more evidence of psychiatric disorder than criminality.

Second, there does not appear to be any fixed and identifiable XYY syndrome, which means the concept is not useful in predicting criminal behaviour. Third, the offending behaviour of some young males with an extra X chromosome may be due to anxiety in adolescence about an apparent lack of masculinity. Fourth, all the young male offenders with an identified extra Y chromosome have come from working class backgrounds. It is thus possible that because young males with an extra Y chromosome are usually tall and well built, they may be defined as 'dangerous' by judges and psychiatrists, and more likely to be incarcerated than fined. Finally, and crucially, there are thousands of perfectly, normal and harmless people in the general population who have either an extra X or Y chromosome.

Advances in genetic science in recent years have led to a revival of claims that aspects of criminality can be accounted for by genetic factors. Ellis (1990) thus looked to processes of natural selection operating on genetic evolution to explain some aspects of criminal behaviour and has argued that some criminal activities – especially rape, assault, child abuse, and property offences – are linked to powerful genetic forces. He nevertheless offers no proof of genetic connections with crime and criminal behaviour, merely presenting a hypothesis based on assumptions of inherent animal-like behaviour.

It has however become increasingly apparent that a tendency to contract many diseases is strongly affected by inherited factors and the particular genes related to specific ailments are currently being identified. Moreover, there have been suggestions in recent years that insurance companies might wish to examine the genetic characteristics of potential clients. Geneticists have been cautious in claiming that human behaviour is primarily determined by inherited characteristics but the discovery that some personality traits can be explained by a genetic component (Jones, 1993) does greatly strengthen the possibility that some criminal behaviour can be explained by a genetic susceptibility triggered by environmental factors and this point is revisited in Chapter 13.

Criminal body types

A further category of the biological variant of the predestined actor model has its foundations directly in the Lombrosian tradition of concentrating on body type. Kretschmer (1964, originally 1921) identified four criminal body types: first, *asthenics* are lean and narrowly built, flat-chested and skinny with their ribs easily counted; second, *athletics* have broad shoulders, deep chests, flat stomachs and powerful legs; third, *pyknics* are of medium build with an inclination to be rotund with rounded shoulders, broad faces and short stubby hands; and fourth, *mixed types* are those which are unclassifiable. Kretschmer argued that the asthenic and athletic builds are associated with schizophrenic personalities, while pyknics are manic-depressives.

Hooton (1939) conducted a detailed analysis of the measurements of more than 17,000 criminals and non-criminals and concluded that the former are organically inferior to other people, that low foreheads indicate inferiority, and that 'a depressed physical and social environment determines Negro and Negroid delinquency to a much greater extent than it does in the case of Whites' (Hooton, 1939, Vol.1: 329). Hooton was not surprisingly widely condemned for the racist overtones of his work and his failure to recognise that the prisoners he studied represented only those who had been caught, convicted or imprisoned. Moreover, his control group appeared to be representative of no known population of humanity.

Sheldon (1949) produced the first modern systematic linking of body traits with criminal behaviour but was at the same time highly influenced by his predecessors in this tradition. He significantly shifted attention from adults to offending male youths, studying 200 between 15 and 21 years of age in an attempt to link physique to temperament, intelligence and offending behaviour, classifying the physiques of the boys by measuring the degree to which they possessed a combination of three different body components. First, *endomorphs* tended to be soft, fat people; second, *mesomorphs* were of muscular and athletic build; and third, *ectomorphs* had a skinny, flat and fragile physique. Sheldon concluded that most offenders tended towards mesomorphy and because the youths came from parents who were offenders, the factors that produce criminal behaviour are inherited.

Glueck and Glueck (1950) conducted a comparative study of offenders and non-offenders and gave considerable support to the work of Sheldon, finding that, as a group, offenders tended to have narrower faces, wider chests, larger and broader waists and bigger forearms than non-offenders. Approximately 60 per cent of the offenders were found to be predominantly mesomorphic but the researchers – like their predecessors – failed to establish whether this group were offenders because of their build and disposition, or because their physique and dispositions are socially conceived to be associated with offending. Or indeed whether a third set of factors associated with poverty and deprivation, affected both their body build and offending behaviour.

Body type theories can be criticised for ignoring different aspects of the interaction between the physical characteristics of the person and their social circumstances. People from poorer backgrounds will tend to have a poorer diet and thus be small in stature while young people in manual occupations are likely to acquire an athletic build. The over-representation of such people among convicted criminals may thus be explained by a variety of socio-cultural – rather than biological – factors.

Gibbons (1970) argues that the high proportion of mesomorphy among offenders is due to a process of social selection and the nature of their activities is such that deviants will be drawn from the more athletic members of that age group. Cortes and Gatti (1972), in contrast, propose that such arguments falsely accuse biological explanations of criminal behaviour of being more determinist than they actually are. They propose that as physical factors are essential to the social selection process, human behaviour has both biological and social causes.

Hartl, Monnelly and Elderkin (1982) conducted a thirty year follow-up of Sheldon's research subjects and found that the criminal group still showed significant signs of mesomorphy but, on the other hand, the highly influential longitudinal Cambridge Study in Delinquent Development found no evidence that offenders were in any way physically different from non-offenders (West, 1982). There thus remains much ambiguity in the findings from body-type research although researchers continue to pursue this approach with Raine et al. (2000) finding that three-year-old children (boys or girls) – who were just half an inch taller than their peers – had a greater than average chance of becoming classroom bullies with the ambitious suggestion that they would go on to be violent criminals.

Psychoses and brain injuries

This category of the biological variant of the predestined actor model addresses neurological conditions that supposedly *cause* criminal behaviour but there is little evidence that brain injuries actually lead to criminal behaviour. There have been cases reported, but these are very rare, and studies suggest that the original personality and social background of the person are of greater significance. A brain injury might however accentuate an underlying trend to aggression if it occurs in a specific area of the brain.

There is some evidence of association between criminality and 'minimal brain dysfunction' (MBD) which is a condition that can lead to learning disabilities in school and thus – by various routes – to offending behaviour, although there is little evidence of neurological malfunction in these cases. The usual personality changes associated with brain injury are forgetfulness, impaired concentration and diminished spontaneity in thought.

There are some organic psychoses that are associated with brain lesions or malfunctions. First, *epidemic encephalitis* is a condition that was widespread among children in the 1920s and was often linked to destructiveness, impulsiveness, arson and abnormal sexual behaviour. Second, *senile dementia* is a general organically based deterioration of the personality that affects *some* old people and may be accompanied by arson, paranoid delusions and deviant sexual behaviour. Third, *Huntingdon's chorea* is an inherited disease involving brain decay – characterised by involuntary and disorganised movements, apathy and depression – that may result in vicious assaults in a fit of uncontrollable temper. Fourth, *brain tumours* – especially in the temporal lobe region – can activate the neural systems linked to aggressive behaviour that can result in outbursts of rage, violence and even murder but the condition is reversed with the surgical removal of the tumour. Fifth, much attention has been devoted in the criminological literature – from Lombroso onwards – towards *epilepsy*, particularly temporal lobe epilepsy and it has been found that some but by no means all, victims of this illness do sometimes make violent assaults on people during and occasionally between seizures (Mark and Ervin, 1970).

There does appear to be a relationship between violent and aggressive behaviour and malfunctions of the limbic system which is that part of the brain concerned with mediating the expression of a broad range of emotional and vegetative behaviours such as hunger, pleasure, fear, sex and anger. Various studies have shown that it is possible by electrical stimulation of the brain, to induce aggressive behaviour in otherwise placid subjects (see Shah and Roth, 1974) and removing or burning out that part of the brain that appears to be responsible for aggression can also control it. It is also possible to electrically stimulate other parts of the brain to produce docility.

In a study of unprovoked 'abnormal' killers, Stafford Clark and Taylor (1949 cited in Shah and Roth, 1974) found that 73 per cent had abnormal EEG readings and among 'clearly insane' murderers, the incidence was 86 per cent. EEG – electroencephalogram – is a record of the rhythmical waves of electrical potential occurring in the vertebrate brain, mainly in the central cortex. Other studies have also shown that EEG abnormalities are highest among aggressive psychopathic criminals and lowest among emotionally stable groups (see Mednick and Volavka, 1980; Volavka, 1987).

EEG abnormality is often associated with chromosomal abnormality. Thus, the majority of people who have an extra X or Y chromosome also have EEG abnormalities. Epileptics always have EEG abnormalities and so very frequently do those with a psychiatric condition known as psychopathy, a condition discussed more fully in the following chapter. There are three possible explanations of the link between EEG abnormality and psychopathy: first, psychopaths do not have the same levels of sensory perception as other people; second, the condition may be associated with the malfunction of specific brain mechanisms, particularly those concerned with emotion; and third, the pattern of brainwaves is different in children and adults and thus what may be normal for the child is abnormal for the adult.

It is this last possible explanation that has led to the development of the concept of EEG motivation, and it seems probable that this proceeds in parallel with psychological motivation. Much of the psychiatric abnormality shown in the behaviour disorders of early adult life can be related to emotional immaturity and this tends to significantly reduce or disappear as an individual passes into his or her 30s and 40s. It is among persons of this type that EEG abnormality is most commonly found.

There is undoubtedly a *correlation* between psychopathy and abnormal EEG but, on the one hand, there are criminals diagnosed as psychopathic but with normal EEG patterns, while at the same time, there are many non-criminal people with bizarre EEG patterns. Moreover, anticonvulsant drugs that stabilise brain rhythms have no effect on psychopaths. EEG patterns are therefore *extremely* difficult to interpret and quite often 'experts' will disagree totally. It has thus not been possible to produce the foundations of a general explanation of crime and criminal behaviour from studies of the brain and the central nervous system. Hans Eysenck has however attempted to develop a general theory based on the autonomic nervous system but his work is overwhelmingly psychological and is discussed in the following chapter.

Some childhood behaviour disorders are thought to be caused by brain dysfunction resulting from complications in pregnancy, birth or childhood and this issue is discussed in Chapter 13. A mild form of dysfunction that has been discussed in recent years is attention deficit disorder which is sometimes identified in conjunction with hyperactivity with the symptoms including behavioural problems and poor cognitive responses. Mannuzza *et al.* (1989) tested a sample for hyperactivity both in childhood and later in young adulthood and found that a significantly greater number of hyperactive children than the controls had been arrested, convicted and imprisoned. The researchers nevertheless found that this difference could be almost entirely explained by the presence of an antisocial conduct disorder in young adulthood. Hyperactivity alone could not be considered responsible for the onset of the later criminal behaviour.

The Cambridge Study in Delinquent Development tested a cohort of young males at regular intervals from the age of eight and data was collected on attention deficit, hyperactivity, home background and delinquency (Farrington, Loeber and Van Kammen, 1990) and found that both attention deficit and behavioural problems were associated with high rates of offending. The problems from the former could be linked to a low IQ, an early record of offending, being a member of a large family and having criminal parents. Behavioural problems were thus linked to deficient parenting. The researchers nevertheless considered that the connection between attention deficit and crime was not necessarily biological considering that environmental and social factors could have been influential.

Certain learning disabilities – allegedly arising from a dysfunction in the central nervous system – have also been linked to offending behaviour. There is however a problem in concluding whether such disabilities arise out of biological or social factors. It is not difficult to see how children with learning difficulties can be perceived as being disruptive or lazy at school and such inappropriate behaviour may also serve to alienate potential friends with the outcome that the young person can come to feel rejected, alienated and isolated. At that point they may well stop going to school – either through truancy or exclusion – and start to mix with other disaffected young people on the streets with the disastrous consequences outlined in the discussion of deviant subculture theories in Chapter 7. Ignoring biologically founded conditions in children and young people can be very much to their disadvantage as is suggested by the relatively recent discovery of the large number of children with autistic spectrum disorders.

Autistic spectrum disorders

Eugen Bleuler first used the term 'autism' at the beginning of the twentieth century to refer to what he thought to be a variant of schizophrenia characterised by 'a narrowing of relationships to people and the outside world, a narrowing so extreme that it seemed to exclude everything except the person's own self' (Frith, 2003: 5). In 1943, Leo Kanner distinguished autism from childhood schizophrenia observing the crucial distinction that 'people with schizophrenia withdrew from social relationships while children with autism never developed them in the first place' (cited in Mesibov, Shea and Adams, 2001: 7).

In 1944 Hans Asperger, a Viennese paediatrician, introduced the term 'autistic psychopathy' emphasising the peculiarities of communication and the difficulties in social adaptation of children with autism (Frith, 2003). However, while Kanner had described children with a more extreme debilitating variant of autism, Asperger described more able, indeed sometimes gifted, children (Attwood, 1998) However, while the variant of autism identified by Kanner was to gain worldwide recognition, the condition identified by Asperger was to remain virtually unknown outside of Germany until it was introduced to the English-speaking world by Lorna Wing in 1981 (Rosaler, 2004).

Wing and Gould (1979 cited in Wing 1998) concluded that children with Kanner's autism and Asperger's Syndrome have in common a triad of impairments affecting social interaction, communication and imagination, accompanied by a narrow, rigid, repetitive pattern of activities and developed from this discovery the notion of a continuum or spectrum of disorders held together by this triad. This spectrum runs from clear-cut autism through to subtle variants that shade into traits found within the normal (neurotypical) population. Moreover, it is now thought that 'autistic traits are widely distributed in the normal population and many "normal people" show isolated autistic traits' (Thambirajah, 2007: 133).

Autism and Asperger's Syndrome are two of the five pervasive developmental disorders (PDD) which are more often referred to today as autistic spectrum disorders. They have a 'neurological basis in the brain and genetic causes play a major role. However, precise causes are still not known' (Hill and Frith, 2004: 1). Thus, they are 'defined using behavioural criteria because, so far, no specific biological markers are known' (Hill and Frith, 2004: 2) which demonstrates that the non-specific and variable nature of the autistic spectrum makes it difficult to diagnose.

The risk of becoming an offender is statistically more probable if any child experiences certain risk factors such as peer rejection, low popularity, social isolation (Farrington, 2005), poor social functioning and impulsivity (Pakes and Winstone, 2007) which are common among children and young people on the autistic spectrum. Holland (1997: 270) significantly observes that:

> those people who fall within the autistic spectrum … have very particular difficulties which markedly impair their understanding of the social world, and they may be more prone to problem behaviour and therefore to offending.

There are thus a number of features of autistic spectrum disorders that can predispose those with the condition to criminal behaviour (Berney, 2004). First, some have narrow obsessions and are unaware of the effect that their behaviour has on others. Howlin (1997) cites the case of a young man fascinated by washing machines from a very young age who would enter any house where he could hear one in action without any appreciation of the alarm this would cause the occupant. Second, some have problems with the interpretation of rules, particularly social ones and as a result of this may 'find themselves unwittingly embroiled in offences such as date rape' (Berney, 2004: 7). It is a misinterpretation of social rules that can be linked to social naivety and social relationships. Often eager to be accepted such children can be very 'easy prey' (Howlin, 2004) and as the National Autistic Society (2005) observes this has led some to be befriended by, and become the unwitting accomplices of criminals. They simply do not understand the motives of other people. Third, children on the autistic spectrum like routine and are resistant to changes. If unexpected changes occur, 'it can be so distressing to a person with autism that they may react with an aggressive outburst' (National Autistic Society, 2005: 9) (see also Baron-Cohen, 1988; Ghaziuddin, 2005).

Asperger himself first suggested a possible association between the condition he described as 'autistic psychopathy' and violence while several other studies have documented examples of violence in those with autistic spectrum disorders (see Baron-Cohen, 1988). Howlin (2004: 301) nevertheless pertinently observes that:

> Although there is little evidence of any significant association between autism and criminal offending, occasional and sometimes lurid publicity has led to suggestions that there may be an excess of violent crime amongst more able people with autism or those diagnosed as having Asperger's syndrome.

This all becomes evident with the case of a thirteen-year-old autistic boy who killed his baby brother by cutting off his left hand and stabbing him seventeen times (BBC News, 2001). When asked by the police why he did it he replied, 'I wanted to be with my mum' (BBC News, 2001). Kelly (2006) reports the case of a 21-year-old male who stabbed to death his 57-year-old boss because he thought she was to blame for getting him sacked. Despite the gravity of this offence, it was observed that 'even now [he] believes he acted appropriately'.

There is however a significant possibility that other factors could have influenced the offending behaviour in the above cases and in others involving people on the autistic spectrum. Ghaziuddin (2005) observes that factors such as poor parental control, a chaotic environment and a family history of poor mental health and criminality could predispose such a person to violence.

It is clear that there are many people located somewhere on the autistic spectrum and many of these have symptoms that can clearly dispose them to criminal behaviour. It is thus important that society becomes aware of this condition and the various difficulties that it can pose those who are on the spectrum. On the hand, it is important to recognise that many – if not the great majority – of people on the spectrum do not become involved in criminal behaviour and indeed there are many very famous people past and present who are on the autistic spectrum and it is extremely likely that this condition has actually contributed to their success.[1] The crucial issue here would again seem to be the specific interaction of predisposing biological factors in a particular social context.

Biochemical theories

Biochemical explanations of criminal behaviour are similar to the altered biological state theories discussed in the following section. The difference lies in the fact that biochemical explanations involve substances – or chemical processes – already present in the body while altered state explanations involves the introduction of outside agents. In this section we will consider sexual hormones, blood sugar levels, and adrenaline sensitivity.

Sexual hormones

Glands such as the pituitary, adrenals, gonads, pancreas and thyroid produce hormones. They control – and are themselves controlled by – certain anatomical features that affect the thresholds for various types of responses and have extensive feedback loops with the central nervous system. Schlapp and Smith (1928) first suggested a causal relationship between hormones and criminal behaviour arguing that either an excess or underproduction of hormones by the ductless glands could lead to emotional disturbance followed by criminal behaviour.

It has long been recognised that male animals – of most species – are more aggressive than females and this has been linked to the male sex hormone, testosterone (Rose *et al.*, 1974; Keverne, Meller and Eberhart, 1982). The relationship between sex hormones and human behaviour does appear more complex even though testosterone has been linked with aggressive crime such as murder and rape. However, it does seem that in most men testosterone levels do not significantly affect levels of aggression (Persky, Smith and Basu, 1971; Scarmella and Brown, 1978). Studies of violent male prisoners suggest that testosterone levels have had an effect on aggressive behaviour. However, these results were not as strong as had been expected from the studies of animals (Kreuz and Rose, 1972; Ehrenkranz, Bliss and Sheard, 1974).

Problematically, these studies of humans have not differentiated between different forms of aggression, although later studies sought to address this issue. Olwens (1987) thus conducted a study of young men with no marked criminal record and found a clear link between testosterone and both verbal and physical aggression with a further distinction between provoked and unprovoked aggressive behaviour: provoked aggressive behaviour tended to be more verbal than physical and was in response to unfair or threatening behaviour by another person; unprovoked aggressive behaviour, in contrast, was violent, destructive and involved activities such as starting fights and making provocative comments. The relationship between testosterone and unprovoked violence was nevertheless found to be indirect and would depend on other factors such as how irritable the particular individual was. Schalling (1987) discovered that high testosterone levels in young males were associated with verbal aggression but not with actual physical aggression which suggests a concern to protect status by the use of threats. Low testosterone level boys would tend not to protect their position, preferring to remain silent. Neither study suggests a direct link between testosterone and aggression, but in a provocative situation those with the highest levels of testosterone were found more likely to resort to violence.

Ellis and Crontz (1990) note that testosterone levels peak during puberty and the early 20s and this correlates with the highest crime rates. It is a finding that they claim provides persuasive evidence for a biological explanation of criminal behaviour and argue that it explains both aggressive and property crime observing that sociological researchers have failed to explain why it is that this distribution exists across all societies and cultures. There is nevertheless no evidence of a causal relationship between criminal behaviour and the level of testosterone. The link may be more tenuous with testosterone merely providing the environment necessary for aggressive behaviour to take place.

McBurnett et al. (2000) propose that violent behaviour in male children may be associated with low saliva levels of the stress hormone cortisol finding those with low concentration were three times more likely to show indications of aggression.

Blood sugar levels

Hypoglycaemia or low blood sugar levels – sometimes related to diabetes mellitus – may result in irritable, aggressive reactions, and may culminate in sexual offences, assaults, and motiveless murder (see Shah and Roth, 1974). Shoenthaler (1982) conducted experiments where it was discovered that by lowering the daily sucrose intake of young offenders held in detention it was possible to reduce the level of their antisocial behaviour. A discussion of the effects of under-nutrition on the central nervous system and thus on aggression can be found in Smart (1981). Virkkunen (1987) has linked hypoglycaemia with other activities often defined as antisocial such as truancy, low verbal IQ, tattooing and stealing from home during childhood and alcohol abuse. If alcohol is drunk regularly and in large quantities, the ethanol produced can induce hypoglycaemia and increase aggression.

Clapham (1989) cites the case of a man who stabbed his wife to death and attempted suicide but was acquitted of murder. The man had been on a strict diet for two months preceding the fatal incident – losing three stone in weight – and had been starved of all sugar, bread, potatoes and fried food. On the fateful morning he had consumed two glasses of whisky and was found immediately after the killing to be suffering from amnesia. Blood tests were conducted in prison several weeks later and he was found to be still suffering from reactive hypoglycaemia. The jury accepted the expert medical opinion that the man had been reduced to an automaton and could not be held responsible for his actions.

Adrenaline sensitivity

The relationship between adrenaline and aggressive behaviour is a similar area of study to that involving testosterone with each involving the relationship between a hormonal level and aggressive antisocial behaviour. Schachter (cited in Shah and Roth, 1974) thus found that injections of adrenaline made no difference to the behaviour of normal prisoners but a great difference to psychopaths; while, Hare (1982) found that when threatened with pain, criminals exhibit fewer signs of stress than other people. Mednick *et al.* (1982) discovered that not only do certain – particularly violent – criminals take stronger stimuli to arouse them, but once they are in a stressed state they recover more slowly to their normal levels than do non-criminals. Eysenck (1959) had offered a logical explanation for this relationship some years previously. An individual with low stress levels is easily bored, becomes quickly disinterested in things and craves exciting experiences. Thus, for such individuals normal stressful situations are not disturbing, they are exciting and enjoyable, something to be savoured and sought after.

Baldwin (1990) suggests that the link between age and crime rates can be partially explained by considering arousal rates observing that children can quickly become used to stimuli that had previously excited them and thus seek ever more thrilling inputs. The stimulus received from criminal type activities does nevertheless decline with age, as does the level of physical fitness, strength and agility required to perform many such activities. Baldwin interestingly explains both the learning of criminal behaviour and its subsequent decline in terms of stimuli in the environment which does then pose the question as to whether the production of adrenaline is biologically or socially dictated.

Altered biological state theories

Altered biological state theories are those that link behavioural changes in an individual with the introduction of an external chemical agent. These are here divided into the following categories: allergies and diet; alcohol; and illegal drugs.

Allergies and diet

Links have been proposed between irritability and aggression that may lead individuals in some circumstances to commit criminal assault, and allergic reactions to such things as pollen, inhalants, drugs and food. Research on the criminological implications of allergies continues but studies indicate two main reactions in these patients. First, *emotional immaturity* is characterised by temper tantrums, screaming episodes, whining and impatience, while, second, *antisocial behaviour* is characterised by sulkiness and cruelty.

More recent research has attempted to bring together earlier work on blood sugar levels, allergies and other biochemical imbalances. The basic premise of the theory of 'biochemical individuality' is that each person has an absolutely unique internal biochemistry and we all vary in our daily need for each of the 40-odd nutrients – minerals, vitamins, carbohydrates, etc – required to stay alive and healthy. From this idea flows the concept of 'orthomolecular medicine' that proposes that many diseases are preventable and treatable by the proper diagnosis, vitamin supplementation and avoidance of substances that would bring on an illness or preclude a cure. Prinz, Roberts and Hantman (1980) proposed that some foods – and in particular certain additives have effects that may lead to hyperactivity and even criminality. A low level of cholesterol has been linked with hypoglycaemia, particularly when alcohol use has been involved (see Virkkunen, 1987).

At first sight, it might appear strange to link criminal behaviour with vitamin deficiency but the evidence for an active role for biochemical disturbance in some offences of violence is too great to be ignored. Indeed, some quite impressive results have been obtained in the orthomolecular treatment of some mental disorders. For example, Vitamin B3 (niacin) has been used successfully to treat some forms of schizophrenia (see: Lesser, 1980; Pihl, 1982; Raloff, 1983) and there is some evidence that addiction to both drugs and alcohol may be related to unmet biochemical individual needs.

Substance abuse is usually brought about by the intake of drugs in the widest sense. Some of these drugs are legal and freely available such as alcohol, which is drunk and glues and lighter fluids which are inhaled. The medical profession prescribes some such as barbiturates, while others – such as cannabis, amphetamines, LSD, MDA or 'Ecstasy', opiates (usually cocaine or heroin) – are only available illegally.

Alcohol use

The use of alcohol has probably much closer links with crime and criminal behaviour than most other drugs – with the contemporary exception of crack cocaine and possibly heroin – and this highly significant link is at least partially explained by the reality that alcohol is legal, readily available and in extremely common usage. In short, alcohol has long been associated with antisocial activity, crime and criminality. Saunders (1984) calculated that alcohol was a significant factor in about 1,000 arrests per day or over 350,000 a year, Flanzer (1981) estimated that 80 per cent of all cases of family violence in the USA involved the consumption of alcohol, while De Luca (1981) estimated that almost a third of the cases of violence against children in the home were alcohol related. Other studies have discovered a strong link between alcohol and general levels of violence (Collins, 1988; Fagan, 1990), while Collins (1988) shows that considerable numbers of non-violent offenders claim to have been drinking when they offended. Rada (1975) found that half his study of convicted rapists had been drinking when they had offended. Collins (1986) concluded that prisoners with drinking problems had committed more assaults than those without such problems. Lindqvist (1986) found that two-thirds of convicted murderers in Sweden had been drinking at the time they had committed their offences.

There are significant problems with assuming a direct causal link between alcohol use and crime because the latter does not have the same effect on all people, for example, Native Americans and Eskimos have been found to metabolise more slowly than white people. Goodwin *et al.* (1973) propose that a predisposition to alcoholism can be genetically transmitted and any drug – including alcohol – can accentuate psychological symptoms in individuals.

Ramsay (1996) observes that it is necessary to consider the lifestyle and subculture of an alcoholic that might well be more relevant to their criminal activities than their drinking. Abram (1989) suggests that both alcohol use and the criminal behaviour may be the outcome of a third factor such as antisocial personality disorder.

Research suggests that victims of crime are also likely to have been drinking. Gottfredson (1984) found that in the UK the chances of becoming a crime victim increased from 5 per cent among non-drinkers to 15 per cent among heavy drinkers and this was particularly so in the case of the young (see also Mott, 1990). Hodge (1993) found that two-thirds of a sample of assailants and 50 per cent of their victims said they had been drinking immediately before the offence occurred. The British Crime Survey 1996 found that victims of domestic violence had far higher levels of alcohol consumption than non-victims (Mirrlees-Black, 1999).

Alcohol and young people have become closely linked in the contemporary UK although this has certainly not always been the case. In the interwar period young people aged 18–24 were the lightest drinkers in the adult population and the group most likely to abstain. Nor did alcohol play a significant part in the youth culture that came into existence in the 1950s, this being more likely to involve the coffee bar than the pub. It was not until the 1960s that pubs and drinking became an integral part of the youth scene and by the 1980s, those aged 18-24 years had become the heaviest consumers of alcohol in the population and the group least likely to abstain (Institute of Alcohol Studies, 2005).

By the year 2002, hazardous drinking, that is, a pattern of drinking that brings with it the risk of physical or psychological harm now or in the future, was most prevalent in teenagers and young adults. Among females, hazardous drinking reached its peak in the age-group 16–19, with just under one third (32 per cent) having a hazardous drinking pattern. Among males, the peak was found in the 20–24 age group, with just under two thirds (62 per cent) having a hazardous drinking pattern (Office for National Statistics, 2001). These changes were accompanied by a decline in the age of regular drinking. Thus, nowadays, most young people are drinking regularly – though not necessarily frequently – by the age of fourteen or fifteen. One survey found that more than a quarter of boys aged 9–10 and a third a year older reported drinking alcohol at least once in the previous week, normally at home (Balding and Shelley, 1993).

Most surveys suggest that there is a growing trend of drinking for effect and to intoxication with a related aspect being the partial merging of the alcohol and drug scenes in the context of youth culture. A large survey of teenagers in England, Wales and Scotland found that by the age 15–16 binge drinking is common, as is being 'seriously drunk' (Beinart et al., 2002). In this study, binge drinking was defined as consuming five or more alcohol drinks in a single session. The growth in binge drinking may be regarded as particularly significant as there is evidence that drinking – and especially heavier drinking – in adolescence increases the likelihood of binge drinking continuing through adult life (Jefferis, Power and Manor, 2005).

Alcohol is associated with a wide range of criminal offences in addition to drink driving and drunkenness in which drinking or excessive consumption defines the offence. Alcohol-related crime has thus become a matter of great public concern and, in England and Wales, approximately 70 per cent of crime audits published in 1998 and 1999 identified alcohol to be an issue, particularly in relation to public disorder (Home Office, 2000).

The term 'alcohol-related crime' normally refers to offences a) involving a combination of criminal damage offences, drunk and disorderly and other public disorder offences; b) involving young males, typically 18–30; and c) occurring in the entertainment areas of town and city centres. However, a whole range of offences are linked to alcohol and these do not necessarily occur in the context of the night-time economy. A study conducted for the Home Office in 1990 found that the growth in beer consumption was the single most important factor in explaining crimes of violence against the person while research also shows that a high proportion of victims of violent crime are drinking or under the influence of alcohol at the time of their assault and a minimum of one in five people arrested by police test positive for alcohol (Bennett, 2000).

An All Party Group of MPs investigating alcohol and crime was advised by the British Medical Association that alcohol is a factor in 60–70 per cent of homicides, 75 per cent of stabbings, 70 per cent of beatings and 50 per cent of fights and domestic assaults; the Police Superintendents Association reported that alcohol is a factor in 50 per cent of all crimes committed; and the National Association of Probation Officers advised that 30 per cent of offenders on probation and 58 per cent of prisoners have severe alcohol problems which is a significant factor in their offence or pattern of offending (All-Party Group on Alcohol Misuse, 1995).

Illegal drug use

Illegal drug taking does not have as long an association with criminal behaviour as alcohol consumption and it was only at the beginning of the twentieth century that drugs were labelled as a major social problem and came to be regulated. Drugs are chemicals and once taken alter the chemical balance of the body and brain and this can clearly affect behaviour but the way that this occurs varies according to the type and quantity of the drug taken (see Fishbein and Pease, 1990; Pihl and Peterson, 1993). The biological effects of cannabis and opiates such as heroin tend to reduce aggressive hostile tendencies, while cocaine and its derivative crack are more closely associated with violence. Interestingly, some see both alcohol and drug misuse as intrinsically wrong and thus in need of punishment while others see them as social and personal problems requiring understanding and treatment. The first solution has generally been applied in the case of (illegal) drugs, while the second has tended to be more acceptable in the case of (legal) alcohol.

In 2001/2, 15 per cent of men and 9 per cent of women aged 16–59 in England and Wales said that they had taken an illicit drug in the previous year. Among those aged 16–24, 35 per cent of males and 24 per cent of females said they had done so in the previous year. The most commonly used drug by young people was cannabis, which had been used by 33 per cent of young men and 22 per cent of young women during that time period. Ecstasy was the most commonly used Class A drug, with higher use among the 16–24 year olds than those aged 25–59. In 2001/2, 9 per cent of males and 4 per cent of females aged 16–24 had used Ecstasy in the previous year. Since 1996 there has been an increase in the use of cocaine among young people, especially among males; while, in contrast, the use of amphetamines and LSD has declined (Institute of Alcohol Studies, 2005). Drug use has been found to be widespread among school pupils although there has been a decrease in prevalence since 2003. In that year 21 per cent of pupils admitted having taken a drug during the previous year, this figure had decreased to 18 per cent by 2004 (Department of Health, 2005).

Breaking the link between drugs and other criminal behaviour has been a key feature of government anti-drug strategies since the mid-1990s (CDCU, 1995; UKADCU, 1998). Recent studies estimate the cost of drug offences to the criminal justice system as £1.2 billion (Brand and Price, 2000) and the social costs of class A drugs have been estimated to be nearly £12 billion (Godfrey *et al.*, 2002). Research on offender populations in the UK reveal that acquisitive crime (particularly shoplifting, burglary and fraud) are the primary means of funding drug consumption (Bennett 2000; Coid *et al.*, 2000; Edmunds, Hough and Turnbull, 1999). The evidence points to users of heroin and cocaine (particularly crack) as the most likely to be prolific offenders (Bennett 2000; Stewart *et al.*, 2000).

The NEW-ADAM research programme has found that those who report using heroin, crack or cocaine commit between five and ten times as many offences as offenders who do not report using drugs. Although users of heroin and cocaine/crack represent only a quarter of offenders, they are responsible for more than half (by value) of acquisitive crime (Bennett, Holloway and Williams, 2001). Links between problematic drug use and crime are nonetheless complex. Edmunds, Hough and Turnbull (1999) suggest that experimental drug use can pre-date contact with the criminal justice system and become problematic after extensive criminal activity. For those engaged in crime prior to drug use, their offending behaviour can increase sharply.

There are at least five ways in which drugs can be identified as being linked with crime. First, drug users may commit offences – including violent ones – in order to fund their activities particularly if they are addicted to heroin (Jarvis and Parker, 1989) and in more recent years crack cocaine. Most drug-related offending nevertheless falls into the category of non-violent property offences (Chaiken and Chaiken, 1991) or prostitution (Plant, 1990). Second, there is a possibility that drug use and other criminal behaviour simply occur alongside each other because of the presence of a third factor such as mental health problems (McBride and McCoy, 1982; Auld, Dorn and South, 1986). Third, drug dealers have a tendency to protect their business interests by whatever means necessary and this is increasingly likely to mean violence (Ruggiero and South, 1995). Fourth, drugs are chemicals which alter the balance of both body and brain and can significantly change behaviour (Fishbein and Pease,

1990; Pihl and Peterson, 1993). Fifth, there can be state involvement in the drugs trade and it has been suggested by Dorn and South (1990) that in the USA the Central Intelligence Agency (CIA) has been involved in the illegal drugs trade.

Treating the offender

Central to the biological variant of the predestined actor model of crime and criminal behaviour is the perception that criminality arises from some physical disorder within the individual offender and it is argued that by following a course of treatment, individuals can be cured of the predisposing condition that causes their criminality. We will now briefly consider three forms of individualised treatment: surgical intervention, chemotherapy and electro-control.

Surgical intervention often means pre-frontal leucotomy, a technique that severs the connection between the frontal lobes and the thalamus. It causes some degree of character change – mainly a reduced anxiety level – and has been used with some success to treat the paranoid and paraphrenic types of schizophrenia, but has now been largely replaced by neuroleptic drugs. It has also been used on 'sexually motivated' and 'spontaneously violent' criminals. Castration has been used on sex offenders in Denmark and the USA with indecisive results. Stürup in Denmark claimed 'acceptable' results with sex offenders, but Mueller (1972 cited in Menard and Morse, 1984) tells of a rapist in California who – following castration – turned from rape to child molesting and murder.

Chemotherapy involves the use of drugs in treatment programmes and also for control purposes. Some drugs are used for the treatment of specific behaviour patterns, for example, antabuse has been used in the treatment of alcoholics, cyclozocine for heroin addicts (both are blocking agents), benperidol (cyproterone acetate), an anti-libidinal drug, and stilboestrol (a female hormone) for sex offenders.

Benperidol and stilboestrol constitute 'chemical castration' and their use on prisoners in the UK and USA instigated widespread intense debate. Proponents insist that these chemicals can only be ethically used on people who freely offer their services as volunteers but there is considerable doubt as to whether one can ever find 'free volunteers' in prison. These drugs also have unpleasant side effects, for example, stilboestrol causes atrophy of the genitals, female breast development, nausea, feminisation, obesity and serious psychiatric disorders.

Some drugs are used exclusively for control purposes. Mace and CS gas are routinely used for riot control. Sedatives and tranquillisers are frequently used to keep potential troublesome prisoners calm. In nineteenth century prisons opium was used for this purpose and in the contemporary UK, Valium, Librium and Largactil are generally used. In the USA a heavy tranquilliser (prolixin) is used which reduces hostility, anxiety, agitation and hyperactivity but often produces a zombie-like effect. It has some other unpleasant side effects which according to the manufacturers include automatic reactions, blurred vision, bladder paralysis, glaucoma, faecal impaction, techychardia, liver damage, skin disorders and death. It is extensively used in prisons for the sole purpose of keeping troublemakers quiet.

Electro-control is still a little futuristic since the research programme is still ongoing in the USA with the idea being to plant a telemetric device on – or in – the prisoner. This will transmit data about the physical state of the subject to a central computer programmed to assess from the information the mental state of the subject. If the indications are that he or she is about to commit an offence an impulse is sent to a receiver planted in the brain that has the potential to cause pain, paralysis or even death. These devices could enable a *dangerous* offender to be safely released from prison. The two main obstacles to the implementation of such schemes have been the limited range of the equipment and ethical concerns raised by civil liberty groups.

Conclusions

Each of the attempts to explain crime and criminal behaviour discussed in this chapter follow directly in the biological predestined actor model tradition established by Lombroso. Each theory has sought explanations in the measurable, organic part of individuals, their bodies and their brains and it is certainly impossible to deny that some of these studies really do explain the criminality of a tiny minority of offenders. Closer investigation of individual cases nevertheless demonstrates that social and environmental factors have been equally important. Indeed, it is important to note that most of the researchers – from Lombroso onwards – came to increasingly recognise that reality.

The early biological positivists had proposed that discoveries about the natural world – and natural laws – would find a counterpart within human behaviour. The criminological emphasis of this approach has thus been on the scientist as the detached objective neutral observer who has the task of identifying natural laws that regulate criminal behaviour. Once these natural laws have been discovered, a reduction in offending behaviour is seen as possible by the use of treatment programmes aimed at ameliorating or eliminating the causes of that behaviour. It has also been proposed that investigations should be extended into the lives of individuals who are deemed to be 'at risk' of offending in order that treatment might be instigated and many offences be prevented before they occur. In short, criminal behaviour is perceived to be a sickness – an inherently problematic analysis – that has led to treatments that are intrusive, in some cases unethical, and on occasion with horrendous wider implications.

The early biological positivists replaced the rational calculating individual of the rational actor model with an organism subject to the forces of biological heredity and impulsive behaviour beyond conscious control. From this same source, however, came Social Darwinism, a mode of thought based on the notion that *The Origins of the Species* offered a new evolutionary and scientific basis for the social sciences as well as for biology. It was an idea highly compatible with interests in the wider world and was soon used to give 'scientific' legitimacy to an old idea, namely that the capacity for rational judgement, moral behaviour and, above all, business success was not equally distributed among the various races and divisions of humanity.

Quite prominent figures of late-nineteenth-century social science began to argue that Africans, Indians, the 'negroes' of North America, paupers, criminals and even women had inherited smaller brains and a reduced capacity for rational thought and moral conduct than everyone else. Such ideas were particularly appealing in the USA, which was experiencing an influx of immigrants of diverse ethnic background and where people were particularly ready to equate the biological processes of natural selection with the competition of an unrestricted market. In both Britain and the USA programmes of selective breeding were proposed to encourage progress or to prevent civilisation from degenerating (Jones, 1980). It was a view that was to remain popular into the early decades of the twentieth century and which was to obtain support from the 'science' of *eugenics* and its supporters who were concerned with 'improving' the genetic selection of the human race. The biological variant of the predestined actor model of crime and criminal behaviour was highly compatible with this viewpoint. Goring (1913) was convinced that criminality was passed down through inherited genes and in order to reduce crime, recommended that people with such characteristics should not be allowed to reproduce. The more recent and rigorous research in search of the 'criminal gene' has rather similar implications.

In 1994 a new Centre for Social, Genetic and Development Psychiatry was opened at the Maudsley Hospital in south London to examine what role genetic structure plays in determining patterns of behaviour, including crime (Muncie, 1999). The following year a major conference was held behind closed doors to discuss the possibility of isolating a criminal gene – the basis of which rested on the study of twins and adoptees (Ciba Foundation, 1996). Moreover, one of the best-selling social science books of the 1990s, *The Bell Curve* (Herrnstein and Murray, 1994) claimed that black people and Latinos are over-represented among the ranks of the poor in the USA because they are less intelligent. The suggestion is that inherited genes mainly determine IQ and that people with low intelligence are more likely to commit crime because they lack foresight and are unable to distinguish right from wrong. Muncie (1999) observes that such theories continue to be attractive – at least to some – because they seem to provide scientific evidence that clearly differentiates us from 'them', an out group we feel legitimately entitled to target, outlaw and in the final instance, eradicate. It is an argument that Einstadter and Henry (1995) note to be characteristic of totalitarian regimes whether they are Nazi Germany, the former USSR, and by extension to the more recent forced therapy programmes in the USA.

Morrison (1995) observes that the Holocaust – the systematic extermination of over six million people by Nazi Germany during the Second World War – was undoubtedly the crime of the twentieth century, yet it had provided such a great problem for criminology that it had not previously been mentioned in any textbook. For he observes the essential question to be whether the Holocaust is at odds with modernity or simply the logical consequence of a project of which we might note the biological variant of the predestined actor model of crime and criminal behaviour to simply be a component. There is certainly strong available evidence to support the latter proposition. The Jewish social theorist Hannah Arendt argues that the Holocaust destroyed the semblance of any belief that evil must be motivated by evil and conducted by evil people. She observes that, 'the sad truth of the matter is that most evil is done by people who never made up their mind to be either good or bad' (Arendt, 1964: 438). Morrison (1995: 203) observes that this horrendous and unsurpassable crime can only be explained by 'the weakness of individual judgement in the face of reason, in the face of the claims of organisation, in the face of claims of the normal, in the face of claims for progress ...'.

The outcome was to destroy our belief in the right of experts – whether they are scientists, social engineers or managerial politicians – to think for us unquestioned. It was suddenly no longer possible to take the notion of modernist civilisation for granted or to accept an unilinear image of social progress in human affairs. The biological variant of the predestined actor model had led to the plausibility of ideas such as sterilisation, genetic selection and even death for the biologically untreatable. Such work was now unpalatable for many in the context of the mid-twentieth century experience of mass systematic extermination in death camps of outsider groups whether based on their ethnicity (in the case of the Jews, Slavs and Gypsies), their sexuality (in the case of homosexuals), their health (in the case of the disabled and seriously ill) or their behaviour (in the case of whole categories of criminals).

In more recent years there has been a sustained campaign to rehabilitate biological theories with the recognition that physical and social environment factors are more closely linked. There remains however serious ethical implications surrounding possible treatment regimes and these issues are revisited in Chapter 13.

Suggested further reading

Biological positivism is an extremely wide subject area and there are thus many relevant texts. Students are therefore advised to use the references in the text as a guide to specific interests. Ferri (1968) is nonetheless a timeless original still worth considering as a general introduction to early criminological positivism *per se*, while Shah and Roth (1974) provide an overview of some of the crucial albeit earlier research in this tradition. For some more recent and very different examples of biological positivism see Herrnstein and Murray (1994) from a right realist perspective and Jones (1993), an eminent contemporary geneticist. For a discussion of the wider implications of biological positivism in modern society see Bauman (1989), Morrison (1995) and Taylor, Walton and Young (1973) who provide very different but essential accounts.

Note

1 The following website provides a very extensive list of people past and present who it is said have been – or are – on the autistic disorder spectrum: http://www. geocities.com/richardg_uk/famousac.html.

6. Psychological positivism

We saw in the previous chapter that proponents of the biological variant of the predestined actor model argue that criminal behaviour is the outcome of factors internal to the physical body of the individual human being that predisposes them to criminality. For psychological positivists, the search for the causes of crime is directed to the mind and thus we encounter notions of the 'criminal mind' or 'criminal personality'. For purist proponents of this perspective, there are patterns of reasoning and behaviour that are specific to offenders and these remain constant regardless of their different social experiences.

There are three broad categories of psychological theories of crimes and the first two groupings – psychodynamic and behavioural learning theories – are firmly rooted in the predestined actor tradition. The third group – cognitive learning theories – reject much of that positivist tradition by incorporating notions of creative thinking and thus choice, in many ways more akin to the rational actor model.

Psychodynamic theories

Psychodynamic explanations of crime and criminal behaviour have their origins in the extremely influential work of Sigmund Freud (1856–1939). His assertion that sexuality is present from birth and has a subsequent course of development is the fundamental basis of psychoanalysis and one that has aroused a great deal of controversy. Freud had originally proposed that experiences of sexual seduction in childhood are the basis of all later neurosis but, subsequently, he was to change his mind and conclude that the seductions had not actually taken place, they were fantasies. It is this notion of the repressed fantasy – pushed to the back of our mind and forgotten – that is the core tenet of the psychoanalytic tradition.

Within the psychoanalytical model, developed by Freud, the human personality has three sets of interacting forces. First, there is the *id* or primitive biological drives. Second, there is the superego – or conscience – that operates in the unconsciousness but which is comprised of values internalised through the early interactions of the person, in particular with their parents. Third, there is the ego or the conscious personality and this has the task of balancing the demands of the id against the inhibitions imposed by the superego, as a person responds to external influences (Freud, 1927).

Freud himself proposed two different models of criminal behaviour. The first views certain forms of criminal activity – for example arson, shoplifting and some sexual offences – as essentially reflecting a state of mental disturbance or illness. His theory of psychosexual development proposes a number of complex stages of psychic development that may easily be disrupted, leading to neuroses or severe difficulties in adults. Crucially, a disturbance at one or more of these stages in childhood can lead to criminal behaviour in later life.

Of essential importance to the psychosexual development of the child is the influence of the parents and, importantly, many of these influences are unconscious. Neither parents nor children are in fact aware of how they are influencing each other. This is an important recognition for, in a sense, it reduces the responsibility of parents for producing children that offend.

The second model proposes that offenders possess a 'weak conscience'. Hence, for Freud, the development of the conscience is of fundamental importance in the upbringing of the child. A sense of morality is closely linked to guilt, and those possessing the greatest degree of unconscious 'guilt' are likely to be those with the strictest consciences and such people are therefore the most unlikely to engage in criminal behaviour. Guilt is significantly something that results *not* from committing crimes, but rather from a deeply embedded feeling that develops in childhood, the outcome of the way in which the parents respond to the transgressions of the child. It is an approach that was to lead to a proliferation of tests attempting to measure conscience or levels of guilt, with the belief that this would allow a prediction of whether the child would later become a criminal.

The Freudian approach is clearly firmly embedded in the predestined actor model. Unconscious conflicts or tensions *determine* all actions and it is the purpose of the conscious (ego) to resolve these tensions by finding ways of satisfying the basic inner urges by engaging in activities sanctioned by society. The later Freudian tradition was more concerned with elaborating on the development of the ego.

Aichhorn (1925) argued that at birth a child has certain instinctive drives that demand satisfaction and that he or she is unaware of – and obviously unaffected by – the norms of society around it. It is thus in an 'asocial state' and the task is to bring it into a social state. When the child's development is ineffective he or she remains asocial. Crucially, if the instinctive drives are not acted out they become suppressed and the child is said to be in a state of 'latent delinquency'. When given outside provocation, this 'latent delinquency' can be activated and translated into actual offending behaviour.

Aichhorn concluded that many of the offenders with whom he had worked had underdeveloped consciences which were the result of the absence of an intimate attachment with their parents when they were children. The proposed solution was to locate such children and place them in a happy environment where they could identify with adults in a way they had previously not experienced with the intention of developing their superego.

Aichhorn identified two further categories of criminal. First, there were those with fully developed consciences but who had identified and indeed might well have very close relationships with parents who were themselves criminals. Second, there were those who had been allowed to do whatever they liked by overindulgent parents.

Healy and Bronner (1936) conducted a study of 105 pairs of brothers where one was a persistent offender and the other a non-offender and found that only nineteen of the former and 30 of the latter had experienced good quality family conditions. These findings suggest that circumstances within a household may well be favourable for one child but not the sibling. It was proposed that the latter had not made an emotional attachment to a 'good parent', hence impeding the development of a superego.

Healy and Bronner also found that siblings exposed to similar unfavourable circumstances might react differently. Thus one might become an offender while the others do not. The proposed explanation was that offenders are more emotionally disturbed and express their frustrated needs through deviant activities while the thwarted needs of the non-offenders were channelled into other socially accepted activities. Healy and Bronner emphasised that the growth and effect of conscience are complicated matters that vary between individuals, thus, one might condemn stealing but condone lying, or vice versa.

Friedlander (1947, 1949) argued that some children develop antisocial behaviour or a faulty character that can leave them susceptible to deviant behaviour. Redl and Wineman (1951) similarly argued that some children develop a delinquent ego, the outcome of which is a hostile attitude towards authority because the child has not developed a good ego and superego.

John Bowlby (1952) extremely influentially argued that offending behaviour takes place when a child has not enjoyed a close and continuous relationship with its mother during its formative years. He studied 44 juveniles convicted of stealing and referred to the child guidance clinic where he worked and compared them with a control group of children – matched for age and intelligence – which had been referred to the same clinic, but not in connection with offending behaviour. Problematically, no attempt was made to check for the presence of criminal elements in the control group thus exposing the study to criticism on methodological grounds (Morgan, 1975). Bowlby found that seventeen of those with convictions for stealing had been separated from their mothers for extended periods before the age of five, in contrast to only two of the control group. Fourteen of the convicted group were found to be 'affectionless characters', persons deemed to have difficulty in forming close personal relationships – while none of the controls were thus labelled.

Maternal deprivation theory was to have a major and lasting influence on the training of social workers (Morgan, 1975). While other researchers have sought to test it empirically their findings have tended to suggest that the separation of a child from its mother is not, in itself, significant in predicting criminal behaviour. Andry (1957) and Grygier (1969) both indicated a need to take account of the roles of both parents. Naess (1959, 1962) found that offenders were no more likely to have been separated from their mothers than non-offenders. Little (1963) found however that 80 per cent of a sample of boys who had received custodial sentences had been separated from at least one parent for varying periods, in fact, separations from the father were found to be more common.

Wootton (1959, 1962) argued that there was no evidence that any effects of separation of the child from its mother will be irreversible and she observed that while only a small proportion of offenders may be affected in this way, there was also a lack of information about the extent of maternal deprivation among non-offenders in general. Rutter (1981), in one of the most comprehensive reviews of the maternal deprivation thesis, considered the stability of the child/mother relationship to be more important than the absence of breaks and argued that a small number of substitutes can carry out mothering functions – without adverse effect – provided that such care is of good quality. Rutter considered the quality of child-rearing practices to be the crucial issue.

Glueck and Glueck (1950) found that the fathers of offenders provided discipline that was generally lax and inconsistent with the use of physical punishment by both parents common and the giving of praise rare. The parents of non-offenders, on the other hand, were found to use physical punishment more sparingly and were more consistent in their use of discipline. McCord, McCord and Zola (1959) agreed with the Gluecks that the consistency of discipline was more important that the degree of strictness. Bandura and Walters (1959) found that the fathers of aggressive boys are more likely to punish such behaviour in the home while approving of it outside and also used physical punishments more than the fathers of their control group.

Hoffman and Saltzstein (1967) identified and categorised three types of child-rearing techniques. First, *power assertion* was found to involve the parental use of – or threats to use – physical punishment and/or the withdrawal of material privileges. Second, *love withdrawal* is where the parent withdraws – or threatens to withdraw – affection from the child, for example, by paying no attention to it. Third, *induction* entails letting the child know how its actions have affected the parent, thus encouraging a sympathetic or empathetic response. Essentially, the first technique primarily relies on the instillation of fear, while the other two depend on fostering guilt feelings in the child.

Hoffman and Saltzstein offer five explanations for the association to be found between moral development and the use of child-rearing techniques. First, an open display of anger and aggression by a parent when disciplining a child increases the dependence of the latter on external control. Punishment connected with power assertion dissolves both the anger of the parent and the guilt of the child more rapidly. Second, love withdrawal and induction, and the anxiety associated with them, has a longer-lasting effect so that the development of internal controls are more likely. Third, where love withdrawal is used, the punishment ends when the child confesses or makes reparation which is referred to as engaging in a corrective act. In the case of physical punishment there is likely to be a lapse of time between it being carried out and the child performing a corrective act. Fourth, withholding love intensifies the resolve of the child to behave in an approved manner in order to retain love. Fifth, the use of induction is particularly effective in enabling the child to examine and correct the behaviour that has been disapproved of.

Hoffman and Saltzstein propose that it is people who have been raised through the use of love withdrawal or induction techniques that are less likely to engage in offending behaviour because of the greater effect of internalised controls. People raised on the power assertion method depend on the threat of external punishment to control their behaviour and thus will only remain controlled as long as that risk is present, certain and sufficiently intense. It is of course only internal controls that are likely to be ever present.

A number of studies have gone beyond child-rearing practices to assess the relevance of more general features of the family unit in the causation of criminal behaviour and some of these conducted in both the USA and the UK have suggested that a 'broken home' – where one of the birth parents is not present – may be a factor in the development of offending behaviour.

Glueck and Glueck (1950) measured the frequency of broken homes among its samples and found that 60 per cent of the offenders came from such a home, compared with only 34 per cent of the control group. In Britain, Burt (1945) and Mannheim (1948) found that a high proportion of offenders came from such homes. Others note that the 'broken home' is not a homogenous category and that a range of different factors need to be considered (Bowlby, 1952; Mannheim, 1955; Tappan, 1960). Nye (1958) and Gibbens (1963) observed that offending behaviour is more likely to occur among children from intact but unhappy homes.

While West (1969) echoed the observations of Wootton (1959) about the difficulties of defining a broken home, his study with Farrington (1973) found that about twice as many offenders – compared with controls – came from homes broken by parental separation before the child was ten years old. Comparing children from a home broken by separation with those broken by the death of a parent, more children from the former were found to be offenders. Moreover, 20 per cent of the former group became recidivists, whereas none of those from the second group did.

Monahan (1957) suggested that broken homes were found far more among black than white offenders; while Pitts (1986) claimed a link between criminality and homelessness and found that African Caribbean youths tend to become homeless more than their white counterparts. Chilton and Markle (1972) had previously observed that the rate of family breakdown is in general much higher in the case of black than white families and this may explain why it is that more black young offenders come from broken homes.

Two studies conducted more recently in the UK have reported that broken homes and early separation predicted convictions up to age 33 where the separation occurred before age five (Kolvin et al., 1990) and that it predicted convictions and self-reported offending behaviour (Farrington, 1992). Morash and Rucker (1989) found that although it was single-parent families who had children with the highest rates of deviancy, these were also the lowest income families. Thus, the nature of the problem – broken home, parental supervision, low income – was unclear. These possible explanations of crime and criminal behaviour are revisited in more detail in later chapters.

Behavioural learning theories

The second category of psychological theories we will consider – behavioural learning theories – have their origins in the work of Ivan Petrovich Pavlov and B.F. Skinner. Pavlov famously studied the processes involved in very simple, automatic animal behaviours, for example, salivation in the presence of food and found that those responses that occur spontaneously to a natural (*unconditioned*) stimulus could be made to happen (*conditioned*) to a stimulus that was previously neutral, for example, a light. Thus, if you consistently turn the light on just before feeding the animal, then eventually the animal will salivate when the light comes on, even though no food is present. This conditioning can of course be undone. Thus, if you continue to present the light without the food, eventually the animal will stop salivating, a contrary process that is called *extinction*.

To some extent the conditioning process is specific to the specific stimulus that is presented but it can also be generalised to other similar stimuli. Thus, if the animal has been conditioned to salivate to a red light, for example, it would salivate slightly if a blue light is turned on. However, you could train it to salivate *only* to the red light, by never rewarding it with food when presented with the blue light. For behaviourists, it is this notion of differential conditioning that is the key to understanding how learning works.

Pavlov carried out his work on automatic behaviours occurring in response to stimuli, B.F. Skinner extended the principle to active learning, where the animal has to *do* something in order to obtain a reward or avoid punishment. The same principle nevertheless applies. The occurrence of the desired behaviour is increased by positive reinforcement and eventually extinguished by non-reinforcement.

Learned behaviours are much more resistant to extinction if the reinforcement has only occasionally been used during learning. This makes sense. If you put money in a ticket machine and no ticket comes out, you stop using the machine. On the other hand, many people put money in gaming machines even though they pay out prizes infrequently.

Behaviour can be differentially conditioned so that it occurs in response to one stimulus and not another. Indeed, in a sense all *operant conditioning* – as this type of learning is called – is differential conditioning. The animal learns to produce certain behaviours and not others, by the fact that only these receive reinforcement.

One further process has to be considered in order to explain the behaviour of the animals in conditioning experiments. If learning really happened as described, then the excitation produced by reinforcement would continue to build up over repeated trials, and a rat, for example, would continually press a bar for food, more and more frequently, until it died of exhaustion. What actually happens is that responses to the stimulus become *less* frequent as it is repeated – eventually stopping altogether – but start again at their old level if there is a break between presentations. To explain this phenomenon, behavioural learning theorists have presumed a 'quantity' of inhibition that builds up as the response is repeated, until it exceeds the level of excitation and stops the responses occurring. It reduces when the animal is not responding leaving the level of excitation unchanged and so the response recommences.

Hans Eysenck (1970, 1977) sought to build a *general* theory of criminal behaviour based on the psychological concept of conditioning and central to his thesis is the human conscience which he considers to be a conditioned reflex. We saw above that the Freudians have been interested in the notion of conscience but Eysenck viewed the concept very differently.

Eysenck's theory is not easy to compartmentalise. He argues from the biological predestined actor perspective that individuals are genetically endowed with certain learning abilities that are conditioned by stimuli in the environment but he accepts the rational actor model premise that crime can be a natural and rational choice activity where individuals maximise pleasure and minimise pain. People are said to learn the rules and norms of society through the development of a conscience which is acquired through learning what happens when you take part in certain activities. In short, the virtuous receive rewards while the deviant is punished.

Eysenck describes three dimensions of personality: *extroversion* – which itself consists of two different components, impulsiveness and sociability and which are themselves partly independent of each other – *neuroticism* and *psychoticism*. Each dimension takes the form of a continuum that runs from high to low. Low extroversion is sometimes termed introversion and, in the case of neuroticism, a person with a high score would be regarded as neurotic and someone with a low score, stable. Scores are usually obtained by the administration of a personality questionnaire of which there are several versions and it is usual to abbreviate the descriptions of a person's score, for example, high N (neuroticism), high E (extroversion), and high P (psychoticism).

Each of these personality dimensions has distinct characteristics. Thus, someone with a high E score would be outgoing and sociable, optimistic and impulsive, a high N person is anxious, moody and highly sensitive, while those with low scores on these continuums present the very opposite of these traits. Insensitivity to others, a liking for solitude, sensation seeking and lack of regard for danger are all linked with psychoticism (Eysenck, 1970). Feldman (1977) observes a similarity between this description of psychoticism and antisocial personality disorder – or psychopathy – which is discussed below.

Eysenck (1977) argues that various combinations of the different personality dimensions within an individual affects their ability to learn not to offend and consequently the level of offending. Someone with a high E and a high N score – a neurotic extrovert – will not condition well. A low E and N score – a stable introvert – is the most effectively conditioned. Stable extroverts and neurotic introverts come somewhere between the two extremes in terms of conditioning.

Various researchers have sought to test Eysenck's theory. Little (1963) compared the scores for convicted young offenders on the extroversion and neuroticism dimensions with those for non-offenders and found no difference in relation to extroversion but the offenders scored higher on the neuroticism scale. Neither dimension nevertheless appeared to be related to repeat offending. Hoghughi and Forrest (1970) compared scores for neuroticism and extroversion between a sample of convicted youths and a control group of supposedly non-offenders – or at least those with no convictions – and found that the offenders were rated higher on the neuroticism scale but were actually less extroverted than their controls. This finding could of course be explained by the possibility that it is the experience of detention itself that could make a young person neurotic.

Hans and Sybil Eysenck (1970) tested 178 incarcerated young offenders on all three-personality dimensions and followed up this research on their release finding that 122 had been reconvicted and all of these scored significantly higher in relation to extroversion than the others. Allsopp and Feldman (1975) conducted a self-report study and found a significant and positive association between scores for E, N and P levels of antisocial behaviour among girls between eleven and fifteen years of age with the strongest association found in relation to psychoticism. Their study of schoolboys conducted the following year reached similar conclusions (Allsopp and Feldman, 1976).

Less research has been conducted in relation to adult criminals but where E and N scores for prisoners have been compared with those for non-prisoners, the former have received higher scores for neuroticism, and repeat offenders have been found to be more neurotic than first offenders. Little evidence has been found to suggest that adult criminals are more extrovert than non-criminals (Feldman, 1977). Eysenck has nevertheless responded to his critics by pointing out that extroversion has two components, sociability and impulsiveness and argues that it is the latter which is more significantly associated with criminal behaviour (Eysenck, 1970). Many personality tests simply provide a score for extroversion that combines those for the two components which means that a person who is highly impulsive but very unsociable will receive an E score midway on the personality continuum.

The association between psychoticism and criminal behaviour has been the subject of very little research but Smith and Smith (1977) and McEwan (1983) found a positive relationship between psychoticism and repeat offending. However, the work of Allsopp and Feldman (1975, 1976) and McGurk and McDougall (1981) suggests that combinations or clusters of scores for the three dimensions are more important than scores for individual dimensions.

Research has been conducted in order to test for a relationship between personality types and offence type. Hindelang and Weis (1972) found that with minor offences – such as vandalism and traffic offences – the descending order of offending was as they had predicted; thus, high E plus high N, high E and low N, or low E and high N, then low E and low N. However, this was found not to be the case with offences involving theft or aggression.

Eysenck, Rust and Eysenck (1977) found that thieves or violent offenders had lower N scores than other groups, conmen had lower P scores, and there was no variation for E scores. McEwan and Knowles (1984) simply found no association between offence type and personality cluster. There thus seems to be considerable uncertainty and ambiguity about the validity and veracity of Eysenck's theory, Farrington (1994) nevertheless suggests that this approach seems to at least identify a distinct link between offending and impulsiveness but he found no significant links with personality.

Antisocial personality disorder appears to be a relatively recent term that is interchangeable with that of psychopathy. There are various and not always consistent definitions of this condition but in general these emphasise such traits as an incapacity for loyalty, selfishness, irresponsibility, impulsiveness, inability to feel guilt and failure to learn from experience. One feature common to all descriptions is a lack of empathy or affection (Blackburn and Maybury, 1985). The American Psychiatric Association (1968) had proposed that a person should be diagnosed as having 'antisocial personality disorder' when the above characteristics are 'inflexible, maladaptive, and persistent, and cause significant functional impairment or subjective distress'. Explanations are nevertheless many and varied.

McCord and McCord (1964) had suggested a lack of parental affection to be one of the key contributory factors. Robins (1966) found that children who behaved in a psychopathic manner were more likely to have fathers who were psychopathic or alcoholics but, on the other hand, Cleckley (1964) found that many of his psychopathic patients came from a happy and supportive family background. Indeed, Hare (1970) observes that most people from a disturbed background do not develop antisocial personality disorder.

Some researchers have studied the functioning of the central nervous system by using the electroencephalogram (EEG) which tests for abnormalities in the electrical activity of the brain in psychopaths. Syndulko (1978) suggested that irregularities are frequently shown in the EEG testing of those with antisocial personality disorder but Hare and Jutari (1986) found that the EEGs of psychopaths were normal while they were active but abnormal while they were resting.

Other studies have examined the functioning of the autonomic nervous system (ANS) in those diagnosed as having antisocial personality disorder. The level of activity in the ANS is assessed by measuring the conductivity of the skin (electrodermal reactivity) and the level of cardiac reactivity. Hare and Jutari (1986) found that when psychopaths are resting their level of electrodermal reactivity is exceptionally low and Hollin (1989) suggests that fast heart rate may be a sign that the psychopath is lowering the level of cortical arousal by 'gating out' the sensory input related to unpleasant situational stimuli.

Eysenck (1963) had found that those diagnosed with antisocial personality disorder are mostly extroverted which suggests the possible relevance of the personality characteristics of psychopaths in explaining their antisocial behaviour. Extroverts are said to be more difficult to socialise because of difficulties in learning and this might well apply to psychopaths and their difficulties may well have a physiological foundation. If this is the case, then we might assume that psychopaths will be very poor at learning to avoid the unpleasant stimuli associated with particular acts but Hollin (1989) observes that the findings from such studies vary according to the type of unpleasant stimulus used. Thus, when poor performance was met with physical pain or by disapproval, psychopaths obtained worse results than controls but were found to be better learners when the consequences were a financial penalty.

Some studies have examined the responsiveness of psychopaths to reward learning where correct responses are rewarded by social approval. The findings are mixed but there is no evidence that psychopaths are less amenable than other people to reward learning (Feldman, 1977).

Feldman (1977) observes that the subjects of antisocial personality disorder research may be unrepresentative, merely being those who have been brought to the attention of the authorities. Psychopathic behaviours may be extremely widespread throughout the population and psychopaths might well be found in legitimate occupations such as business, medicine and psychiatry (Cleckley, 1976). It is only when they engage in proscribed activities that the individuals will come to the attention of the authorities. Considering the findings of the different types of learning studies, there is nevertheless some evidence that psychopaths may be undersocialised because of the way that they learn and, moreover, it is also possible that these difficulties arise from physiological factors.

Vold, Bernard and Snipes (1998) suggest that the term 'psychopath' is simply a useful term employed by psychiatrists who wish to describe a certain type of person who exhibits particular types of behaviour and attitudes. They argue that when it is applied to criminals, the term seems to be merely a label attached to particularly serious offenders. It does nothing to help recognise such offenders in advance, to explain their behaviour or prescribe suitable treatment.

Some psychiatrists who have argued that they are able to identify future dangerous offenders have disputed this notion. Vold, Bernard and Snipes (1998: 101) have responded by noting that 'if that is their claim, then their track record so far has been poor'. Kozol, Boucher and Garofalo (1972) sought to predict the future dangerousness of a group of high-risk offenders prior to their release from prison but failed to predict two-thirds of the violent crime that subsequently occurred. Monahan (1981) comprehensively reviewed the clinical techniques used for predicting violent behaviour and concluded that it can only be done within very restricted circumstances arguing that it is not possible to predict violence over an extended period or when a person is moving from one situation to another, for example, being released from prison.

Researchers have subsequently moved away from trying to predict future violent behaviour towards the more general possibility that individuals might engage in any form of offending behaviour (Vold, Bernard and Snipes, 1998). Most of this research has focused on juveniles rather than adults with the strongest predictor of later offending behaviour found to be early childhood problem behaviours such as disruptive classroom conduct, aggressiveness, lying and dishonesty (Loeber and Dishion, 1983). The stability of these behavioural problems over time suggest that these people may have certain personality characteristics associated with antisocial behaviour even if they do not show up on personality tests.

In recent years personality typing – or offender profiling – has been used, particularly in the USA, to help detect particular types of criminals and it is a method found to have been most useful in the detection of serial murders, although we should note that offender profiling is not that new. Dr Thomas Bond produced a profile of Jack the Ripper in 1888 (Rumbelow, 1987). Serial murder is a repetitive event where the perpetrator kills on a number of different occasions, frequently spanning a matter of months or years, and often at different locations. The murders are often brutal and sadistic and the victims strangers. Most people consider such killers to be simply mad. Holmes and De Burger (1989), on the other hand, argue that such murderers are not suffering from any psychological illness, for in this type of case there is characteristically a motive, and proceed to describe four main types of serial killer. First, there is the *visionary motive type* where the killer commits crimes because they hear voices or see visions. The act itself is usually spontaneous and disorganised and committed only in response to the voices. Second, there is the *mission-oriented motive type* where the killer has a goal, usually to rid the world of a particular type of person such as prostitutes or vagrants – indeed terrorists might well be included in this category – but they are not psychotic and have a strong wish to solve a particular problem. The victims are usually strangers, chosen because they fit into a certain category, of what the perpetrator considers to be legitimate targets, and the act is usually well planned and efficiently carried out. Third, there is the *hedonistic type* who kills basically for pleasure and the enjoyment of the act and there are two sub-categories of this typology. The thrill-orientated killer enjoys the excitement of killing and so kills for pleasure, random strangers with no specific characteristics are chosen as victims with the killing spontaneous and disorganised. The lust killer, on the other hand, kills for a sexual motive, obtaining gratification by abusing others, with the victim usually a stranger who possesses the required characteristics. Fourth, there is the *power/control-oriented type* who is very difficult to distinguish from the lust or thrill-seeking types. In order to prove control, the killer may well carry out sexual acts, but the sex is only a form of power over the victim who is a stranger with specific characteristics and the crime – which is often very sadistic – will be organised and planned.

The psychological profile is however only one of many ways of finding a solution to a murder. The science on which it is based is not an exact one and this fact is often overlooked. Omerod (1996) notes the limitations of the methodology and argues that offender profiling is only useful in a few cases such as rape, killing or arson because the profile only describes a type of person and does not identify an individual. The profile can thus only usefully supplement other investigative methods.

Cognitive learning theories

Both psychodynamic and behavioural learning theories have clear foundations in the predestined actor model although later more sophisticated variants of those traditions became more readily accepting of rational actor model notions of albeit limited choice. They both remained nevertheless committed to the central notion of psychological positivism that proposes that there are patterns of reasoning and behaviour specific to offenders that remain constant regardless of their different social experiences. The third psychological tradition has its foundations in a fundamental critique of the predestined actor model.

The behavioural learning theorists had emphasised the role of environmental stimuli and overt behavioural response but failed to satisfactorily explain why people attempt to organise, make sense of and often alter the information they learn. There thus emerged a growing recognition that mental events – or cognition – could no longer be ignored (Kendler, 1985). Cognitive psychologists proposed that by observing the responses made by individuals to different stimuli it is possible to draw inferences about the nature of the internal cognitive processes that produce those responses.

Many of the ideas and assumptions of cognitivism have their origins in the work of the Gestalt psychologists of Germany, Edward Tolman of the USA and Jean Piaget of Switzerland. Gestalt psychologists emphasised the importance of organisational processes in perception, learning, and problem solving and proposed that individuals were predisposed to organise information in particular ways (Henle, 1985). Tolman (1959) had been a prominent learning theorist at the time of the behavioural movement but later – influenced by the Gestalt theorists – developed a distinctively cognitive perspective where he included internal mental phenomena in his perspective of how learning occurs. Piaget (1980) was a Swiss biologist and psychologist renowned for constructing a highly influential model of child development and learning. His theory is founded on the idea that the developing child builds cognitive structures – mental 'maps', schema or networked concepts – for understanding and responding to physical experiences within his or her environment. Piaget further asserted that the cognitive structure of a child increases in sophistication with development, moving from a few innate reflexes such as crying and sucking to highly complex mental activities. His theory identifies four developmental stages of cognitive development each influenced by physiological maturation and interaction with the environment and characterised by qualitatively different forms of thought.

B.F. Skinner (1938) had – as we have seen above – argued from an operant conditioning perspective that the person must actively respond if they are to learn. Cognitivists share that view with Skinner but shift the emphasis to *mental* rather than physical activity. This social learning theory emphasises that behaviour may be reinforced not only through actual rewards and punishments, but also through expectations that are learned by watching what happens to other people. Ultimately the person will make a choice as to what they will learn and how.

An early proponent of the notion that crime is simply a normal learned behaviour was Gabriel Tarde (1843–1904) who argued that criminals are primarily normal people who – by accident of birth – are brought up in an atmosphere in which they learn crime as a way of life. His 'laws of imitation' were essentially a cognitive theory in which the individual learns ideas through an association with others. Behaviour follows from the incorporation of those ideas. Tarde's first law proposes that people imitate one another in proportion to how much contact they have with each other and this is more frequent and changes more rapidly in urban areas. His second law proposes that the inferior usually imitates the superior suggesting that such offences as drunkenness and murder had originated as crimes committed by royalty but had been subsequently imitated by other social classes, while those in rural areas later imitated crimes originating in the city. His third law suggests that newer fashions replace older ones, for example, murder by shooting has come to replace that by knifing. This is an important theoretical development because it is the first attempt to describe criminal behaviour in terms of normal learned behaviour rather than in terms of biological or psychological defects albeit that the model of learning on which the theory is based is relatively simple (Vold, Bernard and Snipes, 1998). Tarde was to significantly influence Edwin H. Sutherland's later differential association theory and the latter was to have a subsequently huge and enduring impact on criminology, particularly in the USA.

Sutherland had originally embarked on this line of enquiry with his research reported in *The Professional Thief* (1937) which consisted of a description of major elements of the criminal profession of theft as related to him by a thief with the alias 'Chic Conwell'. Sutherland thus discovered that thieving has its own techniques, codes, status, organisation and traditions that were imitated in other groups considered non-criminal.

Sutherland first used the term 'differential association' to explain interaction patterns by which thieves were restricted in their physical and social contacts to association with like-minded others and it was at this stage of its development more or less a synonym for a criminal subculture. In 1939 the concept was used to develop a theory of criminal behaviour where it was proposed that crime is a learned activity much like any other. Sutherland argued that it is the frequency and consistency of contacts with patterns of criminality that determine the chance that a person will participate in systematic criminal behaviour. The basic cause of such behaviour is thus the existence of different cultural groups with different normative structures within the same society that have produced a situation of *differential social organisation*.

Certain shortcomings were identified with this early version of differential association theory. Fundamentally, it said little about the processes through which this 'contamination through exposure' could be resisted through a variety of personal or social differences. It was moreover a rather narrow and deterministic version of learning theory particularly as it tended to rule out such psychological factors as conscience and moral understanding.

Sutherland (1947) consequently revised his theory to now argue that criminal behaviour occurs when individuals acquire sufficient sentiments in favour of law violation to outweigh their association with non-criminal tendencies. Those associations or contacts that have the greatest impact are those that are frequent, early in point of origin or are the most intense. He argued that at this level of explanation it was not necessary to explain why a person has particular associations for this involved a complex of social interactions and relationships, but he maintained that it was the existence of differential social organisation that exposed people to varied associational ties. Differential association also remains in contrast to other psychological explanations, in that it retains a dominant sociological argument that the primary groups to which people belong exert the strongest influence on them. This formulation won wide acceptance because it was widely considered to be sufficient to explain the occurrence of all criminal conduct.

Some key questions were nevertheless to remain unanswered. Thus, what kind of associations can be considered intense? What if criminal attitudes are more compelling than others and thus are able to overcome a primary affiliation to conformist behaviour, even though criminal association ties are fewer? It can be argued moreover that the theory neglects personality traits, provides no place for variations in opportunities to engage in law breaking and cannot explain spontaneous crimes of passion. It will nevertheless be seen in the following chapter that sociological delinquent subcultural theories have their foundations in Sutherland's arguments about the content of what is learned.

Sutherland is particularly remembered for his attempts to apply differential association theory to white collar crime or crimes of the powerful. He noted that the vast majority of criminological data had been compiled in relation to offenders from the lower classes but observed that businessmen committed enormous amounts of crime although this was invariably invisible (Sutherland, 1940). He therefore considered traditional explanations of criminality to be based on a false premise and thus misleading. Indeed, there is some empirical support for this position. Geis (1967) examined evidence given to hearings into the illegal price-fixing activities of some companies in the USA and found that people taking up new posts tended to find price-fixing to be an established practice and routinely became involved as part of learning their new job. Baumhart (1961) had previously found unethical behaviour on the part of businessmen to be influenced by superiors and peers with both he and Geis suggesting that the learning process is reinforced by 'rewards' and 'punishments'. Clinard (1952) noted however that differential association does not explain why it is that some individuals exposed to the same processes do not deviate and therefore proposed that the theory should be adapted to consider personality traits.

Others have maintained the view that crime is normal learned behaviour and have sought to explain that this knowledge acquisition does not have to take place in intimate personal groups. These later theories argue that learning can take place through direct interactions with the environment, independent of associations with other people, through the principles of operant learning. Burgess and Akers (1968) thus rewrote the principles of differential association in the language of operant conditioning and proposed that criminal behaviour could be learned both in non-social situations that are reinforcing and through social interaction in which the behaviour of other persons helps to reinforce that behaviour. Akers (1985) later revised the theory and it now focused on four central concepts. First, *differential association* which is considered the most important source of social learning and refers to the patterns of interactions with others that are the source of social learning either favourable or unfavourable to offending behaviour. At the same time, the indirect influence of more distant reference groups – such as the media – is now also recognised. Second, *definitions* reflect the meanings that a person applies to their own behaviour, for example, the wider reference group might not define recreational drug use as deviant. Third, *differential reinforcement* refers to the actual or anticipated consequences of a particular behaviour where it is proposed that people will do things that they think will result in rewards and avoid activities that they think will result in punishment. Fourth, *imitation* involves observing what others do. Whether they actually choose to imitate that behaviour will nevertheless depend on the characteristics of the person being observed, the behaviour the person engages in and the observed consequences of that behaviour for others.

Akers *et al.* (1979) propose that the learning of criminal behaviour takes place through a specific sequence of events. This process starts with the differential association of the individual with other persons who have favourable definitions of criminal behaviour and they thus provide a model of criminal behaviour to be imitated and social reinforcements for that behaviour. Thus, primarily differential association, definitions, imitation and social reinforcements explain the initial participation of the individual in criminal behaviour. After the individual has commenced offending behaviour, differential reinforcements determine whether the person will continue with that behaviour.

Akers (1992) argues that the social learning process explains the link between social structural conditions and individual behaviours, for example, the modernisation process and social disorganisation, strain conditions and economic inequality that have all been linked with criminal behaviour affect the individual's differential associations of the individual, definitions, models and reinforcements. These issues are further discussed in the following chapter and the third part of this book.

The emergence of the early learning theories had led to the development of a range of *behaviour modification* treatment strategies introduced with the intention of changing behaviour. As the early theorists had proposed that behaviour is related both to the setting in which the offence takes place and the consequences of involvement in such activities, strategies were developed to modify both the environment in which the offence took place and the outcomes of the behaviour. Bringing about change through modification of the environment is called *stimulus control* and is a standard technique in behaviour modification (Martin and Pear, 1992) and it is most apparent in situational crime prevention where the intention is to reduce offending by either reducing the opportunity to commit an offence or increasing the chances of detection. Similarly, there are a range of established methods that seek to modify the consequences that follow a given behaviour. The concept of *token economies* is a significant one where positive acceptable behaviour is rewarded by the award of tokens to be later exchanged for something the person finds rewarding. Behaviour modification techniques are widely used not just with convicted offenders, but in most mainstream schools as a means of controlling children, encouraged by books on positive parenting – 'praise is much more potent than criticism or punishment' – and the training of pet dogs, among many applications.

Strategies that focus explicitly on overt behaviour are often termed *behaviour therapy*, although the basic underpinning theory is the same as that which informs behaviour modification. In the 1970s the notion of skills training in health services was developed and quickly became widespread in the form of assertion, life and social skills training, the latter becoming widely used with a range of offenders (Hollin, 1990a).

A number of particular techniques have become associated with more recent cognitive-behavioural practice, including self-instructional training, 'thought stopping', emotional control training, and problem-solving training (Sheldon, 1995). The rationale underpinning this approach is that by bringing about change of internal – psychological and/or physiological – states and processes, this covert change will, in turn, mediate change at an overt behavioural level. Changes in overt behaviour will then elicit new patterns of reinforcement from the environment and so maintain behaviour change. These cognitive-behavioural methods have been widely used with offender groups and, in particular, with young offenders (Hollin, 1990b) where social skills training, training in problem-solving and moral reasoning techniques have been popular and have been shown to have some success in reducing offending (Maguire, 2001).

The main concerns about the use of cognitive-behavioural methods have focused on the abuse – and potential for abuse – of the methods used. First, there is an issue of powerful methods being used inappropriately by untrained – or poorly trained – personnel. Second, there are ethical issues of these methods being used with people such as prisoners – and in particular young offenders – who are in no position to give free and informed consent.

A particularly interesting example of the application of behaviour modification strategies – and the legitimacy of the aforementioned concerns – exists in Tranquility Bay, Jamaica, where 250 children, almost all from the USA, are incarcerated. They have not however been sent to the centre by a court of law or any welfare organisation. Their parents have paid to have them kidnapped and flown there against their will, to be incarcerated for up to three years, sometimes even longer. They will not be released until they are judged to be respectful, polite and obedient enough to rejoin their families. Parents sign a legal contract with the centre granting 49 per cent custody rights. It permits the Jamaican staff – whose qualifications are not required to exceed a high-school education – to use whatever physical force they feel necessary to control the child. The cost of sending a child there ranges from $25,000 to $40,000 a year (The *Observer*, 2003).

Conclusions

Psychological explanations of crime and criminal behaviour have firm foundations in the predestined actor model of crime and criminal behaviour and it is the implication of both the psychodynamic and behaviourist learning traditions that there is such a thing as the criminal mind or personality which in some way determines the behaviour of the individual. The causes are dysfunctional, abnormal emotional adjustment or deviant personality traits formed in early socialisation and childhood development and the individual is, as a result of these factors, destined to become a criminal. The only way to avoid that destiny is to identify the predisposing condition and provide some form of psychiatric intervention that will in some way ameliorate or preferably remove those factors and enable the individual to become a normal law abiding citizen.

The more recent cognitive learning approach involves a retreat from the purist predestined actor model approach. First, there is recognition of the links between the psychology of the individual and important predisposing influences or stimuli available in the social environment, but the behavioural learning theorists accept that point. It is the second recognition that is the important one. For criminals are now seen to have some degree of choice. They can choose to imitate the behaviours of others or they can choose not to. There may be a substantial range of factors influencing their decision and these may suggest to the individual that in the particular circumstances – when the opportunity arises – criminal behaviour is a rational choice to make. Thus we can see the links between recent cognitive learning theories and contemporary variants of the rational actor model. In short, the active criminal can in favourable circumstances make the choice to change their behaviour and cease offending or alternatively the individual living in circumstances where criminal behaviour is the norm can choose not to take that course of action in the first place. From this perspective, crime is not inevitably destiny. There are nevertheless considerable ethical issues raised by the use of some behavioural modification techniques that seek to influence the cognitive decision-making processes of offenders and indeed of others who have not been convicted of any crime.

Suggested further reading

Psychological positivism is again an extremely wide subject area and there are thus many relevant texts. Students are therefore advised to use the references in the text as a guide to specific interests. However, for a general but comprehensive psychological account of criminal behaviour see Feldman (1977) and Hollin (1989). Freud (1920) still provides an excellent introduction to the main tenets of psychoanalysis; while for a discussion and critique of the psychoanalytic tradition of explaining criminal behaviour see Farrington (1992, 1994). For a comprehensive discussion of the research on maternal deprivation theory see Rutter (1981). Eysenck (1977) gives a comprehensive introduction to his notion of the criminal personality. The cognitive psychology perspective is well represented by Sutherland (1947) for the original and highly influential differential association theory and Akers (1985) for more contemporary social learning theory. Holmes and De Burger (1989) is essential reading for those interested in serial killers, while Omerod (1996) is worthy of consultation on offender profiling. Hollin (1990b) provides a comprehensive discussion of cognitive behavioural interventions with young offenders.

7. Sociological positivism

We have seen in the previous two chapters that both the biological and psychological variants of the predestined actor model of crime and criminal behaviour locate the primary impulse for criminal behaviour in the individual. The sociological version rejects these individualist explanations and proposes those behaviours defined as criminal behaviour are simply those that deviate from the norms acceptable to the consensus of opinion in society. This perspective should not be confused with that of the victimised actor model – the focus of the third part of this book – which proposes that it is the weak and powerless who are defined as criminal and targeted by the rich and powerful in an inherently unequal and unfair society. Sociological *positivists* recognise that crime is a socially constructed entity but at the same time acknowledge that it poses a real threat to the continuance of that society and thus needs to be controlled in some way.

The sociological variant of the predestined actor model involves the 'scientific' measurement of indicators of 'social disorganisation' – such as rates of crime, drunkenness and suicide – in specified urban areas. Proponents recommend that once the whereabouts of existing and potential 'trouble spots' are identified, these must be 'treated', controlled or, in future, 'prevented', if serious social disorder is to be avoided. It is a long-established tradition with its roots in the work of the nineteenth century 'moral statisticians', Quételet (in Belgium) and Guerry (in France) and their social campaigning counterparts in England – Mayhew, Colquhoun, Fletcher and others – who used early empirical methods to investigate the urban slums where crime and deviance flourished. It is an enduring tradition that owes much to the important contribution to sociology established by Emile Durkheim.

Emile Durkheim and social disorganisation theory

Emile Durkheim was the founding father of academic sociology in France and a major social theorist working at the turn of the twentieth century. It was because of the strength and rigour of his large and complex sociological theory that he was able to assert powerfully the merits of social factors in explaining individual and group action. For Durkheim it was not just the psychological and biological versions of the predestined actor model that were unable to provide an adequate explanation of social action, he was also strongly opposed to those theoretical ideas – social contract theory and utilitarianism – that had provided the foundations of the rational actor model. In short, a society that is divided into different interest groups on an unequal basis is not one in which 'just contracts between individuals and society could be made' (Durkheim, 1933 originally 1893: 202).

At this point a few words of caution should be indicated. Durkheim is often misrepresented as a conservative indistinguishable from his French predecessor Auguste Comte. Taylor, Walton and Young (1973) – the eminent radical criminologists discussed fully in the third part of this book – and the present author (Hopkins Burke, 1998b, 1999b) consider this orthodox interpretation to be a gross simplification of a significant, radical, social and criminological theorist. Indeed, much of what has been said about Durkheim is more appropriate to the work of his French predecessor Auguste Comte.

Comte had argued that the process whereby with the development of industrialised society people have become increasingly separated into different places of residence and employment has subverted the moral authority of a previously united society. Thus, from this perspective, people are seen to commit criminal acts not because it is in their material interests to do so, but because there is no strong moral authority influencing them to do otherwise. For Comte, it is the purpose of positivist social science to create this higher moral authority.

The essential difference between Comte and Durkheim lies in their differing views of human nature. For the former, the human being has a natural and inherent desire to reach perfection and it is the creation of a moral authority by social scientists that can create the ordered society that will bring about that state of being. Durkheim simply rejects this view. It is utopian and idealistic to argue that a higher moral authority could restrain human desires at all times in history. Thus, Durkheim, in contrast to Comte, proposes a 'dualistic' view of human nature: a duality between the needs of the body and the soul. Human instincts are biologically given, while it is the task of the social world to develop through the human 'soul' an adherence to a *moral consensus* that is the basis of social order and control. With the changing nature of complex modern society that consensus is a shifting and adaptable entity.

It is possible to observe here a similarity between Durkheim and Freud for both argue that an increased repression of the individual conscience is the basis of the development of a civilised society but there are nevertheless substantial differences in their positions. For Durkheim, individual desires have to be regulated not simply because they have certain biological needs and predispositions, but because the failure to control this aspect of the person can lead to a situation of disharmony and despair, culminating in what he terms egoism and anomie. Durkheim did agree with Freud that individuals were not really human until they had been socialised. Freud, however, saw socialisation and the development of a conscience as necessary for individual well-being. For Durkheim, the lack of socialisation and a conscience leads to conflict between the individual and society.

Durkheim was opposed to the utilitarians – because he considered them to be idealists rather than social scientists – and argued that moral authority can only be acceptable to men and women if it is relevant to their particular position in a changing society. If people are caught up in occupations that are unsuitable to their talents – and they recognise this underachievement – they can have little enthusiasm for moral authority. Central to his social theory is a concern with social change and his enthusiasm to eradicate the 'forced division of labour'.

It was in *The Division of Labour in Society*, first published in 1893, that Durkheim described the processes of social change that accompanies the industrial development of society, arguing that earlier forms of society had high levels of mechanical solidarity, while the more developed industrial societies are characterised by an advanced stage of 'organic' solidarity. However, a further note of caution needs to be indicated here: no society is entirely mechanical or organic with any social formation being in a state of development between the two extremes. Indeed, there may well be many pockets of intense mechanical solidarity in highly developed organic societies and this is an important point well worth remembering and which is discussed further below.

For Durkheim societies with high levels of mechanical solidarity are characterised by the conformity of the group. There is thus a likeness and a similarity between individuals and they hold common attitudes and beliefs that bind one person to another. Now this is a form of social solidarity that may at first sight appear attractive – suggesting popular notions of the close-knit community – but at the same time severe restrictions are placed on the ability of an individual to develop a sense of personal identity or uniqueness. Thus, co-operation between individual members of the group is restricted to what can be achieved through the close conformity of each member to a single stereotype.

Durkheim argues that such societies can further be identified by a very intense and rigid collective conscience where members hold very precise shared ideas of what is right and wrong. There are, however, individuals within that group who differ from the uniform ideal and in these cases the law is used as an instrument to maintain that uniformity. Moreover, repressive and summary punishments are used against individuals and minority groups that transgress against the collective conscience of the majority. This punishment of dissenters usefully emphasises their inferiority while at the same time encouraging commitment to the majority viewpoint. In this sense crime is a normal feature of a society with high levels of mechanical solidarity. Punishment performs a necessary function by reinforcing the moral consensus – or world view – of the group where a reduction in behaviour designated as criminal would as a necessity lead to other previously non-criminal activities becoming criminalised. Indeed, Durkheim takes this argument a step further and claims that a society with no crime would be abnormal. The imposition of tight controls that make crime impossible would seriously restrict the potential for innovation and social progress.

Durkheim argues that with greater industrialisation societies develop greater levels of organic solidarity where there is a more developed division of labour and different groups become dependent on each other. Social solidarity now relies less on the maintenance of uniformity between individuals, and more on the management of the diverse functions of different groups. Nevertheless, a certain degree of uniformity remains essential.

It is time to indicate a further cautionary note. There has been a tendency – encouraged by some influential introductory sociology textbooks – for students to confuse the arguments presented by Durkheim on the increasing development of organic society, with those put forward by nineteenth century conservatives, and the German sociologist Ferdinand Tönnies. For those writers, it was precisely this increasing fragmentation of communal beliefs and values that was the problem and the proposed solution thus lies in re-establishing the moral certainties of a society with high levels of mechanical solidarity. This is not the argument presented by Durkheim.

For Durkheim, the division of labour is a progressive phenomenon. Its appearance signals not the inevitable collapse of morality, but the emergence of a new *content* for the collective conscience. In societies dominated by mechanical solidarity the emphasis is on the obligation of the individual to society: with organic formations, the focus is increasingly on the obligation of society to the individual person. Now to give the maximum possible encouragement to individual rights does not mean that altruism – that is, self-sacrifice for others – will disappear; on the contrary, moral individualism is *not* unregulated self-interest but the imposition of a set of reciprocal obligations that binds together individuals (Durkheim, 1933 originally 1893). Here lies the essential originality of Durkheim's interpretation of the division of labour.

For Adam Smith (1910, originally 1776), the founder of free-market economics, and the utilitarians, the specialisation of economic exchange is simply an effect of the growth of wealth and the free play of economic self-interest. For Durkheim, the true significance of the division of labour lies in its *moral* role. It is a source of restraint upon self-interest and thereby renders society cohesive. The idea that unbridled *egoism* – or competitive individualism – could ever become the basis of a civilised order is for Durkheim quite absurd. In short, Durkheim regarded the cohesion of nineteenth century *laissez-faire* society, with its wholly unregulated markets, its arbitrary inequalities, and its restrictions on social mobility and its 'class' wars, as a dangerous condition. Such imperfect social regulation leads to a variety of different social problems, including crime and deviance.

Durkheim provided a threefold typology of deviants. The first typology is the biological deviant who is explained by the physiological or psychological malfunctioning we encountered in the previous two chapters and who can be present in a normal division of labour. The other two typologies are linked to the nature and condition of the social system and are present in those societies which are characterised by an abnormal or forced division of labour. Thus, the second typology, the functional rebel is, therefore, a 'normal' person who is reacting to a pathological society, rebelling against the existing, inappropriate and unfair division of society and indicating the existence of strains in the social system. For Durkheim, such a person expresses the true 'spontaneous' or 'normal' collective consciousness as opposed to the artificial 'forced' or 'pathological' one currently in operation (Taylor, Walton and Young, 1973). The third typology, skewed deviants involves those who have been socialised into a disorganised pathological society and are the usual focus of the student of deviance and criminal behaviour.

Durkheim proposed two central arguments to explain the growth of crime and criminal behaviour in modern industrial societies. First, such societies encourage a state of unbridled 'egoism' that is contrary to the maintenance of social solidarity and conformity to the law. Second, the likelihood of inefficient regulation is greater at a time of rapid modernisation, because new forms of control have not evolved sufficiently to replace the older and now less appropriate means of maintaining solidarity. In such a period, society is in a state of normlessness or 'anomie', a condition characterised by a breakdown in norms and common understandings.

Durkheim claimed that without external controls, a human being has unlimited needs and society thus has a right to regulate these by indicating the appropriate rewards that should accrue to the individual. Except in times of crisis, everyone has at least a vague perception of what they can expect to earn for their endeavours but at a time of economic upheaval, society cannot exert controls on the aspirations of individuals. During a depression, people are forced to lower their sights, a situation which some will find intolerable but, on the other hand, when there is a sudden improvement in economic conditions, social equilibrium will also break down and there is now no limit on aspirations.

A fundamental recurring criticism of Durkheim emphasised in virtually any introductory sociology text refers to his apparently unassailable methodological collectivism or over-determinism as it is usually termed. Individuals, apparently seem to have little, indeed no, choice in their actions, or in terms of the terminology used in this text their lives appear predestined because of the social conditions in which they live. It is without doubt this interpretation of Durkheim – where it appears impossible to locate any acceptable mechanism to explain social change – that has led to his work being almost universally dismissed as methodologically and politically conservative. A more recent methodological individualist reinterpretation of Durkheim contained in the work of his French compatriot Raymond Boudon (1980) recognises that individuals do have choices, come together with others and form coalitions of interest on which they act and that it is in this way that social change can and does occur. Opportunities for conceiving of, and carrying out, that action are nonetheless invariably *constrained* by – sometimes overwhelmingly – structural constraints, not least the more strongly asserted, believed and enforced *conscience collectives* that are the products of the ultra, or intense, mechanical solidarities that dominate not only simple societies but also pockets of varying size within more complex contemporary societies. In short, individual choice – or acceptance or rejection of a particular way of life or apparent destiny – is possible, from this perspective, but the choices available may be limited, or, in some cases, virtually non-existent (Hopkins Burke and Pollock, 2004: 9).

Hopkins Burke and Pollock (2004) adopt this methodological individualist interpretation of Durkheim in their discussion of hate crime motivation – hate crimes being criminal acts motivated by hatred, bias or prejudice against a person or property based on the actual or perceived race, ethnicity, gender, religion or sexual orientation of the victim – and observe that even in a complex post-industrial society characterised by high levels of organic solidarity, and multifarious interdependencies, the concept of mechanical solidarity retains considerable explanatory power. The authors observe that even within complex and diverse societies, mechanical solidarities continue to significantly exist at three levels in the social world. First, there is the *macro* societal level of national identities that may be particularly strong in those societies where the collective conscience is rigidly enforced by reference to a fundamentalist religious or political belief system. Second, there is the *mezzo* or intermediate level of the organisation and institution, for example, organised hate groups. Third, there is the *micro* level of the small group or gang, such as a 'football firm' in Britain or Europe or localised less organised hate groupings.

Hopkins Burke and Pollock (2004) observe that many contemporary hate groups have philosophies based on the notion of a collective society, consisting of common values, culture, identity, attitude and homogeneity. Those who deviate – or are in some way different from the perceived norm – are defined and labelled as being deviant and outsiders. Deviance, is a necessary function of any mechanical solidarity – whether it be at the macro, mezzo or micro level – inhabited by hate groups because its existence and endurance tests the boundaries of tolerance leading to an ongoing evaluation of prevailing norms and values. Transgressors against the dominant world view – 'subaltern' (Perry, 2001) or subordinate groups, those whose sexual, racial, gendered, or ethnic, identities are different to the traditional white, male, heterosexual identity that exist in a 'normal' society – are perceived to have contravened the mechanical solidarity and are consequently censured.

Hopkins Burke and Pollock (2004) observe that this situation whereby a number of mezzo and micro mechanical solidarities co-exist alongside each other in the same geographical space provides a fertile enabling environment for racist hate as a sense of insecurity and uncertainty can arise among at least certain sections of the traditional white majority. Both Enoch Powell (in Britain) and Jean Marie Le Penn (in France) have successfully taken advantage of the political opportunities proffered by this insecurity and dissent during the latter decades of the twentieth century by claiming that non-white immigration would pose a threat to tradition, culture and opportunity for the traditional 'white' community (Heywood: 1992). Thus, hate crime perpetrators motivated by fears of cultural change, construct themselves as victims and demand first class preferential citizenship as they feel alienated from their traditional community or mechanical solidarity.

In concluding this section we might note that although there continues to be controversy about the accuracy of Durkheim's disorganisation theory taken as a whole, his notion that crime is linked to a breakdown in social controls has been a major inspiration to different sociologists in the twentieth century. In particular, his concept of anomie had a marked influence on the later work of Robert Merton discussed below. Moreover, the twin notions of anomie and egoism are extremely useful in helping to explain the nature of crime and criminal behaviour that occurred in the UK during the 1980s and the early 1990s, a more recent period of severe economic and social disruption. The aftermath of that period is still with us and will be examined in later chapters of this book. In the meantime, we will consider the more readily recognised influence that is apparent in the work of the Chicago School.

The Chicago School

In the early part of the twentieth century, the USA underwent a major transition from a predominantly rural and agricultural society to one based on industrial and metropolitan centres. Chicago, for example, grew from a town of 10,000 inhabitants in 1860 to a large city with a population of over two million by 1910. Life was nevertheless hard; wages were low; hours were long; factory conditions were appalling; and living in slum tenements created serious health problems (see Lilly, Cullen and Ball, 1986).

Sociologists working at the University of Chicago reached the conclusion that growing up and living in such negative conditions undoubtedly influenced the outcome of people's lives. Moreover, crime and criminal behaviour in such an environment could not simply be explained in the individualist terms proposed by the biological and psychological versions of the predestined actor model. It made more 'sense' when viewed as a social problem and it was argued that the poor are not simply born into a life of crime but are driven by the conditions of their social environment. Thus, by changing their surroundings it would be possible to reverse the negative effects of the city and transform these people into law-abiding citizens.

Robert Park (1921) contributed two central ideas to the work of the Chicago School. First, he proposed that like any ecological system, the development and organisation of the city is neither random nor idiosyncratic but patterned, human communities, like plants, live together symbiotically. In other words, different kinds of human beings share the same environment and are mutually dependent on each other. At the same time, patterns of change in the city are comparable to changes in the balance of nature, the human population in US cities was migratory, rather than fixed with new immigrants moving into the poor areas and replacing the previous inhabitants as they moved out to the suburbs. Second, Park observed that the nature of these social processes had their impact on human behaviours like crime, and these could be ascertained only through the careful study of city life. It was a research agenda that several researchers were to embrace.

Ernest Burgess (1928) produced a model of the city that provided a framework for understanding the social roots of crime and argued that as cities expand in size, the development is patterned socially. They grow radially in a series of concentric zones or rings. Burgess outlined five different zones and proposed that a competitive process decided how people were distributed spatially amongst these: commercial enterprises were located in the central business district (or loop) in close proximity to the transport systems; the most expensive residential areas were in the outer commuter zones or suburbs, away from the bustle of the city centre, the pollution of the factories and the homes of the poor.

It was the 'zone in transition' – containing rows of deteriorating tenements and often built in the shadow of ageing factories – that was the particular focus of study. The outward expansion of the business district led to the constant displacement of residents. As the least desirable living area, the zone was the focus for the influx of waves of immigrants who were too poor to reside elsewhere. Burgess observed that these social patterns weakened family and communal ties and resulted in 'social disorganisation'. It was this disorganisation thesis that was influentially presented as the primary explanation of criminal behaviour.

Clifford Shaw and Henry McKay (1972, originally 1931) set out to empirically test concentric zone theory, collating juvenile court statistics in order to map the spatial distribution of juvenile offending throughout the city and their analysis confirmed the hypothesis that offending behaviour flourished in the zone in transition and was inversely related to the affluence of the area and corresponding distance from the central business district. They studied court records over several decades and were able to show that crime levels were highest in slum neighbourhoods regardless of which racial or ethnic group resided there and, moreover, as these groups moved to other zones, their offending rates correspondingly decreased. It was this observation that led Shaw and McKay to conclude that it was the nature of the neighbourhoods – not the nature of the individuals who lived within them – that regulated involvement in crime.

Shaw and McKay emphasised the importance of neighbourhood organisation in allowing or preventing offending behaviour by children and young people. In more affluent communities, parents fulfilled the needs of their offspring and carefully supervised their activities but in the zone of transition families and other conventional institutions – schools, churches, and voluntary associations – were strained, if not destroyed, by rapid urban growth, migration and poverty. Left to their own devices, young people in this zone were not subject to the social constraints placed on their contemporaries in the more affluent areas and were more likely to seek excitement and friends in the streets of the city.

Shaw actively promoted appreciative studies of the deviant, using the criminal's 'own story' by means of participant observation in their particular deviant world which became known as the ethnographic or 'life-history' method and led to the publication of titles like *The Jack Roller: A Delinquent Boy's Own Story*, *The Natural History of a Delinquent Career* and *Brothers in Crime* (Shaw, 1930, 1931, 1938). These studies showed that young people were often recruited into offending behaviour through their association with older siblings or gang members.

Shaw and McKay concluded that disorganised neighbourhoods help produce and sustain 'criminal traditions' that compete with conventional values and can be 'transmitted down through successive generations of boys, much the same way that language and other social forms are transmitted' (Shaw and McKay, 1972: 174). Thus, young people growing up in socially disorganised inner city slum areas characterised by the existence of a value system that condones criminal behaviour could readily learn these values in their daily interactions with older adolescents. On the other hand, youths in organised areas – where the dominance of conventional institutions had precluded the development of criminal traditions – remains insulated from deviant values and peers. Thus, for them, an offending career is an unlikely option.

Shaw and McKay fundamentally argued that juvenile offending can only be understood by reference to the social context in which young people live and, in turn, this context itself is a product of major societal transformations brought about by rapid urbanisation and massive population shifts. Young people born and brought up in the socially disorganised zone of transition are particularly vulnerable to the temptations of crime, as conventional institutions disintegrate around them they are given little supervision and are free to roam the streets where they were likely to become the next generation of carriers of the area's criminal tradition. It was this aspect of their work that provided crucial theoretical foundations for Edwin Sutherland's theory of 'differential association' which was discussed in the previous chapter.

The work of the Chicago School has been criticised from a number of standpoints. First, it has been observed that while the deterministic importance of the transmission of a 'criminal culture' is emphasised there is substantially less detail provided on the origins of that culture. Second, there have been criticisms of a tendency to see the spatial distribution of groups in the city as a 'natural' social process. The role that power and class domination can play in the creation and perpetuation of slums and the enormous economic inequality that permeates such areas is ignored. Third, it has been proposed that they provide only a partial explanation of criminality that seems best able to explain involvement in stable criminal roles and in group-based offending behaviour.

The Chicago School criminologists have nevertheless rightly had a substantial influence on the development of sociological explanations of crime and criminal behaviour. Particularly influential has been the recognition that where people grow up – and the people with whom they associate – is closely linked to a propensity for involvement in criminal activity.

The Chicago School has also had a further practical influence. In the 1930s Clifford Shaw established the 'Chicago Area Project' (CAP). The intention was to allow local residents in socially deprived areas the autonomy to organise neighbourhood committees in the fight against crime and the project encompassed several approaches to crime prevention. First, a strong emphasis was placed on the creation of recreational programmes that would divert young people from criminal activity. Second, efforts were made to have residents take pride in their community by improving the physical appearance of the area. Third, CAP staff members would attempt to mediate on behalf of young people in trouble with those in authority, such as schoolteachers. Fourth, local people were employed as 'street credible' workers in an attempt to persuade youths that education and a conventional lifestyle was in their best interest. Schlossman, Zellman and Shavelson (1984) conducted an evaluation of 50 years of the CAP project and reached the conclusion that it had long been effective in reducing rates of reported juvenile offending.

In summary, social disorganisation theory – as developed by Shaw and McKay – called for efforts to reorganise communities. The emphasis on cultural learning suggests that treatment programmes that attempt to reverse the criminal learning of offenders can counteract involvement in crime. Young offenders should thus be placed in settings where they will receive pro-social reinforcement, for example, through the use of positive-peer-counselling.

Robert Merton and anomie theory

Robert Merton's anomie – or strain – theory attempts to explain the occurrence of not only crime but also wider deviance and disorder and in this sense it is a wide-ranging, essentially sociological explanation that promises a comprehensive account of crime and deviance causation, but – while it provides a major contribution to this endeavour – ultimately fails to fulfil this ambition.

Merton borrowed the term anomie from Emile Durkheim in an attempt to explain the social upheaval that accompanied the Great Depression of the 1930s and later the social conflicts that occurred in the USA during the 1960s. His writings are particularly significant because they challenged the orthodoxy of the time that saw the USA as being characterised by the term, 'the American Dream', a vision of a meritocratic society in which hard work and endeavour – in the context of conservative values – would supposedly distribute social and economic rewards equitably.

Merton essentially followed the Chicago School sociologists in rejecting individualistic explanations of crime and criminal behaviour but at the same time took his sociological argument a step further than Durkheim had done previously. Whereas his predecessor had considered human aspirations to be natural, Merton argued significantly that they are usually socially learned. Moreover, there are – and this is the central component of his argument – social structural limitations imposed on access to the means to achieve these goals. His work therefore focuses upon the position of the individual within the social structure rather than on personality characteristics and in his words, 'our primary aim lies in discovering how some social structures exert a definite pressure upon certain persons in the society to engage in nonconformist conduct' (Merton, 1938: 672).

Merton proposed that this central aim could be achieved by distinguishing between *cultural goals* and *institutionalised means*. The former are those material possessions, symbols of status, accomplishment and esteem that established norms and values encourage us to aspire to, and are, therefore, socially learned; the latter are the distribution of opportunities to achieve these goals in socially acceptable ways. Merton observes that it is possible to overemphasise either the goals or the means to achieve them and that it is this that leads to social strains, or 'anomie'.

Merton was mainly concerned with the application of his theory to the USA and proposed that in that society there is an overemphasis on the achievement of goals such as monetary success and material goods, without sufficient attention paid to the institutional means of achievement and it is this cultural imbalance that leads to people being prepared to use any means, regardless of their legality, to achieve that goal (Merton, 1938: 674). The ideal situation would be where there is a balance between goals and means and in such circumstances individuals who conform will feel that they are justly rewarded.

Deviant, especially criminal, behaviour results when cultural goals are accepted, for example, and people would generally like to be financially successful, but where access to the means to achieve that goal is limited by the position of a person in the social structure. Merton outlined five possible reactions – or adaptations – that can occur when people are not in a position to legitimately attain internalised social goals.

Conformity

Conformity is a largely self-explanatory adaptation whereupon people tend to accept both the cultural goals of society and the means of achieving them. Even if they find their social ascent to be limited, they still tend not to 'deviate'. Merton claimed that in most societies this is the standard form of adaptation, for if this were not the case society would be extremely unstable. He did nevertheless note that for many people, whose access to the socially dictated 'good things in life' through established institutionalised means is in some way more difficult than conventionally portrayed, the 'strain' to achieve might well become intolerable. People could alleviate the strain in such instances by either changing their cultural goal and/or by withdrawing their allegiance to the institutionalised means. In following either or both courses, people would be deviating from norms prescribing what should be desired (success) or how this should be achieved (legitimate means such as education, approved entrepreneurship or conscientious employment). The following four 'modes of adaptation' describe various ways of alleviating 'strain' generated by social inequalities.

Retreatism

Merton considered retreatism to be the least common adaptation. Retreatists are those who reject both social goals *and* the means of obtaining them and these are true 'aliens', they are 'in the society but not *of* it' (Merton, 1938: 677). It is a category of social 'dropouts' that includes among others drug addicts, psychotics, vagrants, tramps and chronic alcoholics.

Ritualism

Merton identifies many similarities between 'ritualists' and 'conformists' with an example of the former a person who adheres to rules for their own sake. Bureaucrats who accept and observe the rules of their organisations uncritically provide the classic example. Those in rule-bound positions in the armed services, social control institutions or the public service may be particularly susceptible to this form of adaptation where the emphasis is on the means of achievement rather than the goals. These people, or groups, need not of course be particularly successful in attaining their conventional goals but their overemphasis on the 'means' clouds their judgement on the desirability of appreciating the goals.

Innovation

The innovator – the usual focus for the student of crime and criminal behaviour – is keen to achieve the standard goals of society, wealth, fame or admiration, but, probably due to blocked opportunities to obtain these by socially approved means, embarks on novel, or innovative, routes. Many 'innovative' routes exist in complex organic societies, so much so that some innovators may be seen to overlap with 'conformists'. For example, the sports, arts and entertainment industries frequently attract, develop and absorb 'innovators', celebrating their novelty in contrast to the conformist or ritualist, and providing opportunities for those whose circumstances may frustrate their social ascent through conventionally prescribed and approved routes.

The innovator may be exceptionally talented, or may develop talents, in a field that is restricted or unusual and conventionally deemed worthy of celebration for its novelty but these individuals are relatively unthreatening to conventional views of the acceptable means of social achievement. There are others, on the other hand, who appear to pose a distinctly destabilising influence on conventional definitions of socially acceptable means of achievement and it is, therefore, one of the strengths of anomie – or strain theories – that they appreciate that some of these 'innovations' are merely 'deviant', and subjectable to informal social controls and censure, while others are proscribed by the criminal law of the relevant jurisdiction.

Some activities are usually seen as 'criminally' censurable in most societies, although they may be excusable in certain circumstances. Robbery is usually seen as an offence when committed against an individual or an institution such as a bank. However, this might not be the case when committed in wartime against the persons or institutions of an 'enemy' state. Homicide is regarded as a serious offence in most jurisdictions, yet it is acceptable when promoted by socially or politically powerful interests in times of war. Similarly, where does the financial 'entrepreneur' stretch the bounds of legality or previously established 'acceptable' business means to the achievement of previously determined goals? Lilly, Cullen and Ball (1986) provide the example of stock exchange regulation abusers in the 1980s as an example of innovative business deviants. At a time when business deregulation had generated many fortunes, some people were encouraged by the prevailing economic circumstances to take opportunities to shorten the means to the social goal of wealth through 'insider dealing' and similar practices.

In short, the innovator may be seen to overemphasise the goals of achievement over the means. Conventionally regarded success may be achieved by any means that seem appropriate to the innovator, who strives to overcome barriers to achievement by adopting any available strategies for achieving established goals.

Rebellion

For Merton rebellious people are those who not merely reject but also wish to change the existing social system and its goals. Rebels thus reject both the socially approved means and goals of their society. The emergence of popular images of the potential of both innovative and rebellious modes of adaptation to the standard social and economic patterns of Western life in the 1960s did much to renew an interest in Merton's approach to crime and deviance.

Three main criticisms have been made of anomie theory. First, it has been observed to be a self-acknowledged 'theory of the middle range' that does little to trace the origins of criminogenic circumstances. Merton is thus accused of being a 'cautious rebel' who fails to explain neither the initial existence of inequality, nor the exaggerated emphasis in society on making money (Taylor, Walton and Young, 1973). Indeed, it was criticisms of this kind that instigated the search for a more totalising, historically and politically aware criminology – or 'sociology of deviance' – in the late 1960s and 1970s. The rise – and indeed fall – of this mode of explaining criminal behaviour is the central focus of the third part of this book.

Anomie theory is not as comprehensive an account of crime and deviance as it may at first look for it fails to explain certain behaviours that are commonly labelled 'deviant' – such as recreational drug use – and which are often undertaken by people who otherwise accept the standard cultural goals and the institutionalised means of achieving them.

The second criticism is targeted at Merton's assumption that cultural goals and values are known and shared by all members of society. Lemert (1972), for example, argued that society is more accurately characterised by the notion of a plurality of values and if this is the case, then Merton's 'ends–means' approach becomes problematic and generally insufficient in explaining crime and deviance. He can be partially defended in that he did state that different goals are possible within his scheme, but he does not give sufficient emphasis to different groups and different values. Moreover, the assumption that it is the 'lower classes' who are most likely to suffer from frustrated aspirations and who are subject to strain and commit criminal or deviant acts may not be accurate. Later criminological studies reveal that there is a great deal more deviant behaviour in society than Merton's formula suggests. Anomie theory – we are told – is hard-pressed to account for business fraud and other 'white-collar' crimes, and also for 'lower-class' conformity. Thus, anomie theory predicts both too few deviant activities among the more privileged members of society and too much among those potentially most subject to strain.

In defence of Merton, it would seem that he was motivated to explain those forms of highly visible and immediately apparent crime that have traditionally been committed by the poorer sections of society and which have been of immediate concern to the public and hence politicians and inevitably criminologists. Indeed, later researchers – predominantly working in the victimised actor tradition, which is the focus of the third part of this book – have sought to use the concept of anomie in an attempt to explain corporate crime. From this perspective, it has been argued that explanations based on individual motivations are inadequate and that it is necessary to consider these in the context of corporate goals, the essential one of which is to maximise profit over a long period (Etzioni, 1961; Box, 1983). Box thus identifies five potential sources of 'environmental uncertainty' for the corporation that represent obstacles to the lawful attainment of its main goal; these are: competitors; the government; employees; consumers; and the public, especially as represented by protectionists. Box observes that confronted with such obstacles, the corporation adopts tactics that frequently involve breaking the law, in order to achieve its goal.

Staw and Szwajkowski (1975) compared the financial performance of 105 large firms subject to litigation involving illegal competition with those of 395 similar firms not so involved and concluded that environmental scarcity did appear linked to a whole range of trade violations. Box (1983) goes further and argues that adherence to the profit motive renders the corporation inherently criminogenic with the bulk of corporate crime initiated by high-ranking officials and he suggests, moreover, that the very factors connected with career success in corporations – and the consequences of such success – are themselves criminogenic.

Gross (1978) conducted a survey of several studies of corporate career mobility and noted the relevance of personality differences. He thus found senior managers to be ambitious, easily accepting of a non-demanding moral code, and to regard their own success at goal attainment as being linked to the success of the organisation. Box (1983) took this notion a step further and argued that the very nature of the corporate promotion system means that those who reach the top are likely to have the very personal characteristics required to commit business crime, the greater success they achieve, the more free they feel from the bind of conventional values. In this way, we might observe that Box's interpretation of anomie seems to be closer to that of Durkheim than Merton.

Financial profit is not the only goal relevant to anomie. Braithwaite (1984: 94) has described fraud as 'an illegitimate means to achieving any one of a wide range of organisational and personal goals when legitimate means ... are blocked', for example, he found a widespread willingness among pharmacologists to fabricate the results of safety tests. This behaviour could sometimes be attributed to financial greed but there were other explanations. Some scientists, for example, have an intense commitment to their work and when the value of this is threatened by test results there could be considerable temptation to cover this up in order to defend professional prestige.

Levin and McDevitt (1993) and Perry (2001) have observed the tendency for hate crime offenders to blame their economic instability or lack of job opportunities on the immigration of 'foreigners', while Hopkins Burke and Pollock (2004) argue that it is the actual adaptation of conformity that is problematic in this context. Central to the whole notion of conformity is the sense that adherents in some way buy into the legitimacy of the whole social order and exactly why they do this is not questioned by Merton but adherence to the law, the influence of macro or localised 'correct' thinking, perhaps in the work context in the case of the latter, and a lack of opportunity could all be legitimate reasons why a person with latent – hidden or suppressed – hate crime motivation keeps this under control. It could well be that as an outcome of a change in structural circumstances – for example, the arrival of a group of immigrants or asylum seekers in the locality, the chance meeting of a new friend or colleague with similar latent views, perhaps while on holiday or after the consumption of a few 'social' drinks, or as the outcome of surfing the Internet – that latent hate crime motivation could well be transformed into something more insidious.

These observations suggest a fundamental premise that hate crime motivation is essentially a pathological deviation from societal norms. Hopkins Burke and Pollock (2004) nevertheless argue the converse and observe that hate crime motivation is simply normal and unremarkable in society as currently constituted. The powerful macro, mezzo and micro mechanical solidarities that exist in even the most complex contemporary organic societies – absorbed and internalised during a socialisation process that may well have prioritised notions of hard work, law-abiding behaviour and indeed conformity to the group – legitimate hate motivation as normal. Given the opportunity in the right venue among 'our own kind' where such views are very much the norm it is possible that latent hate motivation might well be actualised, where the at least tacit approval of the (perhaps) silent majority of conformists might provide succour, support and legitimisation for those prepared to act upon their hate motivation.

The third criticism of Merton is that he made no attempt to apply his typology to women and, at first sight it seems totally inapplicable to them. Leonard (1983) proposes that the main goal of US women is to achieve successful relationships with others not the attainment of material wealth and this is an argument to which we return in the following chapter.

Anomie theory has been subjected to many criticisms but is generally sympathetically regarded in the fields of sociology and criminology. Merton did a great deal to broaden the study of crime and criminal behaviour and to introduce the importance of social structure in shaping the life choices of individuals. Some have argued that he did not go far enough with this endeavour; however, it would seem that Merton – along with many liberal or social democratic critics of unrestrained egoism and conservative values both in his native USA and Britain – had no inclination to see a socialist transformation of society. The latter tends to be the ultimate goal of his critics working at the more radical end of the spectrum in the victimised actor model tradition. To criticise the substantial elements of his theoretical concerns on that basis is therefore rather unfair, particularly as many of those critics have since radically modified their views and come themselves to accept the explanatory potential of Merton's notion of anomie (see Chapter 16). In short, his work has provided a useful starting point for subsequent researchers.

Messner and Rosenfeld (1994) have developed an institutional anomie theory where they observe that the 'American Dream' is a broad, cultural ethos that entails a commitment to the goal of material success, to be pursued by everyone, in a mass society dominated by huge multinational corporations. They argue that not only has economics come to dominate our culture but the non-economic institutions in society have become subservient to the economy, for example, the entire educational system appears to have become driven by the employment market (nobody wants to go to college just for the sake of education anymore), politicians get elected on the strength of the economy, and despite widespread political discourses promoting the sanctity of family values, executives are expected to uproot their families at the behest of the corporation. Goals other than material success (such as parenting, teaching, and serving the community) are simply secondary to the needs of the economy.

Messner and Rosenfeld (1994) argue that the dominant cause of crime is anomie which is promoted and endorsed by the American Dream and where the emphasis is on seeking the most efficient way to achieve economic success. In this context, crime is invariably the most effective and efficient way to achieve immediate monetary gain. Beliefs, values, and commitments are the causal variables, and the closer they are linked to those of the marketplace, the more likely the logic of the economy (competitive, individualistic, and materialistic) will dictate a powerful social force that motivates the pursuit of money 'by any means necessary'. Moreover, since this lawlessness-producing emphasis is caught up in the structural emphasis society places on the economy (and little else), none of the many 'wars' on crime (for example, the war against drugs) will ever be successful (since they indirectly attack the economy).

Messner and Rosenfeld (1994) observe that while commitment to the goal of material success is the main causal variable there are significant others such as values and beliefs. The two values that constitute the American Dream are those of achievement and individualism. Achievement involves the use of material success to measure self-worth with individualism referring to the notion of intense personal competition to achieve material success. Other beliefs related to the American Dream include universalism – the idea that chances for success are open to everyone – and this belief creates an intense fear of failure. While another belief, the 'fetishism' of money refers, in this instance, to the notion that there are no rules for establishing when one has enough money (Messner and Rosenfeld, 1994). An area where the enduring influence of anomie theories is most apparent is in the discussion of deviant subcultures below.

Deviant subculture theories

There are different deviant subculture explanations of crime and criminal behaviour but all share a common perception that certain social groups have values and attitudes that enable or encourage delinquency. The highly influential US subcultural tradition was at its peak during the 1940s and 1950s and incorporated five main explanatory inputs.

First, there was Merton's concept of anomie with its proposition that people may either turn to various kinds of deviant conduct in order to gain otherwise unobtainable material rewards or, failing that, seek alternative goals.

Second, there were the case studies conducted by the Chicago School that had suggested that young males living in socially 'disorganised' areas had different moral standards from other people and these helped facilitate their willingness to become involved in offending behaviour. Moreover, some of these patterns of conduct were passed on – or 'culturally transmitted' – from one generation to the next.

Third, there was the 'masculine identity crisis theory' outlined by the then highly influential functionalist sociologist Talcott Parsons (1937) during a period when his work was highly influenced by Freud. Parsons argued that the primary social role of the adult male is job-centred while that of the adult female is home-centred. Consequently the father is absent from the family home for much of the time and is unable therefore to function as a masculine role model for his children. The outcome is that children of both sexes identify with their mother to the exclusion of their father and this is particularly problematic for the male child who encounters strong cultural expectations that he adopt a masculine role but has no real concept of what this involves. But he has, during his childhood, discovered that stealing, violence and destruction provoke the disapproval of his mother and hence identifies these as non-feminine and therefore masculine characteristics. Offending behaviour satisfies these criteria of masculinity.

Fourth, there was the 'differential association theory' that Edwin Sutherland had developed from the social disorganisation thesis of the Chicago School – discussed in the previous chapter – and which proposed that a person was more likely to offend if they had frequent and consistent contact with others involved in such activities. Offending behaviour was likely to occur when individuals acquired sufficient inclinations towards law breaking which came to eclipse their associations with non-criminal tendencies.

Fifth, there were the early sociological studies of adolescent gangs carried out in the social disorganisation–cultural transmission tradition developed by the Chicago School. Thrasher (1947) thus argued that the adolescent gang emerged out of spontaneous street playgroups of young children in relatively permissive and socially disorganised slum areas but the young males involved were neither 'disturbed' or 'psychopathic' nor 'driven' by socio-economic forces beyond their control, they were simply looking for excitement, adventure and fun. This could be found on the streets but not at school or home.

Later studies of adolescent gangs followed in the tradition established by Thrasher and all argued that involvement in the young male gang was a natural response to a socially disorganised environment and deviant behaviour when it did occur had been learned from previous generations of adolescents (see for example, Yablonsky, 1962). These studies continued throughout the 1930s, 1940s and 1950s in the USA with a few minor examples in the UK. At the same time, the concept of the 'delinquent subculture' was emerging in the USA.

Early US deviant subculture theories

Albert Cohen (1955) observed that previous research had tended to focus on the process through which individual young males had come to adopt deviant values and had either ignored – or taken for granted – the existence of deviant subcultures or gangs. By analysing the structure of such subcultures, Cohen argued that juvenile offending was rarely motivated by the striving for financial success proposed by Merton. In contrast, he argued that adolescent gang members in fact stole for the fun of it and took pride in their acquired reputations for being tough and 'hard'. The gang – or subculture – offers possibilities for *status* and the acquisition of respect that are denied elsewhere. Involvement in gang culture is to use contemporary terminology simply cool.

Cohen noted that although society is stratified into socio-economic classes it is the norms and values of the middle class that are dominant and employed to judge the success and status of everybody in society. The young working-class male nevertheless experiences a different form of upbringing and is unlikely to internalise these norms and values. He is thrust into a competitive social system founded on alien and incomprehensible middle-class norms and values with the outcome that he experiences a deficit of respect and *status frustration.*

Since the young male is involved in a process of interaction with others who are faced with the same difficulties, a mutually agreed solution may be reached and a separate subculture with alternative norms and values with which young males can relate is formed. In this way he can achieve status and respect for involvement in all the things the official culture rejects: hedonism, aggression, dishonesty and vandalism. In short, there is a conscious and *active* rejection of middle-class norms and values.

Cohen's delinquent subculture theory has attracted its share of criticism not least because he failed to base his theoretical formulation on empirical data and, indeed, all attempts to test it have failed and it can be argued that it is inherently untestable. Kitsuse and Dietrick (1959) showed there was no real basis for the assertion that the young working-class male experiences 'problems of adjustment' to middle-class values. They observe that middle-class norms and values are simply *irrelevant* to young working-class men because they have absolutely no interest in acquiring status within the dominant social system. Their aspirations are thus *not frustrated.* They simply resent the intrusion of middle-class outsiders who try to impose their irrelevant way of life upon them and offending behaviour should therefore be considered rational and utilitarian in the context of working-class culture.

Walter Miller (1958) develops this theme and argues that offending is simply the product of long-established traditions of working-class life and it is the very structure of that culture that generates offending behaviour not conflicts with middle-class values. The *focal concerns* of working-class society – toughness, smartness, excitement, fate and autonomy – combine in several ways to produce criminality. Those who respond to such concerns automatically violate the law through their behaviour and, thus, the very fact of being working class places the individual in a situation that contains a variety of direct incitements towards deviant conduct. Implicit in this formulation is a significant attack on the notion that subcultures originate as a response to lack of status or thwarted aspirations. On the contrary, delinquency is simply a way of life and a response to the realities of their particular lives.

Miller himself problematically offers no explanation for the origins of these highly deterministic working-class values from which there appears to be no escape. All he does is note their existence and explain that conforming to them will lead to criminal behaviour. His work was strongly influenced by Parson's masculinity identity crisis (Parsons, 1937) where it had been noted that it is common in lower-class households for the father to be absent, often because he has transgressed against the criminal law. The home life is thus a female-dominated environment that leads working-class males to look for 'suitable' role models outside the home and these could be readily found in the street gangs – termed by Miller 'one-sex peer units' – where the adolescent male could take part in activities that uphold working class 'focal concerns' and give him a sense of belonging, status and respect.

Richard Cloward and Lloyd Ohlin's *Delinquency and Opportunity* (1960) was a major development in deviant subculture theory and provided one of the central foundations of labelling theory which itself is a central element of the victimised actor tradition we will encounter in the third part of this book. They essentially argue that it is necessary to have two theories in order to fully explain adolescent criminal behaviour: first, there is a need for a 'push' theory to explain why it is that large numbers of young people offend and second, a 'pull' theory to explain the continuance of this behaviour and how it becomes passed on to others. The originality of their work lies in their use of a combination of Merton's anomie theory to explain the 'push' and Sutherland's differential association theory to explain the 'pull'.

Cloward and Ohlin observe that there is a discrepancy between the aspirations of working-class adolescent males and the opportunities available to them. When an individual recognises that membership of a particular ethnic group or social class and/or lack of a suitable education has seriously restricted his access to legitimate opportunities he will blame an unfair society for his failure and withdraw his belief in the legitimacy of the social order. It is this awareness that leads to a rejection of conventional codes of behaviour.

Cloward and Ohlin followed Cohen in stressing that individuals have to actively seek out and join with others who face the same problems and together these young males will devise a collective solution to their predicament for surrounded by hostile adults they need all the support that they can get from each other. Moreover, they need to develop techniques to neutralise the guilt they feel and this is easier to achieve as the member of a like-minded group.

Underlying this reformulation of anomie theory is the assumption that illegitimate routes to success are freely available to those individuals who 'need' them. Cloward and Ohlin combine the cultural transmission theory of Shaw with the differential association theory of Sutherland to create an 'illegitimate opportunity structure' concept that parallels the 'legitimate opportunity structure' of Merton. From this theory the existence of three separate delinquent subcultures were predicted. First, *criminal* delinquent subcultures are said to exist where there are available illegitimate opportunities for learning the motivations, attitudes and techniques necessary in order to commit crimes. Second, a *conflict* subculture exists where adolescent males – denied access to the legitimate opportunity structure because of their social class, ethnic origin, etc. – have no available criminal opportunity structure and in this scenario, young males work off their frustrations by attacking people (assault), property (vandalism) and each other (gang fights). Third, *retreatist* subcultures tend to exist where drugs are freely available and membership is composed of those who have failed to gain access to either the legitimate or criminal subcultures. These young males retreat into drug misuse and alcoholism and are considered to be 'double failures'.

Cloward and Ohlin predicted – and this was 1960 – that because the organisation within poor inner cities was collapsing and adult crime was becoming too sophisticated for adolescent males to learn easily, the criminal delinquent subculture would decline. The conflict or retreatist subcultures would on the other hand expand, with increased adolescent violence, 'muggings', vandalism and drug addiction.

Three main criticisms have been made of Cloward and Ohlin's work. First, it is observed that their notion of the criminal subculture is modelled on the fairly stable and structured adolescent gangs of the Chicago slum areas of the 1920s and 1930s and which had long since ceased to exist (Jacobs, 1961). Second, there is an inherent assumption that the working class is a relatively homogeneous group and this is simply not the case. Third, they, like their predecessors, provide a grossly simplistic explanation of drug misuse, which is, in reality, fairly common among successful middle-class professional people, particularly, if alcohol consumption is included under the generic term 'drugs'.

Coward and Ohlin's theory was nevertheless the focus of considerable academic debate with a major issue being the extent to which the actions of young males in delinquent gangs are determined by their socialisation and the extent to which they are committed to the delinquent norms of the group.

Ivan Spergel (1964) provided at least a partial answer to these questions, identifying an 'anomie gap' between aspirations measured in terms of aspired to and expected occupation and weekly wage, finding that the size of this gap differed significantly between offenders and non-offenders and between one subculture and another. Spergel consequently rejected Cloward and Ohlin's subculture categories and replaced them with his own three-part typology: first, *a racket subculture* is said to develop in areas where organised adult criminality is already in existence and highly visible; second, *a theft subculture*

– involving offences such as burglary, shoplifting, taking and driving away cars – would develop where a criminal subculture was already in existence but not very well established and third, *conflict subcultures* – involving gang fighting and 'rep'utation would develop where there is limited or no access to either criminal or conventional activities.

Spergel significantly found that drug misuse was common to all subcultures as part of the transition from adolescent delinquent activity to either conventional or fully developed criminal activity among older adolescents and young adults while people involved in drug misuse do not in themselves constitute a subculture. Moreover, the common form of deviant behaviour specific to a particular area depends on the idiosyncratic features of that particular district and not, as Merton – and Cloward and Ohlin – imply, on *national* characteristics.

The general conclusion reached by critics of early US deviant subculture theories is that they fail to provide an adequate explanation of adolescent offending behaviour while a number of more specific criticisms can also be identified. First, descriptions of the 'typical' offender where they are portrayed as being in some way different from non-offenders and driven into offending behaviour by grim social and economic forces beyond their control make little sense. There is simply no attempt to explain why it is that many if not most young males faced with the same 'problems of adjustment' *do not* join delinquent gangs. Second, virtually all-deviant subculture explanations consider adolescent offending to be a gang phenomenon where in reality this is a very doubtful proposition. A lot of adolescent offending behaviour is a solitary activity or involves, at the most, two or three young males together. The fairly stable gangs identified by the deviant subculture theorists were certainly at that time very difficult to find. Third, none of these explanations takes into account the roles of authority figures – the police, parents, social workers and teachers – in labelling these young people as offenders. Fourth, no adequate explanations are provided of how it is that many young males appear to simply outgrow offending behaviour. Fifth, no explanation is provided for the offending behaviour of adolescent females. Sixth, there is an inherent assumption that offending is the preserve of the young male lower working classes and this is clearly not the case.

The deviant subculture concept has nevertheless been subsequently successfully applied elsewhere in the study of deviant and criminal behaviour with some researchers usefully utilising it to explain corporate – or business – crime. Aubert (1952) examined the attitudes of certain Swedish citizens towards violation of wartime rationing regulations and found that two sorts of obligation influenced the behaviour of each research subject. First, 'universalistic' obligations affected their behaviour as a law-abiding citizen and these should have provided sufficient motivation to obey the law, but sanctions against those who transgressed were found to be invariably weak. Second, 'particularistic' obligations were considered to be due to business colleagues, and these were supported by a philosophy that demanded only avoidance of certain 'blatant offences'. The groups to which white-collar criminals belong were described as having 'an elaborate and widely accepted ideological rationalisation for the offences and ... great social significance outside the sphere of criminal activity' (Aubert, 1952: 177). Corporate crimes were found to be sometimes acceptable and endorsed by group norms with certain types of illegal activity seen as normal. Braithwaite (1984) similarly found that bribing health inspectors was normal and acceptable business practice in the pharmaceutical industry.

These subcultural influences are nevertheless not fully deterministic. Executives who violate laws are not pressured into action by irresistible forces beyond their control. Deviance may be encouraged and condoned but it is not automatic or uncontested destiny. Both Geis (1967) and Faberman (1975) found that even within industries where criminal practices are common, some employees were not prepared to get involved in spite of often quite extensive pressure from senior managers. It seems that individual characteristics, variations between groups within a subculture and the degree of exposure to subcultural values seem to be relevant in this context.

Hopkins Burke and Pollock (2004) note the value of the deviant subculture concept in helping to account for hate crime motivation, for being part of a particular ethnic group with its additional transmitted traditions and mechanical solidarities can undoubtedly act as a particular focus for collective belonging and can undoubtedly provide both the fulcrum for the actualisation of hate crime behaviour and protection against it. The authors also note that it is a particularly useful theoretical tool for helping to explain the kind of institutional racist police behaviour identified in the London Metropolitan Constabulary by the Macpherson Report 1999.

There has long been a tough working class police culture – 'canteen culture' as it has been termed (see Holdaway, 1983; Fielding, 1988; Reiner, 2000) – that has been transmitted and adapted to changing circumstances across the generations. Working in a hard, tough environment, invariably at risk of serious violence, notions of always looking after your colleagues in the face of external censure and senior management, has made considerable sense to serving officers brought together in a perceived shared adversity and has rather inevitably led to them looking inwards to the group for a supportive shared world view. The outcome has been a 'stereotyping', separating and labelling of the public into categories deemed worthy of police assistance – the community or 'those like us' – and the 'others', the 'toe-rags', 'slags', 'scrotes', 'scum' and 'animals'. Some have argued that these stereotypes drive the day-to-day nature and pattern of police work (Smith and Gray, 1986; Young, 1991, 1993) and the Macpherson Report 1999 clearly identified a significant issue of institutional racism within the Metropolitan police where young black males were apparently not deemed worthy of victim status even when murdered.

Hopkins Burke (2004b) observes that this subculture was undoubtedly *relatively* non problematic during an era when police intervention against the rougher elements of a predominantly white monocultural working class had undoubted support from most elements of society including the socially aspiring respectable elements within that class who lived cheek-by-jowl with the roughs and sought protection from them. It was with the fragmentation of that society and the emergence of the ethnic and sexual preference diversity discussed in the final part of this book that this macho-police subculture became increasingly problematic.

This early US deviant subcultural tradition has been widely accused of being overly determinist in its apparent rejection of free will and in this variant of the predestined actor model deviants are seen to be not only different from non deviants but in some way committed to an alternative 'ethical' code that makes involvement in deviant activity appear somewhat mandatory. While it is extremely likely that some young people, or police officers and business personnel, for that matter, are so strongly socialised into the mores of a particular world view – or mechanical solidarity – through membership of a particular ethnic group, the upbringing of their parents and the reinforcing influences of neighbourhood groups or gangs that they do not challenge this heritage in any way, it also likely that many others have less consistent socialisation experiences and have a far more tangential relationship to such deviant behaviour, although they may be at considerable risk of being drawn into a far deeper involvement.

David Matza and the anti-determinist critique

The best and most comprehensive critique of the highly determinist early deviant subculture tradition is provided by David Matza and in doing so he provides an influential and crucial link with the later non-determinist explanations discussed in the third part of this book. Matza (1964) observed that all criminologists working in the predestined actor tradition – from Lombroso onwards – have made three basic assumptions about crime which although they have some validity have simply been taken too far. First, there has been a focus on the criminal and their behaviour while the role of the criminal justice system – a significant part of the environment of the criminal – is ignored. Second, the predestined actor model is overly determinist in its rejection of the notion of rational free will and simply fails to recognise that human beings *are* capable of making rational choices but these are limited by structural constraints. Third, the predestined actor model considers criminals to be fundamentally different types of people from non-criminals, although there are, of course, substantial variations on this theme. Lombroso, for example, considered the criminal to have been 'born bad' while the deviant subculture theorist, on the other hand, considered the actions of the offender to be determined by a commitment to an alternative 'ethical' code that makes involvement in delinquent activity seem mandatory.

Matza notes that those working in the predestined actor tradition have simply failed to explain why it is that most young offenders 'grow out' of offending behaviour. From that determinist perspective, offenders would presumably continue to offend all the time, except of course when they have been incarcerated. This is clearly not the case but it is the logical deduction that can be made from the position taken by such writers as Cohen, and Cloward and Ohlin. In response, Matza proposes that delinquency is a *status* and delinquents are *role players* who intermittently act out a delinquent role.

These young men are perfectly capable of engaging in conventional activity and, therefore, the alleged forces that compel them to be delinquent are somehow rendered inactive for most of their lives. They simply 'drift' between delinquent and conventional behaviour. The young person is neither compelled nor committed to delinquent activity but freely chooses it sometimes and on other occasions does not do so.

Matza accepted the existence of subcultures whose members engage in delinquency but, on the other hand, denied the existence of a specific deviant subculture. Theories that propose the existence of such a subculture assume that this involves a contra culture, one that deliberately runs counter to the values of the dominant culture. Matza argued that this position is problematic for the following reasons. First, there is the implication that the young person does not experience feelings of guilt and this is not the case. Second, there is an assumption that young offenders have no respect for conventional morality whereas, in reality, most young people involved in offending behaviour recognise the legitimacy of the dominant social order and the validity of its moral standards. Third, it is argued that young offenders define all people outside their 'delinquent subculture' as potential victims whereas they distinguish special groups – mostly other delinquents – as legitimate targets to victimise. Fourth, it is proposed that delinquents are immune from the demands of the larger culture whereas, in reality, the members of these supposed 'delinquent subcultures' are *children* and cannot escape from disapproving adults and their condemnation of delinquent behaviour must therefore be taken into consideration with the strong probability that their demands for conformity will be internalised.

Matza found that young males could moreover remain within the 'subculture of delinquency' *without* actually taking part in offending behaviour. Thus, when he showed a sample of photographs of various criminal acts to a group of delinquents – some of which they themselves had committed – their reactions ranged from mild disapproval to righteous indignation.

Matza argued that adolescents go through three stages in a process of becoming deviant. The first stage is the nearest the young male comes to being part of an oppositional subculture and such a situation arises when he is in the company of other young males and where there appears to be an 'ideology of delinquency' implicit in their actions and remarks. In these circumstances he is motivated by his anxiety to be accepted as a member of the group and his concerns about his own masculinity and 'grown-up' status. In this condition of anxiety he reaches conclusions, in his own mind, about what will be the 'correct' form of behaviour to adopt, the 'correct' attitude to present and the 'correct' motives for engaging in a particular form of behaviour from the remarks, gestures and behaviour of the other adolescents. He hears and perhaps sees others in the group approving of or doing daring, but illegal, acts and assumes that, to be accepted, he must join in and show that he is just as good (or bad), if not better than, all the others. So he steals things, vandalises things, hits people not because he 'really' wants to but because he feels he 'ought' to want to, because that is what being 'grown up' is all about.

Matza observes that what this young man fails to realise is that the other members of the group feel exactly the same as he does. The others are also plagued by doubts about acceptance, masculinity and adulthood and, indeed, may be taking *their* cues from him. In other words, all the members of the group are trapped in a vicious circle of mutual misunderstandings. This circle can be broken when two young men confess to each other that they do not like offending or when the particular individual is sufficiently old to stop feeling anxieties about masculinity and adult status. At this stage of maturity a young man can decide to leave the group and cease involvement in deviant activity or to continue.

The second stage thus occurs when the young man, having overcome his original anxieties about masculinity, is faced with another problem, he must overcome his initial socialisation that has taught him not to be deviant and hence protect himself from feelings of guilt. He must find extenuating circumstances that will release him from conventional control and leave him free to choose to drift into deviancy and thus, in this way, young males utilise 'techniques of neutralisation' to justify their behaviour. Matza identifies five major types of neutralisation:

- denial of responsibility (I didn't mean it);
- denial of injury (I didn't really harm him);
- denial of the victim (he deserved it);
- condemnation of the condemners (they always pick on us); and
- appeals to higher loyalties (you've got to help your mates).

These techniques are by themselves merely excuses and not explanations of deviant behaviour. Matza argued that at a deeper level there is a commitment to 'subterranean values', which – like Miller's 'focal concerns' which they resemble – exist in the wider culture of normal society. The most important of these values is what psychologists refer to as the 'need for stimulation', which means, in this context, the search for excitement. Young males commit deliberate criminal acts because they *are* criminal, quite simply, being deviant is better than being bored, deviancy is fun, it is exciting.

Matza argued that the operation of the criminal justice system and the actions of social workers might actually convince young people that deviant behaviour does not really matter. Deviant young males are not stupid, they are aware that many social workers, police officers, teachers and magistrates think that the young person is not fully responsible for their actions but will go ahead and punish – or rather 'treat' – them just the same. Deviant children are as quick as – or even quicker than – non-deviants to recognise this contradiction and to exploit it to their own advantage.

The third stage in a deviant career has now been reached with the young male now in a situation of 'drift' where he knows what is required of him and has learned the techniques of neutralisation which justify his deviant behaviour. On the other hand, he is not automatically *committed* to deviant behaviour and he *could* just boast about previous and unverifiable exploits, much as other young people boast about imaginary sexual encounters.

The missing impetus that makes actual deviant behaviour possible is 'free will' and it is this recognition that distinguishes Matza completely from those working in the predestined actor tradition. The deviant is *responsible* for their behaviour. They *know* that their activities are against the law. They *know* that they may be caught and they *know* that they may be punished. They probably accept that they *should* be punished. It is one of the rules of the game. If this is the case the question that remains to be asked is why the young person should continue to be involved in criminal behaviour.

In the first place, the young person has acquired certain skills partly from their older friends and partly from the mass media, for example television, which has made involvement in criminal behaviour possible. They will have learned from their friends how to manage guilt and discount the possibility of capture. They assume that they will not be caught and criminal statistics suggest that they are likely to be correct in this supposition. This state of *preparation* allows the young person to repeat an offence that they have committed before. Less frequently, the young person falls into a condition of *desperation* derived from a mood of *fatalism*, a feeling of being 'pushed around'. This feeling of being pushed around is sufficient for them to lose their precarious concept of their self as a 'real man' and, at that point, they need to 'make something happen' in order to prove that they are a *cause* not merely an effect and it is this feeling that leads them directly to become involved in more serious, previously untried, delinquent behaviour where even if caught they have still made something happen. The whole apparatus of police, juvenile court and social work department is concerned with them and has been activated by what *they them self* did. In a state of desperation the young person needs to do more than simply repeat an old offence. After all, as his or her peers would say, 'anyone can do that'. In the state of desperation, they need to do something that they have not tried before.

Matza's theoretical schema has also been usefully applied to the study of business crime. Corporate executives have thus been found to use 'techniques of neutralisation' to rationalise deviant acts and violate the law without feeling guilty (Box, 1983). Officials can deny responsibility by pleading ignorance, accident, or that they were acting under orders. Vague laws that rest on ambiguous definitions and permit meanings and interpretation to fluctuate help facilitate this and as a result it is difficult to distinguish praiseworthy corporate behaviour from illegal actions. Box (1983: 55) observes that in these circumstances, 'it is convenient for corporate officials to pull the cloak of honest ignorance over their heads and proceed under its darkness to stumble blindly and unwittingly over the thin line between what is condoned and what is condemned'.

Bandura (1973: 13) found that shared decision making in an organisation allows people to contribute 'to cruel practices ... without feeling personally responsible'. 'Denial of the victim' may also be used. The nature of much corporate crime permits an illusion that there is no real person suffering, particularly when the victims are other corporations or people in far off countries, especially if they are less developed countries (Braithwaite, 1984). Swartz (1975) has noted that company spokespersons have been prepared to blame industrial accidents on 'careless and lazy' workers or the development of brown lung in black workers on their 'racial inferiority'. The corporate criminal often denies that any harm has been caused. Geis (1968: 108) quotes an executive who described his activities as 'illegal ... but not criminal ... I assumed that criminal action meant damaging someone, and we did not do that'. Moreover, the corporate employee can 'condemn the condemners', by pointing to political corruption, or describing laws as unwarranted constraints on free enterprise. Acting for the good of the company – or following widespread but illegal business practices – is seen as more important than obeying the law.

Hopkins Burke and Pollock (2004: 31) discuss how techniques of neutralisation can be used by hate crime offenders to excuse, justify and legitimate their actions and use the following all inclusive and somewhat 'upmarket' illustration to make their point:

> Well I know it is rather unpleasant and one doesn't really like getting involved in these things, but they are different from us. They have a different way of life and it is not really what we want here. You really wouldn't want your children to mix with them now would you? I don't really approve of this sort of thing but something has to be done.

The authors note that having absorbed experiences and knowledge at each stage of their socialisation from parents and friends and having had these values reinforced by access to media – however self selecting this might be – provides the race hate perpetrator with choices which for them are very much rational. In a study conducted for the British Home Office, Rae Sibbitt (1999) found that the views held by all kinds of race hate perpetrators are shared very much by the communities to which they belong and perpetrators very much see this as legitimising their actions. In turn, the wider community not only spawn such perpetrators, but fails to condemn them and thus actively reinforce their behaviour. Hate crime perpetrators are invariably very much part of their local deviant subculture or mechanical solidarity.

Early British deviant subcultural studies

Early British deviant subcultural studies tended to follow the lead of the US theories discussed above. The main influences were the work of Miller and Cohen with the work of Cloward and Ohlin appearing to have had little or no application in Britain, well at least at that time.

John Mays (1954) argued that in certain – particularly older urban – areas, the residents share a number of attitudes and ways of behaving that predispose them to criminality. These attitudes have existed for years and are passed on to newcomers. Working-class culture is not intentionally criminal. It is just a different socialisation, which, at times, happens to be contrary to the legal rules. Criminal behaviour – particularly adolescent criminal behaviour – is not therefore a conscious rebellion against middle-class values but arises from an alternative working-class subculture that has been adopted over the years in a haphazard sort of way.

Terence Morris (1957) argued that social deviants are common among the working classes and that it is the actual characteristics of that class that creates the criminality. Forms of antisocial behaviour exist throughout society and in all classes, but the way in which the behaviour is expressed differs. He considered criminal behaviour to be largely a working-class expression. The family controls middle-class socialisation, it is very ordered and almost all activities are centred on the home and the family. In the working classes, in contrast, the socialisation of the child tends to be divided between family, peer group and street acquaintances with the outcome that the latter child is likely to have a less ordered and regulated upbringing. The peer group is a much stronger influence from a much earlier age and they encounter controls only after they commit a crime and when they are processed by the criminal justice system. The whole ethos of the working class, according to Morris, is oriented towards antisocial and criminal, rather than 'conventional', behaviour.

David Downes (1966) conducted a study among young offenders in the East End of London and found that a considerable amount of offending behaviour took place, but this mostly happened in street corner groups, rather than organised gangs. Status frustration did not occur to a significant degree among these young males and their typical response to a lack of success at school or work was one of 'dissociation', a process of opting out rather than reaction formation. The emphasis was on leisure activities – not on school or work – with commercial forms of entertainment the main focus of interest not youth clubs with their middle-class orientation. Access to leisure pursuits was nevertheless restricted by a lack of money and as an alternative means of entertainment youths would take part in offending. Peter Wilmott (1966) also conducted a study of teenagers in the East End of London and reached much the same conclusions as Miller finding that adolescent offending behaviour was simply part of a general lower working-class subculture. Teenagers became involved in petty crime simply for the fun and 'togetherness' of the shared activity experience.

Howard Parker (1974) conducted a survey of unskilled adolescents in an area of Liverpool that official statistics suggested had a high rate of adolescent offending and found that there was a pattern of loosely knit peer groups, not one of tightly structured gangs. Offending behaviour was not a central activity. Young males shared common problems, such as unemployment and leisure opportunities were limited. Some youths had developed a temporary solution in the form of stealing car radios. Furthermore, the community in which the young males lived was one that largely condoned theft, as long as the victims were from outside the area.

Ken Pryce (1979) studied African-Caribbean youngsters in the St Paul's area of Bristol and suggested that the first African-Caribbeans to arrive in the 1950s came to Britain with high aspirations but found on arrival that they were relegated to a force of cheap labour while they and their children were subject to racism and discrimination, which contributed to a pattern of 'endless pressure'. Pryce suggested there were two types of adaptation to this pressure: one was to be stable, conformist and law-abiding while the other was to adopt an expressive, disreputable rebellious attitude. Second and third generation African-Caribbeans were more likely – but not bound – to adopt the second response.

These earlier British deviant subculture studies were important because they drew our attention to specific historical factors, in particular the level of economic activity, and to the importance of a structural class analysis in the explanation of subcultural delinquency (Hopkins Burke and Sunley, 1996, 1998). They also demonstrated that different groups within the working class had identified distinct problems in terms of negative status and had developed their own solutions to their perceived problems. They moreover tended to neglect the involvement of young women in offending behaviour. Thus, where young women are discussed, they tended to be dismissed as 'sex objects' or adjuncts to male offending behaviour, merely 'hangers-on'.

Studies of deviant youth subcultures carried out in the USA since the late 1960s have predominantly focused on issues of violence, ethnicity, poverty and the close links between all three. Wolfgang and Ferracuti (1967) identified 40 years ago a 'sub-culture of violence' where there was an expectation that the receipt of a trivial insult should be met with violence. Failure to respond in this way – and thus walk away from trouble – was greeted with social censure from the peer group. Curtis (1975) adapted this theory to explain violence among American Blacks and found that the maintenance of a manly image was found to be most important in the subculture with individuals unable to resolve conflicts verbally and more likely to resort to violence in order to assert their masculinity. Behaviour is seen to be partly a response to social conditions, and partly the result of an individual's acceptance of the ideas and values that he has absorbed from the subculture of violence. Maxson and Klein (1990) more recently recognised that certain youth groups, for example, racist 'skinheads' and neo-Nazi organisations, engage in group related violent behaviour for ideological-including political and religious-ends.

Recent research in the USA has proposed that poverty is basically the root cause of gangs and the violence they produce. Miller (1958) had argued that lower-class delinquency was a normal response to sociocultural demands but in his later writings he essentially adopts a 'culture of poverty' view to explain the self-perpetuation of gang life, a view that emphasises the adaptational aspects of the gang to changing socio-economic circumstances (Miller, 1990). However, the most popular current theory to explain criminal behaviour among poor young people in the US inner city is William Julius Wilson's 'underclass theory' where it is suggested that groups in socially isolated neighbourhoods have few legitimate employment opportunities. Inadequate job information networks and poor schools not only lead to weak labour force attachment but also significantly increases the likelihood that people will turn to illegal or deviant activities for income (Wilson, 1991).

Wilson has been accused of failing to address the issues of gang formation and explain the development of specific types of gang problems (Hagedorn, 1992) but a number of other observers assume a close correlation between gangs, gang violence and the development of a socially excluded underclass (Krisberg, 1974; Anderson, 1990; Taylor, 1990). Poverty is central to the underclass thesis and various writers recognise that the absence of economic resources leads to compensatory efforts to achieve some form of economic and successful social adjustment (Williams, 1989; Moore, 1991; Hopkins Burke, 1999a). It is in this context that Spergel (1995: 149) argues that, 'a subculture arises out of efforts of people to solve social, economic, psychological, developmental, and even political problems'. This is an argument to which we return in Chapter 16.

Radical deviant subculture theories

The concept of deviant subculture was subsequently revised and revitalised by radical neo-Marxist sociologists and criminologists – working in the 'victimised actor' tradition – and based at the Birmingham Centre for Contemporary Cultural Studies during the 1970s (see Cohen, 1972; Cohen, 1973; Hebdige, 1976, 1979; Brake, 1985). These researchers observed that 'spectacular' youth subcultures – such as Teddy Boys, Mods, Skinheads and Punks – arise at particular historical 'moments' as cultural solutions to the same structural economic problems created by rapid social change identified by Durkheim – and Merton in a rather different way – as an anomic condition.

These researchers recognise that in contemporary societies the major cultural configurations – or we might observe, macro mechanical solidarities – are cultures based on social class, but within these larger entities are *sub*-cultures which are defined as 'smaller, more localised and differentiated structures, within one or other of the larger cultural networks' (Hall and Jefferson, 1976: 13). These subcultures have different focal concerns than the larger cultural configuration from which it is derived but will share some common aspects or core values with the 'parent culture'. Some, like *deviant* subcultures, are persistent features of the parent culture, but others appear only at certain historical moments and then fade away. These latter subcultures are highly visible and, indeed 'spectacular' and although their members may well look very 'different' from their parents or peers, they will still share the same class position, the same life experiences, and generally the same world view or core values of the parent culture. All they are doing, through their distinctive dress, lifestyle, music etc., is producing a different cultural 'solution' to the problems posed for them by their material and social class position and experience. They are invariably articulating a contemporary variant of the parent culture that is in accord with their changed socio-economic circumstances.

The central concern of that collection of studies was to locate the historical and environmental context in which particular youth subcultures arose and the details of 'style' adopted by these. Central to their argument is the notion that style is a form of *resistance* to subordination which is essentially *ritualistic, symbolic* or *magical* as it is not, actually, a *successful* solution to the problem of subordination. Resistance is not a desperate 'lashing out' or a passive adaptation to an anomic situation of disjunction, but a collective response designed to resist or transform dominant values and defend or recapture working class or ethnic group values – to win space, to reclaim community and reassert traditional values. This resistance is nevertheless symbolic rather than real.

Stan Cohen (1973) notes three contexts in which the concepts of ritual, myth, metaphor, magic, and allegory are invoked. First, the target for attack is inappropriate or irrational in the sense of not being logically connected with the source of the problem, for example, it is argued that skinheads beating up Asian and Gay people is in reality a reaction to other things, such as, perceived threats to community, homogeneity, or traditional stereotypes of masculinity. Second, when the solution does not confront the real material basis of subordination and is not a genuinely political response, the activities are seen as merely, albeit violent, 'gestures'. Third, when the subcultural style denotes something beyond its surface appearance, for example, the boots worn by Skinheads, the young people are making oblique coded statements about their relationships to a particular – in that example, white working class – past or present.

The Birmingham researchers focused on two broad but overlapping areas: mainstream youth and delinquency, especially the transition from school to work and expressive or spectacular youth subcultures. The two major studies of mainstream youth subcultures are those of Willis (1977) and Corrigan (1979) and both are concerned with the transition from school to work among urban lower working-class adolescent boys. Their 'problem' is an alien or irrelevant education system followed by the prospect of a boring and dead end job (or, nowadays, training and the benefits queue, see Hopkins Burke, 1999a) and the 'solution' is a 'culture of resistance' manifested in truancy and petty offending. Actions are ritualistic (or magical) but they can never solve the problem. Spectacular' youth subcultures involve the adoption, by young people of both sexes of a distinctive style of dress and way of using material artefacts combined, usually, with distinctive lifestyles, behaviour patterns and musical preferences. Both variants of subculture invariably involve a contemporary manifestation of parent culture values that have been adapted to the changed socio-economic circumstances in which the group finds itself.

The Birmingham studies represented an important development of the earlier deviant subcultural tradition – which had recognised that deviance often occurs in response to economic or status deprivation – and identified that particular subcultures or status groups have arisen in response to the perceived economic problems of distinct groups. Hopkins Burke and Sunley (1996, 1998) nevertheless observe that these studies presume a linear development of history where different subcultures arise, coalesce, fade and are replaced as economic circumstances change. Thus, for example, the 'Mods' were a product of the upwardly mobile working-classes during the optimistic 1960s (Hebdige, 1976; 1979; Brake, 1980), whereas, on the other hand, the Punks were a product of the 'dole-queue' despondency of the late-1970s (Hebdige, 1979; Brake, 1980, 1985).

Hopkins Burke and Sunley (1996, 1998) have more recently observed the co-existence of a number of different subcultures and propose this to be an outcome of a fragmented society where specific groups of young people have coalesced to create solutions to their specific socio-economic problems and central to this account is the possibility of choice. The simultaneous existence of different subcultures enables some young people to *choose* the solution to their problem from the various subcultures available although that choice will undoubtedly be constrained by structural factors.

The early deviant subcultural studies – and indeed the work of the Birmingham School – tended to suggest that young people had limited choices, if any, between *the* subculture available at a particular time and in that geographical location, and a life of conventionality. This more contemporary – or postmodernist – interpretation of youth subcultures enables us to recognise that individuals, and different groups of young people, not all members of the traditional working-class but in existence concurrently at the same historical moment, have had very different experiences of the radical economic change that has engulfed British society since the late 1970s. These very different groups have developed their own subcultural solutions for coping with this transformation and this postmodernist argument is revisited later in this book.

Conclusions

The early sociological variants of the predestined actor model of crime and criminal behaviour have – like the early biological and psychological versions – been accused of being overly determinist. It is nevertheless a form of criminological explanation that has been extremely influential in informing the direction of later – less determinist – approaches. Furthermore, the recognition that social factors external to the human being place significant *constraints* on that person's choice of action, has been particularly influential and, indeed, would be considered by many today to be an almost common-sense, if partial, explanation of criminal behaviour.

We have seen that the later subculture theorists came increasingly to recognise that human beings are able to make choices about the course of action that they will take but it is a recognition that does not signify a return to unbridled purist variants of the rational actor model. From the perspective of these later and more sophisticated versions of the predestined actor model there is recognition of limited constrained human choice. Thus, the choices available to the individual are restricted by their life-chances, such as their education, training and skills, place of upbringing, membership of ethnic group, gender and differential access to material resources. Thus, people do not enjoy free will – as in the rational choice actor conceptualisation – for no human being is ever totally free and they simply make choices that are constrained by their social circumstances. These issues are developed more fully in the third part of this book.

Suggested further reading

Sociological positivism is an extremely wide subject area and there are thus many relevant texts. Students are therefore again advised to use the references in the text as a guide to specific interests. However, for a comprehensive introduction to the increasingly rediscovered and currently highly influential social theory of Emile Durkheim it is well worth consulting the original text, Durkheim (1933). Shaw and McKay (1972) provide a thorough introduction to the work of the Chicago School. Merton (1938) – subsequently reprinted in many different collections – provides a still essential introduction to anomie theory. The early US deviant subculture tradition is well represented by Cloward and Ohlin (1960) Cohen (1955), Miller (1958) and Spergel (1964). Matza (1964) provides, in a text widely regarded as one of the best criminology books ever written, both an excellent critique of that tradition and an excellent link with both the rational actor and victimised actor models. Spergel (1995) provides a comprehensive overview of more recent US work in that tradition. Early UK research is well represented by Downes (1966), Mays (1954), Morris (1957), Parker (1974) and Pryce (1979). A key text representing the later Marxist influenced Birmingham CCCS approach is Hall and Jefferson (eds) (1976), while Hopkins Burke and Sunley (1998) provide a comprehensive but concise overview of the various formulations of deviant subculture theory while introducing the notion of postmodernism into the debate. Hopkins Burke and Pollock (2004) provide a comprehensive and easily available discussion of the relevance of sociologically informed criminological theories for explaining hate crime motivation.

8. Women and positivism

Explaining female criminal behaviour was for many years a neglected area of criminology and a significant justification for that lack of attention centres on their apparently low levels of involvement in crime and the associated assumption that women are predominantly law-abiding. By the age of 28, 33 per cent of males and 6 per cent of females have been convicted of a serious offence and this ratio has remained similar over the years (Coleman and Moynihan, 1996). Even in the case of shoplifting – an offence traditionally associated with women – there are more males than females convicted. In Britain 80 per cent of those convicted of serious crimes are male while only 3 per cent of the prison population consists of women. There are similar ratios in the USA.

The explanations of female criminality that did exist were founded very much in the predestined actor model of crime and criminal behaviour and this chapter considers how each of the three variants discussed in the previous chapters – biological, psychological and sociological positivisms – have sought to explain female crime.

Biological positivism and women

The works of Lombroso – particularly *The Female Offender* – provide a fundamentally biologically determinist account of female criminality and, while his methodology and conclusions have long been discredited, later biological and psychological writings on female crime (see Thomas, 1907, 1923; Davis, 1961, originally 1937; Pollak, 1950 and others discussed here) have relied at least implicitly on assumptions about the physiological and psychological nature of women to be found in his work (Klein, 1973).

Lombroso – as we saw in Chapter 5 – proposed that crime is an atavism explained by the survival of primitive traits in individuals. Based on this assumption he compared the physical characteristics of convicted female criminals and prostitutes with those women considered to be normal. Traits found to be more common in the 'criminal' group were defined as atavistic and those found to possess a number of these were considered potentially criminal. Moreover, it was argued that women share many common traits because there are fewer variations in their mental capacities: 'even the female criminal is monotonous and uniform compared with her male companion, just as in general woman is inferior to man' (Lombroso and Ferrero, 1885: 122) and furthermore this is explained by her being 'atavistically nearer to her origin than the male' (Lombroso and Ferrero, 1885: 107). Lower rates of female criminality were thus attributed to women in general having fewer anomalies – or variations – than men and this was explained by them being close to the lower forms of less differentiated life.

Lombroso proposed that women are inherently passive and conservative because their traditional sex role in the family inherently prepares them for a more sedentary existence, although he did propose a biological basis for this passivity as being related to the nature of the sex act between men and women. He argued that the great majority of women are constrained from involvement in criminal activity by a lack of intelligence and passion, qualities he associates with *criminal* women and all men. In other words, the female offender is seen – within this indisputably biologically determinist characterisation – to be *masculine* and the normal woman *feminine*. Lombroso observed that the skull anomalies he found in female criminals are closer to those of men – either normal or criminal – than they are to normal women. The female offender often has a 'virile cranium' and considerable body hair but this masculinity is in itself an anomaly rather than a sign of development (Lombroso and Ferrero, 1885: 120).

Finally, Lombroso and Ferrero (1885: 217) note that women have a lack of property sense, which they argue contributes to their criminality: 'in their eyes theft is … an audacity for which compensation is due to the owner … as an individual rather than a social crime, just as it was regarded in the primitive periods of human evolution and is still regarded by many uncivilised nations'. It is a notion that has been challenged on different levels: first, there is the simple assumption that women have a different sense of property than men; second, if there is any credibility in that supposition then this must be explained by the lack of female property ownership and non participation in capitalist wealth accumulation, indeed, women have been considered property themselves (Klein, 1973).

Lombroso has nevertheless provided an enduring – albeit invariably implicit – influence on the biological study of female criminality. Many later biological positivists commented on the passivity and lack of aggression on the part of women and readily proposed this as an explanation for their non involvement in criminal behaviour. Money and Ernhardt (1972) and Rose, Holoday and Bernstein (1971) propose – on the basis of studies conducted with rats in cages – that female passivity is related to the fact that men and women have both different brains and hormones, while behaviourists such as Marsh (1978) argued, in contrast, that differences in behaviour between the sexes is purely the outcome of socialisation. In reality it is very difficult to ascertain which – if either – of the social or the genetic has the greatest influence.

The *generative phases of women* theory is based on biological changes connected to the menstrual cycle and from this perspective, it is proposed that at times of menstruation women are reminded that they can never become men and the subsequent distress this engenders makes them increasingly susceptible to offending behaviour. The best known proponent of this thesis is Otto Pollak (1950) – whose predominantly psychological work is discussed in the next section – and who also proposes that the hormonal disturbance resulting from pregnancy and the menopause may be a cause of female criminality. Dalton (1961) discovered that 59.8 per cent of imprisoned women she studied had committed their offences in the sixteen day period covering pre- and post-menstrual hormone imbalance. On the other hand, 40.2 per cent – or nearly half of the women – had committed crimes during the other twelve days. The results therefore appear inconclusive.

While it remains unclear whether women engage in a higher incidence of criminal behaviour during their generative phases, it is clear that the law has accepted the condition as constituting mitigating circumstances in some instances. Susan Edwards (1988) notes that in the nineteenth century pre-menstrual tension (PMT) was frequently discussed as being an important element of a defence in cases of violence, killing, arson and theft. Both she and Luckhaus (1985) refer to cases in the early 1980s where PMT was successfully pleaded in mitigation with the outcome that murder charges were reduced to manslaughter. This is an interesting finding because medical evidence is divided about the existence of any such syndrome. If there are effects, they appear to be mainly psychological – such as tension, irritability, depression, tiredness, mood swings and feelings of loneliness, although Dalton (1984) includes some relevant physical effects such as epilepsy, fainting and even hypoglycaemia. Rose (2000) proposes that women who have such conditions should receive treatment at an early stage to avoid both later criminal behaviour and the need to admit this type of evidence in court.

In the case of post-natal depression there is the special defence of infanticide. If a mother kills her child within its first year as a result of post-natal depression or breastfeeding she has a partial defence to murder which renders it infanticide. Interestingly, this defence is only available to women and is the only sex-specific defence recognised in the criminal law. It is nevertheless clear that some of these killings might possibly be the outcome of exhaustion through caring for the child, guilt through not feeling affection for it, or the effect of other social pressures, all of which could equally be suffered by a man with primary care of a child. Marks and Kumar (1993) show that the rates of killing of children under one have remained constant since 1957 at about 45 per million per year which is higher than for any other age group. They found that women who kill such children are dealt with much more leniently than men even when the level of violence used by the women is greater. Dell (1984) has shown that in cases of manslaughter sentences have become increasingly punitive, but Maier-Katkin and Ogle (1993) suggest that even when women are convicted of manslaughter they are treated leniently – often with probation – which suggests that it is not so much about a special defence being available but more about a greater compassion for these women.

Men were found to receive considerably harsher sentences in relatively similar cases.

Hormonal imbalances suffered by men – and discussed in Chapter 5 – do not normally influence either their conviction or their sentence. Women, on the other hand, can successfully plead such imbalances even in the most serious cases where they kill another human being. This situation is undoubtedly advantageous for the individual woman involved but for women in general it allows the continuation of the enduring biologically positivist notion that has been in existence since at least Lombroso that they are incapable of controlling themselves and that their actions can be explained through – either physical or psychological – medical reasoning (see Wilczynski and Morris, 1993). The implication of this widely used reasoning would be that women should be treated for this 'sickness' rather than being punished. It thus removes from women the possibility that they might rationally choose to commit criminal behaviour in the socio-economic circumstances in which they find themselves.

Psychological positivism and women

The work of W.I. Thomas is significant because it marks a transition from purely biological explanations of female criminality to a more sophisticated variant that embraces physiological, psychological and even sociological factors. These theories are nevertheless founded on implicit assumptions about the *biological* nature of women that are heavily influenced by the work of Lombroso. Thomas (1907) thus explains the inferior status of women based on physiological assumptions that attribute to men high levels of sexual energy, which leads them to pursue women for their sex, and to women maternal feelings which lead them to exchange sex for domesticity. The outcome is that women – who are also the property of men – are domesticated while men assume leadership. The conduct of the two sexes is moreover regulated and controlled in different ways.

Thomas argued that because women occupy a marginal position in the productive sphere outside the home they consequently occupy a subsidiary position with regard to 'contractual' law which regulates property and production. They simply do not constitute a threat to the commercial world and are therefore treated more leniently than men by the authorities in cases involving property. In matters of sexual conduct the opposite is very much the case and women are rigorously prosecuted by the law.

In *The Unadjusted Girl* (1923), Thomas identified four basic 'wishes', which he proposed to be fundamental to human nature – the desire for new experience, for security, for response and recognition – and proposed that these are derived from the biological instincts of anger, fear, love and the will to gain power and status. These instincts are channelled towards gender appropriate goals through socialisation, with women having a stronger desire for the biological instinct of love than men. It is this intense need to give and feel love that leads women into crime, particularly sexual offences like prostitution.

Significantly, the activities of an individual – although driven by these basic 'wishes' – are controlled by the socialisation processes and can thus be made to serve social or antisocial needs. In short, behaviour can be changed and the individual rehabilitated:

> There is no individual energy, no unrest, no type of wish, which cannot be sublimated and made socially useful. From this standpoint, the problem is not the right of society to protect itself from the disorderly and antisocial person, but the right of the disorderly and antisocial person to be made orderly and socially valuable. ... The problem of society is to produce the right attitudes in its members.
>
> (Thomas, 1923: 232–3)

There is here a significant rejection of the Lombrosian biological perspective which proposes that there are criminally predestined individuals who must be incarcerated, sterilised or otherwise incapacitated. Thomas alternatively proposes the manipulation of individuals to prevent antisocial attitudes and to correct the poor socialisation provided in 'slum' families. The response to a criminal woman who is dissatisfied with her conventional sexual roles is not therefore to change the roles – which would of course involve substantial social transformations – but to change her attitudes.

Thomas (1923) proposes that middle class women commit little crime because they are socialised to control their natural desires and to behave well, treasuring their chastity as an investment. The poor woman, conversely, is not immoral but simply *amoral*. She is not driven to commit crime as the purist predestined actor model proponent might suggest, but simply seek it, motivated by the desire for excitement or 'new experience' and has no interest in middle-class notions of 'security'. Thomas thus uses a market analogy to define female virtue. Good women *keep* their bodies as capital to sell in exchange for marriage and security while bad women trade their bodies for excitement. Klein (1973) observes that this is an astonishing – nay obscene – statement to have been made in an era of mass starvation and illness. Thomas nevertheless simply rejects the possibility of economic explanations of female criminality with as much certainty as Lombroso and Freud, Davis and Pollak to whom we now turn our attention.

The Freudian theory of the position of women is grounded in explicit biological assumptions about their nature and this is unequivocally expressed in his famous dictum that 'anatomy is destiny' (see Lerner, 1998). Women are seen to be anatomically inferior to men with a consequential inferior destiny as wives and mothers. At the root of this inferiority is the inferior nature of female sex organs which is apparently recognised by children universally. Thus, girls assume that they have lost their penis as a punishment, become traumatised and grow up envious and revengeful. Boys noting that girls have lost their penis fear their envy and vengeance.

In the Freudian schema, feminine traits are explained by inferior female genitals. Women are exhibitionistic, narcissistic, and attempt to compensate for their lack of a penis by being well dressed and physically beautiful.

They are also masochistic – as Lombroso and Thomas also noted – because their sexual role is one of receptor, and their sexual pleasure consists of pain. In contrast, men are aggressive and pain inflicting (see Millett, 1970).

Women are also considered inferior because they are preoccupied with personal matters and have little sense of the wider world. Freud proposes that civilisation is based on our repression of the sex drive and it is thus the duty of men to repress their strong instincts in order to get on with the worldly business of civilisation. On the other hand, women:

> Have little sense of justice, and this is no doubt connected with the preponderance of envy in their mental life, for the demands of justice are a modification of envy; they lay down the conditions under which one is willing to part with it. We also say of women that their actual interests are weaker than those of men and that their capacity for the sublimation of their instincts is less.
>
> (Freud, 1933: 183)

Men are capable of sublimating their individual needs because they are rational and capable of understanding the need to control their urges in the interests of wider society. Women, in contrast, are emotional and incapable of making rational judgements. It is therefore appropriate that women should only have a marginal relationship to production and property. The deviant woman in this schema is thus one deemed to be going against her inherent nature and trying to be a *man*. She is thus aggressive, rebellious, and her drive for success is simply indicative of her longing for a penis. This is of course a hopeless ambition and the only outcome for the woman can be neurosis. The solution to her predicament is treatment and help so that she can adjust to her natural sex role.

Klein (1973) observes that Freudian notions of the repression of sexual instincts, the sexual passivity of women, and the sanctity of the nuclear family were conservative even in the early twentieth century when they were developed. They were, however, developed into a remarkably enduring and virtually hegemonic perspective in the USA and beyond which helped facilitate the return of women to the home and out of a productive economy with no capacity for them during the depression and post-war years (Millett, 1970). It was given even greater credibility by the status accorded John Bowlby's (1952) 'maternal deprivation thesis' – published by the United Nations – which proposed that to ensure the successful socialisation of a law abiding citizen, the child needs to be looked after closely and predominantly by its mother during it formative years.

Freud also significantly influenced such writers on female deviance as Kingsley Davis (1961, originally 1937), Otto Pollak (1950) and Gisela Konopka (1966), who used concepts of sexual maladjustment and neurosis to explain the criminality of women. These writers were to define healthy women as masochistic, passive and sexually indifferent, criminal women as sexual misfits, and significantly use *psychological* factors to explain female criminal activity while completely ignoring socio-economic factors.

Kingsley Davis' (1961, originally 1937) influential structural functionalist study of prostitution is significantly founded on crucial assumptions about the 'organic nature of man and woman' that have clear origins in the work of Thomas and Freud. Davis argues that prostitution is a structural necessity with its foundations in the sexual nature of human beings and concludes that prostitution is universally inevitable and that there will always be a class of 'bad' women available to provide their services as prostitutes. Prostitution is universal because sexual repression is essential to the functioning of society.

At the time Davis was writing – in the mid twentieth century – sexuality was only legitimately permitted within the structure of the nuclear family, an institution of social stability and a bulwark of morality:

> The norms of every society tend to harness and control the sexual appetite, and one of the ways of doing this is to link the sexual act to some stable or potentially stable social relationship ... Men dominate women in all economic, sexual and familial relationships and consider them to some extent as sexual property, to be prohibited to other males. They therefore find promiscuity on the part of women repugnant.
>
> (Davis, 1961: 264)

The concept of prostitution is thus linked to promiscuity and defined as a sexual crime with prostitutes themselves perceived not as economically motivated but as sexual transgressors taking advantage of marital restraints on sexuality. Davis argues that there will always be a demand for prostitution as long as men seek women. Only the liberalisation of sexual mores could bring about the eradication of prostitution and he was not optimistic that such a situation would ever arise:

> We can imagine a social system in which the motive for prostitution would be completely absent, but we cannot imagine that the system will ever come to pass. It would be a regime of absolute sexual freedom with intercourse practised solely for pleasure by both parties. There would be no institutional control of sexual expression ... All sexual desire would have to be mutually complementary ... Since the basic causes of prostitution – the institutional control of sex, the unequal scale of unattractiveness, and the presence of economic and social inequalities between classes and between males and females – are not likely to disappear, prostitution is not likely to disappear either.
>
> (Davis, 1961: 286)

Thus men unable to attract women to engage in sexual activity for mutual pleasure – or (and Davis does not discuss this point) have the time, predilection or social skills required to engage in the precursors to this activity – may become frustrated and thus sustain the demand for prostitution.

Davis argues that women become prostitutes for good pay *and* sexual pleasure and there thus exists a functional system beneficial for everyone.

He denies the economic oppression of the women involved. They are on the streets through autonomous, individual choice. Klein (1973) observes that the women are merely adjusting to their feminine role in an illegitimate fashion – as Thomas theorised – they are not attempting to be rebels or to be men as Lombroso and Freud would suggest. At a level of generality, Davis observes the main difference between wives and prostitutes to be between legal and illegal roles, in a personal individualised sense he sees the women who *choose* to become involved in prostitution as maladjusted and neurotic. However, given the universal necessity for prostitution, this analysis seems to imply the necessity of having a perpetually ill and maladjusted class of women which Davis is not prepared to question let alone challenge.

Otto Pollak's *The Criminality of Women* (1950) – a further substantially influential text in the immediate post-Second World War period – proposes the theory of 'hidden' female crime to account for what he considers to be unreasonably low official female crime rates. It is – he argues – the very *nature* of women themselves that accounts for this subterranean criminality. They are simply the instigators rather than the perpetrators of much criminal activity. Pollak acknowledges a partly socially enforced role but insists that women are inherently deceitful for *physiological* reasons:

> Man must achieve an erection in order to perform the sex act and he will not be able to hide his failure. His lack of positive emotion in the sexual sphere must become overt to the partner, and pretense of sexual response is impossible for him, if it is lacking. Woman's body, however, permits such pretense to a certain degree and lack of an orgasm does not prevent her ability to participate in the sex act.
>
> (Pollak, 1950: 10)

The nature of women is therefore reduced to the *sex act* – as with Freud – and women are considered to be inherently more capable of manipulation, accustomed to being sly, passive and passionless. Moreover, women are innately deceitful on another level:

> Our sex mores force women to conceal every four weeks the period of menstruation … They thus make concealment and misrepresentation in the eyes of women socially required and must condition them to a different attitude towards veracity than men.
>
> (Pollack, 1950: 11)

A second factor in hidden crime are the roles played by women that provides them with opportunities as domestics, nurses, teachers and housewives to commit undetectable crimes. Pollak moreover argues that the kinds of crimes committed by women are a reflection of their nature. False accusation, for example, is a consequence of treachery, spite or fear and is a sign of neurosis. Shoplifting, it is proposed, can be traced in many cases to a specific psychiatric disorder called kleptomania. Female criminality is thus explained in terms of socio-psychological factors – economic conditions are considered virtually inconsequential – female crime is personalised and a product of mental illness.

The third factor proposed by Pollak to explain the enigma of hidden female crime is the existence of 'chivalry' in the criminal justice system. Developing from Thomas the theme that women are differentially treated by the law he argues that:

> One of the outstanding concomitants of the existing inequality ... is chivalry, and the general protective attitude of man toward women ... Men hate to accuse women and thus indirectly to send them to their punishment, police officers dislike to arrest them, district attorneys to prosecute them, judges and juries to find them guilty, and so on.
>
> (Pollack, 1950: 151)

Klein (1973) observes that the women who become the clients of the criminal justice system are likely to be poor, from ethnic minority backgrounds – or if white middle-class women those who have stepped outside acceptable definitions of female behaviour – and chivalry is unlikely to be extended to them. She observes that chivalry is a racist and classist concept founded on the notion of women as 'ladies' and this only applies to wealthy white women. These 'ladies', however, are the least likely women to ever come into contact with the criminal justice system in the first place. In these various and different psychological positivist explanations of female crime, crime defined as masculine appears to mean violent, overt crime, whereas 'ladylike' crime refers to sexual violations and shoplifting. Klein observes that women are neatly categorised no matter what kind of crime they commit. If they are violent, they are 'masculine' and suffering from chromosomal deficiencies, penis envy, or atavisms. If they conform, they are manipulative, sexually maladjusted and promiscuous. The *economic* and *social* realities of crime – that it is predominantly poor women who commit criminal offences and that most crimes they commit are property offences – are simply overlooked. The behaviour of women must be sexually defined before it will be considered, for women only count in the sexual sphere. We have thus seen that the theme of sexuality is a unifying thread in the various – invariably contradictory – psychological and biologically determinist theories considered above and moreover their influence endures.

Campbell (1981) observes how women shoplifters – but not men who are responsible for the great majority of these offences – have been explained with reference to psychiatric problems and sexuality. Women are supposed to obtain sexual excitement from the act, or commit the crime to appease repressed sexual desires, or in order to be punished for such feelings. The prevalence of these explanations was to continue because of the number of single, divorced or widowed women found to be committing such offences. The possibility that these very groups could be exposed to particularly harsh economic circumstances was ignored. Gibbens and Prince (1962) studied shoplifting and explained young male working class involvement by reference to the gang or peer group pressure. In the case of a small group of middle-class boys, the researchers suggested that these suffered from homosexual tendencies which enabled them to apply the sexuality-based explanations they had used to explain female involvement to this group.

The actions of criminal women have been invariably explained – as we have seen above – with reference to them having breached the dominant societal definition of female behaviour and some claim that this deviation from the norm justifies subjecting them to increasing sanctions as they move through the system (see Carlen, 1983). Most studies have found no evidence of gender bias in sentencing (see Daly, 1994a; Heidensohn, 1996) but Kennedy (1992) has documented a criminal justice system which she observes to be generally biased against women. She found that in the case of young female offenders the system appears ostensibly to want to help them by showing them the error of their ways and to this end attempts to resocialise them into a socially acceptable gender role. The welfare interventions applied to these young women are nevertheless considerably more invasive of their private lives than any applied to young men and they tend to be treated more as sexual miscreants than criminals. It is apparent – from the above discussion – that clinical and sexual explanations of female criminality have been widely accepted even when those crimes have no clear sexual basis. In the case of male criminality such explanations have long been rejected – sometimes even when there is a clear sexual link – and there would appear to be different standards applied to explaining male and female criminality.

Sociological positivism and women

In this section we consider the applicability of sociological positivist theories of crime and criminal behaviour to female criminality. We shall see that although these theories claim to be general explanations of criminal behaviour they invariably tend to be explanations of male patterns of behaviour and appear – at least at first sight – to have little or no relevance for explaining female criminality (Leonard, 1983).

Robert Merton's influential anomie theory sought – as we saw in the previous chapter – to provide a comprehensive explanation of crime and deviance, proposing that social structures pressure certain individuals to engage in nonconformist behaviour. He argues that US society overemphasises its cultural goals without paying sufficient attention to the paucity of institutionalised means of obtaining these ambitions in a legitimate fashion and specifically refers to the overwhelming desire for financial success and material goods in US society and the willingness of some to use any means to obtain these goals.

Merton (1957) later acknowledged that wealth is not the only success symbol in US society, although he continued to emphasise its centrality. He also now recognised that more affluent people can experience pressure to 'innovate' since one can never have enough money, but he continued to insist that it is the lower classes who commit the most crime because they experience the greatest levels of strain. He also expanded his thoughts on ritualism and now claimed that this is most often found in the lower middle class, where children are socialised to obey rules but have limited opportunities for success. Merton (1966) later acknowledged that people in power exercise a crucial role in determining what particular behaviour violates social standards and that punishment may be differentially imposed in terms of class, race, or age. He nevertheless made no attempt to apply his theory to women and at first sight it does not appear applicable to them.

Eileen Leonard (1983) observes that it is arguable whether the dominant goal in US society monetary success is applicable in the case of women. Ruth Morris (1964) had earlier argued that women and girls aim for successful relationships with others rather than the traditional financial goals of men. More specifically, women were socialised to seek marriage and children more than a lucrative career and while a quarter of a century later more women may aspire to careers, marriage and family remain an equally important goal.

Leonard (1983) acknowledges that many women marry and have children and perhaps in doing so avoid the anomic pressure men experience when unable to achieve social goals. It is also possible that anomie theory may help to explain increases in female criminality if the goals of women shift towards those of males with their greater involvement in the world external to the family. The problem with that possibility is that it presupposes a common gaol for all women without any consideration of differential – or subcultural – socialisation (Ladner, 1972; Anderson and Collins, 1992). Thus, anomie theory directs our thinking towards common goals, not class, race, or ethnic variations.

Leonard (1983) also observes that anomie appears an inappropriate explanation of the crime that does occur among women. It is certainly difficult – in terms of the key concept of innovation – to conceive of an illegal means to the goal of marriage and the family. Theft and prostitution are not alternative means to marriage, while many women convicted of criminal offences are married with children.

Thus anomie theory fails to explain why women deviate in the way that they do or what type of strain actually leads to each outcome. The theory – as Leonard observes – applies largely to men and mainly to the goal of financial success. It ignores social variations in terms of gender, race, or ethnicity, and when a group as significant as women is examined, it is not a matter of making minor revisions. The theory fails in important respects and thus, Merton's 'common' symbols of success may not be so common after all (Leonard, 1983).

Theorists of deviant subcultures have played a central role in developing theoretical explanations of criminal behaviour that consider the differential socialisation experiences of separate groups even though these were primarily concerned with urban, working class male delinquency. Cohen (1955) thus proposes that males and females have different problems that require different solutions. Boys are mainly concerned with comparing their achievements with other males while girls are more concerned about their relationship with males. Cohen does not regard this situation as 'natural' – as was the case with the biological and psychological positivists – but he does propose that girls are mainly fulfilled through their relationships with the opposite sex. He concludes that the problems of adjustment that lead to the formation of delinquent gangs are fundamentally male and that the delinquent subculture is completely inappropriate for addressing female needs.

Cohen argues that a female's 'piece of mind' depends on her assurance of sexual attractiveness and that sexual delinquency is one response to the central female problem of establishing satisfying relationships with men. Leonard (1983) observes that it is unclear how female sexual delinquency provides a solution to establishing satisfactory relationships with males. Moreover, it fails to explain why so many women who have not married successful males, or whose personal relationships are less than satisfactory, do not commit crime.

Miller (1958) makes no attempt to consider criminal activity among women and his arguments appear inapplicable to them. His focal concerns are supposed to apply to lower-class life in general, but if this were so, male and female offending rates would be similar. It would seem that trouble, toughness, smartness, excitement, fate and autonomy are predominantly male preoccupations and are far less relevant to the lives of women.

Differential opportunity theory appears more amenable to a consideration of gender because it addresses the unavailability of both legitimate and illegitimate opportunities. Thus, the lower participation of women in crime may be explained by their limited access to illegitimate opportunities (Harris, 1977). Cloward (1959) acknowledged that women are frequently excluded from criminal activities, although he proposed that class is a more important differential than gender. Other researchers have observed that girls are less likely to have subcultural support for delinquent behaviour when compared with boys (Morris, 1965, Campbell, 1984; Figueira-McDonough, 1984; McCormack, Janus and Burgess, 1986; Chesney-Lind, 1989). Cloward and Ohlin's theory is enhanced by their consideration of the availability of illegitimate opportunity but Leonard (1983) observes that they simply ignore societal reactions and fail to explain criminal behaviour among women who have achieved their social goals. Moreover, they do not question – let alone explain – why such profound structural differences exist in the behaviour and expectations of males and females.

Edwin Sutherland contributed substantially to the development of criminology with his theory of differential dissociation where he argued that involvement in crime was similar to any other learned behaviour (Sutherland and Cressey, 1960). Thus, individuals learn to rob a bank in very much the same way that they learn to fix a car, someone teaches them. In short, people become criminal because of frequent contact with criminal rather than law-abiding people. Cohen, Lindesmith and Schuessler (1956) observe that if the primary group for most females is a relatively restrictive family, they may simply be less likely than males to learn criminal behaviour. Females also lack the opportunity for contact with adolescent gangs – or groups that generate white collar crime – and this further limits the possibility of involvement in criminal behaviour. Even within the same groups as males – for example, the family – their social position is unequal and they are frequently taught dissimilar attitudes. The differential treatment of males and females may culminate, then, with women exposed to an excessive number of definitions of behaviour unfavourable to violating the law. Sutherland indicates this in a discussion of the sex ratio in crime when he states that 'probably the most important difference is that girls are supervised more carefully and behave in accordance with anti-criminal behaviour patterns taught to them with greater care and consistency than in the case of boys' (Sutherland and Cressey, 1960: 115).

Females encounter more anti-criminal patterns (within the family, where they are isolated and controlled) over a longer period of time (owing to external supervision) than males. Sutherland suggests these differences might have originated because females become pregnant and, hence, require more supervision. Thus, differential association interprets the low crime rate among women in terms of their associations, which tend to ensure that they will learn patterns of behaviour favouring adherence to the law.

The differential association approach is compatible with the sex role – or masculinity/femininity – theories that first appeared in the USA during the late 1940s and which propose that proper socialisation is explained purely as a function of the physical sexual nature of the individual. In other words, maleness equals masculinity and femaleness equals femininity. It is when this 'natural' process breaks down that women become criminal. Again these writers – like many of their biologically and psychologically determinist predecessors – have a tendency to portray women as passive, gentle, dependent, conventional and motherly.

Talcott Parsons (1947, 1954) – at the time – the pre-eminent sociologist explained different levels of offending behaviour between males and females as the outcome of the social and family structure prevailing in the USA at the time. The father worked outside the home to provide economically for the family, while the mother was involved with the care and upbringing of the children and looking after the home. Boys were expected to grow up like their fathers and consequently assumed that passivity, conformity and being good are behavioural traits that should be avoided. The outcome is an aggressive attitude which can lead to anti-social, rebellious and criminal activities. Girls, however, have a close adult model – their mother – which allows them to mature emotionally and become feminine.

Grosser (1951) argues that boys become interested in power and money which might lead them to steal while girls see that they will become carers and homemakers and so close relationships are more important to them. Girls are thus more likely to become involved in sexual promiscuity and any criminality – such as theft of clothes and make-up – that will make them more attractive to the opposite sex. Reiss (1960) takes up this theme and argues that young women may be willing to participate in sexual activity because having a close relationship with a male can bring prestige. However, if the girl becomes pregnant or a sexually transmitted disease develops she will lose all prestige from her male and female friends. Hoffman Bustamante (1973) notes that females are rewarded for conforming behaviour; males, on the other hand, although taught to conform, are often rewarded when they breach the rules. She argues that this teaches men – but not women – that although conformity is generally desirable, it can be rational to breach the rules in some cases. Women, in contrast, are shown that the only legitimate way forward is conformity. Sex role skills are said to be important because they will determine the type of crimes an individual will be capable of committing. Thus, weapons are less likely to be used by women because they rarely learn how to use them but they may use household implements to threaten their victims.

Hoffman Bustamante notes that amongst children and teenagers in the USA, girls are more likely than boys to be arrested for juvenile crimes such as 'breach of curfew' and 'running away'. She explains this by saying that girls are more likely to be noticed if they are out alone than boys while parents worry more about their daughters than their sons. Subsequent research has found little evidence to show that either property or aggressive crimes are related to masculinity traits but it has been found that women are more likely to be aggressive if less feminine (see Cullen, Golden and Cullen, 1979; Shover *et al.*, 1979; Widom, 1979).

More recent research has alerted us to the possibility that some women may actually learn criminal behaviour within the family (Miller, 1986) and that the home is often a site of violence against women (Dobash and Dobash, 1980; Stanko, 1985). Cressey (1964) noted 40 years ago that the sex ratio is decreasing and that changes have occurred over time and he proposed that as the social position of women begins to approach that of men, the male–female differential will decline. Increasing employment and education for women has brought them into contact with more groups while weakening restrictions on females, combined with the growing number of broken families and increasing urbanisation, may play a role in increasing female crime.

More recently Giordano and Rockwell (2000) have reconsidered the link between differential association and female criminality and proposed that it is the decisive factor. They observe that although many women have suffered social deprivation or physical abuse without turning to offending behaviour, they suggest that all female criminals have had close associations with positive depictions of deviant lifestyles. From a young age many of the women were 'immersed' in these definitions which they learned from mothers, fathers, aunts, cousins and siblings who might be caught up in these activities. Giordano and Rockwell thus suggest that learning theory and differential associations may explain much female activity.

In concluding this section, we should note that the role of many women in society has changed radically from the vision of the happily married and economically dependent housewife on which most of the theories discussed in this chapter has focused. It seems that more women than ever are the only, the major, or the joint-breadwinner and therefore the pressures of economic success are placed on them. As women often inhabit low paid and insecure areas of the labour market – or are unemployed – they have tremendous pressures placed upon them to provide (Box, 1987). These increased strains may help to explain some of the recent increased female criminality, especially that which takes place in traditional male criminal areas (see Box and Hale, 1983). Certainly, there are certain offences which have risen dramatically and which are associated with female poverty with evasion of payment for television licences probably the most dramatic example (Pantazis and Gordon, 1997). The reality is that women still commit substantially less crime than men, even in those social classes overly represented in the official crime statistics.

Conclusions

We should note that there have been no conclusive scientific tests which have been able to establish – or for that matter completely dismiss – any biological or psychological link with crime and criminal behaviour. Thus, while theories based on these ideas have been widely criticised – and may seem to the reader to be both nonsensical and sexist – they cannot be totally dismissed. Behavioural scientists and others in the social sciences have tried to establish other explanations for criminal behaviour and claim that either socialisation or environment has accentuated a previously very small or non-existent biological difference. In general it seems that biological arguments appear to have little contemporary credibility and the more sociologically based theories seem to offer more plausible explanations.

Sociological explanations have nevertheless failed to provide particularly plausible explanations of either female involvement in criminality or why it is that women are more conforming than men. It may be that the tendency to see male crime as normal necessarily overshadows the study of the much less common female offending (Heidensohn, 1996). Studies implicitly based on masculinity and on presumptions that the offender will be male mean that the behaviour of women, if included at all, is – unconsciously – considered from a masculine or 'malestream' perspective. These issues are revisited from a feminist perspective in Chapter 11.

Suggested further reading

Klein (1973) and Leonard (1983) provide excellent and enduring feminist critiques and overviews of biological, psychological and sociological positivism. For those who wish to consult the original theorists the following will be considered useful: Lombroso (1920) for the foundations of biological positivism which have influenced so many later theorists albeit often implicitly; Thomas (1923) and Pollack (1950) establish the main parameters of psychological positivism; while Parsons (1947, 1954) provides an – albeit difficult – but classic account of sex role theory and the division of labour within the nuclear family.

Part Three

The victimised actor model of crime and criminal behaviour

Definitions of serious crime are essentially ideological constructs. They do not refer to those behaviours which objectively and avoidably cause us the most harm, injury and suffering. Instead they refer only to a sub-section of these behaviours, a sub-section which is more likely to be committed by young, poorly educated males who are often unemployed, live in working-class impoverished neighbourhoods, and frequently belong to an ethnic minority.

(Box, 1983: 10)

We saw in the first part of this book that the rational actor model of crime and criminal behaviour understands human beings to possess free will and they therefore have the capacity to make rational decisions to engage in activities of their choice. Criminal behaviour is simply a rationally chosen activity. The predestined actor model, on the other hand, proposes that crime emanates from factors – be they biological, psychological or social – that are outside the control of the offender and which determine their behaviour. Thus, the major concern of this tradition is to identify and analyse what is considered to be the *causes* that drive individuals to commit criminal acts. A major criticism of that tradition has centred on its acceptance of the conventional morality and criminal laws as self-evident truths. In other words, if a particular action is defined as a crime, it is necessarily wrong because the state decreed it to be so.

The third model of crime and criminal behaviour provides a challenge to the predestined actor notion of determined human behaviour and its uncritical acceptance of the socio-political status quo. Thus, the victimised actor model proposes that the criminal is in some way the victim of an unjust and unequal society and it is the behaviour and activities of the poor and disadvantaged that are targeted and criminalised while the actions of the rich and powerful are simply ignored or not even defined as criminal.

The victimised actor model has two theoretical foundations. First, there is the critique of the predestined actor model of human behaviour offered by symbolic interactionists and which was to become increasingly influential during the latter half of the twentieth century. The labelling theories that provide the first and earliest component of the victimised model tradition – and which are the focus of the following chapter – have their roots in symbolic interactionism in general and the work of George Herbert Mead (1934) in particular.

Symbolic interactionism primarily analyses the way individuals conceptualise themselves and others around them with whom they interact. Of central importance in that analysis is the concept of the 'procedural self'. This broadly speaking is the view that a person's self-identity is continuously constructed and reconstructed in interaction with 'significant others' – those who have an influence on the individual – and that human behaviour can only be understood by reference to this process. Moreover, it is proposed that meanings do not reside within objects or within the psychological elements of the individual person, but rather emerge out of the social processes of interpretation by which definitions of objects are created and used (Plummer, 1975).

Symbolic interactionists conclude that deviance is not a property *inherent* in certain forms of behaviour but one that is *conferred* on certain forms of behaviour by an audience. Thus, in this way, the focus of criminological inquiry was to shift away from the qualities and characteristics of the deviant actor and towards that of the audience, that is, the *response* of society to the deviant act. Of particular relevance here are the responses of the various agencies of social control such as the police, courts, psychiatrists, social workers and teachers.

The work of those writers most closely identified with the labelling/interactionist perspective, such as Lemert (1951), Becker (1963) and, in particular, Erikson (1962, 1966), Kitsuse (1962) and Cicourel (1968) were also influenced by *phenomenological* and *ethnomethodological* approaches.

Phenomenology is a philosophical approach that arose out of a general debate about the character, scope and certainty of knowledge. The most influential proponent of the sociological variant was Alfred Schutz, who argued that sociology should not attempt to establish the 'reality' of social phenomena. Such phenomena are only 'real' if they are defined as such by individuals who then act on the basis of those definitions. Since the reality that lies behind the way individuals interpret the world can never be penetrated, the positivist goal of objectivity should be abandoned in favour of a quest to ascertain subjective *meaning*. The focus on deviant meanings involved the recognition that negative or stigmatic responses to a deviant act may well affect the way that deviants see themselves. This in turn led to widening of the focus to include the creation of deviant meanings by agencies of social control (Rock, 1973).

Ethnomethodology draws on and further develops these phenomenological concepts and methods in order to describe social reality. It is a method of sociological study concerned with how individuals experience and make sense of social interaction. Central to this approach is the notion that *all* expressions of reality are 'indexical'; that is, they are based upon a set of assumptions specific only to the social context in which they are used. Perhaps the major significance of this approach to criminology lies in its profound questioning of the utility of criminal statistics. Unlike other perspectives, which viewed these as reasonably objective and independent of theory, ethnomethodologists treated them as social constructions produced, as are all phenomena, by interpretative work and social organisation.

The second theoretical foundation of the victimised actor model is a critique of the orthodox predestined actor model notion that society is fundamentally characterised by consensus (see Talcott Parsons, 1951). That orthodox view was based on the simple assumption that there is fundamental agreement concerning the goals of social life and the norms, rules and laws that should govern the pursuit of these objectives. There is, however, another long established tradition in the social sciences that considers society to be fundamentally conflict-ridden.

Max Weber (1864–1920) had influentially argued that conflict arises in society from the inevitable battle within the economic marketplace over the distribution of scarce resources and his model and its implications for criminal behavior is both pluralistic and pessimistic. Societies are seen to develop in episodic ways conditioned by historically contingent circumstances, the most important of these being inward – or outward – worldly orientation. Weber (1964) held structuralist ideas about political and economic stratification, distinguishing between class, party, and *status*, the last being most strongly related to perception of life-chances but conflict is not limited to these structural features, as people also fight over ideas and values. This focus provides an explanatory space for socialisation and motivational theories which are based on resistance to the *iron cage of rationalisation* or *bureaucracy* an increasingly pervasive trend in society where every area of life becomes subject to calculation and administration. His emphasis on the behaviour of authorities makes the struggle over political, especially legislative, power (to improve the life chances of the status group) his central contribution to conflict criminology. Weber's approach is pessimistic in the sense that capitalism can only hope to remain flexible and constantly adjust in response to the permanence of conflict and its tendency to become routinised.

Georg Simmel (1908) wrote extensively on the sources of conflict and is a neglected founding father of sociology (Frisby, 1984). Some of his perspective can be identified as providing part of the basic foundations of symbolic interactionism but he also fostered a conflict tradition unique for its idealistic tendencies and spontaneous natural tendencies. Simmel considered the basis of human relationships to be one of *homo homini lupus* where people are seen to be wolves by others (Wolff, 1950). Their true selves are only visible as fragments that emerge during the course of group involvement, that is, when they wish to obtain something from somebody. The self is always situated in context and there are as many selves as there are layers of situations or groups in society. Moreover, because the self is social there can be no antisocial interests because this would be simply self-destructive. People experience feelings like love and contempt at the same time and any time they think they are being a loner or outsider they are actually thinking of others. These insights led Simmel to focus on group conflicts where envies, wants, and desires are expressed. Groups thus provide more-or-less enduring interaction and relative constancy of pattern but they do not consume all there is about an individual.

Form, rather than content, is important for Simmel (1900) who studied money and found that the comparison of quite different contexts yielded a number of stable and recurring social types, such as *the stranger*, the enemy, the criminal, and the pauper. It is strangers – or immigrants – who are often the scapegoats of society. Content varies, but forms are the stable, permanent patterns of interaction. Intuitionism is used to find the inner nature of things without being distracted by sensory observation of what goes on in the context in which this is all taking place (Simmel, 1908).

Sociation is the real object of society and is viewed as an art, a game, or play. Social groups are thus everywhere in (internal) conflict because no one group could exhaust their individuality and are therefore constantly in (external) conflict because of boundary-crossing allegiances. Collins (1988: 123) refers to this rather unsympathetically as 'the grid-lock model of social conflict' but it could be more positively seen as the ongoing expression of selves and thus not a conception of conflict. Simmel (1906) proposed that because people deceive themselves and others every time they try to express their individuality, social structures are distinguished by the relative permissibility of lying and society itself is thus a lie and a fiction (Simmel, 1906). A criminal is thus one who has given up too much integrity and lost their real self, or on the contrary, one who is seeking too much individuality or anonymity and, that is, the criminal social type (Simmel, 1900).

Karl Marx (1818-83) had taken a much more radical stance and argued that conflict involves an inherent struggle by people to abolish the social divisions imposed by the material arrangements within society. Marxism as a social scientific tradition is best distinguished by a particular ontology (view of human nature) and epistemology (way of knowing). Marx considered humanity to be *homo faber* not homo sapiens (Engels, 1845) and Quinney (1965) explains this as the idea of human nature being essentially unfinished and constantly seeking to realise its potential. Explanations of crime based on socialisation experiences, normative structures and cultural demands are therefore incompatible with Marxism because humans are never completely socialised, claim higher loyalties than societal norms and are culture-builders not the products of culture. This ontology thus involves a rejection of both the rational actor model (free will) and predestined actor model (determinism) traditions. It is also part of the deep structure of romantic thought in Western philosophy (Gouldner, 1970).

Marxist epistemology is realism but not the philosophical kind of Plato, but the scepticism or disenchantment of the legal realist tradition that exists in jurisprudence. It is a mature epistemological perspective that seeks to make sense of the facts of constant change and the inevitable loss of idealism which emanates from this position and this scepticism is the basis of the idea that nothing is morally neutral, that people retain the right to critique, expose, pass judgement, and demystify (Quinney, 1974). Critique for the sake of critique is thus important to followers of Marx.

The methodology of Marxism is dialectical historical materialism. Hegel was the idealist philosopher who first popularised this method and was interested in looking forward to a progressive future when the final conflict between thesis and antithesis would result in synthesis. Marx famously 'turned Hegel on his head' which means that the starting point for Marxist analysis involves looking backward, and tracing the centuries-old conflict between the group that produces the means of material survival and the group that has appropriated that production (Chambliss and Mankoff, 1976; Reiman and Headlee, 1981). This methodology thus seeks to discover the total, fundamental, and indispensable source of conflict which is observed to be economic class relations. Such economic reductionism is thus at the centre of the Marxist tradition with the emergence of capitalism seen to be inherently contradictory and the point in history where the forces of production (equipment, technology) increases while the relations of production (means of distributing produced goods) remained fixed (Marx, 1859).

For Marxists, social institutions embodied in the state – such as the criminal justice system – as well as ideas and ideologies – are only reflections of economic realities. Because the surplus population created by an increasingly efficient capitalism is seen as a threat to the capitalist mode of production, the economically powerful use the laws and state to protect their interests, while the converse is also true and economic powerlessness translates into political powerlessness. In response to the expropriation of their labour and the exploitation of their potential in commercialised relationships, criminals come to recognise their true objective interests and engage in protorevolutionary action to bring about the end of capitalism and the guaranteed freedom from want and misery which will be brought about by the establishment of a socialist society. Marxist scholars tend to be strongly committed to humanistic values (Kramer, 1985), keenly aware of the dangers of having ideas co-opted by other reformists (Platt, 1974), and thoroughly partisan inasmuch as their theorising is intended to bring about the politicisation of criminals who have not yet recognised their rightful place in history (Quinney, 1977). Treating criminals as protorevolutionaries is sometimes called the primitive rebellion thesis while Marx (1867) summed up this perspective thus:

> The proletariat created by the breaking up of feudalism and the forcible expropriation of people from the soil could not possibly be absorbed by the newly-created capitalist manufacturers. At the same time, the proletariat could not suddenly adapt to the discipline of their new conditions, and so were turned into beggars, robbers, and vagabonds, partly from inclination, but in most cases from the stress of circumstances. Hence, by the end of the 16th century, the whole of Europe engaged in a bloody war against vagrancy, and legislation was created to treat them as criminals. It was also assumed that their criminal behavior was voluntary and the result of free will, when in actuality it was because they could not adapt to the new economic conditions.

The conflict theorists – who are the focus of the earlier sections of Chapter 9 – had little conscious and explicit recourse to these traditions in sociology and preferred to concentrate on examining and commenting on the world around them, even though their explanations are often strongly resonant of this heritage. The one acknowledged influence is the work of the German sociologist Ralph Dahrendorf whose work follows very much in the tradition established by Weber.

Dahrendorf (1959) proposes that there is conflict in society over the control of authority. Writing at a time when there were spectacular signs of disorder emerging in many economically developed countries in both Eastern and Western Europe, and in the USA he accepted the inevitability of conflict but was confident that new accommodations could emerge to moderate and ameliorate the resulting disorder. Conflict in this formulation was seen positively as a motor for change, towards the development of more effective mechanisms and structures to integrate people and groups into society. While he was keen to distance himself from consensus thinkers who refused to accept the validity, and indeed utility, of conflict in society, Dahrendorf was at the same time critical of those 'utopian' Marxist modes of thought that promised an end to crime with the arrival of socialism (Dahrendorf, 1958).

Dahrendorf fundamentally held a pluralist view of society which recognises the many and varied interest groups in society and that these may conflict over who should hold authority. The challenge for the pluralist is to develop institutions that can best accommodate these varied interests. Dahrendorf fundamentally disagreed with Marxism on the question of inequality and located the source of inequity in the power and authority relationships within a society and did not see these factors as necessarily linked to injustices in economic systems. Unlike Marx, who had argued for the abolition of inequality, Dahrendorf was of the view that because cultural norms always exist and have to depend on sanctions if they are to be enforced, some people must have more power than others so as to make these sanctions work. Thus, it is not the economic inequality resulting from capitalism that produces social inequality but it is an inescapable reality of any society where the basic units, the family, or institutions such as the criminal justice system, necessarily involve dominance–subjection relationships.

Many of the founding principles of the USA have led to a deep-rooted aversion to socialist or Marxist forms of analysis and evidence of this can be found in the manner in which many European immigrants to the United States were screened for 'radical sympathies', most notably following the Bolshevik revolution in Russia in 1917. Subsequently, the post-Second World War 'witch hunt' for radical socialist and communist sympathisers in public life spearheaded by Senator Joseph McCarthy produced a climate hostile to theories based on class conflict.

By the late 1950s, there was nevertheless clear evidence of conflict in the USA, despite a high level of general affluence with the Black Civil Rights movement and a steadily rising crime rate were but two examples. In this context a theoretical approach that offered a non-socialist or non-Marxist explanation for conflict appeared welcome to many American social theorists and criminologists. It was at the time that Dahrendorf was writing that George Vold presented his version of conflict theory and subsequently, Austin Turk developed the approach with direct reliance on the work of Dahrendorf. Richard Quinney was to follow. Their work is the focus of the earlier part of Chapter 9.

The later radical criminology tradition has its roots in an attempt to develop an understanding of crime in response to the rapidly changing and chaotic circumstances of the late 1960s and 1970s. Criticisms of Western societies as being overly concerned with wealth creation and material consumption were hardly new in the 1960s, but the decade saw evidence in the West that the apparent political consensus that had typified post-war politics was disintegrating. Concern began to emerge about the quality of life in societies that encourage the pursuit of material acquisition above the fulfilment of human need and satisfaction. The burgeoning student movement was at the forefront of this criticism, although many of its claims could be traced back to the concerns of social reformers and philosophers over the whole of recorded history. Alternative lifestyles were embraced and celebrated and these concerns were reflected in the arts and entertainment industries making anti-materialism appear interesting and even fashionable.

It was a period characterised by anti-authoritarianism with its roots in an increasing recognition of the failings of the modern state in Western countries to cure human ills and address human needs. In countries such as the UK – and to a lesser extent the USA – there had been a dramatic post-war shift towards an acceptance of the role of the state in the provision of welfare services to ameliorate poverty, ill health, poor educational provision and other human wants. Undoubtedly major improvements had been made, but none of these had fully met public expectations. In most cases welfare benefits were distributed according to strict entitlement rules that attached conditions to the delivery of services. Many argued that benefits should be received as rights due to any citizen, rather than being conditional on obeying lifestyle rules. Hence, radical critics came to see the welfare states of many Western countries as being oppressive.

Many critics of the socio-political consensus came to search for broad political, economic and social theories to explain how Western societies had come to be as they were. Hence, there emerged a complex range of minority interest groups concerned with attempting to explain the circumstances in which social inequality came about. These groups began by mounting protests to push for the fulfilment of equal rights in society and gradually developed historical, political, social and economic theories to support their efforts to argue for change. The Black Civil Rights movement in the United States developed and then fragmented into different wings, each holding differing views on the origins and solutions to the problems that faced black people. The Northern Ireland Civil Rights movement similarly began with an assertion of equal rights for Catholic citizens in Northern Ireland, before different interpretations of the nature of the problems facing this group led to divisions based on differing views concerning the range of possible solutions. The movement to secure equal rights for women also began to take on a new momentum in the late 1960s. More recently, we have seen further issues being raised and fragmentation caused by varying interpretations of the problems within the peace movement, animal rights, the environmental movement and an increasing array of interest groups.

9. Labelling theories

Labelling theories have their foundations in the various concepts and insights provided by interactionism, phenomenology and ethnomethodology – we encountered above – and focus on three central concerns. First, there is a consideration of why and how it is that some acts come to be defined as deviant or criminal while others do not. Thus, to this end there is an examination of legal codes and practices, and the social and professional interest groups that shape the criminal law. Second, it is recognised that certain people and groups are more likely to attract deviant, criminal and stigmatising labels than others. There is thus an examination of the differential applications of laws and labels by the various social control agencies and the relationship of this to organisational context. Unfortunately, these early, well-known and highly influential labelling theorists – with the limited exception of Becker (1963), Kitsuse (1962), Piliavin and Briar (1964) and Cicourel (1968) – did not address these concerns as thoroughly as they might have done, although they contributed significantly to the development of the radical criminology discussed in the following chapter, while the later far less well-known and significantly less influential labelling theorists such as Hartjen (1974), Ditton (1979) and Arvanites (1992) focus very much on the issue of state power. Most of the energy of the most active phase of the highly influential earlier labelling theory was nevertheless directed towards the third concern that assesses the experience of being labelled for the recipients of the label. We will consider each of these concerns in turn.

The social construction of crime

Before labelling theories achieved prominence, most criminologists had a non-problematic conception of crime. Criminal behaviour was simply a form of activity that violates the criminal law. Once crime was thus defined, theorists – working in the predestined actor model tradition – could concentrate on their main concern of identifying and analysing its causes. This whole approach was nevertheless far too simplistic for proponents of the labelling perspective who argued that what is defined as 'criminal' is not fixed but varies across time, culture and even from one situation to the next. From this perspective, the conventional morality of rules and criminal laws in any given society should be studied and questioned and not merely accepted as self-evident.

Labelling theorists fundamentally argue that no behaviour is *inherently* deviant or criminal, but only comes to be considered so when others confer this label upon the act. Thus, it is not the intrinsic nature of an act, but the nature of the societal reaction that determines whether a 'crime' has taken place. Even the most commonly recognised and serious crime of murder is not universally defined in the sense that anyone who kills another is everywhere and always guilty of murder. The essence of this position is neatly summarised in a well-known passage by Becker (1963: 4) whom, unlike most other labelling theorists, was concerned with the creators and enforcers of criminal labels and categories:

> Social groups create deviance by making the rules whose infraction constitutes deviance, and by applying those rules to particular people and labelling them as outsiders. From this point of view ... the deviant is one to whom the label has been successfully applied; deviant behaviour is behaviour that people so label.

Becker argued that rules – including criminal laws – are made by people with power and enforced upon people without power. Thus, even on an everyday level, rules are made by the old for the young, by men for women, by whites for blacks, by the middle class for the working class and we might add here, by schools for their students and parents for their children, an observation to which we return later in this chapter. These rules are often imposed upon the recipients against their will and their own best interests and are legitimised by an ideology that is transmitted to the less powerful in the course of primary and secondary socialisation. As a result of this process, most people internalise and obey the rules without realising – or questioning – the extent to which their behaviour is being decided for them.

Becker also argues that some rules may be cynically designed to keep the less powerful in their place while others may have simply been introduced as the outcome of a sincere – albeit irrational and mistaken – belief on the part of high-status individuals that the creation of a new rule will be beneficial for its intended subjects. Becker termed the people who create new rules for the 'benefit' of the less fortunate 'moral entrepreneurs'.

Becker noted two closely interrelated outcomes of a successful 'moral crusade': first, there is the creation of a new group of 'outsiders', those who infringe the new rule; second, a social control agency emerges charged with enforcing the rule and with the power to impose labels on transgressors, although more often this simply means an extension of police work and power. Eventually the new rule, control agency and 'deviant' social role come to permeate the collective consciousness and are taken for granted with the outcome being the creation of negative stereotypes of those labelled 'deviant'.

Becker (1963) cites the campaign by the US Federal Bureau of Narcotics (FBN) to outlaw marijuana use through the Marijuana Tax Act of 1937 which was justified on the grounds of protecting society – particularly young people – from the ill effects of this drug and relied heavily on propaganda of one sort or another to get its message across. In Becker's view the campaign was undertaken primarily as a means of advancing the organisational interests of the FBN. Moreover, the successful conclusion of the campaign led to 'the creation of a new fragment of the moral constitution of society, its code of right and wrong' (Becker, 1963: 145).

Other studies have looked at the process whereby previously 'acceptable' forms of behaviour have been brought within the remit of the criminal law. Platt (1969) showed how contemporary approaches to 'juvenile delinquency' – indeed even the very concept itself – were the outcome of a nineteenth century moral crusade undertaken by largely upper-class women. This successful campaign established juveniles as a separate category of offender with their own courts, which in turn enabled the scope of the powers of intervention enjoyed by the state to be extended beyond mere breaches of the criminal law to cover 'status offences' such as truancy and promiscuity.

Tierney's (1982) analysis of domestic violence also provides evidence of the process of criminalisation. She argues that 'wife battering' only emerged as an important social issue worthy of criminal justice intervention after the mid-1970s, mainly because of the increasing strength of the women's movement and the determination to secure the provision of refuges, legislation and other measures aimed at protecting women.

In short, what these and similar studies show, is not the inherent harm of behaviour or its pervasiveness that prompts changes in the law, but rather the concerted efforts of sufficiently motivated and powerful social groups to redefine the boundaries of what is considered acceptable and legal.

Others have adopted a macro perspective in order to explain these processes. Thus, Erikson (1962) draws upon Durkheim in arguing that all social systems place certain boundaries on culturally permissible behaviour and deviancy is simply that which is defined as crossing these parameters. Indeed, deviant behaviour may be the only way of *marking* these boundaries. Thus, transactions between deviants and social control agents are 'boundary maintenance mechanisms' which attract a good deal of publicity and by acting outside of these system boundaries deviants demonstrate to society where the perimeters lie while, at the same time, giving those inside a sense of identity or 'belongingness'. These processes in turn help to preserve social stability. Thus, in viewing deviance as essentially 'boundary maintenance activity', the work of Erikson marks a point of convergence between the labelling perspective and the functionalism of Durkheim.

Quinney (1970) also employed a macro sociological perspective but one that combined labelling theory with conflict theory, differential association and deviant subculture theories. He was also influenced by Durkheim's notion of mechanical and organic solidarity in proposing two ideal types of society (or social organisation): *singular* and *segmental*. According to Quinney, in a singular or homogeneous society all crime must necessarily occur outside any value system since by definition all members of the society adhere to this value system. In a segmental or heterogeneous society some segments will share common values with others, but because there is unlikely to be a complete consensus, value systems will be in conflict to a certain extent. Thus, the criminal laws and their enforcement are a product of this conflict and the associated unequal distribution of political power.

Quinney argues that society is segmentally organised or pluralistic and, therefore, the criminal law tends to represent the values of politically powerful sections of society. Moreover, he suggests a direct relation between the possibility of someone being labelled as criminal and their relative position in the social structure.

The recipients of deviant labels

It is conventional wisdom that those who break the law will be labelled as criminal. Becker (1963) nevertheless exposed the inadequacy of this perception, noting that the innocent are sometimes falsely accused, and more importantly, only some of those who violate the criminal law are eventually arrested and processed through the system. Kitsuse (1962) found – in a study of homosexuality that has much wider criminological ramifications – that it is not the behaviour *per se* that is the central issue. It is the interactional process through which behaviour is both defined as deviant and through which sanctions are initiated. Thus distinguishing deviants from non-deviants is not primarily a matter of behaviour but is contingent upon 'circumstance or situation, social and personal biography, and the bureaucratically organised activities of social control' (Kitsuse, 1962: 256).

A number of important studies conducted in the USA confirmed that the actual behaviour is not the only factor in determining whether a deviant or criminal label is conferred. Official responses are shaped by a range of extra-legal variables, such as appearance, demeanour, ethnic group and age, for example, Piliavin and Briar (1964) looked at police encounters with juveniles and found that arrest decisions were based largely on physical cues – manner, dress and general appearance – from which the officer inferred the character of the youth. *Structural* factors, such as gender, social class, ethnic group, and time of day were also significant, thus a young, working-class, black male in a 'high delinquency area' at night was seen to have a very high chance of being at least stopped and questioned, if not arrested. The young man is quite simply *assumed* to be delinquent unless he can prove otherwise (Piliavin and Briar, 1964: 206). More recent studies undertaken in the UK have also shown that some police officers show class and/or race bias in the performance of their duties (see for example Smith and Gray, 1986; Institute of Race Relations, 1987).

Cicourel (1968) found that in the course of their interactions with juveniles, the 'background expectations' of the police – that is, their commonsensical theories as to the typical delinquent – led them to concentrate on certain 'types' of individuals. A further factor in determining how that encounter developed was found to be dependent on how the individual officer defined his or her own role. Those who defined their role in terms of a 'due process' model that emphasises the rights of the defendant attempted to follow the *letter* of the law and, therefore, tended to react only to specific, concrete evidence of the commission of a crime. In contrast, when officers perceived their role primarily in terms of a 'crime control' model that considers the control of crime to be of primary importance they were more concerned with the *spirit* of the law. Thus, they were more likely to respond on the basis of their subjective definition of a situation and the personalities involved.

Cicourel found this process to be essentially class-biased, as it was generally working-class areas and their inhabitants that most closely mirrored the typifications and expectations of the police. Moreover, other criminal justice practitioners, such as probation officers, social workers, court officials and the organisational context within which they work reinforced such practices. Cicourel found probation officers and social workers subscribed to a theory of delinquency causation that focused on factors such as 'broken homes', 'permissive parenting' or 'poverty'. Thus, juveniles with this sort of background were seen as the likeliest candidates for a delinquent career and were often, albeit unwittingly, launched upon one. These findings had serious implications for the validity of crime statistics.

Many criminologists from quite different perspectives had previously acknowledged that official statistics were not a wholly accurate reflection of the reality of crime, for example, there was much concern over the hidden figure of unrecorded crime. Official statistics had been widely viewed as reasonably objective and thus providing a reliable basis for discerning patterns in crime and suggesting associations. From a labelling perspective official statistics were seen to be just another interpretation of the world and their only utility lay in the light they inadvertently shed on the agencies of social control that 'constructed' them. Quinney (1970) suggested four societal structures – age, gender, class and ethnic group – that would enhance the likelihood of someone receiving a criminal label and thus, there is a high probability that a young black working-class male will be defined as deviant. Moreover, the reality that this group is over-represented in the official crime statistics is not surprising since these figures are produced by agencies whose personnel, operating criteria and rationale are drawn from the more politically powerful segments of society. What Quinney was essentially arguing is that some people have the facilities for applying stigmatising labels to other people, ostensibly because these other people violate norms the labellers wish to uphold. This is only possible because these others are identified as members of society with little or no political power.

The consequences of labelling for the recipients

It was noted earlier that labelling theories have for the most part concentrated on their third area of concern which is assessing the consequences of the labelling process for the future conduct of the recipient and this aspect is certainly the most widely discussed and best documented.

Frank Tannenbaum (1938) – who is usually regarded as founder of the labelling perspective – noted that of the many young males who break the law only some are apprehended. His 'dramatisation of evil' hypothesis described the process whereby a community first defines the *actions* of an individual as evil, but eventually goes on to define the *individual himself* as evil, thus casting suspicion on all his future actions. The evil is further 'dramatised' by separating the individual from his usual group and administering specialised treatment to 'punish' or 'cure' the evil. This leads to further isolation and the confirmation and internalisation of his new 'tag'. Eventually he will redefine his self-image in line with the opinions and expectations of others in the community and thereby come to perceive himself as criminal. This idea that in reacting to people as 'criminal', society actually encourages them to become so, and that criminal justice intervention can deepen criminality is the central contention of the labelling approach.

Edwin Lemert (1951) made a crucial distinction between *primary* and *secondary* deviance. The former – with affiliations to the predestined actor model – could arise out of a variety of sociocultural, psychological or even physiological factors. However, because these initial acts are often extremely tentative and certainly not part of an organised way of life, offenders can easily rationalise them as a temporary aberration or see it as part of a socially acceptable role, for example, a worker may observe that everyone pilfers a little from work. Thus such behaviour will be of only marginal significance in terms of the status and self-concept of the individual concerned. In short, primary deviants do not view their deviance as central to themselves and do not consider themselves to be deviant.

If, however, these initial activities are subject to societal reaction – and with each act of primary deviance the offender becomes progressively more stigmatised through 'name calling, labelling or stereotyping' – then a crisis may occur. One way of resolving this crisis is for the individual to accept their deviant status and organise their life and identity around the facts of deviance and it is at this stage that the person becomes a 'secondary deviant'. In short, it is proposed that a youth who steals something and is not caught may be less likely to persist in this behaviour than one that is apprehended and officially sanctioned. Deviance is simply the end result of a process of human interaction. Primary deviance may or may not develop into secondary deviance. It is the number of criminal transgressions and the intensity and hostility of societal reaction that determines the outcome.

It was with the influential work of Becker (1963), Erikson (1966) and Kitsuse (1962) – and their use of Merton's concept of the 'self-fulfilling prophecy': a false definition of a situation, evoking a new behaviour that makes the original false assumption come true – that the labelling perspective was to gain widespread popularity. These writers argued that most offenders are falsely defined as criminal. That is not to say that they are innocent in the sense of having not committed offences, but rather that the system, and thus society, not only judges their actions as criminal and 'bad', but extends this judgement to them as people. The consequences are that once someone has been deemed by society to be 'bad', there is an expectation that this 'badness' must again find expression in some way or another, leading to the commission of further offences. Armed with these stereotypes of offenders as wholly criminal and incapable of law-abiding behaviour, the general population reacts to them on this basis and treats them accordingly. Consequently, offenders may face discrimination in employment, often even where their offence bears no relation to the type of work being sought. Moreover, a person's previous social status, such as parent, spouse or worker, is hidden under the criminal label until that becomes their 'master status' or controlling public identification.

In summary, labelling theorists claim that the false definition of offenders as uncompromisingly criminal fulfils this very prophecy by evoking hostile and negative societal reactions that render conformity difficult, and criminality attractive. Thus, the processes and means of social control that are intended to induce law-abiding behaviour can have the ironic and unintended consequence of achieving the very opposite. It would be meaningless to suggest, that in general, labelling theorists view the processes outlined above as in any way deterministic or unavoidable. It is quite possible that some offenders may react to being labelled and stigmatised by refraining from the type of conduct that elicited such a reaction but as Downes and Rock (1998: 183) pertinently observe:

> Interactionism casts deviance as a process which may continue over a lifetime, which has no necessary end, which is anything but inexorable, and which may be built around false starts, diversions and returns. The trajectory of a deviant career cannot always be predicted. However constrained they may seem to be, people can choose not to err further.

The key point from a labelling perspective is that *many* offenders *do* internalise their criminal labels and thus stable or career criminality arises out of the reaction of society to them.

Moral panics and deviance amplification

The labelling perspective has also been applied at the group level and a useful analytical tool in this context is that of the *deviancy amplification* feedback or spiral (Wilkins, 1964) where it is argued that the less tolerance there is to an initial act of deviance, the more similar acts that will be defined as deviant. This process will give rise to more reactions against offenders resulting in more social *alienation* or *marginalisation* of deviants. This state of affairs will generate more crime by deviant groups, leading to decreasing tolerance of deviants by conforming groups.

Deviancy amplification feedback is central to the phenomenon known as the 'moral panic' which Jock Young (1971) first used in his study of recreational drug users in north London and which was later developed by Stanley Cohen (1973) in his study of the societal reaction to the 'mods and rockers' disturbances of 1964. These studies marked a significant break with those approaches to delinquency – favoured by proponents of the predestined actor model – that were primarily concerned with finding the causes of delinquent behaviour. By contrast, definitional and structural questions relating to why certain groups define certain acts as deviant, and the consequences of this process, were asked.

Cohen (1973) found the press to be guilty of exaggeration and distortion in their reporting of the events in Clacton over the Easter bank holiday weekend in 1964. The sense of outrage communicated by such misrepresentation had set in motion a series of interrelated responses. First, there was increased public concern about the issue, to which the police responded by increasing their surveillance of the groups in question – mods and rockers. This resulted in more frequent arrests, which in turn appeared to confirm the validity of the original media reaction. Second, by emphasising the stylistic differences and antagonisms between the groups, the press reaction encouraged polarisation and further clashes between the groups.

Various moral entrepreneurs call for action to be taken against the groups involved in the outbreaks of lawlessness and usually pronounce that current controls are inadequate. Cohen (1973) shows that these entrepreneurs exaggerate the problem in order to make local events seem ones of pressing national concern and an index of the decline of morality and social standards. The extension of control leads to further marginalisation and stigmatisation of deviants which in turn leads to more demands for police action and so on into a deviancy amplification spiral. Cohen located the nature and extent of reaction to the mods and rockers in the social context of Britain during the 1960s. In particular, ambivalence about social change in the post-war period, the new affluence and freedom of young people and their apparent rejection of traditional social norms such as employment and the family are used as a context for the panic.

The concept of moral panic is also central to Hall *et al.*'s (1978) study of 'mugging' although the concept is used within a very different theoretical framework. While conceding that there can be no deviance without an agency of condemnation and control, it is argued that the notion of moral panic is limited if employed without reference to the social and political structures that empower a dominant minority to construct and implement the process of labelling. Within labelling theories moral panic is thus expressed in terms of a 'society' that creates rules and within the Marxism that informs Hall *et al.*'s approach, it is expressed in terms of a 'state' that has the power to criminalise (Cohen, 1985: 272). Given its theoretical basis, this analysis falls more within the scope of the radical theories discussed in the following chapter.

Goode and Ben-Yehuda (1994) have more recently challenged the assumption of earlier theorists that moral panics are in some way engineered at the behest – and in the interests – of dominant élites and distinguish three different models. First, there is the grass roots model where a panic has its origins within the general public and which expresses a genuinely felt – albeit objectively mistaken – concern about a perceived threat. Second, the elite-engineered model is where dominant groups deliberately and consciously generate concerns and fears that resonate with their wider political interests. Third, the interest-group model is where rule-creators and moral entrepreneurs launch crusades that coincide neatly with their own professional concerns and interests. Goode and Ben-Yehuda (1994) identify the following five characteristics of a moral panic: (i) a disproportionate reaction; (ii) concern about the threat; (iii) hostility to the objects of the panic; (iv) widespread agreement or consensus that the threat is real; and (v) the unpredictability – or volatility – of moral panics in terms of scale and intensity.

Others have criticised the whole notion of moral panics as a conceptualisation of social reaction. Left realists – the subject of Chapter 16 in this book – maintain that crime and the fear of crime should be taken seriously and not dismissed as just an expression of media over-reaction or panic. For example, Waddington (1986) criticised the empirical basis of Hall *et al.*'s (1978) influential study of street robberies, arguing that incidents of 'mugging' were increasing at the time and therefore asked what a proportionate response to the problem should have involved. Others have identified problems with the use of the concept of moral panic to capture reaction to diverse themes or issues. For example, Watney (1987) has questioned the use of the concept to characterise media and policy reactions to HIV/Aids. McRobbie and Thornton (1995) argue that the whole idea of a moral panic needs to be reconsidered in an environment where there may be an institutionalised need for the media to generate 'good stories' and that these can easily become part of a promotional culture that 'ironically' uses sensationalism for commercial purposes.

Criticisms of labelling theories

As the labelling approach became more influential during the 1960s and early 1970s it attracted criticism from a variety of sources. Plummer (1979) noted that because the perspective is so loosely defined, it could harbour several diverse theoretical positions and therefore leave itself open to internal contradiction and criticism from all theoretical sides. Such ambiguity and eclecticism thus led some critics to claim that labelling is at best a vague perspective that does not contain consistent and interrelated concepts and which fails to make precise distinctions between mere description and causal statements (Taylor, Walton and Young, 1973). On the other hand, proponents of labelling theory such as Schur (1971) contend that the strength of the approach lies in its ability to analyse aspects of social reality that have been neglected, offer directions for research and thus complement other theoretical approaches.

Others argue that labelling theories fail to clearly define deviance. According to Gibbs (1966), labelling theorists claim that an act is deviant only if a certain reaction follows, yet at the same time refer to 'secret deviants' and 'primary deviants', and suggest that certain groups of people are licensed to engage in deviant behaviour without negative reactions. This implies, it is argued, that deviance can be identified not merely in terms of societal reactions to it but in terms of *existing social norms*. There may be ambiguity about certain kinds of 'soft' deviance – where criminal definitions are relative to time and place – but there can be no such ambiguity regarding 'hard' deviance, such as violent assault, robbery and burglary, which have always been universally condemned. 'Hard' deviants at least are fully aware that what they are doing is deviant or criminal but freely choose this course of action because it is profitable or exciting. Labelling is therefore an irrelevance.

Taylor, Walton and Young (1973) accept the notion that deviance is not simply an inherent property of an act but they do not agree that it is as arbitrary as labelling theorists imply. They take the view that the deviant is not a passive actor but a decision-maker whose rule breaking reflects initial motives and choices, and thus has meaning. This approach overlaps with a further criticism that observes the emphasis to be on the negative repercussions of labelling which implies an individual totally at the mercy of official labellers. A consequence of this overemphasis on societal reaction at the expense of individual choice has been the tendency to elevate the offender to the status of victim. Labelling theories have 'the paradoxical consequence of inviting us to view the deviant as a passive nonentity who is responsible neither for his suffering nor its alleviation – who is more 'sinned' against than sinning' (Gouldner, 1968: 38). Yet, as previously noted, labelling theories do not on the whole argue that the effects of labelling are determinant, but rather that negative societal reaction can, and in many cases will, deepen criminality. Thus as Downes and Rock (1998: 190) quite correctly observe, 'criticisms of the species offered by Gouldner really reflect a response to only the most narrow versions of interactionism'. As for the charge that labelling theorists take the side of the deviant and overlook the 'real' victims of crime some, most notably Becker (1967), make no apologies for this and argue that they are merely balancing out traditional approaches within criminology that are severely biased *against* the deviant.

Many of the criticisms of labelling theories would seem more justified had the approach been promoted as a developed theory rather than as a perspective comprising loosely connected themes. In the light of this, perhaps the most telling criticism of the perspective is that, though it focused on societal reaction, it stopped short of offering a systematic analysis of social structure and power relations. While acknowledging that political interest and social disadvantage influenced societal reaction, labelling theorists failed to make explicit the connection of the criminal justice system to the underlying capitalist economic order and the inequalities of wealth and power rooted therein. Some of these issues are addressed by later more recent labelling theorists and by the radical theorists we will encounter in the following chapter.

Labelling theories revisited

In more recent years the notions and concepts of labelling theories have been modified and developed. First, more recent attention has been devoted to informal labelling such as that carried out by parents, peers, and teachers which it has been argued has a greater effect on subsequent criminal behaviour than official labelling. Ross Matsueda (1992) and Heimer and Matsueda (1994) discuss the reasons why individuals may be informally labelled as delinquents and note that such labels are not simply an outcome of interaction with the criminal justice system – for example, arrest – but are crucially influenced by the individual's offending behaviour *and* their position in society. Powerless individuals such as urban, ethnic-minority, lower-class adolescents are far more likely to be negatively labelled by parents and peers than more affluent middle-class young people. Matsueda (1992) also argues that informal labels affect the subsequent level of crime committed by individuals because these help shape their perceptions of how others see them. Thus, if they believe that others see them as delinquents and troublemakers, they are more likely to act in accord with this perception and engage in offending behaviour.

Some have observed that a shift seems to have occurred around 1974 in which labelling theorists came to retreat from their underdog focus and move away from the study of 'nuts, sluts, and perverts' (Liazos, 1972) and came to accommodate legalistic definitions and focus on state power. Thus, modern labelling theorists came to recognise that societies socially construct and create crime by passing legislation and, therefore, the substantive nature of the law is a legitimate object of study. These are sometimes referred to as criminalisation theories (Hartjen, 1974) and while they have some resemblance to societal reaction – or labelling perspectives – they are more closely linked to a field of study that some call the sociology of law perspective or the study of law as a mechanism of social control. Labelling theories that focus on state power can be considered as branches of contrology (Ditton, 1979) which refers to a group of theories with some interest in crime waves and moral panics but mostly take the view that criminal justice agencies are part of broader social control mechanisms, like welfare, mental health, education, the military, and the mass media, all of which are used by the state to control 'problem' populations (Arvanites, 1992). Contrology has its theoretical foundations in the work of Foucault (1971, 1977) who argued that various instruments of social control – more humane, enlightened, reasonable responses to deviance – are packaged and sold by the state to cover up the inherent coercion and power in the system. The state is thus always trying to portray a 'velvet glove' where its ultimate goal is to exercise its 'iron fist' to control troublesome populations, in other words, the pervasive 'hard' and 'soft' 'policing' strategies of the 'disciplinary-control-matrix' (Hopkins Burke, 2004b; 2008) which is discussed in more detail in the third part of this book.

Link (1987), Link *et al.* (1987), and Link *et al.* (1989) have used labelling theory to understand how we view and respond to the mentally ill and observe that in the USA public attitudes have been conditioned so that such people are perceived in negative and devalued ways with the outcome being that many who need psychiatric help – and those who care for them – will either try to hide this reality from family friends, colleagues and their employers, or will withdraw from groups or people who they think might reject them.

Some have suggested that the criminal justice system and the public are increasing the stigmatisation of – particularly young – offenders and thus heightening the most negative effects of labelling. De Haan (2000) observes that levels of violence in society appear to be rising – even in the Netherlands where previously there had been reasonable tolerance of such behaviour – and explains this occurrence as a process of relabelling previously non-problematic actions as more serious. Indeed, it seems that there is an increasingly universal intolerance of violence and such behaviour is being dealt with much more harshly. Triplett (2000) claims that an increase in violent offences in the USA during the 1980s and 1990s had been accompanied by changes in the criminal justice system moving less serious offences – particularly status offences such as truancy – up the sentencing tariff, and by a change in the way in which (especially young) violent offenders come to be seen as evil. She observes that these judgements have been subsequently attached to all young offenders who have subsequently become isolated and excluded from mainstream society. Meossi (2000) argues that this demonising of offenders – observed both in Italy and the USA – tends to correlate closely with periodic economic downturns and Halpern (2001) asserts that the subsequent rise in crime levels leads to harsher treatment of offenders thus devaluing people through labelling which can itself lead to further acceleration in offending behaviour.

While many studies have been conducted to apply labelling theory to various types of deviance, Kenney (2002) considers it in relationship to the victims of crime and found that sympathy offered to a victim may be received as condescension and may result in a feeling of a loss of power. The victim may lose self-esteem as a result of this loss of power and if he or she seeks help from friends and loved ones, they may fear feeling or being viewed as incompetent. Once the individual has been labelled as a 'victim' they may well find that work colleagues, friends, and even family begin to avoid them due to feelings of guilt or not knowing how to react which can lead to further isolation of the victim. Many victims do not receive the support they seek from loved ones and may wonder if their feelings are normal. Similarly, Li and Dennis Moore (2001) concluded from their study of the relationship between disability and illicit drug use that discrimination against persons with disabilities leads to higher rates of illegal drug use by these people.

Others have utilised the concept of labelling in a more positive mode. Braithwaite (1989) thus introduces the concept of 'reintegrative shaming' where it is proposed that offenders should be shamed not in order to stigmatise them but to make them realise the negative impact of their actions on both individual victims and the wider community and then encourage others to forgive them and accept them back into society. Reintegrative shaming is an influential concept that underpins reparation and restorative justice programmes and has been widely introduced – in particular with young offenders – in New Zealand (see Morris, Maxwell and Robertson, 1993), Australia (see Strang, 1993; Forsythe, 1994; Hudson et al., 1996), parts of the USA (see Alford, 1997) and Britain (see Dignan, 1999, Young and Goold, 1999; Maxwell and Morris, 2001). It is discussed in more detail in Chapter 15. Some have suggested that such a policy would only work in rural communities with strong community bonds but Braithwaite (1993) considers that it could be even more effective in cities which are invariably constituted of many closely-knit micro-mechanical solidarities or communities (see Hopkins Burke and Pollock, 2004). Moreover, Braithwaite (1993) and Simpson, Lyn Exum and

Smith (2000) consider reintegrative shaming to be an appropriate response to some white-collar and corporate violations of the law and propose that its application would be a considerable advance on a long established tradition of ignoring such cases.

Suggested further reading

Becker (1963) still provides an essential introduction to the labelling tradition in criminology, with Erikson (1966), Kitsuse (1962) and Lemert (1972) being other key texts. Quinney (1970) provides an early link with conflict theory. Cohen (1973) is a milestone text on 'moral panics' with the concept importantly developed from a radical/critical perspective by Hall *et al.* (1978) and revised substantially by Goode and Ben-Yehuda (1994).

10. Conflict and radical theories

Conflict and radical theories sought to explain crime and criminal behaviour in terms of the unequal nature of the socio-political structure of society. Again, this is not a homogenous theory but a diverse collection of perspectives united by a common tendency to see societies as being characterised by conflict rather than consensus. Two broad categories or groupings can nevertheless be identified. First, conflict theorists take a *pluralist* stance and propose that society consists of numerous groups all involved in a struggle to promote their socio-economic interests. Second, *radical* accounts are invariably informed by various interpretations of Marxist social and economic theory. Notwithstanding these differences, writers in both camps see social consensus as a temporary situation engineered by those with substantial power in society and the main concern for both groups of writers is with the social struggle for power and authority.

Among the critics of the labelling perspective were those who argued that it had just not gone far enough and failed to account for the origins of the differential power to label or stigmatise people. It was thus in response to that critique that conflict and radical writers came to explore and apply wider ideas from economic and political science to the consideration of crime and criminal behaviour.

Conflict theories

Thorsten Sellin (1938) was influenced by the work of Georg Simmel and was the first to argue that conflict causes crime. He proposed with his *culture conflict theory* that each culture establishes its own norms – or rules of behaviour – which are then embedded into its members through the various processes of socialisation they undergo. Thus, the norms learned by any individual are prescribed by the host culture to which they belong. In a healthy homogenous society, these norms are enacted into laws and upheld by the members of that society because they are accepted as representing the consensual viewpoint but where homogeneity and consensus does not exist the outcome will be culture conflict. Sellin argues that conflicts over *conduct norms* can occur at both the micro and macro level in society.

At the macro level, conflicts occur between two different societal cultures and can arise because of border conflicts, territorial extension or, most typically, through migration. Secondary conflicts at the micro level occur within the macro culture, particularly when subcultures with their own conduct norms develop within the host culture. In the latter case, the laws usually represent the rules or norms of the dominant culture and indeed, the norms – and rules of behaviour – of other groups can be in conflict with the law. Thus, society contains certain unwritten, and often unspoken, rules about what a person is supposed to do in certain circumstances, for example, if a man finds his wife in bed with another man. Thus, while some more pre-modern or traditional societies might specify exactly what a man is supposed to do in this case – kill both his cheating wife and the other man – more modern societies offer less in way of guidance and, for Sellin, this ambiguous state of confusion and contradiction is what leads to crime. This clearly has implications in contemporary multicultural societies where different cultures may clash on how such situations should be dealt with. We should note however that – unlike the deviant subcultural tradition epitomised by Cohen (1955) or Cloward and Ohlin (1960) and discussed in Chapter 7 – the norms of the subcultures in this conceptualisation do not develop in order to question or challenge dominant societal values or, for that matter, represent a different means of achieving the cultural goals of the middle or upper classes, they represent fundamentally different values and norms.

Lewis Coser (1956) was a functionalist sociologist with nevertheless significantly left-wing political leanings who was also clearly influenced by the work of Simmel. Coser presents several propositions surrounding what he considers to be the key issue of the intensity of conflict. Thus, conflict is seen to actually increase when attempts are made to suppress it, when fighting takes place on behalf of a group, and when conflicting parties are in close proximity. Coser observes that closeness creates intensity because that is when love and hate occur alongside each other. Other propositions have to do with the construction of social forms, like stability and rigidity, which are drawn from comparing the membership of groups which are formed by cross-cutting other group memberships. Non-realistic conflict is perceived to have safety-valve functions and Coser observes that the necessity for hierarchy has emerged from a need to manage group size and complexity. He also produces an image of an ever-present and always-emerging offender and this is also clearly consistent with the ideas of Simmel, although Coser follows a more 'crime is functional for the needs of society' approach than his predecessor.

George Vold (1958) developed the above ideas and produced an explanation of crime and criminal behaviour that emphasised the group nature of society and stressed the fact that groups compete with each other in order to secure what they identify as their interests. He argued that groups become ever more wary and watchful of their interests; vis-à-vis other groups and become engaged in a continuous struggle to improve their standing in relation to others. The whole process of lawmaking, lawbreaking and law enforcement directly reflects deep-seated and fundamental conflicts between these group interests and the more general struggle between groups for control of the police power of the state. Since minority groups lack the power to strongly influence the legislative process, their behaviour is that most often defined as criminal, or deviant. This process of criminalisation then legitimises the use of the police and other control agencies to enforce these laws on behalf of the most powerful groups in society.

For Austin Turk, the theoretical problem of explaining crime lies not in understanding the different varieties of criminal behaviour – for he observes that definitions of what is criminal will vary over time and place – but in explaining the actual process of criminalisation. Specifically this involves examining the process of the assignment of criminal status to individuals, which results in the production of criminality. There is an obvious resonance here with labelling theory but Turk was to go much further than those working in that tradition and sought to explain why it is that labels come to be widely accepted as legitimate, often by those who are so labelled.

Turk fundamentally saw the social order as the outcome of powerful social groups who successfully control society in their own interests. He argued that social control is exercised by providing a normative – moral or value-laden – justification for law, which is then enforced by controlling agencies such as the police. In his earlier work, Turk (1969) suggested that those people who have an unclear view of how their behaviour will impact on others, especially on the powerful, and who go on to break rules, norms or laws, will be the most likely to be caught and processed by control agencies. It is an argument that explains why it is that young people are more likely to fall foul of the law than most adults.

In his later work, Turk (1969) described two ways in which control is exercised in society: first by *coercion* and, second, by the *control of legal images* and *living time*. The control of society by *coercion* – or the threat and exercise of physical force – is perhaps the most obvious form of control but the more that force is applied, the less likely it is to be accepted as legitimate and thus the more difficult it will be to control society. The control of legal images, on the other hand, is an altogether more subtle exercise. Legal systems have formal laws, breaches of which are legally punishable, and there are established procedures for exercising those laws but there are also degrees of discretion as to how the law is exercised. Turk argues that the subtle interplay of the formal and informal allows the powerful to manipulate the legal system in their own interests while still preserving an image of due process and impartiality. The control of living time suggests that people will become accustomed to forms of domination and control, especially if it is maintained and legitimised over generations. Later generations will gradually forget that social control conditions were ever any different from those with which they are familiar.

Richard Quinney was originally a traditional conflict theorist – heavily influenced by social reaction/labelling theory but later coming to be identified with a more radical Marxist inspired perspective – who considered crime to be the product of legal definitions constructed through the exercise of political power. In this way, actions that may cause harm to others and be similar to forms of behaviour which are subject to the criminal law, may be dealt with less seriously, or not at all, if they are conventional activities carried out by, or in the interests of, the powerful. Thus, while the causing of death by a less powerful individual may well be defined as murder or manslaughter, if committed by a corporate body, or high status individual, it may be interpreted as a civil law violation, or simply an accident. Quinney pointed to numerous examples of harm-generating activities committed by the powerful that are not investigated, excused or effectively treated as misdemeanours and which fail to come under the auspices of the criminal law.

Quinney – like many of the later radical criminologists – paid a good deal of attention to the role of the mass media in shaping the way in which people perceive crime. He observed that both crime and non-crime definitions are spread throughout the media. With their pervasive effect, the media select and construct a commonly held view of reality where certain actions are naturally crimes and others non-crimes.

Quinney outlined six propositions that summarise his particular version of conflict theory. First, crime is a definition of human conduct which is created by authorised agents in a politically organised society. Second, these criminal definitions are applied by those segments of society which have the power to shape the enforcement of the criminal law. Third, these criminal definitions are applied by those segments of society that have the power to shape the administration of the criminal law. Fourth, behaviour patterns are structured in segmentally organised society in relation to criminal definitions, and within this context people engage in actions that have relative probabilities of being defined as deviant. Fifth, conceptions of crime are constructed and diffused in the segments of society by various means of communication. Sixth, the social reality of crime is constructed by the formulation and application of criminal definitions, the development of behaviour patterns related to criminal definitions and the construction of criminal conceptions (Quinney, 1970: 15–23).

Criticisms of conflict theories

For the later radical criminologists much of early conflict theory, while accepting the inevitability of social conflict, was still seen as essentially conservative and complacent about the possibility of conflict leading to more successful social integration. It was also to an extent founded on predestined actor model notions that denied the possibility that victims of an unfair social and economic system might simply rationally choose offending behaviour as a way of coming to terms with a system which had failed to accommodate their interests. Conflict theorists had simply failed to explain why the law is as it is in the first place and, moreover, they proffered no acceptable explanation as to why it is that those sections of society who do not have their interests represented by established social institutions should choose to accept 'stable authority relationships' out of which they benefit little. In seeking an answer to that last criticism, Turk had argued that it is a 'lack of sophistication' among the subordinate groups that is to blame for the problems that they pose for established society. They may simply choose to break laws or norms that do not fit in with their perceptions of their situation.

By promoting the idea that offenders have a limited capacity to express themselves to authority, we are encouraged to see their subjective accounts of their actions as less valid than those of authority-holders. This is a perspective strongly countered by labelling theorists such as Howard Becker, who argued that it is the task of the social researcher to give voice to the 'underdog' in the face of more than adequate representation of the account of 'superordinate groups'. The essentially predestined actor model 'correctionalist' stance implicit in the work of Turk is illustrated by his view that deviant subcultures should be forcibly broken up by the authorities in order to coerce deviants back into an integrated consensus (Turk, 1969). This should happen apparently, regardless of whether or not the individuals concerned see such integration to be in their interests or not.

This criticism cannot be directed at Quinney who proposes that the actions of those who are criminally labelled are not so much the outcome of inadequate socialisation and personality disorders but conscientious actions taken against the established, unequal social order. Taking this rather more rational actor model oriented approach, Quinney observed that these acts defined as criminal were perhaps the only appropriate means for expressing thoughts and feelings concerning powerlessness and inequality and, he also, somewhat romantically, considered that deviant, or criminal, behaviour provides the only possibilities for bringing about social change.

Radical theories

Radical theories – like their conflict predecessors – encompass a broad range of ideas. The seminal text in the field, Taylor, Walton and Young's *The New Criminology* (1973) was an attempt to link the concerns of labelling theory with Marxism, while in the USA the works of William Chambliss and Richard Quinney were based on somewhat different foundations.

There are many different variants of Marxism and these variants are invariably focused around different interpretations of what Marx said, wrote or meant. The basic two-class model of social stratification which while retaining some popularity as an explanation of the fiscal crisis (O'Connor, 1973) – and might well come back into its explanatory own during the forthcoming economic recession – has been significantly criticised as a form of 'vulgar Marxism' (Poulantzas, 1969). Similarly, only another vulgar variant 'instrumental Marxism' views the law as a simple tool of the ruling class (Chambliss, 1975) with 'structural Marxism' rejecting notions of deliberate intention by the ruling class and proposes that it rules through the creation and control of ideas (Althusser, 1966) or conspiracies (Mills, 1956). The Frankfurt School (Jay, 1973) incorporated Freudian psychoanalysis into Marxism while neo-Marxism (Friedrichs, 1980) makes use of the suggestion that Marx implied most criminals were *lumpenproletariat* – or what we would today call the underclass – who simply could not be counted on for revolutionary purposes.

Wilhelm Bonger (1916) was a traditional Marxist who saw capitalism to be the creator of social irresponsibility with his scholarship focusing on the dialectical interplay between capitalist business cycles and crime rates, thus when unemployment rises during periods of economic recession the crime rate increases. Using a two-class model, Bonger argued that conflict is likely to continue indefinitely because the inherent contradictions of capitalism creates a climate of motivation for crime with offenders motivated by self-interests rather than social interests.

Rusche and Kirchheimer (1939) took a broader historical focus to examine imprisonment rates and the fluctuations of capitalism and observed that the former rates have tended to vary in accordance with our position in the business cycle. This adds some support to the surplus labour hypothesis which proposes that prisons are simply conduits for those – usually men – who are surplus to the requirements of the economy during any given period in time. Marxist penology (Adamson, 1984) shows little interest in abolishing crime but does seek to abolish prisons while the rehabilitation of prisoners is rejected as a strategy because it would only serve bourgeois interests (Scull, 1977).

Gordon's (1971) theory sees crime to be a rational response to the political and economic structure of institutions and claims that what are traditionally viewed as non-economic goals – status, respect – are closely tied into chances of material survival. Taking an instrumentalist view of the state, he argues that the mere token enforcement of 'upper-world crime' – which is a major concern of conflict criminology (Pearce, 1976) – is explained by protection of power and profits.

Bill Chambliss had become interested in the socio-political context in which the criminal law had developed while undertaking a study of the development of the vagrancy laws in Britain, and observed that the origin of this body of legislation could be traced to vested interests: 'There is little question that these statutes were designed for one express purpose: to force labourers to accept employment at a low wage in order to ensure the landowner an adequate supply of labour at a price he could afford to pay' (Chambliss, 1964: 69).

It is an approach influenced by the US school of *legal realism*, which concerned itself with the distinction between the 'law in books' and the 'law in action' and in Chambliss' 1971 work *Law, Order, and Power* – written in collaboration with Robert Seidman – an almost Durkheimian argument is presented. The authors propose that the complexity that comes with technological development and which necessitates more complicated, differentiated and sophisticated social roles actually operates to put people at odds with one another and thus this increasing social complexity requires that sanctioning institutions be designed to keep order among the conflicting interests. In their view, the basis of the sanctioning would be organised in the interests of the 'dominant groups' in society but the actual application of the sanctions are enforced by bureaucratic institutions who have their own interests. The 'law of action' thus comes to reflect a combination of the organisations created to enforce the rules.

Chambliss (1969) had previously argued that criminal justice bureaucracies tend to deal with members of the lower social classes more harshly than other people because the latter have little to offer in return for leniency and, moreover, they are in no position to fight the system. Chambliss and Seidman (1971) later concluded that the police act illegally and breach the norms of due process at every stage of their activities and that this occurs because they are not committed to the notion of due process in the first place while, at the same time, they have an enormous potential for making discretionary decisions. There are also no real safeguards. Bargains struck with the prosecutor before the trial begins tend to reflect the relative political and economic power of the defendant. Additionally, considerable pressure is applied to the accused to plead guilty leading the powerless to surrender the 'right' to trial by jury in nine cases out of ten.

Chambliss (1969) had observed that much of the criminal legal effort is devoted to processing the very people least likely to be deterred by legal sanctions. On the one hand, he observed that the use of lengthy prison sentences against drug addicts and capital punishment against murderers are instances where sanctions have little deterrent effect. On the other hand, there is a reluctance to impose severe sentences against white-collar and professional criminals, the very offenders who are deterred by sanctions. Chambliss argued that such a policy went directly against the formal logic of deterrence, but fits perfectly with the bureaucratic logic of demonstrating 'effectiveness' by harsh treatment of the powerless while avoiding the organisational tensions that would follow from confronting the powerful.

By the mid-1970s – at a time when a number of important social theorists were returning to the Marxist tradition that had virtually disappeared during the 1940s and 1950s in the USA – there was a significant shift in the position of Chambliss. This shift is reflected in his nine propositions. First, acts are defined as criminal because it is in the interests of the ruling class to define them as such. Second, members of the ruling class will be able to violate the laws with impunity while members of the subject class will be punished. Third, as capitalist societies industrialise and the gap between the ruling-class and the working class widens, penal law will expand in an effort to coerce the latter class into submission. Fourth, crime reduces the pool of surplus labour by creating employment not only for the criminals but also for law enforcers, welfare workers, professors of criminology, and a horde of people who live off the fact that crime exists. This is an analysis later developed by Christie (1993), who introduced the term 'the crime industry' to describe this multitude of interested professional groups. Fifth, crime diverts the attention of the lower classes from the exploitation they experience and directs it toward other members of their own class rather than toward the capitalist class or the economic system. Sixth, crime is a reality that exists only inasmuch as those who create it in society have an interest in its presence. Seventh, people involved in criminal behaviour are acting rationally in ways that are compatible with the life conditions of their social class position. Eighth, crime varies from society to society depending on the political and economic structures of society. Ninth, socialist countries should have much lower rates of crime because the less intense class struggle should reduce the forces leading to and the functions of crime (Chambliss, 1975: 152–5).

In a complementary analysis, Spitzer (1975) focuses upon surplus populations created by capitalism and observes that 'skid-row' alcoholics and others who do not pose a threat to the system are called 'social junk' while dangerous acts and people who do pose a threat are called 'social dynamite' or protorevolutionaries. This analysis has led to a variety of loosely-connected studies on the safety net of capitalism – including welfare and mental health reforms – which some have come to term the medicalisation of deviance (Liska, 1992). The contradiction is that the more capitalism seeks to control these populations, the more exposed becomes the fiscal crisis.

At this time during the late 1960s, similar concerns and conclusions were emerging among a group of radical young criminologists in the UK who were beginning to question the role of orthodox criminology in helping to legitimate unequal social relations in capitalist societies. The law, police and social workers in particular were highlighted as having an important role in preserving the *status quo*, and the proponents of the predestined actor model of criminal behaviour that dominated social work and probation training, the British Home Office and the Cambridge Institute of Criminology, were observed to give these crucial criminal justice agencies academic support. There thus developed among these young radicals an increased concern to restore some dignity to the deviant person. They were no longer to be seen as the 'poor wee things' of the predestined actor model, nor the inevitable and terrible pathological creatures deserving of harsh containment – or even death – proposed by a great deal of right-wing criminology. There was a concern to restore meaning to the deviant actors, to regard them as knowing people responding rationally, albeit sometimes rebelliously, to their circumstances.

This concern for the 'authenticity' of the deviant's position was combined with a concern for the nature of the state and its agencies in labelling deviance, in the passing of legislation, apportioning blame and prosecuting individuals, in the interests of those who already hold political power. The ideas were by no means new and many of them can be traced back to the Chicago School. The work of Howard Becker – discussed in the previous chapter – in such work as *Outsiders* (1963), and other symbolic interactionists and labelling theorists, was very influential, as was the entire phenomenological and ethnomethodological tradition. Further influences were the anti-psychiatry movement and radical psychology epitomised by the work of R.D. Laing (1960).

Notable practitioners in this field emerged from a series of meetings held by the New Deviancy Conference at York University in the late 1960s and early 1970s. Those involved included Paul Rock, David Downes, Laurie Taylor, Stan Cohen, Ian Taylor and Jock Young. These new criminologists – or 'sociologists of deviance' – moved from a purely symbolic interactionist, labelling theory position to one more heavily influenced by Marxism but, at the same time, the latter was itself going through something of a revision.

There had been earlier writers as we have seen above – in particular Wilhelm Bonger (1916) – who had attempted to explain crime and criminal behaviour from a Marxist perspective but these had tended to over-predict the amount of crime that would occur in a capitalist system by proposing that an inherently alienating social structure would inevitably lead to criminal and antisocial behaviour. Bonger's work was crudely deterministic and ignored the possible diversity of responses to adverse social conditions – such as drug taking, retreatism, and ritualistic accommodations by those with little stake in society – as described by Merton and others working in the anomie theory tradition. The new criminologists thus sought a 'totalising' explanation of crime and criminal behaviour, one that accounted for social structural power and history. They argued that they had found the solution – 'a fully social view of deviance' – in the combination of a 'sociology of deviance' based on labelling theory and a then new contemporary form of Marxism.

The classic text in this tradition is Taylor, Walton and Young's *The New Criminology* (1973), which provides an impressive summary of previous criminological ideas and a provision of indicators that the authors considered would give rise to a crime-free society. The book is founded on a set of assumptions that can be summarised as follows. First, crime is a two-sided affair – the cause of criminal behaviour *and* the identification of the power to criminalise. Second, capitalism itself is crime producing – or criminogenic – as crime is a product of the material and social inequalities that are inherent to the logic of capitalism. Third, the only way to eliminate crime is to destroy inequality and thus the power and need to criminalise. Drawing heavily on labelling theory, it was argued that the power to criminalise, make laws and prosecute offenders, or particular groups that are perceived as offenders, was a function of the state. The state was seen to vary in form during different historical periods, and the techniques that it employs to maintain social discipline, ultimately in the interests of the powerful, also varies.

In summary, *The New Criminology* represented a 'global', 'macro' approach that locates the causes of crime and criminal behaviour within the social structure. The labelling perspective retains a great deal of importance in this explanatory model and, indeed, it appears to be at least as important as the underlying structural considerations, but this approach does have the advantage of ensuring that there is an appreciation that individuals do possess a great deal of freedom of action within the broad social context in which they find themselves. The decision to act is nevertheless left to the rationality of the individual.

Criticisms of radical theories

The 'new criminology' provides a generalised prescription for a crime-free, socialist 'good society' and from the standpoint of the twenty-first century, it can be seen to be utopian, reflecting the optimistic nature of the times in which it was written, while, the generality of the work itself meant that it could offer very little to substantive theory at all. Indeed, it can be argued that since its publication very little has been achieved to produce a 'truly social view of deviance'. The subsequent text, edited by Taylor, Walton and Young (1975), appears to have marked something of a retreat into smaller concerns and away from the 'grand theory' and meta-vision of the original programme. Five possible not necessarily mutually exclusive explanations as to why this should have been the case can be identified.

First, some have doubted the legitimacy of merging and synthesising labelling theory and Marxist analysis, as the philosophical underpinnings of the two traditions are fundamentally different. Hirst (1980) argues that Taylor *et al.* are simply labelling theorists who have raided the works of Marx in order to provide a synthesis of the two perspectives.

Second, others have argued that the new criminologists have failed to provide an adequate definition of crime and deviance. For proponents of the predestined actor tradition this was not a problem. Crime is either the outcome of 'pathological behaviour' or simply behaviour that transgresses against the law. The notion of crime consisting of any behaviour that causes social harm is nevertheless highly problematic. The fundamental question is whether it is possible to have a theory of crime causation that legitimately encompasses such diverse activities as working-class theft, rape and 'white-collar' fraud. If we accept such an expansive definition of crime, the problem arises as to how we are to accurately measure social harm and some have argued that once the label 'crime' has become a problematic, it becomes clear that separate areas of criminal behaviour require different explanatory frameworks. In that case, the ability to develop any central all-encompassing criminology begins to dissolve and this inevitably leads to a retreat from grand theory.

Third, the retreat from grand theory was encouraged by the diverse accounts of criminal activity emerging from sociologists and social historians. Studies carried out by researchers such as Thompson (1975) and Hay (1981) reveal that criminal behaviour is not a homogenous concept and thus, the 'rule of law' cannot be simply conceptualised as an external coercive force repressing the working class. Indeed, it could possibly offer protection from certain abuses of power while constraining action in the interests of maintaining order. Examples offered by these authors from the eighteenth and nineteenth centuries demonstrate that state power was a far more complex concept than the authors of *The New Criminology* had at first envisaged. In short, there are many parasitic and diverse forms of crime from which the working class seek protection in law and order.

Fourth, changes in Marxist theory during the 1970s left the first wave of new criminologists intellectually stranded. The state had traditionally been seen as the political form of class domination but during the 1970s, the focus of Marxist theorising changed to encompass such areas as culture, ideology and hegemony, a much more complex analysis. The law was no longer conceptualised as an entirely bourgeois concept, but as a more differentiated idea.

New criminology revisionists addressed many of these complex new issues, some working at Birmingham University's Centre for Contemporary Cultural Studies under its charismatic director, Professor Stuart Hall and this group was responsible for producing the controversial *Policing the Crisis* (1978) an attempt to rework many of the utopian aspects of *The New Criminology* into a more modern and sophisticated theoretical package. Thus ideas were incorporated from the recently available work of the Italian Marxist Antonio Gramsci – originally published during the 1920s – in a discussion of the substantive issue of street robbery or 'mugging'. In doing so, they investigated the relationship between ethnicity, class and the state and this body of work forms a crucial element in the intellectual origins of the critical criminology – one of two contemporary variants of the radical tradition – that is the focus of Chapter 12. It is a perspective that to date has had little impact outside academic criminology.

Fifth, in response to an apparent substantial increase in crime rates and a general perception among vast sections of the population that crime levels were at an unacceptable level, a great deal of popularism came to infiltrate criminological debate. We saw in Chapter 3 that the conservative populists – or 'right' realists – came to take seriously the problems that ordinary people, notably working class people, had experienced, and in doing so managed to capture much of the electoral ground that the political left had always regarded as their natural constituency. We shall see in Chapter 16 that in an effort to recapture the issue of crime from the political 'right', the populist socialists – or left realists – influentially came to reconsider radical criminology. This second contemporary variant of the radical tradition recognises that capitalism may well be responsible for the relative inequality and absolute poverty that shapes so much of British culture and provides the root cause of crime. On the other hand, the bulk of that crime is predatory on the very people that they would wish to defend, the working class and the poor.

Suggested further reading

The US conflict and radical theory approach is well represented by Chambliss (1969, 1975), Chambliss and Seidman (1971), Quinney (1970) and Turk (1969). The radical UK tradition is best represented by Taylor *et al.* (1973) and Taylor *et al.* (eds) 1975). Christie (1993) provides an excellent more recent radical discussion of the notion of crime control as industry in a tradition established by Cohen (1985).

11. The gendered criminal

We have seen in the previous three chapters that the victimised actor model of crime and criminal behaviour proposes that the criminal is in some way the victim of an unjust and unequal society. It is the activities of the poorer and less powerful sections of society that are criminalised while the actions of the rich and powerful are simply ignored or not even defined as criminal. From a feminist perspective, it is men who are the dominant group in society and it is they that make and enforce the rules which are invariably to the detriment of women.

Feminism has had a considerable impact on criminology in recent years – using feminist or critical social theories to consider the significance of gender in crime and criminal justice – and has provided both critiques of the traditional explanations of female criminality that we encountered in Chapter 8 while at the same time offering its own perspectives. We should note that a distinction can be made between the biological characteristics that define and distinguish males and females and the cultural expectations inherent in the social roles defined by societies as being applicable to men and women. 'Sex' is a biological term used to describe the anatomical differences between males and females while the term 'gender' refers to learned behaviour associated with men and women which is developed through the socialisation process. Gender is thus the social construction of non-biological differences between men and women and this can be further explained by the identification of at least two sub-groups such as masculinity and femininity which are partially based on physical difference.

Feminist criminologies challenge the androcentrism – or male-centeredness – of criminology (Daly and Chesney-Lind, 1988) and propose that the main weakness of traditional 'malestream' criminological theory is the failure to understand the important significance of gender and sex roles (Gelsthorpe and Morris, 1990). For some, this significance is reflected in the ongoing differential in sex roles and gender inequality; for others, the inequalities are structural within patriarchy – a situation where the rights and privileges of males are superior to those of females – and are a fundamental principle of societal organisation. Labelling and conflict theories – which we encountered in the preceding two chapters – recognise male-female differences in power but feminist theory proposes that the power differential between men and women is at least as important as, if not more important than, the power differentials of race, class and age. Marxists consider class to be the fundamental divisive force in capitalist society but from the feminist perspective, patriarchy is equally as important and may even be the dominant factor. Feminist theories explain criminal justice decisions as reflecting this male dominance and functioning to support patriarchy by discriminating against women and reinforcing traditional sex and family roles (Mann, 1984; Messerschmidt, 1986; Morris, 1987; Chesney-Lind, 1988, 1989; Daly and Chesney-Lind, 1988; Daly, 1989, 1992, 1994a, 1994b; Simpson, 1989, 1991; Gelsthorpe and Morris, 1990, Chesney-Lind and Shelden, 1992).

It is important to recognise that feminism is not a unitary system of thought but a collection of different theoretical perspectives with each explaining the oppression of women in a different way. Consequently, there is no one feminist explanation of female criminality and before examining these debates it will be useful to briefly consider the different variations of feminist thought or feminisms. First, a further word of caution should be noted. The various versions of feminism tend to be united in their rejection of the term 'victim' to describe the oppression of women in a male dominated society and there is a preference for the far more positive term 'survivor'. It is a linguistic device that suggests that by working together in pursuit of the common cause women can successfully contest and overcome male supremacy.

Perspectives in feminist theory

The French term *feminisme* was first used in the late nineteenth century as a synonym for the emancipation of women (Jaggar, 1983; Pilcher, 1983) and referred in the broadest sense to a 'women's movement' made up of a number of diverse groups seeking to advance the position of women in society. In the early twentieth century, when the term was introduced in the USA, its meaning was limited to referring only to a group that asserted the uniqueness of women's experience and their social and sexual purity (Jaggar, 1983). Today, the term is no-longer so restricted, although there is still confusion about its exact meaning and use.

Feminism is generally perceived to have emerged in Western societies in two waves. The first emphasised equality within rational individual rights and was most notably characterised in the British context by the suffrage movement that lasted from the 1860s to the First World War. Subsequently, there was the opening up of educational opportunities, the provision of social legislation providing rights over property and the marital home. In 1928 there was the provision of the vote for those women over the age of 21. Nonetheless, while the social position of women was enhanced they did not enjoy equality with men.

The second wave of feminism emerged in the USA and was brought to the UK in the late 1960s. The emergence of the Women's Liberation Movement in the wake of the civil rights and student movements demanded nothing less than the wholesale transformation of society. Consciousness-raising groups and the development of women's collectives provided the arena for debate and discussion that formed the basis of contemporary feminist thought and action.

Feminist thought has subsequently had a considerable impact on the social sciences and other academic fields and has essentially involved a challenge to traditional male-dominated perspectives and arguments have been proposed both for the integration of women into theoretical perspectives and the development of new approaches that analyse and develop an understanding of issues specifically related to their lives. Essentially new areas of research have been opened up designed to make previously invisible women visible.

The feminist enterprise within academia has not come without criticism or been universally welcomed with its theories, writing and research often criticised, trivialised and, in some instances, openly undermined. It has despite these problems, challenged the dominance of traditional male-centred knowledge and can be understood as a social and political force. There are at least six main contemporary variants of feminism and we will consider each in turn.

Liberal feminism has its roots in the notions of individual rights and freedoms that were central to the rise and consolidation of modern societies in the eighteenth and nineteenth century. From this perspective, the subordination of women is examined as part of an analysis of the wider social structures and inequalities with the central concern to locate discrimination in social practice, specifically within the public sphere, and extend rights to women to equal those enjoyed by men through the process of legal reform. It is a perspective which has nevertheless been criticised for its inability to confront the deep-rooted levels of gender inequality. In short, there is an identified failure to challenge fundamental male values, while the solutions offered are limited and to some extent superficial. The legacy of sex discrimination and equal pay legislation can be attributed however to the influence of liberal feminism and there is recognition of its value to the broader feminist paradigm (Jaggar, 1983; Tong, 1988).

Radical feminism emerged in the 1970s and focuses on the importance of *patriarchy*, or the 'set of hierarchical relations between men, and solidarity between them, which enables them to control women' (Hartmann, 1981: 447). Patriarchy describes a power relationship inherent in the structures and social relations within which the subordination and exploitation of women occurs and it is used to explain the institutionalisation of male power and domination over women (see Walby, 1980: 173–201). The slogan 'the personal is political' has been used to identify the basis of women's oppression within the private realm of personal relationships and private lives. Thus, the need to expose the hidden secrets of personal relationships and social practice within the private sphere is recognised by radical feminists and has led to the examination of issues such as reproductive freedom, pornography, domestic violence and child abuse. Radical feminists advocate separatism from men to different degrees and this can be seen either partially, in the provision of women-only institutions or events, or wholly, including the withdrawal of women from personal and sexual relationships with men.

Radical feminism has been criticised for its biological determinism, that is, the belief that by nature all men are the same and so are all women. Further criticism is directed at the notion that patriarchy is an all-pervasive universal principle operating in the same way in all places at all times and thus fails to recognise differences in the experiences of women across time and space accounting for class and ethnic differences (Jaggar, 1983).

Marxist feminists argue that the subordination of women is located in the capitalist exploitation of their domestic role and they identify the existence of a dominant ideology that presents women as primarily carers within the domestic sphere and which is used to justify low wages, low status and part-time jobs, and is, in turn, used to deny women the right to economic independence (Beechey, 1977). Women are also considered to be part of a reserve army of labour, available to be drawn into the workforce when the needs of capitalism demand it and to be easily rejected when there is surplus labour (Bruegel, 1978).

Marxist feminists have nevertheless been criticised for their overuse of economic explanations of women's oppression while failing to examine the complexity of family relationships. Tong (1988) notes however the increasing relevance of the Marxist feminist critique, as more and more women have become employed in the market economy, a process that has accelerated during the intervening years.

Socialist feminism provides a synthesis of the radical and Marxist feminist perspectives with recognition that both capitalist and patriarchal systems play a part in the subordination of women. This 'dual systems theory' recognises the systems of capitalism and patriarchy to be separate but at the same time mutually accommodating systems of oppression while 'unified system theorists' have developed unifying concepts as central categories of analysis. Jaggar (1983), for example, identified the concept of 'alienation' that provides a theoretical synthesis of Marxist, radical and liberal feminist thought. The potential of socialist feminism to bring together the diverse accounts of different feminist approaches is significant but it has nevertheless been criticised by black feminists for the tendency to deny the diversity of experiences that different women encounter.

Black feminism examines the structures of domination prevalent in the personal, cultural and institutional levels and experiences of the lives of black women and the axes of race, gender and class are identified as forming the basis of their oppression within which, it is argued, there exists a 'more generalised matrix of domination'. This matrix was described by bell hooks (the writer spells her name in the lower case) (1988: 174–6) as a 'politic of domination' which is grounded in a hierarchical, ideological belief system. In their critique of feminist accounts of the family, education, reproduction and patriarchy, black feminist writers have identified the relationship of black women to the structures, ideologies and institutions of oppression. Accusations of racism made by black feminists towards the broader, often white-middle-class feminist movement have been productive for it has opened up a discourse of difference, recognising the diversity of female experience.

The notion of difference is also central to any understanding of the relationship of feminism to postmodernism (see the fifth part of this book). We shall see later that a prominent feminist Carol Smart has welcomed postmodernism while others have found it problematic. Radical feminists have criticised the emphasis on – and celebration of – individual difference by arguing that it is the collective voice that makes women strong but others argue that the challenge is to find a way to think both women and 'women' recognising diversity *and* collective experience.

It has been the purpose of this section to sensitise the reader with little or no knowledge of contemporary feminism to the diversity of thought that co-exists within that paradigm. The main differences between these accounts centre on factors identified as providing the basis of the oppression of women and the proposed solutions. Black feminism and postmodernist feminism provide both critiques of other feminist accounts and also their own perspectives that recognise the different experiences of women and of their subordination. We now return to our discussion of women and criminality.

The feminist critique of early explanations of female criminality

Late twentieth century criminology was described as the 'most masculine of all the social sciences, a speciality that wore six-shooters on its hips and strutted its machismo' (Rafter and Heidensohn, 1985: 5). Thus, the most significant characteristic of feminist work has been its critique of traditional or 'malestream' criminology with the main concern being the 'intellectual sexism in theories of female crime and the institutional sexism in the juvenile and criminal justice systems' (Daly and Chesney-Lind, 1988: 508).

Bertrand (1967), Heidensohn (1968) and Klein (1973) were among the first feminists to draw attention to the relative neglect of women in the study of crime and the stereotypical distortions imposed on females in those studies that did address the issue and we should note that a more traditional woman criminologist – Barbara Wootton (1959) – first made similar observations during the 1950s. It was nevertheless the publication of Carol Smart's *Women, Crime and Criminology* (1977) that is widely acknowledged to be the turning point, highlighting the failure of much traditional criminology to recognise women while – at the same time – identifying the sexual stereotypes imposed on women and girls in those studies that did consider female criminality and which we encountered in Chapter 8 of this book. The agenda was thus set for future feminist work.

Early feminists criticised traditional criminology for assuming women to be controlled by their biology and incapable of rational action observing that while the rest of the criminological world had moved on from a slavish adherence to the prescriptions of the biological variant of predestined actor model, female crime had been cut off from most of this development (Heidensohn, 1994). At the same time, as Downes and Rock (1998:

274–5) note, 'policies and attitudes towards female criminality mirrored such determinisms and lent undue prominence to "sexual deviance" as the focus of enquiry'. Early feminists emphasised these undesirable consequences to be a direct outcome of the approach to the study of female criminality adopted by traditional criminological theorists where the common theme – regardless of whether biological, psychological, anomie, control, differential association, conflict, labelling, social disorganisation or social learning theories – is that they are designed to explain only male criminality and have been tested only with male populations (Einstadter and Henry, 1995). It is acknowledged that there may be certain elements of these theories that are useful, but neither one single theory nor all the theories combined are capable of explaining female criminality or the male/female differences in crime (Leonard, 1983).

Some feminist theorists nevertheless disagree with this general critical assessment of all traditional criminological theories. Alison Morris (1987) argues that although biological and psychological theories are undoubtedly mistaken, traditional sociological explanations of crime have the potential of explaining female crime and why it occurs less frequently than male crime:

> Special theories for women's crimes have not been particularly successful … One implication of this … is that we need to reconsider the relevance to women of general criminological theories. (T)here is no reason to suppose that explanations of women's crime should be fundamentally different from explanations for men's crimes, though gender must play a part in any such explanation … There are a number of criminological theories, however, which, though not originally developed for women, do contribute to our understanding of women's crime.
>
> (Morris, 1987: 75)

Morris thus finds anomie, differential association and social bonding theories to be particularly relevant and concludes that, 'differential opportunity structure, associations, socialisation, and social bonding can aid our understanding of crimes committed both by men and women and can take account of differences in the nature and extent of their crimes' (Morris, 1987: 76).

There is still not a well-developed, uniquely feminist explanation of criminal behaviour that can answer the generalisability or gender ratio questions. Feminist theorists have approached the task of constructing such a theory by paying close attention to the dimensions of gender and sex roles that they believe other theorists have ignored or misunderstood and this includes not only sex-role expectations, but the significance of the underlying patriarchal structures that permeate all aspects of society. As Chesney-Lind (1989: 19) observes:

> It is increasingly clear that gender stratification in patriarchal society is as powerful a system as class. A feminist approach to delinquency means construction of explanations of female behaviour that are sensitive to its patriarchal context. Feminist analysis of delinquency would also examine

ways in which agencies of social control ... act in ways to reinforce women's place in male society.

The impact of feminist critiques

An area where feminism has been particularly influential has been in focusing our attention on the nature of crimes committed against women by men with the two areas most frequently studied being rape and domestic violence. In the former case feminists have campaigned for anonymity and protection for women against having their character tested in court – although in practice it is still possible to agree with Adler (1982) that few women are actually protected – and the setting up of specialist rape suites in police stations where victims can be dealt with in a sympathetic manner. These changes have encouraged some improvement in the reporting of offences to the police although the incidence of rape continues to be greater than officially recorded (Jones, Newburn, and Smith, 1994). In the case of domestic violence the whole issue is now considered far more serious than previously by the criminal justice system. First, there are now special legal provisions established in order to protect women and children from this behaviour, although some critics have argued that this body of legislation has actually made matters worse, for it allows these offences to be dealt with less seriously than would be the case in incidents of street violence. Second, although the greater emphasis than before in dealing with these cases has led to some increased reporting of such offences, it still remains one of the least reported (see Hanmer and Saunders, 1984; Dobash and Dobash, 1992).

Separate studies of women and their experiences of crime have had a threefold influence. First, there has been the development of different explanations of female criminality and conformity. Second, there has been a general gendering of crime and therefore gendered explanations of certain male criminality and indeed, we might note that in some respects men have also been gender-stereotyped in explanations of crime and criminal behaviour and this point is addressed later in this chapter. Third, there has been recognition of a different female 'experience' of crime, victimisation and the criminal justice system and, in particular, feminist criminologists have been very influential in the development of the left realism that is the focus of Chapter 16 of this book, in particular, the emphasis on the use of victim studies, even though the application of the information is not always acceptable to feminists (see Schwatz and DeKeseredy, 1991; Carlen, 1992). Downes and Rock (1998) identify three specific areas where the feminist perspective has contributed to theoretical criminology: (i) the 'female emancipation leads to crime' debate; (ii) the invalidation of the 'leniency hypothesis'; and, (iii) the emergence of gender-based theories.

The 'female emancipation leads to crime' debate

Freda Adler (1975) and Rita Simon (1975) focused their attention on increases in female crime that had occurred during the late 1960s and early 1970s, and the increasing aggression involved in much female offending and they both claimed that such variations could be explained by the influence of the emerging women's liberation movement.

Adler (1975) argued that there is very little actual difference between the potential propensity for criminality between men and women and previous variations in actual criminal involvement can be explained by sex-role differences. Changes in the social position of women in the legitimate sphere have a correlation in the illegitimate social world which has brought about greater involvement in crimes such as robbery and violence previously solely associated with men.

Simon (1975) argued rather differently that female emancipation has led to an increase in opportunities for women to commit crime particularly in the area of financial or property crimes. Simon disagrees with Adler on two important issues: first, she argues that emancipation will make women less violent as the frustration associated with victimisation and exploitation is reduced both inside and outside the home; and, second, instead of arguing that women are competing with men to become criminals, she proposes that increases in criminality are the outcome of increased opportunities that liberation brings.

Regardless of their differences, both Adler and Simon argued that liberation, or emancipation, causes crime. Box and Hale (1983) neatly summarise the many and varied criticisms by noting merely an historical overlap between women's liberation and an increase in female crime. It has also been noted that the rate of male violent crime has continued to rise faster than the female rate (Mukjurkee and Fitzgerald, 1981) and thus, the 'new violent' female is considered to be a myth (Box, 1983). Walklate (1995) concludes that men and women commit similar types of crime although the latter offend at a much lower rate and commit far less serious crimes than men less frequently. Heidensohn (2000/1) observes that offences committed by women tend to be concentrated in the areas of theft, handling stolen goods and drug offences with little involvement in acts of violence while, Graham and Bowling (1995) found that female offending tends to peak at the age of thirteen to fourteen, a much earlier age than for males. We might note that none of the above observations totally refute the propositions of Adler and Simon that, in short, a reduction in the extent of informal social controls for girls and young women has provided them with opportunities to engage in previously less thinkable criminal activities although a simple causal relationship between female emancipation and criminality was never likely to exist.

The invalidation of the 'leniency hypothesis'

The 'leniency hypothesis' was first proposed by Pollak (1950) and subsequently much feminist work has examined how women are dealt with by the criminal justice system to discover whether of not they are treated more leniently for reasons of 'chivalry'. Farrington and Morris (1983), for example, found that court leniency towards women was an outcome of their lesser criminal records while, Carlen (1983) found that Scottish Sheriffs justified imprisonment more readily for female offenders whom they viewed as having 'failed' as mothers. Downes and Rock (1998: 285–6) conclude that rather than being treated leniently by the courts, 'women – by comparison with men – are under-protected and over-controlled'.

The emergence of gender-based theories

Some writers, in seeking to understand female criminality, have modified the 'control theory' originally proposed by Hirschi (1969) – and discussed more fully in Chapter 15 – and applied this to the situation of women. Heidensohn (1985) argues that the reason why there are so few women criminals is because of the formal and informal controls that constrain them within male dominated society and proposes that in order to understand more about the transmission of gender inequality and the control of women by familial roles, it is necessary to consider the practical and ideological constraints imposed by family life. It is these very practices and policies that limit the involvement of women in activities outside of the home and that propel them back into the family where they are subject to greater control. Heidensohn observes that while women can be seen as responsible for the behaviour of others within the home and within the community, they are acting as the agents of male authority when carrying out that control function, there thus exists the stereotype of the mother reprimanding a child by saying 'wait until your father gets home'.

Heidensohn notes that while women may act as agents of control on behalf of men, they are themselves controlled both at home and outside. The sexual division of labour is related to the notion of separate spheres – public and private – for men and women and the latter are expected to function chiefly within the 'private' sphere of the home. Moreover, the privacy afforded this sphere is a contributing factor in the oppression which women experience for it is within the home that they are vulnerable to isolation and its consequences. Lacking alternative definitions of themselves and their roles, they are affected by those around them, particularly their husbands. Male dominance may result in the subtle undermining of the woman's confidence and self-esteem and this may lead to overt violence and bodily harm (Dobash and Dobash, 1980). Wives, who are housebound, isolated and dependent, are also the major victims of neurosis and depression (Brown and Harris, 1978). Furthermore, paid employment for women often means subjection to male power and supervision. Heidensohn argues that, in short, their socialisation and the conditions of their existence effectively control women. It is thus little wonder that so few women engage in criminal activity. An area of criminality in which women are involved while at the same time clearly being controlled by men – although this latter point is challenged by some – is that of prostitution and feminism has been at the forefront of challenging the notion of this being a victimless crime.

Feminism and prostitution

We saw in Chapter 8 that the influential structural functionalist Kingsley Davis (1961, originally 1937) argued from a traditional malestream perspective that prostitution is a structural necessity for society and will continue to be universally inevitable all the while sexual repression remains essential to the functioning of society. Liberal feminists are not entirely antagonistic to this traditional perspective and observe that prostitution involves choice for women and indeed often some form of 'liberation' (economic or sexual). The contract between the prostitute and her client is seen as a consensual relationship between two adults and these writers highlight the fact that many women work independently from pimps. Any violence and oppression which they experience can be seen to be exacerbated by the present legal system of regulation which stigmatises, marginalises and criminalises the prostitute. Thus, for liberal feminists prostitution is perceived as being a private business transaction. Where radical feminists view the prostitute as a human being who has been reduced to a piece of merchandise or a commodity, liberals propose that a woman is free to enter into contracts or not, as she so wishes. Radical feminists nevertheless do not believe that the desire of a prostitute to enter into such a 'contract' is done of her own free will and argue that prostitution is an exploitative relationship in which the customer is interested only in the services of the prostitute and has no interest in her personal welfare. But the liberal responds to this by pointing out that when one seeks out a professional such as a doctor, lawyer, plumber, or mechanic, one is not centrally concerned in the person doing the professional work – only his or her services (Weisberg, 1996).

Liberal feminists believe that personal 'rights' should predominate over concerns for the social good and this is a political view that goes back to the utilitarianism of John Stuart Mill, who argued that government should stay out of the private affairs of its citizens (Weisberg, 1996). The oppression identified by liberal feminists focuses on the injustices fostered by gender roles which favour men to the disadvantage of women but this does not necessarily mean that they all approve of prostitution in a moral sense.

Marxist feminists identify poverty as the crucial motivation for women involved in prostitution. Thus, the extreme economic misery under capitalism and within the system of marriage which provides it with crucial support makes prostitution a rational choice for women (see Bonger, 1916). Prostitution is identified as a particular corrupt form of labour and Marx himself asserted that 'prostitution is only a specific expression of the general prostitution of the labourer' (cited by Pateman, 1995) and, therefore, can be seen as standing as a symbol of all that is wrong with capitalist society. Prostitutes may well feel that they are free to make rational choices but in objective terms they are oppressed workers reinforcing and perpetuating an exploitative capitalist scheme. Carol Pateman (1995: 191) nevertheless – and perhaps rather surprisingly – appears to agree with the liberal feminists and argues that prostitutes are not wage labourers but rather independent contractors:

The objection that the prostitute is harmed or degraded by her trade misunderstands the nature of what is traded. The body and the self of the prostitute are not offered in the market; she can contract out use of her services without detriment to herself.

Marxists and Marxist feminists observe a significant reduction in the spiritual qualities of life in the capitalist system with people reduced to being mere cogs in an invariably economically determined machine. There is, moreover, a tendency in some feminist writings to discuss the relationship between feminism and prostitution in very much the same terms, thus removing the transcendent and spiritual qualities of prostitutes and leaving only a mechanistic view of their involvement in prostitution (Bromberg, 1997).

Radical feminists argue that prostitution is the product of patriarchal society and point to the inequality and unequal power relations which structure interaction between the sexes. Women are thus exploited by pimps, clients, and sometimes official agencies like the police, in a patriarchal society dominated by male privilege. Prostitution is evidence of the sexual and economic oppression and exploitation of all women by men. Edwards (1993: 113) observes that with radical feminism 'the focus of attention has been turned on its head, and the obsession with prostitutes' sexuality has been abandoned for a concern with the sexuality and psychology of men'.

Radical feminists thus do not view prostitution as a harmless private transaction and victimless crime but, on the contrary, they argue that it reinforces and perpetuates the objectification, subordination, and exploitation of women (Weisberg, 1996) while, at the same time, men are perceived to universally believe two significant myths regarding their own sexuality. The first myth is that men need more sex than women and second, that they are genetically the stronger sex and should therefore be dominant in relationships with women (Jaggar, 1980). Men believe that they have no choice but to respond to their sexual urges which thus creates a self-validating tautology of belief predicated on the notion that their aggressive behaviours are linked to inherited traits. Radical feminists disagree with this male mythology and view the source of male sexuality to be derived in part from culture and not exclusively from biology. Prostitution and pornography as factors in male experience only exacerbate his self-serving belief in the primacy of his sexuality and thus, his role as the 'dominant' sex is reinforced in his mind as something very real, when in fact it is not. In this sense, influences such as prostitution and pornography can be viewed as degrading to all women as acceptance of these events reinforces and perpetuates a cruel fantasy of women as weak and submissive. Weisberg (1996: 71) observes that:

According to the radical feminist view, men are socialised to have sexual desires and to feel entitled to have those desires met, whereas women are socialised to meet those desires and to internalise accepted definitions of femininity and sexual objectification.

As men cling to the idea that their sexuality is an absolute expression of their need and dominance, they prevent women from effecting new attitudes, self-realisations, and behaviours (Bromberg, 1997). The issue of male masculinity is discussed in some detail in the final section of this chapter.

Is there a feminist criminology?

Some writers have observed the existence of an identifiable feminist criminology (Brown, 1986) while others have argued that to have a few writers calling their work feminist does not constitute a 'feminist criminology' (Smart, 1977). Moreover, where attempts to create such a 'feminist criminology' have been made, there has not been any consensus about its success. Pat Carlen (1988) identified two problems with the endeavour first, most feminists, she suggests, identify crime as a male problem, ironically agreeing with the great body of traditional criminology; and second, where there has been an attempt to identify a universal explanation of crime that applies to both men and women, it has been theoretically unsound.

Other feminist writers have identified the wider feminist debate as the ideal location for examining the position of women in society and their social control. They argue that a feminist analysis should be central to any examination of women and crime, rather than the development of a 'feminist criminology' as a separate discipline (Heidensohn, 1985). Alison Morris (1987) takes this point further, suggesting that since the nature of feminism, like criminology itself, is diverse the very idea of a unified feminist criminology is suspect. Gelsthorpe and Morris (1988) suggest that a more appropriate position is to talk about feminist perspectives within criminology, thereby recognising the diversity within both feminism itself and among the writers examining women as subjects within criminology.

For postmodern feminists, all-encompassing feminist theory is itself of concern as it draws together and attempts to provide, in some instances, a universalistic account or grand theory of the experience of all women. However, the rejection of malestream assumptions of truth and reality – an essential feature of feminist postmodernism – has been identified as a potential weakness.

We have seen that Carol Smart (1977) had considered the possibility of creating a 'feminist criminology' but a few years later she had decided that this was an unnecessary task as there were 'more important goals to achieve than the one of constructing a sub-discipline to rank alongside other criminologies' (Smart, 1981: 86). She was however to take this argument a step further in a later article entitled *'Feminist Approaches to Criminology or Postmodern Woman Meets Atavistic Man'* (1990) where she argues that feminism has actually transgressed, or gone beyond, criminology. Smart observes the positive and emancipatory advances made in feminist thought and contrasts these with the perceived limited horizons of criminology and argues that 'the core enterprise of criminology is problematic, that feminists' attempts to alter criminology have only succeeded in revitalising a problematic enterprise'

(Smart, 1990: 70). She focuses on 'the continuing "marriage" of criminology to ... positivistic paradigms' and 'highlights criminology's isolation from some of the major theoretical and political questions which are engaging feminist scholarship elsewhere' and observes that 'for a long time we have been asking "what does feminism have to contribute to criminology?"' when the question should be 'rephrased to read "what has criminology got to offer feminism?"' (Smart, 1990: 83). In this case her reply is that criminology actually has very little to offer.

Gender issues have nevertheless broadened the field of criminological enquiry, opening up opportunities for the examination of female criminality but at the same time the useful possibility of an examination of masculinity, male power and violence drawing upon broader feminist debates. Pat Carlen (1992) – although critical of what she describes as the anti-criminology and libertarian, gender-centric and separatist tendencies of contemporary feminist 'criminologists' – also recognises the benefits of a feminist perspective to an understanding of women, law and order. She advocates the recognition of women's crimes as those of the powerless, of the stereotypical notions of femininity integral to women's oppression and observes the active contributions of some feminist writers to campaigns around women and crime and the influence of these can be observed in the 'left realism' that is the focus of Chapter 16.

Crime and masculinities

Maureen Cain (1989, 1990) agrees with Smart (1990) that feminism has 'transgressed criminology' and thus proposed from that perspective a significant need to answer the fundamental question of what it is about 'maleness' that leads a disproportionate number of men to become criminals. It was thus in response to this feminist discourse that a growing literature began to emerge that sought to 'take masculinity seriously'. Central to this development was the work of the Australian academic Bob Connell (1987, 1995) who – in response to the one-dimensional notion of male dominance presented by radical feminism – recognised the existence of 'multiple masculinities'. In short, he argued that masculinities could be black as well as white, homosexual or heterosexual, working class or middle class, with all subject to challenge and change over time. Connell accepts that there is a dominant masculinity in society which is based on the notions of heterosexual power and authority but proposes that other forms can challenge this and that male power is not absolute but is historically variable and thus a social construction.

James Messerschmidt (1993) applied this analysis of diverse and contested masculinities to youth crime, arguing that the types of offences committed by young males are patterned through various interpretations of masculinity generated by 'structures of labour and power in class and race relations'. In an apparent development of Robert Merton's anomie theory, he argues that crime provides a means of 'doing masculinity' when there is no access to other resources. The nature of the actual offence committed takes on different forms according to how different class and ethnic groups define their masculinities. Thus, for white working-class youth, masculinity is constructed around physical aggression and, for some, hostility to all groups considered to be inferior in a racist and heterosexual society. Lower working-class ethnic minorities, on the other hand, find their masculinity in the street gang. Whereas, the white middle class may envisage a future in mental labour and the white working class in manual labour, both of these routes are seen as inaccessible to many youths from ethnic minority backgrounds and, therefore, offences, such as robbery, provide the opportunity to accomplish a particular form of masculinity based on toughness and physical power. Messerschmidt argues that each form of masculinity represents an attempt to meet the cultural ideal of the dominant form of masculinity that is denied to young people elsewhere whether it is in the home, school, or even work.

Jefferson (1997) is nevertheless critical of such structurally determinist arguments which he observes tell us little of why it is that only a particular minority of young men from a given ethnic group or social class choose to accomplish their masculinity by 'doing crime' while the majority do not. He follows Katz (1988) and Presdee (1994) in noting that criminological knowledge has repeatedly failed to recognise the pleasure that is involved in 'doing masculinity' and 'doing crime'. Both these writers argue that unless we come to understand these pleasures we will never have a complete picture of why it is that particularly young people become involved in criminal behaviour. The work of these cultural criminologists and notions of the attractions and seduction of criminal behaviour is explored in more depth in the final part of this book. However, if masculinity – or at least different variants of masculinity – is a social construction and hence not characteristics biologically inherent in the male *sex* it follows logically from this recognition that there is a false duality between the male and female *gender* with the outcome that women may well do masculinity. Connell (2000: 16) observes that 'unless we subside into defining masculinity as equivalent to men, we must acknowledge that sometimes masculine conduct or masculine identity goes together with a female body'. If this is the case it therefore becomes necessary to analyse how crime and violence committed by women and girls is related to masculinities.

Messerschmidt (2005) argues that both traditional malestream pre-feminist and liberal feminist criminological theories create an artificial dualism in gender constructions and reduce all masculinities and femininities to one normative standard case for each – the 'male sex role' and the 'female sex role' – with the outcome bring a reification of gender. He observes that these criminological theories require that we examine masculinity exclusively done by men and boys and femininity by women and girls while ignoring the creation of *masculinities and femininities by people*. Messerschmidt observes that as masculinities and femininities are not determined biologically, it is important to identify and examine possible *masculinities by women and girls* (and femininities by men and boys) and their relation to crime. Indeed, there remains a necessity in criminological research to uncover not only gender diversity among girls/women, but girls'/women's relations to crime and violence and whether or not such social action constructs masculinity or femininity. Thus, Jody Miller (2001, 2002) shows that certain girls involved in gangs identify with the boys and describe such groupings as 'masculinist enterprises':

> To be sure, 'one of the guys' is only one part of a complex tapestry of gender beliefs and identities held by the gang girls I spoke with – and is rarely matched by gendered actions – but it remains significant nonetheless.
>
> (Miller, 2002: 442)

Miller observes that while gender inequality is rampant in the mixed-gender gangs of which the girls were members – for example, male leadership, a double standard with regard to sexual activities, the sexual exploitation of some girls, and the exclusion of most of the girls from serious gang crime – some of the girls differentiated themselves from others through a construction of being 'one of the guys'. In other words, the notion 'one of the guys' is not fashioned by being *similar* to boys (because of the inequalities) but, rather, certain girls are perceived and perceive themselves as being *different* from other girls.

Messerschmidt (2004) conducted a life-history study of adolescent involvement in violent assault and found numerous gender constructions by violent girls and that some of them 'do' masculinity by in part displaying themselves in a masculine way, by engaging primarily in what they and others in their milieu consider to be authentically masculine behaviour, and by an outright rejection of most aspects of femininity. Messerschmidt (2005) observes that the task of contemporary criminologists is not therefore to reify gender by concentrating research and theory solely on gender differences in crime but proposes that the goal should be to examine and explain both gender differences and gender similarities – that is, gender diversity – in the commission of crime.

Suggested further reading

Key feminist texts in the field of explaining crime and criminal behaviour are Carlen (1988, 1992), Gelsthorpe and Morris (1988), Heidensohn (1985, 1994), Leonard (1983) and Smart (1977, 1981, 1990). Dobash and Dobash (1992) and Hanmer and Saunders (1984) are essential reading on violent crime against women. For key texts on masculinity and crime consult Connell (1987, 1995), Messerschmidt (1993, 2004, 2005), Miller (2001, 2002) and Jefferson (1997).

12. Critical criminology

There are two contemporary manifestations of the radical criminological tradition we encountered in Chapter 10. One variant 'left realism' is the focus of Chapter 16. The other, critical criminology – or 'left idealism' as it has been termed by their former colleagues and now 'realist' opponents – is the only version that can be argued to have unequivocal foundations in the victimised actor model of crime and criminal behaviour. There are a number of different variations of critical criminology but in general it can be said to be a perspective where crime is defined in terms of the concept of oppression. Thus, some groups in society – the working class (in particular, the poorer sections), women (especially, those who are poor, sole parents and socially isolated) and ethnic minority groups (especially, those from non English-speaking backgrounds and refugees) – are seen to be the most likely to suffer oppressive social relations based upon class division, sexism and racism.

Critical criminologists focus their attention on both the crimes of the powerful and those of the less powerful. Crime is viewed to be associated with broad processes of the political economy that affect both groups but in quite different ways. For the powerful, there are pressures associated with the securing and maintenance of state and corporate interests in the context of global capitalism. In the case of the less powerful, criminal behaviour is seen to be the outcome of the interaction between the marginalisation or exclusion from access to mainstream institutions and that of criminalisation by the state authorities with particular attention paid to the increasing racialisation of crime, in which the media and police, in the 'war against crime' and public disorder, target certain invariably ethnic minority communities. In short, critical criminologists link offending behaviour to a social context that is structurally determined by the general allocation of societal resources and by the specific nature of police intervention in the lives of its citizens.

The origins of critical criminology

From the late 1960s onwards, many radical criminologists in the UK came to develop an idealist view of the working class that allowed them to appreciate and even condone deviant acts committed by members of this group. It was thus argued that offenders do not respond mindlessly to stimuli as suggested by the then dominant predestined actor model inspired criminology, but are engaged in activity which is meaningful to them and which so-happens to have been labelled as criminal by the dominant groups in society. Thus, Stan Cohen (1980: 1) argued that 'our society as presently structured, will continue to generate problems for some of its members – like working class adolescents – and then condemn whatever solution these groups find'.

The labelling and deviant subculture perspectives with their tradition of ethnographic observation were a considerable influence on this 'new idealism'. Actual day-to-day contact with so-called deviant adolescents convinced researchers that these young people were simply involved in activities regarded as legitimate by the perpetrators, but which had been prohibited by the state. In stigmatising sections of young people, the legislature was responding to a moral panic fanned by sensational and exaggerated media reporting. Cohen (1973) had written about the stigmatisation of mods and rockers and exaggerated newspaper and television reports of their behaviour, the damage they caused and the holidaymakers they terrorised back in 1964. Today, critical criminologists might claim that diverse groups ranging from recreational drugs users and 'binge' consumers of alcohol to asylum seekers and a welfare dependent underclass are the new 'folk devils' and the targets of an overly enthusiastic and criminalising criminal justice intervention. Thus, critical criminologists have argued that crime rates are far from being a perfect measure of the actual amount of criminality in society – being more a measure of the level of police activity – and thus can create a misleading image of horrific rises in certain types of crime. Figures purporting to show that black people are responsible for a disproportionate number of street robberies, for example, may be seen to reflect racist police stereotyping rather than reality (Hall *et al.*, 1978).

During the 1970s, orthodox criminology with its roots firmly founded in the predestined actor model was undergoing a crisis of confidence or aetiology (Young, 1994) because it had failed to explain why it was the case that the crime statistics appeared to increase ever upwards even during periods of societal affluence. Criminologists had as we have seen in this book proposed many – varied, apparently incompatible and sometimes even more impractical – solutions to an ever-increasing crime problem for many years without any visible success. A cynic might have observed that the numbers of books offering explanations of crime and criminal behaviour – and indeed ways of successfully responding to the crime problem – had grown accordingly on the shelves of academia in direct proportion to the ever-increasing crime figures. Indeed, one of their own had influentially noted that 'nothing works' (Martinson, 1974) an observation subsequently eagerly seized upon at the British Home Office (Mayhew *et al.*, 1976) and which was to become the new official orthodoxy. This new 'administrative criminology' (Young, 1994) was to supposedly bring an end to grandiose projects to change and rehabilitate criminals with the emphasis – highly influenced by contemporary manifestations of the rational actor model discussed in the first part of this book – now on reducing the opportunity to offend while catching and incarcerating those who still managed to transgress. A new and 'useful' role was nevertheless found for academic criminologists who could now be employed in assessing and evaluating the success of these usually small-scale situational crime prevention schemes. Explaining crime and criminal behaviour – and thus developing extravagant and expensive proposals for its elimination – was now dismissed as an academic exercise without practical application and not worthy of support.

If the 'nothing works' argument was becoming increasingly popular with politicians, critical criminologists nevertheless had their own answers to the aetiological crisis. They argued that an analysis of the processes and situations within which the labelling of certain individuals and groups takes place simply does not go far enough. It is necessary to examine the structural relations of power in society and to view crime in the context of social relations and political economy (Scraton and Chadwick, 1996, originally 1992) and it was at this point that much work was done from a Marxist perspective to identify the causal basis of crime, and to make the link between dominant institutions and ruling-class interests. There was, nevertheless, a tendency either to romanticise crime – as acts of rebellion or resistance – or to see the issue solely in economic terms. Later work was to explore in more detail the specific contexts and lived experiences of people involved with the criminal justice system (Hall and Scraton, 1981). The issues of racism, sexism and masculinity had been virtually ignored by much of academic Marxism while, at the other end of the spectrum, there was a perceived need to keep the focus on the actions of those in power, not only in relation to those marginalised in society but more generally in the area of what has come to be known as white-collar crime or crimes of the powerful.

Crimes of the powerful

We saw in Chapter 6 that Edwin Sutherland (1940) had been the first person to use the term 'white collar crime' when he launched an attack on the actions of the respectable in society – which had they been performed by the less powerful in a different context – would have been labelled as criminal. Sutherland basically observed a need to address the inequalities in the treatment of people who engaged in harmful behaviour between those in power and those without power. This pioneering work was to lead to a steady increase in research and writing – in particular, as we have seen, among those working in the differential association, anomie and deviant sub-culture traditions – initially in the USA and then worldwide (Geis and Goff, 1983). Critical criminology subsequently identified and built upon that earlier tradition but has situated it firmly in the context of a contemporary critique of the nature of global capitalist society.

Swartz (1975: 115) has observed that because capitalism involves the maximisation of corporate profits, 'its normal functioning produces ... deaths and illnesses' and the commission of business crime is linked to the values of capitalism and legitimate business goals. In the same vein, Mars (1982) observes that there is only a fine line between 'entrepreneurialism and flair' and 'sharp practice and fraud'. Indeed, many such activities are not greeted with widespread disapproval, for example, an electrician who overcharges for services is often not perceived as a thief but an entrepreneur, and in this way such behaviour is excused and distinguished from the activities of 'real' criminals. Corporations can practise a policy of law evasion and this may include the setting up of factories in countries that do not have pollution controls or stringent safety legislation – for example, the Union Carbide plant in Bhopal (Pearce and Tombs, 1993) – or the selling of goods that have been banned by the developed nations to markets in the developing world (Braithwaite, 1984). An example of this involved the Dalkon Shield intrauterine (contraceptive) device that was sold overseas for a considerable period when it had been declared unsafe in the USA (Hagan, 1994). In other words, multinationals dump some of their products, plants and practices, illegal in industrialised countries, onto undeveloped or underdeveloped countries (Box, 1987).

Such practices occur because the recipient nations are dependent on the capital investment of multinationals, they have fewer resources to check the claims of manufacturers and their government officials are more susceptible to bribery and corruption (Braithwaite, 1984). Corporations therefore export their illegal behaviour to where it is legal or at least where laws are not so rigorously enforced. In addition, multinational corporations often have sufficient economic resources and political influence to instigate or curtail legislation or at least its enforcement. In fact, many of the world's multinationals are wealthier than some of the less developed countries where they have a subsidiary, which means that they hold tremendous economic and political influence in those locations (Carson, 1980; Box, 1983). Box (1983) observes a need to penetrate the process of mystification that perpetuates the myth that corporate crime is both not serious and harmless and which protects the powerful segments of society who benefit from such crime. He himself provides a readable account of the ability of corporate crime to kill, injure and rob while arguing forcefully that the competitive environment in which businesses operate actively encourages employees to break the law:

> Not only does the promotion system mean that people who rise to the top are likely to have just those personal characteristics it takes to commit corporate crime, but these are reinforced by the psychological consequences of success itself, for these too free a person from the moral bind of conventional values.
>
> (Box, 1983: 39)

In short, critical criminologists argue that working-class crime is insignificant when compared to the 'crimes of the powerful' that largely go unpunished. Price-fixing, tax evasion, white-collar crime, environmental pollution, deaths at work and other offences, they contend, cost society far more than, for example, youth offending, a regular source or societal condemnation and moral panic. Moreover, the powerful perpetrators of these offences stand to gain far more material advantage from their misdemeanours while fewer resources are used to combat white-collar crime and some questionable activities are not even criminalised, but are instead portrayed as examples of wealth-creation and enterprise. In addition, offenders in this category can hire accountants and lawyers to protect them and have powerful friends to lobby on their behalf.

Crimes of the less powerful

Critical criminologists recognised that – although the general level of affluence as measured by gross domestic product per head, public spending and welfare benefits had increased – relative deprivation still existed among a substantial minority of society, who were well below 'the average' and accepted standard of living of the majority. Now the definition of relative deprivation changes over time and between societies. Absolute poverty was admittedly being eliminated, but relative poverty continued to exist as the rich claimed a seemingly unfair slice of the larger cake. Thus, according to critical criminologists, attempts by the less powerful to claim their just rewards, or to protest about their lot, were simply criminalised. Reiman (1979) claimed that 'the rich get richer and the poor get prison'.

Critical criminologists explain crime among the less powerful in society by reference to an interaction between *marginalisation*, or the exclusion from access to mainstream institutions, and *criminalisation*, which occurs with the intervention of the state authorities. The latter involves a process in which the law, agencies of social control and the media come to associate crime with particular groups who are subsequently identified, sought out and targeted as a threat. Scraton and Chadwick (1996) argue that this process is used to divert attention from economic and social conditions, particularly at times of acute economic change that could provide the impetus for serious political unrest. Moreover, overtly political protests are criminalised and political terrorists termed 'common criminals' in order to neutralise the political nature of their actions. Hillyard (1987) observes that this criminalisation process helps to engender public support for anti-terrorist measures, as it is easier to mobilise state intervention against criminal acts than for the repression of what might be seen as a just political cause.

Criminalisation can therefore be used to justify harsher social control measures that are often taken against economically and politically marginalised groups who have few means of resisting these initiatives. Major economic changes occurred during the last quarter of the twentieth century in most advanced industrial societies and in particular in the UK that were to impoverish many in the lower, and less powerful social classes, while critical criminologists observe that it is this group that has always been seen, since at least the beginning of the modern era, as the 'dangerous classes'. It is through the criminalisation of their activities that their situation can be attributed to their own weaknesses, thus justifying harsher control measures.

Crime, according to some critical criminologists, is, therefore, a reassuring sign that the perpetual struggle against inequality continues and this is an idea with its origins in the writings of Durkheim (1964: 72) who claimed that crime could be 'functional' for the needs of society:

> Crime must no longer be conceived as an evil that cannot be too much suppressed. There is no occasion for self-congratulation when the crime rate drops noticeably below the average level, for we may be certain that this apparent progress is associated with some social disorder.

Durkheim's concept of the functionality of crime has survived in 'conflict theories' that depict crime as symptomatic of an ongoing struggle between powerful groups and the weak. This conflict essentially needs to take place so that social control does not become an unchecked oppression of citizens by the state.

Critical criminology or 'left idealism'

For critical criminologists – such as Scraton and Chadwick (1996) – the growing disparities between rich and poor, and the expansion in the sheer number of the latter constitute a legitimation crisis for the capitalist system as a whole. *Actual* deprivation is again seen as the cause of working-class crime with the perceived state response involving a substantial move toward 'law-and-order' politics, which has exacerbated the process of identifying and punishing members of particular groups within the working class and ethnic minorities.

Critical criminologists propose that a legitimate response to crime must be built upon a strategy of social empowerment. This means involving people directly in decisions about their future through direct participatory democracy but also crucially requires a redistribution of economic resources to communities on the basis of social need and equity. To counter crimes committed by the powerful, there must be open and public accountability of all state officials and as part of wealth redistribution, there has to be a transfer of wealth from private hands to public ownership under community control. As a general crime prevention measure, and to reduce the prevalence of certain crimes, there needs to be anti-racist and anti-sexist campaigns, including the re-education and retraining of agents of the state such as the police. Strong emphasis is given to extending and protecting basic human rights and institutionalising these by means of watchdog agencies and developmental policies.

Critical criminologists argue that the true function of the criminal justice system is not to solve crime but to unite the people against a rump in their midst – defined as deviant – and hence in this way maintain the legitimacy of the existing social order. The true function of prisons, it is argued, is not to reform criminals but rather to stigmatise them and cause them to be seen as the enemy in our midst (Foucault, 1980). Likewise, it is not the real function of the police to prevent crime and apprehend criminals but rather to

maintain the social order, being used to control industrial disputes, political demonstrations or any other activities that may threaten the community. They are also used to widen the net of social control so that the state – in the form of the criminal justice system – brings under surveillance and control more of those individuals and groups that can be considered potentially deviant (Cohen, 1985). In order to achieve this overall intention, the authorities, in particular the police will require the necessary powers and be relatively free of control by local and central governments (Scraton, 1985).

Many would consider this view of social order, the law and the criminal justice system to be too simplistic and a denial of the reality that most people experience and, moreover, the individual nature of criminality cannot simply be regarded as a construction of the state. Critical criminologists have nevertheless posed a number of important questions and have attempted to critically interrogate dominant and orthodox perceptions of crime and criminal behaviour arguing that crime should not be perceived as a problem of individual offenders in society but as a process related to the wider economic and social structures of power. This is nevertheless a problematic analysis. Most criminal behaviour is not targeted against the dominant social order, while the criminal law is not just directed at keeping the less powerful in their place. Indeed, many of the weaker and poorer sections of our society need both the law and its agents in the criminal justice system to protect them from criminal elements living in their midst (Hopkins Burke, 1998b) and other former radical criminologists were to come to recognise that reality and eventually came to reconsider their stance and the very meaning of radicalism. These subsequently highly influential 'left realists' came to constitute the second variant of the former radical tradition – terming their former radical colleagues as 'left idealists' – and are themselves the focus of attention in Chapter 16.

Critical criminology and the challenge of zemiology

A significant contemporary variant of critical criminology has been zemiology or the study of social harm. The intention from this perspective is to significantly extend the legitimate parameters of criminological study away from a limited focus on those injurious acts defined as such by the criminal law, for example, theft, burglary, criminal damage, and to establish that a vast range of *harms*, for example, sexism, racism, imperialism and economic exploitation, could and should be included as the focal concern of criminological investigation (Schwendinger and Schwendinger, 1970) and these contemporary critical criminologists observe that their former colleagues and now left realists remain trapped within a legal definition of 'crime'. It is the intention of these new zemiologists to look beyond 'crime' to discover where the most dangerous threats and risks to our person and property lie, for example, poverty, malnutrition, pollution, medical negligence, breaches of workplace health and safety laws, corporate corruption, state violence, genocide and human rights violations all have more widespread and damaging consequences than most of the behaviours and incidents that currently make up the 'problem of crime' (Muncie, 2000).

By the 1990s recognition of these social harms was beginning to be identified as a legitimate focus of criminological inquiry (Muncie and McLaughlin, 1996) and the issue of human rights denial was entered on the agenda, not simply through extending definitions of what actually constitutes crime but through recognition of the legal transgressions routinely employed by those wielding political and economic power and their ability to deny or conceal the harms they unleash under the protection of the law (Cohen, 1993). Similarly, it had taken some twenty years of feminist enquiry to establish that violence, danger and risk lie not just on the streets or in the corridors of power, but in the sanctity of the home. Recognising male violence and opening up the vexed question of 'violent masculinities' further extended our conception of what actually does constitute the 'crime problem' (Segal, 1990; Campbell, 1993; Jefferson, 1997).

In other areas, we can witness an at least partial emergence of 'hidden crime' onto the mainstream agenda. The murder of Stephen Lawrence and the unrelenting campaign by his family to expose police and judicial racism was to catapult racial violence and hate crime to the forefront of issues to be addressed by law enforcement and community safety agencies in the early twenty-first century. The concept of state crime – in the form of illegal arms dealings, genocide and torture has been consistent front page news following successive wars in the Balkans, Afghanistan, Iraq and the establishment of the War Crimes Tribunal in The Hague. A long campaign against the transportation of live animals from Britain to Europe entered the issue of animal rights into legitimate crime discourse, as has the recognition of the culpable negligence of tobacco and food companies in knowingly marketing unsafe and life threatening substances. It has also become increasingly likely to find numerous aspects of social policy (in particular housing policy and youth homelessness), environmental policy (in particular road building and pollution) and economic policy (in particular third world debt, the arms trade and corporate greed) being described within a crime discourse.

For zemiologists, a conception of crime without a corresponding conception of power is meaningless. The power to cause certain harmful acts to become visible and define them as 'crime', while maintaining the invisibility of others – or defining them as beyond criminal sanction – lies at the heart of the problem of working within notions of 'the problem of crime'. It is perceived to be a notion with a particularly limited vision of the range of misfortunes, dangers, harms, risks and injuries that are a routine part of everyday life. If the criminological intent is to reveal such misfortunes, risks and harms then the concept of 'crime' has to be rejected as its sole justification and object of inquiry.

Muncie (2000) observes that the first stage in what he terms 'decriminalising criminology' is to recognise that a great number of damaging events are far more serious than those that make up the 'crime problem'. Moreover, many of these incidents – such as petty theft, shoplifting, recreational drug use, vandalism, brawls, antisocial behaviour – would not seem to score particularly high on a scale of serious harm. It is nevertheless these 'minor' events that take up much of the time and preoccupation of law enforcement agencies and the criminal justice system. Conversely, the risk of suffering many of those crimes defined by the state as 'serious' would seem negligible compared to such everyday risks as workplace injury and avoidable disease. What has remained unclear is how far the zemiological project of recoding crime as harm is capable of challenging and overthrowing legal definitions. Nelken (1994) has argued that campaigns to extend the criminal label so that it includes new forms of injury, continually run the risk of reinforcing the concept of crime even when it is seemingly being attacked. From a different, left realist, perspective, Matthews and Young (1992) observed that a comprehensive expansion of the notion of criminality can only lead to nihilism and cynicism and that by removing the principal object of criminology (crime) the subject is evaporated into larger disciplines such as sociology. Henry and Lanier (1998) respond by proposing the need for an integrated definition of crime which recognises the legally defined and the legally ignored, the serious and the trivial, and the visible and the invisible located on a continuum dependent on the seriousness of the harm.

Critical criminologists argue that the redefining of crime as harm opens up the possibility of dealing with pain, suffering and injury as conflicts and troubles deserving negotiation, mediation and arbitration rather than as criminal events deserving guilt, punishment and exclusion. Bianchi (1986) proposed that crime should be defined in terms of tort and dispute with the criminal law replaced by reparative law. From this perspective, questions of crime control are subordinated to those of a wider social justice agenda in which governments and the wider community recognise disadvantage, difference and diversity and acknowledge that they have a responsibility for enhancing personal and social development. Whilst a concept of harm encourages conceptions of victimisation as universal it enables recognition of its most damaging forms beyond those which are currently recognised by media, law and the state. Perceptions of seriousness frequently reveal the differential placed on human life dependent on social status and position within the hierarchy of power. Muncie (2000) thus observes that, for example, the death of Princess Diana and the TV presenter Jill Dando were portrayed in the media to be more serious than the regular and continuing murders experienced by Nationalist and Loyalist communities in Northern Ireland at the time.

Zemiologists propose that the concept of harm enables injury to be addressed by a wide variety of social responses and without necessarily the involvement of the criminal justice system. Thus, the concept of *redress* has an extensive set of formal definitions and meanings from 'to put right, repair, rectify something suffered or complained of' to 'correct, amend, reform or do away with a bad or faulty state of things' (De Haan, 1990: 158). It provides an opportunity for dealing with social problems or conflicts – such as crime – through neighbourhood rather than criminal courts and the pursuit of compensation or reconciliation, rather than retaliation or blame allocation:

To claim redress is merely to assert that an undesirable event has taken place and that something needs to be done about it. It carries no implications of what sort of reaction would be appropriate, nor does it define reflexively the nature of the initial event … It puts forth the claim for a procedure rather than a specific result. Punitive claims already implied in defining an event as a 'crime' are opened up to rational debate.

(De Haan, 1990: 158)

In short, the zemiological aim is to integrate, rather than exclude; to reduce, or if possible, abolish deliberately inflicted pain; to seek restoration rather than retribution (Cohen, 1994). Muncie (1998) observes that working within established criminological or criminal justice discourses essentially excludes any possibility of imaginative rethinking and, therefore, important work needs to be done to expose the ways that these orthodox 'knowledges' of 'crime', criminal justice and criminology are constructed and used in order to open up challenging alternatives.

Muncie (2000) sounds a note of caution for the zemiological project by observing that the successful incorporation of a social harm agenda into mainstream criminological discourse could lead to the unwelcome and totally unintended criminalisation of all 'undesirable behaviour' by the criminal justice system noting that, for example, notions of community safety were first promoted as a means of liberalising crime prevention policy but have been subsequently appropriated by New Labour as a means of targeting the 'antisocial' and used to justify all manner of punitive interventions from curfews to custody. From a zemiological perspective these emergent discourses do not challenge the notion of 'crime', but have become incorporated by it because they continue to fail to recognise the multifaceted nature of harm.

While the concept of harm has clear potential for broadening what for critical criminologists is a traditionally conservative criminological agenda it nevertheless continues to operate within a negative discursive framework. Harm is not only a source of fear, but also a source of *fascination, pleasure* and *entertainment*. Simple observation of television programme listings, the contents of mass circulation newspapers or the shelves of fiction in bookshops will confirm the extent to which an audience perceives crime not just as a social problem but as a major source of entertainment. The way *we* enjoy violence, humiliation and hurt, casts doubt on the universal applicability of harm as always connoting trouble, fear and loss. For participants, too, the pleasure in creating harm, or doing wrong or breaking boundaries is also a significant part of the equation and is the focus of study for cultural criminologists which we will examine further in Chapter 18.

Critical criminology revisited

Critical criminology had been able to respond to the suggestion that criminology was unable to offer a convincing explanation of the ever-increasing crime problem but with the arrival of mass unemployment at the end of the 1970s and the beginning of the 1980s, these radical criminologists were able to return to their traditional argument that it is deprivation which is the main cause of working-class crime. At the time of writing, the major economies of the world are undergoing a major 'correction' which could well turn into a slump not seen since the 1930s and which seems to be the outcome of a 'credit crunch' where boom conditions have been artificially sustained for some years by banks loaning large sums of money that do not really exist to people with a dubious ability to repay. The Chancellor of the Exchequer, Alistair Darling, felt it his duty to tell the public that the UK faces its worst economic crisis in 60 years (BBC News, 2008a) and not long afterwards a leaked draft letter from the Home Office advised that crime levels will inevitably increase because of the downturn. Rising property crime and violent crime, and increased hostility to migrants, were also considered likely. Home Office minister Tony McNulty told the media that the letter was a 'statement of the blindingly obvious' as it was clear that crime would probably go up during the economic slowdown and this argument about property crime, such as burglary, and violent crime was based on the experience of the recession in the early 1990s (BBC News, 2008b) when we might observe that conditions were nowhere near as severe as those that existed during the 1930s.

Such changed socio-economic circumstances should provide fruitful conditions for critical criminological research and analysis and indeed provides support for recent arguments for a return to traditional Marxist analysis. Russell (2006) observes that since the early 1990s, the 'new directions' in critical criminology that we encountered above have simply excluded Marxism on the grounds that it is an outdated mode of analysis. He argues that Marxism remains as relevant as ever for analysing crime, criminal justice, and the role of the state and we might observe that the forthcoming economic crisis where whole groups of 'white collared' professionals, among many others, previously not considered to be members of the working class, not least by themselves, and thus immune to the negative extremes of the trade cycle will in fact become increasingly proletarianised victims of the downturn with both their homes and jobs at risk. The affect on the psyche of those with strong bonds to the conventional social order and socio-economic status world suddenly cast adrift in unfamiliar and significantly impoverished changed circumstances could have major implications for crime and criminality.

Suggested further reading

Box (1987), Cohen (1980, 1985), Hall *et al.* (1978), Reiman (1979), Scraton and Chadwick (1996) and Van Swaaningen (1997) all make essential contributions to critical criminological explanation of crime and criminal behaviour. Those interested in the crimes of the powerful should consult the following body of work not necessarily written by those identifying themselves as critical criminologists: Braithwaite (1984), Geis (1968), Mars (1982) and Pearce and Tombs (1993). Schwendinger and Schwendinger (1970) provide an early and paradigm forming introduction to notions of social harm with Shearing (1989) and Tifft (1995) more recently providing significant discussions. Russell (2006) and Cowling (2008) provide a good discussion of the continuing relevance of Marxism for critical criminology – and indeed criminology in general – while the latter provides an interesting 'toolkit' for utilising Marxist theories in the analysis of crime and criminal justice.

Part Four

Integrated theories of crime and criminal behaviour

As positivism evolved, it eventually encompassed, under the term 'deviance', the many forms of behaviour left behind by the Classical tradition. Lacking the Classical theory of behaviour, however, positivists have not been able to deal with the connections among the many acts that make up deviance and crime. Consequently, they have tended to develop behaviour-specific theories and to treat the relations between deviance and crime as cause and effect rather than as manifestations of a single cause. One purpose of this [theory] is to reunite deviance and crime under a general theory of behaviour.

(Gottfredson and Hirschi, 1990: 3–4

The first three parts of this book each considered a different model of explaining crime and criminal behaviour. The first, the rational actor model proposed that people choose to engage in criminal behaviour in the same way that they choose to become involved in any other form of activity. The second, the predestined actor model proposed that the behaviour of the person is in some way determined by factors, either internal or external to them, in ways over which they have very little or no control. Criminal behaviour is thus the destiny of that person. The third, the victimised actor model proposes that the offender is the victim of an unequal society that has in some way chosen to target and criminalise his or her activities while ignoring those of other invariably more powerful individuals and groups.

Within the parameters of these models there are a range of different theories that have sought to explain criminality and there are essentially three principal ways in which these can be developed and their predictability value validated. The first is to consider each theory on its own. The data obtained by empirical research confirms the predictions of the theory then it is generally accepted. If the data fails to support those predictions then the theory can be either modified or rejected.

The second, theory competition, involves the logical, conceptual, or empirical comparison of two or more theories to determine which offers the best explanation of the phenomenon to be studied (Liska, Krohn and Messner, 1989). In the first three parts of this book, the focus has been on single-theory explanation, albeit in the context of the particular model – or tradition – of criminal behaviour in which it can be best located. Moreover, it should be noted that theory building – like the development and acquisition of knowledge, in general – is usually incremental, each theory thus building on its predecessors that went before.

Evaluation of the evidence on a single theory has rarely led to its total rejection but, on the other hand, no one theory cited has been able to explain all incidences or forms of crime. In reality, the evidence to support, or challenge, most theories lies somewhere in between these two extremes.

The central issue is how well a theory performs when compared with others either internal or external to its model of behaviour. Criticism of one approach from the perspective of another is common, and direct competitive testing of rival perspectives often occurs. For example, the older biological variants of the predestined actor model of criminality have been largely discredited. Even the more recent and sophisticated biological explanations of criminal behaviour have tended to perform badly in comparison with sociological theories. Psychological approaches that rely on emotional disturbance or personality traits have also been found to be less successful than sociological or social-psychological explanations (Akers, 1997).

The third way to assess and construct an explanation of crime and criminal behaviour is through theoretical integration. The objective is to identify commonalties in two or more theories to produce a synthesis that is superior to any one individual theory (Farnsworth, 1989). However, while theory integration often involves such deliberate attempts to fuse together two closely related theories, it may well also stem from theory competition.

Upon closer examination, two theories may not be as compatible as at first thought.

Certainly, all of the theories discussed in the first three parts of this book have been subjected, to some degree, both to competition and integration. For example, there has long been competition between the proponents of biological, sociological and social learning theories as to which approach best provides an explanation of criminal families. On the other hand, most theories have come to at least tacitly – but usually more explicitly – incorporate concepts and notions from their supposed competitors. For example, Cesare Lombroso, that much-maligned early biological positivist, came to accept social factors to such an extent that by the fifth edition of *L'Uomo Delinquente (On Criminal Man)* they account for 80 per cent of his explanation of criminal behaviour.

Moreover, when a theory is first formulated, it tends to build upon other explanations within the context of the particular model of criminal behaviour in which it is situated; for example, critical criminologists provide a radical reworking of labelling perspectives incorporating structural concepts. At the same time, each theory tends to draw upon a range of different sources, for example, labelling theorists incorporate ideas and concepts from symbolic interactionism, phenomenology and ethnomethodology.

All theories have been revised to some degree after their original formulations. These revisions almost always borrow from the insights and explanations found in other theories and the sources can be both internal and external to their host model of criminal behaviour. For example, later criminologists working within the predestined actor tradition came increasingly to recognise that people are capable of making – albeit limited – choices. On the other hand, the converse is also true, later rational actor model theorists came to recognise the limitations of individual rationality. At the same time, the proponents of each theory implicitly or explicitly compare its explanatory power with that of alternative explanations.

Liska, Krohn and Messner (1989) identify different types of theoretical integration. First, there is conceptual integration where concepts from one theory are shown to have meanings similar to those within another theory, for example, there has been a long debate about the similarities between Durkheim's concept of anomie and Marx's notion of alienation. Second, *propositional* integration relates propositions from different theories. This can be accomplished by showing how two or more theories make the same predictions about crime, even though each begins with different concepts and assumptions, for example, both anomie theory and conflict theories predict higher crime rates among the lower social classes. This form of integration can also be achieved by placing the explanatory variables from different theories into some kind of causal or explanatory sequence. The sequence starts with the variables from one theory (for example social disorganisation) to explain the variations in variables from another theory (for example, attachment to family) that can be used to explain offending behaviour.

Theoretical integration can be *within level* (only micro-level or only macro-level), *across level* (micro–macro) as well as *within model* or *across model*. The following chapters in this fourth part of the book consider some of those explanations of crime and criminal behaviour where theorists have deliberately set out to integrate different approaches in order to provide a stronger explanatory tool than that offered by one individual theory.

13. Socio-biological theories

Biology is the key to human nature, and social scientists cannot afford to ignore its rapidly tightening principles. But the social sciences are potentially far richer in content. Eventually they will absorb the relevant ideas of biology and go on to beggar them by comparison.

(Wilson, 1990: 260)

We saw in Chapter 5 that proponents of the biological variant of the predestined actor model sought explanations of crime and criminal behaviour in the measurable physiological part of individuals, their bodies and brains. It was acknowledged that some of the studies reviewed in that chapter really do point to biological explanations of criminality but only in a *tiny* minority of offenders, for a closer investigation of individual cases suggests that social and environmental background is at least equally as important. Consequently, in recent years there has been a concerted attempt to rehabilitate biological explanations by incorporating social and environmental factors into a 'multi-factor' approach to explaining crime and criminal behaviour (Vold, Bernard and Snipes, 1998; Walsh and Ellis, 2006). Thus, from this contemporary perspective, it is argued that the presence of certain biological factors may increase the likelihood, but not determine absolutely, that an individual will engage in criminal behaviour. These factors generate criminal behaviours when they interact with psychological or social factors.

Biosocial theory

Biosociology is an emerging paradigm which seeks to understand human behaviour by integrating relevant insights from the natural sciences into traditional sociological thinking. It is not a 'biological' perspective but conversely a biosocial perspective that recognises 'the continuous, mutual, and inseparable interaction between biology and the social environment' (Lancaster *et al.*, 1987: 2). Biosociology proposes no ultimate causes of human behaviour but rather seeks to understand how biological factors interact with other factors to produce observed behaviour. It does not seek to 'reduce' complex behaviour to the level of biological processes in isolation from environmental influences but merely insists that such processes must be recognised and included in any analysis of behaviour and that such an analysis be consistent with those processes.

The work of Sarnoff Mednick and associates (1977, 1987) provides a good example of the orientation of more recent criminological biologists working in the context of the biosocial paradigm. Mednick, Moffit and Stack (1987) thus argue that the biological characteristics of an individual are only part of the explanation of criminal behaviour with other factors involved being the physical and social environment:

> Where the social experiences of the antisocial individual are not especially antisocial, biological factors should be examined. The value of the biological factors is more limited in predicting antisocial behaviour in individuals who have experienced criminogenic social conditions in their rearing.
>
> (Mednick, Moffit and Stack, 1987: 68)

Mednick proposes in his *biosocial theory* that all individuals must learn to control natural urges that drive us toward antisocial and criminal behaviour. It is acknowledged that the learning process takes place in the context of the family and during the course of interaction with peer groups, and is based on the punishment of undesirable behaviours. The punishment response is mediated by the autonomic nervous system. If the reaction is short-lived, the individual is said to have rewarded him or herself, and criminal behaviour is inhibited. A slow physiological recovery from punishment nevertheless does little to teach the individual to refrain from undesirable behaviour. Mednick ultimately proposes that criminals are those who have slow autonomic nervous system responses to stimuli.

Jeffery (1977) has argued strongly that this new biological criminology is not 'neo-Lombrosian' and is highly critical of those criminological theories that ignore or reject biological components. He proposes that biological, psychological and sociological characteristics should be seen as interacting together in a systems model to produce criminal behaviour. Central to his argument is the notion that individuals are born with particular biological and psychological characteristics that not only may predispose them to, but also may actually cause certain forms of behaviour. This 'nature' is independent of the socialisation process present in the social environment. There is, however, a good deal of interaction between nature and nurture through the physical environment and the feedback mechanisms that exist in human biochemical systems.

Jeffery notes furthermore that poor people tend to experience a poor quality diet and are more likely to be exposed to pollutants. The resulting nutrients and chemicals are transformed by the biochemical system into neurochemical compounds within the brain. Poverty, therefore, leads to behavioural differences through the interaction of individual and environment. It is an argument that has been taken up and developed by key 'right realist' criminological theorists in sometimes highly contentious formulations.

Biosocial theory and the 'new right'

James Q. Wilson was – as we noted in Chapter 3 – a major influence on the development of the 'right realist' perspective on crime and criminal behaviour that was so influential in the rehabilitation of the rational actor model after many years in the explanatory wilderness. It was his work with Richard Herrnstein (Wilson and Herrnstein, 1985) that offers a more definitive account of what they consider to be the underlying causes of crime.

Three elements are defined. First, there are constitutional factors which although not necessarily genetic have some biological origin. Observing that crime is an activity disproportionately undertaken by young men, Wilson and Herrnstein (1985: 69) observe that:

It is likely that the effect of maleness and youthfulness on the tendency to commit crime has both constitutional and social origins: that is, it has something to do with the biological status of being a young male and with how that young man has been treated by family, friends and society.

It is therefore an explanation of criminal behaviour which is not solely rooted in biology. There is a concern to construct an explanation in which factors such as gender, age, intelligence, body type and personality are inserted as potential biological givens of human beings projected into a social world. But these factors are not necessarily determiners of human action. It is a social world in which the individual learns what kind of behaviour is rewarded in what circumstances. This is the second element of the theory.

Wilson and Herrnstein are heavily influenced by the psychological behaviourism of B.F. Skinner – introduced in Chapter 6 – and thus propose that individuals learn to respond to situations in accordance with how their behaviour has been rewarded and punished on previous occasions. From this 'operant conditioning' perspective, it is proposed that the environment can be changed to produce the kind of behavioural response most wanted from an individual. Thus, in order to understand the propensity to commit crime it is important therefore to understand the ways in which the environment might operate on individuals – whose constitutional make-up might be different – to produce this response. Within this general learning framework the influence of the family, the school and the wider community is located.

The third element in the theory is that of the conscience. Wilson and Herrnstein (1985: 125) support the conjecture made by Eysenck that 'conscience is a conditioned reflex' by proposing that some people during childhood have so effectively internalised law-abiding behaviour that they could never be tempted to behave otherwise. For others, breaking the law might be dependent upon the particular circumstances of a specific situation suggesting less effective internalisation of such rules. For yet others, the failure to appreciate the likely consequences of their actions might lead them into criminal behaviour under any conditions. In other words, the effectiveness of something termed 'the conscience' may vary in terms of the particular constitution of the individual and the learning environment in which people find themselves.

These three elements – constitutional factors, the presence and/or absence of positive and negative behavioural reinforcement alongside the strength of the conscience – provide the framework in which Wilson and Herrnstein seek to explain crime. For them the interplay between these factors can explain why crime rates may increase both in times of prosperity and recession since the equation between the social and the individual is a complex one. They suggest that:

> Long-term trends in crime rates can be accounted for primarily by three factors. First, shifts in the age structure of the population will increase or decrease the proportion of persons – young males in the population who are likely to be temperamentally aggressive and to have short horizons. Second, changes in the benefits of crime … and in the cost of crime will change the rate at which crimes occur, especially property crimes … Third, broad social and cultural changes in the level and intensity of society's investment (via families, schools, churches, and the mass media) inculcating an internalised commitment to self control will affect the extent to which individuals at risk are willing to postpone gratification, accept as equitable the outcomes of others, and conform to rules.
>
> (Wilson and Herrnstein, 1985: 437)

Sociobiological theories of rape

Probably the most contentious sociobiological criminological theories to emerge in recent years have been those proposed to explain the act of rape. These explore what role, if any, evolutionary-psychological adaptations play in causing the act of rape in animals and humans and are highly controversial, as traditional sociologically-based theories do not consider rape to be a behavioural adaptation. Furthermore, and perhaps not surprisingly, some have objected to such theories on ethical, religious, feminist or political as well as scientific grounds. Evolutionary psychology proposes that human and primate cognition and behaviour should be understood in the context of human and primate evolutionary history.

It has long been observed that some animals appear to show behaviour resembling rape in humans, such as combining sexual intercourse with violent assault, often observed in ducks and geese (Abele and Gilchrist, 1977; Barash, 1977). Sometimes an animal is sexually approached and penetrated while it is clear that it does not want to be but it is not these observations which are controversial but the interpretation of these – and the extension of the theories based on them – to human beings. It is because rape sometimes results in reproduction that some sociobiologists have argued that rape may be genetically advantageous for rapists and thus prospers as a psychological adaptation.

The idea that rape evolved as a genetically advantageous behavioural adaptation was popularised by Thornhill and Palmer (2000) who propose that all human behaviours are, no matter how indirectly, the result of some evolutionary adaptation (see also Thornhill and Thornhill, 1983). They argue that since the human brain itself, and thus all capacities for any kind of action whatsoever, evolved from natural selection, the only point of dispute is whether rape is only a by-product of some other unrelated adaptation – such as a desire for aggression, domination, etc. – or if rape itself is an adaptation favoured because it increases the number of descendants of rapists. It is argued that the latter is true.

Thornhill and Palmer (2000) argue that the underlying motivations of rapists evolved because they were at one time conducive to reproduction and observe that the overwhelming majority of rape victims are of childbearing age and suggest that childbearing ability is involved in the victims chosen by rapists. Women, they argue, have evolutionary-psychological adaptations that protect their genes from would-be rapists and cite a study which claims that victims of childbearing age suffer more emotional trauma from rape than older women. They present this case as evidence consistent with their theory and propose that women beyond their reproductive years have less to lose – in terms of genetic progeny – by being raped.

Thornhill and Palmer (2000) present rape as an evolutionary inclination but they stress that they are doing so primarily to reveal better ways to combat rape and not to excuse rapists in contemporary society. Rape can only be eliminated, they argue, once a society is fully aware of its evolutionary origins and they discuss a range of rape-prevention methods – including chemical castration – and advocate harsher sentences for rapists than those currently used (see also Chavanne and Gallup, 1998).

Many biologists have declared themselves to be strongly opposed to these sociobiological theories of rape and three crucial arguments can be identified. First, it is difficult to determine to what extent the idea of rape can be extended to intercourse in other animal species, as the defining attribute of rape in humans is the lack of informed consent which is a legal condition whereby a person can be said to have given their permission for the act to take place based upon an appreciation and understanding of the facts and implications of any actions. This concept is difficult to determine in other animals and it is thus argued that these theories are founded on anthropomorphic interpretations of animal behavior which means the attribution of a human form, characteristics, or behaviour to non-human things. Second, it is claimed that forced sex in animals is ineffective as a means of reproduction because males will attack other males, or groups of males will attack lone females, killing them in the process. Third, others do not deny the generally observed attempts to control female sexuality and reproduction, but see these as being culturally conditioned, rather than as a product of evolution (Fausto-Sterling, 1992; Travis, 2003).

Recent sociobiological explanations of childhood delinquency

There has been substantial interest among sociobiological researchers in the USA in recent years in antisocial behavior that is seen to emerge early in childhood in some individuals and persists into adulthood. Contributing to that research interest has been the growing evidence that 5–6 per cent of the most persistent offenders are responsible for 50 per cent of known crimes (Aguilar *et al.*, 2000) and that these individuals are difficult – if not impossible – to rehabilitate and most likely to become recidivists (Kazdin, 1987; Moffitt, 1993a). It is argued that identifying risk factors of early antisocial behavior has important implications for improving both intervention and prevention.

Raine (2002) has proposed the development of a biosocial model to account for the contribution of both biologically and environmentally related risk factors in the development of antisocial behaviour. One group of studies that has sought to test this model has focused on perinatal complications and environmental adversity, noting a consistent interaction between the presence of both of these factors and the development of serious antisocial behavior in adulthood (Raine, Brennan and Mednick, 1997; Piquero and Tibbetts, 1999; Arseneault *et al.*, 2002).

Research has suggested that there are multiple risk factors and pathways associated with the development of antisocial behavior during early and middle childhood (Cicchetti and Rogosch, 1996). One such risk factor is the health status of the mother, which when compromised during pregnancy, has been associated with impaired functioning of the central nervous system of the child and subsequent problems in its well-being (Moffitt, 1993a, 1993b). Complications during the prenatal (conception to seventh month of pregnancy) and perinatal (seventh month of pregnancy through to 28 days after birth) periods have been found to be early factors affecting the development of the central nervous system and have been tested individually as predictors of deviant outcomes (see Brennan and Mednick, 1997). The most consistent correlation has been found between complications during the perinatal stage and later antisocial behaviour (Kandel and Mednick, 1991). Direct relations between perinatal complications and antisocial behaviour have not typically been demonstrated (Cohen *et al.*, 1989; Rantakallio, Koiranen and Moettoenen, 1992). However, in the context of family adversity, high levels of perinatal complications have been associated with increased risk of child antisocial behaviour (Drillien, 1964; Werner, Bierman and French, 1971; Broman, Nichols and Kennedy, 1975).

Recent empirical research testing the biosocial interaction hypothesis has clearly suggested that the correlation between perinatal complications and later anti-social behaviour is moderated by environmental adversity (Brennan and Mednick, 1997; Piquero and Tibbetts, 1999; Laucht *et al.*, 2000; Arseneault *et al.*, 2002). In their study of a Danish male birth cohort, Raine, Brennan, and Mednick (1997) found that boys who suffered both perinatal complications and early maternal rejection were most likely to become violent offenders in adulthood. Arseneault *et al.* (2002) also found support for the biosocial model in a low-income sample of 849 boys with their results suggesting that a combination of perinatal complications posing imminent harm to the infant predicted increased rates of physical aggression at ages six to seventeen years when the children were reared in impoverished environments.

A whole body of research has linked aspects of the environment inhabited by the child – such as the quality of parenting and marital conflict – to the development of antisocial behaviour. Several studies suggest that the quality of early parental care – such as unresponsiveness and rejection – plays a significant role in the development of early-onset antisocial behaviour (Campbell, Shaw and Gilliom, 2000; Shaw et al., 2003). Parental responsiveness, sensitivity to social cues and emotional availability are all associated with positive outcomes in young children, such as behavioural regulation and social competence (Martin, 1981; Bost et al., 1998; Wakschlag and Hans, 1999). A lack of parental responsiveness during infancy, however, has been associated with negative outcomes, such as antisocial behaviour later in childhood (Shaw, Keenan and Vondra, 1994a; Shaw et al., 1998b; Wakschlag and Hans, 1999). Parental rejection, the combination of harsh and controlling parenting practices coupled with unacceptance of the child, also has been linked with the development of later antisocial behaviour (Dishion, 1990; Dodge, Pettit and Bates, 1994; Campbell et al., 1996; Younge, Oetting and Deffenbacher, 1996).

A number of studies support a 'cumulative risk hypothesis' wherein the number of environmental stressors rather than the particular combination of stressors has been associated with child behaviour problems both in the short and long-term (Rutter et al., 1975a; Rutter et al., 1975b; Sameroff et al., 1987; Sanson et al., 1991; Shaw et al., 1994b; Shaw et al., 1998a; Deater-Deckard et al., 1998). In what is now widely considered to be a classic study, Rutter and his colleagues (1975a, 1975b) found a dramatic rise in the probability of child adjustment difficulties as the number of family stressors increased. Sameroff et al. (1987) thus tested the impact of three sets of variables on the behaviour of the children in their sample and found that those with high multiple environmental risk scores had much worse outcomes than children with low multiple risk scores.

There thus does seem to be research evidence to demonstrate a close correlation between biological factors, multiple environmental factors, in particular, poor parenting skills, poverty and inadequate living conditions and the onset and persistence of antisocial behaviour. Whether possession of these factors can be legitimately considered to be the fault or responsibility of the family involved – as would be suggested by right realists such as Wilson and Herrnstein (1985) or at least partially the responsibility of wider society and government is considered in the discussion of the left realists in Chapter 16.

Conclusions

Biologically oriented and sociologically oriented criminologists have in the past been in fundamental disagreement. Both have tended to defend their own positions and disciplines while completely refusing to acknowledge those of their adversaries. Increasingly, there has, however, been recognition of the need for biological theories that examine the interaction of sociological, psychological and biological phenomena in the production of criminal behaviour. Vold, Bernard and Snipes (1998: 87) pertinently observe that:

> This emerging synthesis of perspectives will probably benefit biological criminology, since extreme biological views often raise images of determinism among some audiences, who subsequently react negatively to the furthering of such research and to any policies based on it.

In short, the future of biological explanations of crime and criminal behaviour probably only lies in its rejection of its old predestined actor model pretensions and a willingness – however grudgingly – to incorporate notions from the other two models.

Suggested further reading

Jeffery (1977), Mednick (1977) and Mednick, Moffit and Slack (1987) are essential introductory readings for those interested in socio-biology. Wilson and Herrnstein (1985) provide the links between this approach and right realism. Thornhill and Palmer (2000) provide a contentious biosociological argument for rape as an adaptive behaviour for those with interests in that area while Travis (2003) edits a collection of critiques of that argument.

14. Environmental theories

The environmental criminologists Brantingham and Brantingham (1981) have argued that criminal incidents essentially occur when four different dimensions of crime – a law, an offender, a target and a place – are all in concurrence. They describe environmental criminology as the study of the fourth dimension, the study of where and when crimes occur. However, while academic interest in environmental explanations of crime and criminal behaviour has grown considerably since the 1970s, the recognition of the relevance of geographical setting to levels of crime is far from new.

Early environmental theories

The earliest environmental explanations of crime and criminal behaviour appeared during the nineteenth century. In France, Guerry (1833) and Quételet (1842) had analysed conviction rates for crimes committed in different geographical areas and had made a number of important findings. First, they found that crime rates varied greatly in different geographical areas. Second, when violent crimes and property crimes were separated, a further variation in patterning was found. Third, these patterns remained stable over time. Similar studies were carried out in England and these also showed variations in crime rates between different counties, towns and villages (Plint, 1851; Mayhew, 1968 originally 1862).

Mayhew (1968) conducted a study of parts of London and identified the existence of areas – known as 'rookeries' – with a high proportion of criminal residents and, moreover, the tendency of crime levels to persist over time in these areas was confirmed by later studies. In short, the significance of geographical settings to the incidence of crime was confirmed, while, the tendency for spatial patterns to persist suggested an element of predictability and therefore the possibility of adopting preventive policies.

The later Chicago School variant of environmental criminology – that we encountered in Chapter 7 – also proposed that social disorganisation and social pathology tend to be more prevalent in certain geographical areas.

Researchers in that tradition argued that crime and delinquency are transmitted by frequent contact with criminal traditions that have developed over time in disorganised areas of the city (see Shaw and McKay,1972 originally 1931).

British environmental theories

A number of British studies conducted during the 1950s – Mays (1954), Morris (1957), Wootton (1959) – made repeated attempts to explain the relatively high incidence of crime in urban working class areas. What was distinctive about this approach was the attempt to combine three different sociological explanatory perspectives. First, there was the ecological approach that considers why it is that people live where they do. Second, there was the deviant sub-culture approach that considers the development of distinctive life-patterns and their relationship to local and environmental factors. Third, there was the social reaction, or labelling, approach which considers the effects of classifying certain individuals and residential groups as being different or simply bad (Gill, 1977).

In reality, this integrated theoretical perspective had rather unequivocal theoretical foundations in the predestined actor model. The notion that aspects of social disorganisation and anomie characterised the 'criminal areas' led to the familiar determinist tautology that proposed crime to be caused by levels of social pathology already in existence in these areas but this was by no means a simple or crude environmental determinism. It was rendered more 'open' and complex by adding the rational actor model notion of 'free will' to the environmental predestined actor model 'influences' affecting the city, and ordering and disordering its behaviour patterns. In short, from this perspective influences such as the varying indices of social disorganisation are seen to affect group and individual action but in the last resort it is the individuals themselves who decide whether or not to become criminal. Thus, they can choose to disregard the surrounding influences, even if – as Rex and Moore (1967) have shown – there is little real choice over their area of residence in the ecological struggle between the city 'housing classes'.

A summary of the significant features of this post-Second World War reconstitution of the ecological approach to crime in a British context includes the following points. First, there was a modified use of the core Chicago School concept of the 'struggle for space' in studies of city life. Second, the focus of this concept was on studies of housing allocation and 'housing classes', thus in ecological terms the competition and differential access to residential space (Morris, 1957). Third, there was an emphasis on the importance of market situation, race relations and the 'class struggle for housing' in the work of Rex and Moore (1967) in Sparkbrook, Birmingham, a study which broke with the determinism of the Chicago School while still retaining its distinction of differential urban areas.

Fourth, there was the further theoretical refinement of Lambert (1970), who revealed how high crime rates in inner-Birmingham were not primarily instigated by the arrival of new and unemployed black immigrants, but through the activities of the permanent black and white residents. Newcomers merely adjusted the nature of their activities to fit in with those already taking place in the locality. Again, explanations for crime are located in the market for jobs, housing and leisure. The problems culminating in the Bristol, Brixton and Toxteth (Liverpool) disturbances in 1981 provide good examples of this type of explanation.

Fifth, there was the existence by the early 1970s of two further significant theoretical developments. Taylor, Walton and Young (1973) proposed that criminal area delinquency reflects the availability of opportunities/gratifications that exist in particular urban contexts, rather than being a natural outgrowth of the demoralisation of the less able, the biologically inferior or the individually pathological. At the same time, a more dynamic view of culture was being developed where the notions of change, conflict and struggle were coming to replace the static, predestined actor model notion of a social disorganisation-induced 'pathology' disturbing a harmonious and monolithic 'normal' culture.

Sixth, area studies conducted since the mid-1970s show a changed focus on 'the manufacture of neighbourhood reputation', notably in the work by Damer (1974) and Gill (1977). The focus of these studies remains on the housing area and the neighbourhood unit but now includes new notions such as, 'hierarchies of desirability' of housing area 'types' and types of tenant, the ideology of manufactured reputation, as in Damer's (1974) 'dreadful enclosures', and the differential policing of such areas as prime agents in the production of offending behaviour.

These British ecological analyses did not in themselves purport to provide a causal explanation. Morris (1957) thus stresses their importance as a method of calculating the likelihood of offending behaviour taking place in a particular area, while Baldwin and Bottoms (1976) critically observe studies strong on description without providing theoretical explanation. Later North American studies sought a more sophisticated explanation of the geographical distribution of crime and criminals.

North American environmental theories

Brantingham and Brantingham (1981) observe a distinct break between the earlier ecological research and the later environmental criminology which is characterised by at least three shifts in perspective. First, there has been a significant move away from the tendency for academics to keep their research contained within the parameters of their own specific discipline with environmental criminologists now prepared to incorporate techniques and knowledge from different perspectives. Second, there has been a move away from the traditional predestined actor model search for causes of criminal motivation. Environmental criminologists simply assume that some people are criminally motivated with the focus now on the actual criminal event, to find patterns in where, when and how crimes occur. Third, there has been a shift in emphasis away from the sociological imagination to the geographical imagination. This does not mean, however, a simple replacement of the former by the latter but the two are now used together in an attempt to gain a more comprehensive understanding of crimes, and ultimately an increased capacity to control them.

The contemporary field of environmental criminology includes studies of: the spatial patterning of crime at different levels of aggregation; the 'journey to crime', or the processes by which potential offenders recognise potential crime sites and specific opportunities; and the creation and maintenance of areas of criminal residence. Moreover, environmental criminology should not be equated with a crude environmental determinism; rather, the sequence by which potential criminals recognise and act on criminal opportunities is seen as a 'multistaged decision process situated within a more general environmental learning and evaluation process' (Brantingham and Brantingham, 1981: 25).

Contemporary environmental criminology incorporates elements from three theoretical perspectives: first, routine activities theory (Cohen and Felson, 1979); second, rational choice theory (Cornish and Clarke, 1986); and, third, crime pattern theory (Brantingham and Brantingham, 1984). The first two perspectives were both identified as contemporary variants of the rational actor model and were discussed in detail in Chapter 4 and will be briefly revisited here.

Cohen and Felson (1979) developed routine activities theory in order to explain the changing nature of predatory crimes, in particular burglary. They propose that there are three elements necessary for a crime to occur – a motivated offender, a suitable target and the absence of a capable guardian – and these must converge 'in time and space' (Felson and Clarke, 1998). They argue that crime is dependent on the changing routine activities of victims and changes to the durability and manufacture of products; for example, televisions, computers and stereos have become commonplace in most homes as they are manufactured in large quantities and readily available to consumers. Moreover, these products have become more attractive targets because they are lighter and easier to steal, for example, during the 1970s a computer occupied an entire room whereas in the early twenty-first century, a laptop computer with more power than its predecessor can be easily carried. At the same time, the changing routine activities of people in the last quarter of the twentieth century – for example, women entering the workforce in unprecedented numbers which has left a great number of homes unoccupied during the day – has led to a temporal change in the distribution of burglary and this has now become a daytime rather night-time phenomenon.

Felson and Clarke (1998: 7) explain that 'the rational choice perspective focuses upon the offender's decision making. Its main assumption being that offending is purposive behavior, designed to benefit the offender in some way'. The emphasis is on the need to consider the cost-benefit analysis process of the offender although it is recognised that the decisions reached are not often purely rational because offenders do not factor in all possible risks, relative to rewards, involved in committing a criminal act. There is a long tradition of ethnographic research that has focused on this issue and the recognition that offenders use limited risk cues has led some researchers to propose that offenders operate in terms of a constrained or limited rationality invariably heavily influenced by illicit drugs and alcohol use (Bennett and Wright, 1984; Cromwell, Olson and Avary, 1991; Feeney, 1999; Jacobs, 2000; Wright and Decker, 1997).

Although offenders demonstrate a limited form of rationality in the planning and execution of their offences – for example, many offenders are opportunists – there is much research to support the proposition that they do develop and utilise cues and crime templates in the selection of targets/victims (Brantingham and Brantingham, 1978, 1981; Bennett and Wright, 1984; Cromwell, Olsen and Avary, 1991; Wright and Decker, 1997; Feeney, 1999; Jacobs, 2000).

Brantingham and Brantingham (1978) propose a five-part model of victim selection. First, offenders undertake a 'multi-staged decision process which seeks out and identifies, within the general environment, a target or victim positioned in time and space' (1978: 107). Second, the cues used to make these decisions are taken from the environment in which an offender is operating. Third, an offender uses these cues for target selection and these are learned 'through experience' or 'social transmission' from other experienced offenders. Fourth, through experience, an offender develops 'individual cues, clusters of cues, and sequences of cues associated with "good" targets' (1978: 108) and these develop into crime templates. Crime targets are accepted when they correspond strongly to a crime template. Fifth, although a single offender may possess a multitude of crime selection templates, 'once the template is established, it becomes relatively fixed and influences future searching behaviour' (1978: 107).

Much of the research dedicated to the understanding of cue and template use in target selection has focused on robbery offenders (Wright and Decker, 1997; Feeney, 1999; Jacobs, 2000) and burglary offenders (Bennett and Wright, 1984; Cromwell, Olsen and Avary, 1991). Research on robbery shows that repeat offenders prefer to select targets that are vulnerable, have an outward appearance that indicates the highest potential pay-off and are in specific density areas with good escape routes (Wright and Decker, 1997). Burglary research shows that burglars use similar cues when selecting a residence to victimise. Cromwell, Olsen and Avary (1991: 40) found that the burglars in their study used cues 'to indicate the surveillability of the target', used occupancy probes to avoid personal contact, a substantial proportion preferred to burgle a residence during the day – to avoid personal contact – and they used cues that signified 'the degree of difficulty that might be expected' in entering a home. Although these ethnographic studies indicate that offenders use cues and develop crime templates for victim/target selection, it is shown that offenders rarely incorporate all preferred cues. Instead, due to drug use and cash-intensive lifestyles, offenders chose victims that 'appeared to meet their minimal subjective criteria for an acceptable victim' (Wright and Decker, 1997: 87–8).

Crime Pattern Theory was originally developed by Brantingham and Brantingham (1984) and proposes that crime is the result of the interaction of people – both offenders and potential victims – and movement in the urban landscape in space or time. The researchers note that different crime types, offenders and victims/targets are not evenly distributed across the urban landscape in space or time and the importance of zoning and population flows in a city is observed. Thus, offenders interested in commercial burglary have a limited area to search for suitable attractive establishments, as these tend to cluster along major transportation routes in commercial zones. Moreover, offenders must take time into account as shops have definitive hours of operation which determine when a target will be left unguarded.

Brantingham and Brantingham (1984) emphasise three interrelated concepts to explain the pattern of personal and property crimes and these focus on the movement patterns of both potential victims and offenders. First, *activity nodes* are centres of high activity where individuals 'spend the majority of their time', such as, the home, school, work, places of entertainment and shopping areas (Brantingham and Brantingham, 1998: 36). Second, *pathways* are the routes that connect the activity nodes of a person, such as, streets, pavements or sidewalks and footpaths that may be travelled by foot, public transport or automobile. As people travel these paths from activity nodes with some regularity, the 'paths and narrow areas surrounding them become known spaces to the people who travel them' (1998: 36). Third, an *edge* is a boundary that cannot easily be traversed and this can be both physical and perceptual. A physical edge includes rivers, forests and bridges. A perceptual edge includes areas that people are afraid of, such as, a rival gang territory or areas with a large discrepancy in socio-economic status, for example, a middle class person may experience discomfort when entering high crime inner city areas, while conversely, an inner city offender might wish to target lucrative targets in affluent areas, but generally would not venture into such localities because anonymity is absent (Brantingham and Brantingham, 1995).

These three concepts interact to form what Brantingham and Brantingham refer to as an awareness space, or cognitive map, where people – offender and non-offender – feel most comfortable because they have intimate knowledge of the area. This is the case with offenders and non-offenders. Crime pattern theory predicts that all else being equal, offenders will commit crimes in their awareness spaces, either along a path, along an edge or around an activity node. An offender who commits offences outside their awareness space runs the risk of becoming lost because they are not familiar with escape routes, they are unaware of the location of attractive targets and they would have to devote much time and attention to the routines of guardians. All these tasks are accomplished by committing crimes within the awareness space of an offender because this knowledge is developed through their daily routines.

Contemporary environmental criminology has focused its attention on repeat or chronic offenders who research has shown commit a disproportionate amount of crime (Cromwell, Olsen and Avary, 1991; Horney and Marshall, 1991; Wright and Decker, 1997) while studies indicate that some offenders develop a preference for certain offences (Cromwell, Olsen and Avary, 1991; Wright and Decker, 1997; Schwaner, 2000). These findings are significant for environmental criminologists because it is proposed that these offenders have the most developed and fixed crime templates for target selection. Moreover, by targeting law enforcement resources on these offenders, it should be possible to significantly increase detection rates.

Environmental criminologists have found that certain places experience a disproportionate amount of crime (Sherman, Gartin and Buerger, 1989; Brantingham and Brantingham, 1995; Spelman, 1995). Spelman (1995: 142) found that 'the worst 10 per cent of locations reliably account for some 30 per cent of all calls' for police service. Brantingham and Brantingham (1995) refer to places with a disproportionate level of criminal activity as crime generators and crime attractors. *Crime generators* are places or areas 'to which large numbers of people are attracted for reasons unrelated to any particular level of criminal motivation they might have or to any particular crime they might end up committing' (Brantingham and Brantingham, 1995: 7). These areas or places 'produce crime by creating particular times and places that provide appropriate concentrations of people and other targets in settings that are conducive to particular types of criminal acts' (1995: 7). Examples include the development of new rapid transit routes and stations, the opening of a new bar or new shopping centre. *Crime attractors*, on the other hand, 'are particular places, areas, neighborhoods, districts which present well-known criminal opportunities to which strongly motivated intending criminal offenders are attracted because of the known opportunities for particular types of crime' (1995: 8). These places or areas include inner city ghettos and the opening of a needle exchange clinic in a high crime area. Often the difference between these two concepts is blurred. However, the major differentiator is that a crime generator produces crime in an area that was absent prior to the establishment of the place, while a crime attractor intensifies criminal activities already present in a particular area.

The concepts of environmental criminology have significantly informed crime mapping and analysis which has become increasingly central to the work of the police service and analogous agencies during the past 30 years. In the early days, most agencies used maps with coloured pins to visualise individual crime events and crime plagued areas. Today, with the rapid advancement of technology, computer-based techniques for exploring, visualising and explaining the occurrences of criminal activity have been essential. One of the more influential tools facilitating exploration of the spatial distribution of crime has been Geographical Information Systems or GIS (Ratcliffe and McCullagh, 1999; Harries, 1999). Murray *et al.* (2001) observe that it is the ability to combine spatial information with other data that makes GIS so valuable. Moreover, the considerable quantity of information available to most analysts necessitates an intelligent computational system, able to integrate a wide variety of data and facilitate the identification of patterns with minimal effort.

The research cited above indicates that certain areas are more prone to higher concentrations of crime than others. Widely labelled as 'hot spots', such areas are often targets of increased resources from law enforcement agencies in an effort to reduce crime. The identification of hot spots is helpful because most police departments have limited resources and the ability to prioritise intervention through a geographic lens is appealing (Levine, 1999).

Operationally, the delineation of hot spot boundaries is somewhat arbitrary. Levine (1999) notes that crime density is measured over a continuous area and the boundaries separating hot spots of crime from areas without enough activity to merit that label are perceptual constructs. Moreover, depending on the scale of geographic analysis, a hot spot can mean very different things (Harries, 1999).

Recent studies by the Crime Mapping Research Center at the National Institute of Justice in the USA categorise hot spot detection and methods of analysis as follows: *visual interpretation, choropleth mapping, grid cell analysis, spatial autocorrelation, and cluster analysis.* Furthermore, twelve different variations on the five classes of hot spot identification techniques were systematically documented and evaluated. However, while there are a variety of methods for detecting hot spots in crime event data, no single approach has been found to be superior to others. What has become apparent is that combining cartographic visualisation of crime events with statistical tools provides valuable insights.

Environmental design

Closely linked with environmental criminology are the notions of environmental design and environmental management. It is through the work of writers like Jane Jacobs (1961), Oscar Newman (1972, 1976) and C. Ray Jeffery (1977) that the concept of preventing crime through environmental design was to become influential. These various writers propose that the nature of the built environment can affect the level of crime both by influencing potential offenders and by affecting the ability of a person to exercise control over their surroundings. There is essentially a powerful belief in the capacity of surveillance to help control crime.

Jane Jacobs (1961) was the first person to propose a new way of looking at the relationship between the physical environment and crime and her work was essentially an attack on the urban planning practices in the USA during the 1950s such as the urban renewal and slum clearance programmes which she perceived to be the unnecessary destruction of a number of the older urban neighbourhoods. Jacobs argued that these structures provided a number of natural security techniques – such as being close to the street, with porches and street level windows – that could be useful for enabling a sense of community and social bonding. She argued that the removal of such structures would decrease the social interaction, the ability to identify strangers and the overall sense of security felt by inhabitants.

Oscar Newman (1972, 1976) likewise suggests that part of the explanation for urban crime lies in a breakdown of the social mechanisms that once kept crime in check, while the inability of communities to come together in collective action hampers crime prevention. In his study of low-cost housing projects in New York City he found that higher crime rates were associated with high-rise apartment buildings rather than those with three or five storeys in comparable social settings. In the former, 55 per cent of the crimes were committed in interior public spaces, such as, hallways, lifts, stairwells and lobbies, as opposed to only 17 per cent in the low-rise buildings (Newman, 1972). The proposed solution was to restructure 'the residential environments of our cities so they can again become liveable and controlled ... not by the police but by a community of people sharing a common terrain' (Newman, 1976: 2).

Newman advocated action to foster (i) territoriality, (ii) natural surveillance, (iii) a safe image and (iv) a protected milieu. First, the notion of *territoriality* is defined as the 'capacity of the physical environment to create perceived zones of influence' (Newman, 1976: 51) and, that is, the ability and desire of legitimate users to claim control of an area. It is claimed that the design of buildings and their sites can encourage residents to adopt ownership attitudes, and also that certain layouts inform outsiders that particular areas are for the private use of residents. Newman argues that such design features as narrowed street entrances – real and psychological boundaries – and the use of cul-de-sacs to project a 'private' image, can enhance the environment. The use of raised, coloured paving on residential streets provides such an example. Territoriality is diminished by the existence of public thoroughfares and open spaces that provide access to and from residential areas while giving the impression that they are owned and cared for by nobody.

Second, design features such as overlooked entrance lobbies and well-placed windows, which allow residents to identify and observe strangers, provide *natural surveillance*. Newman urged the avoidance of high-rise blocks to which outsiders can gain easy access, and enclosed entrances where offenders can operate unseen.

Third, the *safe image* good design should seek to convey an impression of a safe and invulnerable neighbourhood in which residents know and look after each other. Where the distinctive image is negative 'the project will be stigmatised and its residents castigated and victimised' (Newman, 1976: 102). It is suggested that public sector housing is particularly affected because such estates or projects are designed to stand out. This image combines with other design features that reduce territoriality and surveillance opportunities and with the socio-economic characteristics of the population to make this type of housing particularly vulnerable to crime.

Fourth, a *safe milieu* is a neighbourhood situated in the middle of a wider crime-free area, which is thus insulated from the outside world by a 'moat' of safety. Jacobs (1961) had suggested that residential areas should be sited alongside commercial areas in the expectation of enhancing safety because of increased activity. Newman (1976: 112) argued that the success of a particular mixture of land uses 'depends as much on the degree to which residents can identify with and survey activity in the related facility as it does on the nature of the users of that facility and the activities they indulge in'.

Attempts by researchers to evaluate the effectiveness of the 'defensible space' thesis have often proved problematic because environmental design usually involves the simultaneous implementation of a number of measures. One initiative that was tested – in Hartford, Connecticut – featured enhanced police patrols and citizen mobilisation as well as design improvements. Large reductions in the relative rates of burglary and robbery were achieved in the redesigned area (Fowler, McCall and Mangione, 1979), but a follow-up study found that the effects of the scheme on offence rates were short-lived (Fowler and Mangione, 1982).

Other studies have found even less support for the effectiveness of environmental design schemes (Evans, Fyfe and Herbert, 1992). Merry (1981), for example, has noted that the advantages of 'defensible space' are largely dependent on the residents who must report or challenge strangers. Thus, in order to reduce crime, 'defensible' space must actually be defended.

Other features of environmental design may have a secondary impact on crime. Traffic calming measures, increasingly seen in residential areas, prevent a quick exit for offenders as well as giving the impression of ownership. Moreover, systems of barriers and one-way schemes to prevent traffic using residential areas as short cuts have the same effect. They also reduce easy and casual access to the area and reduce the chance that a burglar, for example, will select a house in the area while passing through.

The idea of offenders being products of their environment has – as we have seen – firm foundations in the predestined actor model but it has enjoyed a renaissance through collaboration between 'routine activity theorists' and rational choice/opportunity theorists located theoretically within the rational actor tradition (Felson, 1998). Brantingham and Brantingham have commented extensively on Canadian experiments that have sought to curb crime through environmental design and have noted – as we have seen above – that many of these initiatives have stemmed from the observation that people travelling from one place to another, normally between home, school/work and place of entertainment commit much crime.

Similar to environmental design is the notion of Design Against Crime (DAC) which as an approach to innovation emerged at the University of the Arts London during the first decade of this century. DAC has four stated aims. First, to reduce the incidence and adverse consequences of crime through the design of products, services, communications and environments which are 'fit for the purpose' and that are contextually appropriate in all other respects. Second, equip design practitioners with the cognitive and practical tools and resources to design out crime. Third, prove and promote the social and commercial benefits of designing out crime to manufacturing and service industries, as well as to local and national government, and society at large. Fourth, to address environmental complicity with crime in the built environment and to reduce crime and improve individual and community well-being.

DAC thus brings together designers, researchers, criminologists, manufacturers, the police and other stakeholders to design out opportunities for crime and is theoretically informed by the notions of situational crime prevention and opportunity theory which considers 'opportunities' (linked to objects/ environments and sources as well as users and abusers) to be among the main explanations of crime (Felson and Clarke, 1998). Closely linked to these notions are the recent 'hot products' theory (Clarke, 1999).

Clarke (1999) had argued that significant benefits for crime prevention could arise from focusing policy and research attention on 'hot products' or those items that are most likely to be stolen by criminals, which he observes include not just manufactured goods, but also food, animals and works of art. The ultimate hot product is nevertheless cash which helps determine the distribution of many kinds of theft, including commercial robberies, muggings, burglaries and thefts from ticket machines and public phone boxes. Clarke argues that a better understanding, of which products are 'hot', and why, would help businesses protect themselves from theft and would help the police in advising them how to do this. It would help governments in seeking to persuade business and industry to protect their property or to think about ways of avoiding the crime waves that are sometimes generated by new products and illegal use of certain drugs. It would furthermore help consumers avoid purchasing items (such as particular models of car) that put them at risk of theft and might well lead them to demand greater built-in security. Finally, improved understanding of hot products would assist police in thinking about ways to intervene effectively in markets for stolen goods.

Clarke (1999) conducted a review of the most stolen items for a variety of theft types and this led to some important conclusions. First, for each kind of theft, specific items are consistently chosen by criminals. In residential burglaries, for example, criminals are most likely to pick jewellery, videos, cash, stereos and televisions. In shoplifting, the items at risk depend on the store but bookshops in the USA were most likely at the time to lose magazines and cassette tapes, while groceries, supermarkets and convenience stores were most likely to lose cigarettes, video tapes, beauty aids and non-prescription medicines. Second, there was some consistency across the different settings in the goods stolen. Certain items were at risk of being shoplifted wherever they were sold and these included cassettes, cigarettes, alcoholic drinks, and fashion items such as Hilfiger jeans and Nike training shoes. Third, the type of car which is most likely to be stolen will depend on the motivation for the theft. Thus, 'joyriders' (or 'twockers' in the British context) tend to prefer sporty models. Those criminals stealing cars to sell prefer expensive luxury models. Offenders, who were looking to steal components to sell, preferred models with easily-removable, good-quality, radios. Fourth, vehicle body-type helped determine which commercial vehicles were stolen. Vehicles used by the construction industry, such as tippers, seemed to be particularly at risk which might well be the result of a thriving second-hand market, which would make these vehicles easier for thieves to sell. Fifth, it was concluded that relatively few hot products may account for a large proportion of all thefts. For example, theft insurance claims for new cars in the USA were twenty times higher for models with the worst theft record than those with the best. Clarke (1999) observes that policymakers need research assistance help in anticipating and assessing technological developments that could result in new hot products and new ways of preventing theft. Moreover, the existence of large quantities of unprotected attractive property might both encourage habitual thieves to steal more, and tempt more people to try their hands at theft. If theft is made easy, there is likely to be more of it, and making it more difficult may lead to a more orderly, law-abiding society.

Environmental management

The concept of 'environmental management' rests largely on the premise that – apart from encouraging offending by their 'indefensibility' – certain districts may suffer simply because they give the impression that their residents no longer care. The difference between environmental design and environmental management is subtle but nevertheless important. The former requires implementation at the planning stage, before a district is built or developed while the latter can be practised on an existing neighbourhood and also commercial environments where there is less prospect of using informal surveillance.

Essentially, the theory that informs the notion of environmental management proposes that evidence that crime has been committed, if allowed to remain in place, will lead to further offences being committed. The argument is applied especially to such offences as vandalism, public drunkenness, vagrancy and begging: offences which are collectively known as 'incivilities'. Wilson and Kelling (1982: 3) describe the problem as witnessed in urban America in their 'broken windows' thesis:

> A piece of property is abandoned, weeds grow up, and a window is smashed. Adults stop scolding rowdy children; the children, emboldened, become more rowdy. Families move out, unmarried adults move in. Teenagers gather in front of the corner store. The merchant asks them to move, they refuse. Fights occur. Litter accumulates. People start drinking in front of the grocery store, in time; an inebriate drunkard slumps to the sidewalk and is allowed to sleep it off. Pedestrians are approached by panhandlers.
>
> (Wilson and Kelling, 1982: 32)

Incivilities, according to this hypothesis, lead to crime, the evidence of which causes further incivilities. Environmental management involves striving to remove the evidence of incivilities by, for example, cleaning up graffiti and other signs of vandalism, cleaning the streets and avoiding property falling into decay. This thesis has relevance beyond residential areas, for example, refusing to allow its effects to accumulate could reduce vandalism in schools (Knights, 1998). The attraction of broken windows theory has been its plausibility. In fact, it is so plausible that it has been accepted despite very little research support. One study, nevertheless, suggested that the immediate removal of graffiti from subway cars in New York deprived the 'artists' of the expressive benefits of seeing their work travelling around the system, and substantially reduced the problem (Felson, 1998).

Matthews (1992) questions whether the Wilson and Kelling hypothesis should have been so readily accepted and observes that, according to British Crime Survey data, incivilities such as drunks, beggars, litter and vandalism seem to be linked more to the fear of crime than its actuality. He also notes that some inner-city areas have attracted young professional people searching for an exciting and vibrant place in which to live, with street musicians and performers, noisy bars and the other trappings of inner-city life being as attractive to some people as they are a cause of fear to others.

Hopkins Burke (1998c, 2000) nevertheless notes the ambiguity surrounding the issue of street incivilities. Beggars invariably choose specific urban areas where their close proximity to the public enables them to use tacit intimidation as an aid to their activities and different groups undoubtedly differentially receive the resultant aura of menace. Old people may be fearful and genuinely scared while cosmopolitan young professionals might consider it to be just a colourful segment of the rich tapestry of life. Likewise drunken vagrants gathered menacingly in a bus shelter may force by their presence – albeit silently – young mothers with pushchairs outside into the rain. Those openly urinating in the street after a hard day's drinking in the full view of mothers collecting their young children from a nearby nursery should surely experience some regulation, management and restriction placed upon their activities (Hopkins Burke, 1998c). Radical proponents of the victimised actor model would recognise that these people are among the poorest and disadvantaged people in society and are invariably targeted by agents of the criminal justice system; on the other hand the wider public surely deserve some protection from their more antisocial activities. This latter 'left realist' perspective is revisited in Chapter 16.

Broken windows theory was to become very influential in the introduction and implementation of 'zero tolerance' and 'problem-oriented policing' with the former receiving considerable attention from politicians and the media both in the USA and the UK during the last years of the twentieth century. This version of 'broken windows' theory proposed that the police can arrest a tendency towards serious criminal behaviour in a neighbourhood by proactively and assertively confronting antisocial behaviour, minor offenders and 'quality of life' offences (Hopkins Burke, 1998b) but was to go out of favour in most constituencies because of identified difficulties in sustaining hard-line strategies in the long-term (Hopkins Burke, 2002).

Problem-oriented policing (POP) is an altogether more subtle and sustainable policing strategy which requires police forces to analyse the problems that they are routinely called upon to deal with and to devise more effective ways to respond to them. It was first introduced by Herman Goldstein (1977, 1979) during the 1970s and developed during the 1990s (Goldstein, 1990) who argued most influentially for the replacement of the reactive, law enforcement based model of police work by proactive 'bottom-up' approaches which emphasise tackling the underlying conditions which create the problems that the police have to deal with. Police forces should thus analyse patterns of crime incident clusters to identify underlying causes and problems and formulate appropriate responses most successfully in partnership with other criminal justice, welfare and voluntary groups in the locality (Leigh, Read and Tilley, 1998).

Suggested further reading

Key texts in environmental criminology are Brantingham and Brantingham

(1981, 1984), Jacobs (1961), Jeffery (1977) and Newman (1972, 1976). Felson (1998) provides links between this approach and routine activities theory. Wilson and Kelling (1982) provide a classic text on environmental criminology with a left realist critique from Matthews (1992). Hopkins Burke (1998c, 2000) discusses this approach in terms of the policing of begging and vagrancy. Ekblom (2005) provides a good introduction to designing products against crime. Hopkins Burke (1998a, 2004a) provides comprehensive discussions of 'zero tolerance' policing and Leigh, Read and Tilley (1998) a good introduction to 'problem-oriented' policing in practice.

15. Social control theories

Social control theories of crime and criminal behaviour have a long and distinguished pedigree with strong foundations in both the rational actor and predestined actor models of crime and criminal behaviour. Later variants have entailed explicit attempts to integrate notions from both models while even more recently elements from the victimised actor model have been incorporated.

The origins of social control theories

The origins of – or at least the underlying assumptions on – which social control theories are founded can be traced back to the work of Hobbes (1968 originally 1651) in the rational actor tradition, Freud (1927) and Durkheim (1951 originally 1897) from respectively the psychological and sociological variants of the predestined actor model.

Hobbes had been concerned with the apparent incompatibility between human nature and the notion of legal restraint. The answer to his question, 'why do men obey the rules of society?' was however simple enough. 'Fear ... it is the only thing, when there is appearance of profit or pleasure by breaking the laws that makes men keep them' (Hobbes, 1968: 247).

One of the central ideas of Freud that deviant impulses arise naturally when the id is not sufficiently constrained by the other components of the personality, the ego and superego, is also apparent in much of the work on control theory. This is particularly true of those earlier models that draw more explicitly on psychological rather than sociological factors (Reiss, 1951; Nye, 1958; Reckless, 1961).

The roots of the more sociologically oriented control theories can be found partly in the work of Durkheim (1951) who had argued that needs, desires or aspirations arise naturally within the individual; are unlimited and restrained only by the socialised moral norms of a given society. At the same time, it is society itself that creates needs and ambitions that are incapable of realisation in the particular social framework of the time. Merton (1938) later developed this idea in his analysis of *anomie* as a cause of crime.

Social control theory is fundamentally derived from a conception of human nature that proposes that there are no natural limits on elementary human needs and desires. People will always want and seek further economic reward and it is thus not necessary to look for special motives for engaging in criminal activity. Human beings are born free to break the law and will only refrain from doing so under particular circumstances. It is these fundamental assumptions that provide the foundations of later social control theories.

Most of the explanations of crime and criminal behaviour that we have encountered previously in this book view conformity as the normal or natural state of humanity. Criminal behaviour is simply abnormal. It is this orthodox way of thinking about crime that social control theory seeks to challenge. Therefore, in taking deviance for granted and treating conformity as problematic, social control theory offers not so much a theory of *deviance* but one of *conformity*. The central question asked is not the usual, 'why do some people commit crimes?' but rather, 'why do most of us conform?'

The unifying factor in the different versions of control theory is thus the assumption that crime and deviance is only to be expected when social and personal controls are in some way inadequate. Primacy is given to relationships, commitments, values, norms and beliefs that, it is proposed, explain why people do not break laws, in contrast to those theories we have seen in this book that accord primacy to motivating forces thought to explain why people do break laws. From this perspective it is thus recognised that lawbreaking is often the most immediate source of gratification or conflict resolution, and that no special motivation is required to explain such behaviour. Human beings are active, flexible organisms who will engage in a wide selection of activities, unless the range is limited by processes of socialisation and social learning

Some writers in the rational actor tradition, for example Hobbes (1588–1678) and Bentham (1748–1832) had viewed human nature in general as essentially amoral and self-serving but later social control theories do not, on the whole, depict people in this way. They merely reject the underlying assumption contained in many of the theories discussed earlier in this book – for example, anomie and subcultural theories – that people are basically moral as a result of having internalised pro-social norms and values during socialisation.

Because they remove the assumption of morality and the positively socialised individual, control theories are not dependent on explanations such as 'relative deprivation', 'blocked opportunities', 'alienation' or 'status-frustration' to account for the motivated deviant. Crime is seen as a product of the weaknesses of the forces restraining the individual rather than of the strength of the impulse to deviate. It is the *absence* of control and the fact that delinquent or criminal behaviour 'usually results in quicker achievement of goals than normative behaviour' that leaves the individual free to calculate the costs of crime (Hirschi, 1969). Again, the influence of the rational actor model is apparent in this core idea of the 'rational' individual choosing crime only after a careful appraisal of the costs and benefits of such activity.

Early social control theories

It was observed above that social control theories draw on both social and psychological factors in order to explain conformity and deviance. Probably the earliest sociological control theory was Durkheim's theory of anomie where it is proposed that inadequate forms of social control are more likely during periods of rapid modernisation and social change because new forms of regulation cannot evolve quickly enough to replace the declining force of social integration. The outcome is *anomie* – or even the complete collapse of social solidarity – when the insatiable desires and aspirations of individuals can no longer be adequately regulated or controlled by society.

Many of Durkheim's central concerns and ideas were also present in the work of the Chicago School – particularly in its use of the concept of social disorganisation – and itself a theoretical perspective that influenced many of the later theories encountered in this book. There have nevertheless been fundamental differences in how these different theorists have used the concept. For example, anomie theorists argued that social disorganisation generates pressure, which in turn, *produces* crime and deviance (a predestined actor model argument). Social control theorists, on the other hand, consider that social disorganisation causes a weakening of social control, making crime and deviance more *possible* (a rational actor model argument).

The early control theories reviewed in the remainder of this section attach much more importance to psychological factors in their analysis of deviance and conformity. Albert Reiss (1951) thus distinguished between the effects of 'personal' control and 'social' control proposing that the former comes about when individuals internalise the norms and rules of non-deviant primary groups to such an extent that they become their own. The latter are founded in the ability of social groups or institutions to make rules or norms effective. Thus, conformity derived from social control tends to involve mere submission to the norms in question and does not necessarily require the internalisation of these within the value system of the individual. Reiss tested his theory on 1,110 children between the ages of eleven and seventeen who were subject to probation orders and found that personal controls were much more important in preventing deviance than social controls. He did not specify the specific control mechanisms which lead to conformity but did identify the failure of such primary groups as the family to provide reinforcement for non-delinquent roles and values as being crucial to the explanation of delinquency. His perspective was nevertheless true to control theory logic in that no specific motivational sources leading to delinquency were identified.

Jackson Toby (1957) argued that the adolescent without commitment to conventional society is a candidate for 'gang socialisation' which he acknowledged to be part of the causal, motivational, dynamic leading to delinquency, but introduced the concept of 'stakes in conformity' to explain 'candidacy' for such learning experiences. Thus, young people who had few stakes or investments in conformity were more likely to be drawn into gang activity than those who had more to lose. A variety of conventional social relationships and commitments could be jeopardised by involvement in delinquency and thus young people without such stakes were free to be recruited into gangs. This notion of 'stakes in conformity' was to be similar to concepts developed in later versions of social control theory.

Ivan Nye (1958) developed a much more systematic version of control theory and in attempting to locate and identify the factors that encourage conformity in adolescents, he focused on the family, which, because of the affectional bonds established between members, were considered to be the most important mechanism of social control. He identified four modes of social control generated by the family. First, *direct control* is imposed through external forces such as parents, teachers and the police using direct restraint and punishment. Second, individuals themselves in the absence of external regulation exercise *internalised control*. Third, *indirect control* is dependent upon the degree of affection that an individual has for conventional significant others. Fourth, *control through alternative means of needs satisfaction* works by reducing the temptation for individuals to resort to illegitimate means of needs satisfaction. Though independent of each other, these four modes of control were considered mutually reinforcing and to work more effectively in tandem. The focus on the family as a source of control was in marked contrast to the emphasis on economic circumstances as a source of criminogenic motivation at the time. Although he acknowledged motivational forces by stating that '*some* delinquent behaviour results from a *combination* of positive learning and weak and ineffective social control', he nevertheless adopts a control-theory position when he proposes that 'most delinquent behaviour is the result of insufficient social control' (Nye, 1958: 4). Hirschi (1969) was critical of Nye's use of concepts such as internal control, but (together with Gottfredson [Gottfredson and Hirschi, 1990]) was to propose 'self-control' as a key explanatory variable over 30 years later. Nye's work was the first major presentation of research from a social control perspective and most of his findings were to be found consistent with subsequent research using survey data.

Walter Reckless's (1967) containment theory sought to explain why – despite the various 'push' and 'pull' factors that may tempt individuals into criminal behaviour – for example, psychological factors such as restlessness or aggression, or adverse social conditions such as poverty and unemployment – most people resist these pressures and remain law-abiding citizens. Reckless argued that a combination of control factors, both internal and external to the individual, serve as insulators or 'containments' against these 'push' and 'pull' factors. The factors involved in outer containment were identified as being a) reasonable limits and expectations, b) meaningful roles and activities, and c) several complementary variables, such as, a sense of belonging and identity, supportive relationships especially in the family and adequate discipline.

Reckless nevertheless attached much more importance to factors in inner containment as he argued that these would tend to control the individual irrespective of the extent to which the external environment changed. Four key components of inner containment were identified. First, individuals with a strong and favourable *self-concept* are better insulated against those 'push' and 'pull' factors that encourage involvement in criminal activity. Second, *goal orientation* is the extent to which the individual has a clear direction in life oriented towards the achievement of legitimate goals such as educational and occupational success. Third, *frustration tolerance* is where contemporary society – with its emphasis on individualism and immediate gratification – might generate considerable frustration and, moreover, individuals were observed to have different capacities for coping with this factor. Fourth, *norm retention* is the extent to which individuals accept, internalise and are committed to conventional laws, norms, values and rules and the institutions that represent and uphold these. Reckless described the process, by which norm retention is undermined, thus making deviance more possible, as one of norm erosion which involves 'alienation from, emancipation from, withdrawal of legitimacy from and neutralisation of formerly internalised ethics, morals, laws and values' (Reckless, 1967: 476).

This idea of individuals being able to neutralise formerly internalised norms and values to facilitate deviant or offending behaviour had been a prominent element in Matza's drift theory (see Chapter 7) where it was proposed that delinquent youth were 'neither compelled nor committed to' their offending activities but were 'partially unreceptive to other more conventional traditions' (Matza, 1964: 28). In short, delinquent youth could be depicted as 'drifters' who were relatively free to take part in offending behaviour and this was to become a significant challenge to other theories in the 1960s which emphasised status frustration and the adoption of oppositional values by delinquent youth. Matza proposed in contrast to the previous orthodox determinism that the delinquent merely 'flirts' with criminal and conventional behaviour while drifting among different social worlds. No specific constraints or controls were identified that keep young people from drifting, but those that did do were those who have few stakes in conformity and are free to drift into delinquency.

Scott Briar and Irving Piliavin (1965) presented one of the clearest statements of control theory rationale and they specifically challenged other theoretical perspectives of the 1960s by emphasising transitory, situational inducements as the motivating forces for involvement in delinquency in contrast to deviant subcultural or contracultural value systems and socially structured status problems. They found that motivation did not differentiate delinquent and non-delinquent young people as much as variable commitments to conformity and argued that the 'central process of social control' was 'commitments to conformity' and they included fear of material deprivations if apprehended, self-image, valued relationships, current and future statuses and activities. In his version of social control theory to which we now turn our attention, Hirschi (1969) was to limit the concept of commitment to the rational and emotional investments that people make in the pursuit of shared cultural goals

Later control theories

Travis Hirschi (1969) made the most influential contribution to the development of later social control theory and asserts that at their simplest level all share the assumption that 'delinquent acts result when an individual's bond to society is weak or broken (Hirschi, 1969: 16). He identified four elements of the social bond: *attachment, commitment, involvement* and *belief* but unlike other control theorists who had emphasised the internal psychological dimension of control, these terms were employed in a much more sociological sense. The idea that norms and attitudes can be so deeply internalised as to constitute part of the personality is simply rejected and an individual's bonds to conventional society are much more superficial and precarious.

First, *attachment* refers to the capacity of individuals to form effective relationships with other people and institutions, in the case of adolescents, with their parents, peers and school. When these attachments are sufficiently strong, individuals are more likely to be concerned with the opinions and expectations of others and thus more likely to behave in accordance with them. Since this bond of attachment is considered by Hirschi to lie not in some psychological 'inner state', but in ongoing social relationships with significant others, the strength of these attachments can and may vary over time.

Second, *commitment* refers to the social investments made by the individual to conventional lines of action that could be put at risk by engaging in deviant behaviour. This is essentially a rational actor model cost–benefit type of argument where it is proposed that those investing most in conventional social life have a greater stake in conformity, and thus most to lose by breaking the rules. Third, *involvement* again refers not to some psychological or emotional state but to the more mundane reality that a person may be too busy doing conventional things to find time to engage in deviant activities. Fourth, *beliefs* are not – as we might expect – a set of deeply held convictions but rather a set of impressions and convictions in need of constant reinforcement. In this context, beliefs are closely bound up with – and dependent upon – the pattern and strength of attachments an individual has with other people and institutions. These four variables, though independent, are also highly interrelated and are theoretically given equal weight: each helps to prevent law-breaking activities in most people.

For many the main strength of Hirschi's work is empirical rather than theoretical (see Box, 1981; Downes and Rock, 1998). This view tends to be based on the results of a large-scale study conducted by Hirschi of over 4,000 adolescents from mixed social and ethnic backgrounds where a variety of propositions derived from control, strain and cultural diversity theories were tested and for the most part it was the control variables that appeared to correlate most closely and consistently with offending behaviour. Hirschi's data indicates that the closer a relationship a child enjoyed with its parents, the more it is attached to and identifies with them, the lesser the likelihood of involvement in delinquent behaviour. Moreover, it is those who do not like school and do not care what teachers think of them who are more likely to commit delinquent acts. Not that attachment to delinquent peers is, in itself, found to undermine conventional bonds and lead to offending behaviour. It is rather, weak social bonds and a low stake in conformity that leads to the acquisition of delinquent friends. The data showed that high aspirations give a stake in conformity that ties an individual to the conventional social order, and not the reverse suggested by the anomie theory tradition. Moreover, social class and ethnic background were found to be 'very weakly' related to offending behaviour.

Numerous other attempts have been made to test the theoretical and empirical adequacy of Hirschi's original theory and the models derived from it. One notable example is Thomas and Hyman's (1978) study, which is particularly illuminating as it employed a much more sophisticated methodology than Hirschi's original. The authors concluded that, 'while control theory does not appear to provide anything like a full explanation, its ability to account for a significant proportion of delinquency cannot be ignored' (1978: 88–9). Thompson, Mitchell and Doddler (1984) later conducted a survey among hundreds of high school students and juveniles in correctional institutions and found that variations in offending behaviour between the two groups were better explained when the role of delinquent peers was introduced as a variable to the original theoretical formulation. Indeed, their findings were found to be more representative of social learning or differential association theory than social control theory.

Overall, subsequent research has tended to find that the aspects of the social bond most consistently related to offending behaviour are those of the family and the school. There is substantial evidence that juveniles with strong attachments to their family are less likely to engage in delinquency. The evidence on the association between attachment and commitment to the school, particularly poor school performance, not liking school and low educational and occupational aspirations and delinquency, is even stronger.

Despite its impressive empirical support, Hirschi's original formulation of control theory has not escaped criticism. He himself conceded that it overestimated the significance of involvement in conventional activities and underestimated the importance of delinquent friends. Moreover, both of these problems appeared to have stemmed from the same conceptual source, the taken-for-granted assumption of a natural motivation towards offending behaviour (Box, 1981; Downes and Rock, 1998). There have been other criticisms. First, the theory cannot account for the specific form or content of deviant behaviour, or 'why some uncontrolled individuals become heroin users, some become hit men, and others price fixing conspirators' (Braithwaite, 1989: 13). Second, there is a failure to consider the underlying structural and historical context in which criminal behaviour takes place (Elliot, Ageton and Canter, 1979; Box, 1981, 1987). Third, while it plainly considers primary deviance among adolescents, habitual 'secondary deviance' appears to be outside its conceptual boundaries (Box, 1981). Subsequently, other researchers have sought a remedy for these various identified defects by integrating control theory with other theoretical perspectives.

Integrated theoretical perspectives

Elliot, Ageton and Canter (1979) developed a model that sought to expand and synthesise anomie theories, social learning and social control perspectives into a simple explanatory paradigm. They begin with the assumption that individuals have different early socialisation experiences, leading to variable degrees of commitment to, and integration into, the conventional social order, in other words, strong and weak social bonds. These initial bonds can be further reinforced or attenuated by such factors as positive experiences at school and in the wider community, positive labelling in these new settings and continuing stability in the home.

The structural dimension of Elliot *et al.*'s model is most explicit in their analysis of the factors that serve to loosen social bonds. Limited or blocked opportunities, negative labelling experiences at school, for example streaming, social disorganisation at home and in the wider community – high rates of geographic mobility, economic recession and unemployment – are all identified as experiences that may weaken or break initially strong ties to the conventional order.

Such structural impediments to achieving conventional success goals will constitute a source of strain and can of themselves – where commitment to conventional goals is strong enough – provide *the* motivational stimulus to delinquency. In most cases, however, and specifically for those whose ties and commitments to conventional groups and goals are weak in the first place, then some further motivation is necessary for sustained involvement in delinquent behaviour. For Elliot, Ageton and Canter (1979: 15), it is 'access to and involvement in delinquent learning structures that provides this positive motivation and largely shapes the form and content of delinquent behaviour'.

Elliot *et al.* propose two primary explanatory routes to delinquency. The first and probably most frequent represents an integration of control theory and social learning theory and involves weak bonds to conventional society and exposure and commitment to groups involved in delinquent activity. The second path represents an integration of traditional strain and social learning perspectives and this involves strong bonds to conventional society, conditions and experiences that accentuate those bonds and in most cases exposure and commitment to groups involved in delinquency.

Stephen Box (1981, 1987) sought to explain the discrepancy between the findings of self-report studies – such as those conducted by Hirschi – and which suggest only a weak relationship between social class and delinquency, and official statistics that show strong links. By integrating control theory with a labelling/conflict perspective – incorporated from the victimised actor model of crime and criminal behaviour – Box showed how the 'primary' deviants of the self-report studies become the largely economically disadvantaged and minority group 'secondary' deviants of the official statistics. He argues that differential policing practices and institutional biases at different stages of the criminal justice system all operate in favour of the most advantaged sections of society and to the detriment of its less favoured citizens. However, this is not merely a product of discriminating decision-making criteria made on the basis of the individual characteristics of the suspect. Employing a more macro and historical view of the criminalisation process, Box (1981: 20) suggested that it may be plausible to view such outcomes as a response to social problems of which the individual is merely a symbol:

Thus, the economically marginalised and the oppressed ethnic minorities – because they will also be economically marginalised – will be treated more harshly by the judicial system not simply because of who they are, but also because of what they symbolise, namely the perceived threat to social order posed by the growth of the permanently unemployed.

This relationship is viewed as being fully interactive as the stigma, disadvantage and sense of injustice engendered by the criminalisation process, particularly when it is perceived as discriminatory, provides a further impetus towards criminal behaviour.

In his later work, Box (1987) showed how the impact of economic recession – such as that experienced in Britain during the 1980s – could lead to an increase in criminal activity. First, by further reducing legitimate opportunities and increasing relative deprivation, recession produces more 'strain' and thus more individuals with a motive to deviate, particularly among the economically disadvantaged. Thus, the commitment of a person to society is undermined because his or her access to conventional modes of activity has been seriously reduced. Second, by undermining the family and conventional employment prospects the ability and motivation of an individual to develop an attachment to other human beings, who might introduce a controlling influence in his or her life, is substantially reduced.

John Braithwaite's (1989) theory of 'predatory' crime – that is, crimes involving the victimisation of one party by another – builds upon and integrates elements of control, labelling, strain and subcultural theory and argues that the key to crime control is a cultural commitment to shaming in ways that are described as 'reintegrative'; thus, 'societies with low crime rates are those that shame potently and judiciously' (1989: 1). Braithwaite makes a crucial distinction between shaming that leads to stigmatising 'to outcasting, to confirmation of a deviant master status' and shaming that is: 'reintegrative, that shames while maintaining bonds of respect or love, that sharply terminates disapproval with forgiveness. The latter controls crime while the former pushes offenders toward criminal sub-cultures' (1989: 12– 13).

Braithwaite argues that criminal subcultures become attractive to those who have been stigmatised by their shaming because they can provide emotional and social support. Participation in these groups can also supply criminal role models, knowledge on how to offend and techniques of 'neutralisation' (see Matza, 1964, discussed in Chapter 7) that taken together can make the choice to engage in crime more attractive and likely. Therefore, a high level of stigmatisation in a society is a key factor in stimulating the formation of criminal subcultures. The other major societal variable that encourages this configuration is the 'systematic blockage of legitimate opportunities for critical fractions of the population' (1989: 103).

Braithwaite claims that individuals are more susceptible to shaming when they are enmeshed in multiple relationships of *interdependency* and, furthermore, societies shame more effectively when they are *communitarian*. It is such societies or cultures – constituted of dense networks of individual interdependencies characterised by mutual help and trust – rather than individualistic societies that are more capable of delivering the required more potent shaming and more shaming that is reintegrative. This is a crucial observation.

Both Box and Braithwaite have significantly sought to rescue the social control theory perspective from its emphasis on the individual – or more accurately family – culpability that had made it so popular with conservative governments both in the UK and the USA during the 1980s. Box (1981, 1987) located his radical reformulation of social control theory within the victimised actor model but it is the notion of 'reintegrative shaming' developed by Braithwaite that has been central to the populist socialist perspective that is the focus of the following chapter. Significantly, neither Box nor Braithwaite – like Hirschi whom they sought to improve upon – manage to offer a satisfactory explanation of all crime and criminal behaviour. Hirschi sought subsequently – in collaboration with Michael Gottfredson – to do just that.

A general theory of crime

In their *General Theory of Crime*, Gottfredson and Hirschi (1990) manage to combine rational actor model notions of crime with a predestined actor model theory of criminality. In line with the hedonistic calculus of rational actor model thinking, crime is defined as acts of force or fraud undertaken in the pursuit of self-interest. The authors propose that the vast bulk of criminal acts are trivial and mundane affairs that result in little gain and require little in the way of effort, planning, preparation or skill, and their 'versatility construct' points to how crime is essentially interchangeable. The characteristics of ordinary criminal events are simply inconsistent with notions of specialisation or the 'criminal career'. Since the likelihood of criminal behaviour is also closely linked to the availability of opportunity, the characteristics of situations and the personal properties of individuals will also affect the use of force or fraud in the pursuit of self-interest. This concept of criminality – low self-control – is not confined to criminal acts but is also causally implicated in many 'analogous' acts, such as promiscuity, alcohol use and smoking where such behaviour is portrayed as the impulsive actions of disorganised individuals seeking quick gratification.

Gottfredson and Hirschi turn to the predestined actor model in order to account for the variation in self-control among individuals, arguing that the main cause is 'ineffective parenting' and this failure to instil self-control early in life cannot easily be remedied later, any more than effective control, once established, can be later undone. According to this 'stability postulate', levels of self-control will remain stable throughout the life course and 'differences between people in the likelihood that they will commit criminal acts persist over time' (1990: 107).

The *General Theory of Crime* is essentially a radical restatement of the control theory set out by Hirschi in his earlier work successfully addressing many of the key criticisms aimed at the original. It is more explicitly grounded in a rational actor model conception of crime and thus offers a more consistent notion of criminal motivation than has been the case with previous control theories. By asserting that crime is essentially interchangeable while the propensity to commit crime remains stable throughout the life course, the theory has no need to provide separate explanations for different *types* of crime, nor for *primary* or persistent *secondary* deviation.

The theory does nevertheless deny the relevance of structural or sociological variables, including those in Hirschi's original theory. The types of bonds an individual establishes with other people and institutions are now said to be a function of that same individual's level of self-control. Thus, those who have self-control are more likely to form constraining social relationships, whereas those who lack it will tend to 'avoid attachments to or involvement in all social institutions' (1990: 168).

Gottfredson and Hirschi describe their theory as 'general', claiming that it 'is meant to explain all crime, at all times' (1990: 117). Whether it does, or not, depends on the extent to which the observed nature of crime corresponds with that presented as typical by the authors. Depicting all crime as impulsive, unplanned and of little or no real benefit to the perpetrator poses particular problems in the case of white-collar – or business – crime. There is much evidence that high-ranking governmental and corporate officials, acting independently or on behalf of the organisations they serve, use fraud and force in carefully planned ways to enrich themselves and maintain their positions. Barlow (1991: 238) observes that, 'compared to low-end crime, high-end crime is much more likely to involve planning, special expertise, organisation, delayed gratification, and persistence – as well as considerably larger potential gains'.

The existence of high-level crime also seems to cast considerable doubt on Gottfredson and Hirschi's 'stability postulate', that is, the notion that levels of self-control remain constant throughout the life course. Since low self-control is also incompatible with the discipline and effort normally required to attain high office, it is difficult to see how corporate offenders managed to climb the corporate ladder in the first place!

Even if the proposition that low self-control is a causal factor in some – or even most types of crime – is accepted, can we also accept the straightforward association Gottfredson and Hirschi propose between low self-control and ineffective parenting? Although the literature discussed elsewhere in this book does suggest a relationship between parenting and delinquency, this is compromised and complicated when structural factors are considered; for example, while her study of socially deprived families in Birmingham did find that parental supervision was an important factor in determining adolescent offending behaviour, Harriet Wilson (1980: 233–4) warned against the misinterpretation of her findings:

> The essential point of our findings is the very close association of lax parenting methods with severe social handicap. Lax parenting methods are often the result of chronic stress ... frequent or prolonged spells of unemployment, physical or mental disabilities amongst members of the

family, and an often-permanent condition of poverty. It is the position of the most disadvantaged groups in society, and not the individual, which needs improvement in the first place.

These findings show quite clearly that even by relocating the source of control from the nature of an individual's bond to society back to within the individual him- or herself, Gottfredson and Hirschi cannot escape the need to incorporate some sense of underlying structural context into their analysis. Their work has however been influential and Hirschi has himself subsequently outlined the policy implications of the general theory. Hirschi (1995) argues that policies designed to deter (the rational actor model) or rehabilitate (the predestined actor model) will continue to have little success in reducing criminal behaviour. Effective state policies are those that support and enhance socialisation within the family by improving the quality of child-rearing practices with the focus on the form, size, and stability of the family unit. Thus, there should always be two parents for every child, no more than three children in a family and the relationships between parents and children strong and durable. Furthermore, it is not young teenage mothers who are a problem that causes delinquency in children. It is having a mother without a father. Therefore, effective policies are those that focus not on preventing teenage pregnancies, but on maintaining the involvement of the father in the life of the child. It is proposed that these policy reforms would strengthen family bonds, increase socialisation and create greater self-control in the child that will make it unlikely that they will become involved in offending behaviour (1995: 138–9).

Developments in social control theories

Various developments in and modifications to social control theories have occurred in the USA in the later decades of the twentieth and the first decade of the twenty-first centuries. We will here consider three of the most significant: power control theory, control balance theories and differential coercion theory.

Power control theory developed by John Hagan (Hagan, Gillis and Simpson, 1985, 1987, 1990; Hagan, 1989) combines social class and control theories of criminal behaviour in order to explain the effects of familial control on gender differences in crime. Hagan, Gillis and Simpson (1987) argue that parental position in the workforce affects patriarchal attitudes in the household and these, in turn, result in different levels of control placed on boys and girls in the home. Moreover, differing levels of control affect the likelihood of the children taking risks and ultimately becoming involved in deviant behaviour. In other words, because of the greater levels of control placed on girls in patriarchal households, boys are more delinquent than girls.

Power control theory begins with the assumption that mothers constitute the primary agents of socialisation in the family. In households in which the mother and father have relatively similar levels of power at work – 'balanced households' – the former will be less likely to differentially exert control over their daughters, and both sons and daughters will experience similar levels of control thus leading them to develop similar attitudes regarding the risks and benefits of engaging in deviant behaviour. It is thus assumed that balanced households will experience fewer gender differences in deviant behaviour. In contrast, households in which mothers and fathers have dissimilar levels of power in the workplace – 'unbalanced households' – are more 'patriarchal' in their attitudes to gender roles and parents will place greater levels of control on their daughters than their sons. Therefore, the former will develop attitudes unfavourable towards deviant behaviour identifying higher levels of apparent risk and fewer supposed benefits of engaging in such activities. Thus, significant gender differences in unbalanced households are predicted with male children more likely than females to engage in deviant activity.

Research studies suggest that gender differences in criminal behaviour arise because girls are differentially controlled in the household. Thus, in other words, female offending increases or decreases depending on the level of patriarchy (see Bates, Bader and Mencken, 2003). McCarthy, Hagan and Woodward (1999) suggest that gender differences in delinquency and offending behaviour probably decrease because *both* male and female delinquents are affected. Moreover, in less patriarchal households, sons are shown to have more controls placed on them thus decreasing their levels of delinquency.

Charles Tittle (1995, 1997, 1999, 2000) proposes a general theory of deviant behaviour – control balance theory – which provides a definition of deviancy that goes well beyond that of criminality and into the realm of social harms that preoccupies zemiologists. From this perspective, deviancy is simply any activity which the majority find unacceptable and/or disapprove of and occurs when a person has either a surplus or deficit of control in relation to others. Those, whose position in society allows them to exert more control over others and their environment than is exerted over them, enjoy a control surplus. A control deficit arises where people are controlled more by others than they are able to control. Tittle proposes that any control imbalance – surplus or deficit – is likely to lead to deviancy. A deficit of control could well lead to resentment, envy and the loss of any stake in society thus removing any incentive to conform; a surplus can lead to corruption, a desire to extend the surplus, enhance autonomy and increase domination. The link with criminal behaviour is founded on the supposition that the subservience of others largely removes the risk of being caught. A more specific claim is that any breakdown of subservience provokes angry outbursts and this has been used to explain some incidents of domestic violence (see Hopkins and McGregor, 1991). The dual aspect of the theory seems to provide explanations of street crime (most likely to be associated with a control deficit) and corporate crime (most likely to be associated with a control surplus).

Tittle does not assume that an imbalance alone will inevitably lead to criminality but emphasises the drive for autonomy. Criminal motivation arises for those with a control surplus because they want to extend it (greed) and for those with a deficit (need) because they want to alleviate it. For criminal behaviour to occur, motivation has to be triggered by provocation and facilitated by both opportunity and an absence of constraint.

Linking crime with power is not new. Violent crime invariably involves an element of control or power over the victim and sex crimes have often been explained in this way (see Lansky, 1987; Scheff and Retzinger, 1991). Property offences can also be explained in this manner, thus burglars have power over their victims, the power to decide what to take and leave, how much mess and trauma to cause, and for some this is part of the attraction of burglary (Katz, 1988). Control balance theory is nevertheless helpful in explaining gender differentials in offending rates for there is still a tendency for women to be controlled to a greater extent than men and in more spheres of their lives. Women experience control deficits more frequently than men and become easily enmeshed in the full range of submissive deviancy without access to predatory criminal opportunity. In contrast, fewer women are presumed to have a control surplus so that they would be under-represented in the areas of exploitation, plunder and decadence, the converse being true for a considerably higher proportion of males.

Braithwaite (1997) proposes a policy strategy of redistributing control imbalances and argues that a more egalitarian society will reduce both control surplus and deficit with the outcome that deviance in general and offending behaviour in particular will be reduced. He acknowledges that some form of control will be inevitable to maintain order in even the most equal of societies but proposes that this should be exercised in ways which respect those who are subjected to the control.

Differential coercion theory developed by Mark Colvin (2000) seeks to extend our existing understanding of the coercion-crime relationship. Other recent criminological theories have also highlighted the theme of coercion. Athens (1997) thus describes coercive interpersonal relations as primary forces in the creation of dangerous violent criminals. Regoli and Hewitt (1994) argue that coercive acts by adults in their quest for order play a major role in creating an oppressive environment for young people that produces delinquency. Tittle (1995) contends that repression – a concept similar to coercion – creates control deficits that, depending on the strength and consistency of the repression produce predatory, defiant, or submissive forms of deviance. Hagan and McCarthy (1998) focus on the coercive forces in both the background and foreground in their explanation of delinquency among homeless, street youth.

Colvin (2000) observes that coercion has multiple sources – including families, schools, peer relations and neighbourhoods – and then specifies how each of these coercive experiences foster criminal involvement. He uses the term differential because individuals vary in the extent to which they are exposed to coercion and it is a central premise of his perspective that criminal involvement will be positively related to the degree of duress experienced by individuals.

There are two proposed dimensions of differential coercion: the *degree* of the coercive force – on a continuum from none to very strong coercion – and the *consistency* with which it is applied or experienced. In most ordinary circumstances – in families, schools, peer groups and a neighbourhood, for example – coercion is most likely to be experienced on an inconsistent basis, in which case, the extent, or degree, of the coercion is the most significant element in producing delinquency.

Coercion, it is argued, produces a set of 'social-psychological' deficits that are conducive to greater involvement in delinquency. Thus, to the degree that individuals experience coercion, they are more likely to have higher levels of anger, lower self–control, weaker social bonds, and a high degree of 'coercive ideation' (Colvin, 2000). The latter concept refers to a world view in which the individual perceives that the social environment is filled with coercive forces that can only be overcome through coercion. This set of 'social-psychological deficits' mediates the relationship between coercion and delinquency.

Colvin (2000) differentiates between interpersonal and impersonal forms of coercion: the former occurs within direct interpersonal relations of control in various settings, such as, the family, while the latter is connected to pressures from impersonal forces that create an indirect experience of coercion. Interpersonal coercion involves the use or threat of force and intimidation aimed at creating compliance in an interpersonal relationship. These micro-level coercive processes of control can involve the actual or threatened use of physical force and/or the actual or threatened removal of social supports. Impersonal coercion is experienced as pressure arising from larger circumstances beyond the control of the individual and these macro-level sources of coercion can include economic and social pressures created by structural unemployment, poverty, or violent competition among groups.

An example of impersonal coercion discussed by Colvin (2000: 124) is the violent environment within neighbourhoods created by gang rivalries. Such neighbourhoods – perceived as dangerous and violent by the young people who live in them – are a strong, impersonal force that creates an environment of threat (Decker and Van Winkle, 1996) which enhances 'coercive ideation' and other social-psychological deficits that Colvin (2000) argues are conducive to delinquency. Moreover, the school setting can be perceived as coercive if school administrators fail to curtail a threatening school environment created by bullying and other forms of aggression at school.

In summary, for Colvin (2000), the accumulated coercion that juveniles experience in their families, schools, peer relations, and neighbourhoods creates social-psychological deficits that makes involvement in delinquent activities more likely. The logic of differential coercion theory is that the effects of coercion are general and thus are implicated in most, if not all, forms of criminality, including white-collar and corporate crime.

Unnever, Colvin and Cullen (2004) sought to test the core propositions of differential coercion theory and collected data from 2,472 middle school students at six different public schools in a metropolitan area of Virginia. Variables included demographic information including gender, measures of economic status, race, and grade level, as well as various measures of coercion, such as parental coercion, peer coercion, school coercion, and neighbourhood coercion. Other variables included four measures of social-psychological factors: anger, parental social bonds, school social bonds, and coercive ideation.

Their results largely supported the general proposition that different types of coercion would be positively associated with delinquent involvement. Parental coercion, including verbal abuse, threats, and physical punishment, were significantly related to delinquency. School and neighbourhood coercion were also significantly related to delinquency, although the associations were less strong than parental coercion. Peer coercion was found to have no relationship to delinquency. Unnever, Colvin and Cullen (2004) conclude from their data that students exposed to coercive environments develop social-psychological deficits which may lead them to engage in delinquent activities.

Conclusions

In the forty years since Hirschi introduced his control theory it has gained in popularity and influence and this is not difficult to understand. First, social control theory lends itself remarkably well to empirical research and has become *the* most tested theory of crime causation. Moreover, it is very well supported empirically. Second, because it has avoided implicating social structural issues such as poverty and unemployment as a cause of criminal behaviour, it has become very popular with the 'right wing' in the USA and thus extremely attractive for research funds. It was on the basis of these factors that Box (1987) justified his inclusion of control theory in his integrated theory.

While 'popular' support for a particular perspective on crime is, of itself, no proof of worth, extensive empirical support clearly is. Despite its impressive empirical support *vis-à-vis* other theories one could nevertheless argue, as Downes and Rock (1998) have done, that control theory is not addressing the same problems as its rivals. Alternative sociological theories attempt to account for the character of offending behaviour and to construct models of motivation that account for its typical forms. In control theory, by contrast, deviance has no meaning other than as a means of gratifying basic appetites, be they acquisitive, aggressive or sexual.

Even if we can accept the underlying assumptions of control theory about human nature, that we would all be deviant but for the controls that rein in our natural tendencies, the question still remains: 'in what ways would we be deviant?' By redefining the problem of motivation out of existence, it becomes difficult, if not impossible, for control theory to account for the very phenomena that other theories specifically set out to address. In other words, 'why delinquency is so often non-utilitarian; why aggression is so frequently ritualised and non-violent in its outcome; why sexual gratification takes such complex forms. In short, control theorists make far too little of both deviance and conformity' (Downes and Rock, 1998: 238).

There is little doubt that in redirecting attention to the previously overlooked issue of conformity, and how this is 'caused' and sustained, control theory has made a significant contribution to the project of explaining crime and criminal behaviour. It nevertheless fails to supply the complete explanation claimed by Gottfredson and Hirschi but there is however research evidence to suggest that some of the more recent developments in social control theories such as power control theories, control balance theory and differential coercion theory have helped extend the parameters of explanation without necessarily being able to provide a comprehensive explanation of all forms of deviancy and criminal behaviour.

Suggested further reading

Key texts in social control theory written from a US perspective are Gottfredson and Hirschi (1990) and Hirschi (1969). Wilson (1980) provides a classic use of the theory in a UK context. Box (1981, 1987), Braithwaite (1989) and Elliot, Ageton and Canter (1979) have all produced important texts that have integrated social control theory with other theoretical perspectives. Heidensohn (1985) discusses the value of social control theory in the study of women and crime. For more recent developments in social control theory, Hagan, Gillis and Simpson (1985) provides an excellent introduction to their power control theory, Tittle (2000) outlines his control balance theory and Colvin (2000) his differential control theory.

16. Left realism

Left realism is not like the theoretically integrated approaches discussed previously in this fourth part of the book for it is not really an attempt to integrate and synthesise elements from different theories in order to provide a stronger comprehensive theoretical tool. It is more recognition of the validity of explanatory elements contained in each of the three models of crime and criminal behaviour that we have so far encountered, and their practical value as part of a comprehensive strategy for understanding and responding to crime both at a macro societal level and at the level of practice. There is, nevertheless, a predominant emphasis on sociological explanations of criminality with recently more focus on developing an integrated theory synthesising traditions such as labelling and subcultural theories and bringing them together within a socialist feminist framework that stresses class and gender inequality (see Mooney, 2000).

The origins of left realism

Left realism has its origins in the writings of a group of British criminologists some of whom had been in the forefront of the radical criminology of the 1970s and these texts emerged principally in response to four closely interconnected factors. First, there was a reaction among this group to what they considered to be 'left idealism' the utopian positions that their previous confederates in the radical/critical criminological tradition had now taken up. In the USA Elliot Currie (1992) referred to 'progressive minimalists' or left-wing academics frightened of entering the law and order debate for fear of adding to the prejudices of the public and thus promoting support for conservative crime control strategies with the unintended outcome that in ignoring the real problems of serious crime and drug use in the USA:

> they help to perpetuate an image of progressives as being both fuzzy-minded and, much worse, unconcerned about the realities of life for those ordinary Americans who are understandably frightened and

enraged by the suffering and fear crime brings to their communities and families

(Currie, 1992: 91)

Second, there was a response to the rising tide of criminal victimisation that was becoming increasingly apparent in British society and where poor people were overwhelmingly the victims. It nevertheless seems extremely unlikely that these writers and researchers would have so readily discovered this new reality but for the important impetus provided by the other two factors. Thus, third, there was the rise to prominence and power of the populist conservatives or the 'new right' and, fourth, the simultaneous rediscovery by right realist criminologists of the rational actor model of crime and criminal behaviour.

This significant shift in the intellectual climate of radical criminology had centred on a debate around the issue of policing the inner city and the notion of moral panics. Critical criminology, it was acknowledged, had made important contributions to the study of the crimes of the powerful, such as corporate crimes, government wrongdoings, and white-collar crimes but most of these criminologists, it was observed, had simply chosen to ignore the causes and possible control of crime committed by members of the working class against other members of the working class with, of course, the exception of violence against women, children and members of ethnic groups. This failure to acknowledge working-class crime had, however, come at a great price to the political left because it had allowed right-wing politicians – and right-realist criminologists – in several countries to claim opposition to street crime as their own issue, giving them room to generate ideological support for harsh law and order policies.

It was in this context that a new perspective was to emerge amongst some left criminologists that a 'new realist' view on crime was necessary and that it was time to 'take crime seriously' (Lea and Young, 1984). From this viewpoint it was argued that crime is not purely a social construction, nor is the fear of crime shared by many people. To put the latter down solely to the manipulations of the 'capitalist media' or 'the system' is, again, politically and morally irresponsible. Moreover, as was becoming readily apparent from the findings of victimisation studies – such as the British Crime Surveys – to regard criminal statistics as mere inventions is not acceptable either. Broad patterns of offences can be established after all, and a disproportionate amount of personally hurtful crime is undeniably committed by the more 'marginalised' sectors of the urban working class, for example, young black males. Quite simply, the lives of many ordinary citizens are seriously disrupted by this kind of offence, and it is not 'pro-state' to argue for effective policing in these areas.

This group of criminologists on the left of the political spectrum – such as Jock Young, John Lea and Roger Matthews – thus became increasingly worried during the 1980s that the debate on crime control was slipping away from them. Critical criminologists were – by denying that working-class crime was a real problem and concentrating instead on 'crimes of the powerful' – ignoring the plight of working-class victims of predatory crime. Successive

263

defeats of the British Labour Party furthermore convinced them that they had allowed the political high ground to be captured by the new populist conservative theorists. The rediscovered rational actor model was gaining favour with government, while administrative criminologists in the Home Office were – as we have seen elsewhere in this book – concentrating on small-scale empirical investigation.

Young detected a need for a 'radical realist' response: one, which recognised the impact of crime, but which at the same time, addressed the context in which it occurred. The first statement of his dissatisfaction with radical orthodoxy came in a book written with his contemporary John Lea, *What is to be Done About Law and Order?* (Lea and Young, 1984). In this text they stressed the evidence of victim studies, which showed that official statistics presented an incomplete and even inaccurate picture of the impact of crime. Victim studies had two major advantages: first, they revealed offences and incivilities, which, although not reported to the police, nevertheless caused great misery to those who suffered them; second, because many of the studies were localised, they gave a truer impression of the situation in particular areas where offending might be concentrated.

Lea and Young were concerned to highlight differences in victimisation levels within groups. For example, national statistics suggest that women as a group are far less likely than men to be victims of homicide, but a closer examination shows that the chances of a black woman being murdered are greater than that of a white male. They also drew attention to the disparity between the impacts of crime on different groups: thus, men generally feel anger towards aggressors, whereas women tend to suffer shock and fear. Moreover, the impact of crime cannot be measured in absolute terms: £50 stolen from a middle-class home is likely to have less effect on the victims than the same sum taken from a poor household.

For left realists, crime is a real problem that must be addressed. Lea and Young deal with the argument that corporate crime is more important: yes, 'crimes of the powerful' do exist and are to be condemned, but the effects of corporate crime are generally widespread, while those of direct-contact crime are concentrated. Corporate crime may indeed cause financial loss and even death and danger, but the real problem for those living in high-crime areas is posed by predatory offenders in their midst. Left realism thus takes into account the immediate fears that people have and seeks to deal with them.

Lea and Young were also keen to address the peripheral problems around the central issue. People living in high-crime areas suffer individual offences that they may or may not report to the police, but they also suffer a range of incivilities, such as vandalism where they are not directly victimised, threats, vulgarity, sexual harassment, noise and swearing, all of which taken together further reduce quality of life and increase despair.

Police excesses are also identified as causing crime. First, police harassment of minority groups causes resentment and feelings of helplessness that may actually encourage offending. Second, 'military-style policing', such as that noted in the run-up to the Brixton riots in April 1981, creates a siege mentality among the residents of an area that discourages them from assisting the police in their investigations. Moreover, aggressive policing further brutalises crime areas, which in turn leads to more crime.

Left realists have also responded to the claim of critical criminologists that the apparent propensity of black youths to commit predatory crime is solely the outcome of racist police stereotyping and targeting. While recognising that such stereotyping does exist, and deploring it, Lea and Young observe that young black males do in fact commit more of these offences. In the USA they are more represented in this category of offenders than Asians, Hispanics and Mexicans who suffer comparative levels of poverty and discrimination. In fact, in Britain, the police had at first refused to accept that there was a 'black crime problem', instead pointing out that young black males were over-represented in areas where crime tended to be highest.

Left realism, however, draws on the lessons of anomie theory and proposes that young second-generation African Caribbeans in Britain commit more crime than other ethnic groups because they have been fully integrated into the surrounding culture and have consequently been led to expect a fair slice of the economic cake. Not being able to achieve their promised position through legitimate means – because of discrimination – they turn to crime. Other ethnic minorities – having integrated less – retain strong family and cultural ties that subject them to stronger social control and help them to achieve without offending.

Moreover, left realists doubt the existence of the simple relationship between crime and unemployment that has been so central to the critical criminology perspective. Women, who have been unable until recently to enter the workplace in large numbers, have always been massively under-represented in the ranks of offenders. It is only now, when women are finding opportunities for work, that the female crime rate is starting to rise more quickly.

Critical criminologists are accused of being 'schizophrenic' about crime. It is observed that feminists have forced them to take seriously the fear of women about rape and sexual assault, while racial attacks are naturally deplored, but other crime is depicted as being understandable and a symptom of the class struggle. Nevertheless:

> The tide is turning for radical criminology. For over two decades it has neglected the effect of crime upon the victim and concentrated on the impact of the state – through the process of labelling – on the criminal ... It became an advocate for the indefensible: the criminal became the victim, the state the solitary focus of attention, while the real victim remained off-stage.
>
> (Matthews and Young, 1986: Introduction)

Young also turned his sights on the limited adequacy of the 'new administrative criminology' that had come to dominate the British Home Office and the research departments of the larger universities:

> the new administrative criminologists seek to construct a system of punishment and surveillance which discards rehabilitation and replaces

> it with a social behaviourism worthy of the management of white rats
> in laboratory cages.
>
> (Young, 1986b: 28)

While criminologists had often been arguing amongst themselves in the pursuit of the 'holy grail' of an all-encompassing explanation of crime and criminal behaviour, there is evidence that governments had lost patience with a discipline that seemed no closer than ever to solving the crime problem. One of the world's leading criminologists, the Australian John Braithwaite had perceptively observed as recently as 1989:

> The present state of criminology is one of abject failure in its own terms.
> We cannot say anything convincing to the community about the causes
> of crime; we cannot prescribe policies that will work to reduce crime; we
> cannot in all honesty say that societies spending more on criminological
> research get better criminal justice policies than those that spend little or
> nothing on criminology.
>
> (Braithwaite, quoted in Matthews and Young, 1992: 3–4)

In Britain – as we have seen elsewhere in this book – government pessimism at ever being able to solve the crime problem through understanding, and being able to deal with the origins and motivations for offending, had shifted the focus of research. Spending since the late 1970s had been devoted more to finding and evaluating pragmatic solutions to particular offences than to developing criminological theory. Most professional crime prevention practitioners enjoying government patronage had come to accept that crime is a function of opportunity. Whatever motives offenders might have, removal of opportunities for offending will, says the assumption, reduce the incidence of crime. The response of the left realists was in reality an attempt to develop an all-encompassing crime control strategy that while accepting the need for the practical, pragmatic and certainly the empirical, managed to locate this all within both a macro and micro theoretical context.

A balance of intervention

Central to the left realist crime control strategy is the proposition that crime requires a comprehensive solution where there must be a 'balance of intervention'. Both crime and the causes of crime must thus be tackled and their argument is illustrated with the 'Square of Crime' (see below).

The Square of Crime is designed as a reminder that crime is the outcome of a number of lines of force and intervention to prevent it must take place at different levels in order to be effective. Left realists propose that crime is a function of four factors. First, there is *the state*, principally through the capacity of its front-line agents to label individuals and groups as offenders which is a major factor in recidivism. Second, there is *the victim* who may actually encourage offenders through inadequate defence or may even precipitate crime

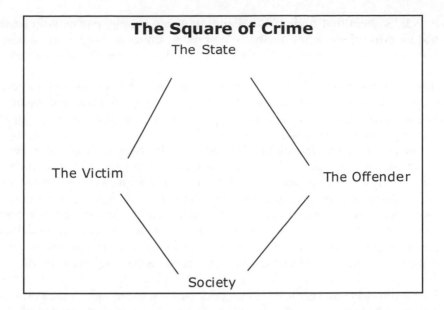

The Square of Crime

The State

The Victim

The Offender

Society

through his or her lifestyle or personality all which determine the impact of crime. Third, there is *society*, through which the various forces of informal and formal social control are exercised. Fourth, there are *the offenders* themselves (their number, their rate of offending, the type of crimes they commit, etc).

Crime occurs not only as a product of these individual four factors, but also as an outcome of the relationship between them. The relationship between the police and the public that left — and indeed right – realists argue, determines the effectiveness of the former in preventing crime, can be described as state–society interplay. The actions of the criminal justice system are state–offender interplay. Fundamentally, all crime prevention efforts, of whatever type, involve some relationship between the four corners of the square. In short,

> To control crime from a realist perspective involves intervention at each part of the square of crime: at the level of the factors which give rise to the putative offender (such as structural unemployment), the informal system (such as lack of public mobilisation), the victim (such as inadequate target hardening), and the formal system (such as ineffective policing).
>
> (Young, 1986b: 41)

Essentially, all the left realists are really saying is that there is something to be said for most explanations of crime and criminal behaviour. The problem with most theorists, they argue, is that by occupying entrenched positions on the causes of crime, they are not able to step back and look at the wider picture.

Critical criminologists accept that the 'new realist' perspective has much in common with both Engels' (1845) and Bonger's (1916) much earlier Marxist versions of 'demoralisation' theory where it had been argued that capitalism is a social system that dehumanises and alienates people, particularly sections of the working class, who inevitably become at times desperate and antisocial in their strategies for personal survival. From that perspective, crime statistics are considered to be an index of the general moral malaise of a society that – in its legitimate as well as illegitimate business – thrives on greed and self-interest. It thus follows that certain kinds of crime, criminal and victim are not to be 'explained away' as if they are somehow unreal or merely a product of repressive bourgeois law.

Consequently, both the older Marxists and the new realists see a positive element in the 'rule of law' and in particular, some need is recognised for effective policing, for example, in declining urban areas. More positively, a socialist strategy is held to require the extension and defence of certain civil rights, which are, nominally at least, available within liberal capitalist society (Hirst, 1980). Thus, the politics of law and order, for the left, should be less to do with the denial of street crime and sympathy with marginalised groups, and more to do with the elaboration of a responsible, rights-based notion of order.

Left realism has nevertheless been criticised for presenting a caricature of a supposedly antagonistic 'left idealist' position. The equation is made that 'the police are part of the state, are a part of capitalism', or that in 'true socialism, when it comes, there will be no problems of order, crime or dissent'. Critical theorists such as Phil Scraton and Joe Sim acknowledge that elements of that position crept into 1960s and 1970s theorising but assert that virtually no one would maintain these caricatured assertions in the early twenty-first century. At the same time, they have quite serious and legitimate reservations about the drift into left realism that requires a response.

Critical criminologists have argued that in a phase of capitalism which displays increasingly harsh traits, it is not at all 'idealist' to argue that the main focus and priority should be on the nature of police coercion and authoritarian tendencies in the state (Scraton, 1985; Sim, Scraton and Gordon, 1987). They argue that the most striking fact about law and order today is not so much the fear of crime and street offences. Rather, we are seeing – if only we look in the right places – a massive growth in the powers of the armed and surveillance branches of the state, limbs of the body politic that are becoming dangerously unaccountable (see Hopkins Burke, 2004c). To concentrate on the 'problem of crime' in this context is to reverse the proper order of priorities.

It would be wrong to say nevertheless, and despite some parallels, that left and right realism are the same. The left would thus strenuously dispute references to Victorian values and the virtues of traditional authority – highlighted by the right – on the grounds that a restricted conception of human autonomy has been based on historical myth. Yet the political right instigated a moral climate during its long period of electoral dominance in the 1980s and 1990s that established an apparent new social consensus. The 'New' Labour Government elected in 1997 was subsequently widely criticised by many traditionalists on the political left – in particular by critical criminologists – for merely carrying on with the law and order project instigated by their predecessors and supposedly political opponents.

Left realism and 'New' Labour

We have seen above and elsewhere in this book that during the 1980s the British Home Office came to promote what Jock Young has termed the new 'administrative criminology'. The emphasis on reducing the opportunity to offend through small-scale situational crime prevention schemes was in perfect accord with the ideological viewpoint of a Conservative Government 1979–97 committed to notions of rational choice and making people take responsibility for their actions but there had also been good practical reasons for this shift in emphasis.

The previous rehabilitative orthodoxy of the predestined actor model of criminal behaviour and its emphasis on treatment and changing criminals (the biological or psychological versions) or their environment (the sociological version) had been widely seen not to work. A considerable sum of money had been spent over the years on rehabilitative measures while at the same time the ever-increasing official crime statistics painted a picture of expensive failure.

The new administrative orthodoxy proposed that if none of these causal explanations of criminal behaviour and their corresponding policy interventions worked then there was little point in pursuing this approach. Conservative populists – or 'right realists' – proposed reducing the opportunity to offend, while catching, incarcerating and incapacitating those who did transgress. Nonetheless, this had not been an entirely successful strategy.

The jury is still unquestionably out on the success of situational crime prevention measures for evaluations of schemes suggest ambiguous outcomes (Hughes, 1998) but crime has definitely been reduced on occasion in certain situations. Problematically, while there remains a population of potentially determined and available criminals there will continue to be an issue of crime displacement. In short, locking all doors and bolting all windows might be a good idea but it is apparently no universal panacea for the problem of crime. Situational crime prevention is undoubtedly a sensible but incomplete crime control strategy.

If we accept the latter point then we have to recognise that some attempt has to be made to address the motivations of offenders or – to use the language of the predestined actor model – to locate the causes of crime and do something about them. The solution for the left realists is a 'balanced intervention' that addresses all sides of the crime problem. For the British 'New' Labour Government – or the populist socialists – unquestionably influenced by this criminological discourse, it is an approach to crime and criminal behaviour summarised and popularised by the oft-quoted sound bite of Prime Minister Tony Blair when Shadow Home Secretary 'tough on crime, tough on the causes of crime'.

Being 'tough on crime' suggests that offenders should take responsibility for their actions and is in theoretical accordance with the prescriptions of the rational actor model. Taking a tough stance on the causes of crime suggests both a targeting of both those individual and structural factors that in some way encourage criminality and is thus in accordance with not only the predestined actor model but *also* – and most appropriately for a socialist political party, however much they might like to disguise that fact – rooted most firmly in the victimised actor model. The theoretical justification for that governmental approach – and it is one that sets it apart from its political opponents and predecessors in government – is offered by the following realist case study of an apparently criminal 'underclass'.

Social exclusion and the 'underclass': a case study

An analysis of a socially excluded 'underclass' whose members are over represented among the ranks of convicted offenders conducted from a left realist perspective requires that we consider theoretical inputs from each of the three models of crime and criminal behaviour introduced in this book. Two principal academic explanations can be found for the existence of this 'underclass' (Crowther, 1998) and these encompass theoretical insights from each of the three models.

Structural accounts – for example, those offered by Dahrendorf (1985), Field (1989), Jordan (1996) and from the USA, William Julius Wilson (1987, 1991) – are normally associated with the political 'left' and have their theoretical foundations firmly located in both the conflict, radical and critical variants of the victimised actor tradition *and* the sociological tradition within the predestined actor model. Primarily various forms of social exclusion, poverty, material deprivation and patterns of inequality are highlighted. Entry into and membership of this class is explained by the inadequacy of state provided welfare services, changes in the labour market and exclusion from full citizenship.

Behavioural accounts, on the other hand – for example, Wilson and Herrnstein (1985), Murray (1990, 1994), and Herrnstein and Murray (1995) – are normally associated with the new political 'right' or populist conservatives and have their theoretical foundations in the rational actor model *and* the biological variant of the predestined actor model (see Chapter 13). This form of explanation came to prominence during the 1980s following the rise in the number of long term unemployed, the burgeoning lone parent population, increased welfare dependency and rising crime and disorder. From this perspective it is argued that the provision of state welfare erodes individual responsibility by giving people incentives not to work and provide for themselves and their family. Moreover, it is argued that those 'controls' – identified in the previous chapter (see Hirschi, 1969) – that stop individuals and communities from behaving badly, such as, stable family backgrounds and in particular positive male role models – do not exist for many members of this 'underclass'.

There is no evidence to suggest that non-participation in the labour market leads to inevitable involvement in a distinctive subculture (Westergaard, 1995; Marshall, Roberts and Burgoyne, 1996; Levitas, 1996; Crowther, 1998). People can remain unemployed for many years, surviving on a very limited income while remaining law-abiding citizens. On the other hand, it has to be recognised that there has been a real problem of crime and antisocial behaviour inflicted on some invariably poor working class communities by gangs of socially excluded males living in their midst (Campbell, 1993; Jordan, 1996) and this situation has been exacerbated during the early years of the twenty-first century in isolated and brutalised communities where young men have become embroiled in criminal lifestyles, amidst the detritus of collapsed economic and community structures and in a wider world where consumerism has triumphed (Hall, Winlow and Ancrum, 2008).

This author has proposed elsewhere that a left realist analysis requires the development of a process model that both locates the *structural* preconditions for the emergence of this social grouping while at the same time examining the nature of their *behavioural* response to their found predicament (Hopkins Burke, 1999a). It is an analysis that provides a theoretical justification for a balanced intervention in their lives.

The structural preconditions for the emergence of an underclass were undoubtedly the collapse of the unwritten post-war social contract between governments and the unskilled working class in advanced industrial societies. This had been founded on the provision of full employment and a fallback position – or safety net – of a relatively generous welfare state. However, with the major economic restructuring that occurred during the late 1970s and the 1980s non-skilled young people – in particular young males – entering into the labour market became increasingly over-represented among the ranks of the unemployed. At the same time, changes to social security entitlement in 1988 – instigated by the populist conservatives with the conscious intention of eradicating welfare dependency – had meant that sixteen and seventeen year olds lost their automatic right to benefits while eighteen to 24 year olds saw a dramatic reduction in the amount of money they could claim. Caroline Adams from the charity 'Action for Children' estimated that this was a contributory reason why 75,000 sixteen to seventeen year olds had no source of income whatsoever (Hopkins Burke, 1998c). In short, the collapse of the economic basis of their existence provides the structural element of a process model of the creation of an underclass (Hopkins Burke, 2000).

The behavioural response of this group has its origins in changes to familial living arrangements encouraged by that economic upheaval. The ideal type nuclear family of industrial modernity (Parsons, 1951) had been based on a division of labour and interdependency between men and women that had made considerable sense. The man had invariably been the main breadwinner while the woman had provided the home conditions to support him while nurturing and socialising the next generation. It was a rational arrangement because there were very few – if any – realistic alternatives available to either man or woman but in changed socio-economic circumstances it was to become a form of social arrangement that was less of a rational choice for the potential participants.

Feminists have observed that stripped of their role as the breadwinner 'workless' men now had little to offer women and their children other than the erratic affection, violence and child abuse that had often been present in working-class families (Campbell, 1993). Moreover, in a situation where the modernist state was quite understandably prepared to place women and children at the head of the queue for welfare benefits and 'social' housing provision, the former had relinquished their economic dependency on men to become dependent upon an increasingly inadequate welfare state (Field, 1989).

Many young men were now stripped of the informal controls of waged employment and family responsibilities that had previously restrained their wilder excesses and brought them back into the fold of conforming non-offending by their early twenties. Unskilled and poorly educated, they were now completely superfluous to the long-term requirements of post-industrial society. Excluded from legitimate employment opportunities and presenting themselves as unattractive propositions to young women as partners in long-term relationships many of these young men found themselves 'frozen in a state of persistent adolescence' (Pitts, 1996: 260). These restricted life chances had important implications for their involvement in crime because all the evidence suggests that 'growing up' also means growing out of crime (Rutherford, 1992). Stripped of legitimate access to adulthood these young men were trapped in a limbo world somewhere between childhood and adulthood long after the 'developmental tasks' of adolescence had been completed (Graham and Bowling, 1995). Now into their second – or even third – generation of what is a workless underclass in some geographical localities, this widely ostracised grouping – 'would you let your children play, or even go to school, with them, *now be honest*' – has become stereotyped as inherently criminogenic and drug-ridden with images that are frequently racialised (see Rose, 1999; Parenti, 2000; Bauman, 1998, 2000).

'New' Labour criminal justice policy revisited

Left realism was to be extremely influential with the 'New' Labour Government elected in 1997. There was a readily identified need for a balanced intervention that tackles both offending behaviour and the social and environmental conditions that support and encouraged that behaviour. The bottom-line would nevertheless be an attempt to reintegrate back into included society the socially excluded 'underclass' identified above, as part of a major government project – or 'big idea' – that this author has elsewhere termed 'reintegrative tutelage' (Hopkins Burke, 1999a, 2008). In order to achieve that ambition it was necessary to incorporate theoretical insights from each of the three substantive models of crime and criminal behaviour outlined in this book and it is the youth justice provisions, in particular, contained in that government's initial flagship criminal justice legislation – The Crime and Disorder Act 1998 – that provides us with an unequivocal demonstration of that strategy.

The influence of the rational actor model is indicated in that legislation by the emphasis on the notion that the young offender must take responsibility for their actions. First, the rule of 'doli incapax' that had presumed that a child under the age of fourteen does not know the difference between serious right and wrong was revised. Second, the courts were given powers to impose a new reparation order, requiring young offenders to make some form of reparation to their victims. It was the crucial intention of these legislative changes that young offenders would encounter the consequences of their actions and recognise the harm they had caused their victims (Home Office, 1997).

Evidence of the influence of the predestined actor model is contained in legislative strategies to identify young people at risk of becoming involved in criminal activity. First, the child safety order was introduced to intervene in the lives of children aged under ten who are considered to be at risk of becoming involved in crime; for example, if they are found wandering the streets unsupervised late at night, or are failing to attend school. Second, local authorities are empowered to impose a temporary curfew on children aged under ten in a specified public area.

These legislative initiatives contained in the Crime and Disorder Act 1998 were however located in the context of a range of other policy initiatives devised to tackle the causes of crime and criminality amongst young people, while at the same time recognising their status as victims of serious social and economic exclusion. There is a clear resonance here with the victimised actor model. First, measures were introduced to support families including assistance for single parents to get off benefits and return to work, to help prevent marriage and family breakdown and to deal with such breakdown. Second, policies were introduced with the intention of helping children achieve at school. These measures included the provision of nursery education for all four year olds; an emphasis on higher school standards, with a particular focus on literacy and numeracy skills in primary schools; with steps taken to tackle truancy and prevent exclusions; and the provision of study support out of school hours. Third, there was the provision of opportunities for jobs, training, and leisure, through the New Start strategy aimed at re-engaging in education or training youngsters up to seventeen that have dropped out of the system. Moreover, there was the welfare to work New Deal for unemployed eighteen to 24 year olds. Fourth, action was taken to tackle drug misuse with new initiatives in the criminal justice system, innovative projects showing what schools and the wider community can do and through the work of the new UK Anti-Drugs Co-ordinator in putting forward a new strategy aimed at young people.

In short, there was to be a comprehensive 'balance of intervention' in the lives of young offenders – or those at serious risk of becoming offenders – with the intention of tackling both their offending behaviour while at the same time challenging the socio-economic structural conditions that had contributed to making such behaviour a rational choice for many. Hopkins Burke (2008: 11) observes that:

> ... Left alone these young people face a life of social exclusion, serious offending, probable lengthy periods of incarceration and the likelihood of being involved in the raising of a further generation in their own image. Of course many of these young males may have only a tangential role in parenting their own children.

The New Labour 'reintegrative tutelage' crime control strategy (Hopkins Burke, 1999a) can be situated in the context of a government commitment to the socio-political notion of communitarianism where there is an emphasis on the centrality of informal, communal bonds, networks for the maintenance of social order and the rights of communities rather than the liberal emphasis on the rights of individuals (See Hughes, 1998, 2000). The US sociologist Amitai Etzioni (1993) is the most prominent contemporary proponent of a conservative communitarianism that seeks a 'remoralisation of society' where people are required to accept their responsibilities to society and not just focus on their rights and entitlements. A more radical version emphasises principles of spontaneous solidarity, rules of reciprocity and small-scale communities founded on participatory democracy (Jordan, 1996).

Communitarianism is discussed in significantly more detail in the concluding chapter of this book but it will suffice for our purposes here to observe that New Labour has been invariably associated with the more conservative version and it is the introduction of the Antisocial Behaviour Order (ASBO) that has clearly demonstrated a commitment to the rights of community even when these have impacted negatively on those of the individual (Hopkins Burke and Morrill, 2002, 2004). ASBOs are statutory measures that aim to protect the public from behaviour that causes or is likely to cause harassment, alarm or distress, contain conditions prohibiting the offender from specific antisocial acts or entering defined areas, and are effective for a minimum of two years. They are civil orders applied for by local authorities, police forces and registered social landlords but breach is a criminal offence, which is arrestable and can lead to the imposition of custodial sentences and it is this element that has been widely criticised by libertarians (see Von Hirsch *et al.*, 1999; Squires and Stephen, 2005).

Hopkins Burke and Morrill (2004), in contrast, observe that people – and the communities in which they live – have a right to be protected against harassment, alarm, distress and incivilities and that it is perfectly reasonable that such behaviour is targeted by the authorities to ensure protection. From this perspective, the ASBO is a reasonable measure that has filled a prominent gap in the law; it is not a punishment but a deterrent and its purpose is to curtail behaviour before it reaches a criminal level. The authors do suggest however that the 'balance of intervention' may have shifted too much in favour of 'communities' at the expense of individual liberty and that there is a 'worrying potential to absorb further into a widening net a whole group of relatively non problematic young people who left pretty much alone would grow out of their antisocial activities and become respectable members of society' (2004: 240).

Jock Young (1999, 2001 and 2003) has questioned the capacity of the New Labour reintegrative tutelage project to successfully tackle a crime problem so clearly identified with what is a difficult to empirically isolate socially excluded minority population. Thus, the social exclusion thesis proposes a supposed binary divide between an inclusive and largely satisfied majority and an excluded and despondent minority. Yet, the presumption of a fairly static underclass is nevertheless misleading as there is in reality a great deal of social mobility across categories (see Hills, LeGrand and Pichaud, 2002). Moreover, there is a supposed moral exclusion where exists a vast majority with good habits of work, virtuous conduct, stable family structures and a minority who are disorganised, welfare dependent, criminal and criminogenic, who live in unstable and dysfunctional families. There is a supposed spatial exclusion where the excluded are geographically isolated from the included and the borderlines between the two are rarely crossed. In reality, no such spatial segregation is empirically apparent – physical mobility in and out of the ghetto, for example, is frequent – and the values of its inhabitants are shared with those of the wider society (Nightingale, 1993; Young, 1999); furthermore, the geographical localities themselves have a mixed population many of whom are in work (Hagedorn, 1992; Newman, 1999).

Young nevertheless continues to support political demands for social integration and citizenship noting that such policies have formed the basis of relatively successful French social inclusion policies (see Pitts, 2003) directly targeted at reducing the problems of racism and active social exclusion both within civil society and by the criminal justice system. Social policies which *both* address the problems of economic exclusion, on the one hand, and social and political exclusion on the other, are proposed (Young and Matthews, 2003). These issues are again revisited in the final part of this book.

Left realist theory revisited

Hopkins Burke (2004b, 2004c) has used left realist theory in a historical context in order to explain the development of the public police service in England and Wales. He observes that the orthodox social progress perspective presents the emergence, expansion and consolidation of a bureaucratic service as part of a progressive humanitarian development of institutions necessary to respond to crime and disorder (Reith, 1956). At the other end of the spectrum, the revisionist Marxist-inspired critical criminological view proposes that the police were 'domestic missionaries' with an emphasis on the surveillance, discipline and control of the rough and dangerous working class elements in society with all of this accomplished in the interests of the capitalist class (Storch, 1975). From this perspective contemporary 'hard' policing strategies targeted at socially excluded groups in society are simply a continuation of that tradition (see Crowther, 1998). Hopkins Burke (2004b, 2004c) observes that empirical reality appears to lie somewhere in the middle of these two polar opposite viewpoints.

The revisionist critical criminology account thus considers definitions of crime and criminality to be class-based with the public police service unequivocally the agents of a capitalist society targeting the activities of the socially excluded while at the same time ignoring the far more damaging behaviour of corporate capitalism (see Scraton and Chadwick, 1996 originally 1992). A left realist account, on the other hand, considers the situation to have been far more ambiguous, crucially recognising that crime was as a real problem for ordinary people in the nineteenth century as it is now (Hopkins Burke, 2004b).

Observed from a left realist perspective it is apparent that from soon after the introduction of the new police in the mid-nineteenth century there was a widespread – and admittedly at times tacit and fairly grudging – acceptance and support for the service. The police may well have targeted criminal elements within the working class and they might on occasion have taken the side of capital in trade disputes but at the same time their moralising mission on the streets coincided conveniently with the increasing enthusiasm for self-betterment among the great majority that has been described from differing sociological perspectives as 'embourgeoisement' (Goldthorpe, 1968-9) and 'the civilising process' (Elias, 1978, 1982).

Moreover, this left realist perspective dismisses neither the orthodox nor revisionist accounts but produces a synthesis of the two. For it seems self-evident that the police – in some form or another – are essential to deal with conflicts, disorders and problems of co-ordination necessarily generated by any complex and materially advanced society (Reiner, 2000) and that there is thus a widespread demand for policing throughout society and among all social classes. Recent studies have shown that while during the nineteenth century prosecutions for property crime emanated overwhelmingly from the more affluent groups, poorer sections of society also resorted extensively to the law as victims (see Storch, 1989; Philips and Storch, 1999; Emsley, 1996; Taylor, 1997; Miller, 1999). Indeed, at crucial times these poorer groups had considerable interest in the maintenance of the status quo. For example, the end of the Crimean War and the prospect of a footloose army of unemployed soldiers returning – at the very time that transportation to the colonies had ended – meant that 'an organised race of criminals' would be roaming the countryside looking for criminal opportunities and from who all would need protection (Hopkins Burke, 1998c, 1999b). Thus, while working-class antagonism may have been exacerbated by police intervention in recreational activities and labour disputes, a close reading of the issues suggests a more complex situation than previously supposed (Hart, 1978). There certainly seems to be little doubt that the police were closely linked with the general increase in orderliness on the streets of Victorian society (Gatrell, 1980; Taylor, 1997) and this was again widely welcomed. Indeed, it has been argued that the crucial way in which the police affect law enforcement is not by the apprehension of criminals – for that depends on many factors beyond their control – but by symbolising the existence of a functioning legal order, by having a visible presence on the street and being seen to be doing something (Gatrell, 1980). It is a discourse that coincides neatly with a consistent widespread contemporary public demand for police on the streets frequently expressed in contemporary crime surveys and regardless of the academic policing orthodoxy that has repeatedly stated that the service on its own can have little effect on the crime rate (see Morgan and Newburn, 1997) and has been finally acknowledged by the British Home Office.

Hopkins Burke (2008) has subsequently developed his left realist historical perspective to help explain the increasing surveillance and control of young people on the streets and elsewhere from the nineteenth century onwards. For the moralising mission of the entrepreneurial philanthropists and the reforming zeal of the liberal politician and administrator corresponded conveniently with those of the mill and mine-owners and a government which wanted a fit healthy fighting force, but it also coincides with the ever increasing enthusiasm for self-betterment among the great majority of the working class that we observed above. Those who were resistant to that moralising and disciplinary mission – the 'rough working' class of the Victorian era – have subsequently been reinvented in academic and popular discourse as the socially excluded 'underclass' of contemporary society, with the moral panics of today a reflection of those of the past and demands for action remarkably similar.

Hopkins Burke (2008) observes that neo-Marxist critical criminology accounts demand significant prominence in this hybrid left realist explanation for significantly young people – and indeed all of us – were in the nineteenth century and certainly today subject to the requirements and demands of the economy. This historical version of the left realist perspective briefly explained here provides a variant on the carceral – or surveillance – society thesis we will encounter in the next and final part of this book by acknowledging our own contribution to the pervasive disciplinary-control-matrix that has encroached upon all our lives.

Suggested further reading

For a comprehensive introduction to the basic tenets of left realism you should consult Lea and Young (1984), Matthews and Young (1986, 1992) and Young (1994). Hopkins Burke (1999a) extends the discussion of the process model of the underclass, while Hopkins Burke and Morrill (2004) discuss the ambiguities between the rights of individuals and communities. Hughes (1998, 2000) provides excellent introductions to communitarianism and its links to crime control and community safety. Young (1999) is essential for a contemporary discussion of social exclusion, while Young and Matthews (2003) should be readily consulted on the relationship between the former and New Labour. Hopkins Burke (2004a) outlines his left realist account of the development of the police service and (Hopkins Burke, 2008) discusses the development of the increasing surveillance and control of young people and the emergence of the contemporary youth justice system.

Part Five

Crime and criminal behaviour in the age of moral uncertainty

Neither liberalism, economic or political, nor the various Marxisms emerge from [the last] two centuries untainted by accusations of crimes against humanity. We can make a list of names, names of places, persons, dates, capable of illustrating and substantiating our suspicion. Following Theodor Adorno I have used the name 'Auschwitz' to signify the extent to which recent Western philosophy seems inconsistent as regards the 'modern' project of the emancipation of humanity.

Lyotard (1988: 110)

My argument is that the modern project (of realisation of universality) has not been abandoned, forgotten, but destroyed, 'liquidated'. There are several methods of destruction, several names which are symbols of it Auschwitz can be taken as a paradigmatic name for the tragic incompletion of modernity.

Lyotard (1988: 32)

Grand narratives have become barely credible.

Lyotard (1988: 46)

This book has examined the different ways that crime and criminal behaviour have been explained during the past 200 years. While these explanations have been proposed at various times by among others legal philosophers, biologists, psychologists, sociologists, political scientists and geographers, it is possible to locate these many and varied explanations – or criminological theories – in terms of one of three different general models or traditions that were the focus of the first three parts of this book.

The first tradition – the rational actor model – proposes that human beings enjoy free will and this enables them to choose whether or not to engage in criminal activities. Crime can be controlled by making the costs of offending – that is, punishment – sufficient to discourage the pursuit of criminal rewards. In other words, the choice of criminal activity would be irrational in such circumstances.

The second tradition – the predestined actor model – proposes that criminal behaviour can be explained in terms of factors that exist either within the individual or their environment that cause that person to act in ways over which they have little or no control. Crime can be controlled by identifying and eradicating these factors through some form of treatment process. Thus, biological and psychological variants propose that the individual should be changed, while sociological versions advocate the transformation of the criminogenic environment.

The third tradition – the victimised actor model – denies neither entirely the prescriptions of the rational actor or the predestined actor models but recognises that people make decisions to behave in ways that may well be perfectly rational for them in the circumstances in which they find themselves but that it is the activities of the economically poor and politically powerless that are criminalised, a process which is conducted in the interests of those with power and wealth. At the micro level, individuals can be labelled and criminalised by coming into contact with front-line agents of the state working in the criminal justice and welfare systems; at the macro societal level it is those with economic power and the control of authority that are in a position to influence the legislative agenda. From this perspective, crime is seen to be a social construction; it can be controlled or reduced by not criminalising dispossessed unfortunates and by abolishing legislation that criminalises their activities.

The fourth part of this book has discussed those attempts to produce a synthesis of different theoretical perspectives – some of these being internal to one particular model of criminal behaviour, others incorporating elements that cross model boundaries – with the intention of providing a bigger, better, all-encompassing theory that seeks to explain as much crime and criminal behaviour as possible. Indeed, these integrated perspectives invariably seek to explain *all* criminal behaviour, an approach clearly in line with modernist social science thinking.

It has been explained that each of the theories introduced in this book – and, indeed, their particular host model or explanatory tradition – have a common central characteristic: that is, each is a product of what has come to be termed the modern age. Prior to the rise of modernity, religion and other forms of pre-scientific knowledge had crucially influenced explanations of crime and, at that time, criminal justice and its administration was non-codified, capricious, invariably brutal and at the cynical discretion of the agents of monarchical regimes. In contrast modern societies are secular, industrialised, rationalised, codified and rule-bound with at least some pretence to widely participative democracy. Science is the dominant – and for a long time unchallenged – form of knowledge and thus, crime and criminal behaviour has been invariably explained by reference to scientific discourses or theories while there had been a wider modernist faith in reason which stretches back from the great liberals of the twentieth century back beyond the Enlightenment philosophers of the eighteenth century, to the Greeks:

> Man is in principle at least, everywhere and in every condition, able, if he wills it, to discover and apply rational solutions to his problems. And these solutions, because they are rational, cannot clash with one another, and will ultimately form a harmonious system in which the truth will prevail, and freedom, happiness, and unlimited opportunity for untrammelled self-development will be open to all.
>
> (Berlin, 1969: 8)

In the last decades of the twentieth century there became increasing doubts about the sustainability of the modernist project in an increasingly fragmented and diverse social world and this is a situation that some social scientists have come to refer as the postmodern condition (see Lyotard, 1984; but also Baudrillard 1988; Bauman, 1989, 1991, 1993). Three main sources for the idea of the postmodern can be identified. The first is the emergence and consolidation of an intellectual current articulated by the publication of two books by Daniel Bell, *The End of Ideology* (1960) and *The Coming of Post-Industrial Society* (1973). It was an emerging world view with two sub-currents: there was the ideological exhaustion of the post-war world with the retreat from the pre-war ideologies of communism and National Socialism that had seemed to lead to only totalitarianism, world war and holocaust. At the same time, there was a growing interest in the idea of a post-industrial – or later 'post-Fordist' – society where manufacturing was giving way to the service industry, primary production was being displaced by secondary exploitation – especially of science and technology – and consumers were coming to outperform producers in the economy. In this changed context, the old radical class analyses seemed to make little sense and the intellectual categories around which modernism had been built appeared to have lost their explanatory power.

The second source is poststructuralism, a movement which had flourished mainly in France during the late 1960s and 1970s and, as its name suggests, succeeded structuralism, which had flourished a decade or so earlier, most notably in the work of Claude Levi-Strauss, but which could be traced back to the nineteenth century. While structuralists had been preoccupied with the 'deep structures' of language and society, poststructuralists were sceptical of efforts to attach meanings to words. Michel Foucault significantly contributed to the wider popular influence of poststructuralism by arguing that knowledge and language – and so the categories derived from them – cannot be regarded as anything other than subjective and relative (Foucault, 1980). Thus, by emphasising the subjectivity of language, poststructuralism contributed to the central belief of postmodernism, that no intellectual tradition can have privileged authority over another.

The third source was an aesthetic movement with its foundations in an architectural controversy centred on the rejection of the so-called 'international style' of austere unadorned modernism epitomised by 1960s tower blocks and multi-storey car parks.

In summary, there are three significant characteristics that appear to distinguish postmodernism from modernism. First, there is an aversion to 'metadiscourses' – or grand self-legitimating theories – that it is proposed can lead to intellectual sterility and political oppression. Second, there is an awareness of the indeterminacy of knowledge and the impossibility of absolute truth inherited from poststructuralism. Third, there is an enthusiasm for eclecticism and variety derived from art, architecture and literature but which has come to have much stronger intellectual reverberations.

The idea of the postmodern thus involves claims that modernist features of society are under challenge. This can be seen in the realm of culture, where self-proclaimed modern thinkers and artists were challenged from the mid-1960s by anti-modernist ideas which attacked the dehumanisation of modern society, questioned the authority of technical experts and celebrated human diversity in place of the pressure to encourage rationalised, standardised, human conformity to systems developed by 'experts' and technicians (see Marcuse, 1964). These concerns were furthermore reflected in the social sciences field by the emergence of radical efforts to challenge orthodox, positivist forms of thought whose claims to objective scientific status were questioned and rejected.

Underlying these changes was the beginning of an economic and political transformation manifest in a breakdown of the Keynesian and Fordist practices of the post-war world in the industrial West. This had been prompted by the oil crisis of the early 1970s, an abandonment of full employment policies with a decline in economic competitiveness, and a restructuring of the world economy with the rise in the productive capacity of the nations of the Pacific Rim. Thus, in all three areas, the economy, the political system and culture, there began to emerge increasingly diverse and fragmented social structures that herald the beginning of postmodernism.

Economically, postmodernity is often described as post-Fordism which involves the rejection of mass production-line technology in favour of both flexible working patterns and labour force. This in turn involves a weakening of trade unions, greater reliance on peripheral and secondary labour markets, the development of a low-paid and part-time, often female, labour force, and the shift towards a service, rather than manufacturing, economy. On the side of capital owning and controlling interests, it involves a greater stress on enterprise and entrepreneurialism, corporate restructuring and the growth of small businesses acting as subcontractors to larger firms. These trends are often seen as evidence of deindustrialisation and the disorganisation of capitalism.

Politically, postmodernity is complex and is difficult to categorise in traditional terms. An interesting development has been Michel Foucault's (1980) poststructuralist conceptualisation of power, which he argues is not simply the prerogative of the state. Strategies of power are seen to be pervasive in society with the state only one location of the points of control and resistance and, from this perspective, there should be a move away from a restricted chain of criminological references – 'state-law-crime-criminals' – to a wider chain of associations that need to be addressed. Thus, for Foucault (1971, 1976) particular areas of social life – for example, medicine, law, sexuality – are colonised and defined by the norms and control strategies which a variety of institutions and experts devise and abide by (Foucault, 1971, 1976). These networks of power and control are governed as much by the *knowledge* and concepts that define them as by the definite intentions of individuals and groups.

The state, for its part, is implicated in this matrix of power-knowledge, but it is only part of it and, in this vein, it has been argued that within civil society there are numerous 'semi-autonomous' realms and relations – such as communities, occupations, organisations, families – where certain kinds of 'policing' and 'order' are indeed present, but where the state administration and police force are technically absent. These semi-autonomous arenas are often appropriately negotiated and resisted by their participants in ways over which even now the state has little jurisdiction. To some, it might seem ironic that this emphasis comes at a time when many of the traditional coercive and regulatory roles of the state are being *enhanced* politically and technologically and it is a point to which we return later for more recently many of these previously autonomous locations have been incorporated into multi-agency partnerships delivering the interests of the state from a distance.

Postmodernity has been expressed in neoconservative ideas, such as those promoted by the British Prime Minister, Margaret Thatcher and the US President, Ronald Reagan (and latterly very much so in the USA, by George Bush), and termed *Thatcherism* and *Reaganomics*. These ideologies have included the offering of tax cuts as means to facilitating consumer choice and the dismantling of elaborate state planning and provision in the fields of welfare. At the same time, the diversity of interests that have become apparent in Western societies has placed strains on conventional representative democratic systems. Thus, long-standing democracies have had significant difficulties in representing myriad interest groups as diverse as major industrialists and financiers, small business proprietors, the unemployed and dispossessed, wide-ranging gender and sexual preference interests, environmentalists and the homeless.

Modernity was essentially an era characterised by moral certainty. There was a confidence and belief in the superiority and infallibility of natural science that had filtered through into the social sciences, in particular, social and political theory. There was a confidence in the explanatory power of grand theories to solve the problems of humanity. There may be competing theories – for example, the many criminological theories introduced in this book – but the devotees of each of these had confidence in the fundamental capacity of their doctrine to solve the crime problem. This might well – as we have seen particularly in the fourth part – entail revisions to the theory, the incorporation of concepts from other theoretical perspectives and indeed other models of criminal behaviour but in the final analysis the intention is the same: as was observed earlier, the creation of a criminological theory that explains most – if not all – criminal activity.

Postmodern societies are – in contrast to modern societies – characterised by moral ambiguity. Now this condition should not be confused with a period of moral uncertainty where the reconsideration and rebuilding of theoretical perspectives can rekindle the moral certainty of old. It is a condition characterised by a terminal loss of certainty with absolutely no expectation that it will ever return.

Postmodern social scientists thus recognise the complexity of society and the moral ambiguities that are inherent within it and there is recognition of a range of different discourses that can be legitimate and hence right for different people, at different times, in different contexts. It is a perspective founded on cultural relativism, the notion that there are a series of legitimate discourses on a particular issue and that it is difficult, if not impossible, to objectively choose between them. Essentially, the objective truth – or the competing objective realities – of modernity, is replaced by recognition of the multiple realities or moral ambiguities of postmodernity. These realities are invariably complex, highly susceptible to inconsistent interpretation and are contested by individuals – politicians and members of the general public – who often make short-term, pragmatic and inconsistent judgements without reference to any coherent body of knowledge.

Whereas modernists had attempted to develop large-scale theories to explain society in terms of enduring, identifiable social structures, postmodernists have followed in the poststructuralist tradition emphasising the redundancy and futility of such efforts and contested the entire concept of truth. The social sciences – since their very inception in modern societies – had made efforts to transcend the relativity of social situations and identify 'what is going on' systematically and objectively, while philosophers had attempted to establish some rational standpoint from which reality could be described. Postmodern writers have, on the other hand, celebrated the failure of the modern project to establish rational foundations for knowledge and have themselves embraced the trend towards human diversity and social fragmentation arguing that there is no objective reality behind the plethora of social meanings. Accounts and definitions have no objective or external reference but are merely elements in a free-floating system of images that are produced and reproduced through the medium of popular mass communication that come to define reality to consumers.

To some postmodernism is undoubtedly a nightmare vision but others have embraced and celebrated its implications. The fragmentation of social institutions such as social class and status may have increased our uncertainty in how we understand society but, on the other hand, the same trends allow the expression of the diversity of human needs, interests and sensitivities. By challenging the validity of modern claims to privileged forms of knowledge for the powerful, postmodernism gives a voice to the less powerful and oppressed and it is thus not surprising that some branches of feminism have embraced this approach.

Postmodernists have also celebrated the development of new social movements such as travelling communities as they make efforts to live a lifestyle outside of the constraints and dictates of the modern world. In the Western world, gay and what were formerly regarded as other unconventional sexual interest groups have also been celebrated for their efforts to break down restrictive stereotypes and 'expert' knowledge surrounding the pursuit of sexual pleasure. The ideas and interests of animal rights groups and environmental concerns have also been welcomed. These challenge the adequacy of representation in long-established representative democracies in which party systems commonly only represent the interests of people as members of a social class and, hence, give rise to a restricted form of political agenda which fails to address other interests. The celebration and acceptance of diversity, therefore, is taken as a positive thing.

Lyotard reflects on some of the horrors of the past two centuries of modernist society when people have controlled and killed others in their pursuit of a rational, scientific world order that – in the criminological context – had led us from the biological notions of Lombroso via Goring to Auschwitz:

> The nineteenth and twentieth centuries have given us as much terror as we can take. We have paid a high enough price for the nostalgia of the whole and the one, for the reconciliation of the concept and the sensible, of the transparent and the communicable experience. Under the general demand for slackening and for appeasement, we can hear the mutterings of the desire for a return to terror, for the realisation of the fantasy to seize reality. The answer is: let us wage war on totality; let us be witness to the unrepresentable; let us activate the differences and save the honour of the name.
>
> (Lyotard, 1984: 81–2)

The philosopher of the social sciences, Feyerabend had too celebrated a non-rationalist – even anarchistic – approach to the manner in which we study the world. Highly critical of efforts to unify and control the limits of science and the potential for knowledge as authoritarian and inhumane, he argues that 'science is an essentially anarchistic enterprise: theoretical anarchism is more humanitarian and more likely to encourage progress than its "law and order" alternatives' (Feyerabend, 1975: 17).

Problematically, given this general approach, we might legitimately ask how Feyerabend can legitimately judge what is 'more humanitarian' and more 'progressive'. In comparison to what is it progressive and why is this so? The Feyerabend legacy is nevertheless significant because it alerts us not to be slaves to dominant paradigms of how we see the world but be prepared to take risks – perhaps even be prepared to consider the previously unthinkable at least in terms of contemporary orthodoxy – and be prepared to consider the potential of a whole range of often neglected theoretical perspectives.

17. Crime and the postmodern condition

Postmodernism can appear to be an extremely negative and nihilistic vision for if there is no such thing as the 'truth of the human condition' it is difficult to formulate an argument in support of basic human rights, or to locate legitimate foundations for law, if the human experience is seen to be reflexive and relative. The relativism implied by postmodernism thus denies the possibility of truth, and hence of justice, in anything other than a purely subjective form, which inevitably consigns us to the prospect of conflict.

Politically, postmodernism can carry us right the way across the traditional political spectrum from the libertarian right-wing assumption of a war of all against all, resonant of the work of Thomas Hobbes, to a libertarianism of the left, or even anarchism, which celebrates and tolerates all human diversity and activity. Postmodernism therefore appears contemptuous of the possibility of developing an objective normative (moral) order which human beings can translate into enforceable norms or laws. Thus, while intellectually challenging and providing a possible explanation for the nature of social change in contemporary western societies, postmodernism has appeared extremely problematic for developing a plausible criminological strategy and this will become increasingly apparent throughout this fifth part of the book.

It is by regarding postmodernism in two distinct ways that it is possible we can accept some of its power to explain the enormous diversity in contemporary society without accepting some of the baggage of philosophical relativism. Pauline-Marie Rosenau (1992: 15) offers this option identifying what she terms *sceptical* and *affirmative* postmodernism:

The sceptical postmodernism (or merely sceptic), offering a pessimistic, negative, gloomy assessment, argues that the postmodern age is one of fragmentation, disintegration, malaise, meaninglessness, a vagueness, or even absence of moral parameters and societal chaos ... This is the dark side of postmodernism, the postmodernism of despair, the postmodernism that speaks of the immediacy of death, the demise of the subject, the end of the author, the impossibility of truth. They argue that the destructive nature of modernity makes the postmodern age one of 'radical, unsuppressible uncertainty' ... characterised by all that is grim, cruel, alienating, hopeless, tired and ambiguous. In this period no social or political project is worthy of commitment. If, as the sceptics claim, there is no truth, then all that is left is play, the play of words and meaning.

Acknowledging that there is no clear-cut divide between the approaches, Rosenau (1992: 15–16) identifies an alternative and altogether more positive tendency in the postmodern movement:

> Although the affirmative postmodernists ... agree with the sceptical postmodern critique of modernity, they have a more hopeful, optimistic view of the postmodern age. More indigenous to Anglo-North American culture than to the [European] Continent, the generally optimistic affirmatives are oriented towards process. They are either open to positive political action (struggle and resistance) or content with the recognition of visionary, celebratory, personal, non-dogmatic projects that range from New Age religion to New Wave lifestyles and include a whole spectrum of postmodern social movements. Most affirmatives seek a philosophical and intellectual practice that is non-dogmatic, tentative and non-ideological. These postmodernists do not, however, shy away from affirming an ethic, making normative choices, and striving to build issue-specific political coalitions. Many affirmatives argue that certain value choices are superior to others, a line of reasoning that would incur the disapproval of the sceptical postmodernists.

The essential problem for the development of legislation and explanations of crime and criminal behaviour in the postmodern condition remains the difficulty of making any objective claims for truth, goodness and morality. This is less the case for the affirmatives than for the sceptics. On the issue of the foundations of knowledge (epistemology), Rosenau (1992: 137) notes:

> Postmodern social science ... announces the end of all paradigms. Only an absence of knowledge claims, an affirmation of multiple realities, and an acceptance of divergent interpretations remain. We can convince those who agree with us, but we have no basis for convincing those who dissent and no criteria to employ in arguing for the superiority of any particular view. Those who disagree with us can always argue that different interpretations must be accepted and that in a postmodern world one interpretation is as good as another. Postmodernists have no interest in convincing others that their view is best – the most just, appropriate, or true. In the end the problem with most postmodern social science is that you can say anything you want, but so can everyone else. Some of what is said will be interesting and fascinating, but some will also be ridiculous and absurd. Postmodernism provides no means to distinguish between the two.

There are clearly some fundamental logical intellectual difficulties posed for those seeking to research and explain criminal behaviour. First, there is little available empirical evidence to support the assumption that we have already reached a post ideological climate. To argue that we can achieve the position that no intellectual tradition can be considered to have privileged authority over another is seriously problematic as the only too obvious reality is that particular traditions are usually seen to be more authoritative. We should moreover note at this juncture that many influential social scientists and theorists deny the notion of postmodern society – which for such a social formation to exist would require some substantive rupture with the modernist social formation – and thus emphasising the continuities and following the influential social theorist Anthony Giddens (1990, 1991) use the term late modernity. The term postmodern *condition* is thus used in this book, although we might note that the equally distinguished social theorist Norbert Elias (1978, 1982) had previously observed that we live in a period of late barbarism.

Second, whilst postmodernism may advocate giving a voice to the oppressed and less powerful – and may celebrate diversity – it could be argued that in practice power relations and political decisions are fundamentally important and may restrict this ideal. Indeed, it could be argued that recent criminal justice policy – both in the UK and the USA and beyond – and the politics that have informed it have tended to encourage less tolerance of difference rather than more. We will now consider how constitutive criminology has sought to explain crime and criminal behaviour in the context of the postmodern condition and their proposed solutions.

Constitutive criminology and postmodernity

Mark Cowling (2006) observes while many criminologists have used aspects of postmodernism as a critique – or as a source of inspiration – the only well-developed attempt to rethink the central issues and themes of criminology in terms of postmodern theories is the constitutive criminology originally developed by Stuart Henry and Dragan Milovanovic (1996, 1999, 2000, 2001). In a critical review of their perspective he observes that they actually produce a fairly orthodox account of postmodernism where there are no privileged knowledges and everyone or anyone is an expert, with a celebration of diversity, plurality and the subjugated. We should nevertheless note that the authors themselves actually deny they are postmodernists and that they and their subsequent followers depend on aspects of modernism in order to identify the marginalised and oppressed. The two main theoretical foundations of constitutive criminology can be identified as being an interpretation of the post-Freudian Jacques Lacan and chaos theory which in its original manifestation describes the behaviour of certain dynamic systems.

Jacques Lacan and constitutive criminology

The ideas of Lacan centre on Freudian concepts such as the unconscious, the castration complex and the ego with the focus being on the centrality of language to subjectivity. Lacan has been extremely influential in critical theory, literary studies and twentieth-century French philosophy but it is his interpretation of clinical psychoanalysis that has been influential with constitutive criminologists.

Lacan understands psychoanalysis as a process in which there are four major discourses: (i) the discourse of the master, (ii) the University, (iii) the hysteric; and (iv) the analyst. It is invariably the role of the discourse of the analyst to help develop the discourse of the hysteric in order to assist her through a collaborative process in articulating her desire and in the criminological context this can be a prisoner, an oppressed community or group who are being helped by an expert activist. Williams and Arrigo (2004) cite the example of young offenders involved in restorative justice.

Constitutive criminologists argue that people who are being repressed by the criminal justice system are extremely likely to be suffering oppression and would thus benefit from assistance in articulating their needs while, at the same time, they might well have desires which are not socially acceptable in their current form and which can get them into trouble with the law. This notion is clearly problematic because of the difficulty of reconciling individual needs with those of the group. Henry and Milovanovic (2001: 168) acknowledge this conundrum to some extent and note that 'satisfying positions of desire can occur at another's expense'.

Constitutive criminologists have a strong commitment to social justice rather than merely criminal justice and thus Henry and Milovanovic (1996: 64) aim for a 'constitutive theorising [which] is a contingently and provisionally based humanistic vision of what could be a radical superliberalism' and where justice is held to be specific to particular sites and which cannot be linked to a desire for consensus or universally posited agreement. Tracy Young (1999) adopts a similar approach and observes that modernist criminal justice systems are concerned with the rationality, uniformity and consistency of treatment before the law, whereas the postmodern equivalent is grounded in chaos theory which allows room for creativity. Variation and creativity are thus seen to be desirable and some of this is linked to the idea that different local justice systems can coexist with each other. Young (1997) uses the examples of a Native American system – or one within a professional body – which she observes can coexist within the wider state justice system.

Chaos theory and constitutive criminology

Henry and Milovanovic (1996) observe that chaos theory is a central component in much postmodernist analysis and it is therefore worth exploring this notion a little further. Chaos theory began as a field of physics and mathematics dealing with the structures of turbulence and self-similar forms of fractal geometry. As it is popularly understood, chaos deals with unpredictable complex systems and the theory originates, in part, from the work of Edward Lorenz, a meteorologist, who simulated weather patterns on a computer. Working with a computer which had limited memory and after viewing a particular pattern, he wanted to recover the data and started the program again, except he put in the values rounded off to three places instead of the original six. He was astonished to find a completely different result on his computer than previously which looked like this when it was printed out:

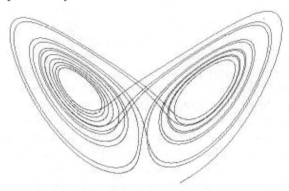

This has become known as the 'butterfly effect' and is often used to refer to complexity and unpredictability and in chaos theory refers to the discovery that in a chaotic system such as the global weather, tiny perturbations (or slight disturbances of a system by a secondary influence within the system) may sometimes lead to major changes in the overall system. It is theoretically possible that a slight rise in temperature in the ocean off the cost of Peru will create tiny changes in the airflow that would eventually lead to different weather in North America and Europe. In most cases the slight change would make no difference whatsoever, but when the system is unpredictable at a certain stage, the future may unfold quite differently, depending upon what little difference occurred. Chaos theory has been subsequently applied to the study of management and organisations – including those within the criminal justice system – and where the constituents of a system are observed to be complex and unpredictable. Some observe parallels between chaos theory and postmodernism even to the extent of proposing that the former is postmodern science (Hayles, 1990, 1991; Brennan, 1995; Bloland, 1995; Markus, 2000) but there is also significant opposition to that notion.

The application of the mathematics of chaos theory to society is inherently problematic (Cowling, 2006). Chaos theory tends to be seen as applicable to physical phenomena governed by deterministic laws which are predictable in principle but which are in reality unpredictable in practice because they are so sensitive to initial conditions. This is famously expressed in the idea that a butterfly flapping its wings in Brazil might cause a hurricane in Florida three weeks from that date and this is why, although it is possible to predict roughly the sort of weather which can be expected in a particular place in three weeks' time, it is not possible to produce an accurate weather forecast. Human societies, in contrast, are complicated systems involving a vast number of variables, for which it is impossible – at least currently – to develop any legitimate equations and thus to speak of systems in terms of chaos takes us no further than the intuition already contained in popular wisdom (Sokal and Bricmont, 1999). Thus the sort of situation in society where a small cause can produce a large effect will also be a highly unpredictable situation and where it is not at all clear what will eventually emerge. Thus, for example, the assignation of Archduke Franz Ferdinand of Austria in Sarajevo in 1914 precipitated a complex chain of events that was to lead to World War 1 and a multitude of subsequent momentous linked events which have changed the history of the world. Few, if any, of these events could have been predicted at the time. Some of those involved in the constitutive criminology project thus use chaos theory simply as a metaphor (Simons and Stroup, 1997; Arrigo 1997; Williams and Arrigo, 2004) but in the main the authors see themselves as *applying* chaos theory (Cowling, 2006).

Constitutive criminologists adopt three main concepts from chaos theory: (i) the notion of undecidability or uncertainty, (ii) the idea that one individual can make a significant difference, and (iii) the analysis of conditions being far from equilibrium. The first two outcomes thus flow from the idea that a very small initial difference can have a massive causal effect but the problem with this is that given the very many possible initial variables the very idea of undecidability means that social science becomes impossible. We simply cannot know what outcome we might expect from an initial set of variables. The constitutive response to this conundrum however is to celebrate the unexpected, surprise, ironic, contradictory, and emergent (Milovanovic, 1997a) but this does seem to occur in a context where there is no background of regularity against which to contrast the unexpected.

Cowling (2006) observes that the idea that one individual can make a difference is found repeatedly in constitutive criminology and the best way of assessing the idea is to consider some ways in which it might be recognised in practice. The examples provided by the constitutive criminologists concern things such as a crossing guard who takes an interest in one particular young person, thus helping him avoid becoming delinquent when his circumstances would make this likely, or going on a demonstration, signing a petition, engaging in civil disobedience or voting (Milovanovic, 1997b).

A further use of chaos theory concerns situations where, following a great deal of replication, far from equilibrium conditions result, and the system itself may thus change dramatically. Young (1997) thus proposes that white-collar crime may be instigated by four or more unmanageable parameters. Thus, for example, a doctor might cope with a general drop in his or her income, the failure of investment portfolios and the reduction in rent payments from tenants if a major corporation was to move from the city, but any further losses such as patients defaulting on bills could well drive them to crime. We might call this the 'straw that broke the camel's back' argument.

A rather different use of chaos theory is the claim that truth values are 'fractal': thus, matters of right or wrong, good or bad, just or unjust are simply matters of degree (Arrigo, 1997). This claim is nevertheless over-optimistic for the practical consequence of the unpredictability which follows from chaos theory is that standard moral judgements become impossible. Cowling (2006) observes that we commend acts of charity because they help people in need while we condemn random unpremeditated violence because it harms people who do not deserve to be harmed. The adoption of chaos theory simply undermines any confidence we might have in typical consequences and thus we have no legitimate basis for making moral judgements.

Henry and Milovanovic (1996) define crime as the power to deny others and they argue that the conventional crime control strategies, in the form of fast expanding criminal justice institutions – the police and prisons – or as political rhetoric rehearsed in the media, fuel the engine of crime. What they seek is the development of 'replacement discourses' that fuel positive social constructions with the intention not to 'replace one truth with another' but instead invoke 'a multiplicity of resistances' 'to the ubiquity of power' (Henry and Milovanovic, 1996: ix–xiii; Milovanovic, 1997b: 91). Constitutive criminologists are thus opposed to imprisonment which they consider to be merely incapacitation and an approach that presents a false separation between inside and outside and observe that the incarcerated actually commit more and worse crimes in their 'new architectural spaces'. They object to expenditure on prisons which they propose is money that might be better spent on education and welfare provision. Prison expansion is, moreover, accompanied by an increased fear of crime with the outcome that incapacitation simply offers the fiction of a safer society but actually offers more freedom for the powerful to commit more crimes (Henry and Milovanovic, 1996: 194; Milovanovic, 1997b). Constitutive criminologists are also opposed to the war on drugs and offer some support for mediation, conflict resolution, and reconciliation programmes and the idea of relating crime more to wider society (Henry and Milovanovic, 2001: 174–75).

Mark Cowling (2006) questions these notions and asks whether the imprisonment of serial killers and rapists simply makes things worse and queries whether it would be better for us all if the state did not interfere in domestic violence. He moreover asks whether it is an appropriate role for 'progressive' criminologists to be supporting 'resistances' by men who have been engaged in battering against the 'ubiquitous' power of the police and courts and propose that such expansive claims need to be revealed and argued rather than merely asserted.

We might observe that in many ways constitutive criminology has considerable similarities to the anarchist criminology to which we now turn although this is part of long-established tradition that clearly precedes postmodernity.

Anarchist criminology

Anarchism is an orientation toward social life and social relations that is ultimately no orientation at all. In fact, anarchism might best be thought of as disorientation; that is, an approach which openly values fractured, uncertain, and unrealised understandings and practices as the emerging essence of social life.

Ferrell, 1998: 5

Unlike most modernist intellectual orientations, anarchism and anarchist criminology do not seek to incorporate reasoned or reasonable critiques of law and legal authority but, in contrast, argue that progressive social change requires the 'unreasonable' and the 'unthinkable'. In other words, reason and 'common sense' notions of the legal and illegal are seen to keep us trapped within the present arrangements of authority and power, and it is thus in our interest to stop making sense, to imagine the unimaginable and think the unthinkable (Ferrell, 1998).

Anarchist criminologists launch aggressive and 'unreasonable' critiques against law and legal authority because they argue that these undermine human community and diversity. Anarchist criminology is thus different from the modernist critical criminological tradition because it is not a careful criticism of criminal justice, a 'loyal opposition' to the state and state law but stands instead as a disloyal and disrespectful attack (Mazor, 1978), a 'counterpunch to the belly of authority' (Ferrell, 1996: 197). Anarchist criminology furthermore aims its disrespectable gaze both high and low: it attacks the state structure and legal authority above us but also encourages those below and beyond this authority to find ways of resisting it and finding more egalitarian alternatives.

Anarchist critiques of law and legality are nothing new and have long established foundations in early anarchism itself with prominent writers and activists like William Godwin (1756–1836), Max Stirner (1806–56), Michael Bakunin (1814–76) and Peter Kropotkin (1842–1921) focusing some of their most significant assaults on state authority and legal control. Kropotkin (1975), for example, criticised the tendency of the law to crystallise that which should be modified and developed on a day-to-day basis and demanded the abolition of prisons and the law itself. Bukanin also called for the destruction of the state and its replacement with the spontaneous and continuous action of the masses.

Ferrell (1998) observes that such anarchist critiques have emerged not as the outcome of theoretical posturing but out of head-on confrontations between state legal authorities and anarchists attempting to construct alternative societal arrangements. Thus, for Bakunin and Kropotkin, anarchist criminology was part of revolutionary activity against the Russian oligarchy and the emerging nation states of capitalism. In fact, Bakunin's notion of 'the spontaneous and continuous action of the masses' referred to an actual case of anarchist revolt: the Paris Commune of 1871. In the USA, anarchists like Emma Goldman (1869–1940) and Alexander Berkman (1870–1936) also mixed labour and social activism with theoretical critique and spent large periods of their lives in prison. Most remarkable were the Wobblies[1] who blended deceptive strategies to avoid legal prosecution with out-and-out defiance of the law. With allied unions they invented strategies to turn the law against itself, and win labour and political victories: thus, for example, on occasion, in the workplace, they obeyed every rule and regulation so precisely as to finally grind all work to a halt and in the streets, they systematically violated unjust laws in such great numbers as to overload courts and jails, and force dismissal of their cases (Ferrell and Ryan, 1985; Kornbluh, 1988; Ferrell, 1991).

Ferrell (1998) observes that anarchist criminology has actually flourished during the previous 30 years in the USA. Harold Pepinsky (1978) published an article advocating 'communist anarchism as an alternative to the rule of criminal law' and later transformed this approach into a 'peacemaking criminology' – which is now almost mainstream in the USA – and is opposed to the violence seen to be inherent in the concept and practice of state law (Pepinsky, 1991; Pepinsky and Quinney, 1991). Larry Tifft (1979) developed an anarchist criminology which argued for replacing state/legal 'justice' with a fluid, face-to-face form of justice grounded in emerging human needs. Bruce DiCristina (1995) has, more recently, constructed a critique of criminology and criminal justice developed from the work of the anarchist philosopher of science Paul Feyerabend (1975) we encountered above. Ferrell (1994, 1995a, 1995b, 1996; Ryan and Ferrell, 1986) has also developed an anarchist criminology aimed especially at examining the interplay between state/legal authority, day-to-day resistance to it, and the practice of criminality.

Anarchist criminology thus incorporates the sort of 'visceral revolt' (Guerin, 1970) that is characteristic of anarchism itself, the passionate sense of 'fuck authority', to quote the old anarchist slogan, that is the outcome of being pushed around by police officers, judges, bosses, priests, and other authorities. Ferrell (1997) notes that anarchists agree with many feminist and postmodernist theorists that intuitive passions are important as methods of understanding and resistance outside the usual confines of rationality and respect while, at the same time, they seek to incorporate a relatively complex critique of state law and legality which begins to explain *why* we might benefit from defying authority, or standing 'against the law'.

Many contemporary critical criminologists agree that state law is so thoroughly lubricated by economic privilege, intertwined with patriarchal arrangements, and protected by racist procedures as to constitute a mailed fist regularly brought down on the heads of women, the poor, ethnic minorities, young people, and other outsiders to economic power or state authority (Ferrell, 1998). Anarchist criminologists agree with this analysis but go further and argue that the practice of centralised state law actually harms people, groups, and the social fabric which joins them together even if it is not aimed directly at 'the powerless'. In other words, they are arguing that the administration of centralised state authority and legality destroys community, exacerbates criminality, and expands the abusive power of the state machinery throughout the contemporary social order and then, through its discriminatory practices, doubles this harm for those pushed to the bottom of the system.

Ferrell (1998) observes four broad harms of state legality. First, there is the 'state-protection racket' (Pepinsky and Jesilow, 1984: 10) where cash and conformity is seen to be extorted from those unlucky enough to be caught up in it:

From speed traps to parking fines, from the plethora of licensing fees to the bureaucratised bungling of the tax authorities, the state operates a vast revenue machine which serves itself and those who operate it and which are enforced by a whole range of state-sanctioned strong-arm tactics such as impoundment, seizure and imprisonment. It is a system designed to perpetuate itself and to protect the powerful in and around it, obscuring its real intentions by an ideological veil of being in the best interests of the community.

(Ferrell, 1998: 13)

Second, this labyrinth of state legality grows in the absence of real human community and once in place suffocates any possibility of fluid and engaged human interaction:

In a social world increasingly fractured by alienated labour and economic inequality, privatised leisure, and the paranoia of the lonely crowd, calls for police assistance and civil litigation multiply as does the sense that such disjointed, externalised tactics somehow constitute appropriate measures for solving disputes and achieving justice.

(Ferrell, 1998: 14)

Third, there is recognition and acknowledgement of the labelling tradition we encountered in the third part of this book with the confinement of people and groups within state-administered categories of criminality and systems of punishment and retribution which, in reality, promotes not rehabilitative humanity but rather a downward spiral of crime, criminalisation, and inhumanity:

This spiral interconnects state and media sponsored fears of crime, an ideology of state-sanctioned retaliation, and thus sudden outbreaks of objectification, dehumanisation, and legal retribution. It is in this way that a system of state law and 'justice' is perpetuated within individual lives and larger social relations.

(Ferrell, 1998: 15)

Fourth, the 'rule of law' continues to proliferate, to penetrate further into all corners of social and cultural life (Cohen, 1979) – as in Max Weber's notion of the 'iron cage of bureaucracy' (Weber, 1964) – while, state legality constitutes a sort of bureaucratic cancer that grows on itself, that produces an ever-expanding maze of legal control, and that in turn generates an ever-expanding body of bureaucratic and legal sycophants employed to obfuscate and interpret it:

This proliferation of legal controls finally suspends what little protection the law once may have afforded. Every facet of social and cultural life is defined by legal control, and thus by state definitions of legality and illegality, we all remain continually vulnerable to the flagrant exercise of state power.

(Ferrell, 1998: 16)

Anarchist criminology thus produces a profoundly radical critique of state law as a system of inherent inhumanity and its sense of standing 'against the law' leads logically to a criminology of crime and resistance. Labour historians and sociologists of work have long documented the pattern by which systems of authoritarian, alienating work generate among workers incidents of sabotage – of intentional rule-breaking and disruption – as a means of resisting these systems and regaining some sense of humanity and control. Anarchist criminologists suggest that this pattern may be found in the interplay of state legal control and criminality. Rather than dismissing criminality as mindless misbehaviour, or worse, simply accepting the social construction of legality and illegality provided by the state as definitive of good and bad human conduct, anarchist criminologists seek to explore the situated politics of crime and criminality. In other words, anarchist criminologists argue that the political – and politically inequitable – nature of state law and criminalisation means that acts of crime under such a system must also carry some degree of political meaning.

Anarchist criminologists thus seek to blur and explore the boundaries between crime and political resistance (Simon, 1991). This exploration does not however assume that all crime constitutes conscious resistance to state authority, nor does it ignore the often, but not always, negative consequences of criminality for people and communities but it does, on the other hand, require that careful attention is paid to various criminal(ised) activities – graffiti writing, 'obscene' art and music performances, pirate radio broadcasts, illegal labour strikes, curfew violations, shoplifting, drug use, street cruising, gangbanging, computer hacking (Ferrell, 1995a, 1996; Ferrell and Sanders, 1995) – as a means of investigating the variety of ways in which criminal or criminalised behaviours may incorporate repressed dimensions of human dignity and self-determination, and lived resistance to the authority of state law.

Anarchist criminology calls for human communities which are decentralised, fluid, eclectic, and inclusive and it is proposed that this sense of inclusive, non-authoritarian community can benefit critical criminology itself. Ferrell (1998) observes that anarchist criminology shares much with the uncertainty and situated politics of feminist criminology, with the decentred authority and textual deconstruction of the postmodern and constitutive criminologies we encountered above, the critical pacifism of peacemaking criminology and of course with the broader critique of legal injustice common to all critical criminologies. He observes that even left realists share with anarchist criminology a concern with identifying and exploring the situated consequences of crime and crime control. In the spirit of eclectic inclusivity, then, anarchist criminology argues against partitioning critical criminology into a series of small intellectual cubicles, and then closing one critical cubicle to the occupants of another (Pepinsky, 1991). It instead calls for an ongoing critical conversation among perspectives, for a multi-faceted critique of legal injustice made all the more powerful by its openness to alternatives. Stan Cohen (1988: 232) writes of his 'lack of commitment to any master plan (such as liberalism, left realism, or abolitionism), a failing, I would like to think, not of my own psyche but of the social world's refusal to correspond to any one theory'. Anarchist criminology shares this postmodern lack of commitment to master plans or grand narratives – including its own – and embraces instead fluid communities of uncertainty and critique.

Suggested further reading

The following texts are recommended for those seeking an introduction to the notion of the postmodern condition: Baudrillard (1988), Bauman (1991, 1993), Harvey (1989) and Lyotard (1984). Rosenau (1992) is essential reading on the relationship of postmodernity to the social sciences. Both Davis (1990) and Young (1999) provide rather different accounts of contemporary post-industrial societies and the significance for criminology. Henry and Milovanovic (1994, 1996, 1999) are the doyens of constitutive criminology and these texts give a thorough introduction to the theory and its applications. Ferrell (1994, 1995a, 1995b) should likewise be consulted on anarchist criminology.

Note

1 The Industrial Workers of the World (IWW or the Wobblies) is an international union currently with headquarters in Cincinnati, Ohio, USA. At its peak in 1923 the organisation claimed some 100,000 members and could marshal the support of perhaps 300,000 workers. Its membership declined dramatically after a 1924 split brought on by internal conflict and government repression. It continues to actively organise but now only numbers about 2,000 members worldwide and membership does not require that one works in a represented workplace, nor does it exclude membership in another labour union.

18. Cultural criminology and the schizophrenia of crime

Cultural criminology seeks to explain crime and criminal behaviour and its control in terms of culture and has very close intellectual links with the postmodern and anarchist criminology we encountered in the previous chapter. From this perspective, crime and the various agencies and institutions of crime control are perceived to be cultural and creative constructs and it is argued that these should be understood in terms of the phenomenological meanings they carry. It is thus a perspective which also has clear links to the labelling tradition which was a central component of the modernist victimised actor model and which has been so influential in providing crucial foundations of critical criminology. Cultural criminology involves a focus upon the continuous generation of meaning around interaction where rules that are created and broken involving a constant interplay of moral entrepreneurship, political innovation and transgression.

The focus of cultural criminology

Cultural criminologists follow in a tradition established by Marx and the later humanist Marxists who argue that the essence of 'humanity' is not that we are rational calculating beings but productive and creative beings who carry with us a 'world vision' and ideology that shapes our own version of what is right and wrong (Lukacs, 1970; Goldmann, 1970). We nevertheless live out the 'everyday' within a social world which is structured at least in part by an economic system that insists on the pursuit of scientific rationalism in order to survive. In this context, 'crime' appears to the dominant political groups in society to be endemic and simply a reflection of their world turned 'upside down'. Mike Presdee (2004: 276) observes that the overwhelming lure of transgression for the cultural criminologist brings with it a 'fascination with the unacceptable' in scientific rational society:

> Culture delivers to us social sites where popular transgression – the breaking through of the constraints created around us – is considered

a crime in itself and where order and its accompanying rationalisations actually herald the death and the destruction of spontaneous life.

That spontaneity – by its very essence – defies and resists order and this dynamic tension between order and disorder in turn creates a cultural energy that is immediately apparent in the culture of 'edge work', 'emotion work' and 'excitement' which provides a central thread in much of the work conducted by cultural criminologists. The history of cultural criminology therefore reflects the history of the discourses of 'limit' and 'transgression'; 'boundary making' and 'boundary breaking'; 'control' and 'hedonism'; 'rationality' and 'irrationality'; alongside the examination of the 'inner' experience of individuals free from moral reasoning and safe from the 'outside' world.

Garland (2001) argues that contemporary life is characterised by a 'culture of control' where we are policed at home, at work, at pleasure and in a surveillance society where we cannot escape the dominant gaze (the gaze of the dominant), as we are watched and tracked, trailed, filmed and photographed, as our 'life-trail' is picked up by the electronic panopticon of rational society. This experience of domination thus produces cultures which are characterised by the process of the dominance through which they are formed. Mainstream criminology has tended to view these cultures as non-cultural, deviant and pathological but cultural criminology approaches human behaviour through an analysis of lived everyday life, and has thus come to understand that humans have the ability to twist, modify and oppose meanings produced by dominant rational groups (Willis, 1978).

Cultural criminology thus studies the way that some cultures have come to be designated as deviant. Cultural activities, whether strategies of resistance or otherwise, represent clear attempts to find meaning in a life lived through rules proscribed by others and provided from above. These are ways of life first 'received' and then 'perceived' and acted upon as 'tastes, feelings, likes and dislikes are developed in minute articulation with the concrete world' (Willis, 1978). Presdee (2004: 281) observes that:

> Now we can begin to see that much crime, but not all; much disorder, but not all, is no more or less than the everyday life of the oppressed and the 'excluded'. From this perspective, crime should be viewed as everyday responses to lives lived out within deprived, brutalised and often lonely social locations. Moreover, the responses from within the structures of domination are often truly masochistic in that the reaction to such disorder is often further acts of cruelty by the dominant over the dominated.

Similar themes are very much in evidence in one of the other major social dynamics explored by cultural criminologists: the changing cultural significance of contemporary consumer cultures and their particular effect on feelings and emotions (see Hayward, 2004a). The desire to own, to have and therefore to 'be' no longer respects the limits and cultural boundaries produced in the past to protect the institution of ownership. This new and all encompassing consumer culture creates a confused consumer psyche where anxiety and its social antidotes are themselves producing much so-called 'social disorder' and 'transgression', as groups and individuals attempt to make sense of a life increasingly mediated through the new and distinct processes associated with consumerism in contemporary society (Presdee, 2000; Hayward, 2004b). The search for the thwarted promise of happiness through consumption thus leads many to hedonism and seemingly irrational acts.

We have seen earlier in this book that a fundamental change has occurred in the economic order during the past 30 years. Thus, where previously 'production' was the dominant culture this has been replaced by the dominance of 'consumption' (Bauman, 1997, 1998) and in this changed world we must all now consume at all costs. Presdee (2004: 283) explains this perspective thus:

> ... it is no longer the creation or the making of 'things' that excites us, but the consumption of things – or more specifically, the *destruction* of 'things'. To destroy, use up, consume, becomes an important daily activity and hangs in our consciousness, peppering our culture and everyday lives. One of the responsibilities of 'citizenship' under contemporary social conditions is to destroy daily. The perfect consumer leaves nothing of the product and is thus made ready for further destruction, emotionally as well as economically.

In a society based on consumption to 'have' is to exist: to have nothing is to be nothing. Presdee asks rhetorically how – in the latter case – can we emotionally live a life that is laden with such shame and observes that it is through crime we can 'have', and therefore 'be'. It is this nothingness and loss of social status that is often the wellspring of social or personal harm, the trigger for violence as self-expression, whether it is directed inwardly (self-mutilation) or outwardly (the mutilation of others):

> Personal social decline isolates us as we learn where we fit; learn that we are poor, that we are ugly, that we are excluded, different, apart. Then a silence descends on the isolated and lonely within a culture of distraction that is part of everyday life and the central question becomes ... social survival or social destruction?
>
> (Presdee, 2004: 286)

Crime and disorder can provide a subjective solution to this conundrum and thus becomes a 'therapeutic action' to alleviate personally perceived loss and translates the nothingness of life into *something* while the pain of life is translated into pleasure.

In the same way that new crimes emerged as feudalism gave way to capitalism, we have now entered a new and largely uncharted phase of globalised capitalism and hyper-consumption and once again crime takes on new meanings that require new criminological understandings. Presdee (2004) observes that individuals work through these new tensions in the turmoil of their everyday lives, then new feelings, emotions and imperatives emerge in their culture and it is somewhere here that the new cultural criminology has established its territory.

The seductions of crime

Cultural criminology uses everyday existences, life histories, music, dance and performance as databases to discover how and why it is that certain cultural forms become criminalised. Ferrell and Sanders (1995) observe that it is the intention to expand and enliven criminology and to push back the boundaries of accepted criminological discourse and it is in this context that Katz (1988) writes about the 'seductions of crime' in which disorder becomes in itself a 'delight' to be sought after and savoured and where the causes of crime are constructed by the offenders themselves in ways which are compellingly seductive. 'Hot-blooded' murder is thus described in terms of a triad of conditions: interpretive, emotional, and practical. Interpretive conditions include the defence of morality, the role of teasing or daring the victim, the role of a supportive audience, and the role of alcohol in casual settings of last resort, for example, in the home. Emotional conditions involve a process of transcending humiliation with rage via the intermediary of righteousness. Practical conditions are a marking, or desecration, of the body of the victim, for example, when offenders can recall precisely the number of stitches it took for a victim to survive. The key term is 'humiliation' which is defined as a 'profound loss of control over one's identity, or soul' (Katz, 1988: 24).

Humiliation is also a key term for analysing other categories of crime and all forms of criminality are considered to be a moral response to this shame. The notion of 'uncertainty' eliminates inevitability in the event. Cursing by the attacker and silent prayers by the victim are treated as priestly omens and sacrificial service honouring the sacred which must be approached by a 'leap into faith' and the final seduction into 'the unknown' (Katz, 1988: 43).

Katz (1988: 51) defines foreground as individual consciousness and associated mental processes while the lesser-important background involves factors such as social class and gender. Background differences can vary the experience of humiliation and open up possibilities for rituals of forgiveness, but foreground, or what is going through the head of the offender at the time of the crime, is more important. Crimes such as shoplifting and pizza theft involve attributing sensual power to an object so that the seduction is like a 'romantic encounter'. Practical conditions involve flirting with the object and a tension of being privately deviant in public places. Emotional conditions involve transcending uncontrollable feelings of thrill. Interpretive conditions involve metaphors of self (bounding immorality), game (timeouts and goal lines), religion (secret defilement), sex (like an orgasm), and the inter-relationship between deviance and charisma (reaching for mysterious forces). The resonating of these metaphors makes the seduction irresistibly compelling and thus, 'it is not the taste for pizza that makes the crime happen but the crime that makes the pizza taste good' (Katz, 1988: 91).

Gang violence requires learning to be a 'badass' by projecting symbols of impenetrability, which Katz relates to the hardness of male phallic imagery and feels that such behaviour requires a commitment to firmness of purpose so that it is left to make the rational choice calculations of costs and benefits. Badasses engage in the 'accidental bump' and hog the pavement when they walk. Practical conditions involve creation of an oppressive background image to emphasise the status of the person as a street survivor, or member of an elite. Emotional conditions involve 'getting over' from 'here' to 'there' and the personal insults involving others' violations of artificial turf space.

Katz (1988) considers robbery to be a prototypical 'breeding ground' for crime and thus those conducting hold-ups with weapons are those that seek 'continuous action' and embrace a death wish (thanatos) and they will commit any degree of violence necessary even to the point where it puts at risk their own lives. These 'stick-up men' also develop a sense of competence at superior perceptual ability – in exploiting contextual weaknesses in a target, be it victim or architecture – and claim a special morality about this. Uncertainty in this example is related to 'chaos', that is, during a hold up, the offender is required to maintain suspense and manage the impression of coming from an alien world.

Katz (1988) argues that it is the desire to seek continuous action – for example, crime, drugs, sex and gambling – which distinguishes the persistent or career criminal. Such offenders – also known as 'heavies' or omnibus felons – will often pursue action to the point of physical and mental exhaustion and they do this by always being available for all spontaneous opportunities, maintaining permeable boundaries for associates, and reckless, super-fast spending with the proceeds from crime.

Katz observes that the main problem for criminals is the transcendence of chaos and this exists as an ongoing project. Chaos is the master dialectic, acting as both a resource and a barrier to action. Katz draws heavily upon Matza (1969) in describing the dizziness of a criminal career where caught up in a lifestyle of frequent intoxication, compounded lies, jealous lovers, and being a constant target for rip-offs and a regular suspect for police, the arrest, or more final end to the project, almost comes as a relief. Katz depicts the project of transcending chaos as a process of imposing discipline and control on one's life and doing this often means the humiliation and physical abuse of women and children. Imposing control is seeking to get caught by sarcastically thanking the authorities, doing some moral accountancy – thus 'got away withs' exceed 'got caughts' – and looking forward to the opportunities for action in prison.

Katz (1988: 247) observes that the attractions of crime are seen as extensions, or 'celebrations' of being male and being black and cites research on childhood socialisation to suggest that the main effect of being male is preparation for a life of pretensions (Lever, 1978). Being black means to live in a culture of continuous insult, even from fellow blacks, and this tradition prepares blacks for becoming 'bad' by overcoming insult with insult. Crime emerges in the process of establishing a gendered, ethnic identity.

The carnival of crime

O'Malley and Mugford (1994) propose that a new phenomenology of pleasure is needed if we are to recognise 'crime' as simply a *transgression* from the impermissible and as *transcendence* of the everyday mundane. Presdee (2000) captures this sense of the inter-relationships between pleasure and pain through his notion of 'crime as carnival' where the latter is a site where the pleasure of playing at the boundaries is clearly catered for. Thus, festive excess, transgression, the mocking of the powerful, irrational behaviour and so on are all temporarily legitimated in the moment of carnival. Breaking rules is a source of joy, of humour, of celebration and many acts that might otherwise be considered criminal are momentarily tolerated. In such acts as sado masachism, raving, joyriding, computer hacking, recreational drug use, reclaim the streets parties, gang rituals and extreme sports, Presdee finds enduring fragments from the culture of the carnival. Moreover, as Thornton's (1995) study of 1990s youth club cultures found, there is a continual and shifting exchange between the boundaries of acceptability and illegality and between subcultural authenticity and media manufacture. Moral panics about deviancy no longer simply signify condemnation, but are something to be celebrated by the subcultural participants themselves.

Cultural criminologists argue that we need to push deeper and deeper to capture the full meaning of social harm. They accept that the traditional concept of crime does have a place but one that is subjugated to, and set against, a multiple series of alternative discourses incorporating transgression, disrespect, disorder, and resistance, as well as loss, injury and troubles. Van Swaaningen (1999: 23) observes that such discourses themselves may also suggest a new sociology of deviance based on difference and 'otherness'. Once more the discursive frame necessary to recognise these elements needs to shift not just from criminal justice to social justice, restoration and reconciliation, but to delight, drama, tolerance, celebration, transcendence and the pursuit of pleasure. It is an ambitious and for some an exhilarating agenda.

The schizophrenia of crime

Hopkins Burke (2007) introduces the term 'the schizophrenia of crime' to refer to the apparently contradictory duality of attitude to criminal behaviour that has become endemic in contemporary societies characterised by the postmodern condition. Thus, on the one hand, it is possible to observe widespread public demand for a rigorous intervention against criminality that has made the 'war against crime' a major political issue and indeed, it is in this context that we can observe an extensive expansion in situational crime prevention strategies epitomised by the ubiquitous existence of closed-circuit television cameras (Hopkins Burke, 2004b), a whole raft of crime control legislation that has placed increasing restrictions on our civil liberties and human rights (Hopkins Burke, 2004c), and the introduction of rigorous 'zero-tolerance-style' policing interventions (see Hopkins Burke, 1998a, 2002, 2004a) that have occurred not as the outcome of the coercive strategies of a totalitarian regime but in response to overwhelming public demand in a liberal democratic society (Hopkins Burke, 2004b). We want it, *we* demand it, and *we* get it (Hopkins Burke, 2007) even though we as individuals are invariably unaware of the ultimate implications for our freedom. Hopkins Burke thus has developed a left realist historical perspective we have encountered elsewhere in this book to incorporate both the embourgeoisement thesis of John Goldthorpe (1968–9) and the 'civilising process' of Norbert Elias (1978, 1982) in order to explain how increasing demands for improved social conditions and material rewards among the respectable working classes – or more recently the new middle-classes – have occurred alongside a fast declining tolerance for the very visible criminality and incivilities in our midst.

On the other hand, we should observe that criminality has become widespread to the virtual point of universality. Many people have consequently committed criminal offences at some stage in their life and a great many continue to do so. There is increasing empirical evidence to show that white-collar, corporate and business crime is extremely widespread as was shown in the introduction to this book and when one considers, for example, recreational drug use (far from the sole prerogative of an unemployed underclass) (see Winlow and Hall, 2006), crimes of disorder and incivility associated with alcohol use (extremely extensive in any location urban or rural in the UK, particularly during weekend evenings) (Hobbs *et al.*, 2000, 2005) and driving cars beyond the legal speed limit (virtually compulsory through peer group pressure on motorways) (Hopkins Burke, 2007) the notion of the virtual universality of criminality is not as implausible as it may at first seem. Hopkins Burke (2007) is clearly influenced by Mike Presdee's notion of 'second lives' where the usually law-abiding and pillars of straight society enjoy alternative part-time existence involving walking on the wild side (Presdee, 2000). There is thus – as Jock Young (1999, 2001) has observed – a considerable 'blurring of boundaries' between the criminal and the legal and, significantly, in our perceptions and understandings of these supposedly polarised opposite behaviours, that enables us to make some sense of 'the schizophrenia of crime' in a world where crime has become both normal and indeed non pathological.

Crime as normal and non pathological

For many years the crime rate rose ever upwards, although it has come down recently in the UK, and more so in the USA, but that fall has been from unprecedented high levels and crime rates remain historically high. David Garland (1996) has pertinently observed that as crime has come to be more frequent it has ceased to be an exceptional or pathological event, which surprises us when it occurs, but has become instead a standard, normal, background feature of our lives.

This increasing blurring of boundaries has become no more apparent than in the realms of organised crime, corporate crime and legitimate business. As Ruggiero (2000) observes, organised crime has become a branch of big business and is simply the illegal sector of capital. Castells (1998) notes that by the middle of the 1990s the 'gross criminal product' of global organised crime had made it the twentieth richest organisation in the world and richer than 150 sovereign states, while De Brie (2000) notes that the total world gross criminal product is estimated at 20 per cent of world trade.

Carter (1997) proposes that the structure of criminal enterprise is no longer characterised by archaic forms of 'family' organisation typified by the old Sicilian Mafia and observes that newer flexible forms of 'entrepreneurial' criminal organisation and methods of operation are highly adaptive to fast moving global networks and achieve increasing integration into the legitimate economy through sophisticated money laundering techniques. The use of encrypted electronic mail, anonymous websites and the myriad of instantaneous transactions which constitute the Internet in general and financial markets in particular, render the legal and the illegal increasingly indistinguishable and where distinguished, beyond the reach of national law enforcement agencies. As both Van Duyne (1997) and Castells (1998) note criminality is thus normalised by these networks.

Ruggiero (1997) further observes that legitimate business both actively seeks relations with criminal organisations and adopts methods akin to those of organised crime. Thus, immigrant smuggling eases labour supply problems in a variety of manufacturing sectors such as clothing and food, construction and agriculture and in 'dirty economies' where semi-legal employment is interspersed with employment in more directly criminal activity. Moreover, as De Brie (2000) notes, the global sphere of multinational corporations enables the export of the most brutal aspects of cheap labour to convenient locations in the southern hemisphere.

Meanwhile, the legal financial sector may go out of its way to attract criminal investments. Kochan and Whittington (1991) note that the closure of the Bank of Credit and Commerce International in 1991 showed how private banks and investment traders openly tout for legal and illegal funds without being too concerned about the distinction between the two. Moreover, legitimate capital has started to use the same tactics as organised crime. Thus, while drugs cartels launder their profits through 'offshore' banking facilities, legitimate capital enhances its power over governments to reduce tax burdens not only with the threat to relocate employment but also by adopting some of the tactics and resources of organised crime (Shelley, 1998). At the same time, for many states criminality acts as a buffer against poverty and economic collapse. Cocaine production, for example, acts as a counter to the impoverishment of thousands of Latin American peasant farmers, reducing the impact of falling world prices for agricultural products and raw materials in these areas. Thus, in a world where the boundaries between criminals and non criminals and legal and illegal activities become increasingly difficult to disentangle, the classic crime control methods of modernity become increasingly more problematic not least with a globalisation of deviance. The globalisation of generic crime and criminal behaviour is considered in more detail in the following chapter which considers new modes of governance in a risk society. We will here consider the globalisation of deviant youth subcultures in the guise of a significant fast growing club culture with clear roots in the notions of the postmodern condition, cultural criminology, the carnival of crime and beyond.

One planet under a groove

Ben Carrington and Brian Wilson (2002) observe that like all youth cultures, and especially those formed through associations with music cultures, the evolution of 'club cultures' around the world can be attributed, in part, to the ongoing global processes of cultural borrowing. The term 'club cultures' refers to the youth cultural phenomenon that is associated with all-night dance parties at nightclubs or other venues, the production and consumption of various dance music genres – music 'mixed' or electronically created by DJs – and with the use of amphetamine drugs – particularly MDMA or 'Ecstasy' – to enhance the dance/music experience. The roots of this culture can be found in the 1970s and early 1980s American dance music scenes of New York, Chicago and Detroit, and more recently in Britain where 'rave culture' emerged in 1988 during what came to be known as the 'second summer of love'. In Britain in particular, the subsequent criminalisation of the rave scene – a partial outcome of moral panics about rave-related drug use – and the incorporation of the rave scene by the mainstream music industry led the culture to become grounded in 'nightclub venues and that is how ravers, in effect, became clubbers' (Carrington and Wilson, 2002). Chambers (1994: 80) argues that:

> The international medium of musical reproduction underlines *a new epoch of global culture contact*. Modern movement and mobility, whether through migration, the media or tourism, have dramatically transformed both musical production and publics and intensified cultural contact.

DJs and promoters thus travel to foreign countries, are exposed to fresh varieties of music and nightclubs, and ultimately integrate ideas gleaned from these experiences into their domestic dance music cultures. Touring DJs and imported albums – in turn – influence local music-makers who combine the new material with their current work, thus creating something 'new again'. Images and ideas extracted from mass and alternative media are incorporated into local music production, fashion styles and club venues. In retrospect, what has emanated from years of this cultural 'cutting and mixing' (Hebdige, 1987) is a fascinating but hazy relationship between a 'global' club culture and various 'local club cultures'.

Carrington and Wilson (2002) observe that the increasing tendency for youth to travel to foreign scenes as 'post-rave tourists' has meant that local cultures are becoming further defined by their diverse and transient membership. These mobile formations might well be described as *reflexive* communities in the extent to which they dissolve the boundary between producers and consumers, are actively entered into by their members rather than being proscribed by social location, are not delimited by simple time–space boundaries, and are based on cultural and symbolic practices.

We observed in Chapter 7 of this book how researchers and scholars at the Centre for Contemporary Cultural Studies (CCCS) in Birmingham, England, had shown how youth 'reactively and proactively' expressed their dissatisfaction with the status quo of post-war British society. By articulating themselves through spectacular forms of 'style' – for example, the extreme fashions of punks and skinheads – youth were believed to be symbolically and creatively resisting, and in so doing, finding 'solutions' to their problems. CCCS theorists referred to these 'magical solutions' as a way of recognising that subcultural involvement is only a temporary form of empowerment and escape that does not (necessarily) substantially challenge the dominance/ hegemony of the ruling classes. Hopkins Burke and Sunley (1996, 1998) more recently observed the co-existence of a number of different subcultures and argued that this is the outcome of the postmodern condition where specific groups of young people have coalesced to create solutions to their specific socio-economic problems with central to their account being the possibility of choice.

Carrington and Wilson (2002) recognise that these studies were to provide significant foundations for later studies of youth culture but among a number of identified limitations was the recognition that insufficient attention had been paid to the ways in which youth cultures were influenced by subcultural traditions in other countries. Others were simply dismissive of such developments and even announced the death of youth subcultures, while Redhead (1990) proposed that subcultural authenticity was now 'impossible' because of the tendency of contemporary culture to be self-referential, shallow, flat and hyper-real or, in other words, a culture of effervescent, spectacular, fast moving, ever-present, 'better than real' images. Muggleton (1997, 2000) thus suggests that the postmodern condition is inhabited by 'postsub-culturalists' whose 'neo-tribal' identities are multiple and fluid, whose consumption is no longer 'articulated through the modernist structuring relations of class, gender or ethnicity' and who are defined by their fragmented/multiple stylistic identities. They have a low degree of commitment to any subcultural group and high rates of subcultural mobility, any fascination with style and image are generally apolitical, and have a 'positive attitude toward media and a celebration of the inauthentic' (Muggleton, 2000: 52). From this perspective dance cultures are invariably seen as the archetypal postmodern youth formation.

Appadurai (1990) provides an alternative perspective and identifies 'five dimensions of cultural flow' in order to describe the dynamics of global cultural transmission. He suggests that these five dimensions – ethnoscapes, mediascapes, technoscapes, finanscapes, and ideoscapes – work in ways that prevent the construction of a homogenous culture. Ethnoscapes refers to the flow of people around the world, for example, tourists, immigrants, refugees, exiles, guest-workers and other moving groups. Technoscapes refers to the flow of technology, for example, the export of technology to countries as part of transnational business relocations. Finanscapes refers to the patterns of global capital transfer and Appadurai (1990: 298) argues that:

> The global relationship between these three scapes is deeply disjunctive and profoundly unpredictable, since each of these landscapes is subject to its own constraints and incentives ... at the same time as each acts as a constraint and a parameter for the other.

Augmenting these first three scapes are mediascapes and ideoscapes. The former refers to mass media images, to the modes of image distribution, for example, electronic or print media and to the ways that these images allow viewers to gain access to other parts of the world and thus become part of 'imagined communities'. The latter refers to images that are invested with political-ideological meaning, for example, the images presented by governmental groups justifying a military action, or images created by social movements attempting to overthrow power groups. The crux of Appadurai's framework is the assumption that the various 'disjunctures' or interactions that occur between global cultural flows – as they relate to the various scapes – provide the analyst with crucial information about the complex ways that local cultures relate to global forces.

Carrington and Wilson (2002) adapt this framework to their discussion of the globalisation of dance music cultures and observe that this more elaborate approach to theorising 'the local' encourages researchers to consider the intricacies of youth tastes, for example, preferences for various genres of dance music, such as house or jungle or trance; interpretations of the music, for example, as an escape, as a form of resistance; and uses of it, for example, making a living in dance-music related occupations. This more flexible and integrated interpretive framework also allows the analyst to consider how youth might simultaneously be interpreters and producers of culture, creating 'alternative' media that both reflects the individuals understandings of global culture, while contributing to this same culture.

Carrington and Wilson (2002) observe that the history of rave and club culture shows how travellers – within the ethnoscape – contributed to the transmission of dance music culture from the USA and Ibiza to Britain, and then, subsequently, back from Britain to the USA and parts of Europe. The 'post-rave tourist' has also emerged, as a clubber who travels to locations around the world with the explicit purpose of experiencing the club/rave culture of the area. It is observed that British satellite and terrestrial television companies continue to make programmes such as *Ibiza Uncovered* (BSkyB) and *Around the World in 80 Raves* (Channel 4) aimed at this newly found constituency of clubbing tourists, who can now enjoy the spectacle related to the post-rave tourist gaze without ever having to engage with the old modernist tradition of actually leaving their front rooms to experience the club sensation.

Carrington and Wilson (2002) argue that it would be a mistake to simply read the consumption – and production – of young people within this scene as an index of cultural manipulation. They argue that there is a sense of agency in the ways in which young people, through their engagement with the dance scene, have developed a degree of scepticism around the truth claims made by the scientific knowledge industries. For example, the attempt to define dance cultures through a public health discourse, as inherently dangerous sites of unknown and indeterminate risk, have spectacularly failed to prevent young people from embracing, adapting and exploring the possibilities of dance culture. It is argued that this is why, despite the attempt of most Western governments to prohibit the consumption of drugs especially amongst the 'vulnerable' young, rates of consumption of Ecstasy – amongst other drugs – have remained high. Carrington and Wilson (2002) suggest that the dance scene, by the extent and degree of its normalisation of drug use, has challenged the hegemony of the anti-drug discourse to the extent that a number of governmental agencies and states are having to radically rethink the effectiveness of the 'war on drugs' citing as an example the dramatic decriminalisation by Portugal of its drug laws in 2001.

Carrington and Wilson (2002) recognise that if social relations are primarily defined as being produced in the last instance by a particular set of (economic) determinants, then formations such as dance music cultures will always be seen as proxies for 'real' oppositional politics. If, however, it is acknowledged that the social field is constituted by multi-various power relations between different social groupings, none of which have an assumed claim to determinacy, then more qualified 'moments of resistance' can be traced by careful and historically situated studies. Gilbert and Pearson (1999: 160) argue that the key questions should not be:

> How likely dance culture is to bring down capitalism or patriarchy, but at what precise points it succeeds or fails in negotiating new spaces. In particular, it is not a simple question of dance culture being 'for' or 'against' the dominant culture, but of how far its articulations with other discourses and cultures – dominant or otherwise – result in *democratisations* of the cultural field, how far they successfully break down existing concentrations of power, and how far they fail to do so.

Thus, in a world where the boundaries between criminals and non criminals and legal and illegal activities have become increasingly difficult to distinguish, the classic crime control methods of modernity become increasingly more problematic not least because these are invariably based on the individual nation-state and are totally inadequate to deal with global phenomena such as the dance culture and its ancillary attached illegal activities. Some criminologists have thus drawn upon the 'governmentality' literature in order to explore the links between contemporary neoliberal political policy and the growing use of 'actuarial' or 'risk-based' strategies of crime control (Stenson and Sullivan, 2001) and these theories are explored in the following chapter.

Suggested further reading

Ferrell and Sanders (1995), Ferrell (1999) and O'Malley and Mugford, (1994), provide a good introduction to cultural criminology, while Ferrell, Hayward and Young (2008) is being published as this book is being written and extremely likely to become a classic. Katz (1988) provides an excellent study of the seductions and pleasures of crime and Presdee (2000) the 'carnival of crime'. Hopkins Burke (2007) provides a more extensive discussion than here of the 'schizophrenia of crime' and Carrington and Wilson (2002) discuss the globalisation of dance culture.

19. Crime, globalisation and the risk society

The previous chapter concluded with the recognition that in a world permeated with the morally ambiguous postmodern condition, where the boundaries between criminals and non criminals, and legal and illegal activities, have become increasingly difficult to distinguish, the classic crime control methods of modernity have become increasingly more problematic. Some criminologists have thus drawn upon the 'governmentality' literature in order to explore the links between contemporary neoliberal political policy and the growing use of 'actuarial' or 'risk-based' strategies of crime control (Stenson and Sullivan, 2001). This is a new governmentality thesis which refers to 'the new means to render populations thinkable and measurable through categorisation, differentiation, and sorting into hierarchies, for the purpose of government' (Stenson, 2001: 22–3). This chapter will commence with a consideration of these new modes of governance, the wider notion of the risk society and the threats contained within it which seem to be a significant outcome of the postmodern condition, and will conclude by considering the internationalisation of crime and risk in terms of globalisation and the morally ambiguous notion of terrorism.

New modes of governance

The concept of governance in contemporary political theory signifies, 'a change in the meaning of government, referring to a *new* process of governing; or a *changed* condition of ordered rule; or the *new* method by which society is governed' (Rhodes, 1997: 46). In criminological theory, the concept has been used to signify changes in the control of crime and to acknowledge similar objects of control such as incivility, harm, safety and security.

The principal feature of the concept of governance is a rupture with traditional perceptions that place the state at the centre of the exercise of political power. In this new Foucauldian conceptualisation, power is thus not simply possessed by the state to be wielded over civil society but is tenuous, unresolved and the outcome of struggles between coalitions of public and private, formal and informal, actors. These struggles are rooted in the central paradox of power: thus, when actors possess the potential to govern they are not powerful because they are not actually governing, but neither are they powerful when they govern because they are dependent on others to carry out their commands (Clegg, 1989).

This all implies a new complex and fragile process of governing through negotiation, bargaining, and other relationships of exchange rather than through command, coercion or normative appeals for support. Thus, in order to accomplish and sustain political authority, would-be political leaders have to appreciate their 'power-dependence' on others and recruit and retain sufficient supporters to maintain a governing coalition (Rhodes, 1997). A criminological example is the attempt to control crime through partnerships of statutory, commercial and voluntary organisations (Crawford, 1997). This multi-agency approach has accompanied official recognition of the limits to the state's capacity to reduce crime, in particular the insufficiency of criminal justice, and the consequent need to enrol expertise and resources from non-state actors including the 'responsibilisation' of private citizens for their own security (Garland, 2001).

This idea of 'joined-up' government to attack multi-faceted and complex problems such as youth offending, through multi-agency partnerships employing a broad spectrum of social policy interventions, represents a definite break with the methods of modern public administration. It challenges the specialisation of government into discrete areas of functional expertise and, in so doing, defines new objects of governance. Youth offending, for example, ceases to be defined only in terms of 'criminality' and thus subject to the expertise of criminal justice professionals but becomes a problem of education, health and, in terms of contemporary terminology, one of 'social exclusion' and 'antisocial behaviour' (Hopkins Burke, 2008).

For most of the twentieth century crime control was dominated by the 'treatment model' prescribed by the predestined actor model of crime and criminal behaviour – we encountered in the second part of this book – and was closely aligned to the powerful and benevolent state which was obliged to intervene in the lives of individual offenders and seek to diagnose and cure their criminal behaviour. It was, as we have seen, the apparent failure of that interventionist modernist project epitomised by chronically high crime rates and the apparent failure of criminal justice intervention that led to a rediscovery of the rational actor model and an increased emphasis on preventive responses.

Crime and the risk society

Garland (1996) observes that the new governmental style is organised around economic forms of reasoning and it is thus reflected in those contemporary rational actor theories which view crime to be simply a matter of opportunity and which requires no special disposition or abnormality. The subsequent outcome has been a shift in policies from those directed at the individual offender to those directed at 'criminogenic situations' and these include 'unsupervised car parks, town squares late at night, deserted neighbourhoods, poorly lit streets, shopping malls, football games, bus stops, subway stations and so on' (Garland, 1999: 19).

For Feeley and Simon (1994: 180) these changes are part of a paradigm shift in the criminal process from the 'old penology' to the 'new penology'. The former was concerned with the identification of the individual criminal for the purpose of ascribing guilt and blame, the imposition of punishment and treatment while the latter is 'concerned with techniques for identifying, classifying and managing groups assorted by levels of dangerousness' based not on individualised suspicion, but on the probability that an individual may be an offender. Justice is thus becoming 'actuarial', its interventions increasingly based on risk assessment, rather than on the identification of specific criminal behaviour and we are therefore witnessing an increase in, and the legal sanction of, such practices as preventive detention, offender profiling and mass surveillance (Norris and Armstrong, 1999).

The past twenty years has witnessed an ever-increasing use of surveillance technologies designed to regulate groups as a part of a strategy of managing danger and these include the ubiquitous city centre surveillance systems referred to above, the testing of employees for the use of drugs (Gilliom, 1994) and the introduction of the blanket DNA testing of entire communities (Nelken and Andrews, 1999). The introduction of these new technologies often tends to be justified in terms of their ability to monitor 'risk' groups who pose a serious threat to society, but, once introduced, the concept of dangerousness is broadened to include a much wider range of offenders and suspects (see Pratt, 1999). Thus, the National DNA Database was originally established in the UK as a forensic source to help identify those involved in serious crimes such as murder and rape, but an amendment to the Criminal Justice and Public Order Act 1994 allows samples to be taken without consent from any person convicted or *suspected* of a recordable offence (Home Office, 1999).

For some these trends are indicative of a broader transition in structural formation from an industrial society towards a risk society (Beck, 1992). This concept is not intended to imply any increase in the levels of risk that exist in society but rather refers to a social formation which is organised in order to respond to risks. As Anthony Giddens observes 'it is a society increasingly preoccupied with the future (and also with safety), which generates the notion of risk' (Giddens, 1998: 3). Beck (1992: 21) himself defines risk in such a social formation as 'a systematic way of dealing with hazards and insecurities induced and introduced by modernisation itself'.

Human beings have always been subjected to certain levels of risk but modern societies are exposed to a particular type that is the outcome of the modernisation process itself and as a result this has led to changes in the nature of social organisation. Thus, there are risks such as natural disasters that have always had negative effects on human populations but these are produced by non-human forces. Modern risks, in contrast, are the product of human activity and Giddens (1998) refers to these two different categories as *external* and *manufactured* risks. Risk society is predominantly concerned with the latter.

Because manufactured risks are the product of human agents there is the potential to assess the level of risk that is being or about to be produced. The outcome is that risks have transformed the very process of modernisation. Thus, with the introduction of human caused disasters such as Chernobyl (in the Ukraine)[1] and the Love Canal Crisis (in New York City)[2] public faith in the modernist project has declined, leaving only variable trust in industry, government and experts (Giddens, 1990). The increased critique of modern industrial practices has resulted in a state of reflexive modernisation with widespread consideration given to issues of sustainability and the precautionary principle that focuses on preventative measures to reduce risk levels. Contemporary debates about global warming and the future of the planet should be seen in the context of debates about the risk society.

Social relations have changed significantly with the introduction of manufactured risks and reflexive modernisation, with risks, much like wealth, distributed unevenly in a population and thus, differentially, influence the quality of life. People will occupy social risk positions they achieve through aversion strategies and which differ from wealth positions which are gained through accumulation. Beck (1992) proposes that widespread risks contain a 'boomerang effect' in that individual producers of risk will at the same time be exposed to them which suggests, for example, that wealthy individuals whose capital is largely responsible for creating pollution will suffer when, for example, contaminants seep into the water supply. This argument might appear to be oversimplified, as wealthy people may have the ability to mitigate risk more easily but the argument is that the distribution of the risk originates from knowledge as opposed to wealth.

Ericson and Haggerty (1997: 450) argue that in the area of criminal justice we are witnessing a transformation of legal forms and policing strategies that reflect the transition to the risk society:

> Risk society is fuelled by surveillance, by the routine production of knowledge of populations useful for their administration. Surveillance provides biopower, the power to make biographical profiles of human populations to determine what is probable and possible for them. Surveillance fabricates people around institutionally established norms – risk is always somewhere on the continuum of imprecise normality.

In these circumstances, policing becomes increasingly more proactive rather than reactive and, given that risk assessment is probabilistic rather than determinist, it requires the assignment of individuals and events to classificatory schemes which provide differentiated assessment of risk and calls for management strategies. Returning to the predestined actor tradition, offenders are now classified as 'prolific' rather than merely opportunistic and having been designated as such, the individual becomes a candidate for targeting by more intensive forms of technical or human surveillance. The emphasis on risk makes everyone a legitimate target for surveillance and 'everyone is assumed guilty until the risk profile assumes otherwise' (Norris and Armstrong, 1999: 25).

Developments in the contemporary youth justice system reflect these wider trends for social policy often focusing on children 'at risk' and the management of that risk pervades every sphere of activity within the contemporary youth justice system. The commencement of intervention itself is regulated through a detailed assessment of risk through the *Asset* profile, which contains a scoring system that predicts the likelihood of offending and will determine the level of intervention and surveillance the young person will experience (Youth Justice Board, 2002; Hopkins Burke, 2008).

Many of the programmes of practical action which flow from strategies of 'risk management' in the criminal justice system are increasingly addressed not by central-state agencies such as the police, 'but *beyond* the state apparatus, to the organisations, institutions and individuals in civil society' (O'Malley, 1992; Fyfe, 1995; Garland, 1996: 451). Following the demise of the Keynesian Welfare State that had epitomised for many the high point in modernity in advanced capitalist nations (Hopkins Burke, 1999a), the emphasis on individuals managing their own risk finds converts from all parts of the political spectrum (Barry, Osborne and Rose, 1996). Thus, Pat O'Malley (1992) has written of the emergence of a new form of 'prudentialism' where insurance against future risks becomes a private obligation of the active citizen. Responsibilisation strategies are thus designed to offload the responsibility for risk management from central government on to the local state and non-state agencies, hence the increasing emphasis on public/private partnerships, inter-agency co-operation, inter-governmental forums and the rapid growth of non-elected government agencies. The composition of such networks allows the state to 'govern-at-a-distance' – to utilise the norms and control strategies of those formerly autonomous institutions identified by Foucault (1971, 1976) – while leaving 'the centralised state machine more powerful than before, with an extended capacity for action and influence' (Garland, 1996: 454).

It is in this context that Hopkins Burke has directed our attention not just to the increasing pervasiveness of policing in its various disguises in society (Hopkins Burke, 2004a) including the development of the contemporary youth justice system (Hopkins Burke, 2008) but also significantly to our own contribution in the legitimisation of this state of affairs and his neo-Foucauldian left realist variation on the carceral surveillance society proposes that in a complex fragmented dangerous global risk society it is *we* the general public – regardless of class location, gender or ethnic origin – that have a significant material interest in the development of that surveillance matrix invariably at an international level.

It is evident that theorists of risk, modernity and postmodernity see many of the processes they are discussing to be global transformations and thus the concept of globalisation is central to these new ways of thinking. The term is however used in different ways. A restricted meaning of globalisation widely used proposes the process to be one of global market liberalisation, the product of the last two decades. Other theorists use the term in a much broader historical perspective and where it refers to a much wider set of processes. We will now examine these processes further in the context of crime and criminal behaviour.

Globalisation and crime

Kinnvall and Jonsson (2002) observe that the concept of globalisation is very difficult to define precisely as it appears to be an all-embracing catchword of the contemporary world covering everything from economic and political issues to the spread of Western culture to all points of the globe. Globalisation is nevertheless invariably discussed in terms of three processes: scale, speed and cognition. Scale involves a discussion of magnitudes and refers to the number of economic, political, social and human linkages between societies at the present which are greater than at any other time in history. Speed has to do with how globalisation is conceptualised in time and space and it is observed that this is not a new phenomenon but does involve a compression of time and space never previously experienced. Cognition refers to an increased awareness of the globe as a smaller place where events elsewhere may have consequences for our everyday political, social and economic lives which may significantly impact on our sense of individual being.

Marfleet and Kiely (1998) define globalisation in reference to a world where societies, cultures, politics and economics have in some sense come closer together. Thus following Giddens (1964) who observed an intensification of worldwide social relations which link distant localities in such a way that local undertakings are shaped by events occurring many miles away and vice versa. Snyder (2002) conceptualises globalisation as an aggregate of multifaceted uneven, often contradictory economic, political, social and cultural processes which are characteristic of our time.

Johannen, Steven and Gomez (2003) note that there appears to be agreement in recent academic discussion that the term globalisation embraces the essence of historical movement, a triumph of neoliberal and characteristically Anglo–US ideology, being a more intense stage of capitalism, a confluence of events and technologies, or some combination of these. This Anglo–US ideology brings with it rapid transformations for business, government and, indeed, ordinary people. Findlay (2000) takes this further and views globalisation in a social context as the progress towards one culture on the planet or a single interdependent society. In this definition, globalisation is seen as a social process whereby the constraints of geography on social and cultural arrangements recede and people become increasingly aware of this recession. The common denominator of all these various different definitions appears to focus on the increasing degree of integration among societies that plays a crucial role in most types of social change.

A review of the literature shows that the following are considered to be critical global crimes: dealing in illicit drugs; illegal trafficking in weapons; illegal trafficking in human beings; money laundering; corruption; violent crimes including terrorism; and war crimes (Braithwaite, 1979; UNDP, 1999; Bequai, 2002). Eduardo (2002) provides an example of the interlinking of transnational crimes where the 'vast poppy fields in eastern Turkey are linked to the heroin dealer in downtown Detroit', 'the banker laundering drug money in Vienna is in league with the thriving cocaine refineries in Colombia', 'the men of the Chinese triads who control gambling and extortion in San

Francisco's Chinatown work the same network as the Singapore gang that turns out millions of fake credit cards' and 'the contract hit man who flies from Moscow to kill an unco-operative store owner in New York, on behalf of the Organisation, gets his fake papers by supplying the Sicilian Mafia with Soviet Army surplus ground-to-air missiles to smuggle into the Balkans to supply the Bosnian Serbs'.

The growing influence of organised crime is estimated to gross $1.5 trillion a year and is a significant rival to multinational corporations as an economic power. Global crime groups have the power to criminalise politics, business and the police, developing efficient networks, extend their reach deep and wide. All have operations extending beyond national borders, and they are now developing strategic alliances which are linked in a global network, reaping the benefits of globalisation (UNDP, 1999). Crime syndicates prefer globalisation, for it creates 'new and exciting opportunities, and among the most enterprising and imaginative opportunists are the world's criminals' (UNDP, 1999: 43). The UNDP (1999: 41) thus observes that:

> The illegal drug trade in 1995 was estimated at $400 billion, about 8% of world trade, more than the share of iron and steel or of motor vehicles, and roughly the same as textiles (7.5%) and gas and oil (8.6%).

There are now 200 million drug users throughout the world and in the past decade the production of opium has more than tripled and that of the coca leaf more than doubled in order to meet the huge demand from this illicit market. The problem of drugs is thus not restricted to a few countries but is a global phenomenon and many armed conflicts taking place in different parts of the world may be financed by illegal sources including a significant element from drugs.

Buchanan (2004) observes that as globalisation has evolved, money launderers have been able to conduct their trade with greater ease, sophistication and profitability. As new financial instruments and trading opportunities have been created and the liquidity of financial markets has improved, it has also allowed money laundering systems to be set up and shut down with greater ease. The latter tend to allocate dirty money around the world on the basis of avoiding national controls and thus flow to countries with less stringent controls. Globalisation has also improved the ability of money launderers to communicate using the Internet and travel allowing them to spread transactions across a greater number of jurisdictions and in doing so increases the number of legal obstacles that may hinder investigations. Underground or parallel banking systems have also attracted the attention of law enforcement and regulatory agencies.

Braithwaite (1979) observes that global money laundering imposes significant costs on the world economy by damaging the effective operations of national economies and by promoting inadequate economic policies. The outcome is that financial markets slowly become corrupted and the confidence of the public in the international financial system is eroded. Eventually, as financial markets become increasingly risky and less stable, the rate of growth of the world economy is reduced.

Eduardo (2000) observes that corruption is a significant trait of global crime with the blurring of the boundary between state and criminal power making the fight against organised crime significantly more difficult. In the countries where organised crime has asserted its political or financial power, whether it be by greed or fear, state illegality has become endemic. Interestingly low levels of corruption are seen to promote economic growth in certain regions but at a higher level it inhibits growth and damages the economy. Bribes are socially damaging and politically destabilising and are harmful for the growth prospects of host countries in that they can undermine the functioning of states, lower the efficiency of production, reduce competitiveness and introduce inequities (Ackerman, 2002). Corruption is not only damaging in itself but it also furthers other criminal activities such as drug production and trafficking and the creation of safe havens for terrorists. Russia is an example of how corruption becomes a main factor in the expansion of organised crime (Eduardo, 2000).

Global crime groups have the power to criminalise politics, business and law enforcement agencies, developing efficient networks and pervasively extending their reach. For example, the United Nations estimates that human trafficking is a $5-7 billion operation annually with four million persons moved from one country to another and within countries (Raymond, 2002). The traffic in women and girls for sexual exploitation – 500,000 a year to Western Europe alone – is estimated to be a $7 billion business (UNDP, 1999) and is a worldwide phenomenon that is becoming the fastest growing branch of organised crime (Raymond, 2002). Reliable estimates indicate that two hundred million people may be under the control of traffickers of various kinds worldwide (Eduardo, 2002).

Globalisation has greatly facilitated the growth of international terrorism. The development of international civil aviation has made hijacking possible, television has given terrorists worldwide publicity and modern technology has provided an impressive range of weapons and explosives (Eduardo, 2002). International terrorist organisations would nevertheless find it hard to operate and pose a challenge to any nation-state without media publicity and requisite funding. It is the money that they obtain from money-laundering, credit card frauds, securities scams, and much more, that enable international terrorists to traverse the globe at will, and buy the requisite equipment and armaments (Bequai, 2002). The threat of international terrorism is multiform. First, there is the traditional state-sponsored terrorism – which is a form of global organised crime – and this is also characterised as socio-political organised crime. Second, there is a new variant of freelance terrorists who constitute an even more frightening possibility because they are not sponsored by any particular state and are loosely affiliated with extremist and violent ideologies. These terrorists have proven to be all the more dangerous precisely because of their lack of organisation and the difficulties associated with identifying them (Eduardo, 2002). Terrorism and terrorist motivations are discussed in more detail below.

Computer and related criminality – cybercrime – has become the phenomenon of the early twenty-first century and this has been created by the vast expansion of computers in the global economy, the rapid increase of their use in households and, in particular, the Internet and public access cable television. There are thus countless individuals with the capacity and intent to use the medium to inflict damage (Bequai, 2002). One of the largest industries utilising the Internet is that of pornography, a business that is estimated to exceed a $100 billion annual turnover and which terrorists have been quick to exploit as a source of income. With a minimal investment of funds, and working though corporate fronts and money men, terrorist organisations have been reaping billions of dollars annually from pornography (Bequai, 2002).

The illegal trafficking of weapons is a fast expanding business which destabilises societies and governments, arming conflicts in Africa and Eastern Europe. Light weapons which have the most immediate impact on the lives of people, have been used in every conflict around the world, and have caused 90 per cent of war casualties since 1945. In El Salvador the homicide rate increased 36 per cent after the end of the civil war and in South Africa machine guns pouring in from Angola and Mozambique are being used increasingly in more and more crimes. In Albania there were five times as many murders in 1997 as in 1996, a rise attributed to the illegal arming of civilians (UNDP, 1999).

Organised crime is not new but criminals have been taking advantage of fast moving technological advances, overall globalisation and the freedom of circulation and the establishment of global markets. The acceleration of the liberalisation of markets has been at least partly technology-driven and with the rapid development of travel, global networks, electronic commerce and the information economy, it has been easy for people to trade and communicate. Financial activity, services and investments are becoming increasingly mobile. These developments provide opportunities for sustained improvements in economic performance but they also raise important new challenges in the form of globalised crime. Globalisation has certainly brought countries closer together through technological innovation and the integration of financial markets. The ability to conduct trade has become substantially quicker and cheaper and the global financial system now operates on a 24-hour basis. Globalisation has increased levels of cross border investment and brought about the transfer of technology, skills and knowledge across countries. It has significantly benefited participants not only in the legal economy but also in the illegal economy (Findlay, 2000).

Findlay (2000) explains the global explosion in crime and criminal activity in terms of the market conditions which are the outcome of the internationalisation of capital, the generalisation of consumerism and the unification of economies that are in a state of imbalance. He observes that power and domination are simply criminogenic. The new rules of globalisation focus on the integration of global markets and the needs of people that markets cannot meet are simply neglected. The process is thus concentrating power in the hands of the rich and already powerful while accentuating the marginalisation of both poor people and poor countries.

Susan George (1999) proposes that globalisation is creating a three-track society, in which there are the exploiters, the exploited and the outcasts, the latter group being people who are not even worth exploiting. She argues that the current 'corporate-driven, neo-liberal globalisation' results in increasing inequalities between rich and poor, both within and between countries. Many are marginalised, specifically in the less developed world with weak state institutions and fragile economies burdened by debt payments. George (1999) observes that those marginalised do not passively wait until they starve to death, but create their own means to survive whether in the legal economy or in the illegal one and more often in the grey area that lies in between.

Globalisation excludes segments of economies and societies from the networks of information available to the dominant society. Unemployment, alienation, and youth abandonment, which make up what Castells (1998) calls the 'black holes of informational capitalism', provide the ideal terrain for criminal recruitment of, for example, global drug traffickers. This phenomenon is even more acute in Russia where following the collapse of the Soviet Union young people became an attractive labour pool for criminal organisations (Findlay, 2000; Eduardo, 2002). Findlay (2000) argues that the globalisation of markets has profoundly transformed the structures of employment, distribution of wealth, and consumption through modernisation, development, and urbanisation. Such macro-economic transformations are moreover accompanied by significant global changes of societal norms and values, which influence the scope and nature of local and global crime (Le Billon, 2001; Eduardo, 2002; Mehanna, 2004). This may be a result of technological transfer, information transfer or immigration.

A further significant link in the globalisation process is that of the media. For example, the globalisation of a culture of violence has spread through the media and has become a major focus of popular culture, from children's cartoons to investigative journalism and has been very influential on the pattern of local crime. The over-representation and legitimisation of violence by the global media is thus compounded locally by the availability of guns, the institutionalisation of violence by criminal justice agencies, lax parental supervision and weak parental bonding. At the cultural level, these phenomena are connected with the general dissolution of traditional norms and values that characterise the current era of globalisation (Funk, 2004).

Terrorism and state violence

On 11 September 2001 the terrorist group al-Qaeda carried out attacks on the World Trade Center in New York City and the Pentagon in Washington DC causing thousands of casualties and in doing so provided inevitable widespread public support for what was to be an extensive authoritarian assault on civil liberties and human rights both in the USA and the UK. Further terrorist attacks on the allies of the USA again involving large numbers of casualties – including those in Bali on 12 October 2002, in Turkey on 20 November 2003 and the London Transport System on 7 July 2005 – and the almost constant warnings by government of failed attempts and successful interventions by the security forces against terrorists invariably living in our midst strengthened support for measures to protect society from such attacks (see Hopkins Burke, 2004c).

There is a well-known adage that 'one man's terrorist is another man's freedom fighter' and it is clear that those involved in the aforementioned al-Qaeda terrorist attacks undoubtedly considered their actions to be justified acts of war, just as the retaliatory strikes against Afghanistan and Iraq were subsequently considered just acts in the 'war against terrorism' by the governments of the USA, UK, and their allies. Contemporary politicians go to great lengths to describe terrorists as being no different from common criminals but this has not always been the case. During the nineteenth century Britain obtained a reputation for being a safe haven for political 'agitators' and refugees from Europe but this situation was to change significantly during the following century when 'political criminals' were to become synonymous with 'terrorists' and abhorred by governments throughout the world.

'Terrorism' is an emotive word which emphasises the extreme fear caused by apparently indiscriminate violent actions of individuals claiming to be operating on behalf of some particular cause. Sometimes terrorist activities are funded by states – state-sponsored terrorism – and the West has been keen to accuse countries such as Libya, Iran, (previously) Iraq and Syria of doing so. Western states have, on the other hand, supported terrorism when it has been in their political interests to do so and thus during the Cold War backed many right-wing-movements invariably as a bulwark against communism.

Israel also readily condemns terrorism but ironically the state itself came into being as the outcome of a terrorist campaign. One of the actions of the Jewish organisation Irgun Zvai Leumi was to blow up the King David Hotel in Jerusalem in July 1946 without giving any warning and killing over 70 people many of them British. The leader of Irgun, Menachem Begin was sought by the British as a terrorist and a murderer and was sentenced to death in his absence. He was later to become Prime Minister of Israel and was awarded the Nobel Peace Prize in 1978. Similarly, Nelson Mandela spent over 25 years in prison for acts of terrorism and subsequently became President of South Africa within five years of his release and a global icon.

Most of the major theories that seek to explain terrorism – and individual and group involvement – are derived from theories of collective violence developed in the field of political science. Terrorism is not a form of governance but anarchism is. Most anarchists reject terrorism but in a theoretical sense, anarchism justifies such actions as a form of criminal action that attacks the values of an organised, complacent society. Anarchism is – as we saw in the previous chapter – a theory of governance that rejects any form of central or external authority, preferring instead to replace it with alternative forms of organisation such as shaming rituals for deviants, mutual assistance pacts between citizens, syndicalism (any non-authoritarian organisational structure that gives the greatest freedom to workers), iconoclasm (the destruction of cherished beliefs), libertarianism (a belief in absolute liberty), and straightforward individualism. Anarchism is often referred to as providing the nineteenth century foundations of terrorism with the actual term first introduced in 1840 by Pierre-Joseph Proudhon. Other major nineteenth anarchist figures – like Karl Heinzen and Johann Most – argued that murder, especially murder-suicide, constituted the highest form of revolutionary struggle and both advocated the use of weapons of mass destruction.

It was minor figures in the history of anarchism, like Charles Gallo, Auguste Vaillantc, Emile Henry, and Claudius Konigstein who advocated the influential idea that to be most effective, the targets must be innocents (in places such as crowded dance halls or shopping centres) or symbols of economic success (like banks and stock exchanges). It is nevertheless important to note that present day anarchists – and certainly not the anarchist criminologists such as Ferrell and Tifft we encountered in the previous chapter – do not support terrorism. Moreover, it is important to recognise that only a small minority of terrorists have ever been anarchists, and only a small minority of anarchists have ever been terrorists.

Passmore (2002) proposes that fascism – a form of government with strong links to state sponsored terrorism – can be defined as the consolidation of an ultranationalist ideology that is unashamedly racist. The word itself comes from the Latin 'fasces' which means to use power to scare or impress people and it generally refers to the consolidation of all economic and political power into some form of super-patriotism that is devoted to genocide or endless war. So called islamo-fascism has links with the birth of Nazi 'national socialist' fascism in 1928 when the Muslim Brotherhood (Al Ikhwan Al Muslimun) – parent organisation of numerous terrorist groups – was formed in reaction to the 1924 abolition of the caliphate by the secularist Turkish Government. Passmore (2002) observes that the term 'Islamic Fascism' is a better term with which to describe the agenda of contemporary radical Islam for this captures the twin thrusts of reactionary fascism. In one sense, fascism is born out of insecurity and a sense of failure, but in another sense it thrives in a once-proud, humbled but ascendant, people. Envy and false grievances are the characteristics of such reactionary fascism while believers are subject to all kinds of conspiratorial delusions that setbacks were caused by others and can be erased through ever more zealous action.

Fascism supports terrorism at home and abroad and its inevitably charismatic leaders are usually given supreme powers to crack down on dissidents. With the frequent wars and militaristic ventures that come with fascism, an effort is made to demonise the enemy as subhumans who deserve extinction while, at the same time, being transformed into scapegoats and blamed for all the past problems a country has experienced. Fascism simply appeals to the frustrations and resentments of an ethnic group of people who think they ought to have a bigger place at the global table. When combined with an anti-western slant (the USA as the Great Satan) fascism becomes a means of social identity (Pan-Africanism, Pan-Arabism, Islamo-Fascism) as well as a facilitator of terrorism.

Hoffman (1993) notes that about a quarter of all terrorist groups and about a half of the most dangerous ones on earth are primarily motivated by religious concerns who believe that God not only approves of their action but demands their action. Their cause is thus sacred and consists of a combined sense of hope for the future and vengeance for the past. Of these two components, the backward-looking desire for vengeance may be the more important trigger for terrorism because the forward-looking component – called apocalyptic thinking or eschatology – tends to produce wild-eyed fanatics who are more a danger to themselves and their own people.

The successful use of terrorism in the name of religion rests upon convincing believers or the converted that a 'neglected duty' exists in the fundamental, mainstream part of the religion. Religious terrorism is therefore, *not* about extremism, fanaticism, sects, or cults, but is instead about a fundamentalist or militant interpretation of the basic tenets. Most religious traditions are filled with plenty of violent images at their core and destruction or self-destruction is a central part of the logic behind religion-based terrorism (Juergensmeyer, 2001). Stitt (2003) observes that evil is often defined as malignant narcissism from a theological point of view and religion easily serves as moral cover for self-centred terrorists and psychopaths. We should note that religion has always absorbed or absolved evil and guilt in what is called theodicy or the study of how the existence of evil can be reconciled with a good and benevolent God (Kraemer, 2004).

Economics has many concepts that are relevant to an understanding of terrorism, such as, supply and demand, costs and benefits and we saw in the first part of this book that rational choice theory has become a significant component of the contemporary variant of the rational actor model of crime and criminal behaviour which proposes that people will engage in crime after weighing the costs and benefits of their actions. Criminals must thus come to believe that their actions will be beneficial – to themselves, their community, or society – and they must come to see that crime pays, or is at least a risk-free way to better their situation (Cohen and Felson, 1979). It is in this theoretical context that the Olson (1982) hypothesis suggests that participants in revolutionary violence base their behaviour on a rational cost-benefit calculus to pursue the best course of action given the social circumstances. Rational choice theory, in political science, follows a similar line, and holds that people can be collectively rational, even when making what appears to be irrational decisions for them as individuals, after perceiving that their participation is important and their personal contribution to the public good outweighs any concerns they may have for the 'free rider' problem (Muller and Opp, 1986).[3]

Martha Crenshaw (1998) is a rational choice theorist who argues that terrorism is not a pathological phenomenon or aberration and that the central focus of study should be on why it is that some groups find terrorism useful and conversely why it is that other groups do not find terrorism useful. Thus, some groups may continue to work with established patterns of dissident action while others may resort to terrorism because they have tried other alternatives. Still other groups may choose terrorism as an early choice because they have learned from the experiences of others that alternative strategies do not work. Crenshaw (1998) calls the latter the contagion effect and claims it has distinctive patterns similar to the copycat effect in other theories of collective violence (Gurr, 1970). There may also be circumstances in which the terrorist group wants to publicise its cause to the world, a process Crenshaw (1995) calls the globalisation of civil war.

Nassar (2004) argues that the processes of globalisation contribute to dreams, fantasies, and rising expectations, but at the same time, lead to dashed hopes, broken dreams, and unfulfilled achievements. He observes that terrorism breeds in the gap between expectations and achievements and this is an argument resonant with Merton's version of anomie theory which we encountered in the second part of this book. Indeed, we might observe that the only thing unique with this version of globalisation theory is that it adds a rich–poor dichotomy. Thus, rich people (or nations) are seen as wanting power and wealth, and poor people (or nations) are seen as wanting justice. From this perspective, rich people are part of the causes of terrorism since they contribute to the conditions which give rise to it while the perpetrators are never seen as being born or socialised with any specific predispositions toward it. In short, globalisation theory proposes that if the oppressed and disgruntled poor people of the world were simply given the chance to find peaceful means for achieving justice, terrorism would not thrive.

Modern sociological perspectives are primarily concerned with the social construction of fear or panic and how institutions and processes, especially the media, primary and secondary groups, maintain that expression of fear. O'Connor (1994) makes use of a neo-functionalist framework to chart the way terrorism impacts on the whole of society by affecting core values of achievement, competition, and individualism. Thus, some societies become 'softer' targets after terrorism (especially after short-term target hardening) and other societies become stronger in the long term. It depends upon interaction patterns, stabilities and interpenetrations among the structural subsystems (economy, polity, religion, law).

O'Connor (1994) identifies five contemporary sociological theories of terrorism. First, the *frustration-aggression hypothesis* proposes that every frustration leads to some form of aggression and every aggressive act relieves that frustration to some extent. Second, the *relative deprivation hypothesis* proposes that as a person goes about choosing their values and interests, they compare what they have and do not have, as well as what they want or do not want, with real or imaginary others. The person then usually perceives a discrepancy between what is possible for them and what is possible for others, and reacts to it with anger or an inflamed sense of injustice. Third, the *negative identity hypothesis* proposes that, for whatever reason, a person develops a vindictive and covert rejection of the roles and statuses laid out for them by their family, community, or society. Thus, a child raised in an affluent family might secretly sabotage every effort to give them a good start in life, until the day comes, with some apparent life-altering experience (like engaging in terrorism) that the long-nurtured negative identity comes to the fore, and the subject can then make it feel more like a total identity transformation. Fourth, the *narcissistic rage hypothesis* is a generic explanation for all the numerous things that can go wrong in child-rearing, such as too much mothering, too little mothering, ineffective discipline, overly stringent

325

discipline, psychological trauma and coming from a broken home which leads to a damaged self-concept and a tendency to blame others for our own inadequacies. Fifth, the *moral disengagement hypothesis* follows the work of David Matza on 'techniques of neutralisation' we encountered in the second part of this book and proposes the ways that a person neutralises or removes any inhibitions they have about committing acts of horrific violence. Thus, some common patterns include imagining oneself to be a hero, portraying oneself as a mere functionary with limited (or diminished) responsibility, minimising the harm done, dehumanising the victim, or insulating oneself in routine activities. O'Connor (1994) observes that organised crime figures, for example, usually hide behind family activities with their wives and children although we should also be aware that there are numerous other ways that violence can be rationalised and neutralised (see Hacker, 1996). Terrorist rationalisations usually involve a complete shift in the way government and civil society is perceived by the individuals and groups concerned.

Psychological explanations of terrorism have tended with a few exceptions (Ross, 1996, 1999) to be clinical and invariably futile attempts to find something pathological in the terrorist personality. Merari (1990) provides a good overview of psychological approaches and factors that have been implicated in the formation of supposedly terrorist personalities and these include the familiar explanations of ineffective parenting, rebellion against parents, a pathological need for absolutism and a variety of other 'syndromes' and hypotheses which it is observed have yielded little valid and reliable information about the psychology of terrorists other than a few generalisations. There have been several promising attempts to merge or combine psychology with sociology – and criminal justice perspectives – into what might be called terrorist profiling (Russell and Bowman, 1977; Bell, 1982; Galvin, 1983; Strentz, 1988; Hudson, 1999). When suicide bombing came to the fore, Merari (1990) conducted interviews with terrorists and found that most who commit suicide attacks are between the ages of sixteen and 28. Most are male, but 15 per cent are female with that proportion increasing. Many come from poor backgrounds and have limited education, but some have university degrees and come from wealthy families.

What sociological and psychological approaches basically tell us is that individuals join terrorist organisations in order to commit acts of terrorism, and that this process is the same as when individuals join criminal subcultures in order to commit acts of crime. Moreover, there appears to be no unique terrorist personality but there does appear to be unique subcultural phenomena which develop, support, and enhance an enthusiasm for cold-blooded, calculated violence which, if not satisfied within a terrorist organisation *might* well be fulfilled elsewhere. Terrorism is a social activity and individuals join a terrorist group usually after they have tried other forms of political involvement. The emotional links between individuals and the strength of commitment to their ideology appear to become stronger by the group living in the underground and facing adversity in the form of counterterrorism.

Socialisation in the terrorist underground is quite intense and the identity of an individual may become tied to the identity of the group but it is just as likely that emotional relationships become as important (if not more) than the purpose of the group. This means that the distribution of beliefs among members in a terrorist group may be uneven and there may be major differences between individual and group ideology (Ferracuti, 1982). Thus, ideology may not necessarily be the main component of motivation.

We have observed in our discussion above how some of the traditional criminological theories that we have encountered in the first four parts of this book – in particular, the US anomie tradition as developed via deviant subculture theories but also social control theories – have helped to explain why it is that people join terrorist groups. In other words, this is part of a long established criminological tradition which proposes that people choose to act in certain criminal ways because of where they are born and who they associate with and this is as much applicable to involvement in terrorism as it is to the white-collar, professional and hate crimes we identified in the second part of this book. Ruggiero (2005) follows in this sociological criminological tradition and commences his discussion with Durkheim and we should observe that the latter's notion of the 'normality of crime' which is functional to requirements of society is commensurate with an understanding of terrorist activity. Terrorist activities seem to make most sense at times of rapid social change – when there is a prevailing sense of normlessness or Durkheimian anomie – and when an unfair or forced division of labour is readily apparent to many.

Terrorism and postmodernism revisited

Whether or not the terrorist activities outlined above can be considered to be 'just' wars in terms of international law and in any objective sense has been widely debated but it does seem that these can be considered perfectly normal, albeit violent and extremely unpleasant activities, which make perfect subjective sense to the participants and the groups supporting them. The significance for our discussion of terrorism is that the events of 11 September 2001 – and those which followed – seemingly signposted the end for any positive notion of a postmodern society. From that date, the very idea of societies being founded on widely accepted and legitimate moral ambiguities where 'there are a range of different discourses that can be legitimate and hence right for different people, at different times, in different contexts' becomes seriously problematic.

Postmodern societies can only function successfully if there is a reciprocal acceptance of diverse values from all participant groups. It was always a deeply problematic notion in societies with a very pronounced 'forced-division-of-labour' (Durkheim, 1933) and it appears seemingly impossible when groups become so totally opposed to the values and activities of others that they are prepared to use any means to destroy them. At that point, such groups become enemies and anyone – however, tangentially associated with them – will become a legitimate target for surveillance and risk assessment. Government cannot afford not to take the issue of state security seriously and the notion of the risk society becomes entrenched and virtually unassailable in public policy discourse.

Suggested further reading

The notion of risk society in general is discussed by Beck (1992) and the significance of this analysis for controlling crime and the notion of governance with the decline of the sovereign state by Garland (1996). For an excellent discussion of 'actuarial justice' and 'risk society' as applied to criminal justice see O'Malley (1992), Feeley and Simon (1994) and Ericson and Haggerty (1997). Giddens (1994, 1998) attempts to square the circle between, the postmodern condition (for him, late modernity), left realism and the 'third way' political strategy of New Labour. Hopkins Burke (2004a) discusses the pervasiveness of multi-agency 'policing' in contemporary societies and apparently contradictory demands for security and human rights. Hopkins Burke (2008) discusses the emergence and establishment of contemporary youth justice system in the context of risk society. Findlay (2000) provides an excellent introduction to the globalisation of crime and criminality and Ruggerio (2005) provides an equally fine socio-criminological discussion of terrorism.

Notes

1 The Chernobyl disaster was an accident at the Chernobyl Nuclear Power Plant on 26 April 1986, consisting of an explosion at the plant and subsequent radioactive contamination of the surrounding geographic area (see Davidson, 2006).
2 Love Canal is a neighbourhood in Niagara Falls, New York, the site of the worst environmental disaster involving chemical wastes in the history of the USA (see Mazur, 1998).
3 The 'free rider' problem is a classic paradox in social science and economics which asks why anybody should do something for the public good when most likely someone else will get credit for it and everybody else will benefit merely by sitting idly and doing nothing.

20. Conclusions: radical moral communitarian criminology

This book has examined the different ways that crime and criminal behaviour has been explained during the past 200 years and while these explanations have been proposed at various times by among others legal philosophers, biologists, psychologists, sociologists, political scientists and geographers, it is possible to locate these many and varied explanations – or criminological theories – in terms of one of three different general models or traditions that were the focus of the first three parts of this book.

The first tradition – the rational actor model – proposes that human beings possess free will and this enables them to choose whether or not to engage in criminal activities. From this perspective, crime can be controlled by making the costs of offending – that is, punishment – sufficient to discourage the pursuit of criminal rewards. In other words, in such punitive circumstances the choice of engagement in criminal activity would be irrational.

The second tradition – the predestined actor model – proposes that criminal behaviour can be explained in terms of factors that exist either within the individual or their environment that cause – or determine – that person to act in ways over which they have little or no control. From this perspective, it is through the identification and eradication of these factors by some form of treatment process that crime can be controlled. Thus, biological and psychological variants of this model propose that the individual should be changed, while sociological versions advocate the transformation of the criminogenic environment.

The third tradition – the victimised actor model – denies neither entirely the prescriptions of the rational actor nor the predestined actor models. It is recognised that people make decisions to behave in ways that may well be perfectly rational for them in the circumstances in which they find themselves but it is the activities of the economically poor and politically powerless that are criminalised and it is thus a process conducted in the interests of those with power and wealth. At the micro level, individuals can be labelled and criminalised by coming into contact with frontline agents of the state working in the criminal justice and welfare systems while at the macro societal level it is those with economic power and the control of authority that are in a position to influence the legislative agenda. From this perspective, crime is seen to be a social construction and can be controlled or reduced by not criminalising dispossessed unfortunates and by abolishing legislation that criminalises their activities.

The fourth part of this book has discussed those attempts to produce a synthesis of different theoretical perspectives – some of these being internal to one particular model of criminal behaviour, others incorporating elements that cross model boundaries – with the intention of providing a bigger, better, all-encompassing theory that seeks to explain as much crime and criminal behaviour as possible and in some cases ambitiously *all* criminal behaviour. It is an approach clearly in line with modernist social science thinking with its emphasis on moral certainty and our ability to successfully social engineer society in the interests of all.

This fifth part of the book has discussed ways of explaining crime and criminal behaviour in a contemporary era permeated by moral ambiguity and where there have been increasing doubts about the sustainability of the modernist project in an increasingly fragmented, complex and diverse social world. Central to the notion of the postmodern condition, there has been the recognition of a range of different discourses that can be legitimate and hence right for different people, at different times, in different contexts and where the notion of the objective truth – or competing objective realities – of modernity, has been replaced by recognition of the multiple realities or moral ambiguities of postmodernity. Many postmodernists have indeed celebrated the failure of the modernist project to establish rational foundations for knowledge and have wholeheartedly embraced this trend towards human diversity and social fragmentation.

It was observed in the previous chapter that postmodern societies can only function successfully if there is reciprocal acceptance of diverse values from all participant groups and it has become perfectly clear that this reciprocity of goodwill does not exist outside of predominantly bourgeois intellectual circles in some of the more affluent societies on this planet. At the same time, a whole range of significant risks, some of which have been chronicled in this fifth part of the book – and of which traditional crime patterns and motivations are only part – have arisen in contemporary global but fragmented society which threaten the health and survival of our social existence in its present form. Global terrorism has significantly focused our thoughts on these issues and – as observed in the previous chapter – government cannot afford to take serious risks with state security in such circumstances and the inevitable outcome is thus an inevitable expansion of the carceral and surveillance society that we collectively not only welcome but actively encourage (Hopkins Burke, 2004a, 2008).

If the regular terrorist atrocities that have occurred throughout the world during the first decade of the twenty-first century have ended any legitimate notion of a postmodern society there would, on the other hand, seem no justifiable basis for a return to the moral certainty of high modernity. Undoubtedly, the governments of the USA and the UK have sought to present to the world a new moral certainty but the many socio-economic and political circumstances that have come to constitute the postmodern *condition* have continued to exist and there are thus legitimate alternative moral certainties available. This author observed four years ago that UK government support for President Bush did not actually embrace the whole neoconservative package of criminal justice interventions – or for that matter, other public policy pronouncements – that had come to dominate official discourse in the USA in the previous few years (Hopkins Burke, 2005). There had been at that time the recent re-election of a neoconservative government with an apparent mandate for the creation of tough right realist policies and thus mounting a challenge to these seemed to be an appropriate strategy for liberal or critical criminologists in the USA and beyond.

The eminent liberal and left realist US criminologist Elliott Currie (1999) had done just that and had questioned the 'triumphalism' which had greeted the supposed fall in crime levels in a number of western countries – but in particular the USA – during the 1990s. He observed that the celebrations were not so much premature as self-delusionary in that the decline in crime levels were in fact measured against baselines that were already astronomically high. Crime in the USA remained very much a reality and had merely returned to levels that were unacceptably high in the mid-1980s. Moreover, the fall in the crime rate could not be simply attributed to the new order in law enforcement exemplified by more imprisonment (deterrence and incapacitation) and tougher policing (crime control and zero tolerance) that had been introduced by the neoconservatives. Evidence of brutality and differential policing practices – particularly in relation to African-Americans and Hispanics in the inner city – not to mention the manipulation of official police statistics had been identified as but some of the negative consequences of these policies (see Hopkins Burke, 2002). Currie observed that this new triumphalism has gradually displaced the idea that socio-economic conditions need to be addressed if social order is to be maintained:

> The flip-side (of triumphalism) being that we've also proven that you don't, after all, need to address such problems as poverty and social exclusion or other supposed 'root causes' of violent crime.
>
> (Currie 1999: 3).

Two ways in which criminologists could play a more effective role in bringing about positive change in the socio-legal domain were thus proposed:

> The first is to push, and push relentlessly, to ensure that this nation makes those preventative social investments that can reduce violent crime in enduring and humane ways, rather than simply suppressing it, hiding it, or denying it … The second is to end the systems abuse in our institutions so that they can be devoted to 'rebuilding' the lives of people in constructive and humane environments.
>
> (Currie, 1999: 6)

Currie thus called for criminologists to encourage the development of more family support programmes, improved programmes for prison inmates and targeted anti-poverty initiatives while clearly challenging the extremes of neo-conservative judicial policy:

> If there's one task that we as professional criminologists should set for ourselves in the new millennium, it's to fight to ensure that stupid and brutal policies that we know don't work are – at the very least – challenged at every forum that's available to us.
>
> (Currie, 1999: 7)

It was observed four years ago that we were living through undoubtedly difficult times and that it was both easy and understandable to be negative and disillusioned in such circumstances but, at the same time, there seemed great possibilities for a reformulated new-liberal criminological agenda – indeed, as part of a wider new-liberal public policy agenda – that could gather support across a wide and diverse section of the population not just in the USA and the UK (Hopkins Burke, 2005). It was also observed that the left realist approach that concluded the fourth part of this book – and endorsed by Elliot Currie – is far from antagonistic to that new-liberal agenda. The theoretical foundations of left realism are of course firmly located in the modernist tradition and it is the undoubted explicit intention of left realists to build a new moral certainty – or even a new teleological project – from the contemporary condition of moral uncertainty. It was observed that a new left realist moral certainty would demand as a baseline a substantial reduction in socio-economic inequality and, at the same time, recognition and celebration of the diversity of the postmodern condition but not the apparent uncontrollable anarchy and acceptable inequalities of moral ambiguity or the rigid authoritarianism and brutalities of neoconservatism.

The left realist strategy *implicitly* suggests an enthusiasm for the postmodern notion of rejecting grand theoretical solutions and a willingness to consider explanatory elements from all perspectives in an attempt to provide a comprehensive intervention against crime. It is thus recognised that most criminological theories have something legitimate to say about *some* forms of crime and criminal behaviour and, thus, due consideration should be given to these in the *appropriate* circumstances.

It was a strategy that seemed to be in harmony with the election of a 'New' Labour Government in 1997 which had proposed a 'new politics' beyond doctrinal dogma and which appeared to be willing to consider policy options from a wide range of perspectives. This strategy which – while not entirely non-ideological and undoubtedly part of a much wider strategy of attempting to build a new moral certainly – fundamentally recognises that good ideas, and for that matter, bad ones, are not the preserve of one side of the traditional left/right political dichotomy. They can emerge from many different sources and there can be a diverse range of motivations for implementing a policy or strategy (Giddens, 1994, 1998). In terms of criminology, this 'third way' would appear to be a sensible long-term approach to both understanding crime and criminal behaviour in all its many manifestations and for the development of flexible strategies for dealing with what this book has clearly demonstrated to be a multifaceted and far from straightforward social problem. For this to be a successful and widely accepted long-term strategy that survives the vagaries of the electoral system it must nevertheless embrace the essential tenets of a contemporary new-liberalism where there is respect for the rights and *responsibilities* of both individuals and *communities* while at the same time recognition that crime is a real problem that impacts hugely and negatively on the lives of real people, be they victims or offenders, and that it is not thus inappropriate or illiberal to intervene in such activities or deal with the consequences of those actions in a rigorous way. These ideas are of course similar to those of the communitarian philosophy that emerged in the USA in the last quarter of the twentieth century.

The communitarian agenda

Communitarianism emerged in the USA during the 1980s as a response to what its advocates considered to be the limitations of liberal theory and practice, but significantly, diverse strands in social, political and moral thought, arising from very different locations on the political spectrum – such as Marxism (Ross, 2003) and traditional 'one-nation' conservatism (Scruton, 2001) – can be identified within this body of thought. Its dominant themes are that the individual rights which have been vigorously promoted by traditional liberals need to be balanced with social responsibilities and autonomous individual selves and do not exist in isolation but are shaped by the values and culture of communities. Communitarians propose that unless we redress the balance toward the pole of community our society will continue to become normless, self-centred, and driven by special interests and power seeking.

This critique of the one-sided emphasis on individual civil or human rights promoted by liberalism is the key defining characteristic of communitarianism for it is observed that rights have tended to be asserted without a corresponding sense of how they can be achieved or who will pay for them. 'Rights talk' is seen to corrupt political discourse by obstructing genuine discussion and is employed without a corresponding sense of responsibilities (see Emanuel, 1991; Glendon, 1991; Etzioni, 1993, 1995a, 1995b). Communitarians do promote the preservation of traditional liberal rights and their extension in non-democratic regimes – or those that practise discrimination – but propose that these rights need to be located in a more balanced framework.

Communitarians argue that the one-sided emphasis on rights in liberalism is related to the individual as a 'disembodied self' who has been uprooted from cultural meanings, community attachments, and the life stories that constitute the full identities of real human beings. Dominant liberal theories of justice, as well as much of economic and political theory, presume such a self (see Etzioni, 1993). Communitarians, in contrast, shift the balance and argue that the 'I' is constituted through the 'We' in a dynamic tension. Significantly, this is not, in terms of this purist form of communitarianism, an argument for the restoration of traditional community with high levels of mechanical solidarity, repressive dominance of the majority or the patriarchal family although some on the conservative fringes do take up that position. Mainstream communitarians are, in fact, critical of community institutions that are authoritarian and restrictive and that cannot bear scrutiny within a larger framework of human rights and equal opportunities and they accept the (post)modern condition that we are located within a complex web of pluralistic communities – or organic solidarity – with genuine value conflicts within them and within selves.

Amitai Etzioni, Mary Ann Glendon and William Galston (1991) outlined the basic framework of communitarianism urging that the focus should be on the family and its central role in socialisation and, therefore, propose that employers should provide maximum support for parents through the creation of work time initiatives, such as the provision of crèche facilities, and they warn us against avoidable parental relationship breakdowns, in order to put the interests of children first:

> The fact is, given the same economic and social conditions, in poor neighbourhoods one finds decent and hardworking youngsters next to antisocial ones. Likewise, in affluent suburbs one finds antisocial youngsters right next to decent hardworking ones. The difference is often a reflection of the homes they come from.
>
> (Etzioni, 1995b: 70)

Etzioni refers to the existence of a 'parenting deficit' in contemporary western societies where self-gratification is considered as much a priority for many parents as ensuring that their children are properly socialised and instilled with the appropriate moral values that act as protection against involvement in criminality and antisocial behaviour. The outcome is both inevitable and disastrous:

> Juvenile delinquents do more than break their parents' hearts. They mug the elderly, hold up stores and gas stations, and prey on innocent children returning from school. They grow up to be useless, or worse, as employees, and they can drain taxpayers' resources and patience ... Therefore, parents have a moral responsibility to the community to invest themselves in the proper upbringing of their children, and communities – to enable parents to so dedicate themselves.
>
> (Etzioni, 1995b: 54)

In the UK Dennis and Erdos (1992) explain the 'parenting deficit' in terms of the liberalisation of sexual mores that has been endemic in western societies since the 1960s. They observe that the illegitimate children of single parents do less well on several fronts with young males becoming involved in criminal behaviour because of the absence of a positive male role model while, at the same time, the whole project of creating and maintaining the skills of fatherhood is being abandoned and lost.

Communitarians, consequently, seek a reversal of these trends and demand a revival of moral education in schools at all levels, including the values of tolerance, peaceful resolution of conflict, the superiority of democratic government, hard work and saving. They also propose that government services should be devolved to an appropriate level, with the pursuit of new kinds of public–private partnerships, and the development of national and local service programmes. These ideas were to become very influential and were to filter into the Clinton administration during the 1990s and beyond and in a pamphlet written shortly after he became Prime Minister of the UK, Tony Blair (1998: 4) demonstrated his communitarian or 'third way' credentials:

> We all depend on collective goods for our independence; and all our lives are enriched – or impoverished – by the communities to which we belong. … A key challenge of progressive politics is to use the state as an enabling force, protecting effective communities and voluntary organisations and encouraging their growth to tackle new needs, in partnership as appropriate.

The most familiar and resonant, of the 'abstract slogans' used by Blair in the promotion of the importance of community was the idea that rights entail responsibilities and this was taken from the work of Etzioni (1993). In contrast to the traditional liberal idea that members of a society may be simply entitled to unconditional benefits or services, it is proposed from this perspective that the responsibility to care for each individual should be seen as lying, first and foremost with the individual themselves. For Blair and his sociological guru Anthony Giddens (1998) community is invoked very deliberately as residing in *civil society*: in lived social relations, and in 'commonsense' notions of our civic obligations. The 'third way' is presented as avoiding what its proponents see as the full-on atomistic egotistical individualism entailed by the Thatcherite maxim that 'there is no such thing as society', and on the other hand, the traditional social-democratic recourse to a strong state as the tool by which to realise the aims of social justice, most notably that of economic equality. For Blair, 'the grievous twentieth century error of the fundamentalist Left was the belief that the state could replace civil society and thereby advance freedom' (Blair, 1998: 4). He thus accepts that the state has a role to play but as a facilitator, rather than a guarantor, of a flourishing community life.

Dissenters have observed that the implementation of the New Labour agenda was to take rather a different course with its character rather more authoritarian – and thus, centred more on the usage of the state apparatus to deliver particular outcomes – than is suggested by the rhetorical appeal to the relatively autonomous powers of civil society to deliver progress by itself (see Driver and Martell, 1997; Jordan, 1998). Hughes (1998) thus refers to the communitarianism of Etzioni and his acolytes – and pursued enthusiastically by governments in both the USA and the UK – as moral *authoritarian* communitarianism and calls for a more radical non-authoritarian variant.

Radical egalitarian communitarianism

Radical egalitarian communitarians such as Bill Jordan (1992, 1996), Elliot Currie (1993, 1996, 1997) and Jock Young (1999) focus on inequality, deprivation and the market economy as causes of crime and promote policies to eliminate poverty which they define as a degree of deprivation that seriously impairs participation in society. Jordan (1992) has argued persuasively that in recent years in the UK and similar western societies we have witnessed deterioration in social relations due to the poor being denied access to material goods and thus their experience of power is simply one of being unjust. He observes that following the major socio-economic transformation that occurred during the last 20 years of the twentieth century there has been the formation of two very different opposing communities of 'choice' and 'fate'. On the one hand, 'communities of choice' are those where individuals and families have developed income security strategies which are associated with comfortable 'safe', convenient, healthy and status giving private environments. On the other hand, 'communities of fate' are those bound together into long-term interdependencies because of lack of opportunities to move geographical location, gain access to good education or healthcare, get decently paid legitimate – 'on-the-cards' – employment or share in the cultural enjoyments of mainstream society.

Jordan argues the need for an unconditional basic income for all citizens as one specific means of sharing out the common good in a more equitable fashion although he accepts that on its own this is no policy panacea. Nevertheless, the provision of a basic income for all would also open up the possibility for individuals and groups to participate in their own chosen projects and commitments and moreover such a scheme would reduce the institutionalised traps and barriers to labour market participation that undermine legitimate efforts by members of 'communities of fate' to rejoin mainstream society. From this perspective we return to the critical criminology agenda we encountered in the third part of this book where it is argued that marginalisation, inequality and exclusion provide the foundations for much crime and antisocial activity. As a consequence the radical *egalitarian* communitarian agenda for crime prevention gives ethical priority to decisions about the redistribution of resources which allows all members an opportunity to share adequately in the life of community on an equal basis. This is clearly a laudable agenda but this contribution does raise the question as to whether the state has to first 'repair' the social wounds before 'the community' can be allowed to participate in an inclusive politics of crime control and social justice.

Elliot Currie (1985, 1993, 1996, 1997) has made a significant contribution to the radical communitarian debate on crime, disorder, the decline of communities in the USA and the left realist programme on crime prevention and argues that the most serious problem in the contemporary USA is that the most disadvantaged communities are sinking into a permanent state of terror and disintegration in a society dominated by the market and consumerism. Currie (1993) outlines the complex deprivations of life in the inner-city and the failure of the state to respond humanely to the drug crisis by instead implementing a mass programme of incarceration and incapacitation while at the same time introducing huge cutbacks in welfare expenditure. He argues that what characterises the 'underclass' in the USA is a 'surplus of vulnerability' exacerbated by the pervasive movement towards a more deprived, more stressful, more atomised and less supportive society, observing that many parents in the deprived communities are overwhelmed by multiple disadvantages and are in no position to counter the effects of family crises on their children.

Currie observes that the 'triumph' of the market society has created deprived communities characterised by the destruction and absence of legitimate livelihoods, significant extremes of economic inequality, the increasing withdrawal of public services, the erosion of informal/communal support networks, the spread of a materialistic and neglectful culture, the unregulated marketing of a technology of violence and a weakening of social and political alternatives:

> The policies of the seventies and eighties, then, did more than merely strip individuals of jobs and income. They created communities that lacked not only viable economic opportunities, but also hospitals, fire stations, movie theatres, stores, and neighbourhood organizations – communities without strong ties of friendship or kinship, disproportionately populated by increasingly deprived and often disorganised people locked into the bottom of a rapidly deteriorating job market. In many cities these disruptive trends were accelerated by the physical destruction left by the ghetto riots of the 1960s or by urban renewal projects and freeways that split or demolished older, more stable neighbourhoods and dispersed their residents.
>
> (Currie, 1993: 70)

Radical communitarians like Currie are thus arguing that behind the growth of crime is a cultural, as well as a, structural transformation of poor communities and in this regard there are some common themes between Etzioni and the radicals. The situation has certainly not improved in the intervening years and in some geographical locations we can observe communities where there are three or four generations of welfare claimants with little or no experience of the legitimate labour market. The reintegration of these socially excluded groups back into mainstream society was an essential and laudable New Labour strategy termed 'reintegrative tutelage' (Hopkins Burke, 1999a) and discussed in Chapter 16. Although clearly there have been some success stories this was ultimately a flawed strategy scuppered not least by the unremitting ravages of the market economy.

Hall, Winlow and Ancrum (2008) have conducted a study of the criminal patterns and criminals living on the alienated housing estates of the North East of England where in some cases there was no-one in employment. The researchers observe that the significant economic downturn of the 1980s was more than a mere structural adjustment for those living in these communities.

337

Rather, it was a radical shift in political economy and culture, a move to the unprecedented domination of life by the market which was to create a large number of locales in permanent recession in both the UK and the USA. Hall, Winlow and Ancrum (2008: 3) observe that:

> The criminal markets developing in these areas now tend to operate in the relative absence of the traditional normal insulation ... regarded as essential to the restraint of the inherently amoral and social logic that lies at the heart of the liberal-capitalist-capitalist market economy.

The researchers pointedly observe that contrary to the arguments presented by some, the 1980s was not a time of vigorous and inherently progressive cultural change, well not in those large brutalised and inherently criminogenic communities in which they conducted their research. Indeed, we might well ask ourselves whether communities are inevitably the supportive protectors and the focus of transformation that is sometimes thought and proposed by some in the literature.

The concept of community reconsidered

Some commentators argue that communities can be restored and revitalised through the provision of community justice and restorative justice mechanisms and thus facilitate strong bonds of social control which are perceived as being legitimate and acceptable to their members. Strang (1995) sums up this viewpoint pertinently 'strong communities can speak to us in moral voices' and they allow 'the policing *by* communities rather than the policing *of* communities' (Strang, 1995: 217). Braithwaite (1989: 100) observes that these informal control processes such as reintegrative shaming – which we have encountered elsewhere in this book – are significantly more effective in communitarian cultures but at the same time observes that in urban, individualistic, and anonymous cultures, such as those that exist in most Western towns and cities, informal control mechanisms simply lack potency. He observes that the appeal to revive or transform community has arisen at exactly the moment when it appears most absent and when Durkheimian anomie or normlessness is rampant and out of control.

The whole notion of community is simply complex and extends well beyond the more traditional definitions based on locality – or neighbourhood – and embraces a multiplicity of groups and networks to which, it is believed we all belong (Strang, 1995: 16). This conception does not rely upon a fixed assumption of *where* a community will be found but builds upon the notion of 'communities of care' – that is, the networks of obligation and respect between the individual and everyone who cares about the person the most – and these are significantly not bounded by geography (Braithwaite and Daly, 1994: 195).

These communities of care are considered more relevant to contemporary modern living in urban societies because they provide a developed notion of 'community' where membership – or social identity – is personal and does not necessarily carry any fixed or external attributes of membership. The fact that such communities do not carry any connotations of coercion or forced membership is one of the distinctive appeals of the concept (Crawford and Clear, 2003) and from this perspective, there is an assumption that people can move freely between communities if they disagree with their practices and values and/or remain within a community but dissent from the dominant moral voice that exists. This is, nevertheless, a significantly problematic situation for, on the one hand, these contemporary 'light' communities are held up as examples of how they can allow sufficient space for individual or minority dissent, innovation and difference but, on the other hand, they are also seen as insufficient with regard to informal control.

Crawford and Clear (2003) observe that this all raises the question of exactly what is meant by the claim to 'restore' or 'reintegrate' communities (see: Van Ness and Strong, 1997; Braithwaite, 1998; Clear and Karp, 1999). The very notion of restoring communities suggests a return to some pre-existing state and appears to involve a nostalgic urge to return to a mythical age of genuine human identity, connectedness, and reciprocity. It certainly does seem questionable that the concept of community constitutes a dynamic force for democratic renewal that challenges existing inequalities of power and the differential distribution of life opportunities and pathways to crime that characterise our society.

Crawford and Clear (2003) argue that it is important that we avoid idealistic notions and confront the empirical realities of most communities. The ideal of unrestricted entry to, and exit from, communities needs to be reconciled with the existence of relations of dominance, exclusion, and differential power. The reality is that many stable communities contain very high levels of mechanical solidarity and tend to resist innovation, creation and experimentation, and shun diversity (Hopkins Burke and Pollock, 2004). These communities may well be able to come together for informal social control but the way these processes play out lacks inclusive qualities and offender-sensitive styles. These communities can be, and often are, pockets of intolerance and prejudice which can be coercive and tolerant of bigotry and discriminatory behaviour. Weaker individuals – and minority groups – within such communities often experience them not as a home of connectedness and mutuality but as the foundations of inequalities that sustain and reinforce relations of dependence (for example with regard to gender role and the tolerance of domestic violence or child abuse). Such communities are, therefore, often hostile to minorities, dissenters and outsiders, and can tolerate and even encourage deviant and offending behaviour. Communities are hierarchical formations which are structured upon lines of power, dominance, and authority, and which are intrinsically exclusive – as social exclusion presupposes processes of exclusion – and many confess and define themselves around notions of 'otherness' that are potentially infused with racialised overtones.

Radical moral communitarian criminology

It is the work of Emile Durkheim that we encountered in the second part of this book and his observations on the moral component of the division of labour in society that provides the theoretical foundations of the 'new' liberalism that was introduced earlier in this chapter and at the same time provides a legitimate social context for community: that is, a political philosophy which actively promotes both the rights and responsibilities of both individuals and communities *but in the context of an equal division of labour.* It is this significant latter element that deviates significantly from the orthodoxy promoted by Amitai Etzioni – and which has been embraced and distorted in the UK by New Labour with its enthusiasm for a strong dictatorial central state apparatus to enforce its agenda – and provides us with the basis of a genuine *radical* moral communitarianism, founded on notions of consensual interdependency with others we all recognise and identify as fellow citizens and social partners, and not as potential legitimate crime targets.

Many of you will be rightly sceptical. Yet another book concludes with the old critical criminological mantra that proposes economic redistribution and a more egalitarian society to be the key to a more peaceful and crime free society and indeed world. How exactly is this to be achieved? Well it has been observed elsewhere in this book that at the time of writing the world is in the process of undergoing a major economic correction that started with the 'credit crunch' where it appears colossal quantities of money that did not really exist – credit or 'funny money' amounting to $1.8 trillion according to some estimates (BBC News, 2008c) – was loaned by banks to a lot of people without the apparent capacity to repay it. It is too early to make definitive judgements on these matters but it would seem that many banking industry judgements over the past few years have veered somewhere along a spectrum from foolishness to criminal incompetency with the outcome that some of the biggest banks throughout the western world would have collapsed without very significant intervention on the part of their governments. Commentators from all political persuasions are in agreement that without this intervention total disaster would have occurred and this crisis has the potential to be the most significant world event since at least the end of the Second World War. The enormity of the situation has been demonstrated by the reality that one of the most right-wing presidents in the history of the USA with an overly zealous enthusiasm for the free market has become perhaps the greatest interventionist president in history. Not even Franklyn D. Roosevelt nationalised banks. At the same time, we have not to date witnessed the independent and isolationist national responses that occurred in similar circumstances during the 1930s with the disastrous outcomes of fascism and war. Indeed, what we have seen is a concerted intervention by all the major economies in reducing interest rates and intervening in their own economies. A moral interdependency of nations it would seem.

Robert Peston the highly respected but controversial BBC Business Editor observes that one of the most striking trends of the past three decades – which became particularly pronounced again in the last few years – has been a widening in the gap between the poor and the rich with the gap between the very poor and the super-rich expanding at an almost exponential rate over the past five years (Peston, 2008). He nevertheless notes that in this grim year of serious economic slowdown and rising inflation, our society is becoming more equal again, on most measures of income and wealth gaps. This is partly explained by the reality that the super-rich have been battered by the turmoil in financial markets and by falls in the prices of shares, commodities, properties and other assets, just like the rest of us. He notes that investment bankers will be lucky if they are still in a job by the end of 2008 and bonuses will be rare. Moreover, the oligarchs and plutocrats of the newer, faster-growing economies are suffering colossal losses on their exposure to markets, such as the Russian stock exchange, which are collapsing.

Thus, a duo of oligarchs, who only recently were giants of global capitalism, Oleg Deripaska and Alisher Usmanov, have faced demands from bank creditors to hand over substantial assets and thus, 'the crunch' is coming to the very top end of the income and wealth spectrum. The news is also not good for those in low paid, insecure jobs where the outlook consists of below-inflation pay rises and possible redundancy but for those living on welfare benefits or dependent on a state pension the news is relatively good. State-funding income will rise in line with the retail prices index or an adapted measure called the Rossi index for September 2008 and both inflation measures have been rising at a faster rate than has been seen since the early 1990s. The RPI, which determines increases in child benefit, incapacity benefit, disability allowance and state pensions, is up 5 per cent and income-related benefits (such as housing benefit, income support and jobseeker's allowance) should be increased by the 6.3 per cent increment in the Rossi index. What this all means is that after many years of receiving a smaller and smaller share of the national cake, those who depend on the state for their income will actually receive bigger pay rises than almost anyone else – and their share of national income will also increase.

Exactly how this economic crisis will develop and conclude is an unknown quantity but it will clearly impact on crime levels and criminal motivation as the leaked Home Office (BBC News, 2008b) memo referred to earlier in this book acknowledged. It would be extremely interesting if the expected increase does not occur and indeed we encounter a reduction in criminal behaviour. Perhaps the expected retreat from the divisive and criminogenic free market might bring about a change in our shared cultural perceptions and a retreat from the materialistic 'ME' consumer society and a constructive return to the collective sentiments that so characterised British society during and in the aftermath of the Second World War. We will have to wait and see.

Suggested further reading

Etzioni (1993, 1995a, 1995b) should be consulted for an introduction to the notion of communitarianism, while Dennis and Erdos (1992) discuss the 'parenting deficit' in a UK context. Jordan (1992, 1996), Currie (1993,

1996, 1997) and Young (1999) should be consulted on radical egalitarian communitarianism. Robert Peston's excellent blog on the BBC website should be consulted by anyone with an interest in the economic downturn and we should all keep a lookout for the inevitable book on the subject that should appear in the not too distant future.

Glossary of terms

actuarial justice: interventions are increasingly based on risk assessment, rather than on the identification of specific criminal behaviour.

administrative criminology: emphasis on reducing the opportunity to offend by the creation and evaluation of usually small-scale situational crime prevention schemes.

altered biological state theories: link behavioural changes in an individual with the introduction of an external chemical agent, that is, allergies and diet, alcohol and illegal drugs.

anarchist criminology: produces a radical critique of state law as a system of inherent inhumanity and its sense of standing 'against the law' leads logically to a criminology of crime and resistance.

'anatomy is destiny': Freudian notion where women are seen to be anatomically inferior to men with a consequential inferior destiny as wives and mothers.

anomie theories: there are two variants: the first developed by Emile Durkheim proposes that anomie is a condition of normlessness experienced by individuals during periods of rapid socio-economic change when previous forms of control and restraint have broken down; the second developed by Robert Merton proposes that individuals use alternative means – including criminal activities – to gain access to socially created needs that they are unable to obtain through legitimate behaviour.

antisocial behaviour orders (ASBOs): statutory measures that aim to protect the public from behaviour that causes or is likely to cause harassment, alarm or distress, contain conditions prohibiting the offender from specific antisocial acts or entering defined areas.

antisocial personality disorder: relatively recent term that it is interchangeable with that of psychopathy. There are various definitions of this condition that in general emphasise such traits as an incapacity for loyalty, selfishness, irresponsibility, impulsiveness, inability to feel guilt and failure to learn from experience.

autistic spectrum disorder: is a relatively new term that includes the sub-groups within the spectrum of autism.

balance of intervention: a left realist notion which proposes that: on the one hand, crime must be tackled and criminals must take responsibility for their actions; on the other hand, the social conditions that encourage crime must also be tackled.

behavioural learning theories: a variant of psychological positivism that proposes that criminal behaviour is conditioned learned behaviour.

behavioural model of the underclass: associated with populist or neo-conservatives and proposes that state welfare erodes individual responsibility by giving people incentives not to work and provide for themselves and their family.

biological positivism: proposes that human beings commit crime because of internal physiological factors over which they have little or no control.

biosocial theory: contemporary biologists who propose that physiological characteristics of an individual are only part of the explanation of criminal behaviour; factors in the physical and social environment are also influential.

'bloody code': a body of legislation that during the seventeenth to the early eighteenth century prescribed the death penalty for a vast number of property crimes.

carnival of crime: festive excess, transgression, the mocking of the powerful, irrational behaviour are all temporarily legitimated in the moment of carnival.

Chicago School: a group of sociologists based at the University of Chicago during the 1920s and 1930s who developed the ecological explanation of crime which proposes that people engage in criminal activities because of determining factors in their immediate environment.

Classical criminology: the foundations of the rational actor model of explaining criminal behaviour, people are rational human beings who choose to commit criminal behaviour and can be dissuaded from doing so by the threat of punishment.

cognitive learning theories: reject much of the positivist psychological tradition of explaining criminal behaviour by incorporating notions of creative thinking and thus choice, in many ways more akin to the rational actor model.

communitarianism: it is proposed that the individual rights promoted by traditional liberals need to be balanced with social responsibilities.

concentric zone theory: analysis confirmed that offending behaviour flourished in the zone in transition and was inversely related to the affluence of the area and corresponding distance from the central business district.

conflict theories: a variant of the victimised actor model that proposes that definitions of criminality – and the decision to act against certain activities and groups – are made by those with control of authority in a pluralist but equal society.

constitutive criminology: crime is defined as the 'power to deny others' and proponents seek the development of 'replacement discourses' that fuel positive social constructions with the intention not to 'replace one truth with another' but instead invoke 'a multiplicity of resistances' 'to the ubiquity of power'.

control balance theories: define deviancy as any activity which the majority find unacceptable and/or disapprove of and occurs when a person has either a surplus or deficit of control in relation to others.

corporate crime: involves illegal acts carried out in the furtherance of the goals of an organisation.

crime control: model of criminal justice that prioritises efficiency and getting results with emphasis on catching, convicting and punishing the offender (see 'due process').

criminalisation: involves a process in which the law, agencies of social control and the media come to associate crime with particular groups who are subsequently identified, sought out and targeted as a threat.

critical criminology: or 'left idealists' to their former cohorts in the radical tradition (see 'left realism') that proposes that crime is defined in terms of the concept of oppression, some groups in society are seen to be the most likely to suffer oppressive social relations based upon class division, sexism and racism.

cultural criminology: crime and the various agencies and institutions of crime control are seen to be cultural and creative constructs and these should be understood in terms of the phenomenological meanings they carry.

cumulative risk hypothesis: where the number of environmental stressors rather than the particular combination of stressors has been associated with child behaviour problems both in the short and long-term.

delinquency and drift: delinquency is a *status* and delinquents are *role players* who occasionally act out a delinquent role, they are nonetheless perfectly capable of engaging in conventional activity.

deterrence: a doctrine that punishment must be both swift and certain in order to dissuade people not to commit crime.

deviancy amplification: a concept which suggests that the less tolerance there is to an initial act of group deviance, the more acts will be defined as deviant (see 'moral panics').

deviant subculture theories: there are many different variants – mostly positivist but latterly incorporating notions of choice – that propose that (predominantly young) people commit crime and deviant behaviour in the company of others for whom this is seen as the normal thing to do.

differential association theory: offending behaviour is likely to occur when individuals acquire sufficient inclinations towards law breaking that outweigh their associations with non-criminal tendencies.

differential coercion theory: seeks to extend our knowledge of the relationship between coercion and crime.

due process: it is the purpose of the criminal justice system to prove the guilt of a defendant beyond a reasonable doubt in a public trial as a condition for the imposition of a sentence, the state has a duty to seek out and punish the guilty but must prove the guilt of the accused (see 'crime control').

environmental criminology: the study of where and when crimes occur.

environmental design theories: the nature of the built environment can affect the level of crime both by influencing potential offenders and by affecting the ability of a person to exercise control over their surroundings.

environmental management theories: the activities of a rational calculating individual can be restricted or curtailed by changing his or her surroundings.

ethnomethodology: is a method of sociological analysis concerned with how individuals experience and make sense of social interaction.

European Enlightenment: philosophical movement that occurred in western Europe during the seventeenth and eighteen century which proposed that the social world could be explained and regulated by natural laws; political systems should be developed that embraced new ideas of individual rationality and free will.

feminism: there are different versions but all observe that it is men who are the dominant group in society and it is privileged males who make and enforce the rules to the detriment of women.

folk devils: see 'moral panic'.

functionalist sociology: society is seen to consist of interdependent sections which work together to fulfill the functions necessary for the survival of society as a whole.

generative phases of women theory: based on biological changes connected to the menstrual cycle.

globalisation: the increasing degree of integration among societies that plays a crucial role in most types of social change.

governmentality: the means to rendering populations thinkable and measurable through categorisation, differentiation, and sorting into hierarchies, for the purpose of government.

hate offenders: those unaccepting of the multicultural nature of contemporary societies in which they live and primarily characterise social groups according to their visible ethnic, racial or sexual identity rather than their personal attributes.

incapacitation: right realist notion that imprisonment is particularly effective in neutralising or incapacitating offenders and frightening others into adopting law abiding lifestyles.

infanticide: if a mother kills her child within its first year as a result of post-natal depression or breastfeeding she has a partial defence to murder.

integrated criminological theories: an incorporation of elements from different approaches in an attempt to provide a stronger explanatory tool than that offered by one individual theory.

Italian School: early biological positivists who developed the influential notion that the criminal is a physical type distinct from the non-criminal.

just deserts: a philosophy that eschews individual discretion and rehabilitation as legitimate aims of the justice system, justice must be both done and seen to be done (see 'due process').

labelling theories: propose that crime is a product of the social reaction to an activity, if the action is ignored or not discovered the person does not become a criminal, this only happens when the person is processed by the criminal justice system and sets off on the path to a criminal career.

latent delinquency theory: proposed that the absence of an intimate attachment with parents could lead to later criminality.

left realism: a response to populist conservatism and right realism that proposes the need for a balance of intervention to address both the crime and the conditions that have caused it, influential with the New Labour Government elected in the UK in 1997.

limited or bounded rationality: offenders will not always obtain all the facts needed to make a wise decision and the information available will not necessarily be weighed carefully.

macro level: at the level of society, the nation state or country.

mainstream youth subcultures: their 'problem' is an alien or irrelevant education system followed by the prospect of a boring and dead end job or, nowadays, training and the benefits queue.

mala in se: acts considered wrong in themselves or 'real' crimes .

mala prohibita: acts prohibited not because they are morally wrong but in order to protect the public .

marginalisation: the exclusion from access to mainstream institutions for the poor and less powerful.

maternal deprivation theory: suggested that a lack of a close mother/child relationship in the early years could lead to criminal behaviour.

mezzo level: the intermediate level of the institution.

micro level: the lowest level of the small group.

modernism or modernity: a secular society based on rationality and reason with science as the dominant form of social explanation.

moral panic: a frenzy of popular societal indignation usually whipped up about a particular activity that is seen to threaten the very fabric of civilisation, once labelled as such, those engaged in the activity, become ostracised and targeted as 'folk devils'.

multiple masculinities: there are different masculinities that are all subject to challenge and change over time.

neo-Classical criminology: the recognition that there is a limitation on the level of rationality enjoyed by some people such as children and the mentally ill and this is a justification for mitigating circumstances in the courtroom.

new criminology: sought an explanation of criminal behaviour based on a theoretical synthesis of Marxism and labelling perspectives.

'new penology': concerned with techniques for identifying, classifying and managing groups assorted by levels of dangerousness based not on individualised suspicion, but on the probability that an individual may be an offender.

'nothing works': agenda at the British Home Office that called into serious question the effectiveness of rehabilitation as a crime control strategy.

offender profiling: used, particularly in the USA, to help detect particular types of criminals, has been most useful in the detection of serial murders.

opportunity theory: a more formalised version of routine activities theory that considers elements of exposure, proximity, guardianship and target attractiveness as variables that increase the risk of criminal victimisation.

Panoptican: a utilitarian prison designed by Jeremy Bentham as a 'mill for grinding rogues honest'. The institution should act as a model for schools, asylums, workhouses, factories and hospitals that could all be run on the 'inspection principle' to ensure internal regulation, discipline and efficiency.

social disorganisation theory: has its origins in the notion developed by Emile Durkheim that imperfect social regulation leads to a variety of different social problems, including crime; as developed by the Chicago School there was call for efforts to reorganise communities to emphasise non-criminal activities.

social evolutionism: the notion that human beings develop as part of a process of interaction with the world they inhabit.

sociological positivism: people commit crime because of determining factors in their environment over which they have little or no control.

'spectacular' youth subcultures: arise at particular historical 'moments' as cultural solutions to the same structural economic problems created by rapid social change.

square of crime: a left realist notion that proposes crime to be the result of a number of lines of force and that intervention to prevent it must therefore take place at different levels in order to be effective.

structural model of the underclass: associated with the liberal left and observes the collapse of manufacturing industry, traditional working class employment and the subsequent retreat of welfare provision as providing the structural preconditions for the creation of a socially excluded class.

subculture of violence: where there is an expectation that the receipt of a trivial insult should be met with violence; failure to respond in this way is greeted with social censure from the peer group.

symbolic interactionism: primarily analyses the way individuals conceptualise themselves and others around them with whom they interact.

techniques of neutralisation: the ways in which offenders may justify their deviant activities to themselves and others.

terrorism: emotive word which emphasises the extreme fear caused by apparently indiscriminate violent actions of individuals claiming to be operating on behalf of some particular cause.

underclass theory: groups in socially isolated neighbourhoods have few legitimate employment opportunities and this increases the chances that they turn to illegal or deviant activities for income.

utilitarianism: assesses the applicability of policies and legislation to promote the 'happiness' of those citizens affected by them.

victimised actor model of crime and criminal behaviour: people commit crime because they have in some way been the victims of an unjust society, they can have choices but these are constrained by their structural situation.

white-collar crime: occurs when an individual commits crime against an organisation within which they work.

zemiology: the study of social harm: for example, sexism, racism, imperialism and economic exploitation.

zone of transition: containing rows of deteriorating tenements and often built in the shadow of ageing factories and home to a transient population of immigrants.

References

Abele, L. and Gilchrist, S. (1977) 'Homosexual Rape and Sexual Selection in Acanthocephalan Worms', *Science*, 197: 81–3.

Abram, K.M. (1989) 'The Effect of Co-occurring Disorders on Criminal Careers: Interaction of Antisocial Personality, Alcoholism, and Drug Disorders', *International Journal of Law and Psychiatry*, 12: 122–36.

Ackerman, R.S. (2002) *Corruption and Government: Human Development Report (UNDP)*. New York: Oxford University Press.

Adamson, E. (1984) 'Toward a Marxian Penology', *Social Problems*, 31: 435–58.

Adler, F. (1975) *Sisters in Crime: The Rise of the New Female Criminal*. New York: McGraw-Hill.

Adler, Z. (1982) 'Rape – The Intention of Parliament and the Practice of the Courts', *Modern Law Review*, 45: 664.

Aguilar, B., Sroufe, A., Egeland, B. and Carlson, E. (2000) 'Distinguishing the Early-onset/Persistent and Adolescent-onset Antisocial Behavior Types: From Birth to 16 Years', *Development and Psychopathology*, 12(2): 109–32.

Aichhorn, A. (1925) *Wayward Youth*. New York: Meridian Books.

Akers, R.L. (1985) *Deviant Behaviour: A Social Learning Approach, 3rd edition*. Belmont, CA: Wadsworth.

Akers, R.L. (1992) 'Linking Sociology and Its Specialities', *Social Forces*, 71: 1–16.

Akers, R.L. (1997) *Criminological Theories: Introduction and Evaluation*. Los Angles, CA: Roxbury.

Akers, R.L., Krohn, M.D., Lanza-Kaduce, L. and Radosevich, M. (1979) 'Social Learning and Deviant Behaviour: A Specific Test of a General Theory', *American Sociological Review*, 44: 635–55.

Alford, S. (1997) 'Professionals Need Not Apply', *Corrections Today*, 59: 98–111.

All-Party Group on Alcohol Misuse (1995) *Alcohol and Crime: Breaking the Link*. London: HMSO.

Allsopp, J.F. and Feldman, M.P. (1975) 'Extroversion, Neuroticism and Psychoticism and Antisocial Behaviour in Schoolgirls', *Social Behaviour and Personality*, 2: 184.

Allsopp, J.F. and Feldman, M.P. (1976) 'Personality and Antisocial Behaviour in Schoolboys', *British Journal of Criminology*, 16: 337–51.

Althusser, L. (1966) *For Marx*. London: Penguin Press.

American Psychiatric Association (1968) *Diagnostic and Statistical Manual of Mental Disorders*. Washington, DC: American Psychiatric Association.

Anderson, E. (1990) *Street Wise*. Chicago, IL: University of Chicago Press.

Anderson, M.L. and Collins, P.H. (1992) *Race, Class and Gender: An Anthology*. Belmont, CA: Wadsworth.

Andry, R.G. (1957) 'Faulty Paternal and Maternal Child Relationships, Affection and Delinquency', *British Journal of Delinquency*, VIII: 34–48.

Appadurai, A. (1990) 'Disjuncture and Difference in the Global Cultural Economy', *Theory, Culture and Society*, 7(2/3): 295–310.

Arendt, H. (1964) *Eichmann in Jerusalem: A Report on the Banality of Evil*. New York: Viking Press.

Arrigo, B.A. (1997) 'Dimensions of Social Justice in a Single Room Occupancy: Contributions from Chaos Theory, Policy and Practice', in D. Milovanovic (ed.) *Chaos, Criminology, and Social Justice: the New Orderly (Dis) Order*. Westport, CT: Praeger.

Arseneault, L., Tremblay, R.E., Boulerice, B. and Saucier, J. (2002) 'Obstetrical Complications and Violent Delinquency: Testing Two Developmental Pathways', *Child Development*, 73(2): 496–508.

Arvanites, T. (1992) 'The Mental Health and Criminal Justice System: Complementary Forms of Coercive Control', in A. Liska (ed.) *Social Threat and Social Control*. Albany, NY: SUNY Press.

Athens, L. (1997) *Violent Acts and Actors Revisited*. Urbana, IL: University of Illinois Press.

Attwood, T. (1998) *Asperger's Syndrome: A Guide for Parents and Professionals*. London: Jessica Kingsley Publishers.

Aubert, W. (1952) 'White Collar Crime and Social Structure', *American Journal of Sociology*, 58: 263–71.

Auld, J., Dorn, N. and South, N. (1986) 'Irregular Work, Irregular Pressure: Heroin in the 1980s', in R. Matthews and J. Young (eds) *Confronting Crime*. London: Sage.

Bakhtin, M. (1984) *Rabelais and His World*. Bloomington, IN: Indiana University Press.

Bakunin, M. (1974) *Selected Writings*. New York: Grove Press.

Balding, J. and Shelley, C. (1993) *Very Young Children in 1991/2*. Exeter: University of Exeter Schools Health Education Unit.

Baldwin, J.D. (1990) 'The Role of Sensory Stimulation in Criminal Behaviour, with Special Attention to the Age Peak in Crime', in L. Ellis and H. Hoffman (eds) *Crime in Biological, Social and Moral Contexts*. New York: Praeger.

Baldwin, J. and Bottoms, A.E. (1976) *The Urban Criminal*. London: Tavistock.

Bandura, A. (1973) *Aggression: A Social Learning Analysis*. Englewood Cliffs, NJ: Prentice Hall.

Bandura, A. and Walters, R.H. (1959) *Adolescent Aggression*. New York: Ronald Press.

Barash, D. (1977) 'Sociobiology of Rape in Mallards (Anas platyrhynchos): Responses of the Mated Male', *Science*, 197: 788–9.

Barlow, H. (1991) 'Review Essay of "A General Theory of Crime"', *Journal of Criminal Law and Criminology*, 1: 82–96.

Baron-Cohen, S. (1988) 'An Assessment of Violence in a Young Man with Asperger's Syndrome', *Journal of Child Psychology and Psychiatry*, 29(3): 351–60.

Barry, A., Osborne, T. and Rose, N. (1996) *Foucault and Political Reason: Liberalism, Neo-Liberalism and Rationalities of Government*. London: UCL Press.

Bates, K.A., Bader, C.D. and Mencken, F.C. (2003) 'Family Structure, Power-Control Theory and Deviance: Extending Power-Control Theory to Include Alternate Family Forms', *Western Criminology Review*, 4(3): 170–90.

Baudrillard, J. (1988) *Selected Writings*. Stanford, CA: Stanford University Press.

Bauman, Z. (1989) *Modernity and the Holocaust*. Cambridge: Polity Press.

Bauman, Z. (1991) *Modernity and Ambivalence*. Cambridge: Polity Press.

Bauman, Z. (1993) *Postmodern Ethics*. Oxford: Blackwell.

Bauman, Z. (1997) *Postmodernity and Its Discontents*. Cambridge: Polity Press.

Bauman, Z. (1998) *Work, Consumerism and the New Poor*. Buckingham: Open University Press.

Bauman, Z. (2000) 'Social Uses of Law and Order', in D. Garland and R. Sparks (eds) *Criminology and Social Theory*. Oxford: Oxford University Press.

Baumhart, R.C. (1961) 'How Ethical are Businessmen', *Harvard Business Review*, 39: 156–76.

BBC News (2001) *Autistic Boy Killed Baby Brother* [Online]. Available at: http://news.bbc.co.uk/1/hi/uk/1165848.stm [accessed 6 January 2009].

BBC News (2002a) *US Condemned for Youth Executions* [Online]. Available at: http://news.bbc.co.uk/1/hi/world/americas/2280250.stm [accessed 6 January 2009].

BBC News (2003) *US Prison Population Peaks* [Online]. Available at: http://news.bbc.co.uk/1/hi/world/2925973.stm [accessed 6 January 2009].

BBC News (2004) *Death Toll on UK Roads Increasing* [Online]. Available at: http://news.bbc.co.uk/1/hi/uk/3835747.stm [accessed 6 January 2009].

BBC News (2008a) *Darling Defends Economy Warning* [Online]. Available at: http://news.bbc.co.uk/1/hi/business/7589739.stm [accessed 6 January 2009].

BBC News (2008b) *Leaked Letter Predicts Crime Rise* [Online]. Available at: http://news.bbc.co.uk/1/hi/uk_politics/7591072.stm [accessed 6 January 2009].

BBC News (2008c) *World Credit Loss '£1.8 trillion'* [Online]. Available at: http://news.bbc.co.uk/1/hi/business/7694275.stm [accessed 6 January 2009].

Beccaria, C. (1963, first English edition 1767) *On Crimes and Punishment*, translated by H. Paolucci. Indianapolis, IN: Bobbs-Merrill Educational.

Beck, U. (1992) *Risk Society*. London: Sage.

Becker, G.S. (1968) 'Crime and Punishment: An Economic Approach', *Journal of Political Economy*, 76(2): 169–217.

Becker, H. (1963) *Outsiders: Studies in the Sociology of Deviance*. New York: Free Press.

Becker, H. (1967) 'Whose Side Are We On?', *Social Problems*, 14(3): 239–47.

Bedau, H. (1964) *The Death Penalty in America*. Garden City, NY: Anchor Books.

Beechey, V. (1977) 'Some Notes on Female Wage Labour in Capitalist Production', *Capital and Class*, (Autumn): 45–66.

Beinart, S., Anderson, B., Lee, S. and Utting, D. (2002) *Youth at Risk? A National Survey of Risk Factors and Problem Behaviour Among Young People in England, Scotland and Wales*. London: Communities that Care.

Bell, B. (1982) 'Psychology of Leaders of Terrorist Groups', *International Journal of Group Tensions*, 12: 84–104.

Bell, D. (1960) *The End of Ideology*. Glencoe, IL: Free Press.

Bell, D. (1973) *The Coming of Post-Industrial Society: A Venture in Social Forecasting*. London: Heinemann.

Bennett, T. (1986) 'Situational Crime Prevention from the Offender's Perspective', in K. Heal and G. Laycock (eds) *Situational Crime Prevention: From Theory into Practice*. London: HMSO.

Bennett, T. (2000) *Drugs and Crime: The Results of the Second Developmental Stage of the New-Adam Programme*, Home Office Research Study 2005. London: Home Office.

Bennett, T., Holloway, K. and Williams, T. (2001) *Drug Use and Offending: Summary Results From the First Year of the NEW-ADAM Research Programme*, Findings 148. London: Home Office.

Bennett, T. and Wright, R. (1984) *Burglars on Burglary*. Brookfield: Gower.

Cohen, A.K. (1955) *Delinquent Boys: The Culture of the Gang.* New York: Free Press.

Cohen, A.K., Lindesmith, A. and Schuessler, K. (eds) (1956) *The Sutherland Papers.* Bloomington, IN: Indiana University Press.

Cohen, L.E. and Felson, M. (1979) 'Social Inequality and Predatory Criminal Victimization: An Exposition and Test of a Formal Theory', *American Sociological Review,* 44: 588–608.

Cohen, L.E., Kluegel, J. and Land, K. (1981) 'Social Inequality and Predatory Criminal Victimisation: An Exposition and Test of a Formal Theory', *American Sociological Review,* 46: 505–24.

Cohen, P. (1972) 'Sub-Cultural Conflict and Working Class Community', *Working Papers in Cultural Studies,* No.2. Birmingham: CCCS, University of Birmingham.

Cohen, P., Velez, C., Brook, J., and Smith, J. (1989) 'Mechanisms of the Relation between Perinatal Problems, Early Childhood Illness, and Psychopathology in Late Childhood and Adolescence', *Child Development,* 60: 701–9

Cohen, S. (1973) *Folk Devils and Moral Panics: The Creation of the Mods and Rockers.* London: Paladin.

Cohen, S. (1979) 'The Punitive City: Notes on the Dispersal of Social Control', *Contemporary Crises,* 3: 339–63.

Cohen, S. (1980, new edition) *Folk Devils and Moral Panics.* Oxford: Martin Robertson.

Cohen, S. (1985) *Visions of Social Control.* Cambridge: Polity Press.

Cohen, S. (1988) *Against Criminology.* New Brunswick, NJ: Transaction.

Cohen, S. (1993) 'Human Rights and Crimes of the State: The Culture of Denial', *Australian and New Zealand Journal of Criminology,* 26(2): 7–115.

Cohen, S. (1994) 'Social Control and the Politics of Reconstruction', in D. Nelken (ed.) *The Futures of Criminology.* London: Sage

Coid, J., Carvell, A., Kittler, Z., Healey, A. and Henderson, J. (2000) *Opiates, Criminal Behaviour and Methadone Treatment,* RDS Occasional Paper. London: Home Office.

Coleman, C. and Moynihan, J. (1996) *Understanding Crime Data.* Buckingham: Open University Press.

Collins, J.J. (1986) 'The Relationship of Problem Drinking in Individual Offending Sequences', in A. Blumstein, J. Cohen, J. Roth and C. Visher (eds) *Criminal Careers and 'Career Criminals',* Vol. 2. Washington, DC: National Academy Press.

Collins, J.J. (1988) 'Alcohol and Interpersonal Violence: Less than Meets the Eye', in A. Weiner and M.E. Wolfgang (eds) *Pathways to Criminal Violence.* Newbury Park, CA: Sage.

Collins, R. (1975) *Conflict Sociology.* New York: Academic.

Colvin, M. (2000) *Crime and Coercion: An Integrated Theory of Chronic Criminality.* New York: St Martin's Press.

Comte, A. (1976) *The Foundations of Sociology* (readings edited and with an introduction by K. Thompson). London: Nelson.

Conklin, J.E. (1977) *Illegal But Not Criminal.* New Jersey: Spectrum.

Connell, R.W. (1987) *Gender and Power.* Cambridge: Polity Press.

Connell, R.W. (1995) *Masculinities.* Cambridge: Polity Press.

Connell, R.W. (2000) *The Men and the Boys.* Sydney: Allen and Unwin.

Cornish, D.B. and Clarke, R.V.G. (1986) *The Reasoning Criminal.* New York: Springer-Verlag.

Corrigan, P. (1979) *The Smash Street Kids.* London: Paladin.

Cortes, J.B. and Gatti, F.M. (1972) *Delinquency and Crime: A Biopsychological Approach.* New York: Seminar Press.

Coser, L. (1956) *The Functions of Social Conflict.* New York: Free Press.

Cowling, M. (2006) 'Postmodern Policies? The Erratic Interventions of Constitutive Criminology', *Internet Journal of Criminology*.

Cowling, M. (2008) *Marxism and Criminological Theory: A Critique and a Toolkit*. Basingstoke: Palgrave Macmillan.

Crawford, A. (1997) *The Local Governance of Crime: Appeals to Community and Partnerships*. Oxford: Clarendon Press.

Crawford, A. and Clear, T.R. (2003) 'Community Justice: Transforming Communities through Restorative Justice?' in E. McLaughlin, R. Fergusson, G. Hughes and L. Westmarland (eds) *Restorative Justice: Critical Issues*. London: Sage/Open University.

Crenshaw, M. (ed.) (1995) *Terrorism in Context*. University Park, PA: Pennsylvania State University Press.

Crenshaw, M. (1998) 'The Logic of Terrorism: Terrorist Behavior as a Product of Strategic Choice' in W. Reich (ed.) *Origins of Terrorism*. New York: Woodrow Wilson Center Press.

Cressey, D. (1964) *Delinquency, Crime and Differential Association*. The Hague: Martinus Nijhoff.

Croall, H. (1992) *White-collar Crime*. Buckingham: Open University Press.

Croall, H. (1998) *Crime and Society in Britain*. Harlow: Longman.

Croall, H. (2001) *Understanding White-collar Crime*, Crime and Justice Series. Buckingham: Open University Press.

Cromwell, P.F., Durham, R., Akers, R.L. and Lanza-Kaduce, L. (1995) 'Routine Activities and Social Control in the Aftermath of a Natural Catastrophe', *European Journal on Criminal Policy and Research*, 3: 56–69.

Cromwell, P.F., Olson, J. and Avary, D. (1991) *Breaking and Entering: An Ethnographic Analysis of Burglary*, Studies in Crime, Law and Justice: Vol. 8. Newbury Park, CA: Sage Publications.

Crowe, R.R. (1972) 'The Adopted Offspring of Women Criminal Offenders', *Archives of General Psychiatry*, 27(5): 600–3.

Crowther, C. (1998) 'Policing the Excluded Society', in R.D. Hopkins Burke (ed.) *Zero Tolerance Policing*. Leicester: Perpetuity Press.

Crowther, C. (2007) *An Introduction to Criminology and Criminal Justice*. Basingstoke: Palgrave Macmillan.

Cullen, F.T., Golden, K.M. and Cullen, J.B. (1979) 'Sex and Delinquency', *Criminology*, 17: 310–25.

Currie, E. (1985) *Confronting Crime: An American Challenge*. New York: Pantheon Books.

Currie, E. (1992) 'Retreatism, Minimalism, Realism: Three Styles of Reasoning on Crime and Drugs in the United States', in J. Lowman and B. MacLean (eds) *Realist Criminology: Crime Control and Policing in the 1990s*. Toronto, ON: Toronto University Press.

Currie, E. (1993) *Reckoning: Drugs, the Cities and the American Future*. New York: Hill and Wang.

Currie, E. (1996) *Is America Really Winning the War on Crime and Should Britain Follow its Example?* NACRO 30th Annual Lecture. London: NACRO.

Currie, E. (1997) 'Market, Crime and Community', *Theoretical Criminology*, 1(2): 147–72.

Currie, E. (1999) 'Reflections on Crime and Criminology at the Millennium', *Western Criminology Review* 2/1 [Online]. Available at: http://wcr.sonoma.edu/v2n2/hil.html [accessed 6 January 2009].

Curtis, L.A. (1975) *Violence, Race and Culture*. Lexington, MA: Heath.

Dahrendorf, R. (1958) 'Out of Utopia: Toward a Reconstruction of Sociological Analysis', *American Journal of Sociology*, 67: 115–27.

Dahrendorf, R. (1959) *Class and Class Conflict in an Industrial Society*. London: Routledge & Kegan Paul.

Dahrendorf, R. (1985) *Law and Order*. London: Stevens.

Dale, D. (1984) 'The Politics of Crime', *Salisbury Review*, October.

Dalgard, S.O. and Kringlen, E. (1976) 'Norwegian Twin Study of Criminality', *British Journal of Criminology*, 16: 213–32.

Dalton, K. (1961) 'Menstruation and Crime', *British Medical Journal*, 2: 1752–3.

Dalton, K. (1964) *The Pre-menstrual Syndrome and Progesterone Therapy*. London: Heinemann Medical.

Daly, K. (1989) 'Neither Conflict Nor Labeling Nor Paternalism Will Suffice: Intersections of Race, Ethnicity, Gender, and Family in Criminal Court Decisions', *Crime and Delinquency*, 35: 136–68.

Daly, K. (1992) 'Women's Pathways to Felony Court: Feminist Theories of Lawbreaking and Problems of Representation', *Review of Law and Women's Studies*, 2: 11–52.

Daly, K. (1994a) *Gender, Crime, and Punishment*. New Haven, CT: Yale University Press.

Daly, K. (1994b) 'Gender and Punishment Disparity;' in G.S. Bridges and M. Myers (eds) *Inequality, Crime and Social Control*. Boulder, CO: Westview Press.

Daly, K. and Chesney-Lind, M. (1988) 'Feminism and Criminology', *Justice Quarterly*, 5(4): 487–535.

Damer, S. (1974) 'Wine Alley: The Sociology of a Dreadful Enclosure', *Sociological Review*, 22: 221–48.

Darwin, C. (1871) *The Descent of Man*. London: John Murray.

Darwin, C. (1872) *The Expression of Emotions in Man and Animals*. Philosophical Library.

Darwin, C. (1968) *On the Origin of the Species*. New York: Penguin.

Davidson, N. (2006) 'Chernobyl's "nuclear nightmares"', *Horizon* [Online]. Available at: http://news.bbc.co.uk/1/hi/sci/tech/5173310.stm [accessed 5 January 2009].

Davis, K. (1961) 'Prostitution', in R.K Merton and R.A. Nesbit (eds) *Contemporary Social Problems*. New York: Harcourt Brace and Jovanovich. Originally published as 'The Sociology of Prostitution', *American Sociological Review*, 2(5) (October, 1937).

Davis, M. (1990) *The City of Quartz: Evacuating the Future in Los Angeles*. London: Verso.

De Brie, C. (2000) 'Thick as Thieves', *Le Monde Diplomatique* (April).

Decker, S.H. and Van Winkle, B. (1996) *Life in the Gang*. New York: Cambridge University Press.

De Haan, W. (1990) *The Politics of Redress*. London: Unwin Hyman.

De Haan, W. (2000) 'Explaining the Absence of Violence: A Comparative Approach', in S. Karstedt and K.-D. Bussman (eds) *Social Dynamics of Crime and Control*. Oxford: Hart.

Deater-Deckard, K., Dodge, K.A., Bates, J.E. and Pettit, G.S. (1998) 'Multiple Risk Factors in the Development of Externalizing Behavior Problems: Group and Individual Differences', *Development and Psychopathology*, 10: 469–93.

Dell, S. (1984) *Murder into Manslaughter*, Maudsley Monograph Series No. 27. London: Institute of Psychiatry.

De Luca, J.R. (ed.) (1981) *Fourth Special Report to the US Congress on Alcohol and Health*. Rockville, MD: National Institute on Alcohol Abuse and Alcoholism.

Dennis, N. and Erdos, G. (1992) *Families Without Fatherhood*. London: Institute for Economic Affairs.

Department of Health (2005) *Smoking, Drinking and Drug Use among Young People in England in 2004*. London: Department of Health.

DiCristina, B. (1995) *Method in Criminology: A Philosophical Primer*. New York: Harrow and Heston.

Dignan, J. (1999) 'The Criminal Justice Act and the Prospect for Restorative Justice', *Criminal Law Review*, 44–56.

Dishion, T.J. (1990) 'The Family Ecology of Boys' Peer Relations in Middle Childhood', *Child Development*, 61: 874–92.

Ditton, J. (1979) *Controlology: Beyond the New Criminology*. London: Macmillan.

Dobash, R.E. and Dobash, R.P. (1980) *Violence against Wives*. London: Open Books.

Dobash, R.E. and Dobash, R.P. (1992) *Women, Violence and Social Change*. London: Routledge & Kegan Paul.

Dodge K.A., Pettit, G.S. and Bates, J.E. (1994) 'Socialization Mediators of the Relation between Socioeconomic Status and Child Conduct Problems', *Child Development*, 65: 649–65.

Dorn, N. and South, N. (1990) 'Drug Markets and Law Enforcement', *British Journal of Criminology*, 30: 165–176.

Downes, D. (1966) *The Delinquent Solution*. London: Routledge & Kegan Paul.

Downes, D. and Rock, P. (1998) *Understanding Deviance, 3rd edition*. Oxford: Oxford University Press.

Drillien, C. M. (1964) *The Growth and Development of the Prematurely Born Infant*. Edinburgh: Livingstone.

Driver, S. and Martell, L. (1997) 'New Labour's Communitarianisms', *Critical Social Policy*, 52: 27–46.

Dugdale, R.L. (1877) *The Jukes*. New York: Putnam.

Durkheim, E. (1933 originally 1893) *The Division of Labour in Society*. Glencoe, IL: Free Press.

Durkheim, E. (1951, originally published in 1897) *Suicide*. New York: Free Press.

Durkheim, E. (1964 originally published 1915) *The Elementary Forms of Religious Life*. Glencoe, IL: Free Press.

Edmunds, M., Hough, M. and Turnbull, P. J. (1999) *Doing Justice to Treatment: Referring Offenders to Drug Treatment Services*, Drugs Prevention Initiative Paper No. 2. London: Home Office.

Eduardo, F. (2000) 'International Money Information Network for Money Laundering Investigators', *Journal of Money Laundering Control*. New York: Cambridge University Press.

Eduardo, F. (2002) 'Combating Money Laundering and Financing of Terrorism' *International Monetary Fund*, 39(3): 126–39.

Edwards, S. (1988) 'Mad, Bad or Pre-Menstrual?', *New Law Journal*, 456.

Edwards, S. (1993) 'England and Wales', in N.J. Davis (ed.) *Prostitution: An International Handbook on Trends, Problems and Policies*. Westport, CT: Greenwood.

Ehrenkranz, J. Bliss, E. and Sheard, M.H. (1974) 'Plasma Testosterone: Correlation with Aggressive Behaviour and Social Dominance in Man', *Psychosomatic Medicine*, 36: 469–83.

Ehrlich, I. (1975) 'The Deterrent Effect of Capital Punishment: A Question of Life or Death', *American Economic Review*, 65: 397.

Einstadter, W. and Henry, S. (1995) *Criminological Theory*. Fort Worth, TX: Harcourt Brace.

Ekblom, P. (2001) 'Situational Crime Prevention', in E. McLaughlin and J. Muncie (eds) *The Sage Dictionary of Criminology*. London: Sage.

Ekblom, P. (2005) 'Designing Products Against Crime', in N. Tilley (ed.) *Handbook of Crime Prevention and Community Safety*. Cullompton: Willan Publishing.

Elias, N (1978) *The Civilising Process, Vol. 1: The History of Manners*. Oxford: Blackwell.

Elias, N. (1982) *The Civilising Process, Vol. 2: State-Formation and Civilisation*. Oxford: Blackwell.

Elliot, D., Ageton, S. and Canter, J. (1979) 'An Integrated Theoretical Perspective on Delinquent Behaviour', *Journal of Research in Crime and Delinquency*, 16: 126–49.

Ellis, L. (1990) 'The Evolution of Violent Criminal Behaviour and its NonLegal Equivalent', in L. Ellis and H. Hoffman (eds) *Crime in Biological, Social and Moral Contexts*. New York: Praeger.

Ellis, L. and Crontz, P.D. (1990) 'Androgens, Brain Functioning, and Criminality: The Neurohormonal Foundations of Antisociality', in L. Ellis and H. Hoffman (eds) *Crime in Biological, Social, and Moral Contexts*. New York: Praeger.

Emanuel, E. (1991) *The Ends of Human Life: Medical Ethics in a Liberal Polity*. Cambridge, MA: Harvard University Press.

Emsley, C. (1996) *The English Police: A Political and Social History*. Harlow: Longman.

Engels, F. (1845) *Karl Marx/Frederick Engels: Collected Works*. New York: International Publishers.

Ericson, R.V. and Haggerty, D. (1997) *Policing the Risk Society*. Oxford: Clarendon Press.

Erikson, K. (1962) 'Notes on the Sociology of Deviance', *Social Problems*, 9: 309–14.

Erikson, K. (1966) *Wayward Puritans: A Study in the Sociology of Deviance*. New York: Wiley.

Escobales, R. (2008) 'Police "Unequivocally" Support Reclassification of Cannabis', *The Guardian*, 5 February.

Etzioni, A. (1961) *A Comparative Analysis of Complex Organisations*. Glencoe, IL: Free Press.

Etzioni, A. (1993) *The Spirit of Community: The Reinvention of American Society*. New York: Touchstone.

Etzioni, A. (ed.) (1995a) *New Communitarian Thinking: Persons, Virtues, Institutions and Communities*. Charlottesville, VA: University of Virginia Press.

Etzioni, A. (1995b) *The Parenting Deficit*. London: Demos.

Etzioni, A., Glendon, M.A. and Galston, W. (1991) *The Responsive Communitarian Platform*. Washington, DC: The Communitarian Network.

Evans, D.J., Fyfe, N.R. and Herbert, D.T. (eds) (1992) *Crime, Policing and Place: Essays in Environmental Criminology*. London: Routledge.

Eysenck, H.J. (1959) *Manual of the Maudsley Personality Inventory*. London: University of London Press.

Eysenck, H.J. (1963) 'On the Dual Nature of Extroversion', *British Journal of Social Clinical Psychology*, 2: 46.

Eysenck, H.J. (1970) *Crime and Personality*. London: Granada.

Eysenck, H.J. (1977) *Crime and Personality, 3rd edition*. London: Routledge & Kegan Paul.

Eysenck, H.J. and Eysenck, S.B.J. (1970) 'Crime and Personality: An Empirical Study of the Three-factor Theory', *British Journal of Criminology*, 10: 225.

Eysenck, S.B.J., Rust, J. and Eysenck, H.J. (1977) 'Personality and the Classification of Adult Offenders', *British Journal of Criminology*, 17: 169–70.

Faberman, H.A. (1975) 'A Criminogenic Market Structure: The Automobile Industry', *Sociological Quarterly*, 16: 438–57.

Fagan, J. (1990) 'Intoxication and Aggression', in M. Tonry and J.Q. Wilson (eds) *Crime and Justice: A Review of Research*, Vol. 13. Chicago, IL: University of Chicago Press.

Farrington, D.P. (1992) 'Juvenile Delinquency', in J.C. Coleman (ed.) *The School Years*, 2nd edition. London: Routledge.

Farrington, D.P. (1994) 'Introduction', in D.P. Farrington (ed.), *Psychological Explanations of Crime*. Aldershot: Dartmouth.

Farrington, D. (2005) 'Introduction to Integrated Developmental and Life-course Theories of Offending' in D. Farrington (ed.) *Integrated Developmental and Life-course Theories of Offending*. Edison, NJ: Transaction Publishers.

Farrington, D.P., Loeber, R. and Van Kammen, W. (1990) 'Long-term Criminal Outcomes of Hyperactivity-Impulsivity-Attention Deficit and Conduct Problems in Childhood', in L. Robbins and M. Rutter (eds) *Straight and Devious Pathways from Childhood to Adulthood*. Cambridge: Cambridge University Press.

Farrington, D.P. and Morris, A.M. (1983) 'Sex, Sentencing and Reconviction', *British Journal of Criminology*, 23(3).

Farnsworth, M. (1989) 'Theory Integration versus Model Building', in S.F. Messner, M.D. Krohn and A.E. Liska (eds) *Theoretical Integration in the Study of Deviance and Crime*. Albany, NY: State University of New York Press.

Fausto-Sterling, A. (1992) 'Putting Woman in Her (Evolutionary) Place' in A. Fausto-Sterling (ed.) *Myths of Gender*. New York: Basic Books.

Feeley, M. and Simon, J. (1994) 'Actuarial Justice: The Emerging New Criminal Law', in D. Nelken (ed.) *The Futures of Criminology*. London: Sage.

Feeney, F. (1999) 'Robbers as Decision Makers', in P. Cromwell (ed.) *In Their Own Words: Criminals on Crime*, 2nd edition. Los Angeles, CA: Roxbury.

Feldman, M.P. (1977) *Criminal Behaviour: A Psychological Analysis*. Bath: Pitman Press.

Felson, M. (1998) *Crime and Everyday Life*, 2nd edition. Thousand Oaks, CA: Pine Forge.

Felson, M. and Clarke, R.V.G. (1998) *Opportunity Makes the Thief*. London: Home Office.

Ferguson, N. (2004) 'The Depressing Reality of This Messianic President's New Empire', *The Independent*, 4 November.

Ferracuti, F. (1982) 'A Sociopsychiatric Interpretation of Terrorism', *Annals of American Academy of Political & Social Science*, 463: 129–41.

Ferrell, J. (1991) 'The Brotherhood of Timber Workers and the Culture of Conflict', *Journal of Folklore Research*, 28: 163–77.

Ferrell, J. (1994) 'Confronting the Agenda of Authority: Critical Criminology, Anarchism, and Urban Graffiti', in G. Barak (ed.) *Varieties of Criminology: Readings from a Dynamic Discipline*. Westport, CT: Praeger.

Ferrell, J. (1995a) 'Urban Graffiti: Crime, Control, and Resistance' *Youth and Society*, 27: 73–92.

Ferrell, J. (1995b) 'Anarchy Against the Discipline', *Journal of Criminal Justice and Popular Culture*, 3: 86–91.

Ferrell, J. (1996) *Crimes of Style: Urban Graffiti and the Politics of Criminality*. Boston, MA: Northeastern University.

Ferrell, J. (1997) 'Criminological *Verstehen*: Inside the Immediacy of Crime', *Justice Quarterly*, 14: 3–23.

Ferrell, J. (1998) 'Against the Law: Anarchist Criminology', *Social Anarchism*, 25: 5–23.

Ferrell, J. (1999) 'Cultural Criminology', *Annual Review of Criminology*, 25: 395–418.

Ferrell, J., Hayward, K. and Young, J. (2008) *Cultural Criminology: An Invitation*. Beverly Hills, CA: Sage.

363

Ferrell, J. and Ryan, K. (1985) 'The Brotherhood of Timber Workers and the Southern Lumber Trust: Legal Repression and Worker Response', *Radical America*, 19: 55–74.

Ferrell, J. and Sanders, C. R. (eds) (1995) *Cultural Criminology*. Boston, MA: Northeastern University Press.

Ferri, E. (1895) *Criminal Sociology*. London: Unwin.

Ferri, E. (1968, originally 1901) *Three Lectures by Enrico Ferri*. Pittsburgh, PA: University of Pittsburgh Press.

Feyerabend, P. (1975) *Against Method: Outline of an Anarchistic Theory of Knowledge*. London: New Left Books.

Field, F. (1989) *Losing Out: The Emergence of Britain's Underclass*. Oxford: Blackwell.

Fielding, N. (1988) *Joining Forces*. London: Routledge.

Figueira-McDonough, J. (1984) 'Feminism and Delinquency: In Search of an Elusive Link', *British Journal of Criminology*, 24: 325–42.

Findlay, M. (2000) *The Globalisation of Crime*. London: Cambridge University Press.

Fishbein, D.H. and Pease, S.E. (1990) 'Neurological Links between Substance Abuse and Crime', in L. Ellis and H. Hoffman (eds) *Crime in Biological, Social and Moral Contexts*. New York: Praeger.

Fishbein, D.H. and Pease, S.E. (1996) *The Dynamic of Drug Abuse*. Boston, MA: Allyn Bacon.

Flanzer, J. (1981) 'The Vicious Circle of Alcoholism and Family Violence', *Alcoholism*, 1(3): 30–45.

Forsythe, L. (1994) 'Evaluation of Family Group Conference Cautioning Program in Wagga, NSW', Conference Paper Presented to the Australian and New Zealand Society of Criminology, 10th Annual Conference.

Foucault, M. (1971) *Madness and Civilisation: A History of Insanity in the Age of Reason*. London: Tavistock.

Foucault, M. (1976) *The History of Sexuality*. London: Allen Lane.

Foucault, M. (1977) *Discipline and Punish – the Birth of the Prison*. London: Allen Lane.

Foucault, M. (1980) *Power/Knowledge: Selected Interviews and Other Writings 1972–77*, edited by C. Gordon. Brighton: Harvester Press.

Fowler, F.J., McCall, M.E. and Mangione, T.W. (1979) *Reducing Residential Crime and Fear: The Hartford Neighborhood Crime Prevention Program*. Washington, DC: US Government Printing Office.

Fowler, F.J. and Mangione, T.W. (1982) *Neighborhood Crime, Fear and Social Control: A Second Look at the Hartford Program*. Washington, DC: US Government Printing Office.

Freisthler, B., Midanik, L. and Gruenewald, P.J. (2004) 'Alcohol Outlets and Child Physical Abuse and Neglect: Applying Routine Activities Theory to the Study of Child Maltreatment', *Journal of Studies on Alcohol*, 65(5): 586–92.

Freud, S. (1920) *A General Introduction to Psychoanalysis*. New York: Boni and Liveright.

Freud, S. (1927) *The Ego and the Id*. London: Hogarth.

Freud, S. (1933) *New Introductory Lectures on Psychoanalysis*. New York: W.W. Norton.

Friedlander, K. (1947) *The Psychoanalytic Approach to Juvenile Delinquency*. London: Kegan Paul.

Friedlander, K. (1949) 'Latent Delinquency and Ego Development', in K.R. Eissler (ed.) *Searchlights on Delinquency*. New York: International University Press, pp. 205–15.

Friedrichs, D. (1980) 'Radical criminology' in J. Inciardi (ed.) *Radical Criminology*. Beverly Hills, CA: Sage.

Frisby, D. (1984) *Georg Simmel*. New York: Tavistock.

Frith, U. (2003) *Autism, Explaining the Enigma, 2nd edition*. Oxford: Blackwell.

Funk, D.G. (2004) *Globalisation and Social Polarisation in Hong Kong*. New York: Routledge.

Fyfe, N.R. (1995) 'Law and Order Policy and the Spaces of Citizenship in Contemporary Britain', *Political Geography*, 14(2): 177–89.

Gabe, J. (2001) *Violence against Professionals in the Community*. London: Royal Holloway.

Galvin, D. (1983) 'The Female Terrorist: A Socio-Psychological Perspective', *Behavioral Science & Law*, 1: 19–32.

Garfinkel, H. (1967) *Studies in Ethnomethodology*. Oxford: Basil Blackwell.

Garland, D. (1996) 'The Limits of the Sovereign State: Strategies of Crime Control in Contemporary Society', *British Journal of Criminology*, 34(4): 445–71.

Garland, D. (1997) 'The Development of British Criminology', in M. Maguire, R. Morgan and R. Reiner (eds) *The Oxford Handbook of Criminology*. Oxford: Clarendon Press.

Garland, D. (1999) '"Governmentality"' and the Problem of Crime', in R. Smandych (ed.) *Governable Places: Readings on Governmentality and Crime Control*. Aldershot: Ashgate.

Garland, D. (2001) *The Culture of Control*. Oxford: Oxford University Press.

Garofalo, R. (1914) *Criminology*. Boston, MA: Little, Brown.

Gatrell, V. (1980) 'The Decline of Theft and Violence in Victorian and Edwardian England', in V. Gatrell, B. Lenman and G. Parker (eds) *Crime and the Law: The Social History of Crime in Europe Since 1500*. London: Europa.

Geis, G. (1967) 'The Heavy Electrical Equipment Anti-trust Cases of 1961', in M.B. Clinard and R. Quinney (eds) *Criminal Behaviour Systems*. New York: Holt, Rinehart & Winston.

Geis, G. (1968) *White-collar Crime: The Offender in Business and the Professions*. New York: Atherton.

Geis, G. and Goff, C. (1983) 'Introduction', in E. Sutherland, *White-Collar Crime: The Uncut Version*. New Haven, CT: Yale University Press.

Geis, G. and Maier, R.F. (eds) (1977) *White-collar Crime: Offences in Business, Politics and the Professions – Classic and Contemporary Views*. New York: Free Press.

Gelsthorpe, L. and Morris, A. (1980) *Feminist Perspectives in Criminology*. Milton Keynes: Open University Press.

Gelsthorpe, L. and Morris, A. (1988) 'Feminism and Criminology in Britain', *British Journal of Criminology*, 28: 83–110.

Gelsthorpe, L. and Morris, A. (eds) (1990) *Feminist Perspectives in Criminology*. Milton Keynes: Open University Press.

George, S. (1999) 'The Crisis of Global Capitalism', *Business Week*, 19 December.

Ghaziuddin, M. (2005) *Mental Health Aspects of Autism and Asperger's Syndrome*. London: Jessica Kingsley Publishers.

Gibbens, T.C.N. (1963) *Psychiatric Studies of Borstal Lads*. Oxford: Oxford University Press.

Gibbens, T.C.N. and Prince, J. (1962) *Shoplifting*. London: Institute for the Study of Delinquency.

Gibbons, D.C. (1970) *Delinquent Behaviour*. Englewood Cliffs, NJ: Prentice-Hall.

Gibbs, J. (1966) 'Conceptions of Deviant Behaviour', *Pacific Sociological Review*, 9: 9–14.

Gibbs, J. (1975) *Crime, Punishment, and Deterrence*. New York: Elsevier.

Giddens, A. (1964) *Structuration and Related Theories of Social Life and Communication*. London: Routledge.

Giddens, A. (1990) *The Consequences of Modernity*. Cambridge: Polity Press.

Giddens, A. (1991) *Modernity and Self-Identity*. Cambridge: Polity Press.

Giddens, A. (1994) *Beyond Left and Right: The Future of Radical Politics*. Cambridge: Polity Press.

Giddens, A. (1998) *The Third Way: The Renewal of Social Democracy*. Cambridge: Polity Press.

Gilbert, J. and Pearson, E. (1999) *Discographies: Dance Music, Culture and the Politics of Sound*. London: Routledge.

Gill, M. and R. Matthews (1994). 'Robbers on Robbery: Offender Perspectives' in M. Gill (ed.) *Crime at Work: Studies in Security and Crime Prevention, Vol. 1*. Leicester: Perpetuity Press.

Gill, O. (1977) *Luke Street: Housing Policy, Conflict and the Creation of the Delinquency Area*. London: Macmillan.

Gilliom, J. (1994) *Surveillance, Privacy and the Law: Employee Drug Testing and the Politics of Social Control*. Ann Arbour, MI: University of Michigan Press.

Giordano, P.C. and Rockwell, S.M. (2000) 'Differential Association Theory and Female Crime' in S.S. Simpson (ed.) *Of Crime and Criminality*. Thousand Oaks, CA: Pine Forge Press.

Glendon, M.A. (1991) *Rights Talk: The Impoverishment of Political Discourse*. New York: Free Press.

Glueck, S. and Glueck, E. (1950) *Unravelling Juvenile Delinquency*. Oxford: Oxford University Press.

Goddard, H.H. (1914) *Feeblemindedness: Its Causes and Consequences*. New York: Macmillan.

Godfrey, C., Eaton, G., McDougall, C. and Culyer, A. (2002) *The Economic and Social Costs of Class A Drug Use in England and Wales, 2000*. London: Home Office.

Goldmann, L. (1970) 'The Sociology of Literature: Status and the Problem of Methods', in M.C. Albrecht, J.H. Barnett and M. Griff, *The Sociology of Art and Literature: A Reader*. London: Duckworth.

Goldstein, H. (1977) *Policing a Free Society*. Cambridge, MA: Ballinger.

Goldstein, H. (1979) 'Improving Policing: A Problem-Oriented Approach', *Crime and Delinquency*, 25: 236–58.

Goldstein, H. (1990) *Problem-Oriented Policing*. New York: McGraw-Hill.

Goldthorpe, J.H. (1968–9) *The Affluent Worker in The Class Structure*, 3 Vols. Cambridge: Cambridge University Press.

Goode, E. and Ben-Yehuda, N. (1994) *Moral Panics: The Social Construction of Deviance*. Oxford: Blackwell.

Goodwin, D., Schulsinger, F., Hermansen, L., Guze, S. and Winokur, G. (1973) 'Alcohol Problems in Adoptees Raised Apart from Alcoholic Biological Parents', *Archives of General Psychiatry*, 28: 238–43.

Gordon, D. (1971) 'Class and the Economics of Crime', *Review of Radical Economics*, 3: 51–75.

Gordon, R.A (1986) 'Scientific Justification and the Race-IQ-Delinquency Model', in T. Hartnagel and R. Silverman (eds) *Critique and Explanation: Essays in Honor of Gwynne Nettler*. New Brunswick, NJ: Transaction.

Goring, C. (1913) *The English Convict: A Statistical Study*. London: HMSO.

Gottfredson, M.R. (1984) *Victims of Crime: The Dimension of Risk*, Home Office Research Study No 81. London: HMSO.

Gottfredson, M.R. and Hirschi, T. (1990) *A General Theory of Crime*. Stanford, CA: Stanford University Press.

Gouldner, A. (1968) 'The Sociologist as Partisan: Sociology and the Welfare State', *The American Sociologist*, May: 103–16.

Gouldner, A. (1970) *The Coming Crisis of Western Sociology*. New York: Basic Books.

Graham, J. and Bowling, B. (1995) *Young People and Crime*, Home Office Research Study No. 145. London: HMSO.

Gramsci, A. (1977, 1978) *Selections from the Political Writings*. London: Lawrence & Wiseheart.

Grasmick, H. and Bursik, R. (1990) 'Conscience, Significant Others and Rational Choice: Extending the Deterrent Model', *Law and Society Review*, 24: 837–61.

Gregory, J. (1986) 'Sex, Class and Crime: Towards a Non-Sexist Criminology', in R. Matthews and J. Young (eds) *Confronting Crime*. London: Sage.

Gross, E. (1978) 'Organisations as Criminal Actors', in J. Braithwaite and P. Wilson (eds) *Two Faces of Deviance: Crimes of the Powerless and the Powerful*. Brisbane: University of Queensland Press.

Grosser, G.H. (1951) quoted in D.C. Gibbons (1981) *Delinquent Behaviour, 3rd edition*. Englewood Cliffs, NJ: Prentice Hall.

Grygier, T. (1969) 'Parental Deprivation: A Study of Delinquent Children', *British Journal of Criminology*, 9: 209.

Guerin, D. (1970) *Anarchism*. New York: Monthly Review.

Guerry, A.M. (1833) *Essai sur la Statisque Morale de la France*. Paris: Crochard.

Gurr, T. (1970) *Why Men Rebel*. Princeton, NJ: Princeton University Press.

Habermas, J. (1989) *The New Conservatism*. Cambridge: Polity Press.

Hacker, F. (1996) *Crusaders, Criminals, Crazies: Terror and Terrorists in Our Time*. New York: Norton.

Hagan, J. (1994) *Crime and Disrepute*. Thousand Oaks, CA: Pine Forge Press.

Hagan, J. (1989) *Structural Criminology*. New Brunswick, NJ: Rutgers University Press.

Hagan, J. Gillis, A.R. and Simpson, J. (1985) 'The Class Structure of Gender and Delinquency: Toward a Power-Control Theory of Common Delinquent Behavior', *American Journal of Sociology*, 90(2): 1151–78.

Hagan, J. Gillis, A.R. and Simpson, J. (1987) 'Class in the Household: A Power-Control Theory of Gender and Delinquency', *American Journal of Sociology*, 92(4): 788–816.

Hagan, J., Gillis, A.R. and Simpson, J. (1990) 'Clarifying and Extending Power-Control Theory', *American Journal of Sociology*, 95(4): 1024–37.

Hagan, J. and McCarthy, B. (1998) *Mean Streets: Youth Crime and Homelessness*. Cambridge: Cambridge University Press.

Hagedorn, J. (1992) 'Gangs, Neighbourhoods, and Public Policy', *Social Problems*, 38(4): 529–42.

Hall, S. and Jefferson, T. (eds) (1976) *Resistance Through Rituals*. London: Hutchinson.

Hall, S. and Scraton, P. (1981) 'Law, Class and Control', in M. Fitzgerald, G. McLennan and J. Pawson (eds) *Crime and Society: Readings in History and Theory*. London: Routledge & Kegan Paul and The Open University Press.

Hall, S., Critcher, C., Jefferson, T., Clarke, J. and Roberts, B. (1978) *Policing the Crisis*. London: Macmillan.

Hall, S., Winlow, S. and Ancrum, C. (2008) *Criminal Identities and Consumer Culture: Crime, Exclusion and the New Culture of Narcissism*. Cullompton: Willan Publishing.

Halpern, D. (2001) 'Moral Values, Social Thrust and Inequality', *British Journal of Criminology*, 41: 230–44.

Hanmer, J. and Saunders, S. (1984) *Well-Founded Fear*. London: Hutchinson.

Hare, D.R. (1970) *Psychopathy: Theory and Research*. New York: Wiley.

Hare, D.R. (1980) 'A Research Scale for the Assessment of Psychopathy in Criminal Populations', *Personality and Individual Differences*, 1: 111–19.

Hare, D.R. (1982) 'Psychopathy and Physiological Activity During Anticipation of An Aversive Stimulus in a Distraction Paradigm', *Psychophysiology*, 19: 266–80.

Hare, D.R. and Jutari, J.W. (1986) 'Twenty Years of Experience with the Cleckley Psychopath', in W.H. Reid, D. Dorr, J.I. Walker and J.W. Bonner (eds) *Unmasking the Psychopath: Antisocial Personality and Related Syndromes*. New York: Norton.

Harries, K. (1999) *Mapping Crime: Principle and Practice*. Washington, DC: National Institute of Justice (NCJ 178919).

Harris, A. (1977) 'Sex and Theories of Deviance: Toward a Functional Theory of Deviant Typescripts', *American Sociological Review*, 42: 3–16.

Hart, J. (1978) 'Police', in W. Cornish (ed.) *Crime and Law*. Dublin: Irish University Press.

Hartjen, C. (1974) *Crime and Criminalization*. New York: Praeger.

Hartl, E., Monnelly, E. and Elderkin, (1982) *Physique and Delinquent Behaviour*. New York: Academic Press.

Hartmann, H. (1981) 'The Family as a Locus of Class, Gender and Political Struggle: The Example of Housework', *Signs*, 6.

Harvey, D. (1989) *The Condition of Postmodernity: An Enquiry into the Origins of Cultural Change*. Oxford: Blackwell.

Hay, D. (1981) 'Property, Authority and the Criminal Law', in M. Fitzgerald, G. McLennan and J. Pawson (eds) *Crime and Society: Readings in History and Theory*. London: Open University Press/Routledge.

Hayles, K. (1990) *Chaos Bound*. Ithaca, NY: Cornell University Press.

Hayles, K. (1991) *Chaos and Order: Complex Dynamics in Literature and Science*. Chicago, IL: University of Chicago Press.

Hayward, K.J. (2004a) *City Limits: Crime, Consumer Culture and the Urban Experience*. London: Glass House Press.

Hayward, K.J. (2004b) 'Crime and Consumer Culture in Late Modernity', in C. Sumner (ed.) *The Blackwell Companion to Criminology*. Oxford: Blackwell.

Heal, K. and Laycock, G. (eds) (1986) *Situational Crime Prevention – From Theory into Practice*. London: HMSO.

Healy, W. and Bronner, A.F. (1936) *New Light on Delinquency and its Treatment*. New Haven, CT: Yale University Press.

Hebdige, D. (1976) 'The Meaning of Mod', in S. Hall and T. Jefferson (eds.) *Resistance Through Rituals: Youth Sub-cultures in Post-war Britain*. London: Hutchinson, pp. 118–143.

Hebdige, D. (1979) *Subculture: The Meaning Of Style*. London: Methuen.

Hebdige, D. (1987) *Cut 'n' Mix: Culture, Identity and Caribbean Music*. London: Comedia.

Heidensohn, F. (1968) 'The Deviance of Women: A Critique and an Enquiry', *British Journal of Criminology*, 19(2): 160–76.

Heidensohn, F.M. (1985) *Women and Crime*. London: Macmillan.

Heidensohn, F. (1987) 'Women and Crime: Questions for Criminology', in P. Carlen and A. Worrall (eds) *Gender, Crime and Justice*. Buckingham: Open University.

Heidensohn, F. (1994) 'Gender and Crime', in M. Maguire, R. Morgan and R. Reiner (eds) *The Oxford Handbook of Criminology*. Oxford: Oxford University Press.

Heidensohn, F. (1996) *Women and Crime*. London: Macmillan.

Heidensohn, F. (2000/2001) 'Women and Violence: Myths and Reality in the 21st Century', *Criminal Justice Matters*, 42: 20.

Heimer, K., and Matsueda, R.L. (1994) 'Role-taking, Role Commitment, and Delinquency: A Theory of Differential Social Control', *American Sociological Review*, 59: 365–90.

Henle, M. (1985) 'Rediscovering Gestalt Psychology', in S. Koch and D.E. Leary (eds), *A Century of Psychology as a Science*. New York: McGraw-Hill.

Henry, S. and Lanier, M.M. (1998) 'The Prism of Crime: Arguments for an Integrated Definition of Crime', *Justice Quarterly*, 15(4): 609–27.

Henry, S. and Milovanovic, D. (1994) 'The Constitution of Constitutive Criminology', in D. Nelken (ed.) *The Futures of Criminology*. London: Sage.

Henry, S. and Milovanovic, D. (1996) *Constitutive Criminology: Beyond Postmodernism*. London: Sage.

Henry, S., and Milovanovic, D. (1999) *Constitutive Criminology at Work: Applications to Crime and Justice*. New York: State University of New York Press.

Henry, S., and Milovanovic, D. (2000) 'Constitutive Criminology: Origins, Core Concepts, and Evaluation', *Social Justice*, 27(2) 260–76.

Henry, S., and Milovanovic, D. (2001) 'Constitutive Definition of Crime: Power as Harm' in S. Henry and M.M. Lanier (eds) *What is Crime? Controversies over the Nature of Crime and What to Do about It*. Lanham, MA: Rowman and Littlefield.

Herrnstein, R.J. and Murray, C. (1994) *The Bell Curve*. New York: Basic Books.

Heywood, A. (1992) *Political Ideologies*. London: McMillan Press.

Hill, E. and Frith, U. (2004) *Autism: Mind and Brain*. Oxford: Oxford University Press.

Hills, J., LeGrand, J. and Pichaud, D. (eds) (2002) *Understanding Social Exclusion*. Oxford: Oxford University Press.

Hillyard, P. (1987) 'The Normalisation of Special Powers: From Northern Ireland to Britain', in P. Scraton (ed.) *Law, Order and the Authoritarian State*. Milton Keynes: Open University Press.

Hindelang, M. (1979) 'Sex Differences in Criminal Activity', *Social Problems*, 27: 15–36.

Hindelang, M.J. and Weis, J.G. (1972) 'Personality and Self-reported Delinquency: An Application of Cluster Analysis', *Criminology*, 10: 268–94.

Hirschi, T. (1969) *Causes of Delinquency*. Berkeley, CA: University of California Press.

Hirschi, T. (1995) 'The Family', in J.Q. Wilson and J. Petersilia (eds) *Crime*. San Francisco, CA: ICS Press.

Hirschi, T. and Hindelang, M.J. (1977) 'Intelligence and Delinquency: A Revisionist Review', *American Sociological Review*, 42: 572–87.

Hirst, P.Q. (1980) 'Law, Socialism and Rights', in P. Carlen and M. Collinson (eds) *Radical Issues in Criminology*. Oxford: Martin Robertson.

Hobbes, T. (1968 originally 1651) *Leviathan*, edited by C.B. Macpherson. Harmondsworth: Penguin.

Hobbs, D., Hadfield, P., Lister, S. and Winlow, S. and Hall, S. (2000) 'Receiving Shadows: Governance and Liminality in the Night-time Economy', *British Journal of Sociology*, 51(4): 701–17.

Hobbs, D., Winslow, S., Lister, S. and Hadfield, P. (2005) 'Violent Hypocrisy: Governance and the Night-time Economy', *European Journal of Criminology*, 42(2): 352–70.

Hodge, J. (1993) 'Alcohol and Violence', in P. Taylor (ed.) *Violence in Society*. London: Royal College of Physicians.

Hoffman, B. (1993) *Holy Terror*. Santa Monica, CA: RAND.

Hoffman, M.L. and Saltzstein, H.D. (1967) 'Parent Discipline and the Child's Moral Development', *Journal of Personality and Social Psychology*, 5: 45.

Hoffman Bustamante, D. (1973) 'The Nature of Female Criminality', *Issues in Criminology*, 8: 117.

Hogg, R. and Brown, D. (1998) *Rethinking Law and Order*. Sydney: Pluto Press.

Hoghughi, M.S. and Forrest, A.R. (1970) 'Eysenck's Theory of Criminality: An Examination with Approved Schoolboys', *British Journal of Criminology*, 10: 240.

Holdaway, S. (1983) *Inside the British Police: A Force at Work*. Oxford: Blackwell.

Holland, T. (1997) 'Forensic Psychiatry and Learning Disability' in O. Russell (ed.) *Seminars in the Psychiatry of Learning Disabilities*. London: The Royal College of Psychiatrists.

Hollin, C.R. (1989) *Psychology and Crime: An Introduction to Criminological Psychology*. London: Routledge.

Hollin, C.R. (1990a) 'Social Skills Training with Delinquents: A Look at the Evidence and Some Recommendations for Practice', *British Journal of Social Work*, 20: 483–93.

Hollin, C.R. (1990b) *Cognitive-Behavioural Interventions with Young Offenders*. Elmsford, NY: Pergamon Press.

Holmes, R.M. and De Burger, J. (1989) *Serial Murder*. Newbury Park, CA: Sage.

Home Office (1997) *Aspects of Crime: Young Offenders*. London: Home Office.

Home Office (1999) *Proposals for Revising Legislative Measures on Fingerprints, Footprints and DNA Samples*. London: Home Office.

Home Office (2000) *British Crime Survey*. London: HMSO.

Home Office (2001) *Confidence in the Criminal Justice System*. London: HMSO.

Home Office (2004) *Anti-social Behaviour Orders and Acceptable Behaviour Orders*. London: HMSO

hooks, b. (1988) *Talking Back, Thinking Feminist, Thinking Black*. Boston, MA: South End Press.

Hooton, E.A. (1939) *The American Criminal: An Anthropological Study*. Cambridge, MA: Harvard University Press.

Hopkins, A. and McGregor, H. (1991) *Working for Change: The Movement Against Domestic Violence*. Sydney: Allen & Unwin.

Hopkins Burke, R.D. (ed.) (1998a) *Zero Tolerance Policing*. Leicester: Perpetuity Press.

Hopkins Burke, R.D. (1998b) 'The Contextualisation of Zero Tolerance Policing Strategies', in R.D. Hopkins Burke (ed.) *Zero Tolerance Policing*. Leicester: Perpetuity Press.

Hopkins Burke, R.D. (1998c) 'Begging, Vagrancy and Disorder', in R.D. Hopkins Burke (ed.) *Zero Tolerance Policing*. Leicester: Perpetuity Press.

Hopkins Burke, R.D. (1999a) *Youth Justice and the Fragmentation of Modernity*. Scarman Centre for the Study of Public Order Occasional Paper Series, The University of Leicester.

Hopkins Burke, R.D. (1999b) 'The Socio-Political Context of Zero Tolerance Policing Strategies', *Policing: An International Journal of Police Strategies & Management*, 21(4): 666–82.

Hopkins Burke, R.D. (2000) 'The Regulation of Begging and Vagrancy: A Critical Discussion', *Crime Prevention and Community Safety: An International Journal*, 2(2): 43–52.

Hopkins Burke, R.D. (2002) 'Zero Tolerance Policing: New Authoritarianism or New Liberalism?' *The Nottingham Law Journal*, 2(1): 20–35.

Hopkins Burke, R.D. (2003) 'Policing Bad Behaviour: Interrogating the Dilemmas', in J. Rowbotham and K. Stevenson (eds) *Behaving Badly? Offensive Behaviour and 'Crime'*. London: Ashgate.

Hopkins Burke, R.D. (ed.) (2004a) *'Hard Cop/Soft Cop': Dilemmas and Debates in Contemporary Policing*. Cullompton: Willan Publishing.

Hopkins Burke, R.D. (2004b) 'Policing Contemporary Society' in R.D. Hopkins Burke, *'Hard Cop/Soft Cop': Dilemmas and Debates in Contemporary Policing*. Cullompton: Willan Publishing.

Hopkins Burke, R.D. (2004c) 'Policing Contemporary Society Revisited' in R.D. Hopkins Burke, *'Hard Cop/Soft Cop': Dilemmas and Debates in Contemporary Policing*. Cullompton: Willan Publishing.

Hopkins Burke, R.D. (2005) *An Introduction to Criminological Theory, 2nd edition*. Cullompton: Willan Publishing.

Hopkins Burke, R.D. (2007) 'Moral Ambiguity, the Schizophrenia of Crime and Community Justice', *British Journal of Community Justice*, 5(1): 43–64.

Hopkins Burke, R.D. (2008) *Young People, Crime and Justice*. Cullompton: Willan Publishing.

Hopkins Burke, R.D. and Morrill, R. (2002) 'Anti-social Behaviour Orders: An Infringement of the Human Rights Act 1998?', *The Nottingham Law Journal*, 2(2): 1–16.

Hopkins Burke, R.D. and Morrill, R. (2004) 'Human Rights v. Community Rights: The Case of the Anti-Social Behaviour Order', in *'Hard Cop/Soft Cop': Dilemmas and Debates in Contemporary Policing*. Cullompton: Willan Publishing.

Hopkins Burke, R.D. and Pollock, E. (2004) 'A Tale of Two Anomies: Some Observations on the Contribution of (Sociological) Criminological Theory to Explaining Hate Crime Motivation', *Internet Journal of Criminology*.

Hopkins Burke, R.D. and Sunley, R. (1996) *'Hanging Out' in the 1990s: Young People and the Postmodern Condition*, Occasional Paper 11, COP Series. Scarman Centre for the Study of Public Order, University of Leicester.

Hopkins Burke, R.D. and Sunley R. (1998) 'Youth Subcultures in Contemporary Britain', in K. Hazelhurst and C. Hazlehurst (eds) *Gangs and Youth Subcultures: International Explorations*. New Brunswick, NJ: Transaction Press.

Horney, J. and Marshall, I. (1991) 'Measuring Lambda through Self-Reports', *Criminology*, 29(3): 471–95.

Hough, M., Clarke, R.V.G. and Mayhew, P. (1980) 'Introduction', in R.V.G. Clarke and P. Mayhew (eds) *Designing Out Crime*. London: HMSO.

Howlin, P. (1997) *Autism: Preparing for Adulthood*. Oxford: Routledge.

Howlin, P. (2004) *Autism and Asperger Syndrome: Preparing for Adulthood, 2nd edition*. Oxford: Routledge.

Hudson, J., Morris, A., Maxwell, G. and Galway, B. (1996) *Family Group Conferences*. Annandale, NSW: Federation Press.

Hudson, R. (1999) *Who Becomes a Terrorist and Why*. Guilford, CT: Lyons Press.

Hughes, G. (1998) *Understanding Crime Prevention: Social Control, Risk and Late Modernity*. Buckingham: Open University Press.

Hughes, G. (2000) 'Communitarianism and Law and Order', in T. Hope (ed.) *Perspective on Crime Reduction*. Dartmouth: Ashgate.

Hurwitz, L. (1981) *The State as Defendant*. London: Aldwych.

Hutchings, B. and Mednick, S.A. (1977) 'Criminality in Adoptees and their Adoptive and Biological Parents: A Pilot Study', in S.A. Mednick and K.O. Christiansen (eds) *Biosocial Bases of Criminal Behaviour*. New York: Gardner.

Ignatieff, M. (1978) *A Just Measure of Pain: The Penitentiary and the Industrial Revolution*. London: Macmillan.

Institute of Alcohol Studies (2005) *Adolescents and Alcohol*. St Ives, Cambridgeshire: IAS.

Institute of Race Relations (1987) *Policing Against Black People*. London: Institute of Race Relations.

Jacobs, B. (2000) *Robbing Drug Dealers*. New York: Aldine de Gruyter.

Jacobs, J. (1961) *The Death and Life of Great American Cities*. New York: Vintage.

Jaggar, A.M. (1980) 'Prostitution' in *Readings in the Philosophy of Sex*. Totowa, NJ: Littlefield, Adams & Co.

Jaggar, A.M. (1983) *Feminist Politics and Human Nature*. Lanham, MD: Rowman and Littlefield.

Jarvis, G. and Parker, H. (1989) 'Young Heroin Users and Crime', *British Journal of Criminology*, 29: 175.

Jay, M. (1973) *The Dialectical Imagination: A History of the Frankfurt School*. Boston, MA: Little, Brown.

Jefferis, B.J.M.H., Power, C. and Manor, O. (2005) 'Adolescent Drinking Level and Adult Binge Drinking in a National Cohort', *Addiction*, 100(4): 543–9.

Jefferson, T. (1997) 'Masculinities and Crime', in M. Maguire, R. Morgan and R. Reiner (eds) *The Oxford Handbook of Criminology, 2nd edition*. Oxford: Clarendon.

Jeffery, C.R. (1977) *Crime Prevention Through Environmental Design*. Beverly Hills, CA: Sage.

Jensen, A.R. (1969) 'How Much Can We Boost IQ and Scholastic Achievement?', *Harvard Educational Review*, 39: 1–23.

Johannen, U., Steven, G. and Gomez, J. (2003) *Social and Economic Impacts of Globalisation in Latin America*. New York: Routledge.

Jones, G. (1980) *Social Darwinism and English Thought – The Interaction between Biological and Social Theory*. Brighton: Harvester Press.

Jones, S. (1993) *The Language of the Genes*. London: Harper Collins.

Jones, T., Newburn, T. and Smith, D. (1994) *Democracy and Policing*. London: Policy Studies Institute.

Jordan, B. (1992) 'Basic Income and the Common Good', in P. van Parisjs (ed.) *Arguing for Basic Income*. London: Verso.

Jordan, B. (1996) *A Theory of Social Exclusion and Poverty*. Cambridge: Polity Press.

Jordan, B. (1998) 'New Labour, New Community?', *Imprints*, 3(2): 113–31.

Juergensmeyer, M. (2001) *Terror in the Mind of God: The Global Rise of Religious Violence*. Berkeley, CA: University of California Press.

Kandel, E. and Mednick, S. (1991) 'Perinatal Complications Predict Violent Offending', *Criminology*, 29(3): 519–29.

Karmen, A. (2004) 'Zero Tolerance in New York City: Hard Questions for a Get-Tough Policy', in R.D. Hopkins Burke *'Hard Cop/Soft Cop': Dilemmas and Debates in Contemporary Policing*. Cullompton: Willan Publishing.

Katz, J. (1988) *Seductions of Crime: Moral and Sensual Attractions in Doing Evil*. New York: Basic Books.

Kazdin, A. E. (1987) *Conduct Disorder in Childhood and Adolescence*. Newbury Park, CA: Sage.

Keane, C., Maxim, P.S. and Teevan, J.T. (1993) 'Drinking and Driving, Self Control, and Gender: Testing a General Theory of Crime', *Journal of Research in Crime and Delinquency*, 30: 30.

Kelling, G. (1999) 'Broken Windows, Zero Tolerance and Crime Control', in P. Francis and F. Penny (eds) *Building Safer Communities*. London: Centre for Crime and Justice Studies.

Kelly, T. (2006) 'Judge Tells McDonald's Killer: You Didn't Know It Was Wrong', *The Daily Mail*, 10 December.

Kendler, H.H. (1985) 'Behaviourism and Psychology: An Uneasy Alliance', in S. Koch and D.E. Leary (eds) *A Century of Psychology as Science*. New York: McGraw-Hill.

Kennedy, H. (1992) *Eve Was Framed*. London: Chatto & Windus.

Kenney, J.S. (2002) 'Victims of Crime and Labelling Theory: A Parallel Process?', *Deviant Behavior: An Interdisciplinary Journal*, 23: 235–65.

Kershaw, C., Budd, T., Kinshott, G., Mattinson, J., Mayhew, P. and Myhill, A. (2000) *The 2000 British Crime Survey*. London: Home Office.

Keverne, F.B., Meller, R.E. and Eberhart, J.A. (1982) 'Social Influences on Behaviour and Neuroendocrine Responsiveness in Talapoin Monkeys', *Scandinavian Journal of Psychology*, 1: 37–54.

King, M. (1981) *The Framework of Criminal Justice*. London: Croom Helm.

Kinnvall, C. and Jonsson, K. (2002) *Globalisation*. New York: Routledge

Kinsey, R., Lea, J. and Young, J. (1986) *Losing the Fight Against Crime*. Oxford: Basil Blackwell.

Kitsuse, J.I. (1962) 'Societal Reaction to Deviant Behaviour: Problems of Theory and Method', *Social Problems*, 9: 247–56.

Kitsuse, J.I. and Dietrick, D.C. (1959) 'Delinquent Boys: A Critique', *American Sociological Review*, 24: 208–15.

Klein, D. (1973) 'The Aetiology of Female Crime: A Review of the Literature', in L. Crites (ed.) *The Female Offender*. Lexington, MA: Lexington Books.

Klepper, S. and Nagin, D. (1989) 'The Deterrent Effect of Perceived Certainty and Severity of Punishment Revisited', *Criminology*, 27(4): 721–46.

Klinefelter, H.F., Reifenstein, E.C., Albright, F. (1942) 'Syndrome Characterized by Gynecomastia, Aspermatogenesis without Aleydigism and Increased Excretion of Follicle-Stimulating Hormone', *Journal of Clinical Endocrinology*, 2: 615–27.

Knights, B. (1998) '"The Slide to Ashes": An Antidote to Zero Tolerance', in R.D. Hopkins Burke (ed.) *Zero Tolerance Policing*. Leicester: Perpetuity Press.

Kochan, N. and Whittington B. (1991) *Bankrupt: The BCCI Fraud*. London: Victor Gollancz.

Koestler, A. and Rolph, C.H. (1961) *Hanged by the Neck*. Harmondsworth: Penguin.

Kolvin, I., Miller, F.J.W., Scott, D.M., Gatzanis, S.R.M. and Fleeting, M. (1990) *Continuities of Deprivation?* Aldershot: Avebury.

Konopka, G. (1966) *The Adolescent Girl in Conflict*. London: Prentice Hall.

Kornbluh, J. (ed.) (1988) *Rebel Voices: An IWW Anthology*. Chicago, IL: Charles H. Kerr.

Kozol, H.L., Boucher, R.J. and Garofalo, R.F. (1972) 'The Diagnosis and Treatment of Dangerousness', *Crime and Delinquency*, 18: 371–92.

Kraemer, E. (2004) 'A Philosopher Looks at Terrorism', in A. Nyatepe-Coo and D. Zeisler-Vralsted (eds) *Understanding Terrorism*. Upper Saddle River, NJ: Prentice Hall.

Kramer, R.C. (1984) 'Corporate Criminality: The Development of an Idea', in E. Hochstetler (ed.) *Corporations as Criminals*. Beverly Hills, CA: Sage.

Kramer, R.C. (1985) 'Humanistic Perspectives in Criminology', *Journal of Sociology and Social Welfare*, 12: 469–87.

Kretschmer, E. (1964) *Physique and Character*, translation by W.J.H. Sprott. New York: Cooper Square.

Kreuz, L.E. and Rose, R.M. (1972) 'Assessment of Aggressive Behaviour and Plasma Testosterone in a Young Criminal Population', *Psychosomatic Medicine*, 34: 321–33.

Krisberg, B. (1974) 'Gang Youth and Hustling: The Psychology of Survival', *Issues in Criminology*, 9: 115–31.

Kropotkin, P. (1975) *The Essential Kropotkin*. New York: Liveright.

Lacey, N., Wells, C. and Meure, D. (1990) *Reconstructing Criminal Law: Critical Social Perspectives on Crime and the Criminal Process*. London: Weidenfeld and Nicolson.

Ladner, J. (1972) *Tomorrow's Tomorrow: The Black Woman*. New York: Doubleday.

Laing, R.D. (1960) *The Divided Self*. Harmondsworth: Penguin.

Lambert, J.R. (1970) *Crime, Police and Race Relations*. London: Institute of Race Relations/ Oxford University Press.

Lancaster, J.B., Sherrod, L., Rossi, A.S. and Altmann, J. (1987) *Parenting Across the Life Span*. Piscataway, NJ: Aldine Transaction.

Lange, J. (1930) *Crime as Destiny*. London: Allen and Unwin.

Lansky, M. (1987) 'Shame and Domestic Violence', in D. Nathanson (ed.) *The Many Faces of Shame*. New York: Guilford.

Laucht, M., Esser, G., Baving, L., Gerhold, M., Hoesch, I., Ihle, W., Steiglieder, P., Stock, B., Stoehr, R., Weindrich, D. and Schmidt, M. (2000) 'Behavioral Sequelae of Perinatal Insults and Early Family Adversity at 8 Years of Age', *Journal of the American Academy of Child and Adolescent Psychiatry*, 39: 1229–37.

Lea, J. and Young, J. (1984) *What is to be Done about Law and Order?* Harmondsworth: Penguin.

Le Billon, P. (2001) 'Fuelling War or Buying Peace: The Role of Corruption in Conflicts', *Journal of International Development*, 13: 951–64.

Leigh, A., Read, T. and Tilley, N. (1998) *Brit Pop 11: Problem Oriented Policing in Practice*, Police Research Series, Paper 93. London: Home Office.

Lemert, E. (1951) *Social Pathology: A Systematic Approach to the Theory of Sociopathic Behavior*. New York: McGraw-Hill.

Lemert, E. (1972) *Human Deviance, Social Problems and Social Control, 2nd edition*. Englewood Cliffs, NJ: Prentice-Hall.

Leonard, E. (1983) *Women, Crime and Society*. London: Longmans.

Lerner, G. (1998) *The Creation of Patriarchy*. Oxford: Oxford University Press.

Lesser, M. (1980) *Nutrition and Vitamin Therapy*. New York: Bantam.

Lever, J. (1978) 'Sex Differences in the Complexity of Children's Play and Games', *American Sociological Review*, 43: 476–88.

Levin, J. and McDevitt, J. (1993) *Hate Crimes: The Rising Tide of Bigotry and Bloodshed*. Boston, MA: Plenum.

Levine, N. (1999) *CrimeStat: A Spatial Statistics Program for the Analysis of Crime Incident Locations*. Washington, DC: Ned Levine & Associates/National Institute of Justice.

Levitas, R. (1996) 'The Concept of Social Exclusion and the New Durkheimian Hegemony', *Critical Social Policy*, 16(1): 5–20.

Li, L., and Moore, D. (2001) 'Disability and Illicit Drug Use: An Application of Labeling Theory', *Deviant Behavior: An Interdisciplinary Journal*, 22: 1–21.

Liazos, A. (1972) 'The Poverty of the Sociology of Deviance: Nuts, Sluts and Perverts', *Social Problems*, 20: 103–20.

Lilly, J.R., Cullen, F.T. and Ball, R.A. (1986) *Criminological Theory: Context and Consequences*. London: Sage.

Lindqvist, P. (1986) 'Criminal Homicide in Northern Sweden, 1970–1981 – Alcohol Intoxication, Alcohol Abuse and Mental Disease', *International Journal of Law and Psychiatry*, 8: 19–37.

Link, B. (1987) 'Understanding Labelling Effects of Mental Disorders: An Assessment of the Effects of Expectations of Rejection', *American Sociological Review*, 54: 395–410.

Link, B., Cullen, F., Frank, J. and Wozniak, J. (1987) 'The Social Reaction of Former Mental Patients: Understanding Why Labels Work', *American Journal of Sociology*, 92: 145–67.

Link, B., Cullen, F., Struening, E., Shrout, P. and Dohrenwend, B. (1989) 'A Modified Labelling Theory Approach to Mental Disorders: An Empirical Assessment', *American Sociological Review*, 54: 400.

Liska, A.E. (1987) *Perspectives on Deviance*. Englewood Cliffs, NJ: Prentice-Hall.

Liska, A. (ed.) (1992) *Social Threat and Social Control*. Albany, NY: SUNY Press.

Liska, A.E., Krohn, M.D. and Messner, S.F. (1989) 'Strategies and Requisites for Theoretical Integration in the Study of Crime and Deviance', in S.F. Messner, M.D. Krohn and A.E. Liska (eds) *Theoretical Integration in the Study of Deviance and Crime*. Albany, NY: University of New York.

Little, A. (1963) 'Professor Eysenck's Theory of Crime: An Empirical Test on Adolescent Offenders', *British Journal of Criminology*, 4: 152.

Locke, J. (1970 originally 1686) *Two Treatise of Government*, edited by P. Laslett. Cambridge: Cambridge University Press.

Locke, J. (1975 originally 1689) *An Essay Concerning Human Understanding*, edited by P.M. Nidditch. Oxford: Clarendon Press.

Loeber, R. and Dishion, T. (1983) 'Early Predictors of Male Delinquency: A Review', *Psychological Bulletin*, 94(1): 68–91.

Lofland, L.H. (1973) *A World of Strangers: Order and Action in Urban Public Space*. New York: Basic Books.

Lombroso, C. (1875) *L'uomo delinquente (The Criminal Man)*. Milan: Hoepli.

Lombroso, C. (1920) *The Female Offender*. New York: Appleton.

Lombroso, C. and Ferrero, W. (1885) *The Female Offender*. London: Unwin.

Luckhaus, L. (1985) 'A Plea for PMT in the Criminal Law', in S. Edwards (ed.) *Gender, Sex and the Law*. London: Croom Helm.

Lukacs, G. (1970) *Writer and Critic*. London: Merlin Press.

Lyng, S. (1990) 'Edgework: A Social Psychological Analysis of Voluntary Risk Taking', *American Journal of Sociology*, 95: 851–86.

Lyons, J. (2005) *Troubled Inside: Meeting the Mental Health Needs of Men in Prison*, Press Release. London: Prison Reform Trust.

Lyotard, J.-F. (1984) *The Post-Modern Condition: A Report on Knowledge*. Manchester: Manchester University Press.

Lyotard, J-F. (1988) *The Differend*. Minneapolis, MN: University of Minnesota Press.

McBride, D. and McCoy, C. (1982) 'Crime and Drugs: The Issues and Literature', *Journal of Drug Issues*, Spring: 128–143.

McBurnett, K., Lahey, B., Rathouz, P. and Loeber, R. (2000) 'Low Salivary Cortisol and Persistent Aggression in Boys Referred for Disruptive Behaviour', *Archives of General Psychiatry*, 57: 38–43.

McCarthy, B., Hagan, J. and Woodward, T. (1999) 'In the Company of Women: Structure and Agency in a Revised Power-Control Theory of Gender and Delinquency', *Criminology*, 37: 761–88.

McCord, W. and McCord, J. (1964) *The Psychopath: An Essay on the Criminal Mind*. New York: Van Nostrand Reinhold.

McCord, W., McCord, J. and Zola, I.K. (1959) *Origins of Crime: A New Evaluation of the Cambridge-Somerville Youth Study*. New York: Columbia University Press.

McCormack, A., Janus, M. and Burgess, A.W. (1986) 'Runaway Youths and Sexual Victimisation: Gender Differences in an Adolescent Runaway Population', *Child Abuse and Neglect*, 10: 387–95.

McEwan, A.W. (1983) 'Eysenck's Theory of Criminality and the Personality Types and Offences of Young Delinquents', *Personality and Individual Differences*, 4: 201–4.

McEwan, A.W. and Knowles, C. (1984) 'Delinquent Personality Types and the Situational Contexts of their Crimes', *Personality and Individual Differences*, 5: 339–44.

McGurk, B.J. and McDougall, C. (1981) 'A New Approach to Eysenck's Theory of Criminality', *Personality and Individual Differences*, 13: 338–40.

McRobbie, A. and Thornton, S. (1995) 'Rethinking "Moral Panic" for Multi-mediated Social Worlds', *British Journal of Sociology*, 46(4): 559–74.

Maguire, J. (2001) *Cognitive Behavioural Approaches: An Introduction to Theory and Research*. London: Her Majesty's Inspectorate of Probation, Home Office.

Maier-Katkin, D. and Ogle, R. (1993) 'A Rationale for Infanticide Laws', *Criminal Law Review*, 903.

Mann, C.R. (1984) *Female Crime and Delinquency*. Birmingham, AL: University of Alabama Press.

Mannheim, H. (1948) *Juvenile Delinquency in an English Middletown*. London: Kegan Paul, Turner, Trubner and Co Ltd.

Mannheim, H. (1955) *Group Problems in Crime and Punishment*. London: Routledge & Kegan Paul.

Mannuzza, S. Klein, R., Konig, P. and Giampino, T. (1989) 'Hyperactive Boys Almost Grown Up: IV. Criminality and its Relation to Psychiatric Status', *Archives of General Psychiatry*, 46: 1073–79.

Marcuse, H. (1964) *One Dimensional Man*. Boston, MA: Beacon.

Marfleet, P. and Kiely, R. (1998) *Globalisation and the Third World*. New York: Routledge.

Mark, V.H. and Ervin, F.R. (1970) *Violence and the Brain*. New York: Harper Row.

Marks, M.N. and Kumar, R. (1993) 'Infanticide in England and Wales', *Medicine Science and the Law*, 33: 324–38.

Markus, M. (2000) 'A Scientist's Adventures in Postmodernism', *Leonardo* 33(3): 179–186.

Mars, G. (1982) *Cheats at Work: An Anthology of Workplace Crime*. London: George Allen and Unwin.

Marsh, P. (1978) *Aggro: The Illusion of Violence*. London: Dent.

Marshall, G., Roberts, S. and Burgoyne, C. (1996) 'Social Class and the Underclass in Britain and the USA', *British Journal of Sociology*, 47(10): 22–44.

Martin, G. and Pear, J. (1992) *Behaviour Modification: What It Is and How to Do It*, 4th edition. Englewood Cliffs, NJ, Prentice-Hall.

Martin, J. (1981) 'A Longitudinal Study of the Consequences of Early Mother–Infant Interaction: A Microanalytic approach', *Monographs of the Society for Research in Child Development*, 190: 46.

Martin, J-P. and Schumann, H. (1997) *The Global Trap: Globalization and the Assault on Democracy and Prosperity*. London: Zed Books.

Martin, J.P. and Webster, D. (1971) *The Social Consequences of Conviction*. London: Heinemann.

Martinson, R. (1974) 'What Works? – Questions and Answers About Prison Reform', *The Public Interest*, 35: 22–54.

Matsueda, R.L. (1992) 'Reflected Appraisals, Parental Labeling, and Delinquency: Specifying a Symbolic Interactionist Theory', *The American Journal of Sociology*, 97(6): 1577–611.

Marx, K. (1859) *Critique of Political Economy*. New York: International Library.

Marx, K. (1867) *Capital*. London: Lawrence & Wishart.

Matravers, M. (ed.) (1999) *Punishment and Political Theory*. Oxford: Hart Publishing.

Matthews, R. (1992) 'Replacing "Broken Windows": Crime, Incivilities and Urban Change', in R. Matthews and J. Young (eds) (1992) *Issues in Realist Criminology*. London: Sage.

Matthews, R. (1996) *Armed Robbery: Police Responses*, Crime Detection and Prevention Series, Paper 78. London: Home Office, Police Research Group.

Matthews, R. and Young, J. (eds) (1986) *Confronting Crime*. London: Sage.

Matthews, R. and Young, J. (eds) (1992) *Issues in Realist Criminology*. London: Sage.

Matza, D.M. (1964) *Delinquency and Drift*. New York: Wiley.

Matza, D.M. (1969) *Becoming Deviant*. Englewood Cliffs, NJ: Prentice Hall.

Maxson, C.L. and Klein, M.W. (1990) 'Street Gang Violence: Twice as Great or Half as Great?' in C.R. Huff (ed.) *Gangs in America*. Newbury Park, CA: Sage.

Maxwell, G. and Morris, A. (2001) 'Putting Restorative Justice Into Practice for Adult Offenders', *Howard Journal of Criminal Justice*, 40: 46–58.

Mayhew, H. (1968 originally 1862) *London Labour and the London Poor, Vol. IV: Those That Will Not Work, Comprising Prostitutes, Thieves, Swindlers and Beggars*. New York: Dover Publications.

Mayhew, P. (1984) 'Target-Hardening: How Much of an Answer?', in R.V.G Clarke and T. Hope (eds) *Coping Burglary*. Boston, MA: Kluwer-Nighoff.

Mayhew, P., Clarke, R.V.G., Sturman, A. and Hough, J.M. (1976) *Crime as Opportunity*. London: HMSO.

Mays, J.B. (1954) *Growing Up in the City: A Study of Juvenile Delinquency in an Urban Neighbourhood*. Liverpool: Liverpool University Press.

Mazor, L.J. (1978) 'Disrespect for Law' in R.J. Pennock and J.W. Chapman (eds) *Anarchism*. New York: New York University.

Mazur, A. (1998) *A Hazardous Inquiry: The Rashemon Effect at Love Canal*. Cambridge, MA: Harvard University Press.

Mead, G. (1934) *Mind, Self and Society*. Chicago, IL: University of Chicago Press.

Mednick, S.A. (1977) 'A Biosocial Theory of the Learning of Law-Abiding Behavior', in S.A. Mednick and K.O Christiansen (eds) *Biosocial Bases of Criminal Behavior*. New York: Gardner.

Mednick, S.A., Pollock, V. Volavka, J. and Gabrielli, W.F. (1982) 'Biology and Violence', in M.E. Wolfgang and N.A. Weiner (eds) *Criminal Violence*. Beverly Hills, CA: Sage.

Mednick, S.A., Gabrielli, T., William, F. and Hutchings, B. (1984), 'Genetic Influences on Criminal Convictions: Evidence from an Adoption Cohort', *Science*, 224.

Mednick, S.A., Moffit, T.E. and Stack, S. (eds) (1987) *The Causes of Crime: New Biological Approaches*. Cambridge: Cambridge University Press.

Mednick, S.A. and Volavka, J. (1980) 'Biology and Crime', in N. Morris and M. Tonry (eds) *Crime and Justice: An Annual Review of Research*, Vol. 2. Chicago, IL: University of Chicago Press.

Mehanna, A. R. (2004) 'Poverty and Economic Development: Not as Direct as it May Seem', *Journal of Socio-Economics*, 33(1): 76–89.

Menard, S. and Morse, B. (1984) 'A Structuralist Critique of the IQ-Delinquency Hypothesis: Theory and Evidence', *American Journal of Sociology*, 89: 1347–78.

Meossi, D. (2000) 'Changing Representations of the Criminal', *British Journal of Criminology*, 40: 290–305.

Merari, A. (1990) 'The Readiness to Kill and Die: Suicidal Terrorism in the Middle East' in W. Reich (ed.) *Origins of Terrorism*. Cambridge: Cambridge University Press.

Merry, S.E. (1981) 'Defensible Space Undefended', *Urban Affairs Quarterly*, 16: 397–422.

Merton, R.K. (1938) 'Social Structure and Anomie', *American Sociological Review*, 3: 672–82.

Merton, R.K. (1957) *Social Theory and Social Structure*. New York: The Free Press.

Merton, R.K. (1966) 'Social Problems and Sociological Theory', in R.K. Merton and R. Nisbet (eds) *Contemporary Social Problems*. New York: Harcourt Brace Jovanovich.

Mesibov, G., Shea, V. and Adams, L. (2001) *Understanding Asperger's Syndrome and High Functioning Autism*. New York: Kluwer Academic/Plenum Publishers.

Messerschmidt, J.W. (1986) *Capitalism, Patriarchy and Crime: Toward a Socialist Feminist Criminology*. Totowa, NJ: Rowman and Littlefield.

Messerschmidt, J.W. (1993) *Masculinities and Crime*. Lanham, MD: Rowman and Littlefield.

Messerschmidt, J.W. (2004) *Flesh and Blood: Adolescent Gender Diversity and Violence*. Lanham, MD.: Rowman and Littlefield.

Messerschmidt, J.W. (2005) 'Masculinities and Crime: Beyond a Dualist Criminology', in C. Renzetti, L. Goodstein, and S. Miller (eds) *Gender, Crime, and Criminal Justice: Original Feminist Readings*. Los Angeles, CA: Roxbury.

Messner, S. and Rosenfeld, R. (1994) *Crime and the American Dream*. Belmont, CA: Wadsworth.

Mill, J.S. (1963–84 originally 1859) *The Collected Works of John Stuart Mill*, edited by F.E.L. Priestly. Toronto, ON: University of Toronto Press.

Miller, E.M. (1986) *Street Women*. Philadelphia, PA: Temple University Press.

Miller, J. (2001) *One of the Guys: Girls, Gangs, and Gender*. New York: Oxford University Press.

Miller, J. (2002) 'The Strengths and Limits of "Doing Gender" for Understanding Street Crime', *Theoretical Criminology*, 6(4): 433–60.

Miller, W.B. (1958) 'Lower Class Culture as a Generalising Milieu of Gang Delinquency', *Journal of Social Issues*, 14: 5–19.

Miller, W.B. (1990) 'When the United States Has Failed to Solve its Youth Gang Problem', in C.R. Huff (ed.) *Gangs in America*. Newbury Park, CA: Sage.

Miller, W. (1999) *Cops and Bobbies, 2nd edition*. Columbus, OH: Ohio State University Press.

Millett, K. (1970) *Sexual Politics*. New York: Doubleday and Company.

Mills, C.W. (1956) *The Power Elite*. New York: Oxford University Press.

Milovanovic, D. (ed.) (1997a) *Chaos, Criminology, and Social Justice: the New Orderly (Dis) Order*. Westport, CT: Praeger.

Milovanovic, D. (1997b) *Postmodern Criminology*. New York: Garland Publishing.

Mind (2004) *Understanding Psychotic Experiences*. London: Mind.

Mind (2006) *Statistics 8: The Criminal Justice System*. London: Mind.

Mirrlees-Black, C. (1999) *Domestic Violence: Findings from a New British Crime Survey Self-completion Questionnaire*. London: HMSO.

Mirrlees-Black, C., Mayhew, P. and Percy, A. (1996) *The 1996 British Crime Survey*, Home Office Statistical Bulletin 19/96. London: Home Office.

Moffitt, T.E. (1993a) 'Adolescent-Limited and Life-Course-Persistent Antisocial Behavior: A Developmental Taxonomy', *Psychological Review*, 100: 674–701.

Moffitt, T.E. (1993b) 'The Neuropsychology of Conduct Disorder', *Development and Psychopathology*, 5: 135–51.

Monahan, T.P. (1957) 'Family Status and the Delinquent Child: A Reappraisal and Some New Findings', *New Forces*, 35: 250–66.

Monahan, J. (1981) *Predicting Violent Behaviour*. Beverly Hills, CA: Sage.

Money, J. and Ernhardt, A.A. (1972) *Man and Woman: Boy and Girl*. Baltimore, MD: John Hopkins University Press.

Mooney, J. (2000) *Gender, Violence and the Social Order*. London: Macmillan.

Moore, J.W. (1991) *Going Down to the Barrio*. Philadelphia, PA: Temple University Press.

Morash, M. and Rucker, L. (1989) 'An Exploratory Study of the Connection of Mother's Age at Childbearing to her Children's Delinquency in Four Data Sets', *Crime and Delinquency*, 35: 45–58.

Morgan, P. (1975) *Child Care: Sense and Fable*. London: Temple Smith.

Morgan, P. (1978) *Delinquent Fantasies*. London: Temple Smith.

Morgan, R. and Newburn, I. (1997) *The Future of Policing*. Oxford: Clarendon Press.

Morris, A. (1987) *Women, Crime and Criminal Justice*. Oxford: Blackwell.

Morris, A., Maxwell, G.M. and Robertson, J.P. (1993) 'Giving Victims a Voice: A New Zealand Experiment', *Howard Journal of Criminal Justice*, 32: 304.

Morris, R. (1964) 'Female Delinquency and Relational Problems', *Social Forces*, 43: 82–8.

Morris, R. (1965) 'Attitudes to Delinquency by Delinquents, Non-Delinquents and Their Friends', *British Journal of Criminology*, 5: 249–65.

Morris, T. and Blom-Cooper, L. (1979) *Murder in England and Wales Since 1957*, The Observer.

Morris, T.P. (1957) *The Criminal Area: A Study in Social Ecology*. London: Routledge & Kegan Paul.

Morrison, W. (1995) *Theoretical Criminology: From Modernity to Post-modernity*. London: Cavendish.

Mott, J. (1990) *Young People, Alcohol and Crime*, Home Office Research Bulletin (Research and Statistics Department), 28: 24–8.

Muggleton, D. (1997) 'The Post-Subculturalist', in S. Redhead (ed.) *The Clubcultures Reader: An Introduction to Popular Cultural Studies*. Malden, MA: Blackwell.

Muggleton, D. (2000) *Inside Subculture: The Postmodern Meaning of Style*. New York: Berg.

Mukjurkee, S.K. and Fitzgerald, M.K. (1981) 'The Myth of Rising Crime', in S.K. Mukjurkee and J.A. Scutt (eds) *Women and Crime*. London: Allen & Unwin.

Muller, E. and Opp, K-D. (1986) 'Rational Choice and Rebellious Collective Action', *American Political Science Review*, 80: 471–87.

Muncie, J. (1998) 'Deconstructing Criminology', *Criminal Justice Matters*, (34): 4–5.

Muncie, J. (1999) *Youth Crime: A Critical Introduction*. London: Sage.

Muncie, J. (2000) 'Decriminalising Criminology', *British Criminology Conference: Selected Proceedings*, Vol. 3.

Muncie, J. and McLaughlin, E. (1996) *The Problem of Crime*. London: Sage/Open University.

Murray, A.T., McGuffog, I., Western, J.S. and Mullins, P. (2001) 'Exploratory Spatial Data Analysis Techniques for Examining Urban Crime', *British Journal of Criminology*, 41: 309–29.

Murray, C. (ed.) (1990) *The Emerging British Underclass*. London: Institute of Economic Affairs Health and Welfare Unit.

Murray, C. (1994) *Underclass: The Crisis Deepens*. London: Institute of Economic Affairs.

Nacro (2003) *Some Facts About Young People Who Offend – 2001*, Nacro Youth Crime Briefing. London: Nacro.

Naess, S. (1959) 'Mother–Child Separation and Delinquency', *British Journal of Delinquency*, 10: 22.

Naess, S. (1962) 'Mother–Child Separation and Delinquency: Further Evidence', *British Journal of Criminology*, 2: 361.

Naffine, N. (1987) *Female Crime*. Sydney: Allen and Unwin.

Nassar, J. (2004) *Globalization and Terrorism*. Lanham, MD: Rowman and Littlefield.

National Autistic Society (2005) *Autism: A Guide for Criminal Justice Professionals* [Online]. Available at: http://www.nas.org.uk/content/1/c4/80/67/cjp_guide.pdf [accessed 6 January 2009].

Platt, A.M. (1969) *The Child Savers: The Invention of Delinquency*. Chicago, IL: University of Chicago Press.

Platt, T. (1974) 'Prospects for a Radical Criminology in the U.S', *Crime and Social Justice*, 1: 2–10.

Plint T. (1851) *Crime in England*. London: Charles Gilpin.

Plummer, K. (1975) *Sexual Stigma*. London: Routledge & Kegan Paul.

Plummer, K. (1979) 'Misunderstanding Labelling Perspectives', in D. Downes and P. Rock (eds) *Deviant Interpretations*. London: Martin Robertson.

Pollak, O. (1950) *The Criminality of Women*. New York: Barnes.

Poulantzas, N. (1969) 'The Problems of the Capitalist State', *New Left Review*, 58: 67–78.

Pratt, J. (1999) 'Governmentality, Neo-Liberalism and Dangerousness', in R. Smandych (ed.) *Governable Places: Readings on Governmentality and Crime Control*. Dartmouth: Ashgate.

Presdee, M. (1994) 'Young People, Culture and the Construction of Crime: Doing Wrong Versus Doing Crime', in G. Barak (ed.) *Varieties of Criminology*. Westport, CT: Praeger.

Presdee, M. (2000) *Cultural Criminology and the Carnival of Crime*. London: Routledge.

Presdee, M. (2004) 'Cultural criminology: The Long and Winding Road', *Theoretical Criminology*, 8(3): 275–85.

Price, W.H. and Whatmore, P.B. (1967) 'Behaviour Disorders and Patterns of Crime Among XYY Males Identified at a Maximum Security Hospital', *British Medical Journal*, 1: 533.

Prinz, R.J., Roberts, W.A. and Hantman, E. (1980) 'Dietary Correlates of Hyperactive Behaviour in Children', *Journal of Consulting and Clinical Psychology*, 48: 760–85.

Prison Reform Trust (2002) *The Prisons League Table 2000–1: Performance Against Key Indicators*. London: Prison Reform Trust.

Prison Reform Trust (2004) *England and Wales – Western Europe's Jail Capital*, Press Release, 2nd February.

Pryce, K. (1979) *Endless Pressure: A Study of West Indian Life-styles in Bristol*. Harmondsworth: Penguin.

Quételet, M.A. (1842) *A Treatise on Man*. Edinburgh: William and Robert Chalmers.

Quinney, R. (1965) 'A Conception of Man and Society for Criminology', *Sociological Quarterly*, 6: 119–27.

Quinney, R. (1970) *The Social Reality of Crime*. Boston, MA: Little, Brown.

Quinney, R. (1974) *Critique of Legal Order*. Boston, MA: Little, Brown.

Quinney, R. (1977) *Class, State and Crime*. New York: David McKay.

Rada, R. (1975) 'Alcoholism and Forcible Rape', *American Journal of Psychiatry*, 132: 444–46.

Radzinowicz, L. (1948–86) *A History of English Criminal Law and its Administration from 1750*, (5 volumes): i) (1948) *The Movement for Reform*; ii) (1956) *The Clash Between Private Initiative and Public Interest in the Enforcement of the Law*; iii) (1956) *Cross Currents in the Movement of the Reform of the Police*; iv) (1968) *Grappling for Control*; v) (with R. Hood, 1986) *The Emergence of Penal Policy in Victorian and Edwardian England*. London: Stevens and Sons.

Rafter, N.H. and Heidensohn, F. (eds) (1985) *International Feminist Perspectives: Engendering a Discipline*. Buckingham: Open University Press.

Raine, A. (2002) 'Biosocial Studies of Antisocial and Violent Behavior in Children and Adults: A Review', *Journal of Abnormal Child Psychology*, 30(4): 311–26.

Raine, A., Brennan, P., and Mednick, S. (1994) 'Birth Complications Combined with Early Maternal Rejections at Age 1 Year Predispose to Violent Crime at Age 18 years', *Archives of General Psychiatry*, 51: 984–8.

Raine, A., Brennan, P., and Mednick, S. (1997) 'Interaction Between Birth Complications and Early Maternal Rejection in Predisposing Individuals to Adult Violence: Specificity to Serious, Early-Onset Violence', *American Journal of Psychiatry*, 154(9): 1265–71.

Raine, A., Lencz, T., Bihrle, S., LaCasse, L. and Colletti, P. (2000) 'Reduced Pre-Frontal Gray Matter Volume and Reduced Autonomic Activity in Antisocial Personality Disorder', *Archives of General Psychiatry*, 57: 119–27.

Raloff, J. (1983) 'Locks – A Key to Violence', *Science News*, 124: 122–36.

Ramsay, M. (1996) *The Relationship Between Alcohol and Crime*, Home Office Research Bulletin 38: 37–44. London: Home Office.

Rantakallio, P., Koiranen, M., and Moettoenen, J. (1992) 'Association of Perinatal Events, Epilepsy, and Central Nervous System Trauma with Juvenile Delinquency', *Archives of Disease in Childhood*, 67: 1459–61.

Ratcliffe, J.H. and McCullagh, M.J. (1999) 'Hotbeds of Crime and the Search for Spatial Accuracy', *Journal of Geographical Systems*, 1: 385–98.

Raymond, G. J. (2002) 'A Comparative Study of Women Trafficked in the Migration Process: Patterns, Profiles and Health Consequences of Sexual Exploitation in Five Countries'. New York: United Nations Convention Against Transnational Organized Crime.

Reckless, W. (1961) *The Crime Problem, 3rd edition*. New York: Appleton Century Crofts.

Reckless, W. (1967) *The Crime Problem, 4th edition*. New York: Appleton Century Crofts.

Redhead, S. (1990) *The End-of-the-Century Party: Youth and Pop Towards 2000*. New York: St Martin's Press.

Redl, F. and Wineman, D. (1951) *Children Who Hate*. New York: Free Press.

Regoli, R. and Hewitt, J. (1994) *Delinquency in Society, 2nd edition*. Boston, MA: McGraw Hill.

Reiman, J. (1979) *The Rich Get Richer and the Poor Get Prison*. New York: John Wiley.

Reiman, J., and Headlee, S. (1981) 'Marxism and Criminal Justice Policy', *Crime and Delinquency*, 27: 24–47.

Reiner, R. (2000) 'Crime and Control in Britain', *Sociology*, 34(1): 71–94.

Reiss, A.J. (1951) 'Delinquency as the Failure of Personal and Social Controls', *American Sociological Review*, 16: 213–39.

Reiss, A.J. (1960) 'Sex Offences: The Marginal Status of the Adolescent', *Law and Contemporary Problems*, 25: 302–23.

Reith, C. (1956) *A New Study of Police History*. London: Oliver and Boyd.

Rex, J. and Moore, R. (1967) *Race, Community and Conflict: A Study in Sparkbrook*. London: Institute of Race Relations/OUP.

Rhodes, R.A.W. (1997) *Understanding Governance: Policy Networks, Governance, Reflexivity and Accountability*. Buckingham: Open University Press.

Robins, L.N. (1966) *Deviant Children Grown Up*. Baltimore, MD: Williams and Wilkins.

Robinson, M.B. and Zaitzow, B.H. (1999) 'Criminologists: Are We What We Study? A National Self-Report Study of Crime Experts', *The Criminologist*, 24(2): 17–19.

Rock, P. (1973) *Deviant Behaviour*. London: Hutchinson.

Rosaler, M. (2004) *Coping with Asperger's Syndrome*. New York: The Rosen Publishing Group.

Rose, N. (1999) *Powers of Freedom: Reframing Political Thought.* Cambridge: Cambridge University Press.

Rose, N. (2000) 'The Biology of Culpability: Pathological Identity and Crime Control in Biological Culture', *Theoretical Criminology*, 4(1): 4–19.

Rose, R.M., Bernstein, I.S., Gorden, T.P. and Catlin, S.E. (1974) 'Androgens and Aggression: A Review and Recent Findings in Primates', in R.L. Holloway (ed.), *Primate Aggression: Territoriality and Xenophobia.* New York: Academia Press.

Rose, R.M., Holoday, J.W. and Bernstein, S. (1971) 'Plasma Testosterone, Dominance, Rank and Aggressive Behaviour in Male Rhesus Monkeys', *Nature*, 231: 366–8.

Rosenau, P.-M. (1992) *Post-Modernism and the Social Sciences: Insights, Inroads and Intrusions.* Princeton, NJ: Princeton University Press.

Ross, J.I. (1996) 'A Model of the Psychological Causes of Oppositional Political Terrorism', *Peace and Conflict: Journal of Peace Psychology*, 2–11.

Ross, J. I. (1999) 'Beyond the Conceptualization of Terrorism: A Psychological-Structural Model' in C. Summers and E. Mardusen (eds.) *Collective Violence.* New York: Rowen and Littlefield.

Ross, P. (2003) 'Marxism and Communitarianism', *Imprints*, 6(3): 215–43.

Rousseau, J. (1964 originally 1762) *First and Second Discourses*, edited by R.D. Masters. New York: St Martin's.

Rousseau, J. (1978 originally 1775) *The Social Contract*, edited by R.D. Masters. New York: St Martin's.

Rowe, D.C. (1990) 'Inherited Dispositions toward Learning Delinquent and Criminal Behaviour: New Evidence', in L. Ellis and H. Hoffman (eds) *Crime in Biological, Social and Moral Contexts.* New York: Praeger.

Rowe, D.C. and Rogers, J.L. (1989) 'Behaviour Genetics, Adolescent Deviance, and "d": Contributions and Issues', in G.R. Adams, R. Montemayor and T.P. Gullotta (eds) *Advances in Adolescent Development.* Newbury Park, CA: Sage.

Ruggiero, V. (1997) 'Trafficking in Human Beings: Slaves in Contemporary Europe', *International Journal of the Sociology of Law*, 25(3): 231–44.

Ruggiero, V. (2000) *Crimes and Markets: Essays in Anti-Criminology.* Oxford: Oxford University Press.

Ruggiero, V. (2005) 'Political Violence: A Criminological Analysis', in M. Natarajan (ed.) *Introduction to International Criminal Justice.* New York: McGraw Hill.

Ruggiero, V. and South, N. (1995) *Eurodrugs: Drug Use, Marketing and Trafficking in Europe.* London: University College London.

Rumbelow, D. (1987) *The Complete Jack Ripper.* London: Star Books.

Rusche, G. and Kirchheimer, O. (1939) *Punishment and Social Structure.* New York: Russell & Russell.

Russell, C. and Bowman, M. (1977) 'Profile of a Terrorist', *Terrorism: An International Journal*, 1(1): 17–34.

Russell, S. (2006) 'The Continuing Relevance of Marxism to Critical Criminology', *Critical Criminology*, 11(2): 113–35.

Rutherford, A. (1992) *Growing Out of Crime, 2nd edition.* London: Waterside Press.

Rutter, M. (1981) *Maternal Deprivation Reassessed.* Harmondsworth: Penguin.

Rutter, M., Cox, A., Tupling, C., Berger, M. and Yule, W. (1975a) 'Attainment and Adjustment in Two Geographical Areas: 1. The Prevalence of Psychiatric Disorder', *British Journal of Psychiatry*, 126: 493–509.

Rutter, M., Yule, B., Quinton, D., Rowlands, O., Yule, W. and Berger, W. (1975b) 'Attainment and Adjustment in Two Geographical Areas: 3. Some Factors Accounting for Area Differences', *British Journal of Psychiatry*, 126: 520–33.

Ryan, K. and Ferrell, J. (1986) 'Knowledge, Power, and the Process of Justice', *Crime and Social Justice*, 25: 178–95.

Sameroff, A., Seifer, R., Zax, M. and Barocas, R. (1987) 'Early Indicators of Developmental Risk: The Rochester Longitudinal Study', *Schizophrenia Bulletin*, 13: 383–94.

Sanson, A., Oberklaid, F., Pedlow, R., and Prior, M. (1991) 'Risk Indicators: Assessment of Infancy Predictors of Pre-school Behavioural Maladjustment', *Journal of Child Psychology and Psychiatry*, 32(4): 609–26.

Saunders, W. (1984) *Alcohol Use in Britain; How Much is Too Much?* Edinburgh: Scottish Health Education Unit.

Scarmella, T.J. and Brown, W.A. (1978) 'Serum Testosterone and Aggressiveness in Hockey Players', *Psychosomatic Medicine*, 40: 262–75.

Schalling, D. (1987) 'Personality Correlates of Plasma Testosterone Levels in Young Delinquents: An Example of Person-Situation Interaction', in S.A. Mednick, T.E. Moffit and S.A. Stack (eds) *The Causes of Crime: New Biological Approaches*. Cambridge: Cambridge University Press.

Scheff, T. and Retzinger, S. (1991) *Emotions and Violence: Shame and Rage in Destructive Conflicts*. Lexington, VA: Lexington Books.

Schlapp, M.G. and Smith, E. (1928) *The New Criminology*. New York: Boni and Liveright.

Schlossman, S., Zellman, G. and Shavelson, R. (1984) *Delinquency Prevention in South Chicago: A Fifty-Year Assessment of the Chicago Area Project*. Santa Monica, CA: Rand.

Schraeger, L.S. and Short, J.F. (1978) 'Towards a Sociology of Organisational Crime', *Social Problems*, 25: 407–19.

Schur, E. (1971) *Labelling Deviant Behaviour: Its Sociological Implications*. New York: Harper and Row.

Schutz, A. (1962) *The Problem of Social Reality*. The Hague: Martinus Nijhoff.

Schwaner, S. (2000) '"Stick'em Up, Buddy": Robbery, Lifestyle, and Specialization within a Cohort of Parolees', *Journal of Criminal Justice*, 28: 371–84.

Schwatz, M.D. and DeKeseredy, W.S. (1991) 'Left Realist Criminology: Strengths, Weaknesses and the Feminist Critique', *Crime, Law and Social Change*, 15: 51.

Schwendinger, H. and Schwendinger, J. (1970) 'Defenders of Order or Guardians of Human Rights', *Issues in Criminology*, 7: 72–81.

Scraton, P. (1985) *The State of the Police*. London: Pluto.

Scraton, P. and Chadwick, K. (1996 originally 1992) 'The Theoretical Priorities of Critical Criminology', in J. Muncie, E. McLaughlin, and M. Langan (eds) *Criminological Perspectives: A Reader*. London: Sage.

Scruton, R. (1980) *The Meaning of Conservatism*. Harmondsworth: Pelican.

Scruton, R. (1985) *Thinkers of the New Left*. London: Longman.

Scruton, R. (2001) *The Meaning of Conservatism, 3rd edition*. Houndmills: Palgrave.

Scull, A. (1977) *Decarceration*. Englewood Cliffs, NJ: Prentice-Hall.

Segal, L. (1990) *Slow Motion: Changing Masculinities, Changing Men*. London: Virago.

Sellin, T. (1938) *Culture, Conflict and Crime*. New York: Social Research Council.

Sellin, T. (1959) *The Death Penalty*. Philadelphia, PA: American Law Institute.

Sellin, T. (1973) 'Enrico Ferri' in H. Mannheim (ed.) *Pioneers in Criminology, 2nd edition*. Montclair, NJ: Patterson-Smith.

Shah, S.A. and Roth, L.H. (1974) 'Biological and Psychophysiological Factors in Criminality', in D. Glaser (ed.) *Handbook of Criminology*. London: Rand McNally.

Shaw, C.R. (1930) *The Jack-Roller: A Delinquent Boy's Own Story*. Chicago, IL: University of Chicago Press.

Shaw, C.R. (1931) *The Natural History of a Delinquent Career*. Chicago, IL: University of Chicago Press.

Shaw, C.R. (1938) *Brothers in Crime*. Chicago, IL: University of Chicago Press.

Shaw, C.R. and McKay, H.D. (1972 originally 1931) *Juvenile Delinquency and Urban Areas*. Chicago, IL: University of Chicago Press.

Shaw, D.S., Keenan, K., and Vondra, J.I. (1994a) 'Developmental Precursors of Externalizing Behavior: Ages 1 to 3', *Developmental Psychology*, 30(3): 355–64.

Shaw, D.S., Vondra, J.I., Hommerding, K., Keenan, K. and Dunn, M. (1994b) 'Chronic Family Adversity and Early Child Behavior Problems: A Longitudinal Study of Low Income Families', *Journal of Child Psychology and Psychiatry*, 35(6): 1109–22.

Shaw, D., Winslow, E., Owens, E., and Hood, N. (1998a) 'Young Children's Adjustment to Chronic Family Adversity: A Longitudinal Study of Low-Income Families', *Journal of the American Academy of Child and Adolescent Psychiatry*, 37(5): 545–53.

Shaw, D., Winslow, E., Owens, E., Vondra, J., Cohn, J., and Bell, R. (1998b) 'The Development of Early Externalizing Problems Among Children from Low-Income Families: A Transformational Perspective', *Journal of Abnormal Child Psychology*, 26(2): 95–107.

Shaw, D.S., Ingoldsby, E., Gilliom, M. and Nagin, D. (2003) 'Trajectories Leading to School-Age Conduct Problems', *Developmental Psychology*, 38, 480–91.

Shearing, C. (1989) 'Decriminalising Criminology', *Canadian Journal of Criminology*, 31(2): 169–78.

Sheldon, B. (1995) *Cognitive-Behavioural Therapy: Research, Practice and Philosophy*. London: Routledge.

Sheldon, W.H. (1949) *Varieties of Delinquent Youth*. London: Harper.

Shelley, L. (1998) 'Crime and Corruption in the Digital Age', *Journal Of International Affairs*, 51(2): 605–20.

Sherman, L., Gartin, P. and Buerger, M. (1989) 'Hot Spots of Predatory Crime: Routine Activities and the Criminology of Place', *Criminology*, 27: 27–55.

Shockley, W. (1967) 'A "Try Simplest Cases" Approach to the Heredity-Poverty-Crime Problem', *Proceedings of the National Academy of Sciences*, 57: 1767–74.

Shoenthaler, S.J. (1982) 'The Effects of Blood Sugar on the Treatment and Control of Antisocial Behaviour: A Double-Blind Study of an Incarcerated Juvenile Population', *International Journal for Biosocial Research*, 3: 1–15.

Shover, N., Norland, S., James, J. and Thornton, W. (1979) 'Gender Roles in Delinquency', *Social Forces*, 58: 158–71.

Sibbitt, R (1999) *The Perpetrators of Racial Harassment and Racial Violence*, Home Office Research Study 176. London: Home Office.

Sim, J., Scraton, P. and Gordon, P. (1987) 'Introduction: Crime, the State and Critical Analysis', in P. Scraton (ed.) *Law, Order and the Authoritarian State: Readings in Critical Criminology*. Milton Keynes: Open University Press.

Simmel, G. (1900) *The Philosophy of Money*. London: Routledge & Kegan Paul.

Simmel, G. (1906) 'The Sociology of Secrecy', *American Journal of Sociology*, 11: 441–98.

Simmel, G. (1908) *Conflict and the Web of Group Affiliations*. New York: Free Press.

Simon, J.K. (1991) 'Michel Foucault on Attica: An Interview', *Social Justice* 18: 26–34.

Simon, R.J. (1975) *Women and Crime*. London: Lexington Books.

Simons, G.L. and Stroup II, W.F. (1997) 'Law and Social Change: The Implications of Chaos Theory in Understanding the Role of the American Legal System', in D. Milovanovic (ed.) *Chaos, Criminology and Social Justice: The New Orderly (Dis) Order*. Westport, CT: Praeger.

Simpson, S.S. (1989) 'Feminist Theory, Crime and Justice', *Criminology*, 27: 605–27.

Simpson, S.S. (1991) 'Caste, Class and Violent Crime: Explaining Differences in Female Offending', *Criminology*, 29: 115–35.

Simpson, S.S., Lyn Exum, M. and Smith, N.C. (2000) 'The Social Control of Corporate Criminals: Shame and Informal Sanction Threats', in S.S. Simpson (ed.) *Of Crime and Criminality: The Use of Theory in Everyday Life*. Thousand Oaks, CA: Pine Forge Press.

Skinner, B.F. (1938) *The Behaviour of Organisms*. New York: Appleton-Century-Crofts.

Skinner, B.F. (1981) 'Selection by Consequences', *Science*, 213: 501–504.

Smart, C. (1977) *Women, Crime and Criminology*. London: Routledge & Kegan Paul.

Smart, C. (1981) 'Response to Greenwood', in A. Morris and L. Gelsthorpe (eds) *Women and Crime*. Cambridge: Cropwood Conference Series.

Smart, C. (1990) 'Feminist Approaches to Criminology; or Post-Modern Woman Meets Atavistic Man', in L. Gelsthorpe and A. Morris (eds) *Feminist Perspectives in Criminology*. Buckingham: Open University Press.

Smart, J. (1981) 'Undernutrition and Aggression', in P.F. Brain and D. Benton (eds) *Multidisciplinary Approaches to Aggression Research*. Amsterdam: Elsevier/North Holland.

Smith, A. (1910) *The Wealth of Nations*. London: Dent.

Smith, D. and Gray, J. (1986) *Police and People in London*. London: Policy Studies Institute.

Smith, D.E. and Smith, D.D. (1977) 'Eysenck's Psychoticism Scale and Reconviction', *British Journal of Criminology*, 17: 387.

Smith, G. (2004) 'What's Law Got to Do With It? Some Reflections on the Police in the Light of Developments in New York City', in R.D. Hopkins Burke (ed.) *Hard Cop, Soft Cop*. Cullompton: Willan Publishing.

Snyder, F. (2002) *Globalisation and Power Disparities*. London: Butterworths Lexis Nexis.

Sokal, A. and Bricmont, J. (1999) *Intellectual Impostures*. London: Profile Books.

Spalek, B. (2004) 'Policing Financial Crime: The Financial Services Authority and the Myth of the "Duped Investor"', in R.D. Hopkins Burke 'Hard Cop/Soft Cop': Dilemmas and Debates in Contemporary Policing. Cullompton: Willan Publishing.

Spelman, W. (1995) 'The Criminal Careers of Public Places' in J. Eck and D. Weisburd (eds) *Crime and Place: Crime Prevention Studies*, Vol. 4. Monsey, NY: Criminal Justice Press.

Spencer, H. (1971) *Structure, Function and Evolution*, readings, edited with an introduction by S. Andreski. London: Nelson.

Spergel, I.A. (1964) *Racketsville, Slumtown, Haulburg*. Chicago, IL: University of Chicago Press.

Spergel, I.A. (1995) *The Youth Gang Problem: A Community Approach*. Oxford: Oxford University Press.

Spitzer, S. (1975) 'Towards a Marxian Theory of Deviance', *Social Problems*, 22: 638–51.

Squires, P. (2006) *Understanding Community Safety*. Bristol: The Policy Press.

Squires, P. and Stephen, D.E. (2005) *Rougher Justice: Anti-social Behaviour and Young People*. Cullompton: Willan Publishing.

Stanko, E. (1985) *Intimate Intrusions: Women's Experience of Male Violence*. London: Routledge & Kegan Paul.

Staw, B.M. and Szwajkowski, E. (1975) 'The Scarcity-Munificence Component of Organizational Environments and the Commission of Illegal Acts', *Administrative Science Quarterly*, 20: 345–54.

Steedman, C. (1984) *Policing the Victorian Community*. London: Routledge & Kegan Paul.

Stenson, K. (2001) 'The New Politics of Crime Control', in K. Stenson and R.R. Sullivan (eds) *Crime, Risk and Justice: The Politics of Crime Control in Liberal Democracies*. Cullompton: Willan Publishing.

Stenson, K. and Sullivan, R.R. (2001) *Crime, Risk and Justice: The Politics of Crime Control in Liberal Democracies*. Cullompton: Willan Publishing.

Stewart, D., Gossop, M., Marsden, J. and Rolfe, A. (2000) 'Drug Misuse and Acquisitive Crime Among Clients Recruited to the National Treatment Outcome Research (NTORS)', *Criminal Behaviour and Mental Health*, 10: 13–24.

Stitt, G.B. (2003) 'The Understanding of Evil: A Joint Quest for Criminology and Theology' in R. Chairs and B. Chilton (eds) *Star Trek Visions of Law and Justice*. Dallas, TX: Adios Press.

Storch, R. (1975) 'The Plague of the Blue Locusts: Police Reform and Popular Resistance in Northern England 1840–57', *International Review of Social History*, 20: 61–90.

Storch, R. (1989) 'Policing Rural Southern England before the Police: Opinion and Practice 1830–1856', in D. Hay and F. Snyder (eds) *Policing and Prosecution*. Oxford: Clarendon Press.

Strang, H. (1993) 'Conferencing: A New Paradigm in Community Policing', Paper delivered to the Annual Conference of the Association of Chief Police Officers.

Strang, H. (1995) 'Replacing Courts With Conferences', *Policing*, 11(3): 21–20.

Strentz, T. (1988) 'A Terrorist Psychological Profile', *Law Enforcement Bulletin*, 57: 11–18.

Stumpfl, F. (1936) *Die Ursprunge des Verbrechans om Lebenshauf Von Zwillengen*. Leipzig: Verlag.

Sullivan, R.F. (1973) 'The Economics of Crime: An Introduction to the Literature', *Crime and Delinquency*, 19: 138–49.

Sutherland, E.H. (1937) *The Professional Thief: By a Professional Thief*. Chicago, IL: University of Chicago Press.

Sutherland, E.H. (1940) 'White-collar Criminality', *American Sociological Review*, 5: 1–12.

Sutherland, E.H. (1947) *Principles of Criminology, 4th edition*. Philadelphia, PA: Lippincott.

Sutherland, E.H. and Cressey, D.R. (1960) *Criminology, 5th edition*. Philadelphia, PA: Lippincott.

Sutherland, E.H. and Cressey, D.R. (1978) *Criminology, 10th edition*. Philadelphia, PA: Lippincott.

Sutton, M. (1995) 'Supply by Theft: Does the Market for Second-hand Goods Play a Role in Keeping Crime Figures High?' *British Journal of Criminology*, 38 (3): 352–65.

Sutton, M. (1998) *Handling Stolen Goods and Theft: A Market Reduction Approach*, Home Office Research Study 178. London: Home Office.

Sutton, M. (2004) 'Tackling Stolen Goods Markets is "Root-Level" Situational Crime Prevention', R.D. Hopkins Burke (ed.) *'Hard Cop/Soft Cop': Dilemmas and Debates in Contemporary Policing*. Cullompton: Willan Publishing.

Swartz, J. (1975) 'Silent Killers at Work', *Crime and Social Justice*, 3: 15–20.

Sykes, G. and Matza, D. (1957) 'Techniques of Neutralization: A Theory of Delinquency', *American Sociological Review*, (22): 664–70.

Syndulko, K. (1978) 'Electrocortical Investigations of Sociopathy', in R.D. Hare and D. Schalling (eds) *Psychopathic Behaviour: Approaches to Research*. Chichester: Wiley.

Tannenbaum, F. (1938) *Crime and the Community*. New York: Columbia University Press.

Tappan, P.W. (1960) *Crime, Justice and Correction*. New York: McGraw-Hill.

Taylor, C.S. (1990) *Dangerous Society*. East Lansing, MI: Michigan State University Press.

Taylor, D. (1997) *The New Police in Nineteenth-Century England: Crime, Conflict and Control*. Manchester: Manchester University Press.

Taylor, I. (1981) *Law and Order: Arguments for Socialism*. London: Macmillan.

Taylor, I., Walton, P. and Young, J. (1973) *The New Criminology: For a Social Theory of Deviance*. London: Routledge & Kegan Paul.

Taylor, I., Walton, P. and Young, J. (eds) (1975) *Critical Criminology*. London: Routledge & Kegan Paul.

Thambirajah, M.S. (2007) *Case Studies in Child and Adolescent Mental Health*. Oxford: Radcliffe Publishing.

Thomas, D.W. and Hyman, J.M. (1978) 'Compliance, Theory, Control Theory and Juvenile Delinquency', in M. Krohn and R.L. Acker (eds) *Crime, Law and Sanctions*. London: Sage.

Thomas, W.I. (1907) *Sex and Society*. Boston, MA: Little, Brown.

Thomas, W.I. (1923) *The Unadjusted Girl*. New York: Harper & Row.

Thompson, E.P. (1975) *Whigs and Hunters*. London: Allen Lane.

Thompson, W.E., Mitchell, J. and Doddler, R.A. (1984) 'An Empirical Test of Hirschi's Control Theory of Delinquency', *Deviant Behavior*, 5: 11–22.

Thornhill, R. and Palmer, C. (2000) *A Natural History of Rape: Biological Bases of Sexual Coercion*. Cambridge, MA: MIT Press.

Thornhill, R. and Thornhill, N. (1983) 'Human Rape: An Evolutionary Analysis', *Ethology and Sociobiology*, 4: 137–73.

Thornton, S. (1995) *Club Cultures*. Cambridge: Polity Press.

Thrasher, F. (1947) *The Gang*. Chicago, IL: University of Chicago Press.

Tierney, K. (1982) 'The Battered Women Movement and the Creation of the Wife Beating Problem', *Social Problems*, 29 (February): 207–20.

Tifft, L. (1979) 'The Coming Redefinition of Crime: An Anarchist Perspective', *Social Problems*, 26: 392–402.

Tifft, L. (1995) 'Social Harm Definitions of Crime', *Critical Criminologist*, 7(1): 9–12.

Tittle, C.R. (1995) *Control Balance: Towards a General Theory of Deviance*. Boulder, CO: Westview Press.

Tittle, C.R. (1997) 'Thoughts Stimulated by Braithwaite's Analysis of Control Balance', *Theoretical Criminology*, 1: 87–107.

Tittle, C.R. (1999) 'Continuing the Discussion of Control Balance', *Theoretical Criminology*, 3: 326–43.

Tittle, C.R. (2000) 'Control Balance', in R. Paternoster and R. Bachman (eds) *Explaining Criminals and Crime: Essays in Contemporary Theory*. Los Angeles, CA: Roxbury.

Toby, J. (1957) 'Social Disorganization and Stake in Conformity: Complementary Factors in the Behavior of Hoodlums', *American Sociological Review*, 22(5): 505–12.

Tolman, E.C. (1959) 'Principles of Purposive Behaviour', in S. Koch and D.E. Leary (eds) *A Century of Psychology as a Science*. New York: McGraw-Hill.

Tolson, N. (2006) *Violence against Clergy in Willesden Archdeaconry*. London: National Churchwatch.

Tolson, N. (2007) *Clergy Lifestyle Theory: Assessing the Risk of Violence to Clergy*. London: National Churchwatch.

Tong, R. (1988) *Feminist Thought: A Comprehensive Introduction*. London: Routledge.

Trasler, G. (1967) *The Explanation of Criminality*. London: Routledge & Kegan Paul.

Trasler, G. (1986) 'Situational Crime Control and Rational Choice: A Critique', in K. Heal and G. Laycock (eds) *Situational Crime Prevention: From Theory into Practice*. London: HMSO.

Travis, C.B. (ed.) (2003) *Evolution, Gender and Rape*. Cambridge, MA: MIT Press.

Triplett, R. (2000) 'The Dramatisation of Evil: Reacting to Juvenile Delinquency During the 1990s', in S.S. Simpson (ed.) *Of Crime and Criminality: The Use of Theory in Everyday Life*. Thousand Oaks, CA: Pine Forge Press.

Turk, A.T. (1969) *Criminality and the Social Order*. Chicago, IL: Rand-McNally.

Tzannetakis, T. (2001) 'Neo-Conservative Criminology', in McLaughlin and J. Muncie (eds) *The Sage Dictionary of Criminology*. London: Sage.

UKADCU (United Kingdom Anti-Drugs Co-ordinating Unit) (1998) *Tackling Drugs to Build a Better Britain: The Government's 10-year Strategy for Tackling Drug Misuse*. London: The Stationery Office.

United Nations Development Programme (UNDP) (1999) *Human Development Report 1999: Globalization with a Human Face*. Oxford: Oxford University Press.

Unnever, J.D., Colvin, M., Cullen, F.T. (2004) 'Crime and Coercion: A Test of Core Theoretical Propositions', *Journal of Research in Crime and Delinquency*, 41(3): 244–68.

Van Den Haag, E. (1975) *Punishing Criminals: Concerning a Very Old and Painful Question*. New York: Basic Books.

Van Duyne, P. (1997) 'Organized Crime, Corruption and Power', *Crime Law and Social Change*, 26: 201–38.

Van Ness, D and Strong, K.H. (1997) *Restoring Justice*. Cincinnati, OH: Anderson Publishing.

Van Swaaningen, R. (1999) 'Reclaiming Critical Criminology', *Theoretical Criminology*, 3(1): 5–28.

Virkkunen, M. (1987) 'Metabolic Dysfunctions Amongst Habitually Violent Offenders: Reactive Hypoglycaemia and Cholesterol Levels', in S.A. Mednick, T.E. Moffit and S.A. Stack (eds) *The Causes of Crime: New Biological Approaches*. Cambridge: Cambridge University Press.

Volavka, J. (1987) 'Electroencephalogram Among Criminals' in S.A. Mednick, T.E. Moffit and S.A. Stack (eds) *The Causes of Crime: New Biological Approaches*. Cambridge: Cambridge University Press.

Vold, G.B. (1958) *Theoretical Criminology*. Oxford: Oxford University Press.

Vold, G.B., Bernard, T.J. and Snipes, J.B. (1998) *Theoretical Criminology, 4th edition*. Oxford: Oxford University Press.

Von Hirsch, A. (1976) *Doing Justice: The Choice of Punishments. Report of the Committee for the Study of Incarceration*. New York: Hill and Wang.

Von Hirsch, A., Ashworth, A., Wasik, M., Smith, A.T.H., Morgan, R. and Gardner, J. (1999) 'Overtaking on the Right', *New Law Journal*, 1501.

Waddington, P.A.J. (1986) 'Mugging as a Moral Panic: A Question of Proportion', *British Journal of Criminology*, 32(2): 245–59.

Wakschlag, L.S. and Hans, S.L. (1999) 'Relation of Maternal Responsiveness during Infancy to the Development of Behavior Problems in High-Risk Youths', *Developmental Psychology*, 35(2): 569–79.

Walby, S. (1980) *Theorizing Patriarchy*. Oxford: Basil Blackwell.

Walker, N. (1980) *Punishment, Danger and Stigma: The Morality of Criminal Justice*. Oxford: Basil Blackwell.

Walker, N. (1985) *Sentencing: Theory, Law and Practice*. London: Butterworths.

Walklate, S. (1995) *Gender and Crime: An Introduction*. Hemel Hempstead: Prentice Hall/Harvester.

Walklate, S. (1998) *Understanding Criminology: Current Theoretical Debates*. Buckingham: Open University Press.

Walsh, A. and Ellis, L. (2006) *Criminology: An Interdisciplinary Approach*. Newbury Park, CA: Sage Publications.

Watney, S. (1987) *Policing Desire: Pornography, Aids and the Media*. London: Methuen.

Weber, M. (1964) *The Theory of Social and Economic Organization*. New York: Free Press.

Weber, M. (1975) 'Religious Rejections of the World and their Directions', in H. Gerth and C.W. Mills (eds) *From Max Weber: Essays in Sociology*. Oxford: Oxford University Press.

Weisberg, D.K. (ed.) (1996) *Applications of Feminist Legal Theory to Women's Lives: Sex, Violence and Reproduction*. Philadelphia, PA: Temple University Press.

Wells, C. (1993) *Corporations and Criminal Responsibility*. Oxford: Clarendon Press.

Werner, E.E., Bierman, J.M. and French, F.E. (1971) *The Children of Kauai: A Longitudinal Study from the Prenatal Period to Age Ten*. Honolulu, HI: University of Hawaii Press.

West, D.J. (1969) *Present Conduct and Future Delinquency*. London: Heinemann.

West, D.J. (1982) *Delinquency: Its Roots, Careers, and Prospects*. London: Heinemann.

West, D.J. and Farrington, D.P. (1973) *Who Becomes Delinquent?* London: Heinemann.

Westergaard, J. (1995) *Who Gets What? The Hardening of Class Inequality in the Late Twentieth Century*. Cambridge: Polity Press.

Widom, C.S. (1979) 'Female Offenders: Three Assumptions About Self-esteem, Sex Role Identity and Feminism', *Criminal Justice Behaviour*, 6: 358–72.

Wilczynski, A. and Morris, A. (1993) 'Parents Who Kill Their Children', *Criminal Law Review*, 26–44.

Wilkins, L. (1964) *Social Deviance*. London: Tavistock.

Williams, C. R. and Arrigo, B. A. (2004) *Theory, Justice and Social Change: Theoretical Integrations and Critical Applications*. New York: Kluwer.

Williams, T. (1989) *The Cocaine Kids: The Inside Story of a Teenage Drug Ring*. Reading, MA: Addison-Wesley Publishing Co.

Willis, P. (1977) *Learning to Labour*. London: Saxon House

Willis, P. (1978) *Profane Culture*. London: Routledge & Kegan Paul.

Wilmott, P. (1966) *Adolescent Boys in East London*. London: Routledge & Kegan Paul.

Wilson, E.O. (1990) *Success and Dominance in Ecosystems: The Case of the Social Insects*. Oldendorf/Luhe: Inter Research.

Wilson, H. (1980) 'Parental Supervision: A Neglected Aspect of Delinquency', *British Journal of Criminology*, 20: 315–27.

Wilson, J.Q. (1975) *Thinking About Crime*. New York: Basic Books.

Wilson, J.Q. (1985) *Thinking About Crime, 2nd edition*. New York: Basic Books.

Wilson, J.Q. and Herrnstein, R.J. (1985) *Crime and Human Nature*. New York: Simon and Schuster.

Wilson, J.Q. and Kelling, G.L. (1982) 'Broken Windows', *Atlantic Monthly*, March: 29–38.

Wilson, J.Q. and Kelling, G.L. (1989) 'Making Neighborhoods Safe', *Atlantic Monthly*, February: 46–58.

Wilson, W.J. (1987) *The Truly Disadvantaged*. Chicago, IL: Chicago University Press.

Wilson, W.J. (1991) 'Public Policy Research and the Truly Disadvantaged', in C. Jencks and P.E. Peterson (eds) *The Urban Underclass*. Washington, DC: The Brookings Institution.

Wilson, W.J. (1996) *When Work Disappears*. New York: Knopf.

Wing, L. (1998) 'The History of Asperger Syndrome' in E. Schopler, G. Mesibov and L. Kunce (eds) *Asperger Syndrome or High-Functioning Autism?* New York: Plenum Press.

Winlow, S. and Hall, S. (2006) *Violent Night: Urban Leisure and Contemporary Culture.* Oxford: Berg.

Witkin, H.A., Mednick, S.A. and Schulsinger, F. (1977) 'XYY and XXY Men: Criminality and Aggression', in S.A. Mednick and K.O. Christiansen (eds) *Biosocial Bases of Criminal Behaviour.* New York: Gardner Press.

Wolff, K. (ed.) (1950) *The Sociology of Georg Simmel.* New York: Free Press.

Wolfgang, M.E. and Ferracuti, F. (1967) *The Sub-culture of Violence: Towards an Integrated Theory in Criminology.* Beverly Hills, CA: Sage.

Wootton, B. (1959) *Social Science and Social Pathology.* London: Allen & Unwin.

Wootton, B. (1962) 'A Social Scientist's Approach to Maternal Deprivation', in M.D. Ainsworth (ed.) *Deprivation of Maternal Care: A Reassessment of its Effects.* Geneva: World Health Organisation.

Wright, M. (1982) *Making Good: Prisons, Punishment and Beyond.* London: Burnett.

Wright, R.A. (1993) 'A Socially Sensitive Criminal Justice System', in J.W. Murphy and D.L. Peck (eds) *Open Institutions: The Hope for Democracy.* Westport, CT: Praeger.

Wright, R.A., and Decker, S. (1997) *Armed Robbers in Action: Stickups and Street Culture.* Boston, MA: Northeastern University Press.

Yablonsky, L. (1962) *The Violent Gang.* New York: Macmillan.

Young, J. (1971) *The Drug Takers: The Social Meaning of Drugtaking.* London: Paladin.

Young, J. (1986a) 'The Failure of Criminology: The Need for a Radical Realism', in R. Matthews and J. Young (eds) *Confronting Crime.* London: Sage.

Young, J. (1986b) 'Ten Points of Realism', in R. Matthews and J. Young (eds) *Issues in Realist Criminology.* London: Sage.

Young, J. (1994) 'Incessant Chatter: Recent Paradigms in Criminology', in M. Maguire, R. Morgan and R. Reiner (eds) *The Oxford Handbook of Criminology.* Oxford: Clarendon Press.

Young, J. (1999) *The Exclusive Society: Social Exclusion, Crime and Difference in Late Modernity.* London: Sage.

Young, J. (2001) 'Identity, Community and Social Exclusion', in R Matthews and J Pitts (eds) *Crime, Disorder and Community Safety.* London: Routledge.

Young, J. (2003) 'Merton with Energy, Katz with Structure', *Theoretical Criminology*, 7(3): 389–414

Young, J. and Matthews, R. (2003) 'New Labour, Crime Control and Social Exclusion' in R. Matthews and J. Young (eds) *The New Politics of Crime and Punishment.* Cullompton: Willan Publishing.

Young, M. (1991) *An Inside Job: Policing and Police Culture in Britain.* Oxford: Oxford University Press.

Young, M. (1993) *In the Sticks.* Oxford: Oxford University Press.

Young, R. and Goold, B. (1999) 'Restorative Police Cautioning in Aylesbury – From Degrading to Shaming Ceremonies', *Criminal Law Review*, 123–34.

Young, T.R. (1997) 'The ABC's of Crime: Attractors, Bifurcations, and Chaotic Dynamics', in D. Milovanovic (ed.) *Chaos, Criminology, and Social Justice: the New Orderly (Dis) Order.* Westport, CT: Praeger.

Young, T.R. (1999) 'A Constitutive Theory of Justice: The Architecture of Affirmative Postmodern Legal Systems' in S. Henry and D. Milovanovic (eds) *Constitutive Criminology at Work: Applications to Crime and Justice.* New York: State University of New York Press.

Younge, S.L., Oetting, E.R. and Deffenbacher, J.L. (1996) 'Correlations Among Maternal Rejection, Dropping Out of School, and Drug Use in Adolescents', *Journal of Clinical Psychology*, 52(1): 96–102.

Youth Justice Board (2002) *Key Elements of Effective Practice–Assessment, Planning Interventions and Supervision*, edition 1. London: Youth Justice Board.

Zimring, F. and Hawkins, G. (1968) 'Deterrence and Marginal Groups', *Journal of Research in Crime and Delinquency*, 5: 110–15.

Zimring, F. and Hawkins, G. (1973) *Deterrence*. Chicago, IL: University of Chicago.

Index

Added to a page number 'g' denotes glossary